MANAGING
PEOPLE AND
ORGANIZATIONS

The Practice of Management Series

HARVARD BUSINESS SCHOOL PUBLICATIONS

The Craft of General Management

Readings selected by Joseph L. Bower

The Entrepreneurial Venture

Readings selected by William A. Sahlman and Howard H. Stevenson

Managing People and Organizations

Readings selected by John J. Gabarro

Strategic Marketing Management

Readings selected by Robert J. Dolan

MANAGING PEOPLE AND ORGANIZATIONS

READINGS SELECTED BY

John J. Gabarro

Harvard Business School

HARVARD BUSINESS SCHOOL PUBLICATIONS
Boston, Massachusetts

Library of Congress Cataloging-in-Publication Data

Managing people and organizations / edited by John J. Gabarro.
    p. cm.—(The Practice of management series)
  Includes index.
  ISBN 0-87584-311-5
  1. Management. I. Gabarro, John J. II. Series.
  HD31.M293918 1991
  658.4--dc20   91-30314
                                                    CIP

The Harvard Business School Publications Practice of Management Series is distributed in the college market by McGraw-Hill Book Company. The readings in each book are available individually through PRIMIS, the McGraw-Hill custom publishing service. Instructors and bookstores should contact their local McGraw-Hill representative for information and ordering.

Printed in the United States of America.

95 94 93 92   5 4 3 2 1

JOHN J. GABARRO

John J. Gabarro is UPS Foundation Professor of Human Resource Management at Harvard Business School, where he has taught in the MBA, Advanced Management, International Senior Management, and the Owner-President Management programs. The author or co-author of four books, he is the recipient of a McKinsey Foundation–*Harvard Business Review* Prize and the Johnson Smith Knisely Foundation Award for research on leadership. At Harvard he has served as Area Chair for Organizational Behavior and Human Resource Management and as Faculty Chairman of Harvard's International Senior Management Program.

CONTENTS

Series Preface   xv

Introduction   John J. Gabarro   1

PART ONE
MANAGING AND LEADING IN ORGANIZATIONS

SECTION A
MANAGING PEOPLE

1   **The Manager's Job: Folklore and Fact**   13
Henry Mintzberg

Contrasting the myths and the facts of managerial life can help answer the basic question, What do managers do?

2   **Power, Dependence, and Effective Management**   33
John P. Kotter

Managers, who are dependent on others, must generate and use power successfully.

3   Management Time: Who's Got the Monkey?   50

William Oncken, Jr., and Donald L. Wass

Effective time management can be achieved through the proper balance of responsibilities in the manager-subordinate relationship.

4   The New Managerial Work   57

Rosabeth Moss Kanter

Changes are occurring in two important aspects of managerial work—sources of power and motivation, as illustrated in the profiles of three managers whose jobs are changing.

5   Managing Without Managers   70

Ricardo Semler

Three key principles of management—work-force democracy, profit sharing, and free access to information—are applied to a thriving company.

SECTION B
LEADING AN ORGANIZATION

6   Managers and Leaders: Are They Different?   85

Abraham Zaleznik

Organizations can foster the development of leaders, whose temperament differs significantly from that of managers.

7   What Leaders Really Do   102

John P. Kotter

Leadership—coping with change—is compared with management—coping with complexity. Organizations can create a culture that promotes leadership.

8   Ways Women Lead   115

Judy B. Rosener

Women's leadership styles differ from those of men in several important elements.

9   How to Choose a Leadership Pattern   126

Robert Tannenbaum and Warren H. Schmidt

Managers must know their own strengths and weaknesses as well as the abilities of their subordinates so that they can choose an appropriate form of leadership.

10   In Praise of Followers   143
Robert E. Kelley

Followers have a specific role, and effective and ineffective followers possess certain traits. An organization can cultivate effective followers using a four-step procedure.

PART TWO
MANAGING INDIVIDUALS AND GROUPS

SECTION A
MOTIVATING AND MANAGING INDIVIDUALS

**11   One More Time: How Do You
Motivate Employees?**   159
Frederick Herzberg

There is a difference between inducements, such as fringe benefits, and genuine motivators, such as greater responsibility. Job enrichment is vital to effective motivation.

12   Pygmalion in Management   179
J. Sterling Livingston

A framework can be used to draw superior performance from employees through the power of expectation. Managers must be sensitive to their own behavior and its impact on subordinates.

13   Making Performance Appraisal Work   195
Michael Beer

Managers and subordinates sometimes have trouble with performance appraisal, but there are several ways to handle these difficulties.

14   Managing Interpersonal Conflict   213
James Ware and Louis B. Barnes

Interpersonal conflict can be managed in three ways. Several relevant action questions can help resolve or control conflict.

15   Managing Your Boss   227
John J. Gabarro and John P. Kotter

For greater effectiveness at work, subordinates must manage their relationship with their boss. This crucial relationship can be developed and maintained in several ways.

SECTION B
MANAGING GROUP EFFECTIVENESS

16   A Framework for Analyzing Work Groups   **241**
Michael B. McCaskey

The factors that influence a work group's behavior and performance are group context, design factors, and group culture.

**17   Problem Solving and Conflict Resolution
in Groups**   **263**
James Ware

Several characteristics of managerial groups enhance and detract from their problem-solving effectiveness. Managers can use basic strategies to influence group behavior.

18   Understanding and Influencing Group Process   **279**
John J. Gabarro and Anne Harlan

There are seven indicators of the effectiveness of a group in accomplishing its formal tasks.

19   How to Run a Meeting   **289**
James Ware

Managers must know how to prepare for and run a meeting effectively.

20   Managing a Task Force   **298**
James Ware

Certain insights can help a manager organize and manage a task force from project conception through completion.

PART THREE
MANAGING ORGANIZATIONAL EFFECTIVENESS

SECTION A
DESIGNING ORGANIZATIONS FOR EFFECTIVENESS

21   Organization Design   **313**
Jay W. Lorsch

Managers face design issues at two organizational levels: the functional unit and the single-business organization.

22 **Organization Design: Fashion or Fit?**   **332**
Henry Mintzberg

An organization's structure can be arranged in five configurations, which serve as an effective tool in diagnosing organizational problems. A misfit results when an organization's design is no longer suited to its task.

23 **Functional Integration: Getting All the Troops
to Work Together**   **353**
Benson P. Shapiro

Six approaches can be taken to achieve functional integration.

24 **Matrix Management: Not a Structure, a Frame of Mind**   **370**
Christopher A. Bartlett and Sumantra Ghoshal

A company can be strategically agile while coordinating complex activities by building a matrix of corporate values and priorities in managers' minds.

25 **In Praise of Hierarchy**   **382**
Elliott Jaques

Hierarchy is praiseworthy when it is a design based on accountability and skill, but it can be misused. There are ways to more properly apply hierarchy to an organization's structure.

SECTION B
MANAGING ORGANIZATIONAL CHANGE

26 **Choosing Strategies for Change**   **395**
John P. Kotter and Leonard A. Schlesinger

People resist change for several reasons. A change strategy should be selected and implemented systematically.

27 **Evolution and Revolution as Organizations Grow**   **410**
Larry E. Greiner

An organization's future is determined less by outside forces than by the organization's own history.

28 **Leading Change**   **424**
Michael Beer

Management can channel change when an organization has a vision that it is working toward. Managers must understand the process, cost, and fears of change.

29 Speed, Simplicity, Self-Confidence: An Interview with Jack Welch   **432**

Noel Tichy and Ram Charan

General Electric is changing its corporate culture and the way its employees think through the innovative tool called Work-Out and through the company's own Value Statement.

**PART FOUR
MANAGING THE HUMAN RESOURCE**

30 Planning with People in Mind   **449**

D. Quinn Mills

A company must incorporate human resource goals into its long-term business planning. A model process can be used to enhance the company's business goals and marketplace success.

31 Career Systems and Strategic Staffing   **464**

Jeffrey A. Sonnenfeld and Maury A. Peiperl

Managers should be familiar with career systems and their basic elements. A four-cell configuration of career systems can be used to link staffing policy with business strategy.

32 Reward Systems and the Role of Compensation   **474**

Michael Beer and Richard E. Walton

Reward systems, which have various designs, affect employee satisfaction and motivation.

33 From Control to Commitment in the Workplace   **487**

Richard E. Walton

A manager must understand the two different strategies for managing a work force—the traditional control model and the newer commitment approach—as well as the transition between the two.

34 From Affirmative Action to Affirming Diversity   **499**

R. Roosevelt Thomas, Jr.

The demographics of the American work force are changing. Ten guidelines can ensure that this new diversity is managed successfully.

35 Management Women and the New Facts of Life   **516**

Felice N. Schwartz

Women cost more to employ than men. Companies can adapt policies and practices to retain talented women and eliminate the extra cost of employing them.

36   Business and the Facts of Family Life   **529**

Fran Sussner Rodgers and Charles Rodgers

Businesses will have to make adjustments to accommodate the new realities of family life. There are a number of ways to lessen the conflict between work and family.

37   Beyond Testing: Coping with Drugs at Work   **543**

James T. Wrich

One approach has proven effective in dealing with the problem of drugs in the workplace.

Index   **555**

SERIES PREFACE

The Harvard Business School has a long and distinguished publishing history. For decades, the School has furnished original educational materials to academic classrooms and executive education programs worldwide. Many of these publications have been used by individual managers to update their knowledge and skills. The Practice of Management Series, developed by Harvard Business School Publications, continues this tradition.

The series addresses major areas of the business curriculum and major topics within those areas. Each of the books strikes a balance between broad coverage of the area and depth of treatment; each has been designed for flexibility of use to accommodate the varying needs of instructors and programs in different academic settings.

These books also will serve as authoritative references for practicing managers. They can provide a refresher on business basics and enduring concepts, and they also offer cutting-edge ideas and techniques.

The main objective of the Practice of Management Series is to make Harvard Business School's continuing explorations into management's best practices more widely and easily available. The books draw on two primary sources of material produced at the School.

Harvard Business School is probably best known for its field research and cases. Faculty members prepare other material for their classrooms, however, including essays that define and explain key business concepts and practices. Like other classroom materials produced at Harvard Business School, these "notes," as they are called at the School, have a consistent point of view—that of the general manager. They have a common purpose—to inform the actual practice of management as opposed to providing a theoretical foundation. The notes are an important source of selections for the books in this series.

The Harvard Business Review has long been recognized by professors and managers as the premier management magazine. Its mix of authors—academics, practicing executives and managers, and consultants—brings to bear a blend of research knowledge and practical intelligence on a wide variety of business topics. Harvard Business Review articles challenge conventional wisdom with fresh approaches and often become a part of enlightened conventional wisdom. The magazine speaks primarily to the practice of management at the level of the general manager. *Harvard Business Review* articles are another essential source of selections for this series.

Finally, this series includes selections published by other distinguished institutions and organizations. In instances where there were gaps in coverage or viewpoint, we have taken the opportunity to tap books and other journals besides the *Harvard Business Review*.

———— ACKNOWLEDGMENTS

The books in this series are the products of a collaborative effort. John J. Gabarro, the Harvard Business School faculty member who wrote the introduction to *Managing People and Organizations*, worked closely with a Harvard Business School Publications editor, John J. Pippa, to select and arrange the best available materials. Professor Gabarro's content expertise, teaching experience, and diligence, together with Mr. Pippa's editorial skill and commitment, have been crucial to the development of the book.

The Harvard Business School faculty whose work is represented in the books have generously taken the time to review their selections. Their cooperation is much appreciated.

Each of the books has been evaluated by practitioners or by professors at other institutions. We would like to thank the following individuals for their careful readings of the manuscript for the collection on organizational behavior and human resource management: Taylor Cox, Jr., School of Business Administration, The University of Michigan; Richard B. Higgins, College of Business Administration, Northeastern University; Robert Drazin, School of Business Administration, Emory University; and Alan L. Wilkins, Graduate School of Management, Brigham Young University. Their evaluations and many useful suggestions have helped us develop and shape this book into a more effective teaching instrument.

We would like to thank Maria Arteta, former Director of Product Management for Harvard Business School Publications; Bill Ellet, Editorial Director of Harvard Business School Publications; and Benson P. Shapiro, Malcolm P. McNair Professor of Marketing and former faculty adviser to Harvard Business School Publications. The Practice of Management Series would not have materialized without their support, guidance, and insight.

INTRODUCTION

This book is about managing people and organizations. The intended audience is practicing managers and MBA students who face the challenges of managing, leading, motivating, and organizing people. The readings have been selected to provide a set of basic concepts and tools for dealing with a range of multifaceted issues that managers must handle to be effective. As such, the book is intended for use not only in MBA and executive education programs—either alone or with an assigned textbook, cases, or other materials—but also as a basic reference for practicing managers.

There have been significant advances in the fields of organizational behavior and management in the last decade. The manager's role, that is, what effective managers really do compared with what theorists have said they should do, is much better understood. Our knowledge of the factors that influence the effectiveness of groups also has expanded, along with our understanding of their potential for self-direction, commitment, and creativity. Similarly, our understanding of organizational design and alternative forms of organization has grown along with our understanding of the management of change. Moreover, developments in human resource management, such as high-commitment work systems and employee involvement, have gone substantially beyond the classic personnel issues of selection, development, and compensation.

The state of both knowledge and practice has grown substantially. So have the challenges, however. If managers have better tools at their disposal today than a decade ago, they also face challenges that are far more demanding.

Much more is expected of managers now than 10 years ago. Being an effective manager requires a deeper level of sophistication and a broader and more versatile set of skills. In most industries the pace of change that organizations (and their people) must cope with is relentless. To be competitive, corporations have had to restructure, downsize, de-layer, and increase spans of control. The simple principles and formulas once found in management texts have become manifestly irrelevant. Companies spawn new organizational forms, such as hybrid organizations, "adhocracies," vendor partnerships, and other kinds of alliances, at a dizzying pace as they scramble for speed and competitive advantage. In addition, the challenges of managing an increasingly diverse work force, the changing role of women in business, and the impact of technology on the nature of work pose human resource issues that simply did not exist to the same extent 10 years ago.

Despite all of this change, some aspects of managing people are fundamental. Certain truths about motivation, group behavior, and organization are as valid today as they were 20 years ago. If anything, the increasing pressures of today's more competitive environment make these basics even more necessary to master. Effective management requires not only dealing with state-of-the-art issues but also handling the essential daily realities of motivating people, solving performance problems, and managing groups efficiently.

The readings in this book were chosen to address both sets of needs: the need for fundamental concepts as well as the newer concepts that address today's emerging imperatives. An important purpose of this book is to bring together a selective set of practice-oriented readings that represent some of the best thinking currently available on both basic and contemporary issues. For this reason, the readings span a broad set of substantive topics and problems in organizational behavior. These include the important question of what constitutes effective management and leadership and whether these two processes are different from each other. At an operational level, the book also addresses the specific aspects of how to manage individuals and groups effectively. Finally, the book examines the broader questions of organizational effectiveness through organizational design choices, organizational change, and the accurate use of human resources.

The readings are distinctly managerial in orientation; they tend to be more problem oriented than theoretical, and they are written for managers from a manager's perspective. In this respect, they are meant to provide frameworks and concepts that ground and supplement existing theory by focusing on practical issues and problems. For this reason, one of the criteria used in choosing these readings is their relevance and usability for managers and MBAs. Many readings were chosen based on the critical reviews and suggestions of business school professors teaching in a variety of programs across the country. Most of the readings that have been included from the *Harvard Business Review* are best-sellers. The background and tool-oriented readings, written by Harvard Business School faculty members, are largely best-selling essays used individually in many classrooms. In this regard, even the most recent readings have passed the tests of user utility and applicability.

───── OVERVIEW OF THE BOOK

The book is organized into four parts, each of which focuses on a different area of management. Each part contains a mix of readings that cover basic issues as well as readings dealing with emergent or controversial issues. The readings have been chosen so that each part contains a mix of concept-oriented and action-oriented readings. Generally, the more conceptual readings provide a framework or way of thinking about problems, while the action-oriented readings tend to offer guidelines for handling specific problems or issues. Readings in each section are arranged so that they begin with basic descriptive frameworks or concepts and then move to issues that are more applied, normative, and contemporary.

MANAGING AND LEADING IN ORGANIZATIONS

Part One focuses on the manager as an instrument of action and is divided into two sections: one focusing on managerial behavior and the other on leadership. Section A, Managing People, begins with "The Manager's Job: Folklore and Fact" by Mintzberg. This reading challenges much of the mythology of what managers "should do" by succinctly describing what Mintzberg's path-breaking research shows they actually do, the different roles they perform, and their inherent dilemmas. "Power, Dependence, and Effective Management" by Kotter takes these roles one step farther by describing the manager's dependent relationships and discussing several ways of establishing power in them. He also discusses several methods of face-to-face and indirect influence. "Management Time: Who's Got the Monkey?" by Oncken and Wass is a widely reproduced reading on time management and delegation, two problems that always have plagued managers.

The last two readings in Part One present provocative ideas on the transformations occurring in the manager's job. Kanter's "The New Managerial Work" builds on the prior readings but details the structural, career, and competitive pressures that are altering the very nature of managerial work, the quandaries these changes create, and what this means in terms of managing for greater innovation and flexibility. This reading also spells out the implications of these changes for the manager's role, the development of a power base, and the motivation of people when traditional rewards and punishments are no longer available. Section A concludes with Semler's "Managing Without Managers." The author, a highly successful entrepreneur, draws on his experience to argue that the manager's role should become more that of coordinator and counselor and that managers should empower employees through real involvement, access to relevant information, and profit sharing.

Section B, Leading an Organization, goes beyond the manager's job to focus explicitly on leadership. This section begins with a controversial reading entitled "Managers and Leaders: Are They Different?" Zaleznik concludes that the answer is emphatically "yes" and that much of what is considered good management stifles true leadership. "What Leaders Really Do" by Kotter continues the theme by explaining how managers and leaders differ. Unlike Zaleznik, however, Kotter concludes that both are needed. The reading describes what organizations (and some individuals) can do to develop the talents and skills of both managers and leaders. The theme of differences is further pursued in "Ways Women Lead" by Rosener. She argues that, based on her research, women lead differently than men. Women's "interactive" style of leadership has several advantages over the "command-and-control" leadership that characterizes the men in her sample, especially in managing professionals and a more diverse work force.

The last reading on leadership, "How to Choose a Leadership Pattern" by Tannenbaum and Schmidt, outlines several factors that managers should consider about themselves, their subordinates, and their context when determining how participative or directive to be. The section concludes with an article by Kelley, "In Praise of Followers." This provides a useful balance to the prior readings by demonstrating the importance of strong, effective followers and what developing them entails.

MANAGING INDIVIDUALS AND GROUPS

In Part Two, the emphasis shifts from the roles of manager and leader to focus more sharply on managing in face-to-face settings. The first group of readings addresses Motivating and Managing Individuals and opens with two readings on motivation and expectations: Herzberg's "One More Time: How Do You Motivate Employees?" and Livingston's "Pygmalion in Management." Both cover basic motivational issues and complement pieces on motivation-and-expectancy theory.

The next three readings are more tactical. Beer's "Making Performance Appraisal Work" examines the reasons why performance appraisals are difficult to conduct and provides several useful and specific guidelines for conducting them more effectively. In the same vein, Ware and Barnes's "Managing Interpersonal Conflict" describes a framework for diagnosing conflict and describes three alternative approaches and diagnostic criteria to use in deciding how to intervene. This section concludes with a widely reprinted reading on "Managing Your Boss" by Gabarro and Kotter, which argues that managing one's boss is as important as managing one's subordinates. This reading provides basic ideas and suggestions on how to do this effectively, even when the boss proves difficult.

The section on Managing Group Effectiveness begins with a popular reading by McCaskey that offers "A Framework for Analyzing Work Groups." This reading presents the basic contextual, situational, and organizational factors that affect a group's informal social structure, culture, and effectiveness. "Problem Solving and Conflict Resolution in Groups" by Ware reviews several aspects of managerial groups that influence their problem-solving effectiveness, the modes that management groups use for resolving conflict, some criteria to use in deciding whether to use a group to solve a problem, and the implications of this for developing effective groups.

The last three readings in this section are distinctly tactical and action oriented. "Understanding and Influencing Group Process" by Gabarro and Harlan provides guidelines for observing the real-time behavior of a group as well as suggestions for when and how to intervene to improve group effectiveness. The section concludes with two readings by Ware that look at how to manage groups. "How to Run a Meeting" describes the mechanics of planning a meeting, creating an agenda, and effectively managing the meeting. The reading includes the pitfalls to avoid and how to identify the work that is needed beforehand. "Managing a Task Force" focuses on the challenges of managing a temporary group (including cross-functional committees) and provides guidance on how to sharpen the group's mandate, create standards to measure progress, achieve coordination, and (very important) how to avoid predictable difficulties.

MANAGING ORGANIZATIONAL EFFECTIVENESS

In Part Three, the emphasis shifts from face-to-face settings to managing effectiveness at the organizational level. The readings are organized into related sections: Designing Organizations for Effectiveness and Managing Organizational Change.

Section A begins with a basic background reading on "Organization Design" by Lorsch that provides a brief historical perspective and then introduces several fundamental concepts, including contingency theory, the notion of "fit," differentiation, and integration. The reading then describes the essentials of organizing basic functional and single-business units. "Organization Design: Fashion or Fit?" by Mintzberg offers more of an overview by describing five basic configurations of organization, their key elements, and the types of situations for which each configuration is best suited. "Functional Integration: Getting All the Troops to Work Together" by Shapiro builds on the Lorsch reading but pays particular attention to the problem of achieving integration across different functions. Shapiro presents six sets of organizational and cultural variables that managers can use to attain cross-functional integration.

The last two readings in this section tend to be more normative. "Matrix Management: Not a Structure, a Frame of Mind" by Bartlett and Ghoshal argues that under many circumstances (such as those faced by transnational, multi-product corporations) traditional structures are insufficient and matrix organizations are too cumbersome. Instead, the authors believe, what is needed are hybrid forms of organization in which matrix is a mind-set, not a formal structure. They propose several nonstructural variables such as vision, staffing, systems, and culture to achieve this. The final reading, "In Praise of Hierarchy" by Jaques, provides a controversial counterpoint to several other readings in this section (as well as earlier parts of the book). The author argues that hierarchy, having survived for 3,000 years, is still the most effective and basic form of organization. Jaques adds that hierarchy can be highly effective if it is not overlayered and is structured according to accountability, skill, and responsibility.

The section on Managing Organizational Change goes beyond organizational design to focus specifically on the dynamics of change and its implementation. In "Choosing Strategies for Change," Kotter and Schlesinger first examine various sources of resistance to change and methods for overcoming them. Then they establish a framework for developing a change strategy and present the key situational variables to consider. "Evolution and Revolution as Organizations Grow" by Greiner argues that as organizations grow, they pass through five predictable phases of change. Each phase includes a unique set of issues; being aware of these issues and taking appropriate actions at each stage can minimize the problems of transition.

The two final readings in this section have a more tactical orientation. "Leading Change" by Beer presents a simple but multifaceted model of critical dimensions that managers should consider when deciding which factors will enhance or impede change. Specific guidelines for implementing change are offered. In "Speed, Simplicity, Self-Confidence: An Interview with Jack Welch" by Tichy and Charan, one of America's most effective CEOs shares his thoughts on the organizational and cultural changes that General Electric is implementing. The motivations behind these changes also are discussed.

MANAGING THE HUMAN RESOURCE

The readings in Part Four focus on the firm's human resource. The first four readings address basic aspects of human resource management that can influence an organization's effectiveness. The last four readings examine current and emerging human resource issues.

"Planning with People in Mind" by Mills argues for incorporating human resource goals into long-term business planning and, drawing on survey and field data, presents a comprehensive analysis of current practices. "Career Systems and Strategic Staffing" by Sonnenfeld and Peiperl looks at career systems as key aspects of organizational effectiveness. The authors present a model of different types of career systems in terms of supply and assignment flow and the types of organizations in which these systems are likely to be found. "Reward Systems and the Role of Compensation" by Beer and Walton provides a basic primer on different types of reward and compensation systems, their strengths and weaknesses, and guidelines for managers to consider in making reward and compensation decisions. "From Control to Commitment in the Workplace" by Walton describes the differences between control and commitment strategies in work-force management, articulating many of the premises underlying effective work restructuring, job design, and self-directed work teams.

The next three readings consider the challenges of managing a more diverse work force. In "From Affirmative Action to Affirming Diversity," Thomas states that today's demographic realities require going beyond affirmative action to affirming diversity. A company accomplishes this by creating an environment that develops qualified, upwardly mobile women and minorities. The reading then discusses 10 guidelines for effectively managing diversity. The next reading is perhaps one of the most controversial on the topic of women in management. "Management Women and the New Facts of Life" by Schwartz suggests that alternative as well as mainstream career tracks should be available to women, once again raising the famous "Mommy track" debate. A related set of issues is addressed in "Business and the Facts of Family Life" by Rodgers and Rodgers. The authors argue that the increasing prevalence of dual-career couples in the work force requires radical changes in workplace rules and conditions, particularly in the areas of flexible work schedules and child care. The final article, "Beyond Testing: Coping with Drugs at Work" by Wrich, realistically assesses the seriousness of substance abuse in the workplace and discusses the advantages of employee assistance programs as an alternative to drug testing.

As this overview demonstrates, the readings in this book span a broad range of topics, issues, and problems. Although it is impossible for any collection of this size to cover every topic exhaustively, an effort has been made to provide broad coverage of major topics as well as depth within each section. In some areas, such as job design, the interested reader may wish to go beyond the scope of the book. For the most part, however, the collection offers as broad a selection of management-oriented readings as is currently available on organizational behavior.

JOHN J. GABARRO

PART ONE

MANAGING AND LEADING IN ORGANIZATIONS

SECTION A

MANAGING PEOPLE

The Manager's Job: Folklore and Fact   1

HENRY MINTZBERG

In this reading, the author answers the basic question, What do managers do? Contrasting the myths with the facts, he examines the various interpersonal, informational, and decisional roles of managers. He also provides prescriptions for more effective management, along with a list of questions for self-study. He then discusses the importance of training managers to manage.

The author has included a retrospective commentary in which he discusses the diverse reactions to the reading since it was first published, his current perspective, and the important issues that still need to be faced.

If you ask managers what they do, they will most likely tell you that they plan, organize, coordinate, and control. Then watch what they do. Don't be surprised if you can't relate what you see to these words.

When a manager is told that a factory has just burned down and then advises the caller to see whether temporary arrangements can be made to supply customers through a foreign subsidiary, is that manager planning, organizing, coordinating, or controlling? How about when he or she presents a gold watch to a retiring employee? Or attends a conference to meet people in the trade and returns with an interesting new product idea for employees to consider?

These four words, which have dominated management vocabulary since the French industrialist Henri Fayol first introduced them in 1916, tell us little about what managers actually do. At best, they indicate some vague objectives managers have when they work.

The field of management, so devoted to progress and change, has for more than a half a century not seriously addressed the basic question: What do managers do? Without a proper answer, how can we teach management? How can we design planning or information systems for managers? How can we improve the practice of management at all?

Our ignorance of the nature of managerial work shows up in various ways in the modern organization—in boasts by successful managers who never spent a single day in a management training program; in the turnover of corporate planners who never quite understood what it was the manager wanted; in the computer consoles gathering dust in the back room because the managers never used the fancy on-line MIS some analyst thought they needed.

Perhaps most important, our ignorance shows up in the inability of our large public organizations to come to grips with some of their most serious policy problems.

Somehow, in the rush to automate production, to use management science in the functional areas of marketing and finance, and to apply the skills of the behavioral scientist to the problem of worker motivation, the manager—the person in charge of the organization or one of its subunits—has been forgotten.

I intend to break the reader away from Fayol's words and introduce a more supportable and useful description of managerial work. This description derives from my review and synthesis of research on how various managers have spent their time.

In some studies, managers were observed intensively; in a number of others, they kept detailed diaries; in a few studies, their records were analyzed. All kinds of managers were studied—foremen, factory supervisors, staff managers, field sales managers, hospital administrators, presidents of companies and nations, and even street gang leaders. These "managers" worked in the United States, Canada, Sweden, and Great Britain.

A synthesis of these findings paints an interesting picture, one as different from Fayol's classical view as a cubist abstract is from a Renaissance painting. In a sense, this picture will be obvious to anyone who has ever spent a day in a manager's office, either in front of the desk or behind it. Yet, at the same time, this picture throws into doubt much of the folklore that has been accepted about the manager's work.

——— FOLKLORE AND FACTS ABOUT MANAGERIAL WORK

There are four myths about the manager's job that do not bear up under careful scrutiny of the facts.

Folklore: The manager is a reflective, systematic planner. The evidence on this issue is overwhelming, but not a shred of it supports this statement.

Fact: Study after study has shown that managers work at an unrelenting pace, that their activities are characterized by brevity, variety, and discontinuity, and that they are strongly oriented to action and dislike reflective activities. Consider this evidence: Half the activities engaged in by the five chief executives of my study lasted less than nine minutes, and only 10% exceeded one hour.[1] A study of 56 U.S. foremen found that they averaged 583 activities per eight-hour shift, an average of 1 every 48 seconds.[2] The work pace for both chief executives and

---

1. All the data from my study can be found in Henry Mintzberg, *The Nature of Managerial Work* (New York: Harper & Row, 1973).
2. Robert H. Guest, "Of Time and the Foreman," *Personnel* (May 1956): 478.

foremen was unrelenting. The chief executives met a steady stream of callers and mail from the moment they arrived in the morning until they left in the evening. Coffee breaks and lunches were inevitably work related, and ever-present subordinates seemed to usurp any free moment.

A diary study of 160 British middle and top managers found that they worked without interruption for a half hour or more only about once every two days.[3]

Of the verbal contacts the chief executives in my study engaged in, 93% were arranged on an ad hoc basis. Only 1% of the executives' time was spent in open-ended observational tours. Only 1 out of 368 verbal contacts was unrelated to a specific issue and could therefore be called general planning. Another researcher found that "in *not one single case* did a manager report obtaining important external information from a general conversation or other undirected personal communication."[4]

Is this the planner that the classical view describes? Hardly. The manager is simply responding to the pressures of the job. I found that my chief executives terminated many of their own activities, often leaving meetings before the end, and interrupted their desk work to call in subordinates. One president not only placed his desk so that he could look down a long hallway but also left his door open when he was alone—an invitation for subordinates to come in and interrupt him.

Clearly, these managers wanted to encourage the flow of current information. But more significantly, they seemed to be conditioned by their own work loads. They appreciated the opportunity cost of their own time, and they were continually aware of their ever-present obligations—mail to be answered, callers to attend to, and so on. It seems that a manager is always plagued by the possibilities of what might be done and what must be done.

When managers must plan, they seem to do so implicitly in the context of daily actions, not in some abstract process reserved for two weeks in the organization's mountain retreat. The plans of the chief executives I studied seemed to exist only in their heads—as flexible, but often specific, intentions. The traditional literature notwithstanding, the job of managing does not breed reflective planners. Managers respond to stimuli and are conditioned by their jobs to prefer live to delayed action.

Folklore: The effective manager has no regular duties to perform. Managers are constantly being told to spend more time planning and delegating and less time seeing customers and engaging in negotiations. These are not, after all, the true tasks of the manager. To use the popular analogy, the good manager, like the good conductor, carefully orchestrates everything in advance, then sits back,

---

3. Rosemary Stewart, *Managers and Their Jobs* (London: Macmillan, 1967); *see also* Sune Carlson, *Executive Behaviour* (Stockholm: Strombergs, 1951).

4. Francis J. Aguilar, *Scanning the Business Environment* (New York: Macmillan, 1967), p. 102.

responding occasionally to an unforeseeable exception. But here again the pleasant abstraction just does not seem to hold up.

Fact: Managerial work involves performing a number of regular duties, including ritual and ceremony, negotiations, and processing of soft information that links the organization with its environment. Consider some evidence from the research:

A study of the work of the presidents of small companies found that they engaged in routine activities because their companies could not afford staff specialists and were so thin on operating personnel that a single absence often required the president to substitute.[5]

One study of field sales managers and another of chief executives suggest that it is a natural part of both jobs to see important customers, assuming the managers wish to keep those customers.[6]

Someone, only half in jest, once described the manager as the person who sees visitors so that other people can get their work done. In my study, I found that certain ceremonial duties—meeting visiting dignitaries, giving out gold watches, presiding at Christmas dinners—were an intrinsic part of the chief executive's job.

Studies of managers' information flow suggest that managers play a key role in securing "soft" external information (much of it available only to them because of their status) and in passing it along to their subordinates.

Folklore: The senior manager needs aggregated information, which a formal management information system best provides. Not too long ago, the words *total information system* were everywhere in the management literature. In keeping with the classical view of the manager as that individual perched on the apex of a regulated, hierarchical system, the literature's manager was to receive all important information from a giant, comprehensive MIS.

But lately, these giant MIS systems are not working—managers are simply not using them. The enthusiasm has waned. A look at how managers actually process information makes it clear why.

Fact: Managers strongly favor verbal media, telephone calls and meetings, over documents. Consider the following:

In two British studies, managers spent an average of 66% and 80% of their time in verbal (oral) communication.[7] In my study of five American chief executives, the figure was 78%.

These five chief executives treated mail processing as a burden to be dispensed with. One came in Saturday morning to process 142 pieces of mail in just over three hours, to "get rid of all the stuff." This same manager looked at

---

5. Unpublished study by Irving Choran, reported in Mintzberg, *The Nature of Managerial Work.*

6. Robert T. Davis, *Performance and Development of Field Sales Managers* (Boston: Division of Research, Harvard Business School, 1957); George H. Copeman, *The Role of the Managing Director* (London: Business Publications, 1963).

7. Stewart, *Managers and Their Jobs*; Tom Burns, "The Directions of Activity and Communication in a Departmental Executive Group," *Human Relations 7*, no. 1 (1954): 73.

the first piece of "hard" mail he had received all week, a standard cost report, and put it aside with the comment, "I never look at this."

These same five chief executives responded immediately to 2 of the 40 routine reports they received during the five weeks of my study and to 4 items in the 104 periodicals. They skimmed most of these periodicals in seconds, almost ritualistically. In all, these chief executives of good-sized organizations initiated on their own—that is, not in response to something else—a grand total of 25 pieces of mail during the 25 days I observed them.

An analysis of the mail the executives received reveals an interesting picture—only 13% was of specific and immediate use. So now we have another piece in the puzzle: not much of the mail provides live, current information—the action of a competitor, the mood of a government legislator, or the rating of last night's television show. Yet this is the information that drove the managers, interrupting their meetings and rescheduling their workdays.

Consider another interesting finding. Managers seem to cherish "soft" information, especially gossip, hearsay, and speculation. Why? The reason is its timeliness; today's gossip may be tomorrow's fact. The manager who misses the telephone call revealing that the company's biggest customer was seen golfing with a main competitor may read about a dramatic drop in sales in the next quarterly report. But then it's too late.

To assess the value of historical, aggregated, "hard" MIS information, consider two of the manager's prime uses for information—to identify problems and opportunities[8] and to build mental models (e.g., how the organization's budget system works, how customers buy products, how changes in the economy affect the organization). The evidence suggests that the manager identifies decision situations and builds models not with the aggregated abstractions an MIS provides but with specific tidbits of data.

Consider the words of Richard Neustadt, who studied the information-collecting habits of Presidents Roosevelt, Truman, and Eisenhower: "It is not information of a general sort that helps a President see personal stakes; not summaries, not surveys, not the *bland amalgams*. Rather . . . it is the odds and ends of *tangible detail* that pieced together in his mind illuminate the underside of issues put before him. To help himself he must reach out as widely as he can for every scrap of fact, opinion, gossip, bearing on his interests and relationships as President. He must become his own director of his own central intelligence."[9]

The manager's emphasis on this verbal media raises two important points. First, verbal information is stored in the brains of people. Only when people write this information down can it be stored in the files of the organization—whether in metal cabinets or on magnetic tape—and managers appar-

---

8. H. Edward Wrapp, "Good Managers Don't Make Policy Decisions," *Harvard Business Review* (September–October 1967): 91. Wrapp refers to this as spotting opportunities and relationships in the stream of operating problems and decisions; in his article, Wrapp raises a number of excellent points related to this analysis.

9. Richard E. Neustadt, *Presidential Power* (New York: John Wiley, 1960), pp. 153–154; italics added.

ently do not write down much of what they hear. Thus the strategic data bank of the organization is not in the memory of its computers but in the minds of its managers.

Second, managers' extensive use of verbal media helps to explain why they are reluctant to delegate tasks. It is not as if they can hand a dossier over to subordinates; they must take the time to dump memory—to tell subordinates all about the subject. But this could take so long that managers may find it easier to do the task themselves. Thus they are damned by their own information system to a dilemma of delegation—to do too much or to delegate to subordinates with inadequate briefing.

Folklore: Management is, or at least is quickly becoming, a science and a profession. By almost any definition of *science* and *profession,* this statement is false. Brief observation of any manager will quickly lay to rest the notion that managers practice a science. A science involves the enaction of systematic, analytically determined procedures or programs. If we do not even know what procedures managers use, how can we prescribe them by scientific analysis? And how can we call management a profession if we cannot specify what managers are to learn? For after all, a profession involves "knowledge of some department of learning or science" (*Random House Dictionary*).[10]

Fact: The managers' programs—to schedule time, process information, make decisions, and so on—remain locked deep inside their brains. Thus, to describe these programs, we rely on words like *judgment* and *intuition,* seldom stopping to realize that they are merely labels for our ignorance.

I was struck during my study by the fact that the executives I was observing—all very competent—are fundamentally indistinguishable from their counterparts of a hundred years ago (or a thousand years ago). The information they need differs, but they seek it in the same way—by word of mouth. Their decisions concern modern technology, but the procedures they use to make those decisions are the same as the procedures used by nineteenth-century managers. Even the computer, so important for the specialized work of the organization, has apparently had no influence on the work procedures of general managers. In fact, the manager is in a kind of loop, with increasingly heavy work pressures but no aid forthcoming from management science.

Considering the facts about managerial work, we can see that the manager's job is enormously complicated and difficult. Managers are overburdened with obligations yet cannot easily delegate their tasks. As a result, they are driven to overwork and forced to do many tasks superficially. Brevity, fragmentation, and verbal communication characterize their work. Yet these are the very characteristics of managerial work that have impeded scientific attempts to improve it. As a result, management scientists have concentrated on

---

10. For a more thorough, though rather different, discussion of this issue, *see* Kenneth R. Andrews, "Toward Professionalism in Business Management," *Harvard Business Review* (March–April 1969): 49.

the specialized functions of the organization, where it is easier to analyze the procedures and quantify the relevant information.[11]

But the pressures of a manager's job are becoming worse. Whereas managers once needed to respond only to owners and directors, they now find that subordinates with democratic norms continually reduce their freedom to issue unexplained orders and that a growing number of outside influences (consumer groups, government agencies, and so on) demand attention. Managers have had nowhere to turn for help. The first step in providing such help is to find out what the manager's job really is.

——— BACK TO A BASIC DESCRIPTION OF MANAGERIAL WORK

Earlier, I defined the manager as that person in charge of an organization or subunit. Besides CEOs, this definition would include vice presidents, bishops, foremen, hockey coaches, and prime ministers. All these "managers" are vested with formal authority over an organizational unit. From formal authority comes status, which leads to various interpersonal relations, and from these comes access to information. Information, in turn, enables the manager to make decisions and strategies for the unit.

The manager's job can be described in terms of various roles, or organized sets of behaviors identified with a position. My description, shown in *Exhibit 1*, comprises ten roles. As we shall see, formal authority gives rise to the three interpersonal roles, which in turn give rise to the three informational roles; these two sets of roles enable the manager to play the four decisional roles.

——— INTERPERSONAL ROLES

Three of the manager's roles arise directly from formal authority and involve basic interpersonal relationships. First is the *figurehead* role. As the head of an organizational unit, every manager must perform some ceremonial duties. The president greets the touring dignitaries. The foreman attends the wedding of a lathe operator. The sales manager takes an important customer to lunch.

The chief executives of my study spent 12% of their contact time on ceremonial duties; 17% of their incoming mail dealt with acknowledgments and requests related to their status. For example, a letter to a company president requested free merchandise for a crippled schoolchild; diplomas that needed to be signed were put on the desk of the school superintendent.

Duties that involve interpersonal roles may sometimes be routine, involving little serious communication and no important decision making.

---

11. C. Jackson Grayson, Jr., in "Management Science and Business Practice," *Harvard Business Review* (July–August 1973): 41, explains in similar terms why, as chairman of the Price Commission, he did not use those very techniques that he himself promoted in his earlier career as a management scientist.

EXHIBIT 1
The Manager's Roles

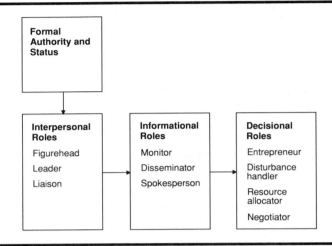

Nevertheless, they are important to the smooth functioning of an organization and cannot be ignored.

Managers are responsible for the work of the people of their unit. Their actions in this regard constitute the *leader* role. Some of these actions involve leadership directly—for example, in most organizations the managers are normally responsible for hiring and training their own staff.

In addition, there is the indirect exercise of the leader role. For example, every manager must motivate and encourage employees, somehow reconciling their individual needs with the goals of the organization. In virtually every contact with the manager, subordinates seeking leadership clues ask, "Does she approve?" "How would she like the report to turn out?" "Is she more interested in market share than in high profits?"

The influence of managers is most clearly seen in the leader role. Formal authority vests them with great potential power; leadership determines in large part how much of it they will realize.

The literature of management has always recognized the leader role, particularly those aspects of it related to motivation. In contrast, until recently it has hardly mentioned the *liaison* role, in which the manager makes contacts outside the vertical chain of command. This is remarkable in light of the finding of virtually every study of managerial work that managers spend as much time with peers and other people outside their units as they do with their own subordinates—and, surprisingly, very little time with their own superiors.

In Rosemary Stewart's diary study, the 160 British middle and top managers spent 47% of their time with peers, 41% of their time with people inside their unit, and only 12% of their time with their superiors. For Robert H. Guest's study of U.S. foremen, the figures were 44%, 46%, and 10%. The chief

EXHIBIT 2
The Chief Executive's Contacts

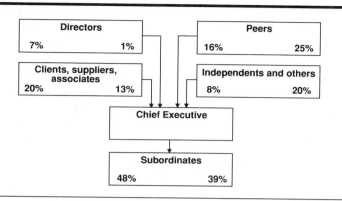

Note: The first figure indicates the proportion of total contact time spent with each group; the second figure indicates the proportion of mail from each group.

executives of my study averaged 44% of their contact time with people outside their organizations, 48% with subordinates, and 7% with directors and trustees.

The contacts the five CEOs made were with an incredibly wide range of people: subordinates; clients, business associates, and suppliers; and peers—managers of similar organizations, government and trade organization officials, fellow directors on outside boards, and independents with no relevant organizational affiliations. The chief executives' time with and mail from these groups is shown in *Exhibit 2*. Guest's study of foremen shows, likewise, that their contacts were numerous and wide-ranging, seldom involving fewer than 25 individuals and often more than 50.

━━━━ INFORMATIONAL ROLES

By virtue of interpersonal contacts, both with subordinates and with a network of contacts, the manager emerges as the nerve center of the organizational unit. The manager may not know everything but typically knows more than subordinates do.

Studies have shown this relationship to hold for all managers, from street gang leaders to U.S. presidents. In *The Human Group*, George C. Homans explains how, because they were at the center of the information flow in their own gangs and were also in close touch with other gang leaders, street gang leaders were better informed than any of their followers.[12] As for presidents,

12. George C. Homans, *The Human Group* (New York: Harcourt, Brace & World, 1950), based on the study by William F. Whyte entitled *Street Corner Society*, rev. ed. (Chicago: University of Chicago Press, 1955).

Richard Neustadt observes: "The essence of [Franklin] Roosevelt's technique for information-gathering was competition. 'He would call you in,' one of his aides once told me, 'and he'd ask you to get the story on some complicated business, and you'd come back after a couple of days of hard labor and present the juicy morsel you'd uncovered under a stone somewhere, and *then* you'd find out he knew all about it, along with something else you *didn't* know. Where he got this information from he wouldn't mention, usually, but after he had done this to you once or twice you got damn careful about *your* information.'"[13]

We can see where Roosevelt "got this information" when we consider the relationship between the interpersonal and informational roles. As leader, the manager has formal and easy access to every staff member. In addition, liaison contacts expose the manager to external information to which subordinates often lack access. Many of these contacts are with other managers of equal status, who are themselves nerve centers in their own organization. In this way, the manager develops a powerful database of information.

Processing information is a key part of the manager's job. In my study, the CEOs spent 40% of their contact time on activities devoted exclusively to the transmission of information; 70% of their incoming mail was purely informational (as opposed to requests for action). Managers don't leave meetings or hang up the telephone to get back to work. In large part, communication *is* their work. Three roles describe these informational aspects of managerial work.

As *monitor,* the manager is perpetually scanning the environment for information, interrogating liaison contacts and subordinates, and receiving unsolicited information, much of it as a result of the network of personal contacts. Remember that a good part of the information the manager collects in the monitor role arrives in verbal form, often as gossip, hearsay, and speculation.

In the *disseminator* role, the manager passes some privileged information directly to subordinates, who would otherwise have no access to it. When subordinates lack easy contact with one another, the manager may pass information from one to another.

In the *spokesperson* role, the manager sends some information to people outside the unit—a president makes a speech to lobby for an organization cause, or a foreman suggests a product modification to a supplier. In addition, as a spokesperson, every manager must inform and satisfy the influential people who control the organizational unit. For the foreman, this may simply involve keeping the plant manager informed about the flow of work through the shop.

The president of a large corporation, however, may spend a great amount of time dealing with a host of influences. Directors and shareholders must be advised about finances; consumer groups must be assured that the organization is fulfilling its social responsibilities; and government officials must be satisfied that the organization is abiding by the law.

---

13. Neustadt, *Presidential Power,* p. 157.

——— DECISIONAL ROLES

Information is not, of course, an end in itself; it is the basic input to decision making. One thing is clear in the study of managerial work: the manager plays the major role in the unit's decision-making system. As its formal authority, only the manager can commit the unit to important new courses of action; and as its nerve center, only the manager has full and current information to make the set of decisions that determines the unit's strategy. Four roles describe the manager as decision maker.

As *entrepreneurs,* managers seek to improve the unit, to adapt it to changing conditions in the environment. In the monitor role, presidents are constantly on the lookout for new ideas. When good ones appear, they initiate development projects that they may supervise or delegate to employees (perhaps with the stipulation that they must approve final proposals).

There are two interesting features about these development projects at the CEO level. First, these projects do not involve single decisions or even unified clusters of decisions. Rather, they emerge as a series of small decisions and actions sequenced over time. Apparently, chief executives prolong each project both to fit it into a busy, disjointed schedule, and so that they can comprehend complex issues gradually.

Second, the chief executives I studied supervised as many as 50 of these projects at the same time. Some projects entailed new products or processes; others involved public relations campaigns, improvement of the cash position, reorganization of a weak department, resolution of a morale problem in a foreign division, integration of computer operations, various acquisitions at different stages of development, and so on.

Chief executives appear to maintain a kind of inventory of the development projects in various stages of development. Like jugglers, they keep a number of projects in the air; periodically, one comes down, is given a new burst of energy, and sent back into orbit. At various intervals, they put new projects on-stream and discard old ones.

While the entrepreneur role describes the manager as the voluntary initiator of change, the *disturbance handler* role depicts the manager involuntarily responding to pressures. Here change is beyond the manager's control. The pressures of a situation are too severe to be ignored—a strike looms, a major customer has gone bankrupt, or a supplier reneges on a contract—so the manager must act.

Leonard R. Sayles, who has carried out appropriate research on the manager's job, likens the manager to a symphony orchestra conductor who must "maintain a melodious performance,"[14] while handling musicians' problems and other external disturbances. Indeed, every manager must spend a considerable amount of time responding to high-pressure disturbances. No

---

14. Leonard R. Sayles, *Managerial Behavior* (New York: McGraw-Hill, 1964), p. 162.

organization can be so well run, so standardized, that it has considered every contingency in the uncertain environment in advance. Disturbances arise not only because poor managers ignore situations until they reach crisis proportions but also because good managers cannot possibly anticipate all the consequences of the actions they take.

The third decisional role is that of *resource allocator*. The manager is responsible for deciding who will get what. Perhaps the most important resource the manager allocates is his or her own time. Access to the manager constitutes exposure to the unit's nerve center and decision maker. The manager is also charged with designing the unit's structure, that pattern of formal relationships that determines how work is to be divided and coordinated.

Also, as resource allocator, the manager authorizes the important decisions of the unit before they are implemented. By retaining this power, the manager can ensure that decisions are interrelated. To fragment this power encourages discontinuous decision making and a disjointed strategy.

There are a number of interesting features about the manager's authorization of others' decisions. First, despite the widespread use of capital budgeting procedures—a means of authorizing various capital expenditures at one time—executives in my study made a great many authorization decisions on an ad hoc basis. Apparently, many projects cannot wait or simply do not have the quantifiable costs and benefits that capital budgeting requires.

Second, I found that the chief executives faced incredibly complex choices. They had to consider the impact of each decision on other decisions and on the organization's strategy. They had to ensure that the decision would be acceptable to those who influence the organization, as well as ensure that resources would not be overextended. They had to understand the various costs and benefits as well as the feasibility of the proposal. They also had to consider questions of timing. All this was necessary for the simple approval of someone else's proposal. At the same time, however, the delay could lose time, while quick approval could be ill-considered and quick rejection might discourage the subordinate who had spent months developing a pet project.

One common solution to approving projects is to pick the person instead of the proposal. That is, the manager authorizes those projects presented by people whose judgment he or she trusts. But the manager cannot always use this simple dodge.

The final decisional role is that of *negotiator*. Managers spend considerable time in negotiations: the president of the football team works out a contract with the holdout superstar; the corporation president leads the company's contingent to negotiate a new strike issue; the foreman argues a grievance problem to its conclusion with the shop steward.

These negotiations are an integral part of the manager's job, for only he or she has the authority to commit organizational resources in "real time" and the nerve-center information that important negotiations require.

———— THE INTEGRATED JOB

It should be clear by now that these ten roles are not easily separable. In the terminology of the psychologist, they form a gestalt, an integrated whole. No role can be pulled out of the framework and the job be left intact. For example, a manager without liaison contacts lacks external information. As a result, that manager can neither disseminate the information that employees need nor make decisions that adequately reflect external conditions. (This is a problem for the new person in a managerial position, since he or she has to build up a network of contacts before making effective decisions.)

Here lies a clue to the problems of team management.[15] Two or three people cannot share a single managerial position unless they can act as one entity. This means that they cannot divide up the ten roles unless they can very carefully reintegrate them. The real difficulty lies with the informational roles. Unless there can be full sharing of managerial information—and, as I pointed out earlier, it is primarily verbal—team management breaks down. A single managerial job cannot be arbitrarily split, for example, into internal and external roles, for information from both sources must be brought to bear on the same decisions.

To say that the ten roles form a gestalt is not to say that all managers give equal attention to each role. In fact, I found in my review of the various research studies that sales managers seem to spend relatively more of their time in the interpersonal roles, presumably a reflection of the extrovert nature of the marketing activity. Production managers, on the other hand, give relatively more attention to the decisional roles, presumably a reflection of their concern with efficient work flow. And staff managers spend the most time in the informational roles, since they are experts who manage departments that advise other parts of the organization. Nevertheless, in all cases, the interpersonal, informational, and decisional roles remain inseparable.

———— TOWARD MORE EFFECTIVE MANAGEMENT

This description of managerial work should prove more important to managers than any prescription they might derive from it. That is to say, *the managers' effectiveness is significantly influenced by their insight into their own work.* Performance depends on how well a manager understands and responds to the pressures and dilemmas of the job. Thus managers who can be introspective about their work are likely to be effective at their jobs. The questions in *Exhibit 3* may sound rhetorical; none is meant to be. Even though the questions cannot be answered simply, the manager should address them.

---

15. *See* Richard C. Hodgson, Daniel J. Levinson, and Abraham Zaleznik, *The Executive Role Constellation* (Boston: Division of Research, Harvard Business School, 1965), for a discussion of the sharing of roles.

EXHIBIT 3
Self-Study Questions for Managers

1. Where do I get my information, and how? Can I make greater use of my contacts? Can other people do some of my scanning? In what areas is my knowledge weakest, and how can I get others to provide me with the information I need? Do I have sufficiently powerful mental models of those things I must understand within the organization and in its environment?

2. What information do I disseminate? How important is that information to my subordinates? Do I keep too much information to myself because disseminating it is time-consuming or inconvenient? How can I get more information to others so they can make better decisions?

3. Do I tend to act before information is in? Or do I wait so long for all the information that opportunities pass me by?

4. What pace of change am I asking my organization to tolerate? Is this change balanced so that our operations are neither excessively static nor overly disrupted? Have we sufficiently analyzed the impact of this change on the future of our organization?

5. Am I sufficiently well-informed to pass judgment on subordinates' proposals? Can I leave final authorization for more of the proposals with subordinates? Do we have problems of coordination because subordinates already make too many decisions independently?

6. What is my vision for this organization? Are these plans primarily in my own mind in loose form? Should I make them explicit to guide the decisions of others better? Or do I need flexibility to change them at will?

7. How do my subordinates react to my managerial style? Am I sufficiently sensitive to the powerful influence of my actions? Do I fully understand their reactions to my actions? Do I find an appropriate balance between encouragement and pressure? Do I stifle their initiative?

Let us take a look at three specific areas of concern. For the most part, the managerial logjams—the dilemma of delegation, the database centralized in one brain, the problems of working with the management scientist—revolve around the verbal nature of the manager's information. There are great dangers in centralizing the organization's data bank in the minds of its managers. When they leave, they take their memory with them. And when subordinates are out of convenient verbal reach of the manager, they are at an informational disadvantage.

The manager is challenged to find systematic ways to share privileged information. A regular debriefing session with key subordinates, a weekly memory dump on the dictating machine, maintaining a diary for limited circulation, or other similar methods may ease the logjam of work considerably. The time spent disseminating this information will be more than regained when decisions must be made. Of course, some will undoubtedly raise the question of confidentiality.

EXHIBIT 3
Self-Study Questions for Managers (Continued)

8. What kind of external relationships do I maintain, and how? Do I spend too much of my time maintaining them? Are there certain people whom I should get to know better?

9. Is here any system to my time scheduling, or am I just reacting to the pressures of the moment? Do I find the appropriate mix of activities or concentrate on one particular function or problem just because I find it interesting? Am I more efficient with particular kinds of work, at special times of the day or week? Does my schedule reflect this? Can someone else schedule my times (besides my secretary)?

10. Do I overwork? What effect does my work load have on my efficiency? Should I force myself to take breaks or to reduce the pace of my activity?

11. Am I too superficial in what I do? Can I really shift moods as quickly and frequently as my work requires? Should I decrease the amount of fragmentation and interruption in my work?

12. Do I spend too much time on current, tangible activities? Am I a slave to the action and excitement of my work, so that I am no longer able to concentrate on issues? Do key problems receive the attention they deserve? Should I spend more time reading and probing deeply into certain issues? Could I be more reflective? Should I be?

13. Do I use the different media appropriately? Do I know how to make the most of written communication? Do I rely excessively on face-to-face communication, thereby putting all but a few of my subordinates at an informational disadvantage? Do I schedule enough of my meetings on a regular basis? Do I spend enough time observing activities firsthand, or am I detached from the heart of my organization's activities?

14. How do I blend my personal rights and duties? Do my obligations consume all my time? How can I free myself from obligations to ensure that I am taking this organization where I want it to go? How can I turn my obligations to my advantage?

But managers would be well advised to weigh the risks of exposing privileged information against having subordinates who can make effective decisions.

If there is a single theme that runs through this reading, it is that the pressures of the job drive the manager to take on too much work, encourage interruption, respond quickly to every stimulus, seek the tangible and avoid the abstract, make decisions in small increments, and do everything abruptly.

Here again, the manager is challenged to deal consciously with the pressures of superficiality by giving serious attention to the issues that require it, by stepping back in order to see a broad picture, and by making use of analytical inputs. Although effective managers have to be adept at responding quickly to numerous and varying problems, the danger in managerial work is that they will respond to every issue equally (and that means abruptly) and that they will never work the tangible bits and pieces of information into a comprehensive picture of their world.

To create this comprehensive picture, managers can supplement their own models with those of specialists. Economists describe the functioning of markets, operations researchers simulate financial flow processes, and behavioral scientists explain the needs and goals of people. The best of these models can be searched out and learned.

In dealing with complex issues, the senior manager has much to gain from a close relationship with the organization's own management scientists. They have something important that the manager lacks—time to probe complex issues. An effective working relationship hinges on the resolution of what a colleague and I have called "the planning dilemma."[16] Managers have the information and the authority; analysts have the time and the technology. A successful working relationship between the two will be effected when the manager learns to share information and the analyst learns to adapt to the manager's needs. For the analyst, adaptation means worrying less about the elegance of the method and more about its speed and flexibility.

Analysts can help the top manager schedule time, feed in analytical information, monitor projects, develop models to aid in making choices, design contingency plans for disturbances that can be anticipated, and conduct "quick and dirty" analyses for those that cannot. But there can be no cooperation if the analysts are out of the mainstream of the manager's information flow.

The manager is challenged to gain control of his or her own time by turning obligations into advantages and by turning those things he or she wishes to do into obligations. The chief executives of my study initiated only 32% of their own contacts (and another 5% by mutual agreement). And yet to a considerable extent they seemed to control their time. There were two key factors that enabled them to do so.

First, managers have to spend so much time discharging obligations that if they were to view them as just that, they would leave no mark on the organization. Unsuccessful managers blame failure on the obligations. Effective managers turn obligations to advantages. A speech is a chance to lobby for a cause; a meeting is a chance to reorganize a weak department; a visit to an important customer is a chance to extract trade information.

Second, the manager frees some time to do the things that he or she—perhaps no one else—considers important by turning them into obligations. Free time is made, not found. Hoping to leave some time open for contemplation or general planning is tantamount to hoping that the pressures of the job will go away. Managers who want to innovate initiate projects and obligate others to report back to them. Managers who need certain environmental information establish channels that will automatically keep them informed. Managers who have to tour facilities commit themselves publicly.

---

16. James S. Hekimian and Henry Mintzberg, "The Planning Dilemma," *The Management Review* (May 1968): 4.

THE EDUCATOR'S JOB

Finally, a word about the training of managers. Our management schools have done an admirable job of training the organization's specialists—management scientists, marketing researchers, accountants, and organizational-development specialists. But for the most part, they have not trained managers.[17]

Management schools will begin the serious training of managers when skill training takes a serious place next to cognitive learning. Cognitive learning is detached and informational, like reading a book or listening to a lecture. No doubt much important cognitive material must be assimilated by the manager-to-be. But cognitive learning no more makes a manager than it does a swimmer. The latter will drown the first time she jumps into the water if her coach never takes her out of the lecture hall, gets her wet, and gives her feedback on her performance.

In other words, we are taught a skill through practice plus feedback, whether in a real or a simulated situation. Our management schools need to identify the skills managers use, select students who show potential in these skills, put the students into situations where these skills can be practiced and developed, and then give them systematic feedback on their performance.

My description of managerial work suggests a number of important managerial skills—developing peer relationships, carrying out negotiations, motivating subordinates, resolving conflicts, establishing information networks and subsequently disseminating information, making decisions in conditions of extreme ambiguity, and allocating resources. Above all, the manager needs to be introspective in order to continue to learn on the job.

No job is more vital to our society than that of the manager. The manager determines whether our social institutions will serve us well or whether they will squander our talents and resources. It is time to strip away the folklore about managerial work and study it realistically so that we can begin the difficult task of making significant improvements in its performance.

* * *

Fifteen years after this reading was published, the author wrote the following commentary.

RETROSPECTIVE COMMENTARY

Over the years, one reaction has dominated the comments I have received from managers who read "The Manager's Job: Folklore and Fact":

---

17. *See* J. Sterling Livingston, "Myth of the Well-Educated Manager," *Harvard Business Review* (January–February 1971): 79.

"You make me feel so good. I thought all those other managers were planning, organizing, coordinating, and controlling, while I was busy being interrupted, jumping from one issue to another, and trying to keep the lid on the chaos." Yet everything in this reading must have been patently obvious to these people. Why such a reaction to reading what they already knew?

Conversely, how to explain the very different reaction of two media people who called to line up interviews after an article based on this one appeared in the *New York Times.* "Are we glad someone finally let managers have it," both said in passing, a comment that still takes me aback. True, they had read only the account in the *Times,* but that no more let managers have it than did this reading. Why that reaction?

One explanation grows out of the way I now see this reading—as proposing not so much another view of management as another face of it. I like to call it the insightful face, in contrast to the long-dominant professional or cerebral face. One stresses commitment, the other calculation; one sees the world with integrated perspective, the other figures it as the components of a portfolio. The cerebral face operates with the words and numbers of rationality; the insightful face is rooted in the images and feel of a manager's integrity.

Each of these faces implies a different kind of knowing, and that, I believe, explains many managers' reaction to this article. Rationally, they "knew" what managers did—planned, organized, coordinated, and controlled. But deep down that did not feel quite right. The description in this article may have come closer to what they really knew. As for those media people, they weren't railing against management as such but against the cerebral form of management, so pervasive, that they saw impersonalizing the world around them.

In practice, management has to be two-faced—there has to be a balance between the cerebral and the insightful. So, for example, I realized originally that managerial communication was largely oral and that the advent of the computer had not changed anything fundamental in the executive suite—a conclusion I continue to hold. (The greatest threat the personal computer poses is that managers will take it seriously and come to believe that they can manage by remaining in their offices and looking at displays of digital characters.) But I also thought that the dilemma of delegating could be dealt with by periodic debriefings—disseminating words. Now, however, I believe that managers need more ways to convey the images and impressions they carry inside of them. This explains the renewed interest in strategic vision, in culture, and in the roles of intuition and insight in management.

The ten roles I used to describe the manager's job also reflect management's cerebral face, in that they decompose the job more than capture the integration. Indeed, my effort to show a sequence among these roles now seems more consistent with the traditional face of management work than an insightful one. Might we not just as well say that people throughout the organization take actions that inform managers who, by making sense of those actions, develop images and visions that inspire people to subsequent efforts?

Perhaps my greatest disappointment about the research reported here is that it did not stimulate new efforts. In a world so concerned with management, much of the popular literature is superficial and the academic research pedestrian. Certainly, many studies have been carried out over the last 15 years, but the vast majority sought to replicate earlier research. In particular, we remain grossly ignorant about the fundamental content of the manager's job and have barely addressed the major issues and dilemmas in its practice.

But superficiality is not only a problem of the literature. It is also an occupational hazard of the manager's job. Originally I believed this problem could be dealt with; now I see it as inherent in the job. This is because managing insightfully depends on the direct experience and personal knowledge that come from intimate contact. But in organizations grown larger and more diversified, that becomes difficult to achieve. And so managers turn increasingly to the cerebral face, and the delicate balance between the two faces is lost.

Certainly, some organizations manage to sustain their humanity despite their large size—as Tom Peters and Robert Waterman show in their book *In Search of Excellence.* But that book attained its outstanding success precisely because it is about the exceptions, about the organizations so many of us long to be a part of—not the organizations in which we actually work.

Fifteen years ago, I stated that "No job is more vital to our society than that of the manager. It is the manager who determines whether our social institutions serve us well or whether they squander our talents and resources." Now, more than ever, we must strip away the folklore of the manager's job and begin to face its difficult facts.

Copyright © 1990; revised 1991.

——— DISCUSSION QUESTIONS

1. The author gives four instances of folklore and fact in managerial work. Give examples that illustrate this folklore/fact dichotomy from your own work experience.

2. The author discusses the ten roles of a manager and the need to establish an integrated whole. He then points out the weaknesses of team management. Do you agree or disagree with this critique of team management?

3. In his description of more effective management, the author presents the challenges a manager must accept and turn to his or her advantage. Give examples from your own life experience in which you have turned challenges to your advantage.

4. Philosophers have admonished us to "Know thyself." Looking at the list of *Self-Study Questions for Managers*, honestly take an inventory of your strengths and weaknesses. (Share them with a classmate and ask for honest feedback. Remember, it's information.)

What are your key strengths? What are weaknesses that you might want to work on?

5. In his retrospective, Mintzberg states, "In practice, management has to be two-faced—there has to be a balance between the cerebral and the insightful." What does the author mean by this assertion?

Power, Dependence, and Effective Management

2

JOHN P. KOTTER

People in general and Americans in particular have always been suspicious of power—the United States was born out of a rebellion, and our political processes were designed to guard against the abuse of power. However, asserts the author of this reading, the negative aspects of power have blinded people to its benefits and uses. Without power, people cannot accomplish very much. This is especially true in management.

As organizations have grown, the author maintains, the number of people that managers need to get their jobs done has increased. As a result, it has become more difficult, if not impossible, for managers to achieve their goals through persuasion or through formal authority alone. They need power. The author describes four different types of power that managers can use, along with persuasion, to influence others. Skillful managers, he concludes, exercise their power with maturity, skill, and sensitivity to the obligations and risks involved.

Americans, as a rule, are not very comfortable with power or with its dynamics. We often distrust and question the motives of people who we think actively seek power. We have a certain fear of being manipulated. Even those people who think the dynamics of power are inevitable and needed often feel somewhat guilty when they themselves mobilize and use power. Simply put, the overall attitude and feeling toward power, which can easily be traced to the nation's very birth, is negative.

One of the many consequences of this attitude is that power as a topic for rational study and dialogue has not received much attention, even in managerial circles. If the reader doubts this, all he or she need do is flip through some textbooks, journals, or advanced management course descriptions. The word *power* rarely appears.

Note: This reading is based on data from a clinical study of a highly diverse group of 26 organizations including large and small, public and private, manufacturing and service organizations. The study was funded by the Division of Research at the Harvard Business School. As part of the study process, the author interviewed about 250 managers.

This lack of attention to the subject of power merely adds to the already enormous confusion and misunderstanding surrounding the topic of power and management. And this misunderstanding is becoming increasingly burdensome because in today's large and complex organizations the effective performance of most managerial jobs requires one to be skilled at the acquisition and use of power.

From my own observations, I suspect that a large number of managers—especially the young, well-educated ones—perform significantly below their potential because they do not understand the dynamics of power and because they have not nurtured and developed the instincts needed to effectively acquire and use power.

In this reading I hope to clear up some of the confusion regarding power and managerial work by providing tentative answers to three questions:

1. Why are the dynamics of power necessarily an important part of managerial processes?
2. How do effective managers acquire power?
3. How and for what purposes do effective managers use power?

I will not address questions related to the misuse of power, but not because I think they are unimportant. The fact that some managers, some of the time, acquire and use power mostly for their own aggrandizement is obviously a very important issue that deserves attention and careful study. But that is a complex topic unto itself and one that has already received more attention than the subject of this reading.

——— RECOGNIZING DEPENDENCE IN THE MANAGER'S JOB

One of the distinguishing characteristics of typical managers is how dependent they are on the activities of a variety of other people to perform their jobs effectively.[1] Unlike doctors and mathematicians, whose performance is more directly dependent on their own talents and efforts, a manager can be dependent in varying degrees on superiors, subordinates, peers in other parts of the organization, the subordinates of peers, outside suppliers, customers, competitors, unions, regulating agencies, and many others.

These dependency relationships are an inherent part of managerial jobs because of two organizational facts of life: division of labor and limited resources. Because the work in organizations is divided into specialized divisions, departments, and jobs, managers are made directly or indirectly dependent on many others for information, staff services, and cooperation in general. Because

---

1. *See* Leonard R. Sayles, *Managerial Behavior: Administration in Complex Organization* (New York: McGraw-Hill, 1964) as well as Rosemary Stewart, *Managers and Their Jobs* (London: Macmillan, 1967) and *Contrasts in Management* (London: McGraw-Hill, 1976).

of their organizations' limited resources, managers are also dependent on their external environments for support. Without some minimal cooperation from suppliers, competitors, unions, regulatory agencies, and customers, managers cannot help their organizations survive and achieve their objectives.

Dealing with these dependencies and the manager's subsequent vulnerability is an important and difficult part of a manager's job because, while it is theoretically possible that all of these people and organizations would automatically act in just the manner that a manager wants and needs, such is almost never the case in reality. All the people on whom a manager is dependent have limited time, energy, and talent, for which there are competing demands.

Some people may be uncooperative because they are too busy elsewhere, and some because they are not really capable of helping. Others may well have goals, values, and beliefs that are quite different and in conflict with the manager's and may therefore have no desire whatsoever to help or cooperate. This is obviously true of a competing company and sometimes of a union, but it can also apply to a boss who is feeling threatened by a manager's career progress or to a peer whose objectives clash with the manager's.

Indeed, managers often find themselves dependent on many people (and things) whom they do not directly control and who are not cooperating. This is the key to one of the biggest frustrations managers feel in their jobs, even in the top ones, which the following example illustrates:

> After nearly a year of rumors, it was finally announced that the president of ABC Corporation had been elected chairman of the board and that Jim Franklin, the vice president of finance, would replace him as president. While everyone at ABC was aware that a shift would take place soon, it was not at all clear before the announcement who would be the next president. Most people had guessed it would be Phil Cook, the marketing vice president.
>
> Nine months into his job as chief executive officer, Franklin found that Phil Cook (still the marketing vice president) seemed to be fighting him in small and subtle ways. There was never anything blatant, but Cook just did not cooperate with Franklin as the other vice presidents did. Shortly after being elected, Franklin had tried to bypass what he saw as a potential conflict with Cook by telling him that he would understand if Cook would prefer to move somewhere else where he could be a CEO also. Franklin said that it would be a big loss to the company but that he would be willing to help Cook in a number of ways if he wanted to look for a presidential opportunity elsewhere. Cook had thanked him but had said that family and community commitments would prevent him from relocating and all CEO opportunities were bound to be in a different city.
>
> Since the situation did not improve after the tenth and eleventh months, Franklin seriously considered forcing Cook out. When he thought about the consequences of such a move, Franklin became more and more aware of just how dependent he was on Cook. Marketing and sales were generally the keys to success in their industry,

and the company's sales force was one of the best, if not the best, in the industry. Cook had been with the company for 25 years. He had built a strong personal relationship with many of the people in the sales force and was universally popular. A mass exodus just might occur if Cook were fired. The loss of a large number of salespeople, or even a lot of turmoil in the department, could have a serious effect on the company's performance.

After one year as chief executive officer, Franklin found that the situation between Cook and himself had not improved and had become a constant source of frustration.

As a person gains more formal authority in an organization, the areas in which he or she is vulnerable increase and become more complex rather than the reverse. As the previous example suggests, it is not at all unusual for the president of an organization to be in a highly dependent position, a fact often not apparent to either the outsider or to the lower-level manager who covets the president's job.

A considerable amount of the behavior of highly successful managers that seems inexplicable in light of what management texts usually tell us managers do becomes understandable when one considers a manager's need for, and efforts at, managing his or her relationships with others.[2] To be able to plan, organize, budget, staff, control, and evaluate, managers need some control over the many people on whom they are dependent. Trying to control others solely by directing them and on the basis of the power associated with one's position simply will not work—first, because managers are always dependent on some people over whom they have no formal authority, and second, because virtually no one in modern organizations will passively accept and completely obey a constant stream of orders from someone just because he or she is the "boss."

Trying to influence others by means of persuasion alone will not work either. Although it is very powerful and possibly the single most important method of influence, persuasion has some serious drawbacks too. To make it work requires time (often lots of it), skill, and information on the part of the persuader. And persuasion can fail simply because the other person chooses not to listen or does not listen carefully.

This is not to say that directing people on the basis of the formal power of one's position and persuasion are not important means by which successful managers cope. They obviously are. But, even taken together, they are not usually enough.

Successful managers cope with their dependence on others by being sensitive to it, by eliminating or avoiding unnecessary dependence and by establishing power over those others. Good managers then use that power to

---

2. I am talking about the type of inexplicable differences that Henry Mintzberg has found; *see* his article "The Manager's Job: Folklore and Fact," *Harvard Business Review* (March–April 1990): 163.

help them plan, organize, staff, budget, evaluate, and so on. *In other words, it is primarily because of the dependence inherent in managerial jobs that the dynamics of power necessarily form an important part of a manager's processes.*

An argument that took place during a middle-management training seminar I participated in a few years ago helps illustrate further this important relationship between a manager's need for power and the degree of his or her dependence on others:

> Two participants, both managers in their thirties, got into a heated disagreement regarding the acquisition and use of power by managers. One took the position that power was absolutely central to managerial work, while the other argued that it was virtually irrelevant. In support of their positions, each described a very "successful" manager with whom he worked. In one of these examples, the manager seemed to be constantly developing and using power, while in the other, such behavior was rare. Subsequently, both seminar participants were asked to describe their successful managers' jobs in terms of the dependence *inherent* in those jobs.
>
> The young manager who felt power was unimportant described a staff vice president in a small company who was dependent only on his immediate subordinates, his peers, and his boss. This person, Joe Phillips, had to depend on his subordinates to do their jobs appropriately, but, if necessary, he could fill in for any of them or secure replacement for them rather easily. He also had considerable formal authority over them; that is, he could give them raises and new assignments, recommend promotions, and fire them. He was moderately dependent on the other four vice presidents in the company for information and cooperation. They were likewise dependent on him. The president had considerable formal authority over Phillips but was also moderately dependent on him for help, expert advice, the service his staff performed, other information, and general cooperation.
>
> The second young manager—the one who felt power was very important—described a service department manager, Sam Weller, in a large, complex, and growing company who was in quite a different position. Weller was dependent not only on his boss for rewards and information, but also on 30 other individuals who made up the divisional and corporate top management. And while his boss, like Phillips's, was moderately dependent on him too, most of the top managers were not. Because Weller's subordinates, unlike Phillips's, had people reporting to them, Weller was dependent not only on his subordinates but also on his subordinates' subordinates. Because he could not himself easily replace or do most of their technical jobs, unlike Phillips, he was very dependent on all these people.
>
> In addition, for critical supplies, Weller was dependent on two other department managers in the division. Without their timely help, it was impossible for his department to do its job. These departments, however, did not have similar needs for Weller's help and cooperation. Weller was also dependent on local labor union officials and on a

federal agency that regulated the division's industry. Both could shut his division down if they wanted.

Finally, Weller was dependent on two outside suppliers of key materials. Because of the volume of his department's purchase relative to the size of these two companies, he had little power over them.

Under these circumstances, it is hardly surprising that Sam Weller had to spend considerable time and effort acquiring and using power to manage his many dependencies, while Joe Phillips did not.

As this example also illustrates, not all management jobs require an incumbent to be able to provide the same amount of successful power-oriented behavior. But most management jobs today are more like Weller's than Phillips's. And, perhaps more important, the trend over the past two or three decades is away from jobs like Phillips's and toward jobs like Weller's. So long as our technologies continue to become more complex, the average organization continues to grow larger, and the average industry continues to become more competitive and regulated, that trend will continue; as it does so, the effective acquisition and use of power by managers will become even more important.

—— ESTABLISHING POWER IN RELATIONSHIPS

To help cope with the dependency relationships inherent in their jobs, effective managers create, increase, or maintain four different types of power over others.[3] Having power based in these areas puts the manager in a position both to influence those people on whom he or she is dependent when necessary and to avoid being hurt by any of them.

SENSE OF OBLIGATION

One of the ways that successful managers generate power in their relationships with others is to create a sense of obligation in those others. When the manager is successful, the others feel that they should—rightly—allow the manager to influence them within certain limits.

Successful managers often go out of their way to do favors for people who they expect will feel an obligation to return those favors. As can be seen in the following description of a manager by one of his subordinates, some people are very skilled at identifying opportunities for doing favors that cost them very little but that others appreciate very much:

---

3. These categories closely resemble the five developed by John R. P. French and Bertram Raven; see "The Base of Social Power," *Group Dynamics: Research and Theory,* Dorwin Cartwright and Alvin Zandler, eds. (New York: Harper & Row, 1968), Chapter 20. Three of the categories are similar to the types of "authority"-based power described by Max Weber in *The Theory of Social and Economic Organization* (New York: Free Press, 1947).

Most of the people here would walk over hot coals in their bare feet if my boss asked them to. He has an incredible capacity to do little things that mean a lot to people. Today, for example, in his junk mail he came across an advertisement for something that one of my subordinates had in passing once mentioned that he was shopping for. So my boss routed it to him. That probably took 15 seconds of his time, and yet my subordinate really appreciated it. To give you another example, two weeks ago he somehow learned that the purchasing manager's mother had died. On his way home that night, he stopped off at the funeral parlor. Our purchasing manager was, of course, there at the time. I bet he'll remember that brief visit for quite a while.

Recognizing that most people believe that friendship carries with it certain obligations ("A friend in need . . ."), successful managers often try to develop true friendships with those on whom they are dependent. They will also make formal and informal deals in which they give something up in exchange for certain future obligations.

BELIEF IN A MANAGER'S EXPERTISE

A second way successful managers gain power is by building reputations as experts in certain matters. Believing in the manager's expertise, others will often defer to the manager on those matters. Managers usually establish this type of power through visible achievement. The larger the achievement and the more visible it is, the more power the manager tends to develop.

One of the reasons that managers display concern about their professional reputations and their track records is that these have an impact on others' beliefs about their expertise. These factors become particularly important in large settings, where most people have only secondhand information about most other people's professional competence, as the following shows:

Herb Randley and Bert Kline were both 35-year-old vice presidents in a large research and development organization. According to their closest associates, they were equally bright and competent in their technical fields and as managers. Yet Randley had a much stronger professional reputation in most parts of the company, and his ideas generally carried much more weight. Close friends and associates claim the reason that Randley is so much more powerful is related to a number of tactics that he has used more than Kline has.

Randley has published more scientific papers and managerial articles than Kline. Randley has been more selective in the assignments he has worked on, choosing those that are visible and that require his strong suits. He has given more speeches and presentations on projects that are his own achievements. And in meetings in general, he is allegedly forceful in areas where he has expertise and silent in those where he does not.

IDENTIFICATION WITH A MANAGER

A third method by which managers gain power is by fostering others' unconscious identification with them or with ideas they stand for. Sigmund Freud was the first to describe this phenomenon, which is most clearly seen in the way people look up to charismatic leaders. Generally, the more a person finds a manager both consciously and (more important) unconsciously an ideal person, the more he or she will defer to that manager.

Managers develop power based on others' idealized views of them in a number of ways. They try to look and behave in ways that others respect. They go out of their way to be visible to their employees and to give speeches about their organizational goals, values, and ideals. They even consider, while making hiring and promotion decisions, whether they will be able to develop this type of power over the candidates:

> One vice president of sales in a moderate-sized manufacturing com-
> pany was reputed to be so much in control of his sales force that he
> could get them to respond to new and different marketing programs
> in a third of the time taken by the company's best competitors. His
> power over his employees was based primarily on their strong iden-
> tification with him and what he stood for. Emigrating to the United
> States at age 17, this person worked his way up "from nothing." When
> made a sales manager in 1965, he began recruiting other young im-
> migrants and sons of immigrants from his former country. When made
> vice president of sales in 1970, he continued to do so. In 1975, 85% of
> his sales force was made up of people whom he hired directly or who
> were hired by others he brought in.

PERCEIVED DEPENDENCE ON A MANAGER

The final way that an effective manager often gains power is by feeding others' beliefs that they are dependent on the manager either for help or for not being hurt. The more they perceive they are dependent, the more most people will be inclined to cooperate with such a manager.

There are two methods that successful managers often use to create perceived dependence.

Finding and Acquiring Resources   In the first, the manager identifies and secures (if necessary) resources that another person requires to perform the job, resources that he or she does not possess, and that are not readily available elsewhere. These resources include such things as authority to make certain decisions; control of money, equipment, and office space; access to important people; information and control of information channels; and subordinates. Then the manager takes action so that the other person correctly perceives that the manager has such resources and is willing and ready to use them to help (or hinder) the other person. Consider the following extreme—but true—example.

> When young Tim Babcock was put in charge of a division of a large manufacturing company and told to "turn it around," he spent the first few weeks studying it from afar. He decided that the division was in disastrous shape and that he would need to take many large steps quickly to save it. To be able to do that, he realized he needed to develop considerable power fast over most of the division's management and staff. He did the following:
>
> 1. He gave the division's management two hours' notice of his arrival.
> 2. He arrived in a limousine with six assistants.
> 3. He immediately called a meeting of the 40 top managers.
> 4. He outlined briefly his assessment of the situation, his commitment to turn things around, and the basic direction he wanted things to move in.
> 5. He then fired the four top managers in the room and told them that they had to be out of the building in two hours.
> 6. He then said he would personally dedicate himself to sabotaging the career of anyone who tried to block his efforts to save the division.
> 7. He ended the 60-minute meeting by announcing that his assistants would set up appointments for him with each of them starting at 7:00 the next morning.
>
> Throughout the critical six-month period that followed, those who remained at the division generally cooperated energetically with Mr. Babcock.

Affecting Perceptions of Resources   A second way effective managers gain these types of power is by influencing other persons' perceptions of the manager's resources.[4] In settings where many people are involved and where the manager does not interact continuously with those he or she is dependent on, those people will seldom possess hard facts regarding what relevant resources the manager commands directly or indirectly (through others), what resources he or she will command in the future, or how prepared he or she is to use those resources to help or hinder them. They will be forced to make their own judgments.

Insofar as managers can influence people's judgments, they can generate much more power than one would generally ascribe to them in light of the reality of their resources.

In trying to influence people's judgments, managers pay considerable attention to the "trappings" of power and to their own reputations and images. Among other actions, they sometimes carefully select, decorate, and arrange their offices in ways that give signs of power. They associate with

---

4. For an excellent discussion of this method, *see* Richard E. Neustadt, *Presidential Power* (New York: John Wiley, 1960).

people or organizations that are known to be powerful or that others perceive as powerful. Managers selectively foster rumors concerning their own power. Indeed, those who are particularly skilled at creating power in this way tend to be very sensitive to the impressions that all their actions might have on others.

FORMAL AUTHORITY

Before discussing how managers use their power to influence others, it is useful to see how formal authority relates to power. By *formal authority*, I mean those elements that automatically come with a managerial job—perhaps a title, an office, a budget, the right to make certain decisions, a set of subordinates, a reporting relationship, and so on.

Effective managers use the elements of formal authority as resources to help them develop any or all of the four types of power previously discussed, just as they use other resources (such as their education). Two managers with the same formal authority can have very different amounts of power entirely because of the way they have used that authority. For example:

> By sitting down with employees who are new or with people who are starting new projects and clearly specifying who has the formal authority to do what, one manager creates a strong sense of obligation in others to defer to her authority later.
>
> By selectively withholding or giving the high-quality service his department can provide other departments, one manager makes other managers clearly perceive that they are dependent on him.

On its own, then, formal authority does not guarantee a certain amount of power; it is only a resource that managers can use to generate power in their relationships.

—— EXERCISING POWER TO INFLUENCE OTHERS

Successful managers use the power they develop in their relationships, along with persuasion, to influence people on whom they are dependent to behave in ways that make it possible for the managers to get their jobs done effectively. They use their power to influence others directly, face to face, and in more indirect ways. (See the *Exhibit* on the next page.)

FACE-TO-FACE INFLUENCE

The chief advantage of influencing others directly by exercising any of the types of power is speed. If the power exists and the manager correctly

EXHIBIT
Methods of Influence

FACE-TO-FACE METHODS	WHAT THEY CAN INFLUENCE	ADVANTAGES	DRAWBACKS
Exercise power based on obligation.	Behavior within zone that the other perceives as legitimate in light of the obligation.	Quick. Requires no outlay of tangible resources.	If the request is outside the acceptable zone, it will fail; if it is too far outside, others might see it as illegitimate.
Exercise power based on perceived expertise.	Attitudes and behavior within the zone of perceived expertise.	Quick. Requires no outlay of tangible resources.	If the request is outside the acceptable zone, it will fail; if it is too far outside, others might see it as illegitimate.
Exercise power based on identification with a manager.	Attitudes and behavior that are not in conflict with the ideals that underlie the identification.	Quick. Requires no expenditure of limited resources.	Restricted to influence attempts that are not in conflict with the ideals that underlie the identification.
Exercise power based on perceived dependence.	Wide range of behavior that can be monitored.	Quick. Can often succeed when other methods fail.	Repeated influence attempts encourage the other to gain power over the influencer.
Coercively exercise power based on perceived dependence.	Wide range of behavior that can be easily monitored.	Quick. Can often succeed when other methods fail.	Invites retaliation. Very risky.
Use persuasion.	Very wide range of attitudes and behavior.	Can produce internalized motivation that does not require monitoring. Requires no power or outlay of scarce material resources.	Can be very time-consuming. Requires other person to listen.
Combine these methods.	Depends on the exact combination.	Can be more potent and less risky than using a single method.	More costly than using a single method.

INDIRECT METHODS	WHAT THEY CAN INFLUENCE	ADVANTAGES	DRAWBACKS
Manipulate the other's environment by using any or all of the face-to-face methods.	Wide range of behavior and attitudes.	Can succeed when face-to-face methods fail.	Can be time-consuming. Is complex to implement. Is very risky, especially if used frequently.
Change the forces that continuously act on the individual: Formal organizational arrangements. Informal social arrangements. Technology. Resources available. Statement of organizational goals.	Wide range of behavior and attitudes on a continuous basis.	Has continuous influence, not just a one-shot effect. Can have a very powerful impact.	Often requires a considerable power outlay to achieve.

understands the nature and strength of it, he or she can influence the other person with nothing more than a brief request or command:

> Jones thinks Smith feels obliged to him for past favors. Furthermore, Jones thinks that his request to speed up a project by two days probably falls within a zone that Smith would consider legitimate in light of his own definition of his obligation to Jones. So Jones simply calls Smith and makes his request. Smith pauses for only a second and says yes, he'll do it.

> Manager Johnson has some power based on perceived dependence over manager Baker. When Johnson tells Baker that he wants a report done in 24 hours, Baker grudgingly considers the costs of compliance, of noncompliance, and of complaining to higher authorities. He decides that doing the report is the least costly action and tells Johnson he will do it.

> Porter identifies strongly with Marquette, an older manager who is not her boss. Porter thinks Marquette is the epitome of a great manager and tries to model herself after her. When Marquette asks Porter to work on a special project "that could be very valuable in improving the company's ability to meet new competitive products," Porter agrees without hesitation and works 15 hours per week above and beyond her normal hours to get the project done and done well.

When used to influence others, each of the four types of power has different advantages and drawbacks. For example, power based on perceived expertise or on identification with a manager can often be used to influence attitudes as well as someone's immediate behavior and thus can have a lasting impact. It is very difficult to influence attitudes by using power based on perceived dependence, but if it can be done, it usually has the advantage of being able to influence a much broader range of behavior than the other methods do. When exercising power based on perceived expertise, for example, one can only influence attitudes and behavior within that narrow zone defined by the expertise.

The drawbacks associated with the use of power based on perceived dependence are particularly important to recognize. A person who feels dependent on a manager for rewards (or lack of punishments) might quickly agree to a request from the manager but then not follow through—especially if the manager cannot easily find out if the person has obeyed or not. Repeated influence attempts based on perceived dependence also seem to encourage the other person to try to gain some power to balance the manager's. And perhaps most important, using power based on perceived dependence in a coercive way is very risky. Coercion invites retaliation.

For instance, in the example in which Tim Babcock took such extreme steps to save the division he was assigned to "turn around," his development and use of power based on perceived dependence could have led to mass resignation and the collapse of the division. Babcock fully recognized this risk, however, and behaved as he did because he felt there was simply *no other way* that he could gain the very large amount of quick cooperation needed to save the division.

Effective managers will often draw on more than one form of power to influence someone, or they will combine power with persuasion. In general, they do so because a combination can be more potent and less risky than any single method, as the following description shows:

> One of the best managers we have in the company has lots of power based on one thing or another over most people. But he seldom if ever just tells or asks someone to do something. He almost always takes a few minutes to try to persuade them. The power he has over people generally induces them to listen carefully and certainly disposes them to be influenced. That, of course, makes the persuasion process go quickly and easily. And he never risks getting the other person mad or upset by making what that person thinks is an unfair request or command.

It is also common for managers not to coercively exercise power based on perceived dependence by itself, but to combine it with other methods to reduce the risk of retaliation. In this way, managers are able to have a large impact without leaving the bitter aftertaste of punishment alone.

INDIRECT INFLUENCE METHODS

Effective managers also rely on two types of less direct methods to influence those on whom they are dependent. In the first way, they use any or all of the face-to-face methods to influence other people, who in turn have some specific impact on a desired person.

Product manager Stein needed plant manager Billings to "sign off" on a new product idea (Product X) which Billings thought was terrible. Stein decided that there was no way he could logically persuade Billings because Billings just would not listen to him. With time, Stein felt, he could have broken through that barrier. But he did not have that time. Stein also realized that Billings would never, just because of some deal or favor, sign off on a product he did not believe in. Stein also felt it not worth the risk of trying to force Billings to sign off, so here is what he did:

> On Monday, Stein got Reynolds, a person Billings respected, to send Billings two market research studies that were very favorable to Product X, with a note attached saying, "Have you seen this? I found them rather surprising. I am not sure if I entirely believe them, but still . . ."
>
> On Tuesday, Stein got a representative of one of the company's biggest customers to mention casually to Billings on the phone that he had

heard a rumor about Product X being introduced soon and was "glad to see you guys are on your toes as usual."

On Wednesday, Stein had two industrial engineers stand about three feet away from Billings as they were waiting for a meeting to begin and talk about the favorable test results on Product X.

On Thursday, Stein set up a meeting to talk about Product X with Billings and invited only people whom Billings liked or respected and who also felt favorably about Product X.

On Friday, Stein went to see Billings and asked him if he was willing to sign off on Product X. He was.

This type of manipulation of the environments of others can influence both behavior and attitudes and can often succeed when other influence methods fail. But it has a number of serious drawbacks. It takes considerable time and energy, and it is quite risky. Many people think it is wrong to try to influence others in this way, even people who, without consciously recognizing it, use this technique themselves. If they think someone is trying, or has tried, to manipulate them, they may retaliate. Furthermore, people who gain the reputation of being manipulators seriously undermine their own capacities for developing power and for influencing others. Almost no one, for example, will want to identify with a manipulator. And virtually no one accepts, at face value, a manipulator's sincere attempts at persuasion. In extreme cases, a reputation as a manipulator can completely ruin a manager's career.

A second way in which managers indirectly influence others is by making permanent changes in an individual's or a group's environment. They change job descriptions, the formal systems that measure performance, the extrinsic incentives available, the tools, people, and other resources that the people or groups work with, the architecture, the norms or values of work groups, and so on. If the manager is successful in making the changes, and the changes have the desired effect on the individual or group, that effect will be sustained over time.

Effective managers recognize that changes in the forces that surround a person can have great impact on that person's behavior. Unlike many of the other influence methods, this one doesn't require a large expenditure of limited resources or effort on the part of the manager on an ongoing basis. Once such a change has been successfully made, it works independently of the manager.

This method of influence is used by all managers to some degree. Many, however, use it sparingly simply because they do not have the power to change the forces acting on the person they wish to influence. In many organizations, only the top managers have the power to change the formal measurement systems, the extrinsic incentives available, the architecture, and so on.

───── GENERATING AND USING POWER SUCCESSFULLY

Managers who are successful at acquiring considerable power and using it to manage their dependence on others tend to share a number of common characteristics:

1. They are sensitive to what others consider to be legitimate behavior in acquiring and using power. They recognize that the four types of power carry with them certain "obligations" regarding their acquisition and use. A person who gains a considerable amount of power based on his perceived expertise is generally expected to be an expert in certain areas. If it ever becomes publicly known that the person is clearly not an expert in those areas, such a person will probably be labeled a "fraud" and will not only lose his power but will suffer other reprimands too.

   A person with whom a number of people identify is expected to act like an ideal leader. If he clearly lets people down, he will not only lose that power, he will also suffer the righteous anger of his ex-followers. Many managers who have created or used power based on perceived dependence in ways that their employees have felt unfair, such as in requesting overtime work, have ended up with unions.

2. They have good intuitive understanding of the various types of power and methods of influence. They are sensitive to what types of power are easiest to develop with different types of people. They recognize, for example, that professionals tend to be more influenced by perceived expertise than by other forms of power. They also have a grasp of all the various methods of influence and what each can accomplish, at what costs, and with what risks. (See the *Exhibit*.) They are good at recognizing the specific conditions in any situation and then at selecting an influence method that is compatible with those conditions.

3. They tend to develop all the types of power, to some degree, and they use all the influence methods mentioned in the *Exhibit*. Unlike managers who are not very good at influencing people, effective managers usually do not think that only some of the methods are useful or that only some of the methods are moral. They recognize that any of the methods, used under the right circumstances, can help contribute to organizational effectiveness with few dysfunctional consequences. At the same time, they generally try to avoid those methods that are more risky than others and those that may have dysfunctional consequences. For example, they manipulate the environment of others only when absolutely necessary.

4. They establish career goals and seek out managerial positions that allow them to successfully develop and use power. They look for jobs, for example, that use their backgrounds and skills to control or manage some critically important problem or environmental contingency that an organization faces. They recognize that success

in that type of job makes others dependent on them and increases their own perceived expertise. They also seek jobs that do not demand a type or a volume of power that is inconsistent with their own skills.

5. They use all of their resources, formal authority, and power to develop still more power. To borrow Edward Banfield's metaphor, they actually look for ways to "invest" their power where they might secure a high positive return.[5] For example, by asking a person to do him two important favors, a manager might be able to finish his construction program one day ahead of schedule. That request may cost him most of the obligation-based power he has over that person, but in return he may significantly increase his perceived expertise as a manager of construction projects in the eyes of everyone in his organization.

   Just as in investing money, there is always some risk involved in using power this way; it is possible to get a zero return for a sizable investment, even for the most powerful manager. Effective managers do not try to avoid risks. Instead, they look for prudent risks, just as they do when investing capital.

6. Effective managers engage in power-oriented behavior in ways that are tempered by maturity and self-control.[6] They seldom, if ever, develop and use power in impulsive ways or for their own aggrandizement.

7. Finally, they also recognize and accept as legitimate that, in using these methods, they clearly influence other people's behavior and lives. Unlike many less effective managers, they are reasonably comfortable in using power to influence people. They recognize, often only intuitively, what this article is all about—that their attempts to establish power and use it are an absolutely necessary part of the successful fulfillment of their difficult managerial role.

---

5. *See* Edward C. Banfield, *Political Influence* (New York: Free Press, 1965), Chapter 11.

6. *See* David C. McClelland and David H. Burnham, "Power Is the Great Motivator," *Harvard Business Review* (March–April 1976): 100.

——— DISCUSSION QUESTIONS

1. The author claims that the manager's need for power arises out of dependency. Do you agree or disagree with this statement?
2. Is acquiring power an art or a skill? Can anyone do it? If so, elaborate.
3. Kotter mentions that there are four different types of power over others. Are there any others that an effective manager could use?
4. The goal of power is to get others to behave in a desired way. There are direct and indirect ways of achieving this. Give an example of how you've used power recently to get someone else to do what you've wanted them to do. How has another person used power recently to get you to do something that they wanted you to do?

3 Management Time: Who's Got the Monkey?

WILLIAM ONCKEN, JR., AND DONALD L. WASS

In any organization, bosses, peers, and subordinates make demands on a manager's scarce time. Because successful leadership hinges on the effective use of time, managers must gain as much control over their time as they can. By cultivating the ability to assign tasks, delegate responsibility, and foster initiative, managers can minimize or do away with subordinates' demands on their time; they are then free to devote their attention to more critical activities. The analogy of a monkey on the back demonstrates the authors' points.

Why is it that managers are typically running out of time while their subordinates are typically running out of work? In this reading, we shall explore the meaning of management time as it relates to the interaction between managers and their bosses, their own peers, and their subordinates.

Specifically, we shall deal with three different kinds of management time:

Boss-imposed time—to accomplish those activities that the boss requires and that the manager cannot disregard without direct and swift penalty.

System-imposed time—to accommodate those requests to the manager for active support from his or her peers. This assistance must also be provided lest there be penalties, though not always direct or swift ones.

Self-imposed time—to do those things that the manager originates or agrees to do. A certain portion of this kind of time, however, will be taken by subordinates and is called *subordinate-imposed time*. The remaining portion will be his or her own and is called *discretionary time*. Self-imposed time is not subject to penalty since neither the boss nor the system can discipline the manager for not doing what they did not know the manager had intended to do in the first place.

The management of time necessitates that managers get control over the timing and content of what they do. Since what their bosses and the system impose on them are backed up by penalty, managers cannot tamper with those requirements. Thus their self-imposed time becomes their major area of concern.

The managers' strategy is therefore to increase the discretionary component of their self-imposed time by minimizing or doing away with the subordinate component. They will then use the added increment to get better control over their boss-imposed and system-imposed activities. Most managers spend much more subordinate-imposed time than they even faintly realize. Hence we shall use a monkey-on-the-back analogy to examine how subordinate-imposed time comes into being and what the superior can do about it.

────── WHERE IS THE MONKEY?

Let us imagine that a manager is walking down the hall and that he notices one of his subordinates, Jones, coming up the hallway. When the two are abreast of one another, Jones greets the manager with, "Good morning. By the way, we've got a problem. You see . . ." As Jones continues, the manager recognizes in this problem the same two characteristics common to all the problems his subordinates gratuitously bring to his attention. Namely, the manager knows (a) enough to get involved, but (b) not enough to make the on-the-spot decision expected of him. Eventually, the manager says, "So glad you brought this up. I'm in a rush right now. Meanwhile, let me think about it and I'll let you know." Then he and Jones part company.

Let us analyze what has just happened. Before the two of them met, on whose back was the "monkey"? The subordinate's. After they parted, on whose back was it? The manager's. Subordinate-imposed time begins the moment a monkey successfully executes a leap from the back of a subordinate to the back of his or her superior and does not end until the monkey is returned to its proper owner for care and feeding.

In accepting the monkey, the manager has voluntarily assumed a position subordinate to his subordinate. That is, he has allowed Jones to make him her subordinate by doing two things a subordinate is generally expected to do for a boss—the manager has accepted a responsibility from his subordinate, and the manager has promised her a progress report.

The subordinate, to make sure the manager does not miss this point, will later stick her head in the manager's office and cheerily query, "How's it coming?" (This is called supervision.)

Or let us imagine again, in concluding a working conference with another subordinate, Johnson, the manager's parting words are, "Fine. Send me a memo on that."

Let us analyze this one. The monkey is now on the subordinate's back because the next move is his, but it is poised for a leap. Watch that monkey. Johnson dutifully writes the requested memo and drops it in his outbasket. Shortly thereafter, the manager plucks it from his inbasket and reads it. Whose move is it now? The manager's. If he does not make that move soon, he will get a follow-up memo from the subordinate (this is another form of supervision). The longer the manager delays, the more frustrated the subordinate will become (he'll be "spinning his wheels") and the more guilty the manager will feel (his backlog of subordinate-imposed time will be mounting).

Or suppose once again that at a meeting with a third subordinate, Smith, the manager agrees to provide all the necessary backing for a public relations proposal he has just asked Smith to develop. The manager's parting words to her are, "Just let me know how I can help."

Now let us analyze this. Here the monkey is initially on the subordinate's back. But for how long? Smith realizes that she cannot let the manager "know" until her proposal has the manager's approval. And from experience, she also realizes that her proposal will likely be sitting in the manager's briefcase for weeks waiting for him to eventually get to it. Who's really got the monkey? Who will be checking up on whom? Wheelspinning and bottlenecking are on their way again.

A fourth subordinate, Reed, has just been transferred from another part of the company in order to launch and eventually manage a newly created business venture. The manager has said that they should get together soon to hammer out a set of objectives for the new job, and that "I will draw up an initial draft for discussion with you."

Let us analyze this one, too. The subordinate has the new job (by formal assignment) and the full responsibility (by formal delegation), but the manager has the next move. Until he makes it, he will have the monkey and the subordinate will be immobilized.

Why does it all happen? Because in each instance the manager and the subordinate assume at the outset, wittingly or unwittingly, that the matter under consideration is a joint problem. The monkey in each case begins its career astride both their backs. All it has to do now is move the wrong leg, and—presto—the subordinate deftly disappears. The manager is thus left with another acquisition to his menagerie. Of course, monkeys can be trained not to move the wrong leg. But it is easier to prevent them from straddling backs in the first place.

WHO IS WORKING FOR WHOM?

To make what follows more credible, let us suppose that these same four subordinates are so thoughtful and considerate of the superior's time that they are at pains to allow no more than three monkeys to leap from each of their backs to his in any one day. In a five-day week, the manager will have picked up 60 screaming monkeys—far too many to do anything about individually. So he spends the subordinate-imposed time juggling his priorities.

Late Friday afternoon, the manager is in his office with the door closed for privacy in order to contemplate the situation, while his subordinates are waiting outside to get a last chance before the weekend to remind him that he will have to "fish or cut bait." Imagine what they are saying to each other about the manager as they wait: "What a bottleneck. He just can't make up his mind. How anyone ever got that high up in our company without being able to make a decision we'll never know."

Worst of all, the reason the manager cannot make any of these "next moves" is that his time is almost entirely eaten up in meeting his own boss-imposed and system-imposed requirements. To get control of these, he needs discretionary time that is in turn denied him when he is preoccupied with all these monkeys. The manager is caught in a vicious circle.

But time is a-wasting (an understatement). The manager calls his secretary on the intercom and instructs her to tell his subordinates that he will be unavailable to see them until Monday morning. At 7:00 P.M., he drives home, intending with firm resolve to return to the office tomorrow to get caught up over the weekend. He returns bright and early the next day only to see, on the nearest green of the golf course across from his office window, a foursome. Guess who?

That does it. He now knows who is really working for whom. Moreover, he now sees that if he actually accomplishes during this weekend what he came to accomplish, his subordinates' morale will go up so sharply that they will each raise the limit on the number of monkeys they will let jump from their backs to his. In short, he now sees, with the clarity of a revelation on a mountaintop, that the more he gets caught up, the more he will fall behind.

He leaves the office with the speed of a person running away from a plague. His plan? To get caught up on something else he hasn't had time for in years: a weekend with his family. (This is one of the many varieties of discretionary time.)

Sunday night he enjoys ten hours of sweet, untroubled slumber, because he has clear-cut plans for Monday. He is going to get rid of his subordinate-imposed time. In exchange, he will get an equal amount of discretionary time, part of which he will spend with his subordinates to see that they learn the difficult but rewarding managerial art called, "The Care and Feeding of Monkeys."

The manager will also have plenty of discretionary time left over for getting control of the timing and content not only of his boss-imposed time but of his system-imposed time as well. All of this may take months, but compared with the way things have been, the rewards will be enormous. His ultimate objective is to manage his management time.

——— GETTING RID OF THE MONKEYS

The manager returns to the office Monday morning just late enough to permit his four subordinates to collect in his outer office waiting to see him about their monkeys. He calls them in, one by one. The purpose of each interview is to take a monkey, place it on the desk between them, and figure out together how the next move might conceivably be the subordinate's. For certain monkeys, this will take some doing. The subordinate's next move may be so elusive that the manager may decide—just for now—merely to let the monkey sleep on the subordinate's back overnight and have him or her return with it at an appointed time the next morning to continue the joint quest for a more substantive move by the subordinate. (Monkeys sleep just as soundly overnight on subordinates' backs as on superiors'.)

As each subordinate leaves the office, the manager is rewarded by the sight of a monkey leaving his office on the subordinate's back. For the next 24 hours, the subordinate will not be waiting for the manager; instead, the manager will be waiting for the subordinate.

Later, as if to remind himself that there is no law against his engaging in a constructive exercise in the interim, the manager strolls by the subordinate's office, sticks his head in the door, and cheerily asks, "How's it coming?" (The time consumed in doing this is discretionary for the manager and boss-imposed for the subordinate.)

When the subordinate (with the monkey on his or her back) and the manager meet at the appointed hour the next day, the manager explains the ground rules in words to this effect:

"At no time while I am helping you with this or any other problem will your problem become my problem. The instant your problem becomes mine, you will no longer have a problem. I cannot help a person who hasn't got a problem.

"When this meeting is over, the problem will leave this office exactly the way it came in—on your back. You may ask my help at any appointed time, and we will make a joint determination of what the next move will be and which of us will make it.

"In those rare instances where the next move turns out to be mine, you and I will determine it together. I will not make any move alone."

The manager follows this same line of thought with each subordinate until at about 11:00 A.M. he realizes that he has no need to shut his door. His monkeys are gone. They will return—but by appointment only. His appointment calendar will assure this.

TRANSFERRING THE INITIATIVE

What we have been driving at in this monkey-on-the-back analogy is to transfer initiative from superior to subordinate and keep it there. We have tried to highlight a truism as obvious as it is subtle. Namely, before developing initiative in subordinates, the manager must see to it that they *have* the initiative. Once the manager takes it back, they will no longer have it and the discretionary time can be kissed good-bye. It will all revert to subordinate-imposed time.

Nor can both manager and subordinate effectively have the same initiative at the same time. The opener, "Boss, we've got a problem," implies this duality and represents, as noted earlier, a monkey astride two backs, which is a very bad way to start a monkey on its career. Let us, therefore, take a few moments to examine what we prefer to call "The Anatomy of Managerial Initiative."

There are five degrees of initiative that the manager can exercise in relation to the boss and to the system: (1) *wait* until told (lowest initiative); (2) *ask* what to do; (3) *recommend*, then take resulting action; (4) *act*, but advise at once, and (5) *act* on own, then routinely report (highest initiative).

Clearly, the manager should be professional enough not to indulge in initiatives 1 and 2 in relation either to the boss or to the system. A manager who uses initiative 1 has no control over either the timing or content of boss-imposed or system-imposed time, and thereby forfeits any right to complain about what he or she is told to do or when. The manager who uses initiative 2 has control over the timing but not over the content. Initiatives 3, 4, and 5 leave the manager in control of both, with the greatest control being at level 5.

The manager's job, in relation to subordinates' initiatives, is twofold; first, to outlaw the use of initiatives 1 and 2, thus giving subordinates no choice but to learn and master "Completed Staff Work"; then, to see that for each problem leaving the office there is an agreed-upon level of initiative assigned to it, in addition to the agreed-upon time and place of the next manager-subordinate conference. The latter should be duly noted on the manager's appointment calendar.

——— CARE AND FEEDING OF MONKEYS

In order to further clarify our analogy between the monkey-on-the-back and the well-known processes of assigning and controlling, we shall refer briefly to the manager's appointment schedule, which calls for five hard-and-fast rules governing the "Care and Feeding of Monkeys" (violations of these rules will cost discretionary time):

Rule 1 Monkeys should be fed or shot. Otherwise, they will starve to death and the manager will waste valuable time on postmortems or attempted resurrections.

Rule 2 The monkey population should be kept below the maximum number the manager has time to feed. Subordinates will find time to work as many monkeys as he or she finds time to feed, but no more. It shouldn't take more than 5 to 15 minutes to feed a properly prepared monkey.

Rule 3 Monkeys should be fed by appointment only. The manager should not have to be hunting down starving monkeys and feeding them on a catch-as-catch-can basis.

Rule 4 Monkeys should be fed face-to-face or by telephone, but never by mail. (If by mail, the next move will be the manager's—remember?) Documentation may add to the feeding process, but it cannot take the place of feeding.

Rule 5   Every monkey should have an assigned next feeding time and degree of initiative. These may be revised at any time by mutual consent, but never allowed to become vague or indefinite. Otherwise, the monkey will either starve to death or wind up on the manager's back.

———— CONCLUDING NOTE

"Get control over the timing and content of what you do" is appropriate advice for managing management time. The first order of business is for the manager to enlarge his or her discretionary time by eliminating subordinate-imposed time. The second is for the manager to use a portion of this new-found discretionary time to see to it that each subordinate possesses the initiative without which he or she cannot exercise initiative, and then to see to it that this initiative is in fact taken. The third is for the manager to use another portion of the increased discretionary time to get and keep control of the timing and content of both boss-imposed and system-imposed time.

The result of all this is that the manager's leverage will increase, in turn enabling the value of each hour spent in managing management time to multiply, without theoretical limit.

Copyright © 1974; revised 1991.

———— DISCUSSION QUESTIONS

1. "Management Time" is one of the most widely read human resource management essays ever published. Can you account for its popularity?
2. Share an instance when you have allowed someone else's "monkey" to jump onto your back. Give an example when you succeeded in passing your monkey on to someone else.
3. Initiative in subordinates is fundamental to managerial time management. What might some stumbling blocks be that would prevent subordinates from having a higher degree of initiative?

The New Managerial Work   4

ROSABETH MOSS KANTER

Downsizing, restructuring, and other organizational changes intended to foster innovation and flexibility have changed the roles and tasks of managers. Collaborative work is increasing, hierarchy fading. To manage effectively in the new organizations, managers need to master change in two critical areas: power and motivation. Rather than exerting direct control over others, managers now and in the future must learn to build relationships, find new sources of ideas and opportunities, and broker deals. Effective managers are no longer watchdogs but integrators and facilitators. Three case histories illuminate the opportunities and dilemmas inherent in these changes.

Managerial work is undergoing such enormous and rapid change that many managers are reinventing their profession as they go. With little precedent to guide them, they are watching hierarchy fade away and the clear distinctions of title, task, department, even corporation, blur. Faced with extraordinary levels of complexity and interdependency, they watch traditional sources of power erode and the old motivational tools lose their magic.

The cause is obvious. Competitive pressures are forcing corporations to adopt new flexible strategies and structures. Many of these are familiar: acquisitions and divestitures aimed at more focused combinations of business activities, reductions in management staff and levels of hierarchy, increased use of performance-based rewards. Other strategies are less common but have an even more profound effect. In a growing number of companies, for example, horizontal ties between peers are replacing vertical ties as channels of activity and communication. Companies are asking corporate staffs and functional departments to play a more strategic role with greater cross-departmental collaboration. Some organizations are turning themselves nearly inside out—buying formerly internal services from outside suppliers, forming strategic alliances and supplier-customer partnerships that bring external relationships inside where they can influence company policy and practice. I call these emerging practices *postentrepreneurial* because they involve the application of entrepreneurial creativity and flexibility to established businesses.

Such changes come highly recommended by the experts who urge organizations to become leaner, less bureaucratic, more entrepreneurial. But so far, theorists have given scant attention to the dramatically altered realities of managerial work in these transformed corporations (see the *Exhibit*). We don't

EXHIBIT
The New Managerial Quandaries

- At American Express, the CEO instituted a program called One Enterprise to encourage collaboration between different lines of business. One Enterprise has led to a range of projects where peers from different divisions work together on such synergistic ventures as cross-marketing, joint purchasing, and cooperative product and market innovation. Employees' rewards are tied to their One Enterprise efforts. Executives set goals and can earn bonuses for their contributions to results in other divisions.

  But how do department managers control their people when they're working on cross-departmental teams? And who determines the size of the rewards when the interests of more than one area are involved?

- At Security Pacific National Bank, internal departments have become forces in the external marketplace. For example, the bank is involved in a joint venture with local auto dealers to sell fast financing for car purchases. And the MIS department is now a profit center selling its services inside and outside the bank.

  But what is the role of bank managers accountable for the success of such entrepreneurial ventures? And how do they shift their orientation from the role

of boss in a chain of command to the role of customer?

- At Digital Equipment Corporation, emphasis on supplier partnerships to improve quality and innovation has multiplied the need for cross-functional as well as cross-company collaboration. Key suppliers are included on product-planning teams with engineering, manufacturing, and purchasing staff. Digital uses its human resources staff to train and do performance appraisals of its suppliers, as if they were part of the company. In cases where suppliers are also customers, purchasing and marketing departments also need to work collaboratively.

  But how do managers learn enough about other functions to be credible, let alone influential, members of such teams? How do they maintain adequate communication externally while staying on top of what their own departments are doing? And how do they handle the extra work of responding to projects initiated by other areas?

- At Banc One, a growing reliance on project teams spanning more than 70 affiliated banks has led the CEO to propose eliminating officer titles because of the lack of correlation between status as measured by title and status within the collaborative team.

even have good words to describe the new relationships. "Superiors" and "subordinates" hardly seem accurate, and even "bosses" and "their people" imply more control and ownership than managers today actually possess. On top of it all, career paths are no longer straightforward and predictable but have become idiosyncratic and confusing.

Some managers experience the new managerial work as a loss of power because much of their authority used to come from hierarchical position. Now that everything seems negotiable by everyone, they are confused about how to mobilize and motivate staff. For other managers, the shift in roles and tasks

EXHIBIT
The New Managerial Quandaries (Continued)

But then what do rank and hierarchy mean anymore, especially for people whose careers consist of a sequence of projects rather than a sequence of promotions? What does "career" mean? Does it have a shape? Is there a ladder?

- At Alcan, which is trying to find new uses and applications for its core product, aluminum, managers and professionals from line divisions form screening teams to consider and refine new-venture proposals. A venture manager, chosen from the screening team, takes charge of concepts that pass muster, drawing on Alcan's worldwide resources to build the new business. In one case of global synergy, Alcan created a new product for the Japanese market using Swedish and American technology and Canadian manufacturing capacity.

But why should senior managers release staff to serve on screening and project teams for new businesses when their own businesses are making do with fewer and fewer people? How do functionally oriented managers learn enough about worldwide developments to know when they might have something of value to offer someplace else?

And how do the managers of these new ventures ever go back to the conventional line organization as middle managers once their venture has been folded into an established division?

- At IBM, an emphasis on customer partnerships to rebuild market share is leading to practices quite new to the company. In some cases, IBM has formed joint development teams with customers, where engineers from both companies share proprietary data. In others, the company has gone beyond selling equipment to actually managing a customer's management information system. Eastman Kodak has handed its U.S. data center operations to IBM to consolidate and manage, which means lower fixed costs for Kodak and a greater ability to focus on its core businesses rather than on ancillary services. Some 300 former Kodak people still fill Kodak's needs as IBM employees, while two committees of IBM and Kodak managers oversee the partnership.

But who exactly do the data center people work for? Who is in charge? And how do traditional notions of managerial authority square with such a complicated set of relationships?

---

offers greater personal power. The following case histories illustrate the responses of three managers in three different industries to the opportunities and dilemmas of structural change.

> *Hank is vice president and chief engineer for a leading heavy equipment manufacturer* that is moving aggressively against foreign competition. One of the company's top priorities has been to increase the speed, quality, and cost-effectiveness of product development. So Hank worked with consultants to improve collaboration between manufacturing and other functions and to create closer alliances

between the company and its outside suppliers. Gradually, a highly segmented operation became an integrated process involving project teams drawn from component divisions, functional departments, and external suppliers. But along the way, there were several unusual side effects. Different areas of responsibility overlapped. Some technical and manufacturing people were co-located. Liaisons from functional areas joined the larger development teams. Most unusual of all, project teams had a lot of direct contact with higher levels of the company.

Many of the managers reporting to Hank felt these changes as a loss of power. They didn't always know what their people were doing, but they still believed they ought to know. They no longer had sole input into performance appraisals; other people from other functions had a voice as well, and some of them knew more about employees' project performance. New career paths made it less important to please direct superiors in order to move up the functional line.

Moreover, employees often bypassed Hank's managers and interacted directly with decision makers inside and outside the company. Some of these so-called subordinates had contact with division executives and senior corporate staff, and sometimes they sat in on high-level strategy meetings to which their managers were not invited.

At first Hank thought his managers' resistance to the new process was just the normal noise associated with any change. Then he began to realize that something more profound was going on. The reorganization was challenging traditional notions about the role and power of managers and shaking traditional hierarchy to its roots. And no one could see what was taking its place.

When George became head of a major corporate department in a large bank holding company, he thought he had arrived. His title and rank were unmistakable, and his department was responsible for determining product-line policy for hundreds of bank branches and the virtual clerks—in George's eyes—who managed them. George staffed his department with MBAs and promised them rapid promotion.

Then the sand seemed to shift beneath him. Losing market position for the first time in recent memory, the bank decided to emphasize direct customer service at the branches. The people George considered clerks began to depart from George's standard policies and to tailor their services to local market conditions. In many cases, they actually demanded services and responses from George's staff, and the results of their requests began to figure in performance reviews of George's department. George's people were spending more and more time in the field with branch managers, and the corporate personnel department was even trying to assign some of George's MBAs to branch and regional posts.

To complicate matters, the bank's strategy included a growing role for technology. George felt that because he had no direct control over the information systems department, he should not be held fully accountable for every facet of product design and implementation. But fully accountable he was. He had to deploy people to learn the new technology and figure out how to work with it. Furthermore, the bank was asking product departments like George's to find ways to link existing products or develop new ones that crossed traditional categories. So George's people were often away on cross-departmental teams just when he wanted them for some internal assignment.

Instead of presiding over a tidy empire the way his predecessor had, George presided over what looked to him like chaos. The bank said senior executives should be "leaders, not managers," but George didn't know what that meant, especially since he seemed to have lost control over his subordinates' assignments, activities, rewards, and careers. He resented his perceived loss of status.

The CEO tried to show him that good results achieved the new way would bring great monetary rewards, thanks to a performance-based bonus program that was gradually replacing more modest yearly raises. But the pressures on George were also greater, unlike anything he'd ever experienced.

For Sally, purchasing manager at an innovative computer company, a new organizational strategy was a gain rather than a loss, although it changed her relationship with the people reporting to her. Less than ten years out of college, she was hired as an analyst—a semiprofessional, semiclerical job—then promoted to a purchasing manager's job in a sleepy staff department. She didn't expect to go much further in what was then a well-established hierarchy. But after a shocking downturn, top management encouraged employees to rethink traditional ways of doing things. Sally's boss, the head of purchasing, suggested that partnerships with key suppliers might improve quality, speed innovation, and reduce costs.

Soon Sally's backwater was at the center of policymaking, and Sally began to help shape strategy. She organized meetings between her company's senior executives and supplier CEOs. She sent her staff to contribute supplier intelligence at company seminars on technical innovation, and she spent more of her own time with product designers and manufacturing planners. She led senior executives on a tour of supplier facilities, traveling with them in the corporate jet.

Because some suppliers were also important customers, Sally's staff began meeting frequently with marketing managers to share information and address joint problems. Sally and her group were now also acting as internal advocates for major suppliers. Furthermore, many of these external companies now contributed performance appraisals of Sally and her team, and their opinions weighed almost as heavily as those of her superiors.

As a result of the company's new direction, Sally felt more personal power and influence, and her ties to peers in other areas and to top management were stronger. But she no longer felt like a manager directing subordinates. Her staff had become a pool of resources deployed by many others besides Sally. She was exhilarated by her personal opportunities but not quite sure the people she managed should have the same freedom to choose their own assignments. After all, wasn't that a manager's prerogative?

Hank's, George's, and Sally's very different stories say much about the changing nature of managerial work. However hard it is for managers at the very top to remake strategy and structure, they themselves will probably retain their identity, status, and control. For the managers below them, structural change is often much harder. As work units become more participative and team oriented, and as professionals and knowledge workers become more prominent, the distinction between manager and nonmanager begins to erode.

To understand what managers must do to achieve results in the postentrepreneurial corporation, we need to look at the changing picture of how such companies operate. The picture has five elements:

1. There are a greater number and variety of channels for taking action and exerting influence.
2. Relationships of influence are shifting from the vertical to the horizontal, from chain of command to peer networks.
3. The distinction between managers and those managed is diminishing, especially in terms of information, control over assignments, and access to external relationships.
4. External relationships are increasingly important as sources of internal power and influence, even of career development.
5. As a result of the first four changes, career development has become less intelligible but also less circumscribed. There are fewer assured routes to success, which produces anxiety. At the same time, career paths are more open to innovation, which produces opportunity.

To help companies implement their competitive organizational strategies, managers must learn new ways to manage, confronting changes in their own bases of power and recognizing the need for new ways to motivate people.

——— THE BASES OF POWER

The changes I've talked about can be scary for people like George and the managers reporting to Hank, who were trained to know their place, to follow orders, to let the company take care of their careers, to do things by the book. The book is gone. In the new corporation, managers have only themselves to count on for success. They must learn to operate without the crutch of hierarchy. Position, title, and authority are no longer adequate tools, not in a world where subordinates are encouraged to think for themselves and where managers have to work synergistically with other departments and even other companies. Success depends increasingly on tapping into sources of good ideas, on figuring out whose collaboration is needed to act on those ideas, on working with both to produce results. In short, the new managerial work implies very different ways of obtaining and using power.

The postentrepreneurial corporation is not only leaner and flatter, it also has many more channels for action. Cross-functional projects, business-unit joint ventures, labor-management forums, innovation funds that spawn activities outside mainstream budgets and reporting lines, strategic partnerships with suppliers or customers—these are all overlays on the traditional organization chart, strategic pathways that ignore the chain of command.

Their existence has several important implications. For one thing, they create more potential centers of power. As the ways to combine resources increase, the ability to command diminishes. Alternative paths of communication, resource access, and execution erode the authority of those in the nominal chain of command. In other words, the opportunity for greater speed and flexibility undermines hierarchy. As more and more strategic action takes place in these channels, the jobs that focus inward on particular departments decline in power.

As a result, the ability of managers to get things done depends more on the number of networks in which they're centrally involved than on their height in a hierarchy. Of course, power in any organization always has a network component, but rank and formal structure used to be more limiting. For example, access to information and the ability to get informal backing were often confined to the few officially sanctioned contact points between departments or between the company and its vendors or customers. Today these official barriers are disappearing, while so-called informal networks grow in importance.

In the emerging organization, managers add value by deal making, by brokering at interfaces, rather than by presiding over their individual empires. It was traditionally the job of top executives or specialists to scan the business environment for new ideas, opportunities, and resources. This kind of environmental scanning is now an important part of a manager's job at every level and in every function. And the environment to be scanned includes various company divisions, many potential outside partners, and large parts of the world. At the same time, people are encouraged to think about what they know that might have value elsewhere. An engineer designing windshield wipers, for example, might discover properties of rubber adhesion to glass that could be useful in other manufacturing areas.

Every manager must think cross-functionally because every department has to play a strategic role, understanding and contributing to other facets of the business. In Hank's company, the technical managers and staff working on design engineering used to concentrate only on their own areas of expertise. Under the new system, they have to keep in mind what manufacturing does and how it does it. They need to visit plants and build relationships so they can ask informed questions.

One multinational corporation, eager to extend the uses of its core product, put its R&D staff and laboratory personnel in direct contact with marketing experts to discuss lines of research. Similarly, the superior economic track record of Raytheon's New Products Center—dozens of new products and patents yielding profits many times their development costs—derives from the connections it builds between its inventors and the engineering and marketing staffs of the business units it serves.

This strategic and collaborative role is particularly important for the managers and professionals on corporate staffs. They need to serve as integrators and facilitators, not as watchdogs and interventionists. They need to sell their services, justify themselves to the business units they serve, literally compete with outside suppliers. General Foods recently put overhead charges for corporate staff services on a pay-as-you-use basis. Formerly, these charges were either assigned uniformly to users and nonusers alike, or the services were mandatory. Product managers sometimes had to work through as many as eight layers of management and corporate staff to get business plans approved. Now these staffs must prove to the satisfaction of their internal customers that their services add value.

By contrast, some banks still have corporate training departments that do very little except get in the way. They do no actual training, for example, yet they still exercise veto power over urgent divisional training decisions and consultant contracts.

As managers and professionals spend more time working across boundaries with peers and partners over whom they have no direct control, their negotiating skills become essential assets. Alliances and partnerships transform impersonal, arm's-length contracts into relationships involving joint planning and joint decision making. Internal competitors and adversaries become allies on whom managers depend for their own success. At the same time, more managers at more levels are active in the kind of external diplomacy that only the CEO or selected staffs used to conduct.

In the collaborative forums that result, managers are more personally exposed. It is trust that makes partnerships work. Since collaborative ventures often bring together groups with different methods, cultures, symbols, even languages, good deal making depends on empathy—the ability to step into other people's shoes and appreciate their goals. This applies not only to intricate global joint ventures but also to the efforts of engineering and manufacturing to work together more effectively. Effective communication in a cooperative effort rests on more than a simple exchange of information; people must be adept at anticipating the responses of other groups. "Before I get too excited about our department's design ideas," an engineering manager told me, "I'm learning to ask myself, 'What's the marketing position on this? What will manufacturing say?' That sometimes forces me to make changes before I even talk to these groups."

An increase in the number of channels for strategic contact within the postentrepreneurial organization means more opportunities for people with ideas or information to trigger action: salespeople encouraging account managers to build strategic partnerships with customers, for example, or technicians searching for ways to tap new-venture funds to develop software. Moreover, top executives who have to spend more time on cross-boundary relationships are forced to delegate more responsibility to lower-level managers. Delegation is one more blow to hierarchy, of course, since subordinates with greater responsibility are bolder about speaking up, challenging authority, and charting their own course.

For example, it is common for new-venture teams to complain publicly about corporate support departments and to reject their use in favor of external service providers, often to the consternation of more orthodox superiors. A more startling example occurred in a health care company where members of a task force charged with finding synergies among three lines of business shocked corporate executives by criticizing upper-management behavior in their report. Service on the task force had created collective awareness of a shared problem and had given people the courage to confront it.

The search for internal synergies, the development of strategic alliances, and the push for new ventures all emphasize the political side of a leader's work. Executives must be able to juggle a set of constituencies rather than control a set of subordinates. They have to bargain, negotiate, and sell instead of making unilateral decisions and issuing commands. The leader's task, as Chester Barnard recognized long ago, is to develop a network of cooperative relationships among all the people, groups, and organizations that have something to contribute to an economic enterprise. Postentrepreneurial strategies magnify the complexity of this task. After leading Teknowledge, a producer of expert systems software, through development alliances with six corporations including General Motors and Procter & Gamble, company chairman Lee Hecht said he felt like the mayor of a small city. "I have a constituency that won't quit. It takes a hell of a lot of balancing." The kind of power achieved through a network of stakeholders is very different from the kind of power managers wield in a traditional bureaucracy. The new way gets more done, but it also takes more time. And it creates an illusion about freedom and security.

The absence of day-to-day constraints, the admonition to assume responsibility, the pretense of equality, the elimination of visible status markers, the prevalence of candid dialogues across hierarchical levels—these can give employees a false sense that all hierarchy is a thing of the past. Yet at the same time, employees still count on hierarchy to shield them when things go wrong. This combination would create the perfect marriage of freedom and support—freedom when people want to take risks, support when the risks do not work out.

In reality, less-benevolent combinations are also possible, combinations not of freedom and support but of insecurity and loss of control. There is often a pretense in postentrepreneurial companies that status differences have nothing to do with power, that the deference paid to top executives derives from their superior qualifications rather than from the power they have over the fates of others. But the people at the top of the organization chart still wield power— and sometimes in ways that managers below them experience as arbitrary. Unprecedented individual freedom also applies to top managers, who are now free to make previously unimaginable deals, order unimaginable cuts, or launch unimaginable takeovers. The reorganizations that companies undertake in their search for new synergies can uncover the potential unpredictability and capriciousness of corporate careers. A man whose company was undergoing drastic restructuring told me, "For all of my ownership share and strategic centrality and voice in decisions, I can still be faced with a shift in direction not of my own making. I can still be reorganized into a corner. I can still be relocated into oblivion. I can still be reviewed out of my special-projects budget."

These realities of power, change, and job security are important because they affect the way people view their leaders. When the illusion of simultaneous freedom and protection fades, the result can be a loss of motivation.

───── SOURCES OF MOTIVATION

One of the essential, unchanging tasks of leaders is to motivate and guide performance. But motivational tools are changing fast. More and more businesses are doing away with the old bureaucratic incentives and using entrepreneurial opportunity to attract the best talent. Managers must exercise more leadership even as they watch their bureaucratic power slip away. Leadership, in short, is more difficult yet more critical than ever.

Because of the unpredictability of even the most benign restructuring, managers are less able to guarantee a particular job—or any job at all—no matter what a subordinate's performance level. The reduction in hierarchical levels curtails a manager's ability to promise promotion. New compensation systems that make bonuses and raises dependent on objective performance measures and on team appraisals deprive managers of their role as the sole arbiter of higher pay. Cross-functional and cross-company teams can rob managers of their right to direct or even understand the work their so-called subordinates do. In any case, the shift from routine work, which was amenable to oversight, to "knowledge" work, which often is not, erodes a manager's claim to superior expertise. And partnerships and ventures that put lower-level people in direct contact with each other across departmental and company boundaries cut heavily into the managerial monopoly on information. At a consumer packaged-goods manufacturer that replaced several levels of hierarchy with teams, plant team members in direct contact with the sales force often had data on product ordering trends before the higher-level brand managers who set product policy.

As if the loss of carrots and sticks was not enough, many managers can no longer even give their people clear job standards and easily mastered procedural rules. Postentrepreneurial corporations seek problem-solving, initiative-taking employees who will go the unexpected extra mile for the customer. To complicate the situation further still, the complexities of work in the new organization—projects and relationships clamoring for attention in every direction—exacerbate the feeling of overload.

With the old motivational tool kit depleted, leaders need new and more effective incentives to encourage high performance and build commitment. There are five new tools:

Mission   Helping people believe in the importance of their work is essential, especially when other forms of certainty and security have disappeared. Good leaders can inspire others with the power and excitement of their vision and give people a sense of purpose and pride in their work. Pride is often a better source of motivation than the traditional corporate career ladder and the promotion-based reward system. Technical professionals, for example, are often motivated most effectively by the desire to see their work contribute to an excellent final product.

Agenda Control   As career paths lose their certainty and companies' futures grow less predictable, people can at least be in charge of their own professional lives. More and more professionals are passing up jobs with glamour and prestige in favor of jobs that give them greater control over their own activities and direction. Leaders give their subordinates this opportunity when they give them release time to work on pet projects, when they emphasize results instead of procedures, and when they delegate work and the decisions about how to do it. Choice of their next project is a potent reward for people who perform well.

Share of Value Creation   Entrepreneurial incentives that give teams a piece of the action are highly appropriate in collaborative companies. Because extra rewards are based only on measurable results, this approach also conserves resources. Innovative companies are experimenting with incentives like phantom stock for development of new ventures and other strategic achievements, equity participation in project returns, and bonuses pegged to key performance targets. Given the cross-functional nature of many projects today, rewards of this kind must sometimes be systemwide, but individual managers can also ask for a bonus pool for their own areas, contingent, of course, on meeting performance goals. And everyone can share the kinds of rewards that are abundant and free—awards and recognition.

Learning   The chance to learn new skills or apply them in new arenas is an important motivator in a turbulent environment because it is oriented toward securing the future. "The learning organization" promises to become a 1990s business buzzword as companies seek to learn more systematically from their experience and to encourage continuous learning for their people. In the world of high technology, where people understand uncertainty, the attractiveness of any company often lies in its capacity to provide learning and experience. By this calculus, access to training, mentors, and challenging projects is more important than pay or benefits. Some prominent companies—General Electric, for example—have always been able to attract top talent, even when they could not promise upward mobility, because people see them as a training ground, a good place to learn, and a valuable addition to a résumé.

Reputation   Reputation is a key resource in professional careers, and the chance to enhance it can be an outstanding motivator. The professional's reliance on reputation stands in marked contrast to the bureaucrat's anonymity. Professionals have to make a name for themselves, while traditional corporate managers and employees stay behind the scenes. Indeed, the accumulation of reputational capital provides not only an immediate ego boost but also the kind of publicity that can bring other rewards, even other job offers. Managers can enhance reputation—and improve motivation—by creating stars, by providing abundant public recognition and visible awards, by crediting the authors of innovation, by publicizing people outside their own departments, and by plugging people into organizational and professional networks.

The new, collaborative organization is predicated on a logic of flexible work assignments, not of fixed job responsibilities. To promote innovation and responsiveness, two of today's competitive imperatives, managers need to see this new organization as a cluster of activity sets, not as a rigid structure. The work of leadership in this new corporation will be to organize both sequential and synchronous projects of varying length and breadth, through which varying combinations of people will move, depending on the tasks, challenges, and opportunities facing the area and its partners at any given moment.

Leaders need to carve out projects with tangible accomplishments, milestones, and completion dates and then delegate responsibility for these projects to the people who flesh them out. Clearly delimited projects can counter overload by focusing effort and can provide short-term motivation when the fate of the long-term mission is uncertain. Project responsibility leads to ownership of the results and sometimes substitutes for other forms of reward. In companies where product development teams define and run their own projects, members commonly say that the greatest compensation they get is seeing the advertisements for their products. "Hey, that's mine! I did that!" one engineer told me he trumpeted to his family the first time he saw a commercial for his group's innovation.

This sense of ownership, along with a definite time frame, can spur higher levels of effort. Whenever people are engaged in creative or problem-solving projects that will have tangible results by deadline dates, they tend to come in at all hours, to think about the project in their spare time, to invest in it vast sums of physical and emotional energy. Knowing that the project will end and that completion will be an occasion for reward and recognition makes it possible to work much harder.

Leaders in the new organization do not lack motivational tools, but the tools are different from those of traditional corporate bureaucrats. The new rewards are based not on status but on contribution, and they consist not of regular promotion and automatic pay raises but of excitement about mission and a share of the glory and the gains of success. The new security is not employment security (a guaranteed job no matter what) but *employability* security—increased value in the internal and external labor markets. Commitment to the organization still matters, but today managers build commitment by offering project opportunities. The new loyalty is not to the boss or to the company but to projects that actualize a mission and offer challenge, growth, and credit for results.

The old bases of managerial authority are eroding, and new tools of leadership are taking their place. Managers whose power derived from hierarchy and who were accustomed to a limited area of personal control are learning to shift their perspectives and widen their horizons. The new managerial work consists of looking outside a defined area of responsibility to sense opportunities and of forming project teams drawn from any relevant sphere to address them. It involves communication and collaboration across functions, across divisions, and across companies whose activities and resources overlap. Thus rank, title, or official charter will be less important factors in success at the new managerial work than having the knowledge, skills, and sensitivity to mobilize people and motivate them to do their best.

⎯⎯ DISCUSSION QUESTIONS

1. This reading is about change and transition. The author lists five elements that characterize the changing picture of postentrepreneurial corporations. Discuss the advantages and disadvantages of change and transition in the workplace. How do people respond? How do you respond?
2. Are the changes discussed in this reading limited to business or are they a reflection of changes elsewhere? Explain.
3. The author advocates a new style of managerial behavior. How easy would you find it to manage in this style? Are there obstacles or problems in managing through influence and collaboration?

5   Managing Without Managers

RICARDO SEMLER

Facing catastrophe, the author, head of a manufacturing company in Brazil, had to make drastic changes in the way the company was managed. The company now operates from three key principles: work-force democracy, profit sharing, and free access to information. Democracy lets employees set their own working conditions; profit sharing rewards them for doing well; access to information tells them how they are doing. The company's management philosophy is antihierarchical and highly unorthodox, but profits are handsome. In this reading, the author explains the obstacles that were overcome to implement these values and the positive results that they caused.

In Brazil, where paternalism and the family business fiefdom still flourish, I am president of a manufacturing company that treats its 800 employees like responsible adults. Most of them—including factory workers—set their own working hours. All have access to the company books. The vast majority vote on many important corporate decisions. Everyone gets paid by the month, regardless of job description, and more than 150 of our management people set their own salaries and bonuses.

This may sound like an unconventional way to run a business, but it seems to work. Close to financial disaster in 1980, Semco is now one of Brazil's fastest-growing companies, with a profit margin in 1988 of 10% on sales of $37 million. Our five factories produce a range of sophisticated products, including marine pumps, digital scanners, commercial dishwashers, truck filters, and mixing equipment for everything from bubble gum to rocket fuel. Our customers include Alcoa, Saab, and General Motors. We've built a number of cookie factories for Nabisco, Nestlé, and United Biscuits. Our multinational competitors include AMF, Worthington Industries, Mitsubishi Heavy Industries, and Carrier.

Management associations, labor unions, and the press have repeatedly named us the best company in Brazil to work for. In fact, we no longer advertise jobs. Word of mouth generates up to 300 applications for every available position. The top five managers—we call them counselors—include a former human resources director of Ford Brazil, a 15-year veteran Chrysler executive, and a man who left his job as president of a larger company to come to Semco.

When I joined the company in 1980, 27 years after my father founded it, Semco had about 100 employees, manufactured hydraulic pumps for ships, generated about $4 million in revenues, and teetered on the brink of catastrophe.

All through 1981 and 1982, we ran from bank to bank looking for loans, and we fought persistent, well-founded rumors that the company was in danger of going under. We often stayed through the night reading files and searching the desk drawers of veteran executives for clues about contracts long since privately made and privately forgotten.

Most managers and outside board members agreed on two immediate needs: to professionalize and to diversify. In fact, both of these measures had been discussed for years but had never progressed beyond wishful thinking.

For two years, holding on by our fingertips, we sought licenses to manufacture other companies' products in Brazil. We traveled constantly. I remember one day being in Oslo for breakfast, New York for lunch, Cincinnati for dinner, and San Francisco for the night. The obstacles were great. Our company lacked an international reputation—and so did our country. Brazil's political eccentricities and draconian business regulations scared away many companies.

Still, good luck and a relentless program of beating the corporate bushes on four continents finally paid off. By 1982, we had signed seven license agreements. Our marine division—once the entire company—was now down to 60% of total sales. Moreover, the managers and directors were all professionals with no connection to the family.

With Semco back on its feet, we entered an acquisitions phase that cost millions of dollars in expenditures and millions more in losses over the next two or three years. All this growth was financed by banks at interest rates that were generally 30% above the rate of inflation, which ranged from 40% to 900% annually. There was no long-term money in Brazil at that time, so all those loans had maximum terms of 90 days. We didn't get one cent from the government or from incentive agencies either, and we never paid out a dime in graft or bribes.

How did we do it and survive? Hard work, of course. And good luck—fundamental to all business success. But most important, I think, were the drastic changes we made in our concept of management. Without those changes, not even hard work and good luck could have pulled us through.

Semco has three fundamental values on which we base some 30 management programs. These values—democracy, profit sharing, and information—work in a complicated circle, with each dependent on the other two. If we eliminated one, the others would be meaningless. Our corporate structure, employee freedoms, union relations, factory size limitations—all are products of our commitment to these principles.

It's never easy to transplant management programs from one company to another. In South America, it's axiomatic that our structure and style cannot be duplicated. Semco is either too small, too big, too far away, too young, too old, or too obnoxious.

We may also be too specialized. We do cellular manufacturing of technologically sophisticated products, and we work at the high end on quality and price. So our critics may be right. Perhaps nothing we've done can be a blueprint for anyone else. Still, in an industrial world whose methods show obvious signs of exhaustion, the merit of sharing experience is to encourage experiment and to plant the seeds of conceptual change. So, what the hell.

——— PARTICIPATORY HOT AIR

The first of Semco's three values is democracy, or employee involvement. Clearly, workers who control their working conditions are going to be happier than workers who don't. Just as clearly, there is no contest between the company that buys the grudging compliance of its work force and the company that enjoys the enterprising participation of its employees.

But about 90% of the time, participatory management is just hot air. Not that intentions aren't good. It's just that implementing employee involvement is so complex, so difficult, and, not uncommonly, so frustrating that it is easier to talk about than to do.

We found four big obstacles to effective participatory management: size, hierarchy, lack of motivation, and ignorance. In an immense production unit, people feel tiny, nameless, and incapable of exerting influence on the way work is done or on the final profit made. This sense of helplessness is underlined by managers who, jealous of their power and prerogatives, refuse to let subordinates make any decisions for themselves—sometimes even about going to the bathroom. But even if size and hierarchy can be overcome, why should workers *care* about productivity and company profits? Moreover, even if you can get them to care, how can they tell when they're doing the right thing?

As Antony Jay pointed out back in the 1950s in *Corporation Man*, human beings weren't designed to work in big groups. Until recently, our ancestors were hunters and gatherers. For more than five million years, they refined their ability to work in groups of no more than about a dozen people. Then along comes the industrial revolution, and suddenly workers are trying to function efficiently in factories that employ hundreds and even thousands. Organizing those hundreds into teams of about ten members each may help some, but there's still a limit to how many small teams can work well together. At Semco, we've found the most effective production unit consists of about 150 people. The exact number is open to argument, but it's clear that several thousand people in one facility makes individual involvement an illusion.

When we made the decision to keep our units small, we immediately focused on one facility that had more than 300 people. The unit manufactured commercial food-service equipment—slicers, scales, meat grinders, mixers— and used an MRP II system hooked up to an IBM mainframe with dozens of terminals all over the plant. Paperwork often took two days to make its way from one end of the factory to the other. Excess inventories, late delivery, and quality problems were common. We had tried various worker participation programs, quality circles, kanban systems, and motivation schemes, all of which got off to great starts but lost their momentum within months. The whole thing was just too damn big and complex; there were too many managers in too many layers holding too many meetings. So we decided to break up the facility into three separate plants.

To begin with, we kept all three in the same building but separated everything we could—entrances, receiving docks, inventories, telephones, as well as certain auxiliary functions like personnel, management information systems, and internal controls. We also scrapped the mainframe in favor of three independent, PC-based systems.

The first effect of the breakup was a rise in costs due to duplication of effort and a loss in economies of scale. Unfortunately, balance sheets chalk up items like these as liabilities, all with dollar figures attached, and there's nothing at first to list on the asset side but airy stuff like "heightened involvement" and "a sense of belonging." Yet the longer-term results exceeded our expectations.

Within a year, sales doubled; inventories fell from 136 days to 46; we unveiled eight new products that had been stalled in R&D for two years; and overall quality improved to the point that a one-third rejection rate on federally inspected scales dropped to less than 1%. Increased productivity let us reduce the work force by 32% through attrition and retirement incentives.

I don't claim that size reduction alone accomplished all this, just that size reduction is essential for putting employees in touch with one another so they can coordinate their work. The kind of distance we want to eliminate comes from having too many people in one place, but it also comes from having a pyramidal hierarchy.

——— PYRAMIDS AND CIRCLES

The organizational pyramid is the cause of much corporate evil because the tip is too far from the base. Pyramids emphasize power, promote insecurity, distort communications, hobble interaction, and make it very difficult for the people who plan and the people who execute to move in the same direction. So Semco designed an organizational *circle*. Its greatest advantage is to reduce management levels to three—one corporate level and two operating levels at the manufacturing units.

It consists of three concentric circles. One tiny, central circle contains the five people who integrate the company's movements. These are the counselors I mentioned before. I'm one of them, and except for a couple of legal documents that call me president, counselor is the only title I use. A second, larger circle contains the heads of the eight divisions—we call them partners. Finally, a third, huge circle holds all the other employees. Most of them are the people we call associates; they do the research, design, sales, and manufacturing work and have no one reporting to them on a regular basis. But some of them are the permanent and temporary team and task leaders we call coordinators. We have counselors, partners, coordinators, and associates. That's four titles and three management layers.

The linchpins of the system are the coordinators, a group that includes everyone formerly called foreman, supervisor, manager, head, or chief. The only people who report to coordinators are associates. No coordinator reports to another coordinator—that feature of the system is what ensures the reduction in management layers.

Like anyone else, we value leadership, but it's not the only thing we value. In marine pumps, for example, we have an applications engineer who can look at the layout of a ship and then focus on one particular pump and say, "That pump will fail if you take this thing north of the Arctic Circle." He makes a lot more money than the person who manages his unit. We can change the manager, but this guy knows what kind of pump will work in the Arctic, and that's worth more. Associates often make higher salaries than coordinators and partners, and they can increase their status and compensation without entering the "management" line.

Managers and the status and money they enjoy—in a word, hierarchy— are the single biggest obstacle to participatory management. We had to get the managers out of the way of democratic decision making, and our circular system does that pretty well.

But we go further. We don't hire or promote people until they've been interviewed and accepted by all their future subordinates. Twice a year, subordinates evaluate managers. Also twice a year, everyone in the company anonymously fills out a questionnaire about company credibility and top management competence. Among other things, we ask our employees what it would take to make them quit or go on strike.

We insist on making important decisions collegially, and certain decisions are made by a companywide vote. Several years ago, for example, we needed a bigger plant for our marine division, which makes pumps, compressors, and ship propellers. Real estate agents looked for months and found nothing. So we asked the employees themselves to help, and over the first weekend they found three factories for sale, all of them nearby. We closed up shop for a day, piled everyone into buses, and drove out to inspect the three buildings. Then the workers voted—and they chose a plant the counselors didn't really want. It was an interesting situation—one that tested our commitment to participatory management.

The building stands across the street from a Caterpillar plant that's one of the most frequently struck factories in Brazil. With two tough unions of our own, we weren't looking forward to front-row seats for every labor dispute that came along. But we accepted the employees' decision because we believe that in the long run, letting people participate in the decisions that affect their lives will have a positive effect on employee motivation and morale.

We bought the building and moved in. The workers designed the layout for a flexible manufacturing system, and they hired one of Brazil's foremost artists to paint the whole thing, inside and out, including the machinery. That plant really belongs to its employees. I feel like a guest every time I walk in.

I don't mind. The division's productivity, in dollars per year per employee, has jumped from $14,200 in 1984—the year we moved—to $37,500 in 1988, and for 1989 the goal is $50,000. Over the same period, market share went from 54% to 62%.

Employees also outvoted me on the acquisition of a company that I'm still sure we should have bought. But they felt we weren't ready to digest it, and I lost the vote. In a case like that, the credibility of our management system is at stake. Employee involvement must be real, even when it makes management uneasy. Anyway, what is the future of an acquisition if the people who have to operate it don't believe it's workable?

——— HIRING ADULTS

We have other ways of combating hierarchy too. Most of our programs are based on the notion of giving employees control over their own lives. In a word, we hire adults, and then we treat them like adults.

Think about that. Outside the factory, workers are men and women who elect governments, serve in the army, lead community projects, raise and educate families, and make decisions every day about the future. Friends solicit their advice. Salespeople court them. Children and grandchildren look up to them for their wisdom and experience. But the moment they walk into the factory, the company transforms them into adolescents. They have to wear badges and name tags, arrive at a certain time, stand in line to punch the clock or eat their lunch, get permission to go to the bathroom, give lengthy explanations every time they're five minutes late, and follow instructions without asking a lot of questions.

One of my first moves when I took control of Semco was to abolish norms, manuals, rules, and regulations. Everyone knows you can't run a large organization without regulations, but everyone also knows that most regulations are poppycock. They rarely solve problems. On the contrary, there is usually some obscure corner of the rule book that justifies the worst silliness people can think up. Common sense is a riskier tactic because it requires personal responsibility.

It's also true that common sense requires just a touch of civil disobedience every time someone calls attention to something that's not working. We had to free the Thoreaus and the Tom Paines in the factory and recognize that civil disobedience was not an early sign of revolution but a clear indication of common sense at work.

So we replaced all the nitpicking regulations with the rule of common sense and put our employees in the demanding position of using their own judgment.

We have no dress code, for example. The idea that personal appearance is important in a job—any job—is baloney. We've all heard that salespeople, receptionists, and service reps are the company's calling cards, but in fact how utterly silly that is. A company that needs business suits to prove its seriousness probably lacks more meaningful proof. And what customer has ever canceled an order because the receptionist was wearing jeans instead of a dress? Women and men look best when they feel good. IBM is not a great company because its salespeople dress to the special standard that Thomas Watson set. It's a great company that also happens to have this quirk.

We also scrapped the complex company rules about travel expenses— what sorts of accommodations people were entitled to, whether we'd pay for a theater ticket, whether a free call home meant five minutes or ten. We used to spend a lot of time discussing stuff like that. Now we base everything on common sense. Some people stay in four-star hotels and some live like spartans. Some people spend $200 a day while others get by on $125. Or so I suppose. No one checks expenses, so there is no way of knowing. The point is, we don't care. If we can't trust people with our money and their judgment, we sure as hell shouldn't be sending them overseas to do business in our name.

We have done away with security searches, storeroom padlocks, and audits of the petty-cash accounts of veteran employees. Not that we wouldn't prosecute a genuinely criminal violation of our trust. We just refuse to humiliate 97% of the work force to get our hands on the occasional thief or two-bit embezzler.

We encourage—we practically insist on—job rotation every two to five years to prevent boredom. We try hard to provide job security, and for people over 50 or who've been with the company for more than three years, dismissal procedures are extra complicated.

On the more experimental side, we have a program for entry-level management trainees called Lost in Space, whereby we hire a couple of people every year who have no job description at all. A "godfather" looks after them, and for one year they can do anything they like, as long as they try at least 12 different areas or units.

By the same logic that governs our other employee programs, we also have eliminated time clocks. People come and go according to their own schedules—even on the factory floor. I admit this idea is hard to swallow; most manufacturers are not ready for factory-floor flextime. But our reasoning was simple.

First, we use cellular manufacturing systems. At our food-processing equipment plant, for example, one cell makes only slicers, another makes scales, another makes mixers, and so forth. Each cell is self-contained, so products— and their problems—are segregated from each other.

Second, we assumed that all our employees were trustworthy adults. We couldn't believe they would come to work day after day and sit on their hands because no one else was there. Pretty soon, we figured, they would start coordinating their work hours with their coworkers.

And that's exactly what happened, only more so. For example, one man wanted to start at 7 A.M., but because the forklift operator didn't come until 8, he couldn't get his parts. So a general discussion arose, and the upshot was that now everyone knows how to operate a forklift. In fact, most people now can do several jobs. The union has never objected because the initiative came from the workers themselves. It was their idea.

Moreover, the people on the factory floor set the schedule, and if they say that this month they will build 48 commercial dishwashers, then we can go play tennis, because 48 is what they'll build.

In one case, one group decided to make 220 meat slicers. By the end of the month, it had finished the slicers as scheduled—except that even after repeated phone calls, the supplier still hadn't produced the motors. So two employees drove over and talked to the supplier and managed to get delivery at the end of that day, the 31st. Then they stayed all night, the whole work force, and finished the lot at 4:45 the next morning.

When we introduced flexible hours, we decided to hold regular follow-up meetings to track problems and decide how to deal with abuses and production interruptions. That was years ago, and we haven't yet held the first meeting.

HUNTING THE WOOLLY MAMMOTH

What makes our people behave this way? As Antony Jay points out, corporate man is a very recent animal. At Semco, we try to respect the hunter that dominated the first 99.9% of the history of our species. If you had to kill a mammoth or do without supper, there was no time to draw up an organization chart, assign tasks, or delegate authority. Basically, the person who saw the mammoth from farthest away was the Official Sighter, the one who ran fastest was the Head Runner, whoever threw the most accurate spear was the Grand Marksman, and the person all others respected most and listened to was the Chief. That's all there was to it. Distributing little charts to produce an appearance of order would have been a waste of time. It still is.

What I'm saying is, put ten people together, don't appoint a leader, and you can be sure that one will emerge. So will a sighter, a runner, and whatever else the group needs. We form the groups, but they find their own leaders. That's not a lack of structure, that's just a lack of structure imposed from above.

But getting back to that mammoth, why was it that all the members of the group were so eager to do their share of the work—sighting, running, spearing, chiefing—and to stand aside when someone else could do it better? Because they all got to eat the thing once it was killed and cooked. What mattered was results, not status.

Corporate profit is today's mammoth meat. And though there is a widespread view that profit sharing is some kind of socialist infection, it seems to me that few motivational tools are more capitalist. Everyone agrees that profits should belong to those who risk their capital, that entrepreneurial behavior deserves reward, that the creation of wealth should enrich the creator.

Well, depending on how you define capital and risk, all these truisms can apply as much to workers as to shareholders.

Still, many profit-sharing programs are failures, and we think we know why. Profit sharing won't motivate employees if they see it as just another management gimmick, if the company makes it difficult for them to see how their own work is related to profits and to understand how those profits are divided.

In Semco's case, each division has a separate profit-sharing program. Twice a year, we calculate 23% of after-tax profit on each division income statement and give a check to three employees who've been elected by the workers in their division. These three invest the money until the unit can meet and decide—by simple majority vote—what they want to do with it. In most units, that's turned out to be an equal distribution. If a unit has 150 workers, the total is divided by 150 and handed out. It's that simple. The guy who sweeps the floor gets just as much as the division partner.

One division chose to use the money as a fund to lend out for housing construction. It was a pretty close vote, and the workers may change their minds next year. In the meantime, some of them have already received loans and have begun to build themselves houses. In any case, the employees do what they want with the money. The counselors stay out of it.

Semco's experience has convinced me that profit sharing has an excellent chance of working when it crowns a broad program of employee participation, when the profit-sharing criteria are so clear and simple that the least-gifted employee can understand them, and perhaps most important, when employees have monthly access to the company's vital statistics—costs, overhead, sales, payroll, taxes, profits.

——— TRANSPARENCY

Lots of things contribute to a successful profit-sharing program: low employee turnover, competitive pay, absence of paternalism, refusal to give consolation prizes when profits are down, frequent (quarterly or semiannual) profit distribution, and plenty of opportunity for employees to question the management decisions that affect future profits. But nothing matters more than those vital statistics—short, frank, frequent reports on how the company is doing. Complete transparency. No hocus-pocus, no hanky-panky, no simplifications.

On the contrary, all Semco employees attend classes to learn how to read and understand the numbers, and it's one of their unions that teaches the course. Every month, each employee gets a balance sheet, a profit-and-loss analysis, and a cash-flow statement for his or her division. The reports contain about 70 line items (more, incidentally, than we use to run the company, but we don't want anyone to think we're withholding information).

Many of our executives were alarmed by the decision to share monthly financial results with all employees. They were afraid workers would want to know everything, like how much we pay executives. When we held the first large meeting to discuss these financial reports with the factory committees and the leaders of the metalworkers' union, the first question we got was, "How much do division managers make?" We told them. They gasped. Ever since, the factory workers have called them "maharaja."

But so what? If executives are embarrassed by their salaries, that probably means they aren't earning them. Confidential payrolls are for those who cannot look themselves in the mirror and say with conviction, "I live in a capitalist system that remunerates on a geometric scale. I spent years in school, I have years of experience, I am capable and dedicated and intelligent. I deserve what I get."

I believe that the courage to show the real numbers will always have positive consequences over the long term. On the other hand, we can show only the numbers we bother to put together, and there aren't as many as there used to be. In my view, only the big numbers matter. But Semco's accounting people keep telling me that since the only way to get the big numbers is to add up the small ones, producing a budget or report that includes every tiny detail would require no extra effort. This is an expensive fallacy and a difficult one to eradicate.

A few years ago, the U.S. president of Allis-Chalmers paid Semco a visit. At the end of his factory tour, he leafed through our monthly reports and budgets. At that time, we had our numbers ready on the fifth working day of every month in super-organized folders, and were those numbers comprehensive! On page 67, chart 112.6, for example, you could see how much coffee the workers in Light Manufacturing III had consumed the month before. The man said he was surprised to find such efficiency in a Brazilian company. In fact, he was so impressed that he asked his Brazilian subsidiary, an organization many times our size, to install a similar system there.

For months, we strolled around like peacocks, telling anyone who cared to listen that our budget system was state-of-the-art and that the president of a Big American Company had ordered his people to copy it. But soon we began to realize two things. First, our expenses were always too high, and they never came down because the accounting department was full of overpaid clerks who did nothing but compile them. Second, there were so damn many numbers inside the folder that almost none of our managers read them. In fact, we knew less about the company then, with all that information, than we do now without it.

Today we have a simple accounting system providing limited but relevant information that we can grasp and act on quickly. We pared 400 cost centers down to 50. We beheaded hundreds of classifications and dozens of accounting lines. Finally, we can see the company through the haze.

(As for Allis-Chalmers, I don't know whether it ever adopted our old system in all its terrible completeness, but I hope not. A few years later, it began to suffer severe financial difficulties and eventually lost so much market share and money that it was broken up and sold. I'd hate to think it was our fault.)

In preparing budgets, we believe that the flexibility to change the budget continually is much more important than the detailed consistency of the initial numbers. We also believe in the importance of comparing expectations with results. Naturally, we compare monthly reports with the budget. But we go one step further. At month's end, the coordinators in each area make guesses about unit receipts, profit margins, and expenses. When the official numbers come out a few days later, top managers compare them with the guesses to judge how well the coordinators understand their areas.

What matters in budgets as well as in reports is that the numbers be few and important and that people treat them with something approaching passion. The three monthly reports, with their 70 line items, tell us how to run the company, tell our managers how well they know their units, and tell our employees if there's going to be a profit. Everyone works on the basis of the same information, and everyone looks forward to its appearance with what I'd call fervent curiosity.

And that's all there is to it. Participation gives people control of their work, profit sharing gives them a reason to do it better, information tells them what's working and what isn't.

——— LETTING THEM DO WHATEVER THE HELL THEY WANT

So we don't have systems or staff functions or analysts or anything like that. What we have are people who either sell or make, and there's nothing in between. Is there a marketing department? Not on your life. Marketing is everybody's problem. Everybody knows the price of the products. Everybody knows the cost. Everybody has the monthly statement that says exactly what each of them makes, how much bronze is costing us, how much overtime we paid, all of it. And the employees know that 23% of the after-tax profit is theirs.

We are very, very rigorous about the numbers. We want them in on the fourth day of the month so we can get them back out on the fifth. And because we're so strict with the financial controls, we can be extremely lax about everything else. Employees can paint the walls any color they like. They can come to work whenever they decide. They can wear whatever clothing makes them comfortable. They can do whatever the hell they want. It's up to them to see the connection between productivity and profit and to act on it.

—— DISCUSSION QUESTIONS

1. The author acknowledges the importance of leadership, but he also points out the value of specialized knowledge and the higher compensation that those who possess this knowledge receive from their companies. Do you agree with this compensation system? Explain. What improvements would you make?

2. The reading mentions several innovative practices such as renaming job descriptions, subordinates hiring and evaluating managers as well as having an important voice in the company's decisions, and abolishing rules, regulations, norms, and manuals. As the author states, "It's never easy to transplant management programs from one company to another." Would this be true for companies you've worked for in the past? Would this program work better in a manufacturing company than in a services company?

3. This reading addresses many of the tensions that exist between labor and management such as salaries. Do you think these tensions are adequately addressed? Explain. Are there other tensions that the author has neglected to mention?

4. There are various theories of leadership (group and exchange theories, contingency, path-goal leadership, and so on). Which, if any, of these theories apply to Semco's style? Support your answer with examples from the reading.

LEADING AN ORGANIZATION

Managers and Leaders: Are They Different?

6

ABRAHAM ZALEZNIK

Most societies, including business organizations, are caught between two conflicting needs: for managers to maintain day-to-day operations and for leaders to create new approaches and envision new areas to explore. Why is there a conflict? Can't both managers and leaders exist in the same society? Even better, can't one person be both a manager and a leader?

The author of this reading suggests that because leaders and managers are basically different types of people, the conditions favoring the growth of one may thwart the growth of the other. Using a variety of individual examples, the author shows how managers and leaders have different attitudes toward their goals, careers, relations with others, and themselves. Bureaucratic organizations, in which managers flourish, may be inimical to the growth of leaders. Organizations that encourage close mentoring relationships between junior and senior executives are more likely to foster leaders.

What is the ideal way to develop leadership? Every society provides its own answer to this question, and each, in groping for answers, defines its deepest concerns about the purposes, distributions, and uses of power. Business has contributed its answer to the leadership question by evolving a new breed called the manager. Simultaneously, business has established a new power ethic that favors collective over individual leadership, the cult of the group over that of personality. While ensuring the competence, control, and the balance of power among groups with the potential for rivalry, managerial leadership unfortunately does not necessarily ensure imagination, creativity, or ethical behavior in guiding the destinies of corporate enterprises.

Leadership inevitably requires using power to influence the thoughts and actions of other people. Power in the hands of an individual entails human risks: first, the risk of equating power with the ability to get immediate results; second, the risk of ignoring the many different ways people can legitimately accumulate power; and third, the risk of losing self-control in the desire for power. The need to hedge these risks accounts in part for the development of collective leadership and the managerial ethic. Consequently, an inherent conservatism dominates the culture of large organizations. In *The Second American Revolution*, John D. Rockefeller 3rd describes the conservatism of organizations:

An organization is a system, with a logic of its own, and all the weight of tradition and inertia. The deck is stacked in favor of the tried and proven way of doing things and against the taking of risks and striking out in new directions.[1]

Out of this conservatism and inertia organizations provide succession to power through the development of managers rather than individual leaders. And the irony of the managerial ethic is that it fosters a bureaucratic culture in business, supposedly the last bastion protecting us from the encroachments and controls of bureaucracy in government and education. Perhaps the risks associated with power in the hands of an individual may be necessary ones for business to take if organizations are to break free of their inertia and bureaucratic conservatism.

——— MANAGER VERSUS LEADER PERSONALITY

Theodore Levitt has described the essential features of a managerial culture with its emphasis on rationality and control:

> Management consists of the rational assessment of a situation and the systematic selection of goals and purposes (what is to be done?); the systematic development of strategies to achieve these goals; the marshalling of the required resources; the rational design, organization, direction, and control of the activities required to attain the selected purposes; and, finally, the motivating and rewarding of people to do the work.[2]

In other words, whether his or her energies are directed toward goals, resources, organization structures, or people, a manager is a problem solver. The manager asks: "What problems have to be solved, and what are the best ways to achieve results so that people will continue to contribute to this organization?" In this conception, leadership is a practical effort to direct affairs; and to fulfill their tasks, managers require that many people operate at different levels of status and responsibility. Our democratic society is, in fact, unique in having solved the problem of providing well-trained managers for business. The same solution stands ready to be applied to government, education, health care, and other institutions. It takes neither genius nor heroism to be a manager, but rather persistence, tough-mindedness, hard work, intelligence, analytical ability and, perhaps most important, tolerance and good will.

---

1. John D. Rockefeller 3rd, *The Second American Revolution* (New York: Harper & Row, 1973), p. 72.

2. Theodore Levitt, "Management and the 'Post-Industrial' Society," *The Public Interest*, (Summer 1976): 73.

Another conception, however, attaches almost mystical beliefs to what leadership is and assumes that only great people are worthy of the drama of power and politics. Here, leadership is a psychodrama in which, as a precondition for control of a political structure, a lonely person must gain control of him- or herself. Such an expectation of leadership contrasts sharply with the mundane, practical, and yet important conception that leadership is really managing work that other people do.

Two questions come to mind. Is this mystique of leadership merely a holdover from our collective childhood of dependency and our longing for good and heroic parents? Or, is there a basic truth lurking behind the need for leaders that no matter how competent managers are, their leadership stagnates because of their limitations in visualizing purposes and generating value in work? Without this imaginative capacity and the ability to communicate, managers, driven by their narrow purposes, perpetuate group conflicts instead of reforming them into broader desires and goals.

If indeed problems demand greatness, then, judging by past performance, the selection and development of leaders leave a great deal to chance. There are no known ways to train "great" leaders. Furthermore, beyond what we leave to chance, there is a deeper issue in the relationship between the need for competent managers and the longing for great leaders.

What it takes to ensure the supply of people who will assume practical responsibility may inhibit the development of great leaders. Conversely, the presence of great leaders may undermine the development of managers who become very anxious in the relative disorder that leaders seem to generate. The antagonism in aim—to have many competent managers as well as great leaders—often remains obscure in stable and well-developed societies. But the antagonism surfaces during periods of stress and change, as it did in the Western countries during both the Great Depression and World War II. The tension also appears in the struggle for power between theorists and professional managers in revolutionary societies.

It is easy enough to dismiss the dilemma I pose—of training managers while we may need new leaders, or leaders at the expense of managers—by saying that the need is for people who can be *both* managers and leaders. The truth of the matter as I see it, however, is that just as a managerial culture is different from the entrepreneurial culture that develops when leaders appear in organizations, managers and leaders are very different kinds of people. They differ in motivation, personal history, and in how they think and act.

A technologically oriented and economically successful society tends to depreciate the need for great leaders. Such societies hold a deep and abiding faith in rational methods of solving problems, including problems of value, economics, and justice. Once rational methods of solving problems are broken down into elements, organized, and taught as skills, then society's faith in technique over personal qualities in leadership remains the guiding conception for a democratic society contemplating its leadership requirements. But there are times when tinkering and trial and error prove inadequate to the emerging problems of selecting goals, allocating resources, and distributing wealth and opportunity. During such times, the democratic society needs to find leaders who use themselves as the instruments of learning and acting, instead of managers who use their accumulation of collective experience to get where they are going.

The most impressive spokesperson, as well as exemplar of the managerial viewpoint, was Alfred P. Sloan, Jr. who, along with Pierre du Pont, designed the modern corporate structure. Reflecting on what makes one management successful while another fails, Sloan suggested that "good management rests on a reconciliation of centralization and decentralization, or 'decentralization with coordinated control.'"[3]

Sloan's conception of management, as well as his practice, developed by trial and error, and by the accumulation of experience. Sloan wrote:

> There is no hard-and-fast rule for sorting out the various responsibilities and the best way to assign them. The balance which is struck . . . varies according to what is being decided, the circumstances of the time, past experience, and the temperaments and skills of the executive involved.[4]

In other words, in much the same way that the inventors of the late nineteenth century tried, failed, and fitted until they hit on a product or method, managers who innovate in developing organizations are "tinkers." They do not have a grand design or experience the intuitive flash of insight that, borrowing from modern science, we have come to call the "breakthrough."

Managers and leaders differ fundamentally in their world views. The dimensions for assessing these differences include managers' and leaders' orientations toward their goals, their work, their human relations, and their selves.

ATTITUDES TOWARD GOALS

Managers tend to adopt impersonal, if not passive, attitudes toward goals. Managerial goals arise out of necessities rather than desires, and, therefore, are deeply embedded in the history and culture of the organization.

Frederic G. Donner, chairman and chief executive officer of General Motors from 1958 to 1967, expressed this impersonal and passive attitude toward goals in defining GM's position on product development:

---

3. Alfred P. Sloan, Jr., *My Years with General Motors* (New York: Doubleday & Co. 1964), p. 429.
4. Ibid., p. 429.

> To meet the challenge of the marketplace, we must recognize changes in customer needs and desires far enough ahead to have the right products in the right places at the right time and in the right quantity.
>
> We must balance trends in preference against the many compromises that are necessary to make a final product that is both reliable and good looking, that performs well and that sells at a competitive price in the necessary volume. We must design, not just the cars we would like to build, but more importantly, the cars that our customers want to buy.[5]

Nowhere in this formulation of how a product comes into being is there a notion that consumer tastes and preferences arise in part as a result of what manufacturers do. In reality, through product design, advertising, and promotion, consumers learn to like what they then say they need. Few would argue that people who enjoy taking snapshots *need* a camera that also develops pictures. But in response to novelty, convenience, a shorter interval between acting (taking the snap) and gaining pleasure (seeing the shot), the Polaroid camera succeeded in the marketplace. But it is inconceivable that Edwin Land responded to impressions of consumer need. Instead, he translated a technology (polarization of light) into a product, which proliferated and stimulated consumers' desires.

The example of Polaroid and Land suggests how leaders think about goals. They are active instead of reactive, shaping ideas instead of responding to them. Leaders adopt a personal and active attitude toward goals. The influence a leader exerts in altering moods, evoking images and expectations, and in establishing specific desires and objectives determines the direction a business takes. The net result of this influence is to change the way people think about what is desirable, possible, and necessary.

CONCEPTIONS OF WORK

What do managers and leaders do? What is the nature of their respective work?

Leaders and managers differ in their conceptions. Managers tend to view work as an enabling process involving some combination of people and ideas interacting to establish strategies and make decisions. Managers help the process along by a range of skills, including calculating the interests in opposition, staging and timing the surfacing of controversial issues, and reducing tensions. In this enabling process, managers appear flexible in the use of tactics. They negotiate and bargain, on the one hand, and use rewards and

---

5. Ibid., p. 440.

punishments, and other forms of coercion, on the other. Machiavelli wrote for managers and not necessarily for leaders.

Alfred Sloan illustrated how this enabling process works in situations of conflict. The time was the early 1920s when the Ford Motor Co. still dominated the automobile industry using, as did General Motors, the conventional water-cooled engine. With the full backing of Pierre du Pont, Charles Kettering dedicated himself to the design of an air-cooled engine, which, if successful, would have been a great technical and market coup for GM. Kettering believed in his product, but the manufacturing division heads at GM remained skeptical and later opposed the new design on two grounds: first, that it was technically unreliable, and second, that the corporation was putting all its eggs in one basket by investing in a new product instead of attending to the current marketing situation.

In the summer of 1923 after a series of false starts and after its decision to recall the copper-cooled Chevrolets from dealers and customers, GM management reorganized and finally scrapped the project. When it dawned on Kettering that the company had rejected the engine, he was deeply discouraged and wrote to Sloan that without the "organized resistance" against the project it would succeed and that unless the project were saved, he would leave the company.

Alfred Sloan was all too aware of the fact that Kettering was unhappy and indeed intended to leave General Motors. Sloan was also aware of the fact that, while the manufacturing divisions strongly opposed the new engine, Pierre du Pont supported Kettering. Furthermore, Sloan had himself gone on record in a letter to Kettering less than two years earlier expressing full confidence in him. The problem Sloan now had was to make his decision stick, keep Kettering in the organization (he was much too valuable to lose), avoid alienating du Pont, and encourage the division heads to move speedily in developing product lines using conventional water-cooled engines.

The actions that Sloan took in the face of this conflict reveal much about how managers work. First, he tried to reassure Kettering by presenting the problem in a very ambiguous fashion, suggesting that he and the executive committee sided with Kettering, but that it would not be practical to force the divisions to do what they were opposed to. He presented the problem as being a question of the people, not the product. Second, he proposed to reorganize around the problem by consolidating all functions in a new division that would be responsible for the design, production, and marketing of the new car. This solution, however, appeared as ambiguous as his efforts to placate and keep Kettering in General Motors. Sloan wrote: "My plan was to create an independent pilot operation under the sole jurisdiction of Mr. Kettering, a kind of copper-cooled-car division. Mr. Kettering would designate his own chief engineer and his production staff to solve the technical problems of manufacture."[6]

While Sloan did not discuss the practical value of this solution, which included saddling an inventor with management responsibility, he in effect used this plan to limit his conflict with Pierre du Pont.

---

6. Ibid., p. 91.

In effect, the managerial solution that Sloan arranged and pressed for adoption limited the options available to others. The structural solution narrowed choices, even limiting emotional reactions to the point where the key people could do nothing but go along, and even allowed Sloan to say in his memorandum to du Pont, "We have discussed the matter with Mr. Kettering at some length this morning and he agrees with us absolutely on every point we made. He appears to receive the suggestion enthusiastically and has every confidence that it can be put across along these lines."[7]

Having placated people who opposed his views by developing a structural solution that appeared to give something but in reality only limited options, Sloan could then authorize the car division's general manager, with whom he basically agreed, to move quickly in designing water-cooled cars for the immediate market demand.

Years later, Sloan wrote, evidently with tongue in cheek, "The copper-cooled car never came up again in a big way. It just died out, I don't know why."[8]

In order to get people to accept solutions to problems, managers need to coordinate and balance continually. Interestingly enough, this managerial work has much in common with what diplomats and mediators do. The manager aims at shifting balances of power toward solutions acceptable as a compromise among conflicting values.

What about leaders, what do they do? Where managers act to limit choices, leaders work in the opposite direction, to develop fresh approaches to long-standing problems and to open issues for new options. Stanley and Inge Hoffmann, the political scientists, liken the leader's work to that of the artist. But unlike most artists, the leader is an integral part of the aesthetic product. One cannot look at a leader's art without looking at the artist. On Charles de Gaulle as a political artist, they wrote: "And each of his major political acts, however tortuous the means or the details, has been whole, indivisible and unmistakably his own, like an artistic act."[9]

The closest one can get to a product apart from the artist is the ideas that occupy, indeed at times obsess, the leader's mental life. To be effective, however, leaders need to project their ideas into images that excite people, and only then develop choices that give the projected images substance. Consequently, leaders create excitement in work.

John F. Kennedy's brief presidency shows both the strengths and weaknesses connected with the excitement leaders generate in their work. In his inaugural address he said, "Let every nation know, whether it wishes us well or ill, that we shall pay any price, bear any burden, meet any hardship, support any friend, oppose any foe, in order to assure the survival and the success of liberty."

---

7. Ibid., p. 91.
8. Ibid., p. 93.
9. Stanley and Inge Hoffmann, "The Will for Grandeur: de Gaulle as Political Artist," *Daedalus* Summer 1968, p. 849.

This much-quoted statement forced people to react beyond immediate concerns and to identify with Kennedy and with important shared ideals. But upon closer scrutiny the statement must be seen as absurd because it promises a position which if in fact adopted, as in the Vietnam War, could produce disastrous results. Yet unless expectations are aroused and mobilized, with all the dangers of frustration inherent in heightened desire, new thinking and new choice can never come to light.

Leaders work from high-risk positions, indeed often are temperamentally disposed to seek out risk and danger, especially where opportunity and reward appear high. From my observations, why one individual seeks risks while another approaches problems conservatively depends more on his or her personality and less on conscious choice. For some, especially those who become managers, the instinct for survival dominates their need for risk, and their ability to tolerate mundane, practical work assists their survival. The same cannot be said for leaders who sometimes react to mundane work as to an affliction.

RELATIONS WITH OTHERS

Managers prefer to work with people; they avoid solitary activity because it makes them anxious. Several years ago, I directed studies on the psychological aspects of career. The need to seek out others with whom to work and collaborate seemed to stand out as important characteristics of managers. When asked, for example, to write imaginative stories in response to a picture showing a single figure (a boy contemplating a violin, or a man silhouetted in a state of reflection), managers populated their stories with people. The following is an example of a manager's imaginative story about the young boy contemplating a violin:

> Mom and Dad insisted that Junior take music lessons so that someday he can become a concert musician. His instrument was ordered and had just arrived. Junior is weighing the alternatives of playing football with the other kids or playing with the squeak box. He can't understand how his parents could think a violin is better than a touchdown.
>
> After four months of practicing the violin, Junior has had more than enough, Daddy is going out of his mind, and Mommy is willing to give in reluctantly to the men's wishes. Football season is now over, but a good third baseman will take the field next spring.[10]

This story illustrates two themes that clarify managerial attitudes toward human relations. The first, as I have suggested, is to seek out activity with other people, that is, the football team, and the second, is to maintain a low level

---

10. Abraham Zaleznik, Gene W. Dalton, and Louis B. Barnes, *Orientation and Conflict in Career* (Boston: Division of Research, Harvard Business School, 1970), p. 316.

of emotional involvement in these relationships. The low emotional involvement appears in the writer's use of conventional metaphors, even clichés, and in the depiction of the ready transformation of potential conflict into harmonious decisions. In this case, Junior, Mommy, and Daddy agree to give up the violin for manly sports.

These two themes may seem paradoxical, but their coexistence supports what a manager does, including reconciling differences, seeking compromises, and establishing a balance of power. A further idea demonstrated by how the manager wrote the story is that managers may lack empathy, or the capacity to sense intuitively the thoughts and feelings of others. To illustrate attempts to be empathic, here is another story written to the same stimulus picture by someone considered by peers to be a leader:

> This little boy has the appearance of being a sincere artist, one who is deeply affected by the violin, and has an intense desire to master the instrument.
>
> He seems to have just completed his normal practice session and appears to be somewhat crestfallen at his inability to produce the sounds which he is sure lie within the violin.
>
> He appears to be in the process of making a vow to himself to expend the necessary time and effort to play this instrument until he satisfies himself that he is able to bring forth the qualities of music which he feels within himself.
>
> With this type of determination and carry through, this boy became one of the great violinists of his day.[11]

Empathy is not simply a matter of paying attention to other people. It is also the capacity to take in emotional signals and to make them mean something in a relationship with an individual. People who describe another person as "deeply affected" with "intense desire," as capable of feeling "crestfallen" and as one who can "vow to himself," would seem to have an inner perceptiveness that they can use in their relationships with others.

Managers relate to people according to the role they play in a sequence of events or in a decision-making *process*, while leaders, who are concerned with ideas, relate in more intuitive and empathetic ways. The manager's orientation to people, as actors in a sequence of events, deflects his or her attention away from the substance of people's concerns and toward their roles in a process. The distinction is simply between a manager's attention to *how* things get done and a leader's to *what* the events and decisions mean to participants.

In recent years, managers have taken over from game theory the notion that decision-making events can be one of two types: the win-lose situation (or zero-sum game) or the win-win situation in which everybody in the action comes out ahead. As part of the process of reconciling differences among people

---

11. Ibid., p. 294.

and maintaining balances of power, managers strive to convert win-lose into win-win situations.

As an illustration, take the decision of how to allocate capital resources among operating divisions in a large, decentralized organization. On the face of it, the dollars available for distribution are limited at any given time. Presumably, therefore, the more one division gets, the less is available for other divisions.

Managers tend to view this situation (as it affects human relations) as a conversion issue: how to make what seems like a win-lose problem into a win-win problem. Several solutions to this situation come to mind. First, the manager focuses others' attention on procedure and not on substance. Here the actors become engrossed in the bigger problem of how to make decisions, not what decisions to make. Once committed to the bigger problem, the actors have to support the outcome since they were involved in formulating decision rules. Because the actors believe in the rules they formulated, they will accept present losses in the expectation that next time they will win.

Second, the manager communicates to the subordinates indirectly, using *signals* instead of *messages*. A signal has a number of possible implicit positions in it while a message clearly states a position. Signals are inconclusive and subject to reinterpretation should people become upset and angry, while messages involve the direct consequence that some people will indeed not like what they hear. The nature of messages heightens emotional response, and as I have indicated, emotionality makes managers anxious. With signals, the question of who wins and who loses often becomes obscured.

Third, the manager plays for time. Managers seem to recognize that with the passage of time and the delay of major decisions, compromises emerge that take the sting out of win-lose situations; and the original "game" will be superseded by additional ones. Therefore, compromises may mean that one wins and loses simultaneously, depending on which of the games one evaluates.

There are undoubtedly many other tactical moves managers use to change human situations from win-lose to win-win. But the point to be made is that such tactics focus on the decision-making process itself and interest managers rather than leaders. The interest in tactics involves costs as well as benefits, including making organizations fatter in bureaucratic and political intrigue and leaner in direct, hard activity and warm human relationships. Consequently, one often hears subordinates characterize managers as inscrutable, detached, and manipulative. These adjectives arise from the subordinates' perception that they are linked together in a process whose purpose, beyond simply making decisions, is to maintain a controlled as well as rational and equitable structure. These adjectives suggest that managers need order in the face of the potential chaos that many fear in human relationships.

In contrast, one often hears leaders referred to in adjectives rich in emotional content. Leaders attract strong feelings of identity and difference, or of love and hate. Human relations in leader-dominated structures often appear turbulent, intense, and at times even disorganized. Such an atmosphere intensifies individual motivation and often produces unanticipated outcomes. Does this intense motivation lead to innovation and high performance, or does it represent wasted energy?

SENSES OF SELF

In *The Varieties of Religious Experience,* William James describes two basic personality types, "once-born" and "twice-born."[12] People of the former personality type are those for whom adjustments to life have been straightforward and whose lives have been more or less a peaceful flow from the moment of their births. The twice-borns, on the other hand, have not had an easy time of it. Their lives are marked by a continual struggle to attain some sense of order. Unlike the once-borns they cannot take things for granted. According to James, these personalities have equally different world views. For a once-born personality, the sense of self, as a guide to conduct and attitude, derives from a feeling of being at home and in harmony with one's environment. For a twice-born, the sense of self derives from a feeling of profound separateness.

A sense of belonging or of being separate has a practical significance for the kinds of investments managers and leaders make in their careers. Managers see themselves as conservators and regulators of an existing order of affairs with which they personally identify and from which they gain rewards. Perpetuating and strengthening existing institutions enhances a manager's sense of self-worth: he or she is performing in a role that harmonizes with the ideals of duty and responsibility. William James had this harmony in mind—this sense of self as flowing easily to and from the outer world—in defining a once-born personality. If one feels oneself as a member of institutions, contributing to their well-being, then one fulfills a mission in life and feels rewarded for having measured up to ideals. This reward transcends material gains and answers the more fundamental desire for personal integrity which is achieved by identifying with existing institutions.

Leaders tend to be twice-born personalities, people who feel separate from their environment, including other people. They may work in organizations, but they never belong to them. Their sense of who they are does not depend upon memberships, work roles, or other social indicators of identity.

---

12. William James, *The Varieties of Religious Experience* (New York: Mentor Books, 1958).

What seems to follow from this idea about separateness is some theoretical basis for explaining why certain individuals search out opportunities for change. The methods to bring about change may be technological, political, or ideological, but the object is the same: to profoundly alter human, economic, and political relationships.

Sociologists refer to the preparation individuals undergo to perform in roles as the socialization process. Where individuals experience themselves as an integral part of the social structure (their self-esteem gains strength through participation and conformity), social standards exert powerful effects in maintaining the individual's personal sense of continuity, even beyond the early years in the family. The line of development from the family to schools, then to career is cumulative and reinforcing. When the line of development is not reinforcing because of significant disruptions in relationships or other problems experienced in the family or other social institutions, the individual turns inward and struggles to establish self-esteem, identity, and order. Here the psychological dynamics center on the experience with loss and the efforts at recovery.

In considering the development of leadership, we have to examine two different courses of life history: (1) development through socialization, which prepares the individual to guide institutions and to maintain the existing balance of social relations; and (2) development through personal mastery, which impels an individual to struggle for psychological and social change. Society produces its managerial talent through the first line of development, while through the second leaders emerge.

——— DEVELOPMENT OF LEADERSHIP

The development of every person begins in the family. Each person experiences the traumas associated with separating from his or her parents, as well as the pain that follows such frustration. In the same vein, all individuals face the difficulties of achieving self-regulation and self-control. But for some, perhaps a majority, the fortunes of childhood provide adequate gratifications and sufficient opportunities to find substitutes for rewards no longer available. Such individuals, the "once-borns," make moderate identifications with parents and find a harmony between what they expect and what they are able to realize from life.

But suppose the pains of separation are amplified by a combination of parental demands and the individual's needs to the degree that a sense of isolation, of being special, and of wariness disrupts the bonds that attach children to parents and other authority figures? Under such conditions, and given a special aptitude, the origins of which remain mysterious, the person becomes deeply involved in his or her inner world at the expense of interest in the outer world. For such a person, self-esteem no longer depends solely upon positive attachments and real rewards. A form of self-reliance takes hold along with expectations of performance and achievement, and perhaps even the desire to do great works.

Such self-perceptions can come to nothing if the individual's talents are negligible. Even with strong talents, there are no guarantees that achievement will follow, let alone that the end result will be for good rather than evil. Other factors enter into development. For one thing, leaders are like artists and other gifted people who often struggle with neuroses; their ability to function varies considerably even over the short run, and some potential leaders may lose the struggle altogether. Also, beyond early childhood, the patterns of development that affect managers and leaders involve the selective influence of particular people. Just as they appear flexible and evenly distributed in the types of talents available for development, managers form moderate and widely distributed attachments. Leaders, on the other hand, establish, and also break off, intensive one-to-one relationships.

It is a common observation that people with great talents are often only indifferent students. No one, for example, could have predicted Einstein's great achievements on the basis of his mediocre record in school. The reason for mediocrity is obviously not the absence of ability. It may result, instead, from self-absorption and the inability to pay attention to the ordinary tasks at hand. The only sure way an individual can interrupt reverie-like preoccupation and self-absorption is to form a deep attachment to a great teacher or other benevolent person who understands and has the ability to communicate with the gifted individual.

Whether gifted individuals find what they need in one-to-one relationships depends on the availability of sensitive and intuitive mentors who have a vocation in cultivating talent. Fortunately, when the generations do meet and the self-selections occur, we learn more about how to develop leaders and how talented people of different generations influence each other.

While apparently destined for a mediocre career, people who form important one-to-one relationships are able to accelerate and intensify their development through an apprenticeship. The background for such apprenticeships, or the psychological readiness of an individual to benefit from an intensive relationship, depends upon some experience in life that forces the individual to turn inward. A case example will make this point clearer. This example comes from the life of Dwight David Eisenhower, and illustrates the transformation of a career from competent to outstanding.[13]

Dwight Eisenhower's early career in the Army foreshadowed very little about his future development. During World War I, while some of his West

---

13. This example is included in Abraham Zaleznik and Manfred F.R. Kets de Vries, *Power and the Corporate Mind* (Boston: Houghton Mifflin, 1975).

Point classmates were already experiencing the war firsthand in France, Eisenhower felt "embedded in the monotony and unsought safety of the Zone of the Interior . . . that was intolerable punishment."[14]

Shortly after World War I, Eisenhower, then a young officer somewhat pessimistic about his career chances, asked for a transfer to Panama to work under General Fox Connor, a senior officer whom Eisenhower admired. The army turned down Eisenhower's request. This setback was very much on Eisenhower's mind when Ikey, his first-born son, succumbed to influenza. By some sense of responsibility for its own, the army transferred Eisenhower to Panama, where he took up his duties under General Connor with the shadow of his lost son very much upon him.

In a relationship with the kind of father he would have wanted to be, Eisenhower reverted to being the son he lost. In this highly charged situation, Eisenhower began to learn from his mentor. General Connor offered, and Eisenhower gladly took, a magnificent tutorial on the military. The effects of this relationship on Eisenhower cannot be measured quantitatively, but, in Eisenhower's own reflections and the unfolding of his career, one cannot overestimate its significance in the reintegration of a person shattered by grief.

As Eisenhower wrote later about Connor, "Life with General Connor was a sort of graduate school in military affairs and the humanities, leavened by a man who was experienced in his knowledge of men and their conduct. I can never adequately express my gratitude to this one gentleman. . . . In a lifetime of association with great and good men, he is the one more or less invisible figure to whom I owe an incalculable debt."[15]

Some time after his tour of duty with General Connor, Eisenhower's breakthrough occurred. He received orders to attend the Command and General Staff School at Fort Leavenworth, one of the most competitive schools in the army. It was a coveted appointment, and Eisenhower took advantage of the opportunity. Unlike his performance in high school and West Point, his work at the Command School was excellent; he was graduated first in his class.

Psychological biographies of gifted people repeatedly demonstrate the important part a mentor plays in developing an individual. Andrew Carnegie owed much to his senior, Thomas A. Scott. As head of the Western Division of the Pennsylvania Railroad, Scott recognized talent and the desire to learn in the young telegrapher assigned to him. By giving Carnegie increasing responsibility and by providing him with the opportunity to learn through close personal observation, Scott added to Carnegie's self-confidence and sense of achievement. Because of his own personal strength and achievement, Scott did not fear Carnegie's aggressiveness. Rather, he gave it full play in encouraging Carnegie's initiative.

---

14. Dwight D. Eisenhower, *At Ease: Stories I Tell to Friends* (New York: Doubleday, 1967), p. 136.

15. Ibid., p. 187.

Mentors take risks with people. They bet initially on talent they perceive in younger people. Mentors also risk emotional involvement in working closely with their juniors. The risks do not always pay off, but the willingness to take them appears crucial in developing leaders.

—— CAN ORGANIZATIONS DEVELOP LEADERS?

The examples I have given of how leaders develop suggest the importance of personal influence and the one-to-one relationship. For organizations to encourage consciously the development of leaders as compared with managers would mean developing one-to-one relationships between junior and senior executives and, more important, fostering a culture of individualism and possibly elitism. The elitism arises out of the desire to identify talent and other qualities suggestive of the ability to lead and not simply to manage.

A myth about how people learn and develop that seems to have taken hold in the American culture also dominates thinking in business. The myth is that people learn best from their peers. Supposedly, the threat of evaluation and even humiliation recedes in peer relations because of the tendency for mutual identification and the social restraints on authoritarian behavior among equals. Peer training in organizations occurs in various forms. The use, for example, of task forces made up of peers from several interested occupational groups (sales, production, research, and finance) supposedly removes the restraints of authority on the individual's willingness to assert and exchange ideas. As a result, so the theory goes, people interact more freely, listen more objectively to criticism and other points of view and, finally, learn from this healthy interchange.

Another application of peer training exists in some large corporations, such as Philips, N.V. in Holland, where organization structure is built on the principle of joint responsibility of two peers, one representing the commercial end of the business and the other the technical. Formally, both hold equal responsibility for geographic operations or product groups, as the case may be. As a practical matter, it may turn out that one or the other of the peers dominates the management. Nevertheless, the main interaction is between two or more equals.

The principal question I would raise about such arrangements is whether they perpetuate the managerial orientation, and preclude the formation of one-to-one relationships between senior people and potential leaders.

Aware of the possible stifling effects of peer relationships on aggressiveness and individual initiative, another company, much smaller than Philips, utilizes joint responsibility of peers for operating units, with one important difference. The chief executive of this company encourages competition and rivalry among peers, ultimately appointing the one who comes out on top for increased responsibility. These hybrid arrangements produce some unintended consequences that can be disastrous. There is no easy way to limit rivalry.

Instead, it permeates all levels of the operation and opens the way for the formation of cliques in an atmosphere of intrigue.

A large, integrated oil company has accepted the importance of developing leaders through the direct influence of senior on junior executives. One chairman and chief executive officer regularly selected one talented university graduate whom he appointed his special assistant, and with whom he would work closely for a year. At the end of the year, the junior executive would become available for assignment to one of the operating divisions, there assigned to a responsible post rather than a training position. The mentor relationship had acquainted the junior executive firsthand with the use of power, and with the important antidotes to the power disease called *hubris*—performance and integrity.

Working in one-to-one relationships, where there is a formal and recognized difference in the power of the actors, takes a great deal of tolerance for emotional interchange. This interchange, inevitable in close working arrangements, probably accounts for the reluctance of many executives to become involved in such relationships. I wonder whether a greater capacity on the part of senior officers to tolerate competitive impulses and challenging behavior of their subordinates might not be healthy for corporations. At least a greater tolerance for interchange would not favor the managerial team player at the expense of the individual who might become a leader.

I am constantly surprised at the frequency with which chief executives feel threatened by open challenges to their ideas, as though the source of their authority, rather than their specific ideas, were at issue. In one case a chief executive officer, who was troubled by the aggressiveness and sometimes outright rudeness of one of his talented vice presidents, used various indirect methods such as group meetings and hints from outside directors to avoid dealing with his subordinate. I advised the executive to deal head-on with what irritated him. I suggested that by direct, face-to-face confrontation, both he and his subordinate would learn to validate the distinction between the authority to be preserved and the issues to be debated.

To confront is also to tolerate aggressive interchange, and has the net effect of stripping away the veils of ambiguity and signaling so characteristic of managerial cultures, as well as encouraging the emotional relationship leaders need if they are to survive.

———— DISCUSSION QUESTIONS

1. Does the author favor either managers or leaders?
2. Does Zaleznik distinguish too sharply between managers and leaders? Is his description of them realistic?
3. Can managers benefit from mentoring relationships? Can they mentor leaders?
4. Are both managers and leaders essential to an organization? Do their roles ever overlap?

7   What Leaders Really Do

JOHN P. KOTTER

Good leadership, asserts the author, is not an accident—it is a talent that can be developed and refined. In this reading, he delineates the differences between management and leadership, explaining the strengths and weaknesses of each and providing examples of leadership tasks such as setting direction and motivating people. The reading closes with suggestions on how to create a corporate culture in which leadership thrives.

Leadership is different from management, but not for the reasons most people think. Leadership isn't mystical and mysterious. It has nothing to do with having charisma or other exotic personality traits. It is not the province of a chosen few. Nor is leadership necessarily better than management or a replacement for it.

Rather, leadership and management are two distinctive and complementary systems of action. Each has its own function and characteristic activities. Both are necessary for success in an increasingly complex and volatile business environment.

Most U.S. corporations today are overmanaged and underled. They need to develop their capacity to exercise leadership. Successful corporations don't wait for leaders to come along. They actively seek out people with leadership potential and expose them to career experiences designed to develop that potential. Indeed, with careful selection, nurturing, and encouragement, dozens of people can play important leadership roles in a business organization.

But while improving their ability to lead, companies should remember that strong leadership with weak management is no better, and is sometimes actually worse, than the reverse. The real challenge is to combine strong leadership and strong management and use each to balance the other.

Of course, not everyone can be good at both leading and managing. Some people have the capacity to become excellent managers but not strong leaders. Others have great leadership potential but, for a variety of reasons, have great difficulty becoming strong managers. Smart companies value both kinds of people and work hard to make them a part of the team.

But when it comes to preparing people for executive jobs, such companies rightly ignore the recent literature that says people cannot manage *and* lead. They try to develop leader-managers. Once companies understand the fundamental difference between leadership and management, they can begin to groom their top people to provide both.

——— THE DIFFERENCE BETWEEN MANAGEMENT AND LEADERSHIP

Management is about coping with complexity. Its practices and procedures are largely a response to one of the most significant developments of the twentieth century: the emergence of large organizations. Without good management, complex enterprises tend to become chaotic in ways that threaten their very existence. Good management brings a degree of order and consistency to key dimensions such as the quality and profitability of products.

Leadership, by contrast, is about coping with change. Part of the reason it has become so important in recent years is that the business world has become more competitive and more volatile. Faster technological change, greater international competition, the deregulation of markets, overcapacity in capital-intensive industries, an unstable oil cartel, raiders with junk bonds, and the changing demographics of the work force are among the many factors that have contributed to this shift. The net result is that doing what was done yesterday, or doing it 5% better, is no longer a formula for success. Major changes are more and more necessary to survive and compete effectively in this new environment. More change always demands more leadership.

Consider a simple military analogy: a peacetime army usually can survive with good administration and management up and down the hierarchy, coupled with good leadership concentrated at the very top. A wartime army, however, needs competent leadership at all levels. No one yet has figured out how to manage people effectively into battle; they must be led.

These different functions—coping with complexity and coping with change—shape the characteristic activities of management and leadership. Each system of action involves deciding what needs to be done, creating networks of people and relationships that can accomplish an agenda, and then trying to ensure that those people actually do the job. But each accomplishes these three tasks in different ways.

Companies manage complexity first by *planning and budgeting*—setting targets or goals for the future (typically for the next month or year), establishing detailed steps for achieving those targets, and then allocating resources to accomplish those plans. By contrast, leading an organization to constructive change begins by *setting a direction*—developing a vision of the future (often the distant future) along with strategies for producing the changes needed to achieve that vision.

Management develops the capacity to achieve its plan by *organizing and staffing*—creating an organizational structure and set of jobs for accomplishing plan requirements, staffing the jobs with qualified individuals, communicating the plan to those people, delegating responsibility for carrying out the plan, and devising systems to monitor implementation. The equivalent leadership activity, however, is *aligning people*. This means communicating the new direction to those who can create coalitions that understand the vision and are committed to its achievement.

Finally, management ensures plan accomplishment by *controlling and problem solving*—formally and informally comparing results to the plan in some detail by means of reports, meetings, and other tools; identifying deviations; and then planning and organizing to solve the problems. But for leadership, achieving a vision requires *motivating and inspiring*—keeping people moving in the right direction, despite major obstacles to change, by appealing to basic but often untapped human needs, values, and emotions.

A closer examination of each of these activities will help clarify the skills leaders need.

──── SETTING A DIRECTION VERSUS PLANNING AND BUDGETING

Since the function of leadership is to produce change, setting the direction of that change is fundamental to leadership.

Setting direction is never the same as planning or even long-term planning, although people often confuse the two. Planning is a management process, deductive in nature and designed to produce orderly results, not change. Setting a direction is more inductive. Leaders gather a broad range of data and look for patterns, relationships, and linkages that help explain things. What's more, the direction-setting aspect of leadership does not produce plans; it creates vision and strategies. These describe a business, technology, or corporate culture in terms of what it should become over the long term and articulate a feasible way of achieving this goal.

Most discussions of vision have a tendency to degenerate into the mystical. The implication is that a vision is something mysterious that mere mortals, even talented ones, could never hope to have. But developing good business direction isn't magic. It is a tough, sometimes exhausting process of gathering and analyzing information. People who articulate such visions aren't magicians but broad-based strategic thinkers who are willing to take risks.

Nor do visions and strategies have to be brilliantly innovative; in fact, some of the best are not. Effective business visions regularly have an almost mundane quality, usually consisting of ideas that are already well known. The particular combination or patterning of the ideas may be new, but sometimes even that is not the case.

For example, when CEO Jan Carlzon articulated his vision to make Scandinavian Airline Systems (SAS) the best airline in the world for the frequent business traveler, he was not saying anything that everyone in the airline industry didn't already know. Business travelers fly more consistently than other market segments and are generally willing to pay higher fares. Thus focusing on business customers offers an airline the possibility of high margins, steady business, and considerable growth. But in an industry known more for bureaucracy than vision, no company had ever put these simple ideas together and dedicated itself to implementing them. SAS did, and it worked.

What's crucial about a vision is not its originality but how well it serves the interests of important constituencies—customers, stockholders, employees—and how easily it can be translated into a realistic competitive strategy. Bad visions tend to ignore the legitimate needs and rights of important constituencies—favoring, say, employees over customers or stockholders. Or they are strategically unsound. When a company that has never been better than a weak competitor in an industry suddenly starts talking about becoming number one, that is a pipe dream, not a vision.

One of the most frequent mistakes that overmanaged and underled corporations make is to embrace long-term planning as a panacea for their lack of direction and inability to adapt to an increasingly competitive and dynamic business environment. Such an approach misinterprets the nature of direction setting and can never work.

Long-term planning is always time-consuming. Whenever something unexpected happens, plans have to be redone. In a dynamic business environment, the unexpected often becomes the norm, and long-term planning can become an extraordinarily burdensome activity. This is why most successful corporations limit the time frame of their planning activities. Indeed, some even consider long-term planning a contradiction in terms.

In a company without direction, even short-term planning can become a black hole capable of absorbing an infinite amount of time and energy. With no vision and strategy to provide constraints around the planning process or to guide it, every eventuality deserves a plan. Under these circumstances, contingency planning can go on forever, draining time and attention from far more essential activities, yet without ever providing the clear sense of direction that a company desperately needs. After a while, managers inevitably become cynical about all this, and the planning process can degenerate into a highly politicized game.

Planning works best not as a substitute for direction setting but as a complement to it. A competent planning process serves as a useful reality check on direction-setting activities. Likewise, a competent direction-setting process provides a focus in which planning then can be realistically carried out. It helps clarify what kind of planning is essential and what kind is irrelevant (see *Exhibit 1*).

———— ALIGNING PEOPLE VERSUS ORGANIZING AND STAFFING

A central feature of modern organizations is interdependence, where no one has complete autonomy, where most employees are tied to many others by their work, technology, management systems, and hierarchy. These linkages

EXHIBIT 1
Setting Direction: Lou Gerstner at American Express

When Lou Gerstner became president of the Travel Related Services (TRS) arm at American Express in 1979, the unit was facing one of its biggest challenges in AmEx's 130-year history. Hundreds of banks were offering or planning to introduce credit cards through Visa and MasterCard that would compete with the American Express card. And more than two dozen financial service firms were coming into the traveler's checks business. In a mature marketplace, this increase in competition usually reduces margins and prohibits growth.

But that was not how Gerstner saw the business. Before joining American Express, he had spent five years as a consultant to TRS, analyzing the money-losing travel division and the increasingly competitive card operation. Gerstner and his team asked fundamental questions about the economics, market, and competition and developed a deep understanding of the business. In the process, he began to craft a vision of TRS that looked nothing like a 130-year-old company in a mature industry.

Gerstner thought TRS had the potential to become a dynamic and growing enterprise, despite the onslaught of Visa and MasterCard competition from thousands of banks. The key was to focus on the global marketplace and, specifically, on the relatively affluent customer American Express had been traditionally serving with top-of-the-line products. By further segmenting this market, aggressively developing a broad range of new products and services, and investing to increase productivity and to lower costs, TRS could provide the best service possible to customers who had enough discretionary income to buy many more services from TRS than they had in the past.

Within a week of his appointment, Gerstner brought together the people running the card organization and questioned all the principles by which they conducted their business. In particular, he challenged two widely shared beliefs—that the division should have only one product, the green card, and that this product was limited in potential for growth and innovation.

present a special challenge when organizations attempt to change. Unless many individuals line up and move together in the same direction, people will tend to fall all over one another. To executives who are overeducated in management and undereducated in leadership, the idea of getting people moving in the same direction appears to be an organizational problem. What executives need to do, however, is not organize people but align them.

Managers organize to create human systems that can implement plans as precisely and efficiently as possible. Typically, this requires a number of potentially complex decisions. A company must choose a structure of jobs and reporting relationships, staff it with individuals suited to the jobs, provide training for those who need it, communicate plans to the work force, and decide how much authority to delegate and to whom. Economic incentives also need to be constructed to accomplish the plan, as well as systems to monitor its implementation. These organizational judgments are much like architectural decisions. It's a question of fit within a particular context.

EXHIBIT 1
Setting Direction: Lou Gerstner at American Express (Continued)

Gerstner also moved quickly to develop a more entrepreneurial culture, to hire and train people who would thrive in it, and to clearly communicate to them the overall direction. He and other top managers rewarded intelligent risk taking. To make entrepreneurship easier, they discouraged unnecessary bureaucracy. They also upgraded hiring standards and created the TRS Graduate Management Program, which offered high-potential young people special training, an enriched set of experiences, and an unusual degree of exposure to people in top management. To encourage risk taking among all TRS employees, Gerstner also established something called the Great Performers program to recognize and reward truly exceptional customer service, a central tenet in the organization's vision.

These initiatives quickly led to new markets, products, and services. TRS expanded its overseas presence dramatically. By 1988, AmEx cards were issued in 29 currencies (as opposed to only 11 a decade earlier). The unit also focused aggressively on two market segments that

had historically received little attention: college students and women. In 1981, TRS combined its card and travel-service capabilities to offer corporate clients a unified system to monitor and control travel expenses. And by 1988, AmEx had grown to become the fifth-largest direct-mail merchant in the United States.

Other new products and services included 90-day insurance on all purchases made with the AmEx card, a Platinum American Express card, and a revolving credit card known as Optima. In 1988, the company also switched to image-processing technology for billing, producing a more convenient monthly statement for customers and reducing billing costs by 25%.

As a result of these innovations, TRS's net income increased a phenomenal 500% between 1978 and 1987—a compounded annual rate of about 18%. The business outperformed many so-called high-tech/high-growth companies. With a 1988 return on equity of 28%, it also outperformed most low-growth but high-profit businesses.

Aligning is different. It is more of a communications challenge than a design problem. First, aligning invariably involves talking to many more individuals than organizing does. The target population can involve not only a manager's subordinates but also bosses, peers, staff in other parts of the organization, as well as suppliers, governmental officials, or even customers. Anyone who can help implement the vision and strategies or who can block implementation is relevant.

Trying to get people to comprehend a vision of an alternative future is also a communications challenge of a completely different magnitude from organizing them to fulfill a short-term plan. It's much like the difference between a football quarterback attempting to describe to his team the next two or three plays versus his trying to explain to them a totally new approach to the game to be used in the second half of the season.

Whether delivered with many words or a few carefully chosen symbols, such messages are not necessarily accepted just because they are understood.

EXHIBIT 2
Aligning People: Chuck Trowbridge and Bob Crandall at Eastman Kodak

Eastman Kodak entered the copy business in the early 1970s, concentrating on technically sophisticated machines that sold, on average, for about $60,000 each. Over the next decade, this business grew to nearly $1 billion in revenues. But costs were high, profits were hard to find, and problems were nearly everywhere. In 1984, Kodak had to write off $40 million in inventory.

Most people at the company knew there were problems, but they couldn't agree on how to solve them. So, in his first two months as general manager of the new copy products group, established in 1984, Chuck Trowbridge met with nearly every key person inside his group, as well as with people elsewhere at Kodak who could be important to the copier business. An especially crucial area was the engineering and manufacturing organization, headed by Bob Crandall.

Trowbridge and Crandall's vision for engineering and manufacturing was simple: to become a world-class manufacturing operation and to create a less bureaucratic and more decentralized organization. Still, this message was difficult to convey because it was such a radical departure from previous communications, not only in the copy products group but throughout most of Kodak. So Crandall set up dozens of vehicles to emphasize the new direction and align people to it: weekly meetings with his own 12 direct reports; monthly Copy Product Forums in which a different employee from each of his departments would meet with him as a group; quarterly meetings with all 100 of his supervisors to discuss recent improvements and new projects to achieve still better results; and quarterly State of the Department meetings, where his managers met with everybody in their own departments.

Once a month, Crandall and all those who reported to him would also meet with 80 to 100 people from some area of his organization to discuss anything they

---

Another big challenge in leadership efforts is credibility—getting people to believe the message. Many things contribute to credibility: the track record of the person delivering the message, the content of the message itself, the communicator's reputation for integrity and trustworthiness, and the consistency between words and deeds.

Finally, aligning leads to empowerment in a way that organizing rarely does. One of the reasons some organizations have difficulty adjusting to rapid changes in markets or technology is that so many people in those companies feel relatively powerless. They have learned from experience that even if they correctly perceive important external changes and then initiate appropriate actions, they are vulnerable to someone higher up who does not like what they have done. Reprimands can take many different forms: "That's against policy" or "We can't afford it" or "Shut up and do as you're told."

Alignment helps overcome this problem by empowering people in at least two ways. First, when a clear sense of direction has been communicated throughout an organization, lower-level employees can initiate actions without the same degree of vulnerability. As long as their behavior is consistent with

EXHIBIT 2
Aligning People: Chuck Trowbridge and Bob Crandall at Eastman Kodak (Continued)

wanted. To align his biggest supplier—the Kodak Apparatus Division, which supplied one-third of the parts used in design and manufacturing—he and his managers met with the top management of that group over lunch every Thursday. More recently, he has created a format called "business meetings," where his managers meet with 12 to 20 people on a specific topic, such as inventory or master scheduling. The goal is to get all of his 1,500 employees in at least one of these focused business meetings each year.

Trowbridge and Crandall also enlisted written communication in their cause. A four- to eight-page *Copy Products Journal* was sent to employees once a month. A program called Dialog Letters gave employees the opportunity to anonymously ask questions of Crandall and his top managers and be guaranteed a reply. But the most visible, and powerful, form of written communication was the chart. In a main hallway near the cafeteria, huge charts vividly reported the quality, cost,

and delivery results for each product, measured against difficult targets. A hundred smaller versions of these charts were scattered throughout the manufacturing area, reporting quality levels and costs for specific work groups.

Results of this intensive alignment process began to appear within six months and still more after a year. These successes made the message more credible and helped get more people on board. Between 1984 and 1988, quality on one of the main product lines increased nearly a hundredfold. Defects per unit went from 30 to 0.3. Over a three-year period, costs on another product line went down nearly 24%. Deliveries on schedule increased from 82% in 1985 to 95% in 1987. Inventory levels dropped by more than 50% between 1984 and 1988, even though the volume of products was increasing. And productivity, measured in units per manufacturing employee, more than doubled between 1985 and 1988.

---

the vision, superiors will have more difficulty reprimanding them. Second, because everyone is aiming at the same target, the probability is less that one person's initiative will be stalled when it comes into conflict with someone else's (see *Exhibit 2*).

—— MOTIVATING PEOPLE VERSUS CONTROLLING AND PROBLEM SOLVING

Since change is the function of leadership, being able to generate highly energized behavior is important for coping with the inevitable barriers to change. Just as direction setting identifies an appropriate path for movement and just as effective alignment gets people moving down that path, successful motivation ensures that they will have the energy to overcome obstacles.

According to the logic of management, control mechanisms compare system behavior with the plan and take action when a deviation is detected. In a well-managed factory, for example, this means the planning process establishes sensible quality targets, the organizing process builds an organization that can achieve those targets, and a control process makes sure that quality lapses are spotted immediately, not in 30 or 60 days, and corrected.

For some of the same reasons that control is so central to management, highly motivated or inspired behavior is almost irrelevant. Managerial processes must be as close as possible to fail-safe and risk-free. That means they cannot be dependent on the unusual or hard to obtain. The whole purpose of systems and structures is to help normal people who behave in normal ways to complete routine jobs successfully, day after day. It's not exciting or glamorous. But that's management.

Leadership is different. Achieving grand visions always requires an occasional burst of energy. Motivation and inspiration energize people, not by pushing them in the right direction as control mechanisms do but by satisfying basic human needs for achievement, a sense of belonging, recognition, self-esteem, a feeling of control over one's life, and the ability to live up to one's ideals. Such feelings touch us deeply and elicit a powerful response.

Good leaders motivate people in a variety of ways. First, they always articulate the organization's vision in a manner that stresses the values of the audience they are addressing. This makes the work important to those individuals. Leaders also regularly involve people in deciding how to achieve the organization's vision (or the part most relevant to a particular individual). This gives people a sense of control. Another important motivational technique is to support employee efforts to realize the vision by providing coaching, feedback, and role modeling, thereby helping people grow professionally and enhancing their self-esteem. Finally, good leaders recognize and reward success, which not only gives people a sense of accomplishment but also makes them feel like they belong to an organization that cares about them. When all this is done, the work itself becomes intrinsically motivating.

The more that change characterizes the business environment, the more that leaders must motivate people to provide leadership as well. When this works, it tends to reproduce leadership across the entire organization, with people occupying multiple leadership roles throughout the hierarchy. This is highly valuable, because coping with change in any complex business demands initiatives from a multitude of people. Nothing less will work.

Of course, leadership from many sources does not necessarily converge. To the contrary, it can easily conflict. For multiple leadership roles to work together, people's actions must be carefully coordinated by mechanisms that differ from those coordinating traditional management roles.

Strong networks of informal relationships—the kind found in companies with healthy cultures—help coordinate leadership activities in much the same way that formal structure coordinates managerial activities. The key difference is that informal networks can deal with the greater demands for coordination associated with nonroutine activities and change. The multitude of communication channels and the trust among the individuals connected by those channels allow for an ongoing process of accommodation and adaptation. When conflicts arise among roles, those same relationships help resolve the conflicts. Perhaps most important, this process of dialogue and accommodation can produce visions that are linked and compatible instead of remote and competitive. All this requires a great deal more communication than is needed to coordinate managerial roles, but unlike formal structure, strong informal networks can handle it.

Of course, informal relations of some sort exist in all corporations. But too often these networks are either very weak—some people are well connected but most are not—or they are highly fragmented—a strong network exists inside the marketing group and inside R&D but not across the two departments. Such networks do not support multiple leadership initiatives well. In fact, extensive informal networks are so important that if they do not exist, creating them has to be the focus of activity early in a major leadership initiative (see *Exhibit 3*).

CREATING A CULTURE OF LEADERSHIP

Despite the increasing importance of leadership to business success, the on-the-job experiences of most people actually seem to undermine the development of attributes needed for leadership. Nevertheless, some companies have consistently demonstrated an ability to develop people into outstanding leader-managers. Recruiting people with leadership potential is only the first step. Equally important is managing their career patterns. Individuals who are effective in large leadership roles often share a number of career experiences.

Perhaps the most typical and most important is significant challenge early in a career. Leaders almost always have had opportunities during their twenties and thirties to actually try to lead, to take a risk, and to learn from both triumphs and failures. Such learning seems essential in developing a wide range of leadership skills and perspectives. It also teaches people something about both the difficulty of leadership and its potential for producing change.

Later in their careers, something equally important happens that has to do with broadening. People who provide effective leadership in important jobs always have a chance, before they get into those jobs, to grow beyond the narrow base that characterizes most managerial careers. This is usually the result of lateral career moves or of early promotions to unusually broad job assignments. Sometimes other vehicles help, like special task-force assignments or a lengthy general management course. Whatever the case, the breadth of knowledge developed in this way seems to be helpful in all aspects of leadership. So does the network of relationships that is often acquired both inside and outside the company. When enough people get opportunities like this, the relationships that are built also help create the strong informal networks needed to support multiple leadership initiatives.

EXHIBIT 3
Motivating People: Richard Nicolosi at Procter & Gamble

For about 20 years after its founding in 1956, Procter & Gamble's paper products division experienced little competition for its high-quality, reasonably priced, and well-marketed consumer goods. By the late 1970s, however, the market position of the division had changed. New competitive thrusts hurt P&G badly. For example, industry analysts estimate that the company's market share for disposable diapers fell from 75% in the mid-1970s to 52% in 1984.

That year, Richard Nicolosi came to paper products as the associate general manager, after three years in P&G's smaller and faster-moving soft-drink business. He found a heavily bureaucratic and centralized organization that was overly preoccupied with internal functional goals and projects. Almost all information about customers came through highly quantitative market research. The technical people were rewarded for cost savings, the commercial people focused on volume and share, and the two groups were nearly at war with each other.

During the late summer of 1984, top management announced that Nicolosi would become the head of paper products in October, and by August he was unofficially running the division. Immediately he began to stress the need for the division to become more creative and market driven, instead of just trying to be a low-cost producer. "I had to make it very clear," Nicolosi later reported, "that the rules of the game had changed."

The new direction included a much greater stress on teamwork and multiple leadership roles. Nicolosi pushed a strategy of using groups to manage the division and its specific products. In October, he and his team designated themselves as the paper division "board" and began meeting first monthly and then weekly. In November, they established Category Teams to manage their major brand groups (such as diapers, tissues, towels) and started pushing responsibility down to these teams. "Shun the incremental," Nicolosi stressed, "and go for the leap."

In December, Nicolosi selectively involved himself in more detail in certain activities. He met with the advertising agency and got to know key creative people.

Corporations that do a better-than-average job of developing leaders put an emphasis on creating challenging opportunities for relatively young employees. In many businesses, decentralization is the key. By definition, it pushes responsibility lower in an organization and in the process creates more challenging jobs at lower levels. Johnson & Johnson, 3M, Hewlett-Packard, General Electric, and many other well-known companies have used that approach quite successfully. Some of those same companies also create as many small units as possible so there are a lot of challenging lower-level general management jobs available.

Sometimes these businesses develop additional challenging opportunities by stressing growth through new products or services. Over the years, 3M has had a policy that at least 25% of its revenue should come from products introduced within the last five years. That encourages small new ventures,

EXHIBIT 3
Motivating People: Richard Nicolosi at Procter & Gamble (Continued)

He asked the marketing manager of diapers to report directly to him, eliminating a layer in the hierarchy. He talked more to the people who were working on new product-development projects.

In January 1985, the board announced a new organizational structure that included not only category teams but also new-brand business teams. By the spring, the board was ready to plan an important motivational event to communicate the new paper products vision to as many people as possible. On June 4, 1985, all the Cincinnati-based personnel in paper plus sales district managers and paper plant managers—several thousand people in all—met in the local Masonic Temple. Nicolosi and other board members described their vision of an organization where "each of us is a leader." The event was videotaped, and an edited version was sent to all sales offices and plants for everyone to see.

All these activities helped create an entrepreneurial environment where large numbers of people were motivated to realize the new vision. Most innovations came from people dealing with new prod-ucts. Ultra Pampers, first introduced in February 1985, took the market share of the entire Pampers product line from 40% to 58% and profitability from break-even to positive. And within only a few months of the introduction of Luvs Delux in May 1987, market share for the overall brand grew by 150%.

Other employee initiatives were oriented more toward a functional area, and some came from the bottom of the hierarchy. In the spring of 1986, a few of the division's secretaries, feeling empowered by the new culture, developed a Secretaries Network. This association established subcommittees on training, on rewards and recognition, and on the "secretary of the future." Echoing the sentiments of many of her peers, one paper products secretary said: "I don't see why we too can't contribute to the division's new direction."

By the end of 1988, revenues at the paper products division were up 40% over a four-year period. Profits were up 66%. And this happened despite the fact that the competition continued to get tougher.

which in turn offer hundreds of opportunities to test and stretch young people with leadership potential.

Such practices can, almost by themselves, prepare people for small- and medium-sized leadership jobs. But developing people for important leadership positions requires more work on the part of senior executives, often over a long period of time. That work begins with efforts to spot people with great leadership potential early in their careers and to identify what will be needed to stretch and develop them.

Again, there is nothing magic about this process. The methods successful companies use are surprisingly straightforward. They go out of their way to make young employees and people at lower levels in their organizations visible to senior management. Senior managers then judge for themselves who has potential and what the development needs of those people are. Executives also discuss their tentative conclusions among themselves to draw more accurate judgments.

Armed with a clear sense of who has considerable leadership potential and what skills they need to develop, executives in these companies then spend time planning for that development. Sometimes that is done as part of a formal succession planning or high-potential development process; often it is more informal. In either case, the key ingredient appears to be an intelligent assessment of what feasible development opportunities fit each candidate's needs.

To encourage managers to participate in these activities, well-led businesses tend to recognize and award people who successfully develop leaders. This is rarely done as part of a formal compensation or bonus formula, simply because it is so difficult to measure such achievements with precision. But it does become a factor in decisions about promotion, especially to the most senior levels, and that seems to make a big difference. When told that future promotions will depend to some degree on their ability to nurture leaders, even people who say that leadership cannot be developed somehow find ways to do it.

Such strategies help create a corporate culture where people value strong leadership and strive to create it. Just as we need more people to provide leadership in the complex organizations that dominate our world today, we also need more people to develop the cultures that will create that leadership. Institutionalizing a leadership-centered culture is the ultimate act of leadership.

DISCUSSION QUESTIONS

1. Kotter points out that setting direction is fundamental to leadership, and strategies spring from setting direction. Devise a vision with strategies that would give direction to a business that you would like to lead.
2. Give examples from your life in which you have had a vision and had to align people who could either help implement your vision or block your vision's implementation. How well did you succeed with both types of people? In retrospect, is there anything that you could have done better?
3. Give instances from your own experience in which you have demonstrated leadership qualities and ability. Also give instances in which your leadership potential was nurtured by others and when you have nurtured the leadership potential of others.

Ways Women Lead

JUDY B. ROSENER

Women managers are succeeding today, but they are not adopting the command-and-control style of leadership traditionally practiced by men. Instead, they are drawing on the skills and attitudes that they have developed from their experience as women.

Because women have historically been expected to play a supportive and cooperative role, they have learned to manage effectively without relying on power and resource control to motivate others. Women managers, for example, are more likely to practice "interactive leadership"—trying to make every interaction with coworkers positive for all involved by encouraging partici-pation, sharing power and information, and making people feel important. The changes occurring in the workplace today may favor this new type of leadership style.

Women managers who have broken the glass ceiling in medium-sized, nontraditional organizations have proven that effective leaders don't come from one mold. They have demonstrated that using the command-and-control style of managing others, a style generally associated with men in large, traditional organizations, is not the only way to succeed.

The first female executives, because they were breaking new ground, adhered to many of the "rules of conduct" that spelled success for men. Now a second wave of women is making its way into top management, not by adopting the style and habits that have proved successful for men but by drawing on the skills and attitudes they developed from their shared experience as women. These second-generation managerial women are drawing on what is unique to their socialization as women and creating a different path to the top. They are seeking and finding opportunities in fast-changing and growing organizations to show that they can achieve results—in a different way. They are succeeding because of—not in spite of—certain characteristics generally considered to be feminine and inappropriate in leaders.

The women's success shows that a nontraditional leadership style is well-suited to the conditions of some work environments and can increase an organization's chances of surviving in an uncertain world. It supports the belief that there is strength in a diversity of leadership styles.

In a recent survey sponsored by the International Women's Forum, I found a number of unexpected similarities between men and women leaders

EXHIBIT
The IWF Survey of Men and Women Leaders

The International Women's Forum was founded in 1982 to give prominent women leaders in diverse professions around the world a way to share their knowledge with each other and with their communities and countries. The organization now has some 37 forums in North America, Europe, Asia, Latin America, and the Middle East. To help other women advance and to educate the public about the contributions women can and are making in government, business, and other fields, the IWF created the Leadership Foundation. The Foundation commissioned me to perform the study of men and women leaders on which this article is based. I conducted the study with the help of Daniel McAllister and Gregory Stephens (Ph.D. students at the Graduate School of Management at the University of California, Irvine) in the spring of 1989.

The survey consisted of an eight-page questionnaire sent to all the IWF members. Each respondent was asked to supply the name of a man in a similar organization with similar responsibilities. The men received the same questionnaire as the IWF members. The respondents were similar in age, occupation, and educational level, which suggests that the matching effort was successful. The response rate was 31%.

The respondents were asked questions about their leadership styles, their organizations, work-family issues, and personal characteristics. The following are among the more intriguing findings, some of which contradict data reported in academic journals and the popular press:

- The women earn the same amount of money as their male counterparts. The average yearly income for men is $136,510; for women it is $140,573. (Most other studies have shown a wage gap between men and women.)

- The men's household income (their own and their spouse's) is much lower than that of the women—$166,454 versus

---

along with some important differences. (For more on the study and its findings, see the *Exhibit*.) Among these similarities are characteristics related to money and children. I found that the men and women respondents earned the same amount of money (and the household income of the women is twice that of the men). This finding is contrary to most studies, which find a considerable wage gap between men and women, even at the executive level. I also found that just as many men as women experience work-family conflict (although when there are children at home, the women experience slightly more conflict than men).

But the similarities end when men and women describe their leadership performance and how they usually influence those with whom they work. The men are more likely than the women to describe themselves in ways that characterize what some management experts call "transactional" leadership.[1] That is, they view job performance as a series of transactions with subordinates—

---

1. Transactional and transformational leadership were first conceptualized by James McGregor Burns in *Leadership* (New York: Harper & Row, 1978) and later developed by Bernard Bass in *Leadership and Performance Beyond Expectations* (New York: Free Press, 1985).

EXHIBIT
The IWF Survey of Men and Women Leaders (Continued)

$300,892. (Only 39% of the men have full-time employed spouses, as opposed to 71% of the women.)

- Both men and women leaders pay their female subordinates roughly $12,000 less than their male subordinates with similar positions and titles.

- Women are more likely than men to use transformational leadership—motivating others by transforming their self-interest into the goals of the organization.

- Women are much more likely than men to use power based on charisma, work record, and contacts (personal power) as opposed to power based on organizational position, title, and the ability to reward and punish (structural power).

- Most men and women describe themselves as having an equal mix of traits that are considered feminine (being excitable, gentle, emotional, submissive, sentimental, understanding, compassionate, sensitive, dependent), mascu-

line (dominant, aggressive, tough, assertive, autocratic, analytical, competitive, independent), and gender-neutral (adaptive, tactful, sincere, conscientious, conventional, reliable, predictable, systematic, efficient).

- Women who describe themselves as predominately feminine or gender-neutral report a higher level of followership among their female subordinates than women who describe themselves as masculine.

- Approximately 67% of the women respondents are married. (Other studies report that only 40% to 50% of women executives are married.)

- Both married men and married women experience moderate levels of conflict between work and family domains. When there are children at home, women experience only slightly higher levels of conflict than men, even though they shoulder a much greater proportion of the child care—61% of the care versus 25% for the men.

---

exchanging rewards for services rendered or punishment for inadequate performance. The men are also more likely to use power that comes from their organizational position and formal authority.

The women respondents, on the other hand, described themselves in ways that characterize "transformational" leadership—getting subordinates to transform their own self-interest into the interest of the group through concern for a broader goal. Moreover, they ascribe their power to personal characteristics like charisma, interpersonal skills, hard work, or personal contacts rather than to organizational stature.

Intrigued by these differences, I interviewed some of the women respondents who described themselves as transformational. These discussions gave me a better picture of how these women view themselves as leaders and a greater understanding of the important ways in which their leadership style differs from the traditional command-and-control style. I call their leadership style "interactive leadership" because these women actively work to make their interactions with subordinates positive for everyone involved. More specifically, the women encourage participation, share power and information, enhance other people's self-worth, and get others excited about their work. All these things reflect their belief that allowing employees to contribute and to feel powerful and important is a win-win situation—good for the employees and the organization.

———— INTERACTIVE LEADERSHIP

From my discussions with the women interviewees, several patterns emerged. The women leaders made frequent reference to their efforts to encourage participation and share power and information—two things that are often associated with participative management. But their self-description went beyond the usual definitions of participation. Much of what they described were attempts to enhance other people's sense of self-worth and to energize followers. In general, these leaders believe that people perform best when they feel good about themselves and their work, and they try to create situations that contribute to that feeling. In general, they do the following:

Encourage Participation   Inclusion is at the core of interactive leadership. In describing nearly every aspect of management, the women interviewees made reference to trying to make people feel part of the organization. They try to instill this group identity in a variety of ways, including encouraging others to have a say in almost every aspect of work, from setting performance goals to determining strategy. To facilitate inclusion, they create mechanisms that get people to participate, and they use a conversational style that sends signals inviting people to get involved.

One example of the kinds of mechanisms that encourage participation is the "bridge club" that one interviewee, a group executive in charge of mergers and acquisitions at a large East Coast financial firm, created. The club is an informal gathering of people who have information she needs but over whom she has no direct control. The word *bridge* describes the effort to bring together these "members" from different functions. The word *club* captures the relaxed atmosphere.

Despite the fact that attendance at club meetings is voluntary and over and above the usual work demands, the interviewee said that those whose help she needs make the time to come. "They know their contributions are valued, and they appreciate the chance to exchange information across functional boundaries in an informal setting that's fun." She finds participation in the club more effective than memos.

Whether or not the women create special forums for people to interact, they try to make people feel included as a matter of course, often by trying to draw them into the conversation or soliciting their opinions. Frieda Caplan, founder and CEO of Frieda's Finest, a California-based marketer and distributor of unusual fruits and vegetables, described an approach she uses that is typical of the other women interviewed: "When I face a tough decision, I always ask my employees, 'What would you do if you were me?' This approach generates good ideas and introduces my employees to the complexity of management decisions."

Of course, saying that you include others doesn't mean others necessarily feel included. The women acknowledge the possibility that their efforts to draw people in may be seen as symbolic, so they try to avoid that perception by acting on the input they receive. They ask for suggestions before they reach their own conclusions, and they test—and sometimes change—particular decisions before they implement them. These women use participation to clarify their own views by thinking things through out loud and to ensure that they haven't overlooked an important consideration.

The fact that many of the interviewees described their participatory style as coming naturally suggests that these leaders do not consciously adopt it for its business value. Yet they realize that encouraging participation has benefits. For one thing, making it easy for people to express their ideas helps ensure that decisions reflect as much information as possible. To some of the women, this point is just common sense. Susan S. Elliott, president and founder of Systems Service Enterprises, a St. Louis computer consulting company, expressed this view: "I can't come up with a plan and then ask those who manage the accounts to give me their reactions. They're the ones who really know the accounts. They have information I don't have. Without their input I'd be operating in an ivory tower."

Participation also increases support for decisions ultimately reached and reduces the risk that ideas will be undermined by unexpected opposition. Claire Rothman, general manager of the Great Western Forum, a large sports and entertainment arena in Los Angeles, spoke about the value of open disagreement: "When I know ahead of time that someone disagrees with a decision, I can work especially closely with that person to try to get his or her support."

Getting people involved also reduces the risk associated with having only one person handle a client, project, or investment. For Patricia M. Cloherty, senior vice president and general partner of Alan Patricof Associates, a New York venture capital firm, including people in decision making and planning gives investments longevity. If something happens to one person, others will be familiar enough with the situation to adopt the investment. That way, there are no orphans in the portfolio, and a knowledgeable second opinion is always available.

Like most who are familiar with participatory management, these women are aware that being inclusive also has its disadvantages. Soliciting ideas and information from others takes time, often requires giving up some control, opens the door to criticism, and exposes personal and turf conflicts. In addition, asking for ideas and information can be interpreted as not having answers.

Further, it cannot be assumed that everyone wants to participate. Some people prefer being told what to do. When Mary Jane Rynd was a partner in a

Big Eight accounting firm in Arizona (she recently left to start her own company—Rynd, Carneal & Associates), she encountered such a person: "We hired this person from an out-of-state CPA firm because he was experienced and smart—and because it's always fun to hire someone away from another firm. But he was just too cynical to participate. He was suspicious of everybody. I tried everything to get him involved—including him in discussions and giving him pep talks about how we all work together. Nothing worked. He just didn't want to participate."

Like all those who responded to the survey, these women are comfortable using a variety of leadership styles. So when participation doesn't work, they act unilaterally. "I prefer participation," said Elliott, "but there are situations where time is short and I have to take the bull by the horns."

Share Power and Information   Soliciting input from other people suggests a flow of information from employees to the boss. But part of making people feel included is knowing that open communication flows in two directions. These women say they willingly share power and information rather than guard it and they make apparent their reasoning behind decisions. While many leaders see information as power and power as a limited commodity to be coveted, the interviewees seem to be comfortable letting power and information change hands. As Adrienne Hall, vice chairman of Eisaman, Johns & Laws, a large West Coast advertising firm, said, "I know territories shift, so I'm not preoccupied with turf."

One example of power and information sharing is the open strategy sessions held by Debi Coleman, vice president of information systems and technology at Apple Computer. Rather than closeting a small group of key executives in her office to develop a strategy based on her own agenda, she holds a series of meetings over several days and allows a larger group to develop and help choose alternatives.

The interviewees believe that sharing power and information accomplishes several things. It creates loyalty by signaling to coworkers and subordinates that they are trusted and their ideas respected. It also sets an example for other people and therefore can enhance the general communication flow. And it increases the odds that leaders will hear about problems before they explode. Sharing power and information also gives employees and coworkers the wherewithal to reach conclusions, solve problems, and see the justification for decisions.

On a more pragmatic level, many employees have come to expect their bosses to be open and frank. They no longer accept being dictated to but want to be treated as individuals with minds of their own. As Elliott said, "I work with lots of people who are bright and intelligent, so I have to deal with them at an intellectual level. They're very logical, and they want to know the reasons for things. They'll buy in only if it makes sense."

In some cases, sharing information means simply being candid about work-related issues. In early 1990, when Elliott hired as employees many of the people she had been using as independent contractors, she knew the transition would be difficult for everyone. The number of employees nearly doubled overnight, and the nature of working relationships changed. "I warned everyone that we were in for some rough times and reminded them that we would be experiencing them together. I admitted that it would also be hard for me, and I made it clear that I wanted them to feel free to talk to me. I was completely candid and encouraged them to be honest with me. I lost some employees who didn't like the new relationships, but I'm convinced that being open helped me understand my employees better, and it gave them a feeling of support."

Like encouraging participation, sharing power and information has its risks. It allows for the possibility that people will reject, criticize, or otherwise challenge what the leader has to say or, more broadly, her authority. Also, employees get frustrated when leaders listen to—but ultimately reject—their ideas. Because information is a source of power, leaders who share it can be seen as naive or needing to be liked. The interviewees have experienced some of these downsides but find the positives overwhelming.

Enhance the Self-worth of Others   One of the by-products of sharing information and encouraging participation is that employees feel important. During the interviews, the women leaders discussed other ways they build a feeling of self-worth in coworkers and subordinates. They talked about giving others credit and praise and sending small signals of recognition. Most important, they expressed how they refrain from asserting their own superiority, which asserts the inferiority of others. All those I interviewed expressed clear aversion to behavior that sets them apart from others in the company—reserved parking places, separate dining facilities, pulling rank.

Examples of sharing and giving credit to others abound. Caplan, who has been the subject of scores of media reports hailing her innovation of labeling vegetables so consumers know what they are and how to cook them, originally got the idea from a farmer. She said that whenever someone raises the subject, she credits the farmer and downplays her role. Rothman is among the many note-writers: when someone does something out of the ordinary, she writes them a personal note to tell them she noticed. Like many of the women I interviewed, she said she also makes a point of acknowledging good work by talking about it in front of others.

Bolstering coworkers and subordinates is especially important in businesses and jobs that tend to be hard on a person's ego. Investment banking is one example because of the long hours, high pressures, intense competition, and inevitability that some deals will fail. One interviewee in investment banking hosts dinners for her division, gives out gag gifts as party favors, passes out M&Ms at meetings, and throws parties "to celebrate ourselves." These things, she said, balance the anxiety that permeates the environment.

Rynd compensates for the negativity inherent in preparing tax returns: "In my business we have something called a query sheet, where the person who reviews the tax return writes down everything that needs to be corrected. Criticism is built into the system. But at the end of every review, I always include a positive comment—your work paper technique looked good, I appreciate the fact that you got this done on time, or something like that. It seems trivial, but it's one way to remind people that I recognize their good work and not just their shortcomings."

Energize Others   The women leaders spoke of their enthusiasm for work and how they spread their enthusiasm around to make work a challenge that is exhilarating and fun. The women leaders talked about it in those terms and claimed to use their enthusiasm to get others excited. As Rothman said, "There is rarely a person I can't motivate."

Enthusiasm was a dominant theme throughout the interviews. In computer consulting: "Because this business is on the forefront of technology, I'm sort of evangelistic about it, and I want other people to be as excited as I am." In venture capital: "You have to have a head of steam." In executive search: "Getting people excited is an important way to influence those you have no control over." Or in managing sports arenas: "My enthusiasm gets others excited. I infuse them with energy and make them see that even boring jobs contribute to the fun of working in a celebrity business."

Enthusiasm can sometimes be misunderstood. In conservative professions like investment banking, such an upbeat leadership style can be interpreted as cheerleading and can undermine credibility. In many cases, the women said they won and preserved their credibility by achieving results that could be measured easily. One of the women acknowledged that her colleagues don't understand or like her leadership style and have called it cheerleading. "But," she added, "in this business you get credibility from what you produce, and they love the profits I generate." While energy and enthusiasm can inspire some, it doesn't work for everyone. Even Rothman conceded, "Not everyone has a flame that can be lit."

━━━ PATHS OF LEAST RESISTANCE

Many of the women I interviewed said the behaviors and beliefs that underlie their leadership style come naturally to them. I attribute this to two things: their socialization and the career paths they have chosen. Although socialization patterns and career paths are changing, the average age of the men and women who responded to the survey is 51—old enough to have had experiences that differed *because* of gender.

Until the 1960s, men and women received different signals about what was expected of them. To summarize a subject that many experts have explored in depth, women have been expected to be wives, mothers, community volunteers, teachers, and nurses. In all these roles, they are supposed to be cooperative, supportive, understanding, gentle, and to provide service to others. They are to derive satisfaction and a sense of self-esteem from helping others, including their spouses. While men have had to appear to be competitive, strong, tough, decisive, and in control, women have been allowed to be cooperative, emotional, supportive, and vulnerable. This may explain why women today are more likely than men to be interactive leaders.

Men and women have also had different career opportunities. Women were not expected to have careers, or at least not the same kinds of careers as men, so they either pursued different jobs or were simply denied opportunities men had. Women's career tracks have usually not included long series of organizational positions with formal authority and control of resources. Many women had their first work experiences outside the home as volunteers. While some of the challenges they faced as managers in volunteer organizations are the same as those in any business, in many ways, leading volunteers is different because of the absence of concrete rewards like pay and promotion.

As women entered the business world, they tended to find themselves in positions consistent with the roles they played at home: in staff positions rather than in line positions, supporting the work of others, and in functions like communications or human resources where they had relatively small budgets and few people reporting directly to them.

The fact that most women have lacked formal authority over others and control over resources means that by default they have had to find other ways to accomplish their work. As it turns out, the behaviors that were natural and/or socially acceptable for them have been highly successful in at least some managerial settings.

What came easily to women turned out to be a survival tactic. Although leaders often begin their careers doing what comes naturally and what fits within the constraints of the job, they also develop their skills and styles over time. The women's use of interactive leadership has its roots in socialization, and the women interviewees firmly believe that it benefits their organizations. Through the course of their careers, they have gained conviction that their style is effective. In fact, for some, it was their own success that caused them to formulate their philosophies about what motivates people, how to make good decisions, and what it takes to maximize business performance.

They now have formal authority and control over vast resources, but still they see sharing power and information as an asset rather than a liability. They believe that although pay and promotion are necessary tools of management, what people really want is to feel that they are contributing to a higher purpose and that they have the opportunity as individuals to learn and grow. The women believe that employees and peers perform better when they feel they are part of an organization and can share in its success. Allowing them to get involved and to work to their potential is a way of maximizing their contributions and using human resources most efficiently.

——— ANOTHER KIND OF DIVERSITY

The IWF survey shows that a nontraditional leadership style can be effective in organizations that accept it. This lesson comes especially hard to those who think of the corporate world as a game of survival of the fittest, where the fittest is always the strongest, toughest, most decisive, and powerful. Such a workplace seems to favor leaders who control people by controlling resources, and by controlling people, gain control of more resources. Asking for information and sharing decision-making power can be seen as serious disadvantages, but what is a disadvantage under one set of circumstances is an advantage under another. The "best" leadership style depends on the organizational context.

Only one of the women interviewees is in a traditional, large-scale company. More typically, the women's organizations are medium-sized and tend to have experienced fast growth and fast change. They demand performance and/or have a high proportion of professional workers. These organizations seem to create opportunities for women and are hospitable to those who use a nontraditional management style.

The degree of growth or change in an organization is an important factor in creating opportunities for women. When change is rampant, everything is up for grabs, and crises are frequent. Crises are generally not desirable, but they do create opportunities for people to prove themselves. Many of the women interviewees said they got their first break because their organizations were in turmoil.

Fast-changing environments also play havoc with tradition. Coming up through the ranks and being part of an established network is no longer important. What is important is how you perform. Also, managers in such environments are open to new solutions, new structures, and new ways of leading.

The fact that many of the women respondents are in organizations that have clear performance standards suggest that they have gained credibility and legitimacy by achieving results. In investment banking, venture capital, accounting, and executive placement, for instance, individual performance is easy to measure.

A high proportion of young professional workers—increasingly typical of organizations—is also a factor in some women's success. Young, educated professionals impose special requirements on their organizations. They demand to participate and contribute. In some cases, they have knowledge or talents their bosses don't have. If they are good performers, they have many employment options. It is easy to imagine that these professionals will respond to leaders who are inclusive and open, who enhance the self-worth of others, and who create a fun work environment. Interactive leaders are likely to win the cooperation needed to achieve their goals.

Interactive leadership has proved to be effective, perhaps even advantageous, in organizations in which the women I interviewed have succeeded.

As the work force increasingly demands participation and the economic environment increasingly requires rapid change, interactive leadership may emerge as the management style of choice for many organizations. For interactive leadership to take root more broadly, however, organizations must be willing to question the notion that the traditional command-and-control leadership style that has brought success in earlier decades is the only way to get results. This may be hard in some organizations, especially those with long histories of male-oriented, command-and-control leadership. Changing these organizations will not be easy. The fact that women are more likely than men to be interactive leaders raises the risk that these companies will perceive interactive leadership as "feminine" and automatically resist it.

Linking interactive leadership directly to being female is a mistake. We know that women are capable of making their way through corporations by adhering to the traditional corporate model and that they can wield power in ways similar to men. Indeed, some women may prefer that style. We also know from the survey findings that some men use the transformational leadership style.

Large, established organizations should expand their definition of effective leadership. If they were to do that, several things might happen, including the disappearance of the glass ceiling and the creation of a wider path for all sorts of executives—men and women—to attain positions of leadership. Widening the path will free potential leaders to lead in ways that play to their individual strengths. Then the newly recognized interactive leadership style can be valued and rewarded as highly as the command-and-control style has been for decades. By valuing a diversity of leadership styles, organizations will find the strength and flexibility to survive in a highly competitive, increasingly diverse economic environment.

DISCUSSION QUESTIONS

1. Think of male and female managers you have known or worked with. Did they conform to the leadership styles described by the author? If not, how did they differ?
2. Based on the author's descriptions of the differences between the leadership styles of men and women, do you feel that this reinforces stereotypes or smashes them?
3. The author asserts that socialization and available career paths associated with gender differences have created women's interactive leadership style. What is the future of this effective leadership style as the differences between the socialization and career potential of men and women lessen?

9 How to Choose a Leadership Pattern

ROBERT TANNENBAUM AND WARREN H. SCHMIDT

The authors of this reading explore the dilemma that today's emphasis on participative decision making creates for modern managers. In relating to subordinates, managers may choose a pattern of leadership that ranges from making all the decisions themselves to allowing their subordinates to make decisions within prescribed limits.

In deciding how to lead, managers must consider their values, their confidence in their subordinates, their leadership inclinations, and their tolerance for ambiguity. They must also determine whether their subordinates have the independence, maturity, interest, and knowledge to share in decision making. Other issues to weigh include the ability of subordinates to work together, the complexity of the task, and the pressures of time. Successful managers are aware of all these factors and are able to act in the organization's best interests. In the retrospective commentary, the authors discuss the changes in organizations and in the world that have affected leadership patterns.

- **I** put most problems into my group's hands and leave it to them to carry the ball from there. I serve merely as a catalyst, mirroring back the people's thoughts and feelings so that they can better understand them."
- "It's foolish to make decisions oneself on matters that affect people. I always talk things over with my subordinates, but I make it clear to them that I'm the one who has to have the final say."
- "Once I have decided on a course of action, I do my best to sell my ideas to my employees."
- "I'm being paid to lead. If I let a lot of other people make the decisions I should be making, then I'm not worth my salt."
- "I believe in getting things done. I can't waste time calling meetings. Someone has to call the shots around here, and I think it should be me."

Each of these statements represents a point of view about good leadership. Considerable experience, factual data, and theoretical principles could be cited to support each statement, even though they seem to be inconsistent when placed together. Such contradictions point up the dilemma in which modern managers frequently find themselves.

DEMOCRACY VERSUS AUTHORITY

The problem of how modern managers can be democratic in their relations with subordinates and at the same time maintain the necessary authority and control in the organizations for which they are responsible has come into focus increasingly in recent years.

Earlier in the century this problem was not so acutely felt. The successful executive was generally pictured as possessing intelligence, imagination, initiative, the capacity to make rapid (and generally wise) decisions, and the ability to inspire subordinates. People tended to think of the world as being divided into leaders and followers.

Gradually, however, from the social sciences emerged the concept of group dynamics with its focus on *members* of the group rather than solely on the leader. Research efforts of social scientists underscored the importance of employee involvement and participation in decision making. Evidence began to challenge the efficiency of highly directive leadership, and increasing attention was paid to problems of motivation and human relations.

Through training laboratories in group development that sprang up across the country, many of the newer notions of leadership began to exert an impact. These training laboratories were carefully designed to give people firsthand experience in full participation and decision making. The designated leaders deliberately attempted to reduce their own power and to make group members as responsible as possible for setting their own goals and methods within the laboratory experience.

It was perhaps inevitable that some of the people who attended the training laboratories regarded this kind of leadership as being truly democratic and went home with the determination to build fully participative decision making into their own organizations. Whenever their bosses made a decision without convening a staff meeting, they tended to perceive this as authoritarian behavior. The true symbol of democratic leadership to some was the meeting—and the less directed from the top, the more democratic it was.

Some of the more enthusiastic alumni of these training laboratories began to get the habit of categorizing leader behavior as democratic or authoritarian. Bosses who made too many decisions themselves were thought of as authoritarian, and their directive behavior was often attributed solely to their personalities.

The net result of the research findings and of the human relations training based upon them has been to call into question the stereotype of an effective leader. Consequently, modern managers often find themselves in an uncomfortable state of mind.

Often they are not quite sure how to behave; there are times when they are torn between exerting strong leadership and permissive leadership. Sometimes new knowledge pushes them in one direction ("I should really get the group to help make this decision"), but at the same time their experience pushes them in another direction ("I really understand the problem better than the group and therefore I should make the decision."). They are not sure when a group decision is really appropriate or when holding a staff meeting serves merely as a device for avoiding their own decision-making responsibility.

The purpose of our reading is to suggest a framework that managers may find useful in grappling with this dilemma. First, we shall look at the different patterns of leadership behavior that managers can choose from in relating to their subordinates. Then, we shall turn to some of the questions suggested by this range of patterns. For instance, how important is it for managers' subordinates to know what type of leadership they are using in a situation? What factors should they consider in deciding on a leadership pattern? What difference do their long-run objectives make as compared to their immediate objectives?

——— RANGE OF BEHAVIOR

Exhibit 1 presents the continuum or range of possible leadership behavior available to managers. Each type of action is related to the degree of authority used by the boss and to the amount of freedom available to subordinates in reaching decisions. The actions seen on the extreme left characterize managers

EXHIBIT 1
Continuum of Leadership Behavior

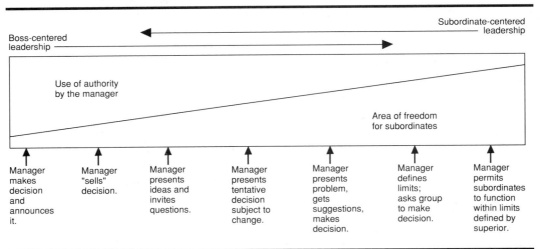

who maintain a high degree of control while those seen on the extreme right characterize managers who release a high degree of control. Neither extreme is absolute; authority and freedom are never without their limitations.

Now let us look more closely at each of the behavior points occurring along this continuum.

The Manager Makes the Decision and Announces It   In this case the boss identifies a problem, considers alternative solutions, chooses one of them, and then reports this decision to the subordinates for implementation. The boss may or may not give consideration to what he or she believes the subordinates will think or feel about the decision; in any case, no opportunity is provided for them to participate directly in the decision-making process. Coercion may or may not be used or implied.

The Manager "Sells" the Decision   Here the manager, as before, takes responsibility for identifying the problem and arriving at a decision. However, rather than simply announcing it, he or she takes the additional step of persuading the subordinates to accept it. In doing so, the boss recognizes the possibility of some resistance among those who will be faced with the decision and seeks to reduce this resistance by indicating, for example, what the employees have to gain from the decision.

The Manager Presents Ideas, Invites Questions   Here the boss who has arrived at a decision and who seeks acceptance of his or her ideas provides an opportunity for subordinates to get a fuller explanation of his or her thinking and intentions. After presenting the ideas, the manager invites questions so that the associates can better understand what he or she is trying to accomplish. This give-and-take also enables the manager and the subordinates to explore more fully the implications of the decision.

The Manager Presents a Tentative Decision Subject to Change   This kind of behavior permits subordinates to exert some influence on the decision. The initiative for identifying and diagnosing the problem remains with the boss. Before meeting with the staff, the manager has thought the problem through and arrived at a decision—but only a tentative one. Before finalizing it, he or she presents the proposed solution for the reaction of those who will be affected by it. He or she says in effect, "I'd like to hear what you have to say about this plan that I have developed. I'll appreciate your frank reactions but will reserve for myself the final decision."

The Manager Presents the Problem, Gets Suggestions, and Then Makes the Decision   Up to this point the boss has come before the group with a solution of his or her own. Not so in this case. The subordinates now get the first chance to suggest solutions. The manager's initial role involves identifying the problem. He or she might, for example, say something of this sort:

"We are faced with a number of complaints from newspapers and the general public on our service policy. What is wrong here? What ideas do you have for coming to grips with this problem?"

The function of the group becomes one of increasing the manager's repertoire of possible solutions to the problem. The purpose is to capitalize on the knowledge and experience of those who are on the firing line. From the expanded list of alternatives developed by the manager and the subordinates, the manager then selects the solution that he or she regards as most promising.[1]

The Manager Defines the Limits and Requests the Group to Make a Decision
At this point the manager passes to the group (possibly taking part as a member) the right to make decisions. Before doing so, however, he or she defines the problem to be solved and the boundaries within which the decision must be made.

An example might be the handling of a parking problem at a plant. The boss decides that this is something that should be worked on by the people involved, so they are called together. Pointing up the existence of the problem, the boss tells them:

"There is the open field just north of the main plant which has been designated for additional employee parking. We can build underground or surface multilevel facilities as long as the cost does not exceed $100,000. Within these limits we are free to work out whatever solution makes sense to us. After we decide on a specific plan, the company will spend the available money in whatever way we indicate."

The Manager Permits the Group to Make Decisions within Prescribed Limits
This represents an extreme degree of group freedom only occasionally encountered in formal organizations as, for instance, in many research groups. Here the team of managers or engineers undertakes the identification and diagnosis of the problem, develops alternative procedures for solving it, and decides on one or more of these alternative solutions. The only limits directly imposed on the group by the organization are those specified by the superior of the team's boss. If the boss participates in the decision-making process, deciding in advance to assist in implementing whatever decision the group makes, he or she attempts to do so with no more authority than any other member of the group.

KEY QUESTIONS

As the continuum in *Exhibit 1* demonstrates, there are a number of ways in which managers can relate to the group or individuals they are supervising.

---

1. For a fuller explanation of this approach, *see* Leo Moore, "Too Much Management, Too Little Change," *Harvard Business Review* (January–February 1956): 41.

At the extreme left of the range, the emphasis is on the manager—on what he or she is interested in, how he or she sees things, how he or she feels about them. As we move toward the subordinate-centered end of the continuum, however, the focus is increasingly on the subordinates—on what they are interested in, how they look at things, how they feel about them.

When business leadership is regarded in this way, a number of questions arise. Let us take four of special importance:

Can bosses ever relinquish their responsibility by delegating it to others?

Our view is that managers must expect to be held responsible by their superiors for the quality of the decisions made, even though operationally these decisions may have been made on a group basis. They should, therefore, be ready to accept whatever risk is involved whenever they delegate decision-making power to subordinates. Delegation is not a way of passing the buck. Also, it should be emphasized that the amount of freedom bosses give to subordinates cannot be greater than the freedom that they themselves have been given by their own superiors.

Should the manager participate with subordinates once he or she has delegated responsibility to them?

Managers should carefully think over this question and decide on their role prior to involving the subordinate group. They should ask if their presence will inhibit or facilitate the problem-solving process. There may be some instances when they should leave the group to let it solve the problem for itself. Typically, however, the boss has useful ideas to contribute and should function as an additional member of the group. In the latter instance, it is important that he or she indicate clearly to the group that he or she is in a *member* role rather than an authority role.

How important is it for the group to recognize what kind of leadership behavior the boss is using?

It makes a great deal of difference. Many relationship problems between bosses and subordinates occur because the bosses fail to make clear how they plan to use their authority. If, for example, the boss actually intends to make a certain decision, but the subordinate group gets the impression that he or she has delegated this authority, considerable confusion and resentment are likely to follow. Problems may also occur when the boss uses a democratic facade to conceal the fact that he or she has already made a decision that he or she hopes the group will accept as its own. The attempt to make them think it was their idea in the first place is a risky one. We believe that it is highly important for managers to be honest and clear in describing what authority they are keeping and what role they are asking their subordinates to assume in solving a particular problem.

Can you tell how democratic a manager is by the number of decisions the subordinates make?

The sheer *number* of decisions is not an accurate index of the amount of freedom that a subordinate group enjoys. More important is the *significance* of the decisions that the boss entrusts to subordinates. Obviously a decision on how to arrange desks is of an entirely different order from a decision involving the introduction of new electronic data-processing equipment. Even though the widest possible limits are given in dealing with the first issue, the group will sense no particular degree of responsibility. For a boss to permit the group to decide equipment policy, even within rather narrow limits, would reflect a greater degree of confidence in them on his or her part.

DECIDING HOW TO LEAD

Now let us turn from the types of leadership which are possible in a company situation to the question of what types are *practical* and *desirable*. What factors or forces should a manager consider in deciding how to manage? Three are of particular importance:

- Forces in the manager
- Forces in the subordinates
- Forces in the situation

We should like briefly to describe these elements and indicate how they might influence a manager's action in a decision-making situation.[2] The strength of each of them will, of course, vary from instance to instance, but managers who are sensitive to them can better assess the problems that face them and determine which mode of leadership behavior is most appropriate for them.

Forces in the Manager   The manager's behavior in any given instance will be influenced greatly by the many forces operating within his or her own personality. Managers will, of course, perceive their leadership problems in a unique way on the basis of their background, knowledge, and experience. Among the important internal forces affecting them will be the following:

1. *Their value system.* How strongly do they feel that individuals should have a share in making the decisions that affect them? Or, how convinced are they that the official who is paid to assume responsibility should personally carry the burden of decision making? The strength of their convictions on questions like these will tend to move managers to one end or the other of the continuum

---

2. *See also* Robert Tannenbaum and Fred Massarik, "Participation by Subordinates in the Managerial Decision-Making Process," *Canadian Journal of Economics and Political Science* (August 1950): 413.

shown in *Exhibit 1*. Their behavior will also be influenced by the relative importance that they attach to organizational efficiency, personal growth of subordinates, and company profits.[3]

2. *Their confidence in subordinates.* Managers differ greatly in the amount of trust they have in other people generally, and this carries over to the particular employees they supervise at a given time. In viewing his or her particular group of subordinates, the manager is likely to consider their knowledge and competence with respect to the problem. A central question managers might ask themselves is "Who is best qualified to deal with this problem?" Often they may, justifiably or not, have more confidence in their own capabilities than in those of subordinates.

3. *Their own leadership inclinations.* There are some managers who seem to function more comfortably and naturally as highly directive leaders. Resolving problems and issuing orders come easily to them. Other managers seem to operate more comfortably in a team role, where they are continually sharing many of their functions with their subordinates.

4. *Their feelings of security in an uncertain situation.* Managers who release control over the decision-making process thereby reduce the predictability of the outcome. Some managers have a greater need than others for predictability and stability in their environment. This tolerance for ambiguity is being viewed increasingly by psychologists as a key variable in a person's manner of dealing with problems.

Managers bring these and other highly personal variables to each situation they face. If they can see them as forces that consciously or unconsciously influence their behavior, they can better understand what makes them prefer to act in a given way. And understanding this, they can often make themselves more effective.

Forces in the Subordinate   Before deciding how to lead a certain group, managers will also want to consider a number of forces affecting their subordinates' behavior. They will want to remember that each employee, like themselves, is influenced by many personality variables. In addition, each subordinate has a set of expectations about how the boss should act in relation to him or her (the phrase "expected behavior" is one we hear more and more often these days at discussions of leadership and teaching). The better managers understand these factors, the more accurately they can determine what kind of behavior on their part will enable subordinates to act most effectively.

Generally speaking, managers can permit subordinates greater freedom if the following essential conditions exist:

---

3. *See* Chris Argyris, "Top Management Dilemma: Company Needs vs. Individual Development," *Personnel* (September 1955): 123–134.

- If the subordinates have relatively high needs for independence. (As we all know, people differ greatly in the amount of direction that they desire.)
- If the subordinates have a readiness to assume responsibility for decision making. (Some see additional responsibility as a tribute to their ability; others see it as passing the buck.)
- If they have a relatively high tolerance for ambiguity. (Some employees prefer to have clear-cut directives given to them; others prefer a wider area of freedom.)
- If they are interested in the problem and feel that it is important.
- If they understand and identify with the goals of the organization.
- If they have the necessary knowledge and experience to deal with the problem.
- If they have learned to expect to share in decision making. (Persons who have come to expect strong leadership and are then suddenly confronted with the request to share more fully in decision making are often upset by this new experience. On the other hand, persons who have enjoyed a considerable amount of freedom resent bosses who begin to make all the decisions themselves.)

Managers will probably tend to make fuller use of their own authority if the above conditions do not exist; at times there may be no realistic alternative to running a "one-man show."

The restrictive effect of many of the forces will, of course, be greatly modified by the general feeling of confidence which subordinates have in the boss. Where they have learned to respect and trust the boss, he or she is free to vary his or her own behavior. The boss will feel certain that he or she will not be perceived as an authoritarian boss on those occasions when he or she makes decisions alone. Similarly, the boss will not be seen as using staff meetings to avoid decision-making responsibility. In a climate of mutual confidence and respect, people tend to feel less threatened by deviations from normal practice, which in turn makes possible a higher degree of flexibility in the whole relationship.

Forces in the Situation   In addition to the forces that exist in managers themselves and in the subordinates, certain characteristics of the general situation will also affect managers' behavior. Among the more critical environmental pressures that surround them are those that stem from the organization, the work group, the nature of the problem, and the pressures of time.

The *type of organization* is one element to consider. Like individuals, organizations have values and traditions that inevitably influence the behavior of the people who work in them. Managers who are newcomers to a company quickly discover that certain kinds of behavior are approved while others are not. They also discover that to deviate radically from what is generally accepted is likely to create problems for them.

These values and traditions are communicated in numerous ways— through job descriptions, policy pronouncements, and public statements by top executives. Some organizations, for example, hold to the notion that the desirable executive is one who is dynamic, imaginative, decisive, and persuasive. Other organizations put more emphasis upon the importance of the executive's ability to work effectively with people—human relations skills. The fact that the person's superiors have a defined concept of what the good executive should be will very likely push the manager toward one end or the other of the behavioral range.

In addition, the amount of employee participation is influenced by such variables as the size of the working units, their geographical distribution, and the degree of inter- and intra-organizational security required to attain company goals. For example, the wide geographical dispersion of an organization may preclude a practical system of participative decision making, even through this would otherwise be desirable. Similarly, the size of the working units or the need for keeping plans confidential may make it necessary for the boss to exercise more control than would otherwise be the case. Factors like these may considerably limit the manager's ability to function flexibly on the continuum.

Before turning decision-making responsibility over to a subordinate group, the boss should consider *group effectiveness*, that is, how effectively its members work together as a unit.

One of the relevant factors here is the experience the group has had in working together. It can generally be expected that a group that has functioned for some time will have developed habits of cooperation and thus be able to tackle a problem more effectively than a new group. It can also be expected that a group of people with similar backgrounds and interests will work more quickly and easily than people with dissimilar backgrounds, because the communication problems are likely to be less complex.

The degree of confidence that the members have in their ability to solve problems as a group is also a key consideration. Finally, such group variables as cohesiveness, permissiveness, mutual acceptance, and commonality of purpose will exert subtle but powerful influence on the group's functioning.

The *nature of the problem* may determine what degree of authority should be delegated by managers to their subordinates. Obviously, managers will ask themselves whether subordinates have the kind of knowledge that is needed. It is possible to do them a real disservice by assigning a problem that their experience does not equip them to handle.

Because the problems faced in large or growing industries increasingly require knowledge of specialists from many different fields, it might be inferred that the more complex a problem, the more anxious a manager will be to get some assistance in solving it. However, this is not always the case. There will be times when the very complexity of the problem calls for one person to work it out. For example, if the manager has most of the background and factual data relevant to a given issue, it may be easier for him or her to think it through than to take the time to fill in the staff on all the pertinent background information.

The key question to ask, of course, is "Have I heard the ideas of everyone who has the necessary knowledge to make a significant contribution to the solution of this problem?"

The *pressure of time* is perhaps the most clearly felt pressure on managers (in spite of the fact that it may sometimes be imagined). The more that they feel the need for an immediate decision, the more difficult it is to involve other people. In organizations that are in a constant state of crisis and crash programming, one is likely to find managers personally using a high degree of authority with relatively little delegation to subordinates. When the time pressure is less intense, however, it becomes much more possible to bring subordinates in on the decision-making process.

These, then, are the principal forces that impinge on managers in any given instance and that tend to determine their tactical behavior in relation to subordinates. In each case their behavior ideally will be that which makes possible the most effective attainment of their immediate goals within the limits facing them.

LONG-RUN STRATEGY

As managers work with their organizations on the problems that come up day to day, their choice of a leadership pattern is usually limited. They must take account of the forces just described and, within the restrictions those factors impose on them, do the best that they can. But as they look ahead months or even years, they can shift their thinking from tactics to large-scale strategy. No longer need they be fettered by all of the forces mentioned, for they can view many of them as variables over which they have some control. They can, for example, gain new insights or skills for themselves, supply training for individual subordinates, and provide participative experiences for their employee group.

In trying to bring about a change in these variables, however, they are faced with a challenging question: At which point along the continuum *should* they act?

Attaining Objectives   The answer depends largely on what they want to accomplish. Let us suppose that they are interested in the same objectives that most modern managers seek to attain when they can shift their attention from the pressure of immediate assignments:

1. To raise the level of employee motivation
2. To increase the readiness of subordinates to accept change
3. To improve the quality of all managerial decisions
4. To develop teamwork and morale
5. To further the individual development of employees

In recent years managers have been deluged with a flow of advice on how best to achieve these longer-run objectives. It is little wonder that they are often both bewildered and annoyed. However, there are some guidelines which they can usefully follow in making a decision.

Most research and much of the experience of recent years give a strong factual basis to the theory that a fairly high degree of subordinate-center behavior is associated with the accomplishment of the five purposes mentioned.[4] This does not mean that managers should always leave all decisions to their assistants. To provide the individual or the group with greater freedom than they are ready for at any given time may very well tend to generate anxieties and therefore inhibit rather than facilitate the attainment of desired objectives. But this should not keep managers from making a continuing effort to confront subordinates with the challenge of freedom.

CONCLUSION

In summary, there are two implications in the basic thesis that we have been developing. The first is that successful leaders are those who are keenly aware of the forces which are most relevant to their behavior at any given time. They accurately understand themselves, the individuals and groups they are dealing with, and the company and broader social environment in which they operate. And certainly they are able to assess the present readiness for growth of their subordinates.

But this sensitivity or understanding is not enough, which brings us to the second implication. Successful leaders are those who are able to behave appropriately in the light of these perceptions. If direction is in order, they are able to direct; if considerable participative freedom is called for, they are able to provide such freedom.

Thus, successful managers of people can be primarily characterized neither as strong leaders nor as permissive ones. Rather, they are people who maintain a high batting average in accurately assessing the forces that determine what their most appropriate behavior at any given time should be and in actually being able to behave accordingly. Being both insightful and flexible, they are less likely to see the problems of leadership as a dilemma.

* * *

The authors wrote the following commentary fifteen years after this reading was first published.

---

4. For example, *see* Warren H. Schmidt and Paul C. Buchanan, *Techniques that Produce Teamwork* (New London, Conn.: Arthur C. Croft Publications, 1954); and Morris S. Viteles, *Motivation and Morale in Industry* (New York: W. W. Norton & Company, Inc., 1953).

——— RETROSPECTIVE COMMENTARY

Since this reading was first published in 1958, there have been many changes in organizations and in the world that have affected leadership patterns. While the article's continued popularity attests to its essential validity, we believe it can be reconsidered and updated to reflect subsequent societal changes and new management concepts.

The reasons for the article's continued relevance can be summarized briefly:

- The article contains insights and perspectives that mesh well with, and help clarify, the experiences of managers, other leaders, and students of leadership. Thus it is useful to individuals in a wide variety of organizations—industrial, governmental, educational, religious, and community.
- The concept of leadership the article defines is reflected in a continuum of leadership behavior (*see Exhibit 1* in original article). Rather than offering a choice between two styles of leadership, democratic or authoritarian, it sanctions a range of behavior.
- The concept does not dictate to managers but helps them to analyze their own behavior. The continuum permits them to review their behavior within a context of other alternatives, without any style being labeled right or wrong.

(We have sometimes wondered if we have, perhaps, made it too easy for anyone to justify his or her style of leadership. It may be a small step between being nonjudgmental and giving the impression that all behavior is equally valid and useful. The latter was not our intention. Indeed, the thrust of our endorsement was for managers who are insightful in assessing relevant forces within themselves, others, and situations, and who can be flexible in responding to these forces.)

In recognizing that our article can be updated, we are acknowledging that organizations do not exist in a vacuum but are affected by changes that occur in society. Consider, for example, the implications for organizations of these recent social developments:

- The youth revolution that expresses distrust and even contempt for organizations identified with the establishment.
- The civil rights movement that demands all minority groups be given a greater opportunity for participation and influence in the organizational processes.
- The ecology and consumer movements that challenge the right of managers to make decisions without considering the interest of people outside the organization.
- The increasing national concern with the quality of working life and its relationship to worker productivity, participation, and satisfaction.

These and other societal changes make effective leadership in this decade a more challenging task, requiring even greater sensitivity and flexibility than was needed in the 1950s. Today's manager is more likely to deal with employees who resent being treated as subordinates, who may be highly critical of any organizational system, who expect to be consulted and to exert influence, and who often stand on the edge of alienation from the institution that needs their loyalty and commitment. In addition, the manager is frequently confronted by a highly turbulent, unpredictable environment.

In response to these social pressures, new concepts of management have emerged in organizations. Open-system theory, with its emphasis on subsystems' interdependency *and* on the interaction of an organization with its environment, has made a powerful impact on managers' approach to problems. Organization development has emerged as a new behavioral science approach to the improvement of individual, group, organizational, and interorganizational performance. New research has added to our understanding of motivation in the work situation. More and more executives have become concerned with social responsibility and have explored the feasibility of social audits. And a growing number of organizations, in Europe and in the United States, have conducted experiments in industrial democracy.

In light of these developments, we submit the following thoughts on how we would rewrite certain points in our original article.

The article described forces in the manager, subordinates, and the situation as givens, with the leadership pattern a result of these forces. We would now give more attention to the *interdependency* of these forces. For example, such interdependency occurs in (a) the interplay between the manager's confidence in subordinates, their readiness to assume responsibility, and the level of group effectiveness; and (b) the impact of the behavior of the manager on that of subordinates, and vice versa.

In discussing the forces in the situation, we primarily identified organizational phenomena. We would now include forces lying outside the organization and would explore the relevant interdependencies between the organization and its environment.

In the original article, we presented the size of the rectangle in *Exhibit 1* as a given, with its boundaries already determined by external forces—in effect, a closed system. We would now recognize the possibility of the manager and/or the subordinates taking the initiative to change those boundaries through interaction with relevant external forces—both within their own organization and in the larger society.

The article portrayed the manager as the principal and almost unilateral actor. He or she initiated and determined group functions, assumed responsibility, and exercised control. Subordinates made inputs and assumed power only at the will of the manager. Although the manager might have taken outside forces into account, it was he or she who decided where to operate on the continuum; that is, whether to announce a decision instead of trying to sell the idea to subordinates, whether to invite questions, to let subordinates decide an issue, and so on. While the manager has retained this clear prerogative in many organizations, it has been challenged in others. Even in situations where managers have retained it, however, the balance in the relationship between managers and subordinates at any given time is arrived at by interaction—direct or indirect—between the two parties.

Although power and its use by managers played a role in our article, we now realize that our concern with cooperation and collaboration, common goals, commitment, trust, and mutual caring limited our vision with respect to the realities of power. We did not attempt to deal with unions, other forms of joint worker action, or with individual workers' expressions of resistance. Today, we would recognize much more clearly the power available to *all* parties and the factors that underlie the interrelated decisions on whether to use it.

In the original article, we used the terms "manager" and "subordinate." We are now uncomfortable with "subordinate" because of its demeaning, dependency-laden connotations and prefer "nonmanager." The titles "manager" and "nonmanager" make the terminological difference functional rather than hierarchical.

We assumed fairly traditional organizational structures in our original article. Now we would alter our formulation to reflect newer organizational modes that are slowly emerging such as industrial democracy, intentional communities, and "phenomenarchy."[5] These new modes are based on observations such as the following:

- Both manager and nonmanagers may be governing forces in their group environment, contributing to the definition of the total area of freedom.
- A group can function without a manager, with managerial functions being shared by group members.
- A group, as a unit, can be delegated authority and can assume responsibility within a larger organizational context.

Our thoughts on the question of leadership have prompted us to design a new behavior continuum (see *Exhibit 2*) in which the total area of freedom shared by manager and nonmanagers is constantly redefined by interactions between them and the forces in the environment.

The arrows in the exhibit indicate the continual flow of interdependent influence among systems and people. The points on the continuum designate the types of manager and nonmanager behavior that become possible with any given amount of freedom available to each. The new continuum is both more

---

5. For a description of phenomenarchy, *see* Will McWhinney, "Phenomenarchy: A Suggestion for Social Redesign," *Journal of Applied Behavioral Science* (May 1973).

EXHIBIT 2
Continuum of Manager-Nonmanager Behavior

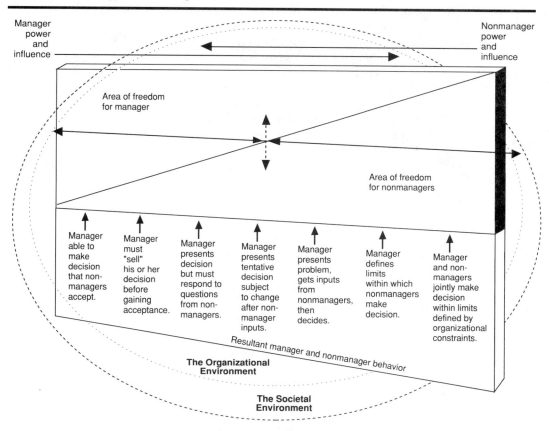

complex and more dynamic than the 1958 version, reflecting the organizational and societal realities of today.

DISCUSSION QUESTIONS

1. The authors offer a range of patterns that a leader can choose to employ. Choose two or three of these patterns and give an example of each pattern's effective use. When is it appropriate to be autocratic? Democratic?

2. Society has an effect on an organization and therefore on leadership patterns. The reading lists some of the social developments that

have had implications for organizations, such as the civil rights movement. What current societal developments may influence the organization and its leadership patterns?

3. As a leader, which leadership style do you prefer? Why? As a subordinate, which leadership pattern do you prefer? Why?

4. The authors provide several factors beyond the manager's control that affect leadership style. Can you name other factors that limit the range of leadership behavior that a manager can employ?

5. The demographics of the American workforce are changing at both the managerial and subordinate levels. What are some of these demographic trends? How might these changes affect the choice of leadership style?

In Praise of Followers   10

ROBERT E. KELLEY

Without good followers to back them up, leaders are irrelevant. This reading examines the role of the follower, comparing the traits of effective and ineffective followers. The best followers manage themselves well; are committed to the organization and to a purpose, principle, or person outside themselves; build their competence for maximum impact; and are courageous and honest.

Although companies often nurture leadership skills, they neglect the importance of "followership" skills. The author describes four steps that organizations can take to cultivate effective followers: 1) redefine the roles of leaders and followers as equal but different, 2) hone followership skills, 3) evaluate follower performance and provide feedback, and 4) build organizational structures that encourage followership.

We are convinced that corporations succeed or fail, compete or crumble, on the basis of how well they are led. So we study great leaders of the past and present and spend vast quantities of time and money looking for leaders to hire and trying to cultivate leadership in the employees we already have.[1]

I have no argument with this enthusiasm. Leaders matter greatly. But in searching so zealously for better leaders we tend to lose sight of the people these leaders will lead. Without his armies, after all, Napoleon was just a man with grandiose ambitions. Organizations stand or fall partly on the basis of how well their leaders lead, but partly also on the basis of how well their followers follow.

For example, declining profitability and intensified competition for corporate clients forced a large commercial bank on the East Coast to reorganize its operations and cut its work force. Its most seasoned managers had to spend most of their time in the field working with corporate customers. Time and energies were stretched so thin that one department head decided he had no choice but to delegate the responsibility for reorganization to his staff people, who had recently had training in self-management.

---

1. Author's note: I am indebted to Pat Chew for her contributions to this article. I also want to thank Janet Nordin, Howard Seckler, Paul Brophy, Stuart Mechlin, Ellen Mechlin, and Syed Shariq for their critical input.

Despite grave doubts, the department head set them up as a unit without a leader, responsible to one another and to the bank as a whole for writing their own job descriptions, designing a training program, determining criteria for performance evaluations, planning for operational needs, and helping to achieve overall organizational objectives.

They pulled it off. The bank's officers were delighted and frankly amazed that rank-and-file employees could assume so much responsibility so successfully. In fact, the department's capacity to control and direct itself virtually without leadership saved the organization months of turmoil, and as the bank struggled to remain a major player in its region, valuable management time was freed up to put out other fires.

What was it these singular employees did? Given a goal and parameters, they went where most departments could only have gone under the hands-on guidance of an effective leader. But these employees accepted the delegation of authority and went there alone. They thought for themselves, sharpened their skills, focused their efforts, put on a fine display of grit and spunk and self-control. They followed effectively.

To encourage this kind of effective following in other organizations, we need to understand the nature of the follower's role. To cultivate good followers, we need to understand the human qualities that allow effective "followership" to occur.

——— THE ROLE OF FOLLOWER

Bosses are not necessarily good leaders; subordinates are not necessarily effective followers. Many bosses couldn't lead a horse to water. Many subordinates couldn't follow a parade. Some people avoid either role. Others accept the role thrust upon them and perform it badly.

At different points in their careers, even at different times of the working day, most managers play both roles, though seldom equally well. After all, the leadership role has the glamour and attention. We take courses to learn it, and when we play it well we get applause and recognition. But the reality is that most of us are more often followers than leaders. Even when we have subordinates, we still have bosses. For every committee we chair, we sit as a member on several others.

So followership dominates our lives and organizations, but not our thinking, because our preoccupation with leadership keeps us from considering the nature and the importance of the follower.

What distinguishes an effective from an ineffective follower is enthusiastic, intelligent, and self-reliant participation—without star billing—in the pursuit of an organizational goal. Effective followers differ in their motivations for following and in their perceptions of the role. Some choose followership as their primary role at work and serve as team players who take satisfaction in helping to further a cause, an idea, a product, a service, or more rarely, a person.

Others are leaders in some situations but choose the follower role in a particular context. Both these groups view the role of follower as legitimate, inherently valuable, even virtuous.

Some potentially effective followers derive motivation from ambition. By proving themselves in the follower's role, they hope to win the confidence of peers and superiors and move up the corporate ladder. These people do not see followership as attractive in itself. All the same, they can become good followers if they accept the value of learning the role, studying leaders from a subordinate's perspective, and polishing the followership skills that will always stand them in good stead.

Understanding motivations and perceptions is not enough, however. Since followers with different motivations can perform equally well, I examined the behavior that leads to effective and less effective following among people committed to the organization and came up with two underlying behavioral dimensions that help to explain the difference.

One dimension measures to what degree followers exercise independent, critical thinking. The other ranks them on a passive/active scale. The *Exhibit* identifies five followership patterns.

Sheep are passive and uncritical, lacking in initiative and sense of responsibility. They perform the tasks given them and stop. Yes People are a livelier but equally unenterprising group. Dependent on a leader for inspiration, they can be aggressively deferential, even servile. Bosses weak in judgment and self-confidence tend to like them and to form alliances with them that can stultify the organization.

Alienated Followers are critical and independent in their thinking but passive in carrying out their role. Somehow, sometime, something turned them off. Often cynical, they tend to sink gradually into disgruntled acquiescence, seldom openly opposing a leader's efforts. In the very center of the diagram we have Survivors, who perpetually sample the wind and live by the slogan "better safe than sorry." They are adept at surviving change.

In the upper right-hand corner, finally, we have Effective Followers, who think for themselves and carry out their duties and assignments with energy and assertiveness. Because they are risk takers, self-starters, and independent problem solvers, they get consistently high ratings from peers and many superiors. Followership of this kind can be a positive and acceptable choice for parts or all of our lives—a source of pride and fulfillment.

Effective followers are well-balanced and responsible adults who can succeed without strong leadership. Many followers believe they offer as much value to the organization as leaders do, especially in project or task-force situations. In an organization of effective followers, a leader tends to be more an overseer of change and progress than a hero. As organizational structures flatten, the quality of those who follow will become more and more important. As Chester I. Barnard wrote 50 years ago in *The Functions of the Executive,* "The decision as to whether an order has authority or not lies with the person to whom it is addressed, and does not reside in 'persons of authority' or those who issue orders."

EXHIBIT
Some Followers Are More Effective

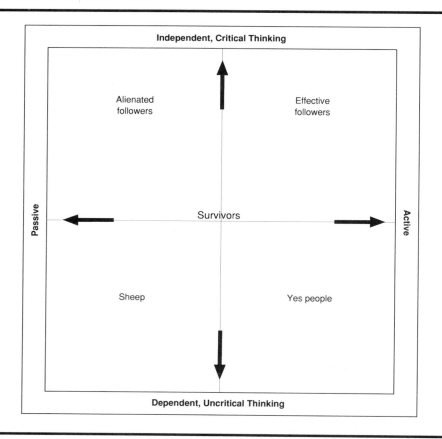

THE QUALITIES OF FOLLOWERS

Effective followers share a number of essential qualities:

1. They manage themselves well.
2. They are committed to the organization and to a purpose, principle, or person outside themselves.
3. They build their competence and focus their efforts for maximum impact.
4. They are courageous, honest, and credible.

Self-management   Paradoxically, the key to being an effective follower is the ability to think for oneself—to exercise control and independence and to work without close supervision. Good followers are people to whom a leader can safely delegate responsibility, people who anticipate needs at their own level of competence and authority.

Another aspect of this paradox is that effective followers see themselves—except in terms of line responsibility—as the equals of the leaders they follow. They are more apt to openly and unapologetically disagree with leadership and less likely to be intimidated by hierarchy and organizational structure. At the same time, they can see that the people they follow are, in turn, following the lead of others, and they try to appreciate the goals and needs of the team and the organization. Ineffective followers, on the other hand, buy into the hierarchy and, seeing themselves as subservient, vacillate between despair over their seeming powerlessness and attempts to manipulate leaders for their own purposes. Either their fear of powerlessness becomes a self-fulfilling prophecy—for themselves and often for their work units as well—or their resentment leads them to undermine the team's goals.

Self-managed followers give their organizations a significant cost advantage because they eliminate much of the need for elaborate supervisory control systems that, in any case, often lower morale. For example, a large midwestern bank redesigned its personnel selection system to attract self-managed workers. Those conducting interviews began to look for particular types of experience and capacities—initiative, teamwork, independent thinking of all kinds—and the bank revamped its orientation program to emphasize self-management. At the executive level, role playing was introduced into the interview process: how you disagree with your boss, how you prioritize your in-basket after a vacation. In the three years since, employee turnover has dropped dramatically, the need for supervisors has decreased, and administrative costs have gone down.

Of course not all leaders and managers like having self-managing subordinates. Some would rather have sheep or yes people. The best that good followers can do in this situation is to protect themselves with a little career self-management; that is, to stay attractive in the marketplace. The qualities that make a good follower are too much in demand to go begging for long.

Commitment   Effective followers are committed to something—a cause, a product, an organization, an idea—in addition to the care of their own lives and careers. Some leaders misinterpret this commitment. Seeing their authority acknowledged, they mistake loyalty to a goal for loyalty to themselves. But the fact is that many effective followers see leaders merely as coadventurers on a worthy crusade, and if they suspect their leader of flagging commitment or conflicting motives they may just withdraw their support, either by changing jobs or by contriving to change leaders.

The opportunities and the dangers posed by this kind of commitment are not hard to see. On the one hand, commitment is contagious. Most people like working with colleagues whose hearts are in their work. Morale stays high. Workers who begin to wander from their purpose are jostled back into line. Projects stay on track and on time. In addition, an appreciation of commitment and the way it works can give managers an extra tool with which to understand and channel the energies and loyalties of their subordinates.

On the other hand, followers who are strongly committed to goals not consistent with the goals of their companies can produce destructive results. Leaders having such followers can even lose control of their organizations.

A scientist at a computer company cared deeply about making computer technology available to the masses, and her work was outstanding. Since her goal was in line with the company's goals, she had few problems with top management. Yet she saw her department leaders essentially as facilitators of her dream, and when managers worked at cross-purposes to that vision, she exercised all of her considerable political skills to their detriment. Her immediate supervisors saw her as a thorn in the side, but she was quite effective in furthering her cause because she saw eye to eye with company leaders. But what if her vision and the company's vision had differed?

Effective followers temper their loyalties to satisfy organizational needs— or they find new organizations. Effective leaders know how to channel the energies of strong commitment in ways that will satisfy corporate goals as well as a follower's personal needs.

Competence and Focus   On the grounds that committed incompetence is still incompetence, effective followers master skills that will be useful to their organizations. They generally hold higher performance standards than the work environment requires, and continuing education is second nature to them, a staple in their professional development.

Less effective followers expect training and development to come to them. The only education they acquire is force-fed. If not sent to a seminar, they don't go. Their competence deteriorates unless some leader gives them parental care and attention.

Good followers take on extra work gladly, but first they do a superb job on their core responsibilities. They are good judges of their own strengths and weaknesses, and they contribute well to teams. Asked to perform in areas where they are poorly qualified, they speak up. Like athletes stretching their capacities, they don't mind chancing failure if they know they can succeed, but they are careful to spare the company wasted energy, lost time, and poor performance by accepting challenges that coworkers are better prepared to meet. Good followers see coworkers as colleagues rather than competitors.

At the same time, effective followers often search for overlooked problems. A woman on a new-product development team discovered that no one was responsible for coordinating engineering, marketing, and manufacturing. She worked out an interdepartmental review schedule that identified the people who should be involved at each stage of development. Instead of burdening her boss with yet another problem, this woman took the initiative to present the issue along with a solution.

Another woman I interviewed described her efforts to fill a dangerous void in the company she cared about. Young managerial talent in this manufacturing corporation had traditionally made careers in production. Convinced that foreign competition would alter the shape of the industry, she realized that marketing was a neglected area. She took classes, attended seminars, and read widely. More important, she visited customers to get feedback about her company's and competitors' products, and she soon knew more about the product's customer appeal and market position than any of her peers. The extra competence did wonders for her own career, but it also helped her company weather a storm it had not seen coming.

Courage   Effective followers are credible, honest, and courageous. They establish themselves as independent, critical thinkers whose knowledge and judgment can be trusted. They give credit where credit is due, admitting mistakes and sharing successes. They form their own views and ethical standards and stand up for what they believe in.

Insightful, candid, and fearless, they can keep leaders and colleagues honest and informed. The other side of the coin of course is that they can also cause great trouble for a leader with questionable ethics.

Jerome LiCari, the former R&D director at Beech-Nut, suspected for several years that the apple concentrate Beech-Nut was buying from a new supplier at 20% below market price was adulterated. His department suggested switching suppliers, but top management at the financially strapped company put the burden of proof on R&D.

By 1981, LiCari had accumulated strong evidence of adulteration and issued a memo recommending a change of supplier. When he got no response, he went to see his boss, the head of operations. According to LiCari, he was threatened with dismissal for lack of team spirit. LiCari then went to the president of Beech-Nut, and when that, too, produced no results, he gave up his three-year good-soldier effort, followed his conscience, and resigned. His last performance evaluation praised his expertise and loyalty, but said his judgment was "colored by naiveté and impractical ideals."

In 1986, Beech-Nut and LiCari's two bosses were indicted on several hundred counts of conspiracy to commit fraud by distributing adulterated apple juice. In November 1987, the company pleaded guilty and agreed to a fine of $2 million. In February 1988, the two executives were found guilty on a majority of the charges. The episode cost Beech-Nut an estimated $25 million and a 20% loss of market share. Asked during the trial if he had been naive, LiCari said, "I guess I was. I thought apple juice should be made from apples."

Is LiCari a good follower? Well, no, not to his dishonest bosses. But yes, he is almost certainly the kind of employee most companies want to have: loyal, honest, candid with his superiors, and thoroughly credible. In an ethical company involved unintentionally in questionable practices, this kind of follower can head off embarrassment, expense, and litigation.

———— CULTIVATING EFFECTIVE FOLLOWERS

You may have noticed by now that the qualities that make effective followers are, confusingly enough, pretty much the same qualities found in some effective leaders. This is no mere coincidence, of course. But the confusion underscores an important point. If a person has initiative, self-control, commitment, talent, honesty, credibility, and courage, we say, "Here is a leader!" By definition, a follower cannot exhibit the qualities of leadership. It violates our stereotype.

But our stereotype is ungenerous and wrong. Followership is not a person but a role, and what distinguishes followers from leaders is not intelligence or character but the role they play. As I pointed out at the beginning of this reading, effective followers and effective leaders are often the same people playing different parts at different hours of the day.

In many companies, the leadership track is the only road to career success. In almost all companies, leadership is taught and encouraged while followership is not. Yet effective followership is a prerequisite for organizational success. Your organization can take four steps to cultivate effective followers in your work force.

1. Redefine Followership and Leadership   Our stereotyped but unarticulated definitions of leadership and followership shape our expectations when we occupy either position. If a leader is defined as responsible for motivating followers, he or she will likely act toward followers as if they needed motivation. If we agree that a leader's job is to transform followers, then it must be a follower's job to provide the clay. If followers fail to need transformation, the leader looks ineffective. The way we define the roles clearly influences the outcome of the interaction.

Instead of seeing the leadership role as superior to and more active than the role of the follower, we can think of them as equal but different activities. The operative definitions are roughly these: people who are effective in the leader role have the vision to set corporate goals and strategies, the interpersonal skills to achieve consensus, the verbal capacity to communicate enthusiasm to large and diverse groups of individuals, the organizational talent to coordinate disparate efforts, and, above all, the desire to lead.

People who are effective in the follower role have the vision to see both the forest and the trees, the social capacity to work well with others, the strength of character to flourish without heroic status, the moral and psychological balance to pursue personal and corporate goals at no cost to either, and, above all, the desire to participate in a team effort for the accomplishment of some greater common purpose.

This view of leadership and followership can be conveyed to employees directly and indirectly—in training and by example. The qualities that make good followers and the value the company places on effective followership can be articulated in explicit follower training. Perhaps the best way to convey this message, however, is by example. Since each of us plays a follower's part at least from time to time, it is essential that we play it well, that we contribute our competence to the achievement of team goals, that we support the team leader with candor and self-control, that we do our best to appreciate and enjoy the role of quiet contribution to a larger, common cause.

2. Honing Followership Skills   Most organizations assume that leadership has to be taught but that everyone knows how to follow. This assumption is based on three faulty premises: 1) that leaders are more important than followers, 2) that following is simply doing what you are told to do, and 3) that followers inevitably draw their energy and aims, even their talent, from the leader. A program of follower training can correct this misapprehension by focusing on topics such as improving independent, critical thinking and self-management, which includes:

- Disagreeing agreeably
- Building credibility
- Aligning personal and organizational goals and commitments
- Acting responsibly toward the organization, the leader, coworkers, and oneself
- Similarities and differences between leadership and followership roles
- Moving between the two roles with ease

3. Performance Evaluation and Feedback   Most performance evaluations include a section on leadership skills. Followership evaluation would include items like the ones I have discussed. Instead of rating employees on leadership qualities such as self-management, independent thinking, originality, courage, competence, and credibility, we can rate them on these same qualities in both the leadership and followership roles and then evaluate each individual's ability to shift easily from the one role to the other. A variety of performance perspectives will help most people understand better how well they play their various organizational roles.

Moreover, evaluations can come from peers, subordinates, and self as well as from supervisors. The process is simple enough: peers and subordinates who come into regular or significant contact with another employee fill in brief, periodic questionnaires where they rate the individual on followership qualities. Findings are then summarized and given to the employee being rated.

4. Organizational Structures That Encourage Followership   Unless the value of good following is somehow built into the fabric of the organization, it is likely to remain a pleasant conceit to which everyone pays occasional lip service but no dues. Here are four good ways to incorporate the concept into your corporate culture:

- In leaderless groups, all members assume equal responsibility for achieving goals. These are usually small task forces of people who can work together under their own supervision. However hard it is to imagine a group with more than one leader, groups with none at all can be highly productive if their members have the qualities of effective followers.

- Groups with temporary and rotating leadership are another possibility. Again, such groups are probably best kept small and the rotation fairly frequent, although the notion might certainly be extended to include the administration of a small department for, say, six-month terms. Some of these temporary leaders will be less effective than others, of course, and some may be weak indeed, which is why critics maintain that this structure is inefficient. Why not let the best leader lead? Why suffer through the tenure of less effective leaders? There are two reasons. First, experience of the leadership role is essential to the education of effective followers. Second, followers learn that they must compensate for ineffective leadership by exercising their skill as good followers. Rotating leader or not, they are bound to be faced with ineffective leadership more than once in their careers.

- Delegation to the lowest level is a third technique for cultivating good followers. Nordstrom's, the Seattle-based department store chain, gives each sales clerk responsibility for servicing and satisfying the customer, including the authority to make refunds without supervisory approval. This kind of delegation makes even people at the lowest levels responsible for their own decisions and for thinking independently about their work.

- Finally, companies can use rewards to underline the importance of good followership. This is not as easy as it sounds. Managers dependent on yes people and sheep for ego gratification will not leap at the idea of extra rewards for the people who make them most uncomfortable. In my research, I have found that effective followers get mixed treatment. About half the time, their contributions lead to substantial rewards. The other half of the time they are punished by their superiors for exercising judgment, taking risks, and failing to conform. Many managers insist that they want independent subordinates who can think for themselves. In practice, followers who challenge their bosses run the risk of getting fired.

In today's flatter, leaner organization, companies will not succeed without the kind of people who take pride and satisfaction in the role of supporting player, doing the less glorious work without fanfare. Organizations that want the benefits of effective followers must find ways of rewarding them, ways of bringing them into full partnership in the enterprise. Think of the thousands of companies that achieve adequate performance and lackluster profits with employees they treat like second-class citizens. Then imagine for a moment the power of an organization blessed with fully engaged, fully energized, fully appreciated followers.

━━━ DISCUSSION QUESTIONS

1. Leaders must be followers, and followers often are leaders as illustrated by Jerome LiCari's courage. Provide an instance from your personal experience when you were a follower who led.
2. Articulate a larger common cause that you are committed to as a follower.
3. In a work group of effective and competent followers, is there any real need for a leader? Should one goal of an organization be to make leaders obsolete?
4. This reading makes an important point about stereotypes and their detrimental effects. How have you allowed stereotypes to control your behavior? How have you overcome them?

MANAGING INDIVIDUALS AND GROUPS

MOTIVATING AND MANAGING INDIVIDUALS

One More Time: How Do You Motivate Employees?

11

FREDERICK HERZBERG

According to conventional wisdom, managers don't motivate employees by (figuratively) kicking them; they motivate them by offering them induce-ments—more money, fringe benefits, shorter hours, comfortable surroundings.

In this reading, the author distinguishes between these inducements, which create dissatisfaction if they're absent but do little to inspire employees when they're present, and genuine motivators: recognition of achievement, greater responsibility, and opportunity for advancement. The secret to motivation, the author says, is job enrichment. Among the ways management can produce job enrichment are to remove some controls (while retaining accountability), increase employees' accountability for their own work, give people complete natural work units, and assign individuals specialized tasks so they can become experts in them. The author updates these concepts in the retrospective commentary.

How many articles, books, speeches, and workshops have pleaded plaintively, "How do I get an employee to do what I want?"

The psychology of motivation is tremendously complex, and what has been unraveled with any degree of assurance is small indeed. But the dismal ratio of knowledge to speculation has not dampened the enthusiasm for new forms of snake oil that are constantly coming on the market, many of them with academic testimonials. Doubtless this reading will have no depressing impact on the market for snake oil, but since the ideas expressed in it have been tested in many corporations and other organizations, it will help—I hope—to redress the imbalance in the aforementioned ratio.

——— "MOTIVATING" WITH KITA

In lectures to industry on the problem, I have found that the audiences are anxious for quick and practical answers, so I will begin with a straight-forward, practical formula for moving people.

What is the simplest, surest, and most direct way of getting someone to do something? Ask? But if the person responds that he or she does not want to do it, then that calls for psychological consultation to determine the reason for such obstinacy. Tell the person? The response shows that he or she does not understand you, and now an expert in communication methods has to be brought in to show you how to get through. Give the person a monetary incentive? I do not need to remind the reader of the complexity and difficulty involved in setting up and administering an incentive system. Show the person? This means a costly training program. We need a simple way.

Every audience contains the "direct action" manager who shouts, "Kick the person!" And this type of manager is right. The surest and least circumlocuted way of getting someone to do something is to administer a kick in the rear—to give what might be called the KITA.

There are various forms of KITA, and here are some of them:

Negative Physical KITA   This is a literal application of the term and was frequently used in the past. It has, however, three major drawbacks: 1) it is inelegant; 2) it contradicts the precious image of benevolence that most organizations cherish; and 3) since it is a physical attack, it directly stimulates the autonomic nervous system, and this often results in negative feedback—the employee may just kick you in return. These factors give rise to certain taboos against negative physical KITA.

In uncovering infinite sources of psychological vulnerabilities and the appropriate methods to play tunes on them, psychologists have come to the rescue of those who are no longer permitted to use negative physical KITA. "He took my rug away"; "I wonder what she meant by that"; "The boss is always going around me"—these symptomatic expressions of ego sores that have been rubbed raw are the result of application of:

Negative Psychological KITA   This has several advantages over negative physical KITA. First, the cruelty is not visible; the bleeding is internal and comes much later. Second, since it affects the higher cortical centers of the brain with its inhibitory powers, it reduces the possibility of physical backlash. Third, since the number of psychological pains that a person can feel is almost infinite, the direction and site possibilities of the KITA are increased many times. Fourth, the person administering the kick can manage to be above it all and let the system accomplish the dirty work. Fifth, those who practice it receive some ego satisfaction (one-upmanship), whereas they would find drawing blood abhorrent. Finally, if the employee does complain, he or she can always be accused of being paranoid; there is no tangible evidence of an actual attack.

Now, what does negative KITA accomplish? If I kick you in the rear (physically or psychologically), who is motivated? *I* am motivated; *you* move! Negative KITA does not lead to motivation, but to movement. So:

Positive KITA   Let us consider motivation. If I say to you, "Do this for me or the company, and in return I will give you a reward, an incentive, more status, a promotion, all the quid pro quos that exist in the industrial organization," am I motivating you? The overwhelming opinion I receive from management people is, "Yes, this is motivation."

I have a year-old Schnauzer. When it was a small puppy and I wanted it to move, I kicked it in the rear and it moved. Now that I have finished its obedience training, I hold up a dog biscuit when I want the Schnauzer to move. In this instance, who is motivated—I or the dog? The dog wants the biscuit, but it is I who want it to move. Again, I am the one who is motivated, and the dog is the one who moves. In this instance all I did was apply KITA frontally; I exerted a pull instead of a push. When industry wishes to use such positive KITAs, it has available an incredible number and variety of dog biscuits (jelly beans for humans) to wave in front of employees to get them to jump.

Why is it that managerial audiences are quick to see that negative KITA is *not* motivation, while they are almost unanimous in their judgment that positive KITA *is* motivation? It is because negative KITA is coercion, and positive KITA is co-option. But in fact, it is worse to be co-opted than to be coerced because coercion is externally imposed while co-option means that you gave your compliance. This is why positive KITA is so popular: it is a tradition; it is the American way. The organization does not have to kick you; you kick yourself.

──── MYTHS ABOUT MOTIVATION

Why is KITA not motivation? If I kick my dog (from the front or the back), he will move. And when I want him to move again, what must I do? I must kick him again. Similarly, I can charge a person's battery, and then recharge it, and recharge it again. But it is only when one has a generator of one's own that we can talk about motivation. One then needs no outside stimulation. One *wants* to do it.

With this in mind, we can review some positive KITA personnel practices that were developed as attempts to instill "motivation":

1. Reducing Time Spent at Work   This represents a marvelous way of motivating people to work—getting them off the job! We have reduced (formally and informally) the time spent on the job over the last 50 or 60 years until we are finally on the way to the "6½-day weekend." An interesting variant of this approach is the development of off-hour recreation programs. The philosophy here seems to be that those who play together, work together. The fact is that motivated people seek more hours of work, not fewer.

2. Spiraling Wages   Have these motivated people? Yes, to seek the next wage increase. Some medievalists still can be heard to say that a good depression will get employees moving. They feel that if rising wages don't or won't do the job, reducing them will.

3. Fringe Benefits   Industry has outdone the most welfare-minded of welfare states in dispensing cradle-to-the-grave succor. One company I know of had an informal "fringe benefit of the month club" going for a while. The cost of fringe benefits in this country has reached approximately 25% of the wage dollar, and we still cry for motivation.

People spend less time working for more money and more security than ever before, and the trend cannot be reversed. These benefits are no longer rewards; they are rights. A 6-day week is inhuman, a 10-hour day is exploitation, extended medical coverage is a basic decency, and stock options are the salvation of American initiative. Unless the ante is continuously raised, the psychological reaction of employees is that the company is turning back the clock.

When industry began to realize that both the economic nerve and the lazy nerve of their employees had insatiable appetites, it started to listen to the behavioral scientists who, more out of a humanist tradition than from scientific study, criticized management for not knowing how to deal with people. The next KITA easily followed.

4. Human Relations Training   More than 30 years of teaching and, in many instances, of practicing psychological approaches to handling people have resulted in costly human relations programs and, in the end, the same question: How do you motivate workers? Here, too, escalations have taken place. Thirty years ago it was necessary to request, "Please don't spit on the floor." Today the same admonition requires three "pleases" before the employee feels that a superior has demonstrated the psychologically proper attitude.

The failure of human relations training to produce motivation led to the conclusion that supervisors or managers themselves were not psychologically true to themselves in their practice of interpersonal decency. So an advanced form of human relations KITA, sensitivity training, was unfolded.

5. Sensitivity Training   Do you really, really understand yourself? Do you really, really, really trust other people? Do you really, really, really, really cooperate? The failure of sensitivity training is now being explained, by those who have become opportunistic exploiters of the technique, as a failure to really (five times) conduct proper sensitivity-training courses.

With the realization that there are only temporary gains from comfort and economic and interpersonal KITA, personnel managers concluded that the fault lay not in what they were doing, but in the employee's failure to appreciate what they were doing. This opened up the field of communications, a whole new area of "scientifically" sanctioned KITA.

6. Communications   The professor of communications was invited to join the faculty of management training programs and help in making employees understand what management was doing for them. House organs, briefing sessions, supervisory instruction on the importance of communication, and all sorts of propaganda have proliferated until today there is even an International Council of Industrial Editors. But no motivation resulted, and the obvious thought occurred that perhaps management was not hearing what the employees were saying. That led to the next KITA.

7. Two-way Communication Management ordered morale surveys, suggestion plans, and group participation programs. Then both employees and management were communicating and listening to each other more than ever, but without much improvement in motivation.

The behavioral scientists began to take another look at their conceptions and their data, and they took human relations one step further. A glimmer of truth was beginning to show through in the writings of the so-called higher-order-need psychologists. People, so they said, want to actualize themselves. Unfortunately, the "actualizing" psychologists got mixed up with the human relations psychologists, and a new KITA emerged.

8. Job Participation Though it may not have been the theoretical intention, job participation often became a "give-them-the-big-picture" approach. For example, if a man is tightening 10,000 nuts a day on an assembly line with a torque wrench, tell him he is building a Chevrolet. Another approach had the goal of giving employees a "feeling" that they are determining, in some measure, what they do on the job. The goal was to provide a *sense* of achievement rather than a substantive achievement in the task. Real achievement, of course, requires a task that makes it possible.

But still there was no motivation. This led to the inevitable conclusion that the employees must be sick, and therefore to the next KITA.

9. Employee Counseling The initial use of this form of KITA in a systematic fashion can be credited to the Hawthorne experiment of the Western Electric Company during the 1930s. At that time, it was found that the employees harbored irrational feelings that were interfering with the rational operation of the factory. Counseling in this instance was a means of letting the employees unburden themselves by talking to someone about their problems. Although the counseling techniques were primitive, the program was large indeed.

The counseling approach suffered as a result of experiences during World War II, when the programs themselves were found to be interfering with the operation of the organizations; the counselors had forgotten their role of benevolent listeners and were attempting to do something about the problems that they heard about. Psychological counseling, however, has managed to survive the negative impact of World War II experiences and today is beginning to flourish with renewed sophistication. But, alas, many of these programs, like all the others, do not seem to have lessened the pressure of demands to find out how to motivate workers.

Because KITA results only in short-term movement, it is safe to predict that the cost of these programs will increase steadily and new varieties will be developed as old positive KITAs reach their satiation points.

——— HYGIENE VERSUS MOTIVATORS

Let me rephrase the perennial question this way: How do you install a generator in an employee? A brief review of my motivation-hygiene theory of job attitudes is required before theoretical and practical suggestions can be offered. The theory was first drawn from an examination of events in the lives of engineers and accountants. At least 16 other investigations, using a wide variety of populations, have since been completed, making the original research one of the most replicated studies in the field of job attitudes.

The findings of these studies, along with corroboration from many other investigations using different procedures, suggest that the factors involved in producing job satisfaction (and motivation) are separate and distinct from the factors that lead to job dissatisfaction. Because separate factors need to be considered, depending on whether job satisfaction or job dissatisfaction is being examined, it follows that these two feelings are not opposites of each other. The opposite of job satisfaction is not job dissatisfaction but, rather, *no* job satisfaction; and similarly, the opposite of job dissatisfaction is not job satisfaction, but *no* job dissatisfaction.

Stating the concept presents a problem in semantics, for we normally think of satisfaction and dissatisfaction as opposites—therefore, what is not satisfying must be dissatisfying, and vice versa. But when it comes to understanding the behavior of people in their jobs, more than a play on words is involved.

Two different needs of human beings are involved here. One set of needs can be thought of as stemming from humankind's animal nature—the built-in drive to avoid pain from the environment, plus all the learned drives that become conditioned to the basic biological needs. For example, hunger, a basic biological drive, makes it necessary to earn money, and then money becomes a specific drive. The other set of needs relates to that unique human characteristic, the ability to achieve and, through achievement, to experience psychological growth. The stimuli for the growth needs are tasks that induce growth; in the industrial setting, they are the job content. *Contrariwise*, the stimuli inducing pain-avoidance behavior are found in the job environment.

The growth or *motivator* factors that are intrinsic to the job are: achievement, recognition for achievement, the work itself, responsibility, and growth or advancement. The dissatisfaction-avoidance or *hygiene* (KITA) factors that are extrinsic to the job include: company policy and administration, supervision, interpersonal relationships, working conditions, salary, status, and security.

A composite of the factors that are involved in causing job satisfaction and job dissatisfaction, drawn from samples of 1,685 employees, is shown in

EXHIBIT 1
Factors Affecting Job Attitudes as Reported in 12 Investigations

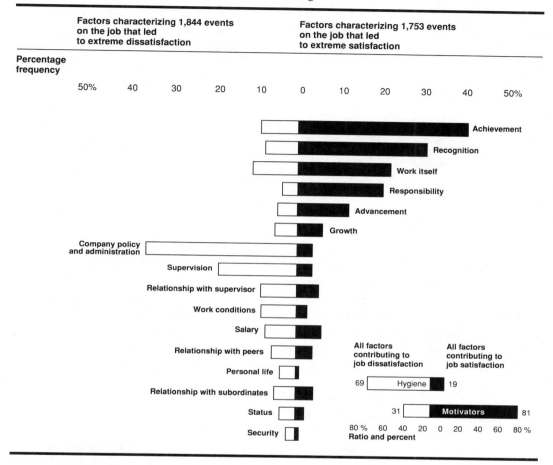

Exhibit 1. The results indicate that motivators were the primary cause of satisfaction, and hygiene factors the primary cause of unhappiness on the job. The employees, studied in 12 different investigations, included lower-level supervisors, professional women, agricultural administrators, men about to retire from management positions, hospital maintenance personnel, manufacturing supervisors, nurses, food handlers, military officers, engineers, scientists, housekeepers, teachers, technicians, female assemblers, accountants, Finnish foreman, and Hungarian engineers.

They were asked what job events had occurred in their work that had led to extreme satisfaction or extreme dissatisfaction on their part. Their responses are broken down in *Exhibit 1* into percentages of total positive job events and of total negative job events. (The figures total more than 100% on both the "hygiene" and "motivators" sides because often at least two factors can be attributed to a single event; advancement, for instance, often accompanies assumption of responsibility.)

To illustrate, a typical response involving achievement that had a negative effect for the employee was, "I was unhappy because I didn't do the job successfully." A typical response in the small number of positive job events in the company policy and administration grouping was, "I was happy because the company reorganized the section so that I didn't report any longer to the guy I didn't get along with."

As the lower right-hand part of *Exhibit 1* shows, of all the factors contributing to job satisfaction, 81% were motivators. And of all the factors contributing to the employees' dissatisfaction over their work, 69% involved hygiene elements.

ETERNAL TRIANGLE

There are three general philosophies of personnel management. The first is based on organizational theory, the second on industrial engineering, and the third on behavioral science.

Organizational theorists believe that human needs are either so irrational or so varied and adjustable to specific situations that the major function of personnel management is to be as pragmatic as the occasion demands. If jobs are organized in a proper manner, they reason, the result will be the most efficient job structure, and the most favorable job attitudes will follow as a matter of course.

Industrial engineers hold that humankind is mechanistically oriented and economically motivated and that human needs are best met by attuning the individual to the most efficient work process. The goal of personnel management therefore should be to concoct the most appropriate incentive system and to design the specific working conditions in a way that facilitates the most efficient use of the human machine. By structuring jobs in a manner that leads to the most efficient operation, engineers believe that they can obtain the optimal organization of work and the proper work attitudes.

Behavioral scientists focus on group sentiments, attitudes of individual employees, and the organization's social and psychological climate. This persuasion emphasizes one or more of the various hygiene and motivator needs. Its approach to personnel management is generally to emphasize some form of human relations education, in the hope of instilling healthy employee attitudes and an organizational climate that is considered to be felicitous to human values. The belief is that proper attitudes will lead to efficient job and organizational structure.

There is always a lively debate about the overall effectiveness of the approaches of organizational theorists and industrial engineers. Manifestly both have achieved much. But the nagging question for behavioral scientists has been: What is the cost in human problems that eventually cause more expense to the

EXHIBIT 2
'Triangle' of Philosophies of Personnel Management

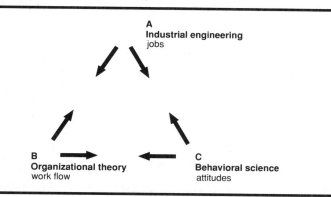

organization—for instance, turnover, absenteeism, errors, violation of safety rules, strikes, restriction of output, higher wages, and greater fringe benefits? On the other hand, behavioral scientists are hard put to document much manifest improvement in personnel management, using their approach.

The three philosophies can be depicted as a triangle, as is done in *Exhibit 2*, with each persuasion claiming the apex angle. The motivation-hygiene theory claims the same angle as industrial engineering, but for opposite goals. Rather than rationalizing the work to increase efficiency, the theory suggests that work be *enriched* to bring about effective utilization of personnel. Such a systematic attempt to motivate employees by manipulating the motivator factors is just beginning.

The term job enrichment describes this embryonic movement. An older term, job enlargement, should be avoided because it is associated with past failures stemming from a misunderstanding of the problem. Job enrichment provides the opportunity for the employee's psychological growth, while job enlargement merely makes a job structurally bigger. Since scientific job enrichment is very new, this reading only suggests the principles and practical steps that have recently emerged from several successful experiments in industry.

JOB LOADING

In attempting to enrich certain jobs, management often reduces the personal contribution of employees rather than giving them opportunities for growth in their accustomed jobs. Such endeavors, which I shall call horizontal job loading (as opposed to vertical loading, or providing motivator factors), have been the problem of earlier job-enlargement programs. Job loading merely enlarges the meaninglessness of the job. Some examples of this approach, and their effect, are:

- Challenging the employee by increasing the amount of production expected. If each tightens 10,000 bolts a day, see if each can tighten 20,000 bolts a day. The arithmetic involved shows that multiplying zero by zero still equals zero.
- Adding another meaningless task to the existing one, usually some routine clerical activity. The arithmetic here is adding zero to zero.
- Rotating the assignments of a number of jobs that need to be enriched. This means washing dishes for a while, then washing silverware. The arithmetic is substituting one zero for another zero.
- Removing the most difficult parts of the assignment in order to free the worker to accomplish more of the less challenging assignments. This traditional engineering approach amounts to subtraction in the hope of accomplishing addition.

These are common forms of horizontal loading that frequently come up in preliminary brainstorming sessions of job enrichment. The principles of vertical loading have not all been worked out as yet, and they remain rather general, but I have furnished seven useful starting points for consideration in *Exhibit 3*.

A SUCCESSFUL APPLICATION

An example from a highly successful job-enrichment experiment can illustrate the distinction between horizontal and vertical loading of a job. The subjects of this study were the stockholder correspondents employed by a very large corporation. Seemingly, the task required of these carefully selected and highly trained correspondents was quite complex and challeng-

EXHIBIT 3
Principles of Vertical Job Loading

PRINCIPLE	MOTIVATORS INVOLVED
A Removing some controls while retaining accountability	Responsibility and personal achievement
B Increasing the accountability of individuals for own work	Responsibility and recognition
C Giving a person a complete natural unit of work (module, division, area, and so on)	Responsibility, achievement, and recognition
D Granting additional authority to employees in their activity; job freedom	Responsibility, achievement, and recognition
E Making periodic reports directly available to the workers themselves rather than to supervisors	Internal recognition
F Introducing new and more difficult tasks not previously handled	Growth and learning
G Assigning individuals specific or specialized tasks, enabling them to become experts	Responsibility, growth, and advancement

ing. But almost all indexes of performance and job attitudes were low, and exit interviewing confirmed that the challenge of the job existed merely as words.

A job-enrichment project was initiated in the form of an experiment with one group, designated as an achieving unit, having its job enriched by the principles described in *Exhibit 3*. A control group continued to do its job in the traditional way. (There were also two "uncommitted" groups of correspondents formed to measure the so-called Hawthorne Effect—that is, to gauge whether productivity and attitudes toward the job changed artificially merely because employees sensed that the company was paying more attention to them in doing something different or novel. The results for these groups were substantially the same as for the control group, and for the sake of simplicity I do not deal with them in this summary.) No changes in hygiene were introduced for either group other than those that would have been made anyway, such as normal pay increases.

The changes for the achieving unit were introduced in the first two months, averaging one per week of the seven motivators listed in *Exhibit 3*. At the end of six months the members of the achieving unit were found to be outperforming their counterparts in the control group, and in addition indicated a marked increase in their liking for their jobs. Other results showed that the achieving group had lower absenteeism and, subsequently, a much higher rate of promotion.

Exhibit 4 illustrates the changes in performance, measured in February and March, before the study period began, and at the end of each month of the study period. The shareholder service index represents quality of letters, including accuracy of information, and speed of response to stockholders' letters of inquiry. The index of a current month was averaged into the average of the two prior months, which means that improvement was harder to obtain if the indexes of the previous months were low. The achievers were performing less well before the six-month period started, and their performance service index continued to decline after the introduction of the motivators, evidently because of uncertainty after their newly granted responsibilities. In the third month, however, performance improved, and soon the members of this group had reached a high level of accomplishment.

Exhibit 5 shows the two groups' attitudes toward their job, measured at the end of March, just before the first motivator was introduced, and again at the end of September. The correspondents were asked 16 questions, all involving motivation. A typical one was, "As you see it, how many opportunities do you feel that you have in your job for making worthwhile contributions?" The answers were scaled from 1 to 5, with 80 as the maximum possible score. The achievers became much more positive about their job, while the attitude of the control unit remained about the same (the drop is not statistically significant).

How was the job of these correspondents restructured? *Exhibit 6* lists the suggestions made that were deemed to be horizontal loading, and the actual vertical loading changes that were incorporated in the job of the achieving unit. The capital letters under "Principle" after "Vertical loading" refer to the

EXHIBIT 4
Shareholder Service Index in Company Experiment

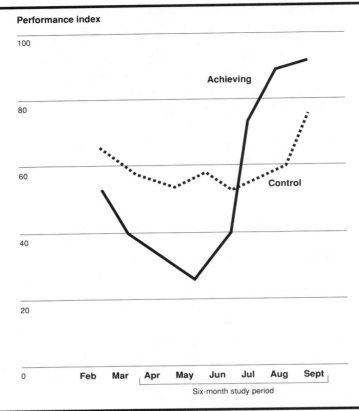

corresponding letters in *Exhibit 3*. The reader will note that the rejected forms of horizontal loading correspond closely to the list of common manifestations I mentioned earlier.

———— STEPS FOR JOB ENRICHMENT

Now that the motivator idea has been described in practice, here are the steps that managers should take in instituting the principle with their employees:

1. Select those jobs in which a) the investment in industrial engineering does not make changes too costly, b) attitudes are poor, c) hygiene is becoming very costly, and d) motivation will make a difference in performance.
2. Approach these jobs with the conviction that they can be changed. Years of tradition have led managers to believe that the content of

the jobs is sacrosanct and the only scope of action that they have is in ways of stimulating people.

3. Brainstorm a list of changes that may enrich the jobs, without concern for their practicality.

4. Screen the list to eliminate suggestions that involve hygiene, rather than actual motivation.

5. Screen the list for generalities, such as "give them more responsibility," that are rarely followed in practice. This might seem obvious, but the motivator words have never left industry; the substance has just been rationalized and organized out. Words like *responsibility*, *growth*, *achievement*, and *challenge*, for example, have been elevated to the lyrics of the patriotic anthem for all organizations. It is the old problem typified by the pledge of allegiance to the flag being more important than contributions to the country—of following the form, rather than the substance.

6. Screen the list to eliminate any *horizontal* loading suggestions.

7. Avoid direct participation by the employees whose jobs are to be enriched. Ideas they have expressed previously certainly constitute a valuable source for recommended changes, but their direct involvement contaminates the process with human-relations *hygiene* and, more specifically, gives them only a *sense* of making a

EXHIBIT 5
Changes in Attitudes Toward Tasks in Company Experiment

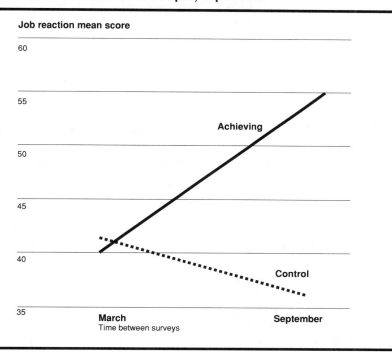

EXHIBIT 6
Enlargement versus Enrichment of Correspondents' Tasks in Company Experiment

HORIZONTAL LOADING SUGGESTIONS *rejected*	VERTICAL LOADING SUGGESTIONS *adopted*	PRINCIPLE
Firm quotas could be set for letters to be answered each day, using a rate which would be hard to reach.	Subject matter experts were appointed within each unit for other members of the unit to consult with before seeking supervisory help. (The supervisor had been answering all specialized and difficult questions.)	G
The secretaries could type the letters themselves, as well as compose them, or take on any other clerical functions.	Correspondents signed their own names on letters. (The supervisor had been signing all letters.)	B
All difficult or complex inquires could be channeled to a few secretaries so that the remainder could achieve high rates of output. These jobs could be exchanged from time to time.	The work of the more experienced correspondents were proofread less frequently by supervisors and was done at the correspondents' desks, dropping verification from 100% to 10%. (Previously, all correspondents' letters had been checked by the supervisor.)	A
The secretaries could be rotated through units handling different customers, and then sent back to their own units.	Production was discussed, but only in terms such as "a full day's work is expected." As time went on, this was no longer mentioned. (Before, the group had been constantly reminded of the number of letters that needed to be answered.)	D
	Outgoing mail went directly to the mailroom without going over supervisors' desks. (The letters had always been routed through the supervisors.)	A
	Correspondents were encouraged to answer letters in a more personalized way. (Reliance on the form-letter approach had been standard practice.)	C
	Each correspondent was held personally responsible for the quality and accuracy of letters. (This responsibility had been the province of the supervisor and the verifier.)	B, E

contribution. The job is to be changed, and it is the content that will produce the motivation, not attitudes about being involved or the challenge inherent in setting up a job. That process will be over shortly, and it is what the employees will be doing from then on that will determine their motivation. A sense of participation will result only in short-term movement.

8. In the initial attempts at job enrichment, set up a controlled experiment. At least two equivalent groups should be chosen, one an experimental unit in which the motivators are systematically introduced over a period of time, and the other one a control group in

which no changes are made. For both groups, hygiene should be allowed to follow its natural course for the duration of the experiment. Pre- and post-installation tests of performance and job attitudes are necessary to evaluate the effectiveness of the job enrichment program. The attitude test must be limited to motivator items in order to divorce employees' views of the jobs they are given from all the surrounding hygiene feelings that they might have.

9. Be prepared for a drop in performance in the experimental group for the first few weeks. The changeover to a new job may lead to a temporary reduction in efficiency.

10. Expect your first-line supervisors to experience some anxiety and hostility over the changes you are making. The anxiety comes from their fear that the changes will result in poorer performance for their unit. Hostility will arise when employees start assuming what the supervisors regard as their own responsibility for performance. The supervisor without checking duties to perform may then be left with little to do.

After successful experiment, however, the supervisors usually discover the supervisory and managerial functions that they have neglected, or that were never theirs because all their time was given over to checking the work of their subordinates. For example, in the R&D division of one large chemical company I know of, the supervisors of the laboratory assistants were theoretically responsible for their training and evaluation. These functions, however, had come to be performed in a routine, unsubstantial fashion. After the job-enrichment program, during which the supervisors were not merely passive observers of the assistants' performance, the supervisors actually were devoting their time to reviewing performance and administering thorough training.

What has been called an employee-centered style of supervision will come about not through education of supervisors, but by changing the jobs that they do.

───── CONCLUDING NOTE

Job enrichment will not be a one-time proposition, but a continuous management function. The initial changes should last for a very long period of time. There are a number of reasons for this:

- The changes should bring the job up to the level of challenge commensurate with the skill that was hired.
- Those who have still more ability eventually will be able to demonstrate it better and win promotion to higher-level jobs.
- The very nature of motivators, as opposed to hygiene factors, is that they have a much longer-term effect on employees' attitudes. Perhaps the job will have to be enriched again, but this will not occur as frequently as the need for hygiene.

Not all jobs can be enriched, nor do all jobs need to be enriched. If only a small percentage of the time and money that is now devoted to hygiene, however, were given to job enrichment efforts, the return in human satisfaction and economic gain would be one of the largest dividends that industry and society have ever reaped through their efforts at better personnel management.

The argument for job enrichment can be summed up quite simply: if you have employees on a job, use them. If you can't use them on the job, get rid of them, either via automation or by selecting someone with lesser ability. If you can't use them and you can't get rid of them, you will have a motivation problem.

* * *

Nineteen years after this reading's original publication, the author wrote the following commentary.

—— RETROSPECTIVE COMMENTARY

I wrote this article at the height of the attention on improving employee performance through various (contrived) psychological approaches to human relations. I tried to redress industrial social scientists' overconcern about how to treat workers to the neglect of how to design the work itself.

The first part of the article distinguishes between motivation and movement, a distinction that most writing on motivation misses. Movement is a function of fear of punishment or failure to get extrinsic rewards. It is the typical procedure used in animal training and its counterpart, behavioral modification techniques for humans. Motivation is a function of growth from getting intrinsic rewards out of interesting and challenging work.

While the immediate behavioral results from movement and motivation appear alike, their dynamics, which produce vastly different long-term consequences, are different. Movement requires constant reinforcement and stresses short-term results. To get a reaction, management must constantly enhance the extrinsic rewards for movement. If I get a bonus of $1,000 one year and $500 the next, I am getting extra rewards both years, but psychologically I have taken a $500 salary cut.

Motivation is based on growth needs. It is an internal engine, and its benefits show up over a long period of time. Because the ultimate reward in motivation is personal growth, people don't need to be rewarded incrementally. I write a book—a big accomplishment. Then I write an article—a lesser accomplishment, but nevertheless an addition to my personal growth.

For this article, I invented the acronym KITA (kick in the ass) to describe the movement technique. The inelegance of the term offended those who consider good treatment a motivating strategy, regardless of the nature of the work itself. In this plain language I tried to spotlight the animal approach to dealing with human beings that characterizes so much of our behavioral science intervention.

EXHIBIT 7
How the Hygiene-Motivator Factors Affect Job Attitudes in Six Countries

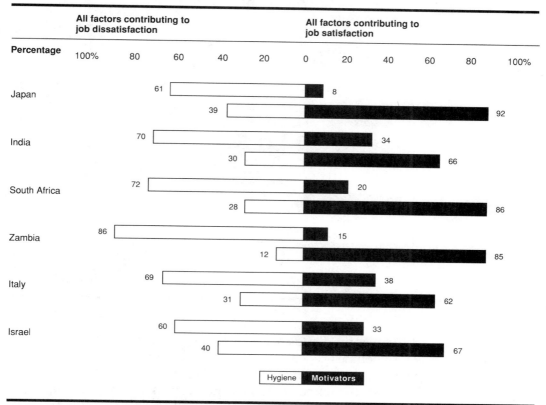

The article's popularity stems in great part from readers' recognition that KITA underlies the assumed benevolence of personnel practices. If I were writing "One More Time" today, I would emphasize the important, positive role of organizational behaviorists more than I did in 1968. We can certainly learn to get along better on the job. Reduced workplace tension through congenial relations is a necessary ingredient of a pleasant environment.

The second part of the article describes my motivation-hygiene theory. It suggests that environmental factors (hygienes) can at best create no dissatisfaction on the job, and their absence creates dissatisfaction. In contrast, what makes people happy on the job and motivates them are the job content factors (motivators). The controversy surrounding these concepts continues to this day.

While the original 12 studies were mostly American (they also included Finnish supervisors and Hungarian engineers), the results have been replicated throughout the world. A sampling of recent foreign investigations, which the reader can compare with the first American studies detailed in *Exhibit 1*, appears in *Exhibit 7*. The similarity of the profiles is worth noting.

EXHIBIT 8
Sensory Ingredients of Job Enrichment

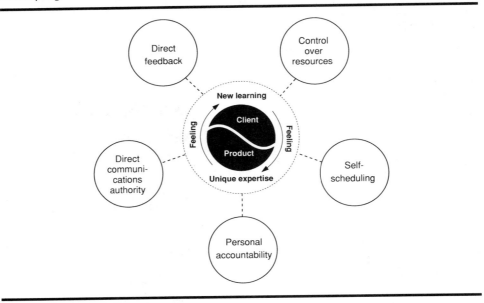

The 1970s was the decade of job enrichment (discussed in the third part of the article), sometimes called job design or redesign by opponents of the motivation-hygiene theory. Since the first trial-and-error studies at AT&T, experience has produced refinements of the procedures for job enrichment and the goals for achieving it. I like to illustrate them in the wheel shown in *Exhibit 8.*

This diagram reflects my conviction that the present-day abstraction of work has shut out feelings from the job content. Finance, for example, has become the focus of attention in most businesses, and nothing is more abstract and devoid of feeling. Part of the blame can be laid to electronic communication, which promotes detachment and abstraction. Job enrichment grows out of knowing your product and your client with feeling, not just intellectually.

With reference to the motivator ingredients discussed in the 1968 article, "recognition for achievement" translates into "direct feedback" in *Exhibit 8.* The wheel in *Exhibit 8* shows this feedback to come chiefly from the client and product of the work itself, not from the supervisor (except in the case of new hires). The motivator factor "responsibility" translates into a number of ingredients: self-scheduling, authority to communicate, control of resources, and accountability. Finally, the motivator factors "advancement" and "growth" translate into the central dynamic of new learning leading to unique expertise. The feeling of satisfaction is also indicated as a dynamic of learning from clients and products.

The key to job enrichment is nurture of a client relationship rather than a functional or hierarchical relationship. Let me illustrate with a diagram of

EXHIBIT 9
Client Relationships in an Air Force Function

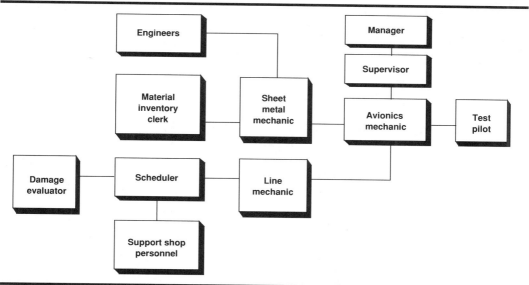

relationships in an airplane overhaul project carried out for the U.S. Air Force (*Exhibit 9*). The avionics mechanic's external client is the test pilot, and although he reports to his supervisor, his supervisor serves him. The sheet metal mechanic and the line mechanic serve the avionics mechanic. And so on back into the system.

By backing into the system, you can identify who serves whom—not who reports to whom—which is critical in trying to enrich jobs. You identify the external client, then the core jobs, or internal client jobs, serving that client. You first enrich the core job with the ingredients shown in *Exhibit 8* and then enrich the jobs that serve these internal clients.

During the 1970s, critics predicted that job enrichment would reduce the number of employees. Ironically, the restructuring and downsizing of U.S. companies during the 1980s have often serendipitously produced job enrichment. With fewer employees performing the same tasks, some job enrichment was inevitable. But the greater efficiency of enriched jobs ultimately leads to a competitive edge and more jobs.

Today, we seem to be losing ground to KITA. It's all the bottom line, as the expression goes. The work ethic and the quality of worklife movement have succumbed to the pragmatics of worldwide competition and the escalation of management direction by the abstract fields of finance and marketing—as opposed to production and sales, where palpable knowledge of clients and products resides. These abstract fields are more conducive to movement than to motivation. I find the new entrants in the world of work on the whole a passionless lot intent on serving financial indexes rather than clients and products. Motivation encompasses passion; movement is sterile.

To return to "One More Time": I don't think I would write it much differently today, though I would include the knowledge gained from recent job enrichment experiments. The distinction between movement and motivation is still true, and motivation-hygiene theory is still a framework with which to evaluate actions. Job enrichment remains the key to designing work that motivates employees.

━━━ DISCUSSION QUESTIONS

1. Give an example from your work history of factors that contributed to your job satisfaction and factors that contributed to any feeling of job dissatisfaction that you may have had.
2. Does motivation or job enrichment discussed in this reading apply to all jobs or only to jobs at a certain level in the organization?
3. The author gives several principles of vertical job loading. Are there other principles you could add? Do you see any potential drawbacks to the principles listed?
4. In the original reading, the author did not find much value in the behavioral science philosophy of personnel management. In his retrospective comments, the author states that he "would emphasize the important, positive role of organizational behaviorists." Why do you suppose he has made this shift?
5. Have developments that you are aware of in the areas of organizational design and human resource management tended to support or oppose the author's approach to motivation? Explain.

Pygmalion in Management 12

J. STERLING LIVINGSTON

This reading focuses on the power of managers' expectations in training, teaching, and preparing subordinates for more responsible and rewarding positions. Because the early years of people's careers deeply influence their self-image and future performance, it is crucial that managers be sensitive to their own behavior and its impact on subordinates. Enthusiasm and interest are key; discouragement, low expectations, and lack of involvement by executives lead to poor employee performance and low self-esteem. A retrospective commentary outlines the author's recent perspectives on the power of self-fulfilling managerial prophecies.

In George Bernard Shaw's *Pygmalion*, Eliza Doolittle explains:

> You see, really and truly, apart from the things anyone can pick up (the dressing and the proper way of speaking, and so on), the difference between a lady and a flower girl is not how she behaves but how she's treated. I shall always be a flower girl to Professor Higgins because he always treats me as a flower girl and always will; but I know I can be a lady to you because you always treat me as a lady and always will.

Some managers always treat their subordinates in a way that leads to superior performance. But most managers, like Professor Higgins, unintentionally treat their subordinates in a way that leads to lower performance than they are capable of achieving. The way managers treat their subordinates is subtly influenced by what they expect of them. If managers' expectations are high, productivity is likely to be excellent. If their expectations are low, productivity is likely to be poor. It is as though there were a law that caused subordinates' performance to rise or fall to meet managers' expectations.

The powerful influence of one person's expectations on another's behavior has long been recognized by physicians and behavioral scientists and, more recently, by teachers. But heretofore the importance of managerial expectations for individual and group performance has not been widely understood. I have documented this phenomenon in a number of case studies prepared during the past decade for major industrial concerns. These cases and other evidence available from scientific research now reveal the following:

- Managers' expectations and treatment of their subordinates largely determine the subordinates' performance and career progress.
- A unique characteristic of superior managers is the ability to create high performance expectations that subordinates fulfill.
- Less-effective managers fail to develop similar expectations, and as a consequence, the productivity of their subordinates suffers.
- Subordinates, more often than not, appear to do what they believe they are expected to do.

IMPACT ON PRODUCTIVITY

One of the most comprehensive illustrations of the effect of managerial expectations on productivity is recorded in studies of the organizational experiment undertaken in 1961 by Alfred Oberlander, manager of the Rockaway district office of the Metropolitan Life Insurance Company. He had observed that outstanding insurance agencies grew faster than average or poor agencies and that new insurance agents performed better in outstanding agencies than in average or poor agencies, regardless of their sales aptitude. He decided, therefore, to group his superior agents in one unit to stimulate their performance and to provide a challenging environment in which to introduce new salespeople.

Accordingly, Oberlander assigned his six best agents to work with his best assistant manager, an equal number of average producers to work with an average assistant manager, and the remaining low producers to work with the least able manager. He then asked the superior group to produce two-thirds of the premium volume achieved by the entire agency during the previous year. He describes the results as follows:

> Shortly after this selection had been made, the people in the agency began referring to this select group as a "superstaff" because of their high esprit de corps in operating so well as a unit. Their production efforts over the first 12 weeks far surpassed our most optimistic expectations . . . proving that groups of people of sound ability can be motivated beyond their apparently normal productive capacities when the problems created by the poor producer are eliminated from the operation.
>
> Thanks to this fine result, our overall agency performance improved by 40%, and it remained at this figure.
>
> In the beginning of 1962 when, through expansion, we appointed another assistant manager and assigned him a staff, we again used this same concept, arranging the agents once more according to their productive capacity.
>
> The assistant managers were assigned . . . according to their ability, with the most capable assistant manager receiving the best group, thus playing strength to strength. Our agency overall production again

improved by about 25% to 30%, and so this staff arrangement remained in place until the end of the year.

Now in this year of 1963, we found upon analysis that there were so many agents . . . with a potential of half a million dollars or more that only one staff remained of those people in the agency who were not considered to have any chance of reaching the half-million-dollar mark.

Although the productivity of the "superstaff" improved dramatically, it should be pointed out that the productivity of those in the lowest unit, "who were not considered to have any chance of reaching the half-million-dollar mark," actually declined, and that attrition among them increased. The performance of the superior agents rose to meet their managers' expectations, while that of the weaker ones declined as predicted.

Self-fulfilling Prophecies   The "average" unit, however, proved to be an anomaly. Although the district manager expected only average performance from this group, its productivity increased significantly. This was because the assistant manager in charge of the group refused to believe that she was less capable than the manager of the superstaff or that the agents in the top group had any greater ability than the agents in her group. She insisted in discussions with her agents that every person in the middle group had greater potential than those in the superstaff, lacking only their years of experience in selling insurance. She stimulated her agents to accept the challenge of outperforming the superstaff. As a result, in each year the middle group increased its productivity by a higher percentage than the superstaff did (although it never attained the dollar volume of the top group).

It is of special interest that the self-image of the manager of the average unit did not permit her to accept others' treatment of her as an average manager, just as Eliza Doolittle's image of herself as a lady did not permit her to accept others' treatment of her as a flower girl. The assistant manager transmitted her own strong feelings of efficacy to her agents, created mutual expectancy of high performance, and greatly stimulated productivity.

Comparable results occurred when a similar experiment was made at another office of the company. Further confirmation comes from a study of the early managerial success of 49 college graduates who were management-level employees of an operating company of AT&T. David E. Berlew and Douglas T. Hall of the Massachusetts Institute of Technology examined the career progress of these managers over a period of five years and discovered that their relative success, as measured by salary increases and the company's estimate of each one's performance and potential, depended largely on the company's expectations of them.

The influence of one person's expectations on another's behavior is by no means a business discovery. More than half a century ago, Albert Moll concluded from his clinical experience that subjects behaved as they believed they were expected to. The phenomenon he observed, in which "the prophecy causes its own fulfillment," has recently become a subject of considerable scientific interest. For example:

- In a series of scientific experiments, Robert Rosenthal of Harvard University has demonstrated that a "teacher's expectation for a pupil's intellectual competence can come to serve as an educational self-fulfilling prophecy."
- An experiment in a summer Headstart program for 60 preschoolers compared the performance of pupils under two groups: teachers who had been led to expect relatively slow learning by their children, and teachers who had been led to believe that their children had excellent intellectual ability and learning capacity. Pupils of the second group of teachers learned much faster.[1]

Moreover, the healing professions have long recognized that a physician's or psychiatrist's expectations can have a formidable influence on a patient's physical or mental health. What takes place in the minds of the patients and the healers, particularly when they have congruent expectations, may determine the outcome. For instance, the havoc of a doctor's pessimistic prognosis has often been observed. Again, it is well known that the efficacy of a new drug or a new treatment can be greatly influenced by the physician's expectations—a result referred to by the medical profession as a "placebo effect."

Pattern of Failure   When salespersons are treated by their managers as superpeople, as the superstaff was at the Metropolitan Rockaway district office, they try to live up to that image and do what they know supersalespersons are expected to do. But when the agents with poor productivity records are treated by their managers as *not* having any chance of success, as the low producers at Rockaway were, this negative expectancy also becomes a managerial self-fulfilling prophecy.

Unsuccessful salespersons have great difficulty maintaining their self-image and self-esteem. In response to low managerial expectations, they typically attempt to prevent additional damage to their egos by avoiding situations that might lead to greater failure. They either reduce the number of sales calls they make or avoid trying to close sales when that might result in further painful rejection, or both. Low expectations and damaged egos lead them to behave in a manner that increases the probability of failure, thereby fulfilling their managers' expectations. Let me illustrate:

Not long ago I studied the effectiveness of branch bank managers at a West Coast bank with over 500 branches. The managers who had had their lending authority reduced because of high rates of loss became progressively less effective. To prevent further loss of authority, they turned to making only safe loans. This action resulted in losses of business to competing banks and a

---

1. The Rosenthal and Headstart studies are cited in Robert Rosenthal and Lenore Jacobson, *Pygmalion in the Classroom* (New York: Holt, Rinehart, and Winston, Inc., 1968), p. 11.

relative decline in both deposits and profits at their branches. Then, to reverse that decline in deposits and earnings, they often reached for loans and became almost irrational in their acceptance of questionable credit risks. Their actions were not so much a matter of poor judgment as an expression of their willingness to take desperate risks in the hope of being able to avoid further damage to their egos and to their careers.

Thus, in response to the low expectations of their supervisors who had reduced their lending authority, they behaved in a manner that led to larger credit losses. They appeared to do what they believed they were expected to do, and their supervisors' expectations became self-fulfilling prophecies.

── POWER OF EXPECTATIONS

Managers cannot avoid the depressing cycle of events that flow from low expectations merely by hiding their feelings from subordinates. If managers believe subordinates will perform poorly, it is virtually impossible for them to mask their expectations because the message usually is communicated unintentionally, without conscious action.

Indeed, managers often communicate most when they believe they are communicating least. For instance, when they say nothing—become cold and uncommunicative—it usually is a sign that they are displeased by a subordinate or believe that he or she is hopeless. The silent treatment communicates negative feelings even more effectively, at times, than a tongue-lashing does. What seems to be critical in the communication of expectations is not what the boss says so much as the way he or she behaves. Indifferent and noncommital treatment, more often than not, is the kind of treatment that communicates low expectations and leads to poor performance.

Common Illusions   Managers are more effective in communicating low expectations to their subordinates than in communicating high expectations to them, even though most managers believe exactly the opposite. It usually is astonishingly difficult for them to recognize the clarity with which they transmit negative feelings. To illustrate again:

- The Rockaway district manager vigorously denied that he had communicated low expectations to the agents in the poorest group who, he believed, did not have any chance of becoming high producers. Yet the message was clearly received by those agents. A typical case was that of an agent who resigned from the low unit. When the district manager told the agent that he was sorry she was leaving, the agent replied, "No you're not; you're glad." Although the district manager previously had said nothing to her, he had unintentionally communicated his low expectations to his agents through his indifferent manner. Subsequently, the agents who were assigned to the lowest unit interpreted the assignment as equivalent to a request for their resignation.

- One of the company's agency managers established superior, average, and low units, even though he was convinced that he had no superior or outstanding subordinates. "All my assistant managers and agents are either average or incompetent," he explained to the Rockaway district manager. Although he tried to duplicate the Rockaway results, his low opinions of his agents were communicated—not so subtly—to them. As a result, the experiment failed.

Positive feelings, however, often do not come through clearly enough. Another insurance agency manager copied the organizational changes made at the Rockaway district office, grouping the salespeople she rated highly with the best manager, the average salespeople with an average manager, and so on. Improvement, however, did not result from the move. The Rockaway district manager therefore investigated the situation. He discovered that the assistant manager in charge of the high-performance unit was unaware that his manager considered him to be the best. In fact, he and the other agents doubted that the agency manager really believed there was any difference in their abilities. This agency manager was a stolid, phlegmatic, unemotional woman who treated her agents in a rather pedestrian way. Because high expectations had not been communicated to them, they did not understand the reason for the new organization and could not see any point in it. Clearly, the way managers *treat* subordinates, not the way they organize them, is the key to high expectations and high productivity.

EXHIBIT
The Relationship of Motivation to Expectancy

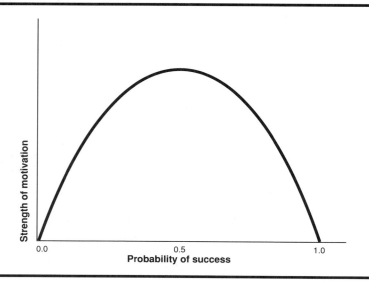

Impossible Dreams   Managerial expectations must pass the test of reality before they can be translated into performance. To become self-fulfilling prophecies, expectations must be made of sterner stuff than the power of positive thinking or generalized confidence in one's subordinates—helpful as these concepts may be for some other purposes. Subordinates will not be motivated to reach high levels of productivity unless they consider the boss's high expectations realistic and achievable. If they are encouraged to strive for unattainable goals, they eventually give up trying and settle for results that are lower than they are capable of achieving. The experience of a large electrical manufacturing company demonstrates this. The company discovered that production actually declined if production quotas were set too high, because the workers simply stopped trying to meet them. In other words, the practice of dangling the carrot just beyond the donkey's reach, endorsed by many managers, is not a good motivational device.

Scientific research by David C. McClelland of Harvard University and John W. Atkinson of the University of Michigan has demonstrated that the relationship of motivation to expectancy varies in the form of a bell-shaped curve (see the *Exhibit*).[2]

The degree of motivation and effort rises until the expectancy of success reaches 50%, then begins to fall even though the expectancy of success continues to increase. No motivation or response is aroused when the goal is perceived as being either virtually certain or virtually impossible to attain.

Moreover, as Berlew and Hall have pointed out, if subordinates fail to meet performance expectations that are close to their own level of aspirations, they will lower personal performance goals and standards, performance will tend to drop off, and negative attitudes will develop toward the activity or job.[3] It is therefore not surprising that failure of subordinates to meet the unrealistically high expectations of their managers leads to high rates of attrition, either voluntary or involuntary.

Secret of Superiority   Something takes place in the minds of superior managers that does not occur in the minds of those who are less effective. While superior managers are consistently able to create high performance expectations that their subordinates fulfill, weaker managers are not successful in obtaining a similar response. What accounts for the difference?

The answer, in part, seems to be that superior managers have greater confidence than other managers in their own ability to develop the talents of their subordinates. Contrary to what might be assumed, the high expectations of superior managers are based primarily on what they think about themselves—about their own ability to select, train, and motivate their subordinates.

---

2. *See* John W. Atkinson, "Motivational Determinants of Risk-Taking Behavior," *Psychological Review*, vol. 64, no. 6 (1957): 365.

3. David E. Berlew and Douglas T. Hall, "The Socialization of Managers: Effects of Expectations on Performance," *Administrative Science Quarterly* (September 1966): 208.

What managers believe about themselves subtly influences what they believe about their subordinates, what they expect of them, and how they treat them. If they have confidence in their ability to develop and stimulate them to high levels of performance, they will expect much of them and will treat them with confidence that their expectations will be met. But if they have doubts about their ability to stimulate them, they will expect less of them and will treat them with less confidence.

Stated in another way, the superior managers' record of success and their confidence in their ability give their high expectations credibility. As a consequence, their subordinates accept these expectations as realistic and try hard to achieve them.

The importance of what a manager believes about his or her training and motivational ability is illustrated by "Sweeney's Miracle," a managerial and educational self-fulfilling prophecy.

James Sweeney taught industrial management and psychiatry at Tulane University, and he also was responsible for the operation of the Biomedical Computer Center there. Sweeney believed that he could teach even a poorly educated man to be a capable computer operator. George Johnson, a former hospital porter, became janitor at the computer center; he was chosen by Sweeney to prove his conviction. In the mornings, George Johnson performed his janitorial duties, and in the afternoons Sweeney taught him about computers.

Johnson was learning a great deal about computers when someone at the university concluded that to be a computer operator one had to have a certain I.Q. score. Johnson was tested, and his I.Q. indicated that he would not be able to learn to type, much less operate a computer.

But Sweeney was not convinced. He threatened to quit unless Johnson was permitted to learn to program and operate the computer. Sweeney prevailed, and he is still running the computer center. Johnson is now in charge of the main computer room and is responsible for training new employees to program and operate the computer.[4]

Sweeney's expectations were based on what he believed about his own teaching ability, not on Johnson's learning credentials. What managers believe about their ability to train and motivate subordinates clearly is the foundation on which realistically high managerial expectations are built.

──── THE CRITICAL EARLY YEARS

Managerial expectations have their most magical influence on young people. As subordinates mature and gain experience, their self-image gradually hardens, and they begin to see themselves as their career records imply. Their own aspirations and the expectations of their superiors become increasingly

---

4. *See* Rosenthal and Jacobson, *Pygmalion in the Classroom*, p. 3.

controlled by the reality of their past performance. It becomes more and more difficult for them and for their managers to generate mutually high expectations unless they have outstanding records.

Incidentally, the same pattern occurs in school. Rosenthal's experiments with educational self-fulfilling prophecies consistently demonstrate that teachers' expectations are more effective in influencing intellectual growth in younger children than in older children. In the lower grade levels, particularly in the first and second grades, the effects of teachers' expectations are dramatic. In the upper grade levels, teachers' prophecies seem to have little effect on children's intellectual growth, although they do affect their motivation and attitude toward school. Although the declining influence of teachers' expectations cannot be completely explained, it is reasonable to conclude that younger children are more malleable, have fewer fixed notions about their abilities, and have less well-established reputations in the schools. As they grow, particularly if they are assigned to "tracks" on the basis of their records, as is now often done in public schools, their beliefs about their intellectual ability and their teachers' expectations of them begin to harden and become more resistant to influence by others.

Key to Future Performance   The early years in a business organization, when young people can be strongly influenced by managerial expectations, are critical in determining future performance and career progress. This is shown by a study at AT&T.

Berlew and Hall found that what the company initially expected of 49 college graduates who were management-level employees was the most critical factor in their subsequent performance and success. The researchers concluded that the correlation between how much a company expects of an employee in the first year and how much that employee contributes during the next five years was "too compelling to be ignored."[5]

Subsequently, the two men studied the career records of 18 college graduates who were hired as management trainees in another of AT&T's operating companies. Again they found that both expectations and performance in the first year correlated consistently with later performance and success.

"Something important is happening in the first year. . . .," Berlew and Hall concluded. "Meeting high company expectations in the critical first year leads to the internalization of positive job attitudes and high standards; these attitudes and standards, in turn, would first lead to and be reinforced by strong performance and success in later years. It should also follow that a new manager who meets the challenge of one highly demanding job will be given subsequently a more demanding job, and his level of contribution will rise as he responds to the company's growing expectations of him. The key . . . is the

---

5. Berlew and Hall, "The Socialization of Managers," p. 221.

concept of the first year as a *critical period for learning,* a time when the trainee is uniquely ready to develop or change in the direction of the company's expectations."[6]

Most Influential Boss   A young person's first manager is likely to be the most influential in that person's career. If managers are unable or unwilling to develop the skills young employees need to perform effectively, the latter will set lower personal standards than they are capable of achieving, their self-images will be impaired, and they will develop negative attitudes toward jobs, employers, and—in all probability—their own careers in business. Because the chances of building successful careers with these first employers will decline rapidly, the employees will leave, if they have high aspirations, in hope of finding better opportunities. If, however, early managers help employees achieve maximum potential, they will build the foundations for successful careers.

With few exceptions, the most effective branch managers at a large West Coast bank were mature people in their forties and fifties. The bank's executives explained that it took considerable time for a person to gain the knowledge, experience, and judgment required to handle properly credit risks, customer relations, and employee relations.

One branch manager, however, ranked in the top 10% of the managers in terms of effectiveness (which included branch profit growth, deposit growth, scores on administrative audits, and subjective rankings by superiors), was only 27 years old. This young person had been made a branch manager at 25, and in two years had improved not only the performance of the branch substantially but also developed a younger assistant manager who, in turn, was made a branch manager at 25.

The assistant had only average grades in college, but in just four years at the bank had been assigned to work with two branch managers who were remarkably effective teachers. The first boss, who was recognized throughout the bank for unusual skill in developing young people, did not believe that it took years to gain the knowledge and skill needed to become an effective banker. After two years, the young person was made assistant manager at a branch headed by another executive, who also was an effective developer of subordinates. Thus it was that the young person, when promoted to head a branch, confidently followed the model of two previous superiors in operating the branch, quickly established a record of outstanding performance, and trained an assistant to assume responsibility early.

For confirming evidence of the crucial role played by a person's first bosses, let us turn to selling, because performance in this area is more easily measured than in most managerial areas. Consider the following investigations:

---

6. David E. Berlew and Douglas T. Hall, "Some Determinants of Early Managerial Success," Alfred P. Sloan School of Management Organization Research Program #81-64 (Cambridge: MIT Press, 1964), p. 13.

- In a study of the careers of 100 insurance salespeople who began work with either highly competent or less-than-competent agency managers, the Life Insurance Agency Management Association found that those with average sales-aptitude test scores were nearly five times as likely to succeed under managers with good performance records as under managers with poor records, and those with superior sales aptitude scores were found to be twice as likely to succeed under high-performing managers as under low-performing managers.[7]
- The Metropolitan Life Insurance Company determined in 1960 that differences in the productivity of new insurance agents who had equal sales aptitudes could be accounted for only by differences in the ability of managers in the offices to which they were assigned. Agents whose productivity was high in relation to their aptitude test scores invariably were employed in offices that had production records among the top third in the company. Conversely, those whose productivity was low in relation to their test scores typically were in the least successful offices. After analyzing all the factors that might have accounted for these variations, the company concluded that differences in the performance of new agents were due primarily to differences in the "proficiency in sales training and direction" of the local managers.[8]
- A study I conducted of the performance of automobile salespeople in Ford dealerships in New England revealed that superior salespersons were concentrated in a few outstanding dealerships. For instance, 10 of the top 15 salespeople in New England were in 3 (out of approximately 200) of the dealerships in this region, and 5 of the top 15 people were in one highly successful dealership. Yet 4 of these people previously had worked for other dealers without achieving outstanding sales records. There was little doubt that the training and motivational skills of managers in the outstanding dealerships were critical.

Astute Selection   Although success in business sometimes appears to depend on the luck of the draw, more than luck is involved when a young person is selected by a superior manager. Successful managers do not pick their subordinates at random or by the toss of a coin. They are careful to select only those who they know will succeed. As Metropolitan's Rockaway district manager, Alfred Oberlander, insisted: "Every man or woman who starts with us is going to be a top-notch life insurance agent, or he or she would not have been asked to join the team."

---

7. Robert T. Davis, "Sales Management in the Field," *Harvard Business Review* (January–February 1958): 91.

8. Alfred A. Oberlander, "The Collective Conscience in Recruiting," address to Life Insurance Agency Management Association annual meeting, Chicago, Illinois (1963), p. 5.

When pressed to explain how they know whether a person will be successful, superior managers usually end up by saying something like, "The qualities are intangible, but I know them when I see them." They have difficulty being explicit because their selection process is intuitive and is based on interpersonal intelligence that is difficult to describe. The key seems to be that they are able to identify subordinates with whom they can probably work effectively—people with whom they are compatible and whose body chemistry agrees with their own. They make mistakes, of course. But they give up on a subordinate slowly because that means giving up on themselves—on their judgment and ability in selecting, training, and motivating people. Less-effective managers select subordinates more quickly and give up on them more easily, believing that the inadequacy is that of the subordinate, not of themselves.

━━━ DEVELOPING YOUNG PEOPLE

Observing that his company's research indicates that "initial corporate expectations for performance (with real responsibility) mold subsequent expectations and behavior," R. W. Walters, Jr., director of college employment at AT&T, contends that "initial bosses of new college hires must be the best in the organization."[9] Unfortunately, however, most companies practice exactly the opposite.

Rarely do new graduates work closely with experienced middle managers or upper-level executives. Normally they are bossed by first-line managers who tend to be the least experienced and least effective in the organization. Although there are exceptions, first-line managers generally are either old pros who have been judged as lacking competence for higher levels of responsibility, or they are younger people who are making the transition from "doing" to managing. Often these managers lack the knowledge and skill required to develop the productive capabilities of their subordinates. As a consequence, many college graduates begin their careers in business under the worst possible circumstances. Since they know their abilities are not being developed or used, they quite naturally soon become negative toward their jobs, employers, and business careers.

Although most top executives have not yet diagnosed the problem, industry's greatest challenge by far is to rectify the underdevelopment, underutilization, and ineffective management and use of its most valuable resource—its young managerial and professional talent.

Disillusion and Turnover   The problem posed to corporate management is underscored by the sharply rising rates of attrition among young managerial

---

9. "How to Keep the Go-Getters," *Nation's Business* (June 1966): 74.

and professional personnel. Turnover among managers one to five years out of college is almost twice as high now as it was a decade ago, and five times as high as two decades ago. Three out of five companies surveyed by *Fortune* magazine reported that turnover rates among young managers and professionals were higher than five years ago.[10] Although the high level of economic activity and the shortage of skilled personnel have made job-hopping easier, the underlying causes of high attrition, I am convinced, are underdevelopment and underutilization of a work force that has high career aspirations.

The problem can be seen in its extreme form in the excessive attrition rates of college and university graduates who begin their careers in sales positions. Whereas the average company loses about 50% of its new college and university graduates within three to five years, attrition rates as high as 40% in the *first* year are common among college graduates who accept sales positions in the average company. This attrition stems primarily, in my opinion, from the failure of first-line managers to teach new college recruits what they need to know to be effective sales representatives.

As we have seen, young people who begin their careers working for less-than-competent sales managers are likely to have records of low productivity. When rebuffed by their customers and considered by their managers to have little potential for success, the young people naturally have great difficulty in maintaining their self-esteem. Soon they find little personal satisfaction in their jobs and, to avoid further loss of self-respect, leave their employers for jobs that look more promising. Moreover, as reports about the high turnover and disillusionment of those who embarked on sales careers filter back to college campuses, new graduates become increasingly reluctant to take jobs in sales.

Thus ineffective first-line sales management sets off a sequence of events that ends with college and university graduates avoiding careers in selling. To a lesser extent, the same pattern is duplicated in other functions of business, as evidenced by the growing trend of college graduates to pursue careers in more meaningful occupations, such as teaching and government service.

A serious generation gap between bosses and subordinates is another significant cause of breakdown. Many managers resent the abstract, academic language and narrow rationalization characteristically used by recent graduates. As one manager expressed it to me, "For God's sake, you need a lexicon even to talk with these kids." Nondegreed managers often are particularly resentful, perhaps because they feel threatened by the bright young people with book-learned knowledge that they do not understand.

For whatever reason, the generation gap in many companies is eroding managerial expectations of new college graduates. For instance, I know of a survey of management attitudes in one of the nation's largest companies that

---

10. Robert C. Albrook, "Why It's Harder to Keep Good Executives," *Fortune* (November 1968): 137.

revealed that 54% of its first-line and second-line managers believed that new college recruits were "not as good as they were five years ago." Because what managers expect of subordinates influences the way they treat them, it is understandable that new graduates often develop negative attitudes toward their jobs and their employers. Clearly, low managerial expectations and hostile attitudes are not the basis for effective management of new people entering business.

Industry has not developed effective first-line managers fast enough to meet its needs. As a consequence, many companies are underdeveloping their most valuable resource—talented young men and women. They are incurring heavy attrition costs and contributing to the negative attitudes young people often have about careers in business.

For top executives in industry who are concerned with the productivity of their organizations and the careers of young employees, the challenge is clear: to speed the development of managers who will treat subordinates in ways that lead to high performance and career satisfaction. Managers not only shape the expectations and productivity of their subordinates but also influence their attitudes toward their jobs and themselves. If managers are unskilled, they leave scars on the careers of young people, cut deeply into their self-esteem, and distort their image of themselves as human beings. But if they are skillful and have high expectations, subordinates' self-confidence will grow, their capabilities will develop, and their productivity will be high. More often than one realizes, the manager is Pygmalion.

* * *

The author wrote the following commentary nineteen years after this reading was first published.

⸺ RETROSPECTIVE COMMENTARY

Self-fulfilling managerial prophecies were a bit mysterious when I documented the phenomenon 19 years ago. At that time, the powerful influence of managers' expectations on the development, motivation, and performance of their subordinates was not widely understood. Since then, however, the "Pygmalion effect" has become well known.

Recent research has confirmed that effective leaders have the ability to create high performance expectations that their employees fulfill. Every manager should understand, therefore, how the Pygmalion effect works.

What managers think about themselves and their abilities, as I explained in "Pygmalion in Management," is crucial to their effectiveness in creating self-fulfilling prophecies. Warren Bennis and Burt Nanus recently reached a similar conclusion after conducting some 90 interviews with CEOs and top public administrators. They wrote: "Our study of effective leaders strongly suggested that a key factor was . . . what we're calling . . . positive self-regard. . . . Positive self-regard seems to exert its force by creating in others a sense of confidence and high expectations, not very different from the fabled Pygmalion effect."[11]

The way managers develop confidence in their abilities and transmit their feelings of efficacy to their employees is illustrated by the success of Lee A. Iacocca of Chrysler—whom, interestingly, Bennis and Nanus used as a model for their theory of leadership. Iacocca's self-assurance can be traced to his prior success as president of Ford. His subsequent prophecy that Chrysler would be saved was accepted as credible by Chrysler's employees because they saw him as a competent automobile executive. They tried hard to meet his expectations and "behaved as they believed they were expected to," which my article indicated would be normal under the circumstances.

It is highly unlikely, however, that Iacocca could have saved Chrysler if he had been an industry outsider who needed two or three years to learn the automotive business. If he had been an outsider, he could not have moved decisively to do what needed to be done, nor could he have created a strong sense of confidence and high expectations among Chrysler's employees. His success was due to his experience and competence. It is doubtful that a prophecy by a less-qualified executive would have been self-fulfilling. So the message for managers is this: to be a Pygmalion, you must acquire the industry knowledge and job skills required to be confident of your high expectations and to make them credible to your employees.

Your organization can help identify the knowledge and skills you need to perform your job effectively. Your supervisors can give you assignments that will spur your development. But you must assume responsibility for your own development and career growth.

A word of caution may be in order, however. As I explained in my article, managers often unintentionally communicate low expectations to their subordinates, even though they believe otherwise. When they communicate low expectations, they become negative Pygmalions who undermine the self-confidence of their employees and reduce their effectiveness. Managers must be extremely sensitive, therefore, to their own behavior and its impact on their subordinates. They must guard against treating their employees in ways that lower their feelings of efficacy and self-esteem and are unproductive.

If I were writing "Pygmalion in Management" today, I might focus more attention on the problems of the negative Pygmalions because there are more of them than positive Pygmalions in U.S. industry. But the dark side of the Pygmalion effect is distressing, and I prefer to think about the bright side. It is a hopeful concept that can help all managers become more effective.

The difference between employees who perform well and those who perform poorly is not how they are paid but how they are treated. All managers

---

11. Reported in their book *Leaders* (New York: Harper & Row, 1985).

can learn how to treat their employees in ways that will lead to mutual expectations of superior performance. The most effective managers always do.

———— DISCUSSION QUESTIONS

1. Relate in detail, from any period in your life, the effects that another person's positive or negative expectations have had on your self-image and performance.
2. In his retrospective commentary, the author states that "negative" Pygmalions are the rule rather than the exception. Offer specific steps that an organization can take to reverse that trend.
3. This reading stresses the influence a superior has on a subordinate. What are some of the responsibilities a subordinate must assume for his or her development and career growth?
4. The author brings out the importance of the early years in a person's career and of developing young people. What relevance does this reading have to people at mid-life who are changing careers?
5. The author mentions a "generation gap" between nondegreed managers and college-educated subordinates. What are other characteristics of the American work force that might create a "generation gap"? What can management do to remedy them?

Making Performance Appraisal Work

13

MICHAEL BEER

This reading explores some of the reasons why managers and subordinates are often ambivalent about performance appraisal. Both the individual and the organization have their own goals, some of which conflict. The most significant conflict, however, is between the individual and the organization: the individual seeks to confirm a positive self-image and to gain rewards, while the organization wants individuals to be open to criticism so they can improve their performance. The author examines various difficulties that arise from this conflict, particularly the problems of avoidance and defensiveness. He concludes by suggesting solutions to performance appraisal problems. Three possible areas for improvement are the appraisal system itself, the interview process, and the ongoing relationship between the boss and the subordinate.

When performance has been good, when superior and subordinates have an open relationship, when promotions or salary increases are abundant, when there is plenty of time for preparation and discussion—in short, whenever it is a pleasure—performance appraisal is easy to do. Most of the time, however, and particularly when it is most needed and most difficult (e.g., when performance is substandard), performance appraisal refuses to go smoothly.[1]

WHAT IS PERFORMANCE APPRAISAL AND WHY IS IT A PROBLEM?

The evaluation of individual performance is an inevitable part of organizational life. Individuals are constantly evaluated by their bosses, peers, and subordinates. Much of the evaluation is informal, but most organizations have a formal appraisal system designed to collect systematic information about the performance of employees. The formal system usually includes a form on which supervisors indicate their evaluations of subordinates' performances. The form may be a blank sheet of paper on which the supervisor notes his or her views,

---

1. Morgan W. McCall and David L. DeVries, "Appraisal in Context: Clashing with Organizational Realities," presented in symposium "Performance Appraisal and Feedback: Flies in the Ointment," at the 84th Annual Convention of the American Psychological Association, Washington D.C., September 5, 1976.

a guide for setting objectives and checking on their attainment (commonly referred to as Management by Objectives or MBO), or a series of ratings on how the subordinate performs on the job. Regardless of the format, appraisals become part of the individual's formal record and are used to make decisions about pay and career. Supervisors usually sit down with the subordinate once a year to discuss the appraisal.

For a number of very important reasons, almost all organizations maintain appraisal systems. They provide data for personnel planning and are a means of influencing employee performance and fulfilling the moral obligation of letting people know where they stand; increasingly, appraisal systems are important as a protection against legal suits by employees who have been fired or demoted.

Managers recognize performance appraisal as a potentially useful tool for improving the performance of subordinates and the effectiveness of their organizational unit; yet they also sense that performance appraisal inherently poses some danger to the motivation of their subordinates and their relationship with them. Like tax payments, performance appraisal is something managers feel obligated to do but would rather avoid. However, subordinates want, and often ask for, feedback about how they are doing, but they prefer feedback that is consistent with their image of themselves as good performers. Thus, both managers and subordinates have ambivalent feelings about performance appraisal and share a natural tendency to underplay or avoid dealing with the negative aspects of the procedure.

Performance appraisal is both a system of papers and procedures designed by the organization for use by its managers (*the appraisal system*) and an interpersonal process in which manager and subordinate communicate and attempt to influence each other (*the appraisal process* or *interview*). Many of the problems in performance appraisal stem from the appraisal system itself—the objectives it is intended to serve, the administrative system in which it is embedded, and the forms and procedures that make up the system. These system-design problems will *not* be discussed in any depth but will be referred to as needed to explain problems in the appraisal process. The focus will be on what is known about this process, the difficulties it presents, and how these might be overcome.

───── GOALS OF PERFORMANCE APPRAISAL

Both the organization and the individual employee have goals they wish fulfilled by performance appraisal. In some cases these objectives are compatible, in others not.[2]

---

2. This discussion of performance-appraisal goals draws extensively on Lyman W. Porter, Edward E. Lawler III, and Richard J. Hackman, *Behavior in Organizations* (New York: McGraw-Hill, 1975).

THE ORGANIZATION'S GOALS

Performance evaluation is an important element in the information and control system of most complex organizations. It provides information about the performance of the organization's members, which is used in decisions about placement, promotions, firing, and pay. Not having the right person available to fill an important job can be as serious as not having the money to expand physical facilities or buy equipment. An evaluation system can help track those people who have potential so that they can be placed in developmental positions. The organization's personnel department is usually responsible for coordinating these activities, and the performance appraisal system serves it in this purpose.

Performance appraisal systems, and more important, the discussions between supervisor and subordinate about performance, can also be aimed at influencing the behavior and performance of individuals. This is true of Management by Objectives Systems, as well as various performance-rating systems. The process of influencing behavior is important to the organization's development of future human resources, and it is of utmost importance to managers' efforts to obtain the results for which they are accountable. The performance appraisal process can motivate employees, point out needed change in the way they do things, and help them grow and develop competence needed now and in the future. It is thus a major tool for changing individual behavior.

From the organization's point of view, then, performance appraisal serves the following two sets of goals:

Evaluation Goals

- To give feedback to subordinates so they know where they stand;
- To develop valid data for pay (salary and bonus) and promotion decisions and to provide a means of communicating decisions;
- To help the manager in making discharge and retention decisions and to provide a means of warning subordinates about unsatisfactory performance.

Coaching and Development Goals

- To counsel and coach subordinates so that they will improve their performance and develop future potential;
- To develop commitment to the larger organization through discussion of career opportunities and career planning;
- To motivate subordinates through recognition and support;
- To strengthen supervisor-subordinate relations;
- To diagnose individual and organizational problems.

The most significant observation to draw from this list is that there are many goals and that they are in conflict.[3] When the goal is evaluation, managers

---

3. Michael Beer and Robert A. Ruh, "Employee Growth Through Performance Management," *Harvard Business Review*, July–August 1976.

use the appraisal system as a tool for making difficult judgments that affect a subordinate's future. In communicating these judgments, managers must justify their appraisal in response to or in anticipation of disagreement by the subordinate. The result can be an adversarial relationship, poor listening, and low trust—conditions that work against the coaching and development objectives of performance appraisal. When coaching and development are the goals, managers must play the role of helper. They must listen, draw out subordinates about their problems, and help subordinates understand their weaknesses. The different communication skills required to achieve the conflicting goals of performance appraisal make the process difficult for the manager.

THE INDIVIDUAL'S GOALS

Like the organization, the individual has conflicting goals in performance evaluation. Individuals want feedback about their performance because it helps them learn about themselves.[4] The performance appraisal is an opportunity for them to get feedback and to learn how they are progressing. If this information is favorable, it helps satisfy their needs for competence and psychological success; if it is not, they tend to experience failure, and the feedback is often difficult to accept. Thus, even when people in organizations ask for and sometimes demand feedback, they are hoping for feedback that will affirm their concept of themselves. When rewards such as pay and promotion are tied to the evaluation, employees have a further reason for wanting to avoid unfavorable evaluations. They may gloss over problems, if not deny them. Often without realizing it, the individuals may present themselves in a favorable light to gain valued organizational rewards.

There are obvious conflicts between an individual's desire for personal development and the wish for rewards and feedback consistent with self-image. Self-development requires openness to feedback and receptiveness to alternative approaches to the job. However, this openness may not always serve the subordinate's objective of gaining raises, bonuses, and promotions when these are scarce.

CONFLICTING INDIVIDUAL AND ORGANIZATION GOALS

Because the organization is pursuing the conflicting objectives of evaluation and development, the manager must use performance appraisal

4. Leon Festinger et al., *Social Pressures in Informal Groups* (Stanford: Stanford University Press, 1950); T. F. Pettigrew, "Social Evaluation Theory: Convergences and Applications," in J. D. Levine (ed.), *Nebraska Symposium on Motivation* (Lincoln: University of Nebraska Press, 1967).

EXHIBIT 1
Conflicts in Performance Appraisal

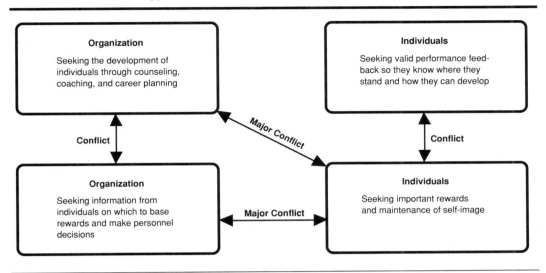

Source: Adapted from Porter, Lawler, and Hackman, *Behavior in Organizations*, 1975.

in two quite contradictory ways. Similarly, individuals have conflicting objectives as they approach a performance appraisal. The most significant conflict, however, is that between the individual and the organization. The individual desires to confirm a positive self-image and to obtain organizational rewards of promotion or higher pay. The organization wants individuals to be open to negative information about themselves so they can improve their performance and also wants individuals to be helpful in supplying this information. The conflict arises over the exchange of valid information. As long as individuals see the appraisal process as having an important effect on their rewards, career, and self-image, they will be reluctant to engage in the open dialogue required for valid evaluation and personal development. The poorer the individual's performance, the worse the potential conflict and the less likely the exchange of valid information. *Exhibit 1* depicts the several kinds of conflict involved in performance appraisal.

PROBLEMS IN PERFORMANCE APPRAISAL

AMBIVALENCE AND AVOIDANCE

Given the inherent conflicts, it is not surprising that supervisors and subordinates are often ambivalent about participating in the performance appraisal process.[5] Superiors are uncomfortable because their organizational role places them in the position of being both judge and jury. They must make decisions that significantly affect people's careers and lives. Furthermore, most managers are not trained to handle the interpersonally difficult situations that often arise with negative feedback. This is particularly a problem because managers would like to maintain good relations with their subordinates in order to carry on with their own jobs. All this leads to uncertainty about their subjective judgments and anxiety about meeting with subordinates to discuss performance. Yet supervisors also know that both the organization and the subordinate want such a discussion to be held. Finally, supervisors often feel personally bound to let people know where they stand. If they are not open with their subordinates, the knowledge that they have been less than truthful keeps them from building a relationship of mutual trust.

At the same time, subordinates are likely to be ambivalent about receiving negative feedback. They may want to discuss negative aspects of their performance so they can improve and develop but will not want to jeopardize promotions, pay, or their own self-image.

The ambivalence of both superiors and subordinates has led to the vanishing performance appraisal.[6] In many organizations, supervisors report that they hold periodic appraisal interviews and give honest feedback, while their subordinates report that they have not had a performance appraisal for many years or that they have heard nothing negative.[7] Probably the supervisors, fearful of the appraisal process, have expressed themselves so that the subordinates do not receive the unwelcome messages. The supervisor may carefully package negative feedback between heavy doses of positive feedback (the sandwich approach) or may make only general statements, without referring to specific problems. That is, supervisors provide negative feedback, but immediately counterbalance it with positive statements when their own anxiety or the subordinate's defensiveness signals potential problems. Because of their fear of awareness that will affect their self-image, subordinates collude with the supervisor in avoiding negative feedback. This sometimes results in long conversations only marginally related to the purpose of the appraisal interview. Sometimes avoidance manifests in small talk or humor that conveys an oblique message, or in the use of phrases that do not have clear meaning to either the supervisor or subordinate. Thus, negative feedback is often not explored in depth and is not fully understood and internalized by the subordinate.

As a result, no real appraisal occurs or, more likely, the appraisal just skims the surface. Both parties collude in meeting the organization requirement for appraisal but avoid the tough issues.

---

5. Douglas T. Hall and Edward E. Lawler III, "Job Design and Job Pressures as Facilitators of Professional-Organization Integration," *Adminstrative Science Quarterly*, 15 (1970), pp. 271–281.

6. Porter et al., *Behavior in Organizations*.

7. Hall and Lawler, "Job Design and Job Pressures."

FEEDBACK AND DEFENSIVENESS

The conflict between the organization's evaluation objectives and its coaching and development objectives tends to place the manager in the incompatible roles of judge and helper. Some managers feel obligated to fulfill their organizational role as judge by communicating to the subordinates all facets of the evaluation. They want to be sure they fulfill their obligation of letting subordinates know where they stand by detailing all shortcomings in performance. This naturally can elicit resistance from subordinates as they defend against threats to their self-esteem. The defensiveness may take various forms.[8] Subordinates may try to blame their unsatisfactory performance on others or on uncontrollable events; they may question the appraisal system itself or minimize its importance; they may demean the source of the data; they may apologize and promise to do better in the hope of shortening their exposure to negative feedback; or they may agree too readily to the feedback while inwardly denying its validity or accuracy.

Supervisors find themselves giving negative feedback while trying to create an open dialogue that will lead to information exchange and development. The defensiveness that results may be expressed as open hostility and denial or may be masked by passivity and surface compliance. In neither case does the subordinate really accept or understand the feedback. Thus, the very subordinates who need development most may learn least.

AVOIDANCE AND DEFENSIVENESS COMBINED

The worst situation is one in which the problems created by ambivalence and avoidance of performance appraisal combine with the problems of feedback and defensiveness. This can happen when managers go through a pro forma performance appraisal simply to fulfill their duty as supervisors. Their ambivalence leads them to avoid direct and meaningful talk about performance. However, because of their need to fulfill their role, they go through a mechanical yet complete review of the evaluation form. Without going deeply into problems of subordinates' performance, they nevertheless elicit defensive behavior by covering the evaluation form in detail. Thus, neither the benefits of avoidance (i.e., maintenance of good relations and personal comfort), nor the benefits of accurate feedback (i.e., clear understanding and development) are realized, while all the problems of avoidance and defensiveness remain.

---

8. Alvin Zander, "Research on Self-Esteem, Feedback and Threats to Self-Esteem," in A. Zander (ed.), *Performance Appraisals: Effects on Employees and Their Performance* (Ann Arbor, Mich.: The Foundation for Research in Human Behavior, 1963).

EXHIBIT 2
Factors Influencing Appraisal Outcomes

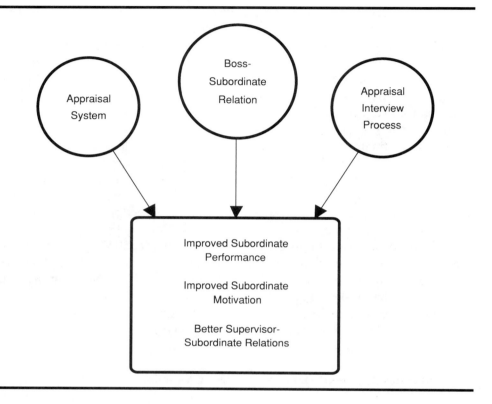

NONEVALUATIVE EVALUATION

The central dilemma in the appraisal process is how to have an open discussion of performance that meets the individual's need for feedback and the organization's personnel development objectives while preventing damage to the individual's self-esteem and confidence about organizational rewards.

POTENTIAL SOLUTIONS TO APPRAISAL PROBLEMS

Several approaches to the problems are possible. A manager seeking to improve performance appraisal should examine each of the three major factors influencing appraisal outcomes (*Exhibit 2*), to see where changes might be helpful. First, the appraisal system can be designed to minimize negative dynamics. The manager often has only marginal control over these matters. Second, the ongoing relationship between boss and subordinate will have a major influence on the appraisal process and outcome. Third, the quality of the communication during the interview process can help minimize problems.

THE APPRAISAL SYSTEM

Uncoupling Evaluation and Development   Less defensiveness and a more open dialogue are likely if the manager distinguishes his or her roles as helper and judge.[9] Two separate performance appraisal interviews can be held: one focused on evaluation and the other on coaching and development. The open, problem-solving dialogue required for building a relationship and developing subordinates comes at a different time of the year from the meeting in which the supervisor informs the subordinate of the overall evaluation and its implications for retention, pay, and promotion. This split recognizes that a manager cannot be simultaneously a helper and a judge, because the behavior required by one role interferes with the behavior required by the other.

Choosing Appropriate Performance Data   A manager can minimize defensiveness and avoidance by narrowly focusing feedback on specific behaviors or specific performance goals. For example, an unsatisfactory rating on a characteristic as broad as motivation is likely to be perceived as a personal attack and could threaten self-esteem. Individuals are more likely to attend to feedback about specific incidents or aspects of job performance than to broad generalizations. Specific feedback is also more helpful to the individual in terms of changing behavior. Thus, an appraisal discussion that relies on a report-card rating of traits or performance is doomed to failure because it leads the supervisor into general evaluative statements that threaten the subordinate.

Fortunately, some appraisal techniques can guide the supervisor toward more specific behavioral observations. A behavioral rating scale, for example, asks supervisors to indicate the degree to which subordinates fulfill certain behavioral requirements of their job (e.g., participating actively in meetings or communicating sufficiently with other departments). In the Critical Incident Method, the supervisor records important examples of effective or ineffective performance.[10] Similarly, various Management by Objectives (MBO) techniques can help guide the appraisal discussion toward reviewing specific accomplishments. Some experts on performance appraisal have suggested that a comprehensive performance management system should include both MBO and behavioral ratings.[11] They see these techniques as complementary tools in managing and appraising performance: MBO is a means of managing *what* employees should do, while behavioral ratings are a means of helping them see *how* they should do it.

---

9. Herbert Henry Meyer, Emanuel Kay, and John R. P. French Jr., "Split Roles in Performance Appraisal," *Harvard Business Review*, January–February 1965; Beer and Ruh, "Employee Growth."

10. John C. Flanagan and Robert K. Burns, "The Employee Performance Record," *Harvard Business Review*, September–October 1955.

11. Beer and Ruh, "Employee Growth."

Upward Appraisal   One of the appraisal dynamics that contributes most to both defensiveness and avoidance is the authoritarian character of the supervisor-subordinate relationship. The simple fact that one person is the boss and is responsible for evaluation places him or her in a dominant role and induces submissive behavior in the subordinate. Furthermore, the boss holds and controls rewards. To develop the open two-way dialogue required for coaching and employee development, power must be equalized or at least brought into better balance during the interview. Physical arrangements can contribute to this goal, but the adoption of an upward, or rate-your-boss, appraisal process may be even more effective. Before the interview, the subordinate is given a form on which to rate the supervisor's performance, with a clear understanding that the ratings will be discussed in the appraisal meeting.

An upward appraisal can help a supervisor create the conditions needed for an effective performance appraisal interview. This gives subordinates a real stake in the appraisal interview and an opportunity to influence a part of their environment that ultimately affects their performance. Thus, upward appraisal makes subordinates more equal, less dependent, and more likely to enter the appraisal process with an open mind. The supervisor also has an opportunity to model nondefensive behavior and to demonstrate a willingness to engage in a real two-way dialogue.

Most organizations do not have such rate-your-boss forms, but supervisors can develop their own or seek informal feedback sometime during the appraisal interview.

SUPERVISOR-SUBORDINATE RELATIONS

Not surprisingly, the quality of the appraisal process depends on the nature of the day-to-day boss-subordinate relationship. In an effective relationship, the supervisor is providing ongoing feedback and coaching. Thus, the appraisal interview is merely a review of issues that have already been discussed. Moreover, expectations for the appraisal interview are likely to be shaped by the broader supervisor-subordinate relationship of which the appraisal is only a small part. If a relationship of mutual trust and supportiveness exists, subordinates are more apt to be open in discussing performance problems and less defensive in response to negative feedback.

There are no easy techniques for changing a boss-subordinate relationship, but the appraisal interview itself, if appropriately conducted, can help build a relationship of mutual trust.

THE APPRAISAL INTERVIEW

The best techniques for conducting a particular appraisal interview depend on the mix of objectives pursued and the characteristics of the subordinate. Employees differ in age, experience, sensitivity to negative feedback, attitude toward the supervisor, and desire for influence and control over their destiny. If the subordinate is young, inexperienced, and dependent, and looks up to the supervisor, and if the supervisor's objective is to let the subordinate know that performance improvement is needed, it may be appropriate to have the supervisor do most of the talking. However, if the subordinate is older, more experienced, sensitive about negative feedback, and has a high need for controlling his or her destiny, a less directive approach to the interview will better meet the objectives.

Norman Maier describes three types of appraisal interviews, each with a specific and slightly different objective.[12] The differences are important in determining the skills required by the supervisor and the outcomes for employee motivations and supervisor-subordinate relationships. The three methods—termed *tell and sell, tell and listen,* and *problem-solving*—can be combined if several objectives must be met by the same interview.

The Tell-and-Sell Method   The aim of the tell-and-sell method is to communicate to employees their evaluation as accurately as possible. The fairness of the evaluation is assumed and the manager seeks (a) to let the subordinates know how they are doing, (b) to gain their acceptance of the evaluation, and (c) to get them to follow the manager's plan for improvement. In the interview, supervisors are in complete control; they do most of the talking. They decide what subordinates need to do to improve and attempt to persuade subordinates that their observations and recommendations are valid. Clearly, this method can lead to defensiveness, lack of trust, lack of open communication, and exchange of invalid information. Supervisor-subordinate relations can be hurt because the employees feel hostile and angry when they must accept a supervisor's views that are inconsistent with their self-perceptions. This method may not motivate employees to change because they are placed in a dependent position and do not contribute to the plan.

Nevertheless, there may be situations in which this approach is the only way. For example, a supervisor may decide to use this approach for an employee who remains resistant to change after less directive approaches have been used.

The Tell-and-Listen Interview   The purpose of this interview method is to communicate the evaluation to the subordinate and then let him or her respond to it. The supervisor describes the subordinate's strengths and weaknesses during the first part of the interview, postponing points of disagreement until later. The second part of the interview is devoted to exploring the subordinate's feelings about the evaluation. Thus, the supervisor functions as a judge but also listens to objections from the subordinate without refuting

12. Norman R. F. Maier, "Three Types of Appraisal Interviews," *Personnel*, March–April 1958.

them. In fact, the supervisor encourages the subordinate to disagree in order to drain off any negative feelings the appraisal arouses. The verbal expression of frustration is assumed to reduce the hostility resulting from negative feedback.

The tell-and-listen interview differs substantially from the tell-and-sell method in how disagreement and resistance are handled. Although both interviews start with a one-way communication from the supervisor to the employee, in the tell-and-listen interview the supervisor then sits back and assumes the role of a nondirective counselor.[13] This role requires the supervisor to (a) *listen actively*—accepting and trying to understand the employee's attitudes and feelings; (b) *make effective use of pauses*—waiting patiently without embarrassment for the subordinate to talk; (c) *reflect feelings*—responding to and restating feelings in a way that shows understanding of them; and (d) *summarize feelings*—helping subordinates understand themselves. This approach is not intended to communicate agreement or disagreement with subordinates. Rather, it acknowledges the subordinates' viewpoints and helps them decide which part of the feedback to accept.

The tell-and-listen approach is apt to result in better understanding between supervisor and subordinate than is the tell-and-sell. The subordinate is less likely to be defensive and therefore more likely to accept feedback. Through listening supervisors can learn a great deal about subordinates. However, the interview may not give subordinates a clear understanding of where they stand and how to improve, and may not inspire a commitment to improving behavior.

The Problem-Solving Interview   This interview approach takes the manager out of the role of judge and puts him or her in the role of helper. The objective is to help subordinates discover their own performance deficiencies and lead them to take the initiative in developing a joint plan for improvement. The problem-solving interview is best suited to coaching and development objectives. It has no provision for communicating the supervisor's evaluation. The assumption is that subordinates' self-understanding and motivation to improve performance can best be achieved in a climate of open communication and mutual influence.

Because the objective is to allow subordinates to discover their own developmental needs, the manager cannot specify areas for improvement—that would be an evaluative judgment. The supervisor helps employees examine themselves and their jobs and must be willing to consider their ideas for performance improvement. In this regard, the skills required in the problem-solving interview are similar to those required in the latter half of the tell-and-listen interview. However, the objective is to go well beyond listening and help subordinates discover and explore alternative solutions to problems identified. Supervisors may suggest their own ideas for solution but in the pure problem-

13. Carl R. Rogers, "Releasing Expression," *Counseling and Psychotherapy* (Cambridge: Houghton Mifflin Co., 1942).

solving interview, the supervisor works from the subordinates' initiatives. Supervisors may stimulate subordinate initiative by asking questions about how to eliminate a job problem. The questions should not put subordinates on the spot but should indicate an interest in helping them develop the best plan. Maier gives the following examples:

"Can this plan of yours deal with an emergency situation, if one arises?"

"Would you have other people at your level participate in the plan?"

"What kinds of problems do you anticipate in a changing market?"[14]

Exploratory questions can draw the person out, help clarify thinking, and direct analysis to areas that may have been overlooked.

The problem-solving interview eliminates defensiveness because the issues raised and the ideas for solution are primarily the subordinate's. He or she is therefore more willing to accept problems and better motivated to accomplish personal and job-related plans for improvement. This interview method also encourages creative thinking by the subordinate, and both supervisor and employee are more likely to arrive at new discoveries about the job and themselves. Thus, there is the potential for changes in the job, the organization, and the supervisor's own style. All of these can affect an individual's performance.

The Mixed-Model Interview   These three interview models are a convenient way of categorizing stylistic strategies for an appraisal interview. As noted earlier, the ideal way of dealing with the inherent conflict between evaluation (judging) and development (helping) is to separate the interviews and choose the appropriate method for each. If this were done, the tell-and-sell or tell-and-listen interview would be used for evaluation and the problem-solving interview would be used for developmental objectives. However, such factors as time, organizational practice, and subordinate expectations may dictate that one interview serve both purposes.

The most effective way to implement a mixed-model appraisal interview is to begin with the open-ended problem-solving interview and end with the more directive tell-and-sell or tell-and-listen approach. The reverse order is unlikely to work.[15] If the supervisor starts off with one-way communication, two-way communication and in-depth exploration of personal and job performance issues are unlikely to follow. Thus, as *Exhibit 3* shows, the interview should start with an open-ended exploration of perceptions and concerns, with the subordinate taking the lead, and finish with a more narrowly defined agreement on what performance improvements are expected. If a mutual

---

14. Maier, "Three Types of Appraisal Interviews."

15. Ibid.; Herbert H. Meyer, "The Annual Performance Review Discussion—Making It Constructive," unpublished and undated paper, University of South Florida.

EXHIBIT 3
Mixed-Model Interview

Interview Begins

Open-ended discussion and
exploration of problems.
The subordinate leads
and the supervisor listens.

Problem-solving interview.
The subordinate leads, but the
supervisor takes a
somewhat stronger role.

Agreement on performance
problems and a plan
for improvements needed.

The supervisor summarizes
his or her views, using
tell-and-listen or tell-and-sell
methods if the subordinate
has not dealt
with important issues.

Interview Ends

agreement on performance problems and improvements is not possible, ultimate responsibility for telling the subordinate what is expected rests with the supervisor.

A mixed-model interview can be implemented in many ways. One possible pattern for an effective appraisal interview with multiple purposes is outlined here. This procedure, which assumes an interview similar to that shown in *Exhibit 3*, makes the climate of the interview more conducive to coaching and problem solving but also allows the supervisor to play a directive role if needed. The goal is to improve employee performance and motivation as well as boss-subordinate relations, while leaving subordinates with a clear understanding of what is expected and where they stand. The 10 steps are described in order.

1. *Scheduling.* Notify the subordinate well before the meeting date that an appraisal discussion is scheduled. The time of the interview should be such that both parties are alert and undisturbed by external organizational or family matters. The side effects of unrelated upsetting events can affect the interview process needlessly.
2. *Agreeing on content.* Discuss with the subordinate the nature of the interview, and work toward agreement on what will be discussed

in the interview (i.e., rating forms to be used or performance issues to be discussed). This gives the subordinate a chance to prepare for the meeting (including rating the supervisor if this is to be part of the session), and to come into the interview on a more equal footing with the boss.

3. *Agreeing on process.* Before the interview, agree with the subordinate on the process for the appraisal discussion. For example, agreement should be reached on the sequencing of interview phases (e.g., an open exploratory discussion, followed by problem solving, action planning, and upward appraisal). Similarly, ground rules for communication can be established that will ensure constructive feedback and good listening. The important point is that both parties understand and agree to the interview process before the interview starts.

4. *Location and space.* If possible, meet on neutral territory or in the subordinate's office. This helps establish a relationship of more equal power, which is crucial to open communication. Using the supervisor's office gives him or her an edge. Similarly, it is best that the supervisor not sit behind a desk, which often symbolizes authority and can be a barrier to communication.

5. *Opening the interview.* Review the objectives of the appraisal interview as previously agreed to. This sets the stage and allows supervisor and subordinate to prepare themselves psychologically. It is a warm-up for the more important communication to come.

6. *Starting the discussion.* Give the initiative to the subordinate in the discussion that follows the opening statement. Specifically, start the discussion by asking, "How do you feel things are going on the job? What's going well and what problems are you experiencing? How do you see your performance?" Such general questions will stimulate the subordinate to take the initiative in identifying and solving problems. A useful technique may be to ask the subordinate to appraise his or her own performance on the form provided by the organization. (It has been found that subordinates usually evaluate themselves and their performance realistically.) If the manager starts by expressing views about the employee's performance, the interview almost inevitably develops into a tell-and-sell session in which the subordinate participates very little. Only an unusually strong and skilled subordinate could regain the initiative.

7. *Exchanging feedback.* Follow well-accepted ground rules for giving and receiving feedback.[16] A supervisor who models these methods for effective communication encourages the exchange of valid information. In giving feedback, a supervisor can reduce employee defensiveness by being specific about the performance and behavior causing the problems. Citing examples of observed behavior and describing the effects of that behavior on others,

---

16. John Anderson, "Giving and Receiving Feedback," Procter & Gamble Co., unpublished paper.

on the supervisor's feelings, and on the performance of the department can help an employee identify what needs to be changed. Following this procedure allows the supervisor to give feedback without being overly evaluative. To prevent defensive reactions, the supervisor should avoid blaming, accusing, making general statements, and imputing motives to behavior (e.g., you aren't committed).

The supervisor should also model and encourage the subordinate to follow ground rules for receiving feedback. When signs of defensiveness appear in the receiver of negative feedback, the giver will often pull back from the process and thus hold back important information. Active listening, however, can enhance the value of negative feedback. Receivers of feedback can maintain openness and keep information coming by exploring negative feedback and showing a willingness to examine themselves critically. They can paraphrase what is being said, request clarification, and summarize the discussion periodically. In contrast, justifying actions, apologizing, blaming others, explaining, or building a case tends to cut off feedback and reduce understanding.

It is impossible and undesirable, of course, to prevent receivers of feedback from giving any explanation of their behavior. The timing of explanations is critical, however, in signaling openness versus defensiveness. Active listening should precede explanations. The communication in an appraisal interview can be much improved if both boss and subordinate follow these ground rules, which should be agreed to before the interview begins.

8. *The manager's views.* Provide a summary of the subordinate's major needs for improvements based on the previous discussion. This summary sets the agenda for jointly developing plans for improvement. This should also include the subordinate's strengths—those assets that should be maintained.

9. *Developing a plan for improvement.* Let the subordinate lead with what he or she thinks is an adequate plan for improvement, given the previous discussion and summary. The supervisor is more likely to prevent defensiveness by reacting to and perhaps expanding on the subordinate's plans for changing rather than by making such suggestions directly. A problem-solving rather than blame-placing approach should be maintained. However, if the subordinate cannot formulate good action plans, or seems to be unmotivated to do so, the supervisor can take a more directive approach at this point. The interview should end with a concrete plan for performance improvement; otherwise, no change is likely to occur. A plan may include certain task assignments, training programs, subordinate experimentation with new approaches in specific settings, a change in the subordinate's role, working closely with others who are skilled in a certain area, or a shift of goals and objectives.

10. *Closing the discussion*. Close the interview by discussing what the future might hold for the individual. (This assumes that opportunities for promotion exist and the employee clearly has potential, or that the individual raises the issue.) If the employee needs to be told where he or she stands, this should occur at the very end of the interview by way of a summary of the appraisal discussion. As stated earlier, such a judgment should ideally be delivered in a separate interview or review.

This proposed interview sequence assumes that the primary objective of the appraisal discussion is counseling and coaching, with a secondary goal of letting subordinates know where they stand. It is also assumed that the appraisal interview is a culmination of ongoing performance discussions. The most effective coaching of behavior takes place immediately and directly on a day-to-day basis. The formal interview is an attempt to improve working relations, encourage upward communication, develop deeper understanding, and define developmental plans.

GUIDELINES FOR ASSESSING THE APPRAISAL PROCESS INTERVIEW

After the interview, participants should ask themselves several questions as a check on the effectiveness of the appraisal process. Indeed, an effective appraisal interview should probably also include at least one examination of the process sometime during the interview. The following questions might be helpful:

At the beginning

1. Did the supervisor create an open and accepting climate?
2. Was there agreement on the purpose and process for the interview?
3. Were both parties equally well prepared?

During the interview

4. To what extent did the supervisor really try to understand the employee?
5. Were broad and general questions used at the outset?
6. Was the supervisor's feedback clear and specific?
7. Did the supervisor learn some new things—particularly about the feelings and values of the subordinate?
8. Did the subordinate disagree with and confront the supervisor?
9. Did the interview end with mutual agreement and understanding about problems and goals for improvement?

Appraisal outcomes

10. Did the appraisal session motivate the subordinate?
11. Did the appraisal build a better relationship?

12. Did the subordinate come out with a clear idea of where he or she stands?
13. Did the supervisor arrive at a fairer assessment of the subordinate?
14. Did he or she learn something new about the subordinate?
15. Did the subordinate learn something new about the supervisor and the pressures he or she faces?
16. Does the subordinate have a clear idea of what actions to take to improve performance?

——— SUMMARY

This reading has explored the underlying causes of problems organizations experience with performance appraisal. The main barriers to effective appraisals are avoidance by the supervisor and defensiveness in the subordinate. This reading has illustrated how supervisors and subordinates can overcome these problems by discussing performance evaluations in a nonevaluative manner.

——— DISCUSSION QUESTIONS

1. Can you name any drawbacks or flaws to performance appraisal other than the difficulties mentioned in the reading? Do you think performance appraisals are necessary? Is there a better solution to evaluating performance?
2. This reading touches on the latent hostility that can exist within an organization. What are some ways that an organization can prevent the buildup of such hostilities?
3. The concept of subordinates evaluating their supervisors is mentioned in the reading. Do you think this is a useful practice? How much weight should such a concept be given in an organization that decides to operate that way?
4. According to the reading, effective performance appraisal is "an inevitable part of organizational life." In organizations where you have been employed, have managers been well prepared to deliver effective evaluations? What can organizations do to ensure that their managers possess this important skill?

Managing Interpersonal Conflict   14

JAMES WARE AND LOUIS B. BARNES

This reading explores the nature, sources, and dynamics of interpersonal conflict. After setting forth some definitions to guide the discussion, the authors consider positive and negative outcomes, substantive and emotional issues, and underlying and background contributors to conflict. They suggest three approaches for managing conflict—bargaining, controlling, and constructive confrontation—and offer a set of action questions to use in developing a strategy to manage conflict.

Few managers enjoy dealing with conflicts that involve themselves, their bosses, peers, or subordinates. Whether the conflict is openly hostile or subtly covert, strong personal feelings may be involved. Furthermore, there are often valid veiwpoints on both sides, making the process of finding an acceptable solution mentally exhausting and emotionally draining. Yet the ability to productively manage such conflict is critical to managerial success. Interpersonal differences often become sharpest when the organizational stakes seem to be high, but almost all organizations include their share of small issues blown into major conflicts. The manager's problem is to build on human differences of opinion, while not letting them jeopardize overall performance, satisfaction, and growth.

ASSUMPTIONS AND DEFINITIONS

Interpersonal conflict typically involves a relationship in which a sequence of conditions and events moves toward aggressive behavior and disorder. Conflict can also be viewed, however, in terms of its background conditions, the perceptions of the parties involved, their feelings, their actual behavior, and the consequences or outcomes of their behavior.

Conflict is an organizational reality that is inherently neither good nor bad. It can be destructive, but it can also play a productive role both within a person and between persons. Problems usually arise when potential conflict is artificially suppressed, or when it escalates beyond the control of the adversaries or third-party intermediaries. Whereas most managers will seek to reduce conflict when it occurs, because of its negative repercussions, some will seek to use it for its positive effects on creativity, motivation, and performance. The management of conflict usually entails maintaining a delicate balance between these positive and negative attributes.

There is no one best way for managing interpersonal conflict, either as an involved adversary or as a third party. Rather, there are a number of strategies and tactics involving the external conditions, differing perceptions, internal feelings, behavior, and outcomes. The present relationships of the parties involved (superior–subordinates, peers, representatives) and their past histories as adversaries, allies, or relatively neutral third parties, are other key variables. The relative power of the parties involved is another factor to consider in deciding whether to withdraw from conflict, to compromise, to work toward controlling a conflict within certain boundaries, to seek constructive confrontations, to force conflict into a win/lose pattern, to smooth it over with friendly acts, or to try other subtle or forceful approaches.

Conflict experienced as an involved participant is emotionally different from conflict seen as a relatively objective third party. One advantage of third parties is their ability to add a different perspective to the perceptions, feelings, and behavior of the involved adversaries. This reading examines the management of conflict from the vantage points of both the involved adversaries and an outside third party, which might be a boss, colleague, friend, or subordinate. Each of these different roles has its own strengths and weaknesses.

QUESTIONS FOR THE ANALYSIS OF CONFLICT

A manager may become concerned about conflict when it leads to lower productivity, satisfaction, or growth, be it individual or organizational. The manager might begin an analysis of the conflict by examining such consequences or outcomes. A second area for analysis includes the behavior patterns of the involved parties. A third area entails differing feelings and perceptions. A fourth area consists of underlying or background conditions that helped initiate and now perpetuate the conflict. Each area provides an appropriate point for dealing with a conflict situation. A manager might pose these four questions, which are discussed in the sections that follow:

1. What are the important personal and organizational consequences of the conflict? What are possible future consequences?
2. What behavior patterns characterize the conflict?
3. What substantive issues are involved? To what extent are they colored by each side's perceptions and feelings? Who in the organization might be an objective third party?
4. What are the underlying or background conditions leading to the conflictual feelings, perceptions, behavior, and outcomes?

OUTCOME CONSIDERATIONS

Conflicts generally have both positive and negative consequences. An awareness of both kinds of outcomes complicates the diagnosis but can lead to more effective intervention decisions.

Positive Outcomes   The competitiveness within a conflict can increase the participants' motivation and creativity. A manufacturing manager who becomes angry at being pushed around by a sales vice president, for example, may respond by trying harder to produce a workable production schedule ("just to show that I can do it"). This competitive dynamic—the urge to win—often leads to innovative breakthroughs, because of the effort and willingness to consider new approaches. Interpersonal conflicts frequently clarify persistent underlying organizational problems. Furthermore, intense conflict can focus attention on basic issues and lead to the resolution of long-standing difficulties that can no longer be smoothed over or easily avoided.

Involvement in a conflict can also sharpen an individual's personal approaches to bargaining, influencing, and competitive problem solving. In addition, participants often increase their understanding of their own values and positions on important issues. For example, a manager may clarify an idea by explaining it to someone who clearly disagrees with it.

Thus conflicts can be useful, or at least can lead to positive outcomes, for the organization and for one or more of the individuals involved. There are often negative consequences, however, and conflict can escalate to a level where negative outcomes outweigh the positive ones.

Negative Outcomes   Interpersonal conflicts are often unpleasant emotional experiences for the individuals involved. A subordinate who suppresses anger with a boss, a pair of managers who exchange angry words with each other, two colleagues who avoid each other because of previous tensions, two other associates who "play games" by not sharing relevant and important information—all of these patterns penalize the organization and have an emotional impact on the people involved. The organizational landscape is littered with managers who could not get along with their bosses, colleagues, or subordinates. In one sense, they were not good people managers, but we could also say that the firm had failed to help them develop effective procedures for dealing with conflict.

When a person is involved in a conflict relationship, negative outcomes spill out as emotions of anger, frustration, fear of failure, and a sense of personal inadequacy. Careers can be sidetracked or ruined. The stress of conflictual relationships can make life miserable for people, disrupt patterns of work, and consume an inordinate amount of time for those involved as well as for those affected or indirectly concerned. The direct loss of productivity is but one negative business outcome; the danger of continued poor decision making because of withheld information is yet another. The irony is that the parties determined to win their own limited battles often cause major losses for themselves and the organization.

Short-term negative outcomes can also lead to worsening relationships unless some remedial action is taken. Both the involved and third-party managers have the problem of deciding when to act. Although managers sometimes maintain tensions over time for their positive outcomes, most managers try to change the situation before the schisms become too great. Before they can take appropriate steps, however, managers need to understand the behavior taking place.

BEHAVIOR PATTERNS

Interpersonal conflicts tend to develop patterns. That is, the two parties first engage in open conflict over a particular issue, then separate and gather forces before coming together and going at each other again. Often an organizational procedure, such as budgeting, scheduling, or assigning work, precipitates the conflict and serves as part of the background. Sometimes an apparently trivial issue sets off one party against the other. There may even be periods of time when two people seem to work relatively well together or are effectively buffered from one another. Then, once again, some event or change in circumstances sets them off. Although these events are not always predictable, they often follow an identifiable pattern. Poor listening, one-upmanship, power plays for resources, perceived putdowns, and overcontrolling comments can all serve as triggering devices. The initial behaviors can set in motion the reactions and reciprocal behaviors that start a conflict cycle. Careful attention to when and how a conflict heats up is an important part of developing a conflict-management strategy.

Equally important is how the principals involved express their differences. When the conflict is open and active, the conflictual behaviors are usually obvious: shouting, sulking, repeated sniping, heated debate, unwillingness to listen, hardening of positions, and so on. When the conflict is latent, however, or underground, the signs are not so evident. Then the behaviors are usually more subtle: writing memos to avoid face-to-face contact, delaying decisions to block the other party, interacting through subordinates or third parties, avoiding direct exchanges, or changing times of daily arrivals and departures to avoid meeting. Detecting suppressed conflict requires great sensitivity but is important because many conflicts are expressed indirectly.

Understanding the behavior patterns in a particular conflict is an important prelude to planning its management. If particular events trigger open conflict, then those events may be either stopped or actively constrained. Understanding behavior patterns can also help participants or third parties make more effective choices about when and where to enter the conflict. Finally, the patterns of a conflict can provide important clues to the underlying reasons for the conflict.

SUBSTANTIVE ISSUES, PERCEPTIONS, AND FEELINGS

Most conflicts include two distinctively different kinds of issues. Substantive issues involve disagreements over policies, procedures, decisions, use of resources, roles and responsibilities, or other organizational practices. Emotional issues, in contrast, involve the highly personal perceptions and feelings that people can have about each other and about the substantive issues in contention. Because social customs and the norms of most organizations discourage open expression of negative personal feelings, intense emotional conflicts are often expressed and rationalized as substantive issues. People often drum up disagreements on trivial issues to provide justification for an emotional conflict with another individual.

This tendency to distort and magnify differences means that conflicts often escalate rapidly in intensity and importance. Each person builds a grievance list of real and perceived problems. People seek support wherever they can find it, repeatedly citing evidence to justify their feelings as a means of gaining sympathy. Worse yet, people attribute all kinds of negative motives and intentions to other persons, while thinking of themselves as the injured "good guys."

Conflicts also escalate because each time the two people interact they may try to "score points," and each interaction then becomes part of the history of the conflict. Whenever a person thinks that he or she has lost one round, the effort to win the next one can become even more intense as the following example demonstrates.

> A product manager and an inventory control manager had to meet regularly to review and update sales forecasts. Their interests conflicted somewhat because the product manager wanted to minimize unit costs and avoid stockouts, while the inventory control manager wanted to minimize total purchasing costs and inventory levels. When their forecasts became inaccurate, the two managers had several disagreements over the forecasting procedures and their divergent goals. Gradually, the two managers lost sight of each other's different basic assumptions and organizational needs; rather, they began to personalize their differences. Each felt threatened and attacked by the other, and these feelings intensified each time they interacted. Their growing distrust and lack of respect spilled over into personal antagonism, with each manager seeing ulterior motives and unpleasant personality traits in the other. Hostilities escalated with personal threats, name-calling, and accusations of stupidity, self-interest, and dishonesty. Thus, a legitimate set of substantive differences became transformed into the vicious cycle of an emotional battle.

Some managers involved in a dispute are determined to work out an agreement, through bargaining, control procedures, constructive confrontation, or other forms of negotiation. Still other managers will see conflict as something to avoid, withdraw from, or smooth over. Colleagues and bosses are probably more willing to take the first approach than are subordinates, who may feel forced to fall back on the second approach; and all parties may prefer a third-party mediator. A manager's choice has much to do with individual tolerance for conflict and the accompanying uncertainties. Through experience, managers can learn how much to trust their own perceptions and feelings during such stressful times. Although a certain amount of stress may be a productive motivator, most people have difficulty remaining open-minded and flexible during times of high stress. In addition, performance shortcomings may challenge one's assumptions about personal abilities and self-concept. The most natural response is to look elsewhere for a scapegoat—"If they would give me more accurate sales forecasts, I wouldn't have all this excess inventory." It is much easier to change perceptions about someone else's ability ("she just doesn't know how to forecast") or motives ("he's feeding me false data to make me look bad") than it is to admit personal failure or the need for help. Scapegoating is thus another personal characteristic that contributes to escalation in a conflict.

The advantage of third parties, trusted by both adversaries, is that their outside perceptions and feelings can serve as a reality check for both adversaries. If the third party can help work out a procedure for coping with the conflict, then that may be a major step toward further agreement or resolution. A boss acting as a third party has the added power of being able to arbitrate or to tip the power balance one way or the other; however, even this apparent advantage can have negative effects in the long run if the boss is perceived as taking sides too often. One of the hardest yet most important challenges for the third party is to stay in touch with the perceptions and feelings of both adversaries and simultaneously maintain his or her own views; that is, the third party must deal with the conflict *relationship* rather than be pulled toward either adversarial viewpoint.

UNDERLYING AND BACKGROUND CONDITIONS

The underlying causes of interpersonal conflict are just as numerous and varied as the ways in which conflicts are expressed. Assessing the factors causing or reinforcing a particular conflict is difficult because multiple forces are usually involved. Separating out the primary causes is often impossible because most serious conflicts become self-reinforcing: These conflicts have such a powerful history and have become so personalized that their original sources are irrelevant to the present situation. Nevertheless, attempts to understand a conflict must consider the forces behind the adversaries' actions. Managing the conflict then means changing the situational factors surrounding it, or altering the ways in which the adversaries respond to the situation and to each other.

These causal factors are divided into two categories: (1) situational or external characteristics and (2) personal or internal characteristics. These distinctions are somewhat arbitrary, however, and will be treated more distinctively here than they usually are in practice.

Situational—External Characteristics   This category includes all of the external conditions surrounding the two people—the organizational rules and procedures that affect their interactions; the pressures of time and deadlines; competition for budgetary funds, staff, organizational influence, and other scarce resources; performance pressures from bosses, peers, and other departments; and promotion opportunities.

When two people from different departments (such as the market analyst and inventory control manager described earlier) must interact, they may represent and reflect their own reference group's differences in goals, values, and priorities. Thus *interdepartmental* conflict frequently becomes *interpersonal* conflict unless the two representatives can rise above the special interests of the groups they represent.

But even two people from the same department can become competitive for scarce resources, whether these are budgetary funds, subordinates, control over key procedures and decisions, office space, or the boss's time or job. The pressure to perform can make the personal stakes so high that individual managers become inflexible and defensive. These stakes are particularly important when middle managers must compete for promotion opportunities that include individual responsibilities and rewards. Because most organizations reward successful managers both formally (promotions and salary increases) and informally (influence, status, credibility), the social pressures to compete and win can be extremely intense.

Personal—Internal Factors   The personal goals, styles, and abilities of two people in conflict can also affect their behavior and their relationship. Personal career goals and ambitions can develop in response to the organizational pressures just described. People may experience feelings of rivalry and interpersonal competition, however, even when there is little external basis for such emotions. Sometimes there is a poor fit between a person and the job requirements, and his or her poor performance may create serious problems for someone else. More frequently, however, conflict erupts and escalates because one manager sees another manager as actively blocking a personally important goal. Whether that perception is accurate or not is almost irrelevant. The resulting anger, frustration, and anxiety contribute to the emotional escalation of conflict. These kinds of feelings are often strong among ambitious, competitive, achievement-oriented individuals.

"Bad chemistry" between two people is also spoken of as a cause of conflict. If people have different personal values, styles, or work habits, then they may also disagree on how to accomplish important tasks. Consider the possible tensions between an aggressive, high-energy manager and a careful, methodical analyst; or between a talkative, easy-going plant manager and a quiet, reserved manufacturing manager. Sometimes personal styles are complementary, but sometimes they are basically incompatible. When the people involved feel strongly about their ways of doing things, conflict is almost inevitable.

One of the most critical personal characteristics feeding a conflict is a limited capacity for coping with stress. When personal and organizational stakes are high, people may develop "short fuses" and become intolerant of others' mistakes or even of their legitimate needs. When two people under extreme pressure must interact frequently, they may find it difficult to avoid blaming each other for the problems they are experiencing.

When a high-pressured situation is exacerbated by each person's internal anxieties and stress, conflict usually surfaces in the areas of perception, feeling, and behavior. Confronted with these conditions and with the outcomes of a conflict, a manager—either as adversary or as onlooker—must face a series of choices. The first is whether to avoid the conflict or to try to manage it. Although the choice may seem clear-cut on paper—managers should manage—many managers are better at conflict avoidance, or smoothing over, than they are at conflict management. The skills and strength for managing a conflict, either as an involved participant or as a third party, do not come easily for most people. At the same time, there are instances when avoidance or smoothing over stress and negative outcomes makes sense, if satisfaction is valued more highly than performance or growth. This is often true in family businesses and in close partnerships. But in situations where management is trying to optimize the balance of the three outcomes— performance, satisfaction, and growth—there is a greater need for managing conflict.

───── MANAGING THE CONFLICT

A manager who chooses to manage a conflict and not withdraw or smooth it over must first of all take stock of his or her place in the situation: adversary or third party? boss or subordinate? representative or free agent? with power and dependencies or, relatively speaking, without them? Any one of these roles poses its own set of demands and choices. Some of these demands and choices also depend on the manager's comfort with using power in this fashion and willingness to take on this conflict. The following sections briefly discuss three general approaches to conflict management and then raise several questions that a manager might ask before choosing an approach.[1]

The three approaches can be roughly categorized as (1) bargaining, (2) controlling, and (3) confrontation. *Bargaining behavior* is probably most prevalent under conditions of required interdependence and a rough balance of power. *Controlling behavior* is more apt to be used when one party or the other (including the third party) has relatively higher power and when the interdependence requirements are more flexible. *Confrontation behavior* may be used under either of the above conditions but appears to depend more on the personal attributes of the parties involved and on the assumptions they make about the setting and time pressures. (Confrontation behavior may be intended to be either destructive or constructive. The focus here is on constructive confrontation.) As each of these approaches is discussed, the assumption is made that the acting manager understands the conflict situation's outcomes and consequences; the behavior, the perceptions and feelings related to the substantive issues; and the underlying background conditions. Each approach offers an entry point for either an adversary or a third-party mediator, but the choice of approach depends on the individual's position, skills, and personal preferences.

BARGAINING

For a manager involved in a conflict, as either adversary or mediator, negotiating or bargaining on the substantive issues often appears to be the reasonable approach. The assumption here is that the conflict involves a situation in which one party would gain at the other's expense. If the two parties come to the bargaining table in union-management fashion, however, they signal that they will consider new ways to resolve the conflict.

The advantage of a bargaining approach is that the motive of compromise provides an incentive to go beyond conflict. In approaching the bargaining table, the two parties, with or without a third-party mediator, usually prepare to lose as well as to win some points. The goal is to reach a solution acceptable to both sides. Many bargaining situations, however, involve games such as bluffing, behind-the-scenes negotiations, an attempt to marshal outside power sources, a tendency to overstate one's initial demands, and the heavy use of legalistic procedures that preserve the appearance of a rational process. Each of these bargaining tactics involves risks as well as rewards. Another problem with a bargaining approach is that the parties often place a higher premium on

1. Ideas in this section are drawn from the following sources: Richard Walton, *Interpersonal Peacemaking* (Reading, MA: Addison-Wesley, 1969); Louis R. Pondy, "Organizational Conflict: Concepts and Models," *Administrative Science Quarterly* (vol. 12, no. 2, September 1967), pp. 296–320; Robert R. Blake and Jane S. Mouton, *The New Managerial Grid* (Houston: Gulf Publishing Co., 1978).

acceptable compromises than on sound solutions. A manager who engages in a bargaining approach, either as an adversary or as a third party, can lose sight of the organization's well-being and become consumed in the limited goal of reaching an acceptable solution.

CONTROLLING

There are four strategies for controlling interpersonal conflict. They may come into play when a power imbalance enables one party to exert pressure on the situation. Other times, two adversaries will tire of the controls or a third party will appear who gains the trust of both adversaries. Conflict control can also be a temporary approach used until the crisis is over or conditions improve enough to permit bargaining or confrontation. The four strategies are (1) preventing interaction or reducing its frequency, (2) structuring the forms and patterns of interaction, (3) reducing or changing the external situational pressures, and (4) personal counseling to help the two parties accept and deal with the process and realities of the conflict. This last strategy, counseling, is different from mediation and can be used with bargaining and confrontation approaches.

Preventing Interaction or Reducing Its Frequency   This strategy is often useful when emotions are high. It controls conflict by reducing the possibility of triggering events. If the two people are physically separate and no longer need to interact with each other, then there is little opportunity for them to express differences. Although the differences continue to exist, the intense feelings are likely to dissipate without recurring run-ins, or at least to cool down enough to permit other approaches.

There are many ways to reduce or eliminate interaction. Sometimes operating procedures can be modified to eliminate the necessity of two people working together. If that option is impossible, then peers or subordinates can substitute for one or both parties. If the conflict stems from an underlying conflict of interest, however, it is just as likely to flare up in the new relationship. One or both of the people could be transferred to a new job or even to a new physical location.

Several of these options are relatively expensive and time-consuming. They may be useful, however, if there is no other way to work out the differences, or if the hostility has reached a level where confrontation would be either impossible or inordinately drawn out. Separating the two parties may create more serious long-term problems or only delay an eventual confrontation. When adversaries are separated, their hostilities sometimes merely go underground and may become more intense because of the absence of an opportunity to express them. When that happens, the eventual confrontation may be even more serious, as the pent-up emotions finally come tumbling out. In these instances, trusted third parties can help judge whether reducing interaction makes sense.

Structuring the Forms of Interaction   The separation options listed above are sometimes not feasible. When the two parties must continue to interact, the conflict can be controlled by adopting clear guidelines of behavior. These procedures can be as specific and narrow as the parties wish. For example, the procedures might specify the time and place of meetings, the allowable discussion topics, the specific information to be provided by each individual, or even the types of questions or comments not allowed. Alternatively, the procedures might specify or imply new channels of communication: meetings could be replaced with memos, messages, or telephone calls.

How these ground rules are established depends on the specific situation and on the relationships between the people involved. A manager can generally impose these kinds of procedures on subordinates or on other adversaries with less organizational authority. In the absence of such a clear mandate, however, the ground rules are often arrived at by negotiation or mutual agreement or with the help of a third party.

This strategy permits the continued exchange of vital information and prevents the exchange of hostile and judgmental emotions that would interfere with needed communication. Like physical separation, this strategy should be a temporary strategy, since the suppression of strong emotions can easily lead to more violent and destructive flare-ups later on. Involved adversaries may find that their own perspectives need the objectivity of outsiders to reduce distortion in making judgments and to help learn when to use and when to abandon this approach.

Reducing or Changing External Pressures   Changing the conditions that feed the conflict is often more effective than focusing on the interactions that characterize the conflict. When situational factors are largely responsible for the problem, dealing with those factors directly can control the conflict or even eliminate it.

The factors that should be changed will depend on the specific circumstances, each manager's power to affect the critical factors, and the organizational consequences of the changes (sometimes a change that might control the conflict would not be appropriate for other, more important reasons). Situational factors that could be changed include extending deadlines, adding new project personnel, modifying organizational policies or making temporary exceptions, setting up periodic informational meetings, increasing budget allocations, and protecting the principals from harassment by peers or by organizational superiors. Sometimes these mechanisms are in the hands of one of the adversaries and can be acted upon; at other times they need actions from outside or from above the conflict.

Personal Counseling   In contrast to the other control strategies, this approach does not address the conflict itself but focuses on how the two people are reacting to it. The underlying assumption here is that providing counseling, reassurance, and emotional support will help make their conflict more tolerable. In addition, the process of ventilating feelings about an adversary to a colleague or friend usually releases pent-up tensions and may become a first step toward discovering new ways to deal directly with the conflict. Alternatively, talking out the problem with the third party can lead an individual to invent new procedures or personal goals that make him or her less dependent on the other party, thus reducing the inherent stress in the conflict.

Controlling a conflict can be a useful short-term strategy, because it often brings about positive changes in either the situation or the parties. When this approach is not likely to succeed or when interdependence needs are high, managers should think about ways to constructively confront the conflict.

CONSTRUCTIVE CONFRONTATION

Constructive confrontation is potentially the most difficult and the most rewarding of all the approaches to conflict management. It should begin with a serious and well-communicated attempt to understand and explore the other party's perceptions and feelings. A third party can aid this process by helping to build an exploratory climate. This party must be careful to avoid the initial temptation to support one of the two adversaries. It is important to remember that a constructive confrontation does not usually begin with a confrontation but with an attempt to understand.

Constructive confrontation has the advantage, once a climate of exploration has been established, of conveying the possibility of a win/win solution. It seeks an exchange of information—substantive as well as perceptions and feelings—that provides new definitions of the problem and new motives for a common solution. Both mediators and adversaries need skill, patience, persistence, and commitment to listening to each other while constantly looking for ways to move out of a deadlock. Asking the simple question What if . . . ? can be helpful in searching for new alternatives.

A confrontation may initially have to move carefully while the two adversaries seek ways to release their emotions and feelings. Once again a third party can help legitimize these expressions while monitoring the ways in which negative or hostile feelings are expressed. For example, the third party—or even one of the adversaries—may suggest that the parties agree to express and explore feelings that result from actual behavior rather than those based upon inference and speculation of the other's motives and perceptions. Without these ground rules for the expression of feelings, confrontation can easily become more destructive than constructive. Such ground rules help the parties involved move to new stages of exchanging information and problem solving.

——— SOME RELEVANT ACTION QUESTIONS

A manager involved either as an adversary or as a third party in a conflict might use the following questions in deciding on an approach for conflict management. These questions are especially important when considering a confrontation strategy, but they are also applicable to the other approaches.

1. To what extent is there a productive level of tension and motivation in the conflict relationship? Or has the conflict become highly destructive?

If conflict resolution is to be successful, there typically must be enough stress in the situation for the participants to desire a resolution, but not so much that they are unable to deal with the issues or each other. Too little tension may require alerting participants to the personal or organizational outcomes that make the latent conflict dangerous or dysfunctional. Too much tension may require cooling-off steps or temporary controlling measures.

Interpersonal conflict often persists because only one party is motivated to do anything about it. When this happens, little can be done until the tension level is again high enough for both adversaries to at least say they want to work toward a resolution. Such stated motivation can serve as a starting point.

2. What are the balances of status and power positions among the two or three parties?

The balance of power configurations can play a big part in determining appropriate paths to conflict resolution or avoidance. For example, there may be less chance for successful resolution when one party in a two-party relationship is much more powerful or influential than the other. It is often harder to get third-party involvement in such situations, paticularly when the power imbalance involves a superior and a subordinate. At the same time, third-party mediation can be most helpful in these instances, because it can help rebalance the power equation. The advantage for controlling is clearly on the side of the person with higher status, whether that person is an adversary or a third party, although constructive confrontation will more likely thrive when a rough power balance is achieved.

3. To what extent are time and flexible resources available?

Conflict resolution in almost any form can require considerable time, new procedures, off-site meetings, outside help, painful adjustments, restructuring of relationships, and tolerance for uncertainties. As conflict conditions develop and change, so might the participants' needs for time and resources. It may be easier to change situational or external variables, such as new procedures, than it is to change the internal perceptions of all parties in the conflict arena, particularly those who identify with or support the two adversaries. Under these conditions, active counseling by a number of managers may be useful to provide new perspectives throughout the conflict arena. Changing the feelings and perceptions of the two adversaries may not be enough if their supporters will not allow them to relinquish the conflict. The conflict-resolution process may need more time to work for all involved parties.

—— CONCLUSION

Managers must recognize that interpersonal conflict is inevitable in any human organization. It can be both a constructive and a destructive force. A manager's first choice is whether to ignore or avoid such realities or whether to find ways to manage the complexities of the conflict. The first alternative is often easier in the short run but more costly in the long run. The management of conflict requires some understanding of its outcomes, its destructive behavior and reciprocity patterns, the perceptions and feelings that drive the behavior, and the underlying and background conditions that help to perpetuate the conflict. Each of these areas provides an entry point for managing the conflict—whether the approach is bargaining, controlling, confronting, or some combination. Understanding these areas can help a manager explore his or her options in handling the realities of a conflict. Most managers will have ample opportunity to view conflict both as outsiders and as involved adversaries.

—— DISCUSSION QUESTIONS

1. The authors suggest several ways of managing conflict such as bargaining, controlling, and confronting. What other ways of managing conflict can you suggest?
2. Give an example of a conflict situation (either real or imagined) that has a win-win solution. Now think of a situation (again, real or imagined) that has a win-lose outcome. How might this situation have been managed to achieve a win-win result?
3. The authors mention the idea of conflict enhancing the participants' motivation and creativity. Give an example from your experience in which conflict increased your motivation and creativity.
4. The authors focus on the potential gains that conflict can have for individuals. What benefits might an organization gain from conflict?
5. Give an example when conflict avoidance or smoothing over might be more beneficial than conflict management.

Managing Your Boss   15

JOHN J. GABARRO AND JOHN P. KOTTER

It is just as important to manage your relationship with your boss as it is to manage subordinates, products, markets, and technologies, argue these authors. If the relationship is rocky, neither managers nor their bosses can do their jobs effectively; the responsibility for the relationship should not and cannot rest entirely with the boss. This reading offers suggestions for ways that managers can develop and maintain healthy working relationships with their bosses.

To many the phrase *managing your boss* may sound unusual or suspicious. Because of the traditional top-down emphasis in organizations, it is not obvious why you need to manage relationships upward—unless, of course, you would do so for personal or political reasons. But in using the expression managing your boss, we are not referring to political maneuvering or apple-polishing. Rather, we are using the term to mean the process of consciously working with your superior to obtain the best possible results for you, your boss, and the company.

Studies suggest that effective managers take time and effort to manage not only relationships with their subordinates but also those with their bosses.[1] These studies show as well that this aspect of management, essential though it is to survival and advancement, is sometimes ignored by otherwise talented and aggressive managers. Indeed, some managers who actively and effectively supervise subordinates, products, markets, and technologies, nevertheless assume an almost passively reactive stance vis-à-vis their bosses. Such a stance practically always hurts these managers and their companies.

If you doubt the importance of managing your relationship with your boss or how difficult it is to do so effectively, consider for a moment the following sad but telling story:

Frank Gibbons was an acknowledged manufacturing genius in his industry and, by any profitability standard, a very effective executive. His strengths propelled him into the position of vice president of manufacturing for the second-largest and most profitable company in its industry. Gibbons was

---

1. *See,* for example, John J. Gabarro, "Socialization at the Top: How CEOs and Their Subordinates Develop Interpersonal Contracts," *Organizational Dynamics* (Winter 1979); and John P. Kotter, *Power in Management,* AMACOM (1979).

not, however, a good manager of people. He knew this, as did others in his company and his industry. Recognizing this weakness, the president made sure that those who reported to Gibbons were good at working with people and could compensate for his limitations. The arrangement worked well. Two years later, Philip Bonnevie was promoted into a position reporting to Gibbons. In keeping with the previous pattern, the president selected Bonnevie because he had an excellent track record and a reputation for being good with people. In making that selection, however, the president neglected to notice that, in his rapid rise through the organization, Bonnevie himself had never reported to anyone who was poor at managing subordinates. Bonnevie had always had good-to-excellent bosses. He had never been forced to manage a relationship with a difficult boss. In retrospect, Bonnevie admits he had never thought that managing his boss was a part of his job.

Fourteen months after he started working for Gibbons, Bonnevie was fired. During that same quarter, the company reported a net loss for the first time in seven years. Many of those who were close to these events say that they don't really understand what happened. This much is known, however: while the company was bringing out a major new product—a process that required its sales, engineering, and manufacturing groups to coordinate their decisions very carefully—a whole series of misunderstandings and bad feelings developed between Gibbons and Bonnevie.

For example, Bonnevie claims Gibbons was aware of and had accepted Bonnevie's decision to use a new type of machinery to make the new product; Gibbons swears he did not. Furthermore, Gibbons claims he made it clear to Bonnevie that introduction of the product was too important to the company in the short run to take any major risks.

As a result of such misunderstandings, planning went awry: a new manufacturing plant was built that could not produce the new product designed by engineering, in the volume desired by sales, at a cost agreed on by the executive committee. Gibbons blamed Bonnevie for the mistake. Bonnevie blamed Gibbons.

Of course, one could argue that the problem here was caused by Gibbons's inability to manage his subordinates. But one can make just as strong a case that the problem was related to Bonnevie's inability to manage his boss. Remember, Gibbons was not having difficulty with any other subordinates. Moreover, given the personal price paid by Bonnevie (being fired and having his reputation within the industry severely tarnished), there was little consolation in saying the problem was that Gibbons was poor at managing subordinates. Everyone already knew that.

We believe that the situation could have turned out differently had Bonnevie been more adept at understanding Gibbons and at managing his relationship with him. In this case, an inability to manage upward was unusually costly. The company lost $2 to $5 million, and Bonnevie's career was, at least temporarily, disrupted. Many less costly cases like this probably occur regularly in all major corporations, and the cumulative effect can be very destructive.

—— MISREADING THE BOSS-SUBORDINATE RELATIONSHIP

People often dismiss stories like the one we just related as being merely cases of personality conflict. Because two people can on occasion be psychologically or temperamentally incapable of working together, this can be an apt description. But more often, we have found, a personality conflict is only a part of the problem—sometimes a very small part.

Bonnevie did not just have a different personality from Gibbons, he also made or had unrealistic assumptions and expectations about the very nature of boss-subordinate relationships. Specifically, he did not recognize that his relationship to Gibbons involved *mutual dependence* between two *fallible* human beings. Failing to recognize this, a manager typically either avoids trying to manage his or her relationship with a boss or manages it ineffectively.

Some people behave as if their bosses were not very dependent on them. They fail to see how much the boss needs their help and cooperation to do his or her job effectively. These people refuse to acknowledge that the boss can be severely hurt by their actions and needs cooperation, dependability, and honesty from them.

Some see themselves as not very dependent on their bosses. They gloss over how much help and information they need from the boss in order to perform their own jobs well. This superficial view is particularly damaging when a manager's job and decisions affect other parts of the organization, as in Bonnevie's situation. A manager's immediate boss can play a critical role in linking the manager to the rest of the organization, in making sure the manager's priorities are consistent with organizational needs, and in securing the resources the manager needs to perform well. Yet some managers need to see themselves as practically self-sufficient, as not needing the critical information and resources a boss can supply.

Many managers, like Bonnevie, assume that the boss will magically know what information or help their subordinates need and provide it to them. Certainly, some bosses do an excellent job of caring for their subordinates in this way, but for a manager to expect that from all bosses is dangerously unrealistic. A more reasonable expectation for managers to have is that modest help will be forthcoming. After all, bosses are only human. Most really effective managers accept this fact and assume primary responsibility for their own careers and development. They make a point of seeking the information and help they need to do a job instead of waiting for their bosses to provide it.

Thus, it seems to us that managing a situation of mutual dependence among fallible human beings requires the following:

- You must have a good understanding of the other person and yourself, especially regarding strengths, weaknesses, work styles, and needs.
- You must use this information to develop and manage a healthy working relationship—one that is compatible with both persons' work styles and assets, is characterized by mutual expectations, and meets the most critical needs of the other person. And that is essentially what we have found highly effective managers doing.

UNDERSTANDING THE BOSS AND YOURSELF

Managing your boss requires that you gain an understanding of both the boss and his context as well as your own situation and needs. All managers do this to some degree, but many are not thorough enough.

THE BOSS'S WORLD

At a minimum, you need to appreciate your boss's goals and pressures, his or her strengths and weaknesses. What are your boss's organizational and personal objectives, and what are the pressures on him, especially those from his boss and others at his level? What are your boss's long suits and blind spots? What is his or her preferred style of working? Does he or she like to get information through memos, formal meetings, or phone calls? Does your boss thrive on conflict or try to minimize it?

Without this information, a manager is flying blind when dealing with his boss, and unnecessary conflicts, misunderstandings, and problems are inevitable.

Goals and Pressures   In one situation we studied, a top-notch marketing manager with a superior performance record was hired into a company as a vice president "to straighten out the marketing and sales problems." The company, which was having financial difficulties, had been recently acquired by a larger corporation. The president was eager to turn it around and gave the new marketing vice president free rein—at least initially. Based on previous experience, the new vice president correctly diagnosed that greater market share was needed and that strong product management was required to bring that about. As a result, the vice president made a number of pricing decisions aimed at increasing high-volume business.

When margins declined and the financial situation did not improve, however, the president increased pressure on the new vice president. Believing that the situation would eventually correct itself as the company gained back market share, the vice president resisted the pressure.

When by the second quarter margins and profits had still failed to improve, the president took direct control over all pricing decisions and put all items on a set level of margin, regardless of volume. The new vice president began to be shut out by the president, and their relationship deteriorated. In fact, the vice president found the president's behavior bizarre. Unfortunately, the president's new pricing scheme also failed to increase margins, and by the fourth quarter both the president and the vice president were fired.

What the new vice president had not known until it was too late was that improving marketing and sales had been only *one* of the president's goals. The most immediate goal had been to make the company more profitable—quickly.

Nor had the new vice president known that the boss was invested in this short-term priority for personal as well as business reasons. The president had been a strong advocate of the acquisition within the parent company, and the boss's personal credibility was at stake.

The vice president made three basic errors. Taking information at face value, the vice president made assumptions in certain areas despite having no information, and—most damaging—never actively tried to clarify what the boss's objectives were. As a result, the vice president ended up taking actions that were actually at odds with the president's priorities and objectives.

Managers who work effectively with their bosses do not behave this way. They seek out information about the boss's goals and problems and pressures. They are alert for opportunities to question the boss and others around him or her to test their assumptions. They pay attention to clues in the boss's behavior. Although it is imperative that they do this when they begin working with a new boss, effective managers also continue to do this because they recognize that priorities and concerns change.

Strengths, Weaknesses, and Work Style   Being sensitive to a boss's work style can be crucial, especially when the boss is new. For example, a new president who was organized and formal in approach replaced someone who was informal and intuitive. The new president worked best with written reports and also preferred formal meetings with set agendas.

One of the division managers realized this need and worked with the new president to identify the kinds and frequency of information and reports the president wanted. This manager also made a point of sending background information and brief agendas for their discussions. The manager found that with this type of preparation their meetings were very useful. With adequate preparation, the new boss was even more effective at brainstorming problems than the boss's more informal and intuitive predecessor had been.

In contrast, another division manager never fully understood the new boss's work style, objecting to its excessive control. As a result, the manager seldom sent the new president the necessary background information, and the president never felt fully prepared for meetings with the manager. In fact, the president spent a great deal of time when they met trying to get what should have been supplied beforehand. The boss experienced these meetings as frustrating and inefficient, and the subordinate often was thrown off guard by the questions that the president asked. Ultimately, this division manager resigned.

The difference between the two division managers just described was not so much one of ability or even adaptability. Rather, the difference was that one of them was more sensitive to the boss's work style than the other and to the implications of the boss's needs.

YOU AND YOUR NEEDS

The boss is only half of the relationship. You are the other half, as well as the part over which you have more direct control. Developing an effective working relationship requires, then, that you know your own needs, strengths and weaknesses, and personal style.

Your Own Style   You are not going to change either your basic personality structure or that of your boss. But you can become aware of what it is about you that impedes or facilitates working with your boss and, with that awareness, take actions that make the relationship more effective.

For example, in one case we observed, a manager and his superior ran into problems whenever they disagreed. The boss's typical response was to harden his position and overstate it. The manager's reaction was then to raise the ante and intensify the forcefulness of his argument. In doing this, he channeled his anger into sharpening his attacks on the logical fallacies in his boss's assumptions. His boss in turn would become even more adamant about holding his original position. Predictably, this escalating cycle resulted in the subordinate avoiding whenever possible any topic of potential conflict with his boss.

In discussing this problem with his peers, the manager discovered that his reaction to the boss was typical of how he generally reacted to counterarguments—but with a difference. His response would overwhelm his peers, but not his boss. Because his attempts to discuss this problem with his boss were unsuccessful, he concluded that the only way to change the situation was to deal with his own instinctive reactions. Whenever the two reached an impasse, he would check his own impatience and suggest that they break up and think about it before getting together again. Usually when they renewed their discussion, they had digested their differences and were more able to work them through.

Gaining this level of self-awareness and acting on it are difficult but not impossible. For example, by reflecting over his past experiences, a young manager learned that he was not very good at dealing with difficult and emotional issues where people were involved. Because he disliked those issues and realized that his instinctive responses to them were seldom very good, he developed a habit of touching base with his boss whenever such a problem arose. Their discussions always surfaced ideas and approaches the manager had not considered. In many instances, they also identified specific actions the boss could take to help.

Dependence on Authority Figures   Although a superior-subordinate relationship is one of mutual dependence, it is also one in which the subordinate is typically more dependent on the boss than the other way around. This dependence inevitably results in the subordinate feeling a certain degree of frustration, sometimes anger, when his or her actions or options are constrained by the boss's decisions. This is a normal part of life and occurs in the best of relationships. The way in which a manager handles these frustrations largely depends on his or her predisposition toward dependence on authority figures.

Some people's instinctive reaction under these circumstances is to resent the boss's authority and to rebel against the boss's decisions. Sometimes a person will escalate a conflict beyond what is appropriate. Seeing the boss almost as an institutional enemy, this type of manager will often, without being conscious of it, fight with the boss just for the sake of fighting. The manager's reactions to being constrained are usually strong and sometimes impulsive. He or she sees the boss as someone whose role is to hinder progress, an obstacle to be circumvented or at best tolerated.

Psychologists call this pattern of reactions counterdependent behavior. Although a counterdependent person is difficult for most superiors to manage and usually has a history of strained relationships with superiors, this sort of manager is apt to have even more trouble with a boss who tends to be directive or authoritarian. When the manager acts on his or her negative feelings, often in subtle and nonverbal ways, the boss sometimes *does* become the enemy. Sensing the subordinate's latent hostility, the boss will lose trust in the subordinate or his or her judgment and behave less openly.

Paradoxically, a manager with this type of predisposition is often a good manager of his or her own people. The manager will often go out of the way to get support for them and will not hesitate to go to bat for them.

At the other extreme are managers who swallow their anger and behave in a very compliant fashion when the boss makes what they know to be a poor decision. These managers will agree with the boss even when a disagreement might be welcome or when the boss would easily alter his or her decision if given more information. Because they bear no relationship to the specific situation at hand, their responses are as much an overreaction as those of counterdependent managers. Instead of seeing the boss as an enemy, these people deny their anger—the other extreme—and tend to see the boss as if he or she were an all-wise parent who should know best, should take responsibility for their careers, train them in all they need to know, and protect them from overly ambitious peers.

Both counterdependence and overdependence lead managers to hold unrealistic views of what a boss is. Both views ignore that most bosses, like everyone else, are imperfect and fallible. They don't have unlimited time, encyclopedic knowledge, or extrasensory perception; nor are they evil enemies. They have their own pressures and concerns that are sometimes at odds with the wishes of the subordinate—and often for good reason.

Altering predispositions toward authority, especially at the extremes, is almost impossible without intensive psychotherapy (psychoanalytic theory and research suggest that such predispositions are deeply rooted in a person's personality and upbringing). However, an awareness of these extremes and the range between them can be very useful in understanding where your own predispositions fall and what the implications are for how you tend to behave in relation to your boss.

If you believe, on the one hand, that you have some tendencies toward counterdependence, you can understand and even predict what your reactions and overreactions are likely to be. If, on the other hand, you believe you have some tendencies toward overdependence, you might question the extent to which your overcompliance or inability to confront real differences may be making both you and your boss less effective.

━━━━ DEVELOPING AND MANAGING THE RELATIONSHIP

With a clear understanding of both your boss and yourself, you can—usually—establish a way of working together that fits both of you, that is characterized by unambiguous mutual expectations, and that helps both of you to be more productive and effective. We have already outlined a few traits such a relationship consists of, which are itemized in the *Exhibit*, and here are a few more.

COMPATIBLE WORK STYLES

Above all else, a good working relationship with a boss accommodates differences in work style. For example, in one situation we studied, a manager (who had a relatively good relationship with the boss) realized that during meetings the boss would often become inattentive and sometimes brusque. The subordinate's own style tended to be discursive and exploratory. The manager would often digress from the topic at hand to deal with background factors, alternative approaches, and so forth. The boss, instead, preferred to discuss problems with a minimum of background detail and became impatient and distracted whenever the subordinate digressed from the immediate issue.

Recognizing this difference in style, the manager became terser and more direct during meetings with the boss. To prepare to do this, before meetings with the boss the manager would develop brief agendas to be used as a guide. Whenever a digression was needed, the manager explained why. This small shift in personal style made these meetings more effective and far less frustrating for them both.

EXHIBIT
Managing the Relationship with Your Boss

Make sure you understand your boss and the boss's context, including his or her:
  Goals and objectives
  Pressures
  Strengths, weaknesses, blind spots
  Preferred work style

Assess yourself and your needs, including:
  Your own strengths and weaknesses
  Your personal style
  Your predisposition toward dependence on authority figures

Develop and maintain a relationship that:
  Fits both your needs and styles
  Is characterized by mutual expectations
  Keeps your boss informed
  Is based on dependability and honesty
  Selectively uses your boss's time and resources

Subordinates can adjust their styles in response to their bosses' preferred method for receiving information. Peter Drucker divides bosses into "listeners" and "readers." Some bosses like to get information in report form so that they can read and study it. Others work better with information and reports presented in person so that they can ask questions. As Drucker points out, the implications are obvious. If your boss is a listener, you brief him or her in person, *then* follow it up with a memo. If your boss is a reader, you cover important items or proposals in a memo or report, *then* discuss them with him or her.

Other adjustments can be made according to a boss's decision-making style. Some bosses prefer to be involved in decisions and problems as they arise. These are high-involvement managers who like to keep their hands on the pulse of the operation. Usually their needs (and your own) are best satisfied if you touch base with them whenever necessary. A boss who has a need to be involved will become involved one way or another, so there are advantages to including him or her at your initiative. Other bosses prefer to delegate—they don't want to be involved. They expect you to come to them with major problems and inform them of important changes.

Creating a compatible relationship also involves drawing on each other's strengths and making up for each other's weaknesses. Because he knew that his boss—the vice president of engineering—was not very good at monitoring his employees' problems, one manager we studied made a point of doing it himself. The stakes were high: the engineers and technicians were all union members, the company worked on a customer-contract basis, and the company had recently experienced a serious strike.

The manager worked closely with his boss, the scheduling department, and the personnel office to ensure that potential problems were avoided. He also developed an informal arrangement through which his boss would review with him any proposed changes in personnel or assignment policies before taking action. The boss valued his advice and credited his subordinate for improving both the performance of the division and the labor-management climate.

MUTUAL EXPECTATIONS

The subordinate who passively assumes that he or she knows what the boss expects is in for trouble. Of course, some superiors will spell out their expectations very explicitly and in great detail. But most do not. And although many corporations have systems that provide a basis for communicating expectations (such as formal planning processes, career planning reviews, and performance appraisal reviews), these systems never work perfectly. Also, between these formal reviews expectations invariably change.

Ultimately, the burden falls on the subordinate to find out what the boss's expectations are. These expectations can be both broad (regarding, for example, what kinds of problems the boss wishes to be informed about and when) as well as very specific (regarding such things as when a particular project should be completed and what kinds of information the boss needs in the interim).

Getting a boss who tends to be vague or nonexplicit to express his expectations can be difficult. But effective managers find ways to get that information. Some will draft a detailed memo covering key aspects of their work and then send it to their bosses for approval. They then follow this up with a face-to-face discussion in which they go over each item in the memo. This discussion often surfaces virtually all of the boss's relevant expectations.

Other effective managers will deal with an inexplicit boss by initiating an ongoing series of informal discussions about "good management" and "our objectives." Still others find useful information more indirectly through those who used to work for the boss and through the formal planning systems in which the boss makes commitments to his or her superiors. Which approach you choose, of course, should depend on your understanding of your boss's style.

Developing a workable set of mutual expectations also requires that you communicate your own expectations to the boss, find out if they are realistic, and influence the boss to accept the ones that are important to you. Being able to influence the boss to value your expectations can be particularly important if the boss is an overachiever. Such a boss will often set unrealistically high standards that need to be brought into line with reality.

A FLOW OF INFORMATION

How much information a boss needs about what a subordinate is doing will vary significantly depending on the boss's style, the situation the boss is in, and the confidence the boss has in the subordinate. But it is not uncommon for a boss to need more information than the subordinate would naturally supply or for the subordinate to think the boss knows more than he or she really does. Effective managers recognize that they probably underestimate what the boss needs to know and make sure they find ways to keep the boss informed through a process that fits his or her style.

Managing the flow of information upward is particularly difficult if the boss does not like to hear about problems. Although many would deny it, bosses often give off signals that they want to hear only good news. They show great displeasure—usually nonverbally—when someone tells them about a problem. Ignoring individual achievement, they may even evaluate more favorably subordinates who do not bring problems to them.

Nevertheless—for the good of the organization, boss, and subordinate— a superior needs to hear about failures as well as successes. Some subordinates deal with a good-news-only boss by finding indirect ways to get the necessary information to him, such as a management information system in which there is no messenger to be killed. Others see to it that potential problems, whether in the form of good surprises or bad news, are communicated immediately.

DEPENDABILITY AND HONESTY

Few things are more disabling to bosses than subordinates on whom they cannot depend, whose work they cannot trust. Almost no one is intentionally undependable, but many managers are inadvertently so because of oversight or uncertainty about the boss's priorities. A commitment to an optimistic delivery date may please a superior in the short term but be a source of displeasure if not honored. It's difficult for a boss to rely on a subordinate who repeatedly slips deadlines. As one president described a subordinate: "When he's great, he's terrific, but I can't depend on him. I'd rather he be more consistent even if he delivered fewer peak successes—at least I could rely on him."

Nor are many managers intentionally dishonest with their bosses. But it is so easy to shade the truth a bit and play down concerns. Current concerns often become future surprise problems. It's almost impossible for bosses to work effectively if they cannot rely on a fairly accurate reading from their subordinates. Because it undermines credibility, dishonesty is perhaps the most troubling trait a subordinate can have. Without a basic level of trust in a subordinate's word, a boss feels constrained to check all of a subordinate's decisions, which makes it difficult to delegate.

GOOD USE OF TIME AND RESOURCES

Your boss is probably as limited in his or her store of time, energy, and influence as you are. Every request you make of your boss uses up some of these resources. For this reason, common sense suggests drawing on these resources with some selectivity. This may sound obvious, but it is surprising how many managers use up their boss's time (and some of their own credibility) over relatively trivial issues.

In one instance, a vice president went to great lengths to get his boss to fire a meddlesome secretary in another department. His boss had to use considerable effort and influence to do it. Understandably, the head of the other department was not pleased. Later, when the vice president wanted to tackle other more important problems that required changes in the scheduling and control practices of the other department, he ran into trouble. He had used up many of his own as well as his boss's blue chips on the relatively trivial issue of getting the secretary fired, thereby making it difficult for him and his boss to meet more important goals.

—— WHOSE JOB IS IT?

No doubt, some subordinates will resent that on top of all their other duties, they also need to take time and energy to manage their relationships with their bosses. Such managers fail to realize the importance of this activity and how it can simplify their jobs by eliminating potentially severe problems. Effective managers recognize that this part of their work is legitimate. Seeing themselves as ultimately responsible for what they achieve in an organization, they know they need to establish and manage relationships with everyone on whom they are dependent, and that includes the boss.

—— DISCUSSION QUESTIONS

1. This reading focuses on what an individual can do to manage his or her relationship with the boss. What can an organization do to incorporate the concept of managing bosses into its culture?
2. The *Exhibit* in the reading advises you to assess yourself and your needs. What are your strengths and weaknesses when working with a boss? What is your personal style? What is your predisposition toward dependence on authority figures?
3. Describe a situation in which you felt empowered by managing the relationship with your boss. Explain how you managed the relationship in this situation. Describe a situation in which you neglected to manage the relationship with your boss. What would you have done differently?
4. What can a boss do to encourage his or her subordinates to manage the relationship between them constructively?

SECTION B

MANAGING GROUP EFFECTIVENESS

A Framework for Analyzing Work Groups

16

MICHAEL B. McCASKEY

The author describes work groups *as those groups to which a manager may be assigned as either a leader or a member. Using a case example to illustrate the concepts presented, the author explores the features of work groups and the factors that influence their behavior and performance. Topics covered include the significance of context and the role of people, tasks, and formal organization in influencing group design and group culture.*

Work groups can be a forum for enhancing self-identity, a protection against excessive stress and uncertainty, and a home base in an otherwise impersonal corporation. However, more often, managers complain about the time wasted in committee meetings, the indecisiveness of the other person's work group and the red tape of one's own. Throughout this reading, the question addressed is What do managers need to know about groups? The concern is on what managers need to know to participate effectively in, as well as lead, work groups.

Work groups here refer to those groups that a manager might be assigned to as either a leader or a member, including such diverse gatherings as a company's sales force and a division operating committee. Membership can number from three up to dozens of people, but not every collection of people is a group.

The factors that can influence a group's behavior and performance include the people in the group, the task(s) they are asked to perform, the organizational constraints placed on the group, and so forth. To assist the reader, an actual work group situation will be presented here and analyzed: The Merit Corporation case will be given in several installments, thus providing a continuous example to ground the concepts of how work groups operate.[1] You may want to move back and forth between the case and the concepts, letting each enrich your understanding of the other.

---

1. The Merit Corporation case used as an illustration is a revised version of a case written by Anthony G. Athos and Diana Barrett. It is meant to serve as the basis for class discussion rather than to illustrate either effective or ineffective handling of an administrative situation.

———— MERIT CORPORATION: PART 1

The Merit Corporation was a medium-sized firm that manufactured and sold children's furniture nationally. From its inception the company had been family owned and operated, and John Kirschner was now the president of Merit. His grandfather and uncle had started the company, and control eventually passed to his father and then to him. At age 54 Kirschner was considering early retirement but was still actively involved with every aspect of the company's operations. He felt that it was time for a close look at his organization.

Merit's headquarters and the largest of its three manufacturing plants were located in an industrial park 10 miles outside of Boston. Merit shared the building with a number of other firms and had offices on the second and third floors of the six-story building. All employees worked a 40-hour, five-day week. Work began promptly at 8:30 A.M. and ended at 4:30 P.M. Coming in early or leaving late was generally considered to be a sign of ineffectiveness by Kirschner. He set the pattern himself (just as his father and grandfather had before him), parking his car next to the front entrance of the building at precisely 8:30 A.M. and, with rare exception, leaving at 4:30 P.M.

In a departure from the company's conservative philosophy and practice, Kirschner had brought in new managers from outside. Some of them had MBAs, and most had backgrounds in plastics or in consumer marketing. Kirschner emphasized continuing technical and managerial education and sent a number of his top people to Harvard's Advanced Management Program. Kirschner also advocated managing by committee, and he shared the CEO function with two other executives. Merit had generous fringe benefits and a pension plan that was a model in its area. Thus labor disputes had never been a significant problem. Turnover was generally low, and employee morale was high. Merit enjoyed a dominant position in the juvenile furniture market. Kirschner felt that the company's only troubling problem was the development of new products.

New products had traditionally been developed by a series of temporary task forces. On a rotating basis, managers would spend six months on a task force to develop a new product. This system had been used for years, since Kirschner's father and grandfather had both felt that line managers should have experience in the new-products area.

Over the past 10 years, however, several changes warranted a new look at an area so fundamental to Merit's success. The birth rate was declining, and people seemed less inclined to spend a great deal of money on juvenile furniture. The consumers' movement was vocal about product imperfections and poor design features, such as sharp corners and toxic paints. Responding to these concerns increased production costs. The field had also become increasingly competitive as manufacturers of household furniture began to use their excess capacity to produce children's furniture. As a result of these and other factors, obtaining adequate financing had become increasingly difficult. The higher cost of debt had led to price increases, which did not help attract customers in a highly competitive market where product differentiation was difficult. The company's sales had leveled off at approximately $120 million.

Kirschner had always been especially interested in the new-products area because he had started there at Merit. He decided that before retiring he wanted to improve significantly the new-products area because strength here would help ensure the firm's continued success.

After giving the matter considerable thought and briefly discussing it with his top managers, Kirschner decided that a radical change was necessary. He decided to form a group of six to eight people with diverse and possibly even unorthodox backgrounds to work full time on developing new products. Kirschner felt that if he could find the right people and give them a good deal of encouragement, the company would strengthen its new-products development. Consequently, he set about finding and hiring the kind of people who could give real impetus to the company's new-products development. Kirschner also began looking for office space to house the new group. Although no space was available on the second and third floors, some office space was available on the fourth floor. It seemed desirable for the group to have an area of its own.

——— GROUP CONTEXT

Whatever actions Kirschner takes in initiating a group at Merit will occur within the context of the existing organization and its wider environment. Even though he is the company's president, he does not have complete freedom. Any changes made must recognize the existing structure and people, the company's history and traditions, what the economy and competitors are doing, and many other features as well. If Kirschner wants to initiate a new group, background factors such as these will influence the size, independence, and behavior of the group. To study how a work group operates, the following aspects of the context or background should be considered:

- Purposes for which the group was created
- Physical setting in which the group works
- Company size, nature of business, location, past history, and proposed future
- Competitors, suppliers, and regulators
- Political, social, economic, and legal systems.

Background factors like these will influence efforts by Kirschner to begin a new group. For example, some of the older executives might value their experience on the rotating task forces of line managers that Merit had used to develop new products and therefore resist any changes in existing procedures.

This does not appear to be the case at Merit, but if such feelings and outlooks arise, Kirschner will have to deal with them. Failing to do so would endanger the ability of the group to carry out its mission or to survive after Kirschner retires.

Contextual factors, then, are the background factors out of which a group arises and in which a group operates. Context will affect the way a group behaves, and these factors must be part of any analysis of how a work group operates. Turning to the case, what do you notice about Merit? What features are likely to be important for how the new work group or any other group performs at Merit?

One of the primary considerations affecting the proposed group is the purpose it will serve. Kirschner seems to like to introduce changes; his assessment of the company's strengths and weaknesses leads him to feel that the new-products area is where the company needs the most improvement. He would like to retire and may want to leave a vital new-products group as a legacy. Since the proposed group will have his support, it may enjoy unusual advantages in securing information and getting resources, but the group's success is not guaranteed. If there is a contest among aspirants to succeed Kirschner as president, some competitive dynamics may endanger or support the fledgling group.

Locating the group on a different floor from the rest of the corporation headquarters may also turn out to be important. The group's mission will be to create new products, and it may want to set up procedures different from those geared to produce and sell existing lines. The physical separation of the group may allow for this.

The company's history of being family owned and managed through three presidents may influence other executives to go along with Kirschner's wishes. He has successfully introduced other changes, and this record may also provide *social capital,* the credibility necessary to introduce further changes. At the same time the leveling off of company growth, and the expectations of future development created by bringing MBAs into the firm, may fuel a desire to create new and better products. Pride in being #1 in its industry and the threat of new competition from general-purpose furniture manufacturers may also fuel a willingness to break with Merit's ways of developing new products. These contextual factors will influence the degree and kind of support group members are likely to receive from the rest of the organization.

—— MERIT CORPORATION: PART 2

Within six months Kirschner hired eight new people, described below, who he felt had diversity of background, intelligence, enthusiasm, and imagination. They were all between the ages of 27 and 29 and had been educated at some of the country's best technical and liberal arts schools.

Christopher Kane, 28, BA Math, Tufts; MBA, Stanford
Worked for McKinsey & Co. in a variety of areas, including marketing diversification and systems analysis.

Andrew Jacobson, 29, BS Math, M.I.T.
Systems Analyst for Mitre Corp. for one year. Founder of a Public Interest Research Group under the auspices of Ralph Nader. Heavily involved with environmental and consumer issues.

John O'Hara, 28, BA, Oberlin
Sculptor and painter. Had a one-artist show at the Cleveland Art Museum. Taught art and metal sculpting in United States and abroad.

Robert Vidreaux, 28, BA Social Relations, Harvard
Led two archeological digs to Iran and spent two years working at the Museum of Natural History in New York. Has three patents and a variety of inventions in the area of water filtration and purification.

Susanne Tashman, 27, BA English, Hollins; JD, Yale
Worked for Davis, Marshall and Polk, a law firm, for two years, specializing in Securities and Exchange Commission work.

Joan Waters, 27, BA Chemistry, Wellesley; MBA, Harvard
Worked for Sloan-Kettering Laboratories in New York City for two years in the area of chromosomal aberrations and viruses. After receiving MBA, worked in the financial office of Lily Laboratories on long-range planning for one year.

Matthew Kiris, 29, BS Chemistry, Cal Tech
Spent three years investigating the effect of high concentrations of pesticides in tidal regions both in the U.S. and in the Far East. Was a consultant in the Dept. of Public Health both in the U.S. and in Japan.

Raynor Carney, 29, BA Political Science, Northwestern; MBA Columbia
Has had extensive political experience, organizing a major gubernatorial campaign and fund raising for the state Democratic party. Served as the primary developer and contractor for modular low-cost housing project in Maryland.

Kirschner wanted one person reporting directly to him but decided against imposing any further structure on the group. He appointed Kane as group head, partly because he was the first to be hired and partly because Kane had made such a positive impression.

When the eight people began work at Merit, they did not know each other, and they did not know what they would be doing on a day-to-day basis. Their training and skills were very different. For example, Jacobson, who had worked as a systems analyst and was also interested in consumer and environmental issues, tended to be comfortable about the implications of the data in light of his other interests. His previous experience in a large company had led him to expect a way of doing things that he guessed was probably quite different from what others in the group expected. O'Hara, for his part, had never worked in a business environment, and although he was used to working long hours and being committed to a project for an extended length of time, he brought fewer expectations than Jacobson did about the job at Merit. Vidreaux, on the other hand, because of his interest in inventing new ways of doing things, tended to approach a procedure by first looking for other ways in which it might be done.

Not only were their backgrounds and interests very different but their personal characteristics were also quite varied. Kane, who had always worn a coat and tie to work, contrasted sharply with O'Hara, who was more comfortable in jeans. Tashman had worked in a law firm before coming to Merit, and thus she had become quite comfortable dressing more formally every day. In contrast, Waters preferred to dress informally; she saw the opportunity to dress even more informally as a major advantage of her new job.

The work styles of the eight were also quite different. O'Hara was extremely untidy and could work comfortably only with stacks of paper cluttering his desk and immediate area. Meanwhile, Jacobson, as he put it, was "compulsively neat." Kiris felt that he worked better with low music in the room, while both Waters and Tashman had strong preferences for quiet when working.

Kirschner believed that the new group would be creative if given lots of freedom and encouragement. He made it clear that his only requirements of the group were a biweekly progress report for the executive committee and a monthly financial report. Kirschner emphasized that group members were free to work as they wished, as long as they focused their energies on developing new products that met the need for durable, but inexpensive, multipurpose children's furniture.

━━━ GROUP DESIGN FACTORS

In part 2 of the Merit case, several factors appear that are important to the behavior developing in the New Products Development (NPD) group. These factors include the people who formed the group, the tasks they are required to perform, and the formal structure and operating mechanisms of the organization where they work. Part of a manager's job in managing a group is to arrange these factors in such a way as to enhance an organization's effectiveness.

The task for the NPD group is to develop new products that meet the need for durable, but inexpensive, multipurpose children's furniture. Kirschner has hired people he thinks are suited to this task. He also has set the group apart from the rest of the organization, both physically and in their reporting relationship to him. So Kirschner is making decisions about what have been called the three *design factors*—people, task requirements, and formal organization. He is trying to fit these design factors together in the strongest combination to increase the group's chances of success.

PEOPLE

First, there are the people who have been named to the NPD group; they are a diverse collection of people, many without much business experience. Because human beings are composed of a myriad of subtle and shifting characteristics, the possibilities for categorizing them are endless. Research on group behavior and organizational design, however, has found some characteristics more useful to focus on than others:

- Skills and interests possessed by individual members of the group;
- What the members' learning styles are. Some people learn by actually doing things, while others learn by reflecting and analyzing;
- Values and assumptions individual members hold. Particularly important in a group setting are members' expectations about leadership;
- Members' preferences for variety, for definition and structure, and for individual challenge. Some people feel more comfortable with loosely structured situations, where they have a great deal of autonomy. Other people strongly prefer clarity and definition in tasks and roles.

To effectively manage the NPD group, Kirschner will need to consider the rich mix of people and how they might best work together. Included among the eight are people who have sculpted, invented, performed research, and organized campaigns. They are all young and well educated and so may expect to work together in a more or less democratic style. Leadership may emerge slowly and is unlikely ever to be dictatorial.

It may also make a difference to the group's operation that O'Hara and Jacobson have quite different working styles. One is exploratory and messy, the other systematic and neat. Jacobson and Tashman are used to a corporate way of doing things; O'Hara, the sculptor, is not. Vidreaux, who has spent time on archeological digs and inventing, may well be a maverick on procedures. These dispositions and skills must be taken into account in trying to manage the group effectively.

TASK REQUIREMENTS

The second major design factor that influences a group's behavior is the tasks that individuals or the group must perform. Research on designing social systems has identified a group's task requirements:

- Interactions required among people
- Variety of activities involved
- Novelty or routineness of the tasks
- Degree to which the work pace is under an individual's control.

Kirschner has deliberately kept the list of task requirements short and open-ended for the NPD group: develop new products for children's furniture within certain constraints. The fact that the group is to be innovative means that the task is more novel than routine and calls for a breadth of skills. The new product must appeal to parents, not offend consumer watchdogs, be low in cost and durable, and capable of being manufactured by Merit.

Kirschner has not specified or required any pattern of interaction among the eight group members, but the nature of the task suggests they will probably have to interact with those who know marketing and with those who understand engineering and manufacturing. O'Hara, Kane, Waters, and others will have to find ways to divide up the work and then bring all the parts together. Group members have high individual control over their work pace and work activities because the task is relatively unspecified when compared, for example, with an assembly line work group.

FORMAL ORGANIZATION

The third factor is the organizational structure and operating systems, or the formal organization within which the group operates, including

- Hierarchy of authority
- Pattern of reporting relationships
- Formal measurement, evaluations, and control systems
- Reward systems
- Selection and recruitment procedures.

Because he wants to foster innovation, Kirschner has taken special pains to shield the NPD group from most of the structure and procedures that apply to the rest of the organization. He has appointed Kane to be head of the group for reporting purposes, and the only required reviews are a progress report every other week and a monthly financial report. The group reports directly to him and not, as might be true in other organizations, to a vice president of research and development or marketing vice president. Kirschner personally recruited and selected the eight members of the group into the organization, thus making it clear to the rest of the organization that this is a special project, high on his list of priorities. Although little is known about other organizational systems that might affect the NPD group, the point here is that there are few organizational procedures and very little structure to constrain or guide the group's behavior.

Care must be taken not to presume that a manager can readily change structure and procedures. Because Kirschner is the company's president and is starting up a new group, he has more freedom than most managers. However, even he must operate within the context of company history and traditions, the economic outlook, competitors' behavior, and so forth.

In a given situation a manager will have varying degrees of control over the three design factors, depending on his or her formal authority. He or she may influence those things that a manager (1) has complete control over; (2) requires help from others to change; and (3) has little or no control over. In the case of the NPD group, for example, Kane is unlikely to have direct control over how the members of the group are rewarded or where it reports to in the organization hierarchy. But he can go to Kirschner and argue for changes in these factors. For a wide range of other matters, Kane and the group have a great deal of control. This is due to the newness of the group, Kirschner's shielding efforts, and the fact that the task is relatively unspecified on required activities and interactions. In other, well-established groups, long embedded in a particular organizational structure, the degrees of freedom about division of activities, required interactions, pace of the work, and so forth, will often be substantially less. In analyzing what a manager *should do* versus what a manager *can do* to improve the performance of a work group, these three levels of control should be kept firmly in mind.

The eight people named to the NPD group are not yet a group; rather, they are a collection of people who will have to build a group. They are required to perform certain activities and interactions, such as developing a new product and reporting on their progress every other week. However, beyond a few minimal requirements, the eight are free to evolve whatever patterns of thought and behavior meet their needs. The emergence of those patterns is one of the most interesting and, for a manager, important aspects of group life. In reading the next installment of the Merit case, keep close track of behaviors that emerge—those activities, interactions, and rules that are not required but that group members devise over time. Keep track also of how these emerging activities and interactions might affect the group's performance.

——— MERIT CORPORATION: PART 3

On January 2 the eight members of the NPD group arrived at Merit and reported to Kirschner's office. Kirschner had planned an informal orientation day. He presented each person with a packet of information about the company, data about the products that Merit manufactured, and information about compensation and fringe benefits. Then they toured the offices and the plant with "Mr. K.," as they quickly came to call Kirschner.

After lunch, which was held in a restaurant a few miles away, the group members were introduced to the executives with whom they would come into contact. Then Kirschner took them to the fourth floor of the building, where he had rented three offices next to one another. He explained that they would have one secretary who would be working directly with them and that they could use additional support staff if necessary. He apologized for the condition of the offices, which were sparsely furnished and not air-conditioned. He encouraged the group members to get to know one another and to organize the space as they wished.

After Kirschner left, the group spent the rest of the afternoon organizing the work space. The three offices were adjacent to one another and were interconnected. Each office had enough room for two or three desks. The middle office was the largest and contained three desks and a large table. Kane, whom Kirschner introduced as the group's head for reporting and administrative purposes, moved into the first office. Carney took the next desk because he wanted to be near a window. Tashman and Waters had already discovered the middle office. Kiris took the remaining desk in this room because he thought he would occasionally work at the large table. The three others shared the last office where the group decided to put the coffee machine that Jacobson had found in a storage closet (see *Exhibit 1* for a diagram of the office layout).

The group members spent the next few weeks familiarizing themselves with the company. Kirschner usually came upstairs once or twice a week, and he often brought new information that he thought the members might be able to use. They informally organized themselves into functional areas, on the basis of individual interest, training, and expertise. For example, although the group as a whole developed cash flow projections, Tashman usually took responsibility for coordinating this activity. O'Hara used his artistic ability to translate ideas into three-dimensional drawings. And Jacobson proved to be particularly adept at synthesizing complex data because of his background in systems analysis. Vidreaux was first seen as an antagonist, because of the disorderly way in which he worked. Then others began to see him as very helpful because his background and interest in social relations enabled him to bring up potentially disruptive issues about the group's process of working together. Kane was the nominal group head, but Waters soon became a coleader, partly because she had the technical expertise to communicate with engineers in the production department and also because of the organizational ability she had acquired in her MBA training.

The group quickly developed some routines. Group members got into the habit of bringing their lunch and eating around the large table in the middle room. Almost daily over lunch they would brainstorm to elicit new ideas. Anyone could start a lunch session; however, because Waters, Tashman, and Kiris shared the middle office, they tended to initiate the sessions. Because the physical layout brought the eight in contact with one other so easily, they interacted regularly.

Although working an eight-hour day was not specifically required of the group, individuals tended to come in at 8:30 A.M. and leave at 4:30 P.M. As ideas were gradually turned into viable products, however, they began working after hours and on weekends. After a while some of them began to come in late in the mornings and work until 6 P.M. or 7 P.M., while others preferred to come in before work hours and leave early. It became the norm to work late or on

EXHIBIT 1
Office Layout

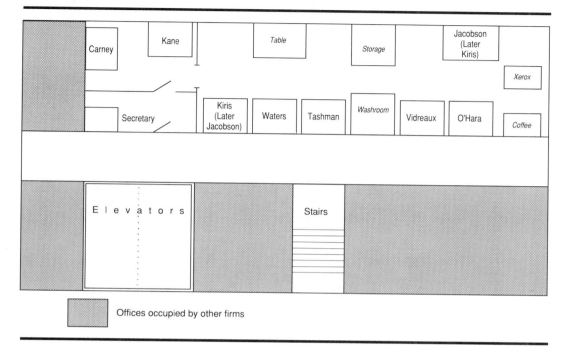

Offices occupied by other firms

weekends if a task was left unfinished. People were almost always in the office between 10 A.M. and 3 P.M., since it was during these hours that the brainstorming sessions and lunch tended to occur. As subgroups formed, and people tended to work together in twos or threes, tension and sometimes friction occurred.

One source of tension was Carney, who preferred to work alone much of the time. He was often in the middle of something when the other members of the group wanted to begin a brainstorming session. Carney felt that it was more important to finish what he was doing than to work with the group. He eventually missed so many sessions that the other group members kidded him about his antisocial behavior. When this seemed to have no effect, they began to exclude him from informal conversations. At lunch one day when Carney was absent, Vidreaux suggested that the group discuss the purpose and frequency of the sessions and the importance of everyone being present. As a result of this discussion, group members realized that exceptions to regular attendance could be made without affecting productivity. Subsequently, Carney was included in more informal conversations, but he still remained at the edge of the group.

A similar incident occurred around the issue of work space. O'Hara was extremely untidy and could work comfortably only in the midst of clutter. Jacobson, one of his office mates, was very orderly and found the clutter disturbing. Considerable antagonism developed between the two until

Vidreaux kiddingly brought up the issue at a group session. As a result of the discussion, Jacobson agreed to change places with Kiris, who was indifferent to messiness.

——— GROUP CULTURE

Part 3 of the Merit case shows the eight people of the NPD group busy with the process of building a group. Individuals are finding out who they can be in the group, what aspects of self others will value and confirm. Simultaneously, each person is confirming certain aspects of others' self-presentation and also learning the particular social and task skills others bring to the group. The eight are dividing the work, developing patterns of interacting, and establishing norms for behaving. In short, they are building a group culture.

PATTERNS EMERGE

The patterns of behavior and values that members create for themselves constitute a group's culture. These are the ways of thinking and behaving that a group evolves over time. Even in the first weeks of their being together, members of the NPD group developed several characteristic patterns that were not required of them. These emerging patterns of behavior are the members' interpretation of what they have been asked to do. More important, the emerging patterns of behavior are the members' inventions to fit their individual needs to the task and social context. For example, they have developed a pattern of working as many hours as needed to complete their tasks, even if it means coming in on weekends or staying late. They have also developed patterns of mutual helping on the job. These activities and interactions are not required, but nonetheless, they affect the group's performance for better or worse.

Because the group members are young and close in age, it is not surprising that informal, loosely structured interaction has emerged. The members interact frequently and easily and do not seem to emphasize status differences, although some are emerging. They have found lunchtime brainstorming sessions useful, and these sessions are becoming a pattern. Some who previously never brought lunch to work now regularly do to visit and eat together as a group.

NORMS

The patterns outlined are emerging, and some are being enforced as norms of the group. *Norms* are the expectations and guidelines that are shared by group members for how members should behave. Over time, group members define what is fair and what is appropriate behavior. Almost all groups will develop their own norms given enough time. Not to follow the group's norm threatens the cohesiveness of the group, and people who deviate from the group's norms will suffer some form of social censure. For example, in the NPD group, Carney prefers working alone to attending many of the group's brainstorming sessions. At first he is kidded; when this proves ineffective for changing his behavior, he is excluded more and more from ordinary social contact. This could become a serious clash, but Vidreaux initiates explicit discussion. The result is that Carney remains on the periphery of the group, a deviant from the group's norms. The episode illustrates a group's attempt to bring a member's behavior into line. In some groups kidding may even be followed by physical intimidation, and eventually one may be totally cut off from the group's social life. This ultimate sanction treats such a member as a social isolate.

Even though they are enforced by group members, norms are not applied monolithically; they are far more subtle than that. Not all behaviors are covered by norms, and norms do not apply equally to everyone. Some members may be given leeway because of their personal needs or unique contribution. At Merit, Carney is allowed some deviation from group norms, although at the cost of remaining on the social periphery. Research on groups shows that leaders, more than other group members, tend to embody the group's central values and norms. Leaders may be allowed some exceptions from group norms because of their high status, but in so doing they use up a certain amount of the social capital they have accumulated. If, as happens in most groups, members largely conform to the group's norms, the norms help regularize interactions between members. It is much easier, for example, for everyone in the NPD to attend impromptu brainstorming sessions if everyone follows the norm of being in the office between 10 A.M. and 3 P.M.

This does not mean that a manager entering a group for the first time has to conform absolutely to the group's norms. It does mean that he or she must approach the task of possibly changing group norms with care and understanding of how they work.

Take David King, the new principal of Robert F. Kennedy High School, as another example. In his first staff meeting he was surprised that people, who in private meetings with him were highly critical of one another, were extremely polite and considerate with each other in a public meeting. King was uncovering a norm for courteous conduct and the avoidance of open conflict. When King pushed against this norm in his first meeting with his staff, some group members reacted explosively. Norms serve an important function for group members in stabilizing their interactions along predictable paths. When a manager decides that some norms are blocking group effectiveness, he or she must examine the purpose the norms serve before attempting to change them. Similarly, other features of group culture, such as roles, help give stability and predictability to the interactions of group members.

ROLES

A *role* is the characteristic and expected social behavior of an individual. In addition to the role of formally appointed group leader, other informal roles may also develop. For example, Waters has emerged as an *informal coleader* of the group. And Carney has become a *deviant* because of his unwillingness to follow an important norm of the group. Carried further, a member who fails to follow several group norms where other members are less tolerant, may become a *social isolate*. Roles such as these are often helpful in defining what the norms are in a group. At one end of the continuum, informal leaders are likely to adhere to group norms, while at the other end, extreme social isolates violate some, perhaps many, of the group's norms.

In the NPD group several roles have developed based on the special skills and interests of different members. For example, Tashman coordinates the development of cash flow projections and O'Hara does the drawings. Less is known about roles connected to how the group works, except that Kane and Waters are coleaders—Kane is the formal leader and Waters is an informal leader. Vidreaux has become another informal leader because he raises process issues for discussion and can successfully conclude discussions.

People in a group develop patterns of behavior that contribute or detract from the group's ability to achieve its social and task functions. Take a group, for example, where one person consistently cracks a joke to break tensions and to reharmonize relationships. In the same group another person often supplies technical information, while a third person typically keeps an eye on the clock and returns the group to its agenda when discussion strays too far. Behaviors like these, often bundled into specialized roles, are important to the level of effectiveness a group achieves.

RITUALS, STORIES, AND LANGUAGE

As part of its cultural ways, a work group may also develop rituals, stories about past deeds, and language shorthand. In the NPD group, members already have one ritual in the lunchtime discussions along with a norm of consistent attendance. This young group does not have sagas or myths to relate about previous heroic efforts, but when those develop, they will also serve to reinforce the social ties among members. As is typical of work groups, members of the NPD group use their own language shorthand to talk about different parts of their world, such as Mr. K., brainstorming, and antisocial behavior. Language shorthand offers clues to what is emotionally significant in a group's way of working together, or what shared sentiments help hold the group together. For example, *Mr. K.* conveys a mixture of deference and special relationship to the company's president, especially if no one else in the company addresses him this way. It may signal their feeling that, if they are refused a hearing lower down in the organization, they can take their case to the top. Quite likely, members of the NPD group have other phrases and code words that make sense to themselves but are puzzling to outsiders. Like rituals and stories, special language conventions serve to draw boundaries around the group, differentiating group members from others.

MAPS

One feature of group culture is the most invisible and often the most difficult for group members to articulate. It is the *map* that group members create of what is important to notice in the world around them. The eight people in the NPD group do not face a predefined reality that is fixed, objective, and composed of hard facts. Their work world consists of much that is overwhelming. Like individuals who must selectively perceive the world, group members must also selectively perceive aspects of their world. Furthermore, out of what they notice they must build some kind of coherent picture that makes sense to themselves and provides a common base of understanding within the group. Rather quickly, group members tacitly evolve agreements on what is most important and on what the cause-and-effect linkages are. The process of formulating a shared map is not always smooth, and some group members can map only part of their world in common. This version of reality is treated as real; it is real for group members and is slow to change.

A map guides a group member's daily decisions about what to do and how to interact with others, and it facilitates predicting the likely outcomes of one action versus another. With the information provided so far about the NPD group, we know little about its map. But the map of a sales group, for example, may stress the importance of frequently "pressing the flesh" with customers because it appears to be important in a customer's continuing willingness to buy the product. Mapping is the mental process by which members of the group interactively comprehend and deal with the world around them. For a new member coming into a group, this means that a group has the power to influence how she or he sees the world.

Thus far several features of group culture have been distinguished. Its components—emergent activities, norms, roles, rituals, stories, language, and mapping—are an ongoing social construction of reality. The group's culture is not immediately obvious but can be inferred through change in its major outlines, as over time the group makes small modifications and adjustments. What is most important to know for managing groups is that the culture a group forms is outside the direct control of a manager. It can only be influenced by the manager's actions, example, and the arrangement of the various design factors. Appreciating the constructed quality of group culture, however, opens new possibilities for leading and participating in groups. It separates what is easily changed from what is not, and focuses attention on what a manager can directly influence and what is more in the province of group members. Because group culture is closely connected to group performance, managers need to understand the process of forming a group culture and develop the ability to analyze it.

——— MERIT CORPORATION: PART 4

After the NPD group had been operating for six months, Kirschner and the executive committee saw that the group had developed a variety of innovative and unique product ideas. They could also see that group members were enthusiastic about their work. At the end of the first year the group came out with a new product. Within six months the product had won a 20% share of an extremely competitive market and had been widely acclaimed for its low manufacturing costs, durability, and consumer appeal. To celebrate, the group had lunch away from the office one Friday, and the celebration lasted all afternoon.

——— OUTCOMES AND FEEDBACK

Although managers may be tempted to think of what a group produces solely in terms of its work productivity, the outcomes of a group are actually multidimensional. Consider the various outcomes that a group produces under three headings: (1) productivity, (2) satisfaction, and (3) individual growth.

The productivity of the NPD group was quite high. The group produced a variety of new product ideas and successfully introduced a new product into a competitive marketplace. The group had achieved its major purpose.

Beyond work productivity, an important outcome for the group was its sense of satisfaction with how it operated and what it achieved. The term *satisfaction* is a shorthand for the rich mixture of feelings that a member can experience as a result of being part of a successful group. These feelings can include strong negative as well as positive, ambivalent, and sometimes even contradictory emotions. They are part of what fuels each member's participation or lack of it in the group. Think, for a moment, of the groups in which you have especially enjoyed working. What were the characteristics of those groups? How did you feel during the group meetings? How did that add to the amount and the quality of the work you did?

Emotions, feelings of satisfaction or dissatisfaction, can be powerful stimuli for behavior in groups. As some scholars have phrased it, groups run on emotion. The feelings that result from a period of work have reinforcing effects on existing aspects of group life. As group members see the group producing certain outcomes, this reinforces or weakens features in the group culture. For example, those in the NPD group who championed the product idea that proved to be a market success probably saw their standing increased. The success of the group and the attendant positive feelings reinforced the map and the group's norms about what was to be valued and what was not. In addition, feedback can reinforce or weaken the patterns of interaction between people, task, and formal organization. Because the feedback in this instance is positive, patterns are strengthened. If the outcomes had been negative, the pattern of working together, which the group had evolved, would be questioned.

Crucial for managing the group's long-term health is the extent to which individuals feel they are learning and growing. No direct information exists on the NPD group, but it appears that many of the eight see themselves as learning and growing. O'Hara and Kiris, with nonbusiness backgrounds, are learning to operate successfully in a business setting. In exercising leadership skills, Waters is growing and developing as a manager. Such individual growth keeps a member involved and committed to the group's activities and provides a basis for even better performance over the long run. If individual commitment were found lacking, the manager of a group would have to resort to increasingly heavy external pressures that would eventually be self-defeating.

WORK-GROUP BEHAVIOR MODEL

The concepts introduced to this point can now come together in a model of work-group behavior. This model, devised for managers, focuses on the dominant features of how a group operates and the action available to a manager for managing a group. The model does not aim for conceptual elegance, nor is it totally inclusive; rather, it tries to distill the number of categories down to those that accurately portray the main features of group life (see *Exhibit 2* for the major elements of the model).

The model indicates that what a group produces, its outcomes, are influenced by a set of factors called group culture. Group culture refers to the patterns of behaving and thinking that develop in the group. Group culture arises from the interaction of the three design factors—the people in the group, the tasks they are required to perform, and the structure and systems of the organization in which the group operates. The design factors and how they interact are in turn shaped by a set of factors called context. The company, its history and traditions, its size and economic clout, the physical setting in which the group works, the state of the economy, government action, consumer attitudes, the actions of competitors are all contextual factors that could ulti- mately affect a given work group. Theoretically, arrows could be drawn be- tween all parts of the model. Group behavior is a complex and subtle phenomenon in which everything, to some degree, is interconnected. But

EXHIBIT 2
Model for Analyzing a Work Group

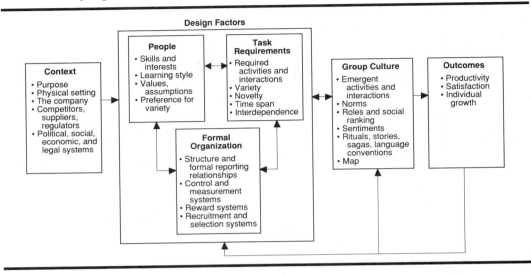

because it is more useful to concentrate on the typical patterns of interaction, arrows describe only the most important relationships.

It is important to note that the whole system is dynamic. Changes in any part of the model can eventually lead to changes throughout the model. For example, when the economy hits a severe downturn (a change in a contextual factor), top management may decide to lay off people. Some of these will be members of a work group. Remaining members may respond by attempting to increase production and lower costs, or they may go on strike or look for other jobs. In response to a downturn, organizational systems, particularly budgeting and auditing systems, are likely to be tightened. This will affect the group's norms about how much they should try to produce and how efficiently. It may well alter patterns of interaction and give new prominence to those group members who have special skills for dealing with the crisis. All the changes and adjustments percolate through and result in altered outcomes—perhaps higher productivity, higher or lower satisfaction, and a mixture of other feelings. The outcomes are multidimensional and have effects on the group culture and on design factors.

You should be able to fill out a chart for the NPD group, using the major categories—context, design factors, group culture, outcomes—of the model in *Exhibit 2*. More important, you should also understand some of the interrelationships between the concepts.

Few social systems stand still, and events continued to change at Merit. Part 5 describes what happened to the NPD group over the next several months. Partway through the case history, there will be a chance to test your understanding of the model.

──── MERIT CORPORATION: PART 5

Three months later Kirschner retired. The executive committee brought in Joe Donaldson as vice president of marketing, a man with 15 years of experience in a large consumer-product organization. The NPD group would now report to him.

Donaldson was extremely interested in the work the group had done, but he was concerned that no additional new products appeared to be imminent. Two months after his arrival at Merit, Donaldson asked Kane to come down to his office to discuss this problem. Kane explained that it had taken some time for the group to adjust to Merit but that things seemed to be going quite well; in fact, Kane was enthusiastic about the group's future. Donaldson continued to express concern about the viability of such a group at Merit. Kane, somewhat flustered, finally told him that he could attribute some of the problems to the poor secretarial help and the lack of support staff on the fourth floor. Kane also stressed that creativity in work groups tends to occur in cycles. He was confident that the group was in a trough now and would soon be out of it.

Two weeks after Donaldson's meeting with Kane, the group heard of his decision. The NPD group would move downstairs with the rest of the staff. Donaldson hoped that with better administrative assistance, closer contact with line executives, and with his personal involvement, the group could repeat its first success.

Within 30 days of Donaldson's decision the NPD group moved downstairs to the second floor and reported directly to Donaldson. Although the offices could not be located next to one another, they were redecorated, and each person was given ample secretarial and administrative help. In addition, Donaldson encouraged the group to increase expenses if necessary to quickly bring out another new product. The group was also encouraged to work an 8:30 A.M. to 4:30 P.M. day, because the occupants of the adjoining offices might resent their unpredictable schedules.

Before reading further, use the model shown in *Exhibit 2* to predict what will happen.

──── MERIT CORPORATION: PART 5 *(CONTINUED)*

At first, the new offices and novel atmosphere made up for the distance between offices. Those who preferred to dress informally, however, began to feel quite uncomfortable and changed to more traditional business attire. Within a few weeks, patterns of interaction that had proved successful as well as personally satisfying to individual members had fallen away. Because group members could no longer easily enter and leave each other's offices and because they had no place to hold brainstorming sessions, their sense of what they ought to do on a given day became vague. Certain individuals, especially Carney, were more uncomfortable than others. Carney began to issue working papers on what the competition was likely to do and on social issues, neither of which was seen as particularly relevant to the group's work. Soon he was ostracized from the group. Without a comfortable and accessible place to have lunch together, people began to go out to restaurants in subgroups. It became the exception rather than the rule for the group to meet informally. Individuals began to feel increasingly dissatisfied with their jobs and felt surrounded by people with different personal values. At the same time, the old roles seemed quite inappropriate in the new environment. During an infrequent group lunch at a nearby restaurant, numerous complaints were voiced, ranging from feelings of inadequacy, to a sense of boredom, to dissatisfaction with the rigid work hours.

Within two months, O'Hara left Merit to be married and to live on the West Coast; Tashman and Carney also left. Kane suggested recruiting new people, but Donaldson decided that it would be best to disband the group, assigning the remaining individuals to regular departments and reinstituting the task-force system that had earlier been used for new-product development. After three months, every member of the group had resigned except for Kane.

On one of his rare visits to the office, Kirschner asked Kane what had gone wrong. Kane was reluctant to describe what he thought Donaldson's effect had been, so he told Kirschner that it was difficult to maintain a creative group over a long time and that most members had personal reasons for leaving. Kirschner seemed to accept the explanation and did not pursue the matter further.

Donaldson looked at the NPD group and saw reduced outcomes. In his eyes, the absence of a new product in two months was cause for trying to change the group. He changed the location and work schedule of the group, without careful consideration of what the group's culture was and how it worked. Unknowingly, he disrupted the culture that group members had devised to fit their diverse personalities to the task Kirschner had given them. The map, norms, and roles the group had established broke down. Carney and others became uncertain about what to do. Their previous excitement, satisfaction, and sense of purpose turned to confusion and hostility. The group as a social system floundered and became a collection of individuals once again. Several people quit and eventually the group was disbanded.

Donaldson used a deficient model of how groups operate. His actions seriously weakened and then broke the links between design and culture and between culture and outcomes. He implicitly linked those things he could directly control—such as work schedule, reporting relationships, and physical setting—to group performance. He seemed unaware of the intervening role played by group culture and of how outcomes were multiple in nature. Using a model that overlooked important features of how a group operates led him to make a number of ill-conceived changes.

One of the aims of presenting a managerial mode of group behavior is to focus attention on the intelligent selection of action to be taken:

1. Look at the outcomes of a group. Why do they perform the way they do?
2. Look at the culture of the group. What are their norms and values? What do they do that is not required but nonetheless affects their performance for better or worse? Why is the culture the way it is?
3. Look at the design factors. Which of these are under your direct control and which can you only indirectly influence? How can the design factors be changed in a desirable direction to produce the outcomes you are trying to achieve?
4. Look at the context within which the group operates. Are the proposed changes consonant with contextual factors? Where should you anticipate difficulties?

Had Donaldson thought through such an analysis for the NPD group, he would not have been guaranteed a success. Skills are needed to carry out any plans suggested by analysis. However, Donaldson would have increased his chances of successfully intervening and eventually achieving the results he sought.

——— CONCLUSION

The model of group behavior presented here captures much of what happens in a work group and provides a platform for building further knowledge. Looking at groups in this way allows the reader to identify the multiple causes of a group's behavior and performance. Furthermore, the model in its attention to managerial action, and what is and is not under a manager's control, suggests a way to think about participating in and leading a work group.

By showing how leadership functions can be distributed in a group and how a map is interactively constructed, the model provides a new way to think about leadership in work groups. An informal, or unappointed, leader of a group can help build a culture that brings together members, tasks, and organization. In high-performing groups several members usually share the behaviors that maintain a group socially and those that move it toward task accomplishment. Likewise, although the first attempt usually falls to the formal leader, informal leaders can play a major role in formulating or reformulating the map that guides a group's efforts.

The culture constructed by group members represents their stance vis-à-vis the rest of the world and influences their effectiveness. They act out the various aspects of their emerging culture and subsequent outcomes provide feedback for further action. Feedback from the rest of the world leads to reinforcing, modifying, or in unusual cases, abandoning the map, norms, and roles that make up the group culture. The revised patterns of thinking and interacting go through additional cycles throughout the group's life. A group might continue its growth and development or settle into established routines.

In summary, group culture is closely connected to the outcomes that the group produces, and yet culture is beyond the direct control of a manager. A manager works through three design factors—people, tasks, and formal organization—to influence culture. These are the most readily available areas for actions influencing group behavior. However, managerial action should occur only after a careful analysis of how the culture of the group will be affected and what the consequences will be for the group. It is a mistake to be concerned with productivity without also being concerned about emotional and individual growth. To improve a work group's performance, a manager must understand the multiple causes of the group's behavior. This model provides a practical starting point for acquiring such an understanding.

Copyright © 1979; revised 1991.

——— DISCUSSION QUESTIONS

1. The author mentions a feature of group culture known as maps. Consider the groups that you've belonged to. What were their maps? How did you feel as a new member? How long did it take you to feel like a group member? How did you relate to the members that were there before you? To those that came after you?

2. What has been the context for the groups that you've belonged to? Do you join groups? In what situations? If you don't join groups on your own, how do you feel when you are required to join a group? If you wanted to accomplish a goal, whether at work or elsewhere, and you could only accomplish this goal with group support, how would you go about gaining the support you need?

3. Consider your behavior in a group. Do you interact easily or tend to shy away from interactions? What personal compromises do you make? What personal compromises don't you make?

4. Name five different groups you have been part of that have had an important influence on your life either directly or indirectly. Explain the nature of the influence.

5. The author states that an effective group has several leaders. Does your experience of effective groups agree with the author's assertion? What does the presence of multiple leaders imply—concerning leadership theories?

Problem Solving and Conflict Resolution in Groups

17

JAMES WARE

This reading begins by describing the strengths and weaknesses of groups as problem solvers. According to the author, the decision to use a group for problem solving is determined by balancing the characteristics of a particular problem against the characteristics of a group. The reading also identifies and compares three modes of conflict resolution: smoothing and avoidance, bargaining and forcing, and confronting and problem solving. Interdepartmental conflict and the difficult position of department representatives are also examined. The author closes with a reminder of the importance of careful diagnosis and with several suggestions for managers on how to constructively influence group behavior.

Management groups deal with organizational problems in a wide variety of ways. Clearly, some styles of problem solving are more effective than others, and some management groups are much more capable of handling and resolving internal conflict than others are. Because group decision making is so common in organizations, effective managers must be highly skilled at influencing group processes.

This reading examines the characteristics of managerial groups that enhance and detract from their effectiveness in problem solving and describes the most common ways in which groups handle conflict. The reading explains how styles of problem solving and conflict resolution affect the nature and quality of group decisions. The dynamics of interdepartmental conflict are also examined because most important organizational problems involve two or more departments with differing goals, priorities, and needs. Although many of the ideas covered here refer primarily to interactions in face-to-face meetings, the same processes generally apply to group behavior over extended periods of time.[1]

---

1. The next two sections on the strengths and weaknesses of groups as problem solvers draw heavily, although not exclusively, on "Assets and Liabilities in Group Problem Solving," by Norman R.F. Maier, *Psychological Review* (July 1967): 239–49. The article is a systematic review of research on group problem-solving behavior and effectiveness in a wide variety of contexts.

STRENGTHS OF GROUPS AS PROBLEM SOLVERS

Group problem solving has some distinct advantages over individual problem solving in organizations. The most compelling reasons for using a management group to deal with organizational problems are as follows:

Diversity of Problem-Solving Styles   Different people have different ways of thinking about problems. Although almost any problem can be viewed from several different perspectives, most people have relatively fixed patterns of thinking. Some people (e.g., engineers and accountants) rely on highly quantitative techniques. Other people (e.g., architects and designers) think graphically, using pictures and diagrams, while others (e.g., entrepreneurs and commodity traders) tend to rely on feelings and intuition about what will work in a given situation.

Individual problem solvers too often fall into ruts that prevent them from seeing other productive ways of dealing with a particular problem. When people with different styles interact with others in a group, however, they can stimulate one another to try new ways of approaching the problem.

More Knowledge and Information   Individuals also bring different specialized knowledge and current experiences to a problem-solving discussion. Even when some group members are much more highly skilled or formally educated than others, the diversity of the knowledge, skills, and thinking styles in the group can lead to more innovative solutions than the experts could produce working alone. For example, a sales manager who has worked closely with customers may be able to suggest product-design modifications that would not have occurred to a product engineer.

Furthermore, by exchanging tentative ideas as they explore the problem and possible solutions, group members can challenge and improve one another's thinking. During a discussion, one person's comment often triggers a new idea for someone else. This process of sharing and building increases both the number and the quality of solution ideas.

Greater Understanding and Commitment   By participating in the deliberations that lead to a decision, people gain a more thorough understanding of the problem. Furthermore, even if they disagree with the decision, they are more likely to accept it if they have had an opportunity to express their disagreement during the decision process. Participation is one of the main reasons that task forces are so often successful in achieving organizational changes.

WEAKNESSES OF GROUPS AS PROBLEM SOLVERS

Many management groups develop patterns of behavior that seriously detract from their problem-solving effectiveness. Among the most important weaknesses of group problem solving are the following:

Use of Organizational Resources   Group decision making consumes more time and resources than does individual problem solving. After all, a one-hour meeting of eight people requires as much time as one person working all day on the problem. Furthermore, achieving an equal and adequate understanding of the problem by all members of the group can be difficult and time-consuming.

Pressure to Conform   Groups often develop such strong norms of conformity that members spend more time and energy figuring out the party line than they do analyzing a problem. Agreeing becomes more important than being right, and conforming to the majority point of view becomes a requirement for remaining part of the group. Conformity is a particular danger in management groups whose members differ in their levels of authority, status, and power. Less-powerful members may find it especially difficult to confront or disagree with their organizational superiors.

Extensive research on group decision making has repeatedly shown that the solution or argument mentioned most frequently in a group is almost always the one finally chosen, regardless of its validity. This valence effect is particularly pervasive in overly conforming groups.

Advocacy and Individual Domination   Perhaps the most common weakness of problem-solving groups is their susceptibility to control by individuals or small coalitions. Decision making turns into a contest in which winning becomes more important than being right. Individuals advocate their own points of view, vying for leadership to satisfy personal needs or to achieve organizational influence that benefits one group or department rather than the total organization.

Although a group discussion may appear to focus on substantive issues and the pros and cons of each alternative, the debates may involve underlying issues of power, prestige, and influence. If a domination attempt is being made based on information or ideas directly related to the focal problem, the group may actually benefit. Often, however, those who argue loudest and strongest do so precisely because of the logical weaknesses of their positions.

Diffusion of Responsibility   Group members often lose their individual identities and sense of responsibility during problem-solving deliberations. Discussion may move so swiftly that members forget who initiated certain ideas; most finished ideas are combinations of several peoples' recommendations. Although this process can be highly creative, it also can lead to a group's reaching riskier decisions than any of its members would have agreed to individually. Under these circumstances, a group can make poor decisions. Individual members will usually deny personal responsibility for the decisions and their consequences.

Groups Are Solution Oriented   Most people feel unsettled by problems and dislike being faced with them. Thus, many management groups tend to short-circuit problem analysis, jumping quickly to solution proposals. Experienced managers often feel sure they know what the problem is and thus are opposed to spending time exploring its underlying causes. Often, of course, the problem as it is first defined is only a symptom of a much bigger and more complex situation. Yet when problem-solving groups are formed, they rarely spend enough time exploring the problem.

───── WHEN TO USE A GROUP

In many organizational situations, a manager has little choice about whether to handle a problem alone, assign it to a single subordinate, or involve a group. Organizational traditions frequently restrict the manager's options; almost every company has standing committees, regular staff meetings, and other settings that bring together specialists from different functional or geographic areas to address both recurring and isolated problems. In other situations, the pressures of time and individual responsibility, the need for specific expertise, or the requirements of confidentiality clearly point to an individually determined decision. Between these two extremes, however, are situations in which a manager must decide whether an individual or a group effort will be more productive.

The choice of when to refer a particular problem to a management group depends upon both the characteristics of the problem and the skills and interests of the group. The most important factors in each of these areas are discussed in the following sections.

CHARACTERISTICS OF THE PROBLEM

The nature of the problem and the organizational requirements for a solution define the primary criteria for determining whether to use a group problem-solving process.

Complexity, Uncertainty, and Conflict   Organizational problems can usually be described as involving uncertainty, complexity, or conflict. *Uncertain* problems are those in which the problem solver lacks information about underlying causes, potential solutions, or even solution criteria. *Complex* problems are those in which more is known about related causes and possible choices; however, so many factors affect the situation that their interactions and consequences are difficult to trace and to understand. *Conflict* problems are those in which different individuals or subgroups have differing priorities or goals that cannot be mutually satisfied. In conflict situations both the choices and their consequences may be very clear; the difficulty lies in choosing among the alternatives and in determining how to make that choice when competing goals and interests are at stake.

Most real-world problems involve all three of these elements, although in varying degrees. Defining the problem in terms of its uncertainty, complexity, and conflict potential helps clarify what additional information is needed, who possesses it, and who is affected by the problem (or will be affected by its solution). Generally, the more uncertain, the more complex, and the more conflictful the problem, the more likely it is that involving others in developing a solution will be appropriate and effective.

Business Stakes   The more important the problem, the more appropriate it is to involve others in its solution. Problems with higher organizational stakes (whether tangible outcomes, such as costs, profits, and market share, or intangible ones, such as public reputation, status, and power) call for more thorough analysis, wider awareness of issues, and shared responsibility for solutions and their consequences. A group process is much more likely to be effective when the risks and potential payoffs are large because group members will pay more attention, take more time, and devote more energy to finding a widely acceptable solution.

Task Interdependence   When a work procedure or information system crosses department boundaries, procedural changes are almost impossible without bringing together people from all the affected departments. Imagine a materials-control manager attempting to modify an inventory-control system without involving sales, accounting, purchasing, manufacturing, and production control. Each department will be affected by the system changes and can influence the success of the implementation effort. The problem cannot be resolved by one manager in one functional area.

Need for Acceptance and Commitment   Another reason for using a group process is that those people who have been involved in the group deliberations will better understand the problem and its solution and will more readily accept and support the group decision. This aspect of group problem solving is especially important when the solution includes an implementation effort involving several people. When many of those people are not direct subordinates of the manager who is responsible for making the change, their acceptance and commitment is doubly important.

Deadline Pressures   Group processes consume more managerial time and related organizational resources than does individual problem solving. If a decision deadline is too immediate, involving others may be impossible even though the problem is substantive and calls for their inclusion. However, a tight deadline may be a compelling reason for bringing in more people. If their understanding of the problem is adequate, the group members can divide up the work and attack several aspects of it simultaneously.

To summarize, a group problem-solving process is generally called for when

- the problem is uncertain or complex, and has potential for conflict
- the problem requires interdepartmental or intergroup cooperation and coordination
- the problem and its solution have important personal and organizational consequences
- there are significant but not immediate deadline pressures
- widespread acceptance and commitment are critical to successful implementation.

CHARACTERISTICS OF THE GROUP

Organizational problems do not develop in a vacuum, and management groups differ in their abilities to work on various kinds of problems. Several important characteristics of problem-solving groups also influence the decision to use a group process.

Relevant Knowledge and Skills   The most obvious criterion is whether the group possesses the knowledge and skills to solve the problem productively. This is not a simple issue, however, because individuals often have greater problem-solving capabilities than they have previously demonstrated. Furthermore, groups develop problem-solving skills primarily through practice.

Unfortunately, the immediate need to solve a problem and stabilize the organization often overshadows the longer-term developmental needs of a group. Managers frequently justify individual problem solving through lack of time, group work overload, and the group's lack of knowledge and experience. However, when developing the group's problem-solving skills is an important objective, the manager should consciously submit to the group those problems whose nature might otherwise suggest individual attention.

Current Work Load   If a group is already working at or near its normal capacity, then adding another important problem to the group's agenda will generally be ineffective. Not only would the problem receive inadequate attention and effort, but other group tasks will probably suffer as well. An overloaded group is generally characterized by high levels of stress, and high stress typically leads to brief and shallow diagnosis, a preference for solutions that are simple and certain (rather than creative and effective), and unusually severe and inflexible conflict. Overloaded groups are not effective problem solvers.

Group Expectations   Company norms sometimes value group participation in certain kinds of decisions, regardless of whether that participation improves the quality of the solution. In fact, many of the tensions that develop between managers and subordinates derive from differing assumptions about the appropriateness of group participation in certain types of decisions. Thus, a manager must be concerned not only with the substance of a problem but also with its emotional components. If a group feels strongly about its right to be involved in a decision, the manager must take that into account, whether or not he or she agrees with the group.

Norms for Conflict Resolution   Perhaps the most critical aspect of a group's problem-solving capacity is its approach to handling conflict. Group decision making is especially difficult when group members have different and/or conflicting goals and needs. If the problem can potentially create serious and heated controversy and the group is not skilled at confronting its differences, a group solution will probably not be effective. A group that has developed healthy confronting norms, however, can be an appropriate forum for reviewing an issue with many alternative solutions.

Because conflict-resolution skills are critical to group problem-solving effectiveness, the next section describes alternative modes for handling conflict.

Thus, a management group is more likely to develop an effective solution to an organizational problem if

- group members possess the required knowledge and analytic skills or are capable of developing them
- the group is not already overloaded with other work
- the group's expectations about involvement are taken into account
- the group is skilled at resolving conflict and is characterized by open, confronting norms.

The manager's task is to find the most workable fit between the problem and the problem-solving group. Neither element can be addressed in isolation, and none of the specific characteristics described earlier can be treated independently of the others. Because an ideal fit almost never occurs on its own, much of the manager's work involves trying to modify one or more of these characteristics. Finding the leverage points is not simple, and there are no formulas that will substitute for careful diagnosis of the most important elements in each situation.

—— MODES OF CONFLICT RESOLUTION

Because styles of problem solving and conflict resolution are such important variables in determining group effectiveness, they are among the most frequently studied aspects of group behavior. The literature on management groups contains numerous models of problem solving, group and intergroup conflict, bargaining, and techniques for managing conflict.

Research on styles of group problem solving suggests that there are three primary modes of conflict resolution: bargaining and forcing, smoothing and avoiding, and confronting and problem solving. As the labels indicate, confronting and problem solving is by far the most effective approach (though by no means the most common). This assertion draws on a substantial body of research. For example, Lawrence and Lorsch, in their extensive study of product innovation groups in several different industries, found that the management groups of the more-profitable firms invariably employed confronting styles of decision making more than other modes and generally did so more often than did the management groups of less-profitable competitors.[2] In fact, the mode of conflict resolution that characterized a company's management groups was found to be the most consistent variable that discriminated between profitable and unprofitable companies in the different industries.

The remainder of this section describes each of these three modes in some detail and suggests their relative strengths and weaknesses as styles of conflict resolution.

SMOOTHING AND AVOIDANCE

A group employing smoothing tactics is more interested in maintaining harmony and agreement than in confronting the problem or the individual members' differences. Group members assume that conflict is destructive; because they value membership in the group, they avoid confronting their differences out of fear that the resulting conflict will split the group irreparably. People who favor smoothing over their differences often have little confidence in their own ability to articulate their reasoning or to persuade others of their position. They also assume that the group is generally incapable of dealing with problems that involve conflict.

Groups that develop a smoothing-and-avoidance style tend to favor the status quo; they work on maintaining an even keel and not rocking the boat. Such groups often redefine the problems they face so that minimum disagreement occurs; they develop powerful norms of avoiding conflict, withdrawing from controversial issues, and withholding critical comments. Members of a smoothing group describe their beliefs by quoting proverbs such as "Soft words win hard hearts," "Kill your enemies with kindness," and "Smooth words make smooth ways." (These and similar sayings were actually used to identify smoothing-and-avoiding groups in the Lawrence and Lorsch research and in earlier studies as well.[3])

Group members may privately express sharp criticisms of each other and even of the way they work as a group; however, these criticisms are kept private. Meetings are often perfunctory and always polite, although a sensitive observer can usually pick up nonverbal signals that contrast sharply with the surface verbal behavior. Even when the stakes are high for some members on a

2. Paul R. Lawrence and Jay W. Lorsch, *Organization and Environment* (Homewood, Illinois: Richard D. Irwin, 1969).

3. Robert R. Blake and Jane S. Mouton, *The Managerial Grid* (Houston: Gulf Publishing Company, 1964).

particular issue, the pattern of smoothing is hard to break. Membership in a smoothing group can be extremely frustrating, especially for persons interested in making changes or improving organizational performance.

BARGAINING AND FORCING

In a group characterized by bargaining and forcing, the participants view each other as adversaries and define the problems in terms of what each person, subgroup, or department stands to gain or lose. Decision making is viewed as a win/lose proposition in which it is clearly better to win than to lose. Groups operating in this mode develop norms that justify pushing for one's own point of view regardless of the merits of others' views; forcing when one has an advantage and seeking compromise when one does not; concealing unfavorable information; and digging for data that the opponent is hiding.

The proverbs that typify a bargaining-and-forcing climate include "Tit for tat is fair play," "Might overcomes right," and "You scratch my back, I'll scratch yours." Conflict is viewed as inevitable, necessary, and even desirable; however, it is treated almost like a poker game in which one bluffs, conceals data, and seeks to scare the other participants out of the game. Most decisions are reached by making a series of compromises and trade-offs or by powerful parties forcing the issue. Participants assume the worst about each other, and each party seeks to maximize its own share of the "pot."

The poker analogy is important and appropriate because groups operating in this mode seldom try to increase the total size of the pot or find a solution in which everyone wins. Attention tends to be concentrated on how to divide up limited resources, whether they are budgetary funds, sales territories, management bonuses, or intangibles such as prestige and status.

CONFRONTING AND PROBLEM SOLVING

Groups operating in a confronting mode assume that disagreements are healthy if they are worked through in pursuit of a solution that is good for the total organization. The basic difference between this orientation and the preceding ones is that here the individual parties recognize that their goals are interdependent and that it's to everyone's advantage in the long run if the total organization benefits. A confronting group believes that the solution will be better if each party is open about its needs and objectives and the differences causing the conflict. Emphasizing these differences clarifies goals and interests and leads to creative solutions. Confronting the differences helps individuals find areas of common interest as well; the parties explicitly search for ways to increase the total payoff so that everyone can win rather than merely argue over the relative shares of a fixed outcome.

The proverbs that typify this mode include "Come now and let us reason together," "Try and trust will move mountains," and "By digging and digging the truth is discovered."

A problem-solving group focuses on the needs and objectives of the total organization as well as on those of each member. It also focuses on the relationships between the members, not on the individuals or their personalities. Group members recognize that the problem lies in their differences and interdependencies, rather than with any individuals or their positions. Furthermore, emphasis is on resolving the problem, not on merely accommodating different points of view.

A confronting style is risky and requires participants to challenge one another's underlying values and assumptions and to share personal concerns and criticisms. Trust and integrity are essential to an effective confronting-and-problem-solving climate.

COMPARISONS AMONG THE THREE MODES

The three modes are, of course, prototypes or even stereotypes: Actual management groups often act in ways that contain elements of two or even all three of these modes. Most groups develop a predominant style, but typically each group has its own mixture of styles, which may vary over time or from problem to problem.

The *Exhibit* provides a shorthand means of comparing these three styles. Each style is characterized briefly in terms of the group's way of defining the problem, the role of conflict, the attitudes of the participants, and the nature of the outcomes. The bottom two rows describe characteristic norms and representative proverbs that capture the beliefs and values implicit in the norms.

As noted earlier, the confronting-and-problem-solving mode is generally most effective for resolving group conflicts. However, there are also situations in which either a smoothing or a bargaining orientation is necessary. Consider a group faced with an unavoidable deadline and a decision that involves several mutually exclusive alternatives. The group may be forced to reach a decision without fully confronting all of the individual members' positions and needs. Even if the members are adept at productive confrontation, the group leader may explicitly suppress conflict to reach a quick decision.

Clearly, however, there is a difference between a one-time, short-term strategy of avoiding differences in order to meet a deadline and the longer-term development of norms that continually suppress conflict. Using successive short-term crises to justify a smoothing leadership style can be dangerous: just a few short-term crises can create a long-term pattern.

Bargaining is probably the most common (though not necessarily the most effective) form of conflict resolution when the problem involves scarce resources and two or more departments in an organization. Budgets and sales

EXHIBIT
Modes of Conflict Resolution

	SMOOTHING AND AVOIDING	*CONFRONTING AND PROBLEM SOLVING*	*BARGAINING AND FORCING*
Problem	Define to minimize differences	Define relative to total organization's needs	Define in terms of stakes for each subgroup
Role of Conflict	Destructive	Can be healthy	Good to win; bad to lose
Participants	Accommodators	Collaborators	Adversaries
Outcomes	Maintain status quo	Interdependent; all benefit when total group benefits	Win/lose
Typical Norms	Withdraw when attacked	Confront differences	Push when you have the advantage
	Avoid conflict	Be open and fair	Compromise when you do not
	Keep your tongue in check	Decide questions by reason, not by power	Maximize your own share
Representative Proverbs	Soft words win hard hearts	Come now, and let us reason together	Tit for tat is fair play
	Kill your enemies with kindness	Try and trust will move mountains	Might overcomes right
	Smooth words make smooth ways	By digging and digging the truth is discovered	You scratch my back; I'll scratch yours

Source: Adapted from unpublished materials developed by John J. Gabarro

territories *are* limited; organizational resources that go to one department obviously cannot go to another. In the absence of clear organizational priorities, bargaining is often the only means for resolving interdepartmental conflict. Bargaining can be particularly useful for groups that meet infrequently, when members do not know each other well or when the overall organization does not have a definite direction.

All too often, however, the bargaining climate degenerates into the kinds of forcing tactics described earlier. The game and winning become more important than achieving the best solution. The interests of the total group (and even of the subgroups) are lost in the battle to acquire scarce resources or to achieve organizational prominence.

Thus, even under these special circumstances, an open, confronting climate remains a desirable goal. It is an elusive goal, however, because an active confrontation of differences requires skillful participants. Open discussion of important differences is inherently stressful and productive only when group members possess both analytic and interpersonal skills. An effective problem-solving group continually risks falling apart in disagreement; creative problem solving is almost impossible without creative tension.

——— INTERGROUP AND INTERDEPARTMENTAL DECISION MAKING

Managing group problem solving effectively is a challenge under any circumstances. The process is especially complex when the group is temporary and composed of people from several different primary groups. Most of the difficulties are heightened versions of those that arise within a single group; however, the differing orientations and goals of people from various departments complicate the process significantly.

INTERDEPARTMENTAL CONFLICT

The major sources of interdepartmental conflict include vying for scarce resources; differing interests and priorities; and different personal values, orientations, and styles of thinking and problem solving. Problem-solving groups composed of people from various functional areas clearly begin with a wider range of goals and opinions about the problem. In addition, the stakes are usually higher; the problems are usually more complicated, and individuals' positions on most issues are much less flexible.

Interdepartmental conflict stems from more than just differing goals and priorities, however. Natural differences in departmental size and power also affect the problem-solving process. Larger, more-powerful departments generally exercise greater control over joint operations and decision making. If one department depends on another for a critical resource (raw materials, information, or even people), it may often defer to that department to avoid losing critical resources. This kind of power imbalance frequently leads to decisions being determined by political clout rather than by their merits, and the company suffers as a result. Furthermore, one-sided control usually leads to resentment by the weaker department, and working relationships deteriorate as a result.

Differences in departmental work loads and stress can also contribute to conflict. An overworked department will generally be less open to change, and its members will be especially resentful of other departments' comparative lack of pressure. Furthermore, overworked departments are apt to resort either to bargaining-and-forcing or to smoothing-and-avoidance strategies. They do not have the time to work through differences more carefully.

DEPARTMENT REPRESENTATIVES

Given so many potential sources of conflict, it is easy to understand how difficult interdepartmental problem solving and decision making can be. In most situations what holds the group together is the recognition of a common overriding interest in the success of the total organization. Often, however, that success is so taken for granted that individual departmental interests and prestige become more important. In interdepartmental decision making each group member acts as a representative of his or her home department. This role creates particular difficulties for the representatives, and these difficulties in turn affect their behaviors in the interdepartmental group.

Individual Problems of Department Representatives   Each representative experiences internal conflict as he or she attempts to balance commitments to the home department with those to the interdepartmental group. To maintain membership in both groups each representative must conform to two sets of norms and expectations. Department representatives usually learn rather quickly how to vary their behavior and language depending on the group they are currently interacting with, but there are often times when conforming with one group's expectations places the representative directly at odds with the other group. For example, membership on a task force developing new sales forecasting methods may require a product manager to share marketing department data and procedures that reflect poorly on her own staff. More significantly, the marketing department may have a history of resolving internal conflict via hard-nosed bargaining, while the task-force group is being managed in a more open, confronting style. The product manager is caught in the middle: If she shares data openly with the task force, she risks being ostracized by her own department; yet, if she reflects her department's bargaining stance, she will antagonize other task-force members and perhaps weaken her influence (and thus the marketing department's influence) on the task force's recommendations.

This dual membership problem puts a great deal of stress on department representatives. They must not only live with dual (and often conflicting) sets of goals, norms, and values but must also answer to two constituent groups for the actions they take and the decisions they make. Even when the representative disagrees with the position taken by one group, he or she must offer an explanation to the other group. Furthermore, each constituent group typically holds the representative responsible for *all* the actions and decisions of the other group. The representative is pressured by each group not only to explain its own position to the other group but also to influence the other group. Thus, each representative is a target for influence attempts from both directions, at the same time that he or she is trying to influence both the home department and the problem-solving group.

Relationship Problems of Department Representatives   This internal conflict also contributes to several kinds of relationship problems for department representatives. The pressures they feel often lead them to interpret challenges or criticisms of their home departments as personal attacks. In fact, many managers do express procedural criticisms in a personal fashion. Because the representatives view each other as symbols of their respective departments, substantive departmental conflicts often escalate quickly into emotional interpersonal disputes.

Another relationship problem arises when the representatives feel different levels of commitment to their two constituencies. Although some representatives remain oriented primarily toward their home departments, others develop more loyalty to the interdepartmental group. Group members may also differ in the degree of independence they have to make commitments on behalf of their departments and in the willingness of their departments to accept decisions of the interdepartmental group. These differences in orientation and influence further complicate the way the representatives are able to work with one another.

Personal Skills of Department Representatives   The group and interpersonal skills of the individual department representatives will also affect their ability to work together. The greater the role conflict, the more important personal skills become. Perhaps the most essential characteristic for a representative is a high tolerance for stress, ambiguity, and conflict. Individuals who cannot live with competing goals, irreconcilable values, and unresolved organizational problems should probably avoid interdepartmental assignments. Representatives also must be good listeners. Understanding the needs and motives of others is an essential prerequisite to effective problem solving. Similarly, representatives must be able to explain their own positions and needs articulately and persuasively, and they must be capable of making quick, on-the-spot judgments. Interdepartmental groups usually make decisions that have major implications for individual departments; group members must be able to trace out the consequences of new ideas rapidly in order to influence group decisions as they occur.

——— MANAGERIAL IMPLICATIONS

This reading has identified an extensive and diverse set of ideas for understanding group problem-solving behavior. Up to this point there have been few specific suggestions for how individual managers can develop and reinforce healthy problem-solving norms in groups. The reading has stressed the importance of careful diagnosis because the appropriateness of any particular action depends on the group's present skills and existing norms. However, several basic strategies for effectively influencing group behavior exist and can be employed by managers.

Understand the Sources of Current Behavior   Both individuals and groups develop patterns of behavior that are useful to them. Thus, to change someone's behavior, you must first understand the reasons why that behavior is functional for that person. A manager cannot always change underlying conditions and personal characteristics; however, it is futile to try to influence current behavior without understanding its sources and without considering how it benefits the individuals involved.

Demonstrate Desired Behavior Yourself   Serving as a role model is a powerful way that a manager can affect his or her subordinates' behavior. An obviously capable and successful manager can have a significant impact on peers, and even on superiors, in the organization.

Concerning problem-solving behavior, this principle suggests demonstrating your own commitment to making decisions based on facts and objective criteria. Furthermore, if you stress your own interest in finding solutions that maximize the goals of the total organization, others will also become more aware of their common objectives. You can model problem-solving behavior in the following ways: Suggest several solution alternatives rather than just one; do your homework and present factual support for your suggestions; avoid becoming involved in coalitions and compromises; and define your underlying assumptions so that you and others can question their validity.

Underlying this suggestion is the assumption that a problem-solving orientation will in fact lead to effective decision making. Your own success will encourage others to act similarly and will lead to a more open, confronting set of decision-making norms and procedures.

Monitor the Decision-Making Process   By increasing your sensitivity to the dynamics of a group's decision making, you can improve your ability to influence how the group works together. The counterpart of modeling problem-solving behavior is to insist on it in others as well. Press group members for factual evidence to back up their assertions; do not let minority views get squeezed out; work on achieving a balance of participation, and so on.

One of the most important aspects of group management is varying your style according to the particular phase of problem solving. During problem definition and solution finding, encourage open, nonevaluative exploration. Later, when a decision is required, press individuals to make personal commitments, and again make sure that minority concerns are fully aired before the group decision is considered final.

Although these suggestions are easiest to implement if you are the formal leader of the group, most of them can also be acted on by other members of the group. It may be more difficult for a member to influence group norms, but it is by no means impossible. The principles of effective problem solving that have been discussed in this reading have considerable legitimacy in our society; acting on these ideas will rarely be viewed as inappropriate behavior. In fact, just the opposite is true: By appealing to group members' personal values, you will generally gain much respect. Even when confronting strongly held opinions, you can succeed if you have done your own homework and know you stand on solid ground.

Copyright © 1978; revised 1991.

——— DISCUSSION QUESTIONS

1. What cultural concepts might work against the practice of confronting and problem solving as a mode of conflict resolution?

2. Consider your personality, and using traits that you know define you best, decide which mode of conflict resolution you are most comfortable adopting. Ask your peers for feedback. (Do they see you as you see yourself?)

3. If a company discovered that its approaches to conflict resolution did not include confronting and problem solving, what steps might the organization take to include this mode in its culture?

4. According to the author, there are three modes of conflict resolution. Give an example when it might be advantageous to use smoothing and avoiding. Do the same for confronting and problem solving and for bargaining and forcing.

5. The reading mentions that confronting and problem solving as a mode of conflict resolution is an important characteristic of profitable companies. Why might this behavior characterize a successful organization?

Understanding and Influencing Group Process

18

JOHN J. GABARRO AND ANNE HARLAN

This reading focuses on group process, or how a group goes about achieving its formal tasks. Observing this process, according to the authors, enables a manager to spot the group's covert and overt dynamics and to gain insights that will help make the group's interactions more productive. The authors identify seven aspects of group behavior that indicate how effectively a group is functioning. Suggestions are also given for interventions that a group leader or group member can use to improve group performance.

A camel is a horse put together by a committee" is a saying frequently applied to group decision making. Why are so many groups inefficient, slow, and frustrating, rather than effective in combining the insights and expertise of their members? To some extent the answer may be found in the formal group design. Perhaps the people chosen were not the ones who should have been included in such a group, or perhaps the group's goal was simply unattainable. More often, however, the difficulties encountered have less to do with content of task issues than with the *group process*, or how the group is going about achieving its formal tasks.[1]

Each group member is a unique individual, bringing certain expectations, assumptions, and feelings to the group, not only about his or her own role but also about the roles of other members in the group. As a result of these expectations certain interrelationships develop. These patterns may become either beneficial or detrimental to the group's purpose. Spotting detrimental patterns is the first key to understanding and improving the functioning of any group, but often these patterns are hard to identify because you cannot read each person's mind. For instance, how do you know that everyone understands what the agenda is, or that person X understands it but is likely to deviate from it if possible, or whether person X has the leverage to change the agenda if he or she wants to? By being attentive to what is happening among group members, you can develop a greater awareness of what is and what is not likely to

---

1. Portions of this reading were excerpted from a working paper by Eric H. Nielsen on influencing groups.

happen in a group and of what the group is or is not capable of doing at a given meeting.

Being able to observe and understand a group's process is important for two reasons. First, it enables you to understand what is taking place covertly as well as overtly in the group's behavior. Second, it can provide you with insights into what you and others can do to make the group's interactions more productive.

Listed below are seven aspects of group behavior that can furnish valuable clues on how effectively a group functions. It is unlikely that all of these will be relevant to your concerns at a given point in time, or that you can attend to them all simultaneously. The more adept you are at observing and assessing them, however, the more likely it is that you will spot potential difficulties early and act on them to improve the group's effectiveness.

PARTICIPATION

Participation—who participates, how often, when, and to what effect—is the easiest aspect of group process to observe. Typically, people who are higher in status, more knowledgeable, or simply more talkative, tend to participate more actively. Those who are newer, lower in status, uninformed, or not inclined to express their feelings and ideas verbally, generally speak less frequently. Even in groups composed of people of equal status and competence, some people will speak more than others; this variation is to be expected and is not necessarily a sign of an ineffective group. When great disparity exists among the contributions of individual members, however, it is usually a clue that the process is not effective—particularly when individuals or coalitions dominate the group's discussion.

There are many reasons why unequal participation can reduce a group's effectiveness. Low participators often have good ideas to offer but are reluctant to do so or cannot contribute their ideas because they are squeezed out by high participators who dominate the meeting. This imbalance can be a potential problem because those ideas receiving the most attention inevitably become the ones that are most seriously considered when it is time to make a decision. Considerable research shows that the most frequently stated ideas tend to be adopted by the group, regardless of their quality. Maier calls this the valence effect,[2] and it is one of the reasons groups often make poor decisions. Thus, large imbalance in participation can result in potentially good ideas being underrepresented in the discussion, or perhaps not even expressed.

Another negative consequence of uneven participation, understood through common sense as well as research, is that low participators are likely to tune out, lose commitment to the task, or become frustrated and angry—

---

2. Norman R. F. Maier, "Assets and Liabilities in Group Problem Solving: The Need for an Integrative Function," *Psychological Review*, vol. 74, no. 4 (July 1967), pp. 239–248.

especially if they have tried to enter the discussion but have been ignored or cut off by high participators. These negative attitudes result not only in poorer quality decisions but also in less commitment to implementing the group's decision.

Several factors contribute to uneven participation. One is that people who have the most at stake in a given issue (and may therefore be the least objective) are more motivated to participate than others who may have better ideas to offer. Another is that different people have different internal standards on which they judge whether one of their ideas is worth offering to the group. Thus, people with higher internal standards may be less likely to contribute than those with lower internal standards. The negative consequences for the quality of the group's discussion are obvious.

A marked change in a person's participation during a meeting is also a clue that something important may be going on. If a person suddenly becomes silent or withdraws during part of a meeting, it could suggest a number of possibilities (depending on the person's nonverbal behavior). For example, it might simply mean that the person has temporarily withdrawn to mull over the comments of a prior speaker. It may also be that the person has tuned out, or it may be a sign of hostility or frustration.

Here are some questions to consider in observing participation:

1. Who are the high participators? Why? To what effect?
2. Who are the low participators? Why? To what effect?
3. Are there any shifts in participators, such as an active participator suddenly becoming silent? Do you see any reason for this in the group's interaction, such as a criticism from a higher-status person or a shift in topic? Is it a sign of withdrawal?
4. How are silent people treated? Is their silence taken by others to mean consent? Disagreement? Disinterest? Why do you think they are silent?
5. Who talks to whom? Who responds to whom? Do participation patterns reflect coalitions that are impeding or controlling the discussion? Are the interaction patterns consistently excluding certain people who need to be supported or brought into the discussion?
6. Who keeps the discussion going? How is this accomplished? Why does the group leader want the discussion to continue in such a vein?

Interventions   There are several simple and unobtrusive process interventions that you can make, either as a group leader or as a group member, to bring about a better balance in participation. These interventions are particularly important if you think that potentially valuable minority views are not getting their share of time, that certain people have not had a chance to develop their ideas fully, or that some group members are not part of the discussion. One intervention is to try to *clarify* a point that someone had made earlier and that seemed to fall through the cracks—by saying something like "Tom, let me see if I understood what you said a moment ago." A related technique is to *reinforce* a prior point by asking the person to elaborate on it—"Dana, I was interested in what you were saying earlier; can you elaborate on it?" Similarly, a very direct technique for bringing out silent people is to simply *query* them— "Maria, you haven't said a word during this discussion; what are your ideas on it?" or to make a comment as direct as "We've heard a lot from the marketing people but very little from production scheduling. What do you folks think about the problem?"

—— INFLUENCE

Influence and participation are not the same thing. Some people may speak very little, yet capture the attention of the whole group when they do speak. Others may talk frequently but go unheard. Influence, like participation, is often a function of status, experience, competence, and to some degree personality. It is normal for some people to have more influence on a group's process than others, and this fact is not necessarily a sign that a group is ineffective. However, when one individual or subgroup has so much influence on a discussion that others' ideas are rejected out of hand, it is usually a clue that the group's effectiveness will suffer and that the discussion will fail to probe alternatives. This imbalance is particularly dangerous when minority views are systematically squelched without adequate exploration.

An asymmetry in influence can have several negative consequences on a group's effectiveness. As already noted, it can result in the suppression of potentially valuable minority views; it can contribute to imbalanced participation, and it will inevitably result in hostility and lack of commitment by group members who feel that they have been left out. As with participation, considerable research on group behavior and alienation shows that the more influence people feel they have had on a group's discussion, the more committed they are likely to be to its decisions, regardless of whether their own points of view have been adopted by the group.

One way of checking relative influence is to watch the reactions of the other group members. Someone who has influence is not only likely to have others listening attentively but is also less likely to be interrupted or challenged by the others. He or she may also be physically seated at or near the head of the table or near the center of a subgroup.

Struggles for influence and leadership often characterize the early stages of a group's life, especially in temporary groups such as task forces, project teams, or committees. To some extent these struggles occur in most groups, although usually mildly covert. Vying for leadership can become a problem, however, when it disrupts the group's ability to deal with the task at hand. The disruption occurs when being dominant is an important need for those who are vying for leadership. Under these circumstances, the competition gets played out indirectly with one person disagreeing with the other because of his or her need to establish dominance, regardless of the relative merits of the other's arguments. The hidden agenda then becomes scoring points rather than working on the problem. Often two people engaged in such a power struggle are not even aware of their hidden motives and genuinely think that they are arguing about the problem at hand.

In assessing influence patterns within a group, you may find the following questions useful:

1. Which members are listened to when they speak? What ideas are they expressing?
2. Which members are ignored when they speak? Why? What are their ideas? Is the group losing valuable inputs simply because some are not being heard?
3. Are there any shifts in influence? Why?
4. Is there any rivalry within the group? Are there struggles among individuals or subgroups for leadership?
5. Who interrupts whom? Does this reflect relative power within the group?
6. Are minority views consistently ignored regardless of possible merit?

Interventions   If you observe that the opinions of an individual or subgroup of people appear to be unduly influencing a group's progress, you can intervene to open up the discussion. One strategy is simply to *support or reinforce* the views of minority members—"I think there is some merit to what Jenna was saying earlier, and I'd like to elaborate on it," or "I think that we're not giving enough thought to Jenna and Carlos's position, and I think we should explore it further before dropping it." Another intervention is to actually *point out* that the opinions of certain people are dominating the discussion—"Mary, you've made your point quite forcefully and clearly, but I'd also like to hear the other side of the question before we go further." Similarly, another technique is to ask the group to *open up* the discussion—"So far we've spent a lot of time talking about Jenna and Bill's proposal, but I'd like to hear some differing opinions," or "The managers seem to agree strongly on what needs to be done, but I'd like to hear more about what the customer representatives think are the problems."

GROUP CLIMATE

Members bring with them many assumptions of how groups ought to function generally and how their particular group should function. Frequently, these assumptions will be quite different from one member to another. One person may feel that the way for a group to work effectively is to be strictly business—no socializing and with tight leader control over the group. Others may feel that the only way a group can work creatively is to give each person equal time for suggestions, get together informally, and use relatively loose leadership. After group members have tested each others' assumptions early on in the group, a climate or atmosphere becomes established that may or may not facilitate effective group functioning. Different group climates are effective in different situations.

For example, if the problem to be solved is one that demands a creative, new solution and the collaboration of several experts, then a climate of openness in which everyone has an equal opportunity to participate will be most effective. In other situations, however, a more competitive or structured group climate might encourage a higher-quality solution, especially if expertise is not distributed equally among all group members. To gauge a group's climate, you should make certain observations:

1. Do people prefer to keep the discussion friendly and congenial? Do people prefer conflict and disagreement?
2. Do people seem involved and interested? Is the atmosphere one of work? Play? Competition? Avoidance?
3. Is there any attempt to suppress conflict or unpleasant feelings by avoiding tough issues?

For most task groups an unstructured, laissez-faire, or conflict-free climate is not effective: Important issues and conflicts are not explored sufficiently, and the quality of the group's work is sacrificed for the maintenance of friendly and smooth relations. Conversely, a highly structured climate can impede effective problem solving because members do not allow each other enough freedom to explore alternatives or consider creative solutions. A highly competitive climate can also be dysfunctional; competition can impede thoughtful deliberation and exchange, resulting in failure to build on other people's ideas.

Interventions   Intervening to alter a group's climate is more difficult than the interventions previously described. It can be done, however, by reinforcing and supporting desirable behavior, as well as by raising the issue directly. Where a group is smoothing over and avoiding important problems, for example, a useful intervention would be, "We seem to have a lot of agreement, but I wonder if we have really tackled some of the tougher underlying issues." When a group seems to be tied up by its own structure, often a comment as simple as the following will suffice: "I think that maybe we're looking at the problem too narrowly, and it might be useful to discuss whether we should also consider X, which isn't on the agenda but seems relevant to what we're talking about."

MEMBERSHIP

A major concern for group members is their degree of acceptance or inclusion in the group. Different patterns of interaction may develop in the group, providing clues to the degree and kind of membership. You can use these questions to examine the patterns of interaction:

1. Is there any subgrouping? Sometimes two or three members may consistently agree and support each other or consistently disagree and oppose one another.
2. Do some people seem to be outside the group? Do other members seem to be insiders? How are outsiders treated?
3. Do some members move physically in and out of the group—for example, lean forward or backward in their chairs or move their chairs in and out? Under what conditions do they come in or move out?

The problem of in-groups and out-groups is closely related to the earlier discussion of influence within the group. The interventions described earlier—supporting, querying, and opening up the discussion—are also useful for bringing in marginal members.

FEELINGS

During any group discussion, interactions among members frequently generate feelings. These feelings, however, are seldom talked about. When observing, you will often have to use tone of voice, facial expressions, gestures, and other nonverbal cues to make guesses about feelings:

1. What signs of feelings (anger, irritation, frustration, warmth, affection, excitement, boredom, defensiveness, competitiveness, etc.) do you observe in group members?
2. Are group members overly nice or polite to each other? Are only positive feelings expressed? Do members agree with each other too readily? What happens when members disagree?
3. Do you see norms operating about participation or the kinds of questions that are allowed (e.g., "If I talk, you must talk")? Do members feel free to probe each other about their feelings? Do questions tend to be restricted to intellectual topics or events outside of the group?

Most groups in business develop norms that allow for the expression of only positive feelings or feelings of disagreement and not anger. The problem with suppressing strong negative feelings is that they usually resurface later. For example, a person who is angry about what someone said earlier in the meeting gets back at that person later in the discussion by disagreeing or by criticizing his or her idea regardless of the idea's merit. The person's hidden motive becomes getting even, and he or she will do so by resisting ideas, being stubborn, or derailing the discussion. This retaliation is usually disguised with substantive issues and often has an element of irrationality to it. It is often more effective to bring out the person's anger in the first place and deal with it then.

TASK FUNCTIONS

For any group to function adequately and make maximum progress on the task at hand, certain task functions must be carried out. First, there must be *initiation*—the problem or goals must be stated, time limits laid out, and some agenda agreed upon. This function most frequently falls to the leader but may be taken on by other group members. Next, there must be both *opinion* and *information* seeking and giving on various issues related to the task. One of the major problems affecting group decisions and commitments is that groups tend to spend insufficient time on these phases. *Clarifying* and *elaborating* are vital not only for effective communication but also for creative solutions. *Summarizing* includes a review of ideas to be followed by *consensus testing*—making sure that all the ideas are on the table and that the group is ready to enter into an evaluation of the various ideas produced. The most effective groups follow this order rather than the more common procedure of evaluating each idea or alternative as it is discussed. Different group members may take on these task functions, but each must be covered. Use the following questions to check:

1. Are suggestions made as to the best way to proceed or tackle the problem?
2. Is there a summary of what has been covered? How effectively is this done? Who does it?
3. Is there any giving or asking for information, opinions, feelings, feedback, or searching for alternatives?
4. Is the group kept on target? Are topic jumping and going off on tangents prevented or discouraged?
5. Are all the ideas out before evaluation begins? What happens if someone begins to evaluate an idea as soon as it is produced?

MAINTENANCE FUNCTIONS

Groups cannot function effectively if cohesion is low or if relationships among group members become strained. In the life of any group, there will be periods of conflict, dissenting views, and misunderstandings. It is the purpose of maintenance functions to rebuild damaged relations and bring harmony back to the group. Without these processes, group members can become alienated, resulting in the group's losing valuable resources.

Two maintenance activities that can serve to prevent these kinds of problems are *gate keeping,* which ensures that members wanting to make a contribution are given the opportunity to do so, and *encouraging,* which helps create a climate of acceptance.

Compromising and *harmonizing* are two other activities that have limited usefulness in the actual task accomplishment, but they are sometimes useful in repairing strained relations.

When the level of conflict in a group is so high that effective communication is impaired, it is often useful for the group to suspend the task discussion and examine its own processes in order to define and attempt to solve the conflicts. The following questions will focus attention on a group's maintenance functions:

1. Are group members encouraged to enter into the discussion?
2. How well do members get their ideas across? Are some members preoccupied and not listening? Are there any attempts by group members to help others clarify their ideas?
3. How are ideas rejected? How do members react when their ideas are rejected?
4. Are conflicts among group members ignored or dealt with in some way?

⎯⎯⎯ PROCESS OBSERVATION AND FEEDBACK

This reading has covered seven important aspects of group process that can influence a group's effectiveness. The interventions suggested are relatively simple and can be made naturally and unobtrusively during the normal progress of a meeting. The more people in a group skilled at making process observations, the greater the likelihood that the group will not bog down, waste valuable time, or make poor decisions. For this reason an increasing number of U.S. and foreign firms have developed norms that encourage open discussions of group process. In many companies, meetings are ended with a brief feedback session on the group's process, during which group members evaluate the meeting's effectiveness.

You need not be in such a firm or use terms such as *process feedback* to contribute to a group's effectiveness. Most of the ideas presented in this reading are based on common sense; practicing them does not require using the terms described here. The ideas described are more important than specific labels applied to them.

——— DISCUSSION QUESTIONS

1. Describe your participation in work groups to which you've belonged. Has your participation varied within the same group? From group to group? Why or why not?
2. Relate an experience you've had influencing a group. Explain the important aspects of your personal approach to influence in a group setting. If you've never felt as if you've influenced a group, explain why not.
3. What factors—other than those mentioned in the reading—might affect group process?
4. This reading focuses on group dynamics within a single group. Would these same principles apply to the dynamics between two groups? What would be the same? What would be different?

How to Run a Meeting

19

JAMES WARE

This reading delineates the practical details of running a meeting—"the most overused and underutilized of all management tools." According to the author, careful preparation is essential and includes setting objectives, selecting participants, planning the agenda, collecting relevant information, and setting a time and place for the meeting. The author offers strategies and suggestions for beginning the meeting, encouraging problem solving, keeping the discussion on track, reaching a decision, and ending the meeting.

Meetings are among the most overused and underutilized of all management tools. One study of managerial behavior found that many executives spent over two-thirds of their time in scheduled meetings. More significantly, important organizational decisions are almost always reached in management meetings or as a result of one or more meetings. Given their importance and the amount of management time they consume, it is indeed a tragedy that so many meetings are inefficient and, worse, ineffective.

Yet planning and conducting a meeting is not a difficult task. Although there are no magic formulas to guarantee success, there are a number of simple procedures that effective managers employ to improve the quality of their meetings.

There are, of course, many different kinds of meetings, ranging from two-person interchanges all the way up to industrywide conventions with thousands of participants. Most management meetings, however, involve relatively small groups of people in a single organization. This reading will concentrate on a number of techniques for running these kinds of management meetings more effectively. For further simplicity, the primary focus will be on scheduled meetings of managers who are at approximately the same level in the organization and who have known each other and worked together before.

The suggestions that follow are divided into planning activities to carry out before the meeting and leadership activities to engage in during the meeting. Both kinds of work are essential: The most thorough preparation in the world will be wasted if you are careless during the meeting, while even outstanding meeting leadership rarely overcomes poor planning.

289

——— PREPARING FOR THE MEETING

Perhaps the most useful way to begin is to sit down with a blank sheet of paper and think through what the meeting will be like. Write down all the issues that are likely to come up, what decisions need to be made, what you want to happen after the meeting, and what things have to happen before the meeting can take place. Although the circumstances surrounding each meeting are unique, your planning should include the following activities:

Setting Objectives   Most managers call meetings either to exchange information or to solve organizational problems. Generally your reasons for calling the meeting are fairly obvious, especially to you. It is worth being very explicit about your purposes, however, because they have major implications for who should attend, which items belong on the agenda, when and where you hold the meeting, and what kinds of decision-making procedures you should use.

An information-exchange meeting can be an efficient mechanism if the information to be shared is complex or controversial, if it has major implications for the meeting participants, or if there is symbolic value in conveying the information personally. If none of these conditions is present, it may be more efficient, and just as effective, to write a memo or make several telephone calls.

Problem-solving meetings provide an opportunity to combine the knowledge and skills of several people at once. The ideas that evolve out of an open-ended discussion are usually richer and more creative than what the same people could produce working individually.

The two different objectives—information exchange and problem solving—call for very different kinds of meetings. Thus, you should make your goals clear both to yourself and to the other meeting participants.

Selecting Participants   Invite people to the meeting who will either contribute to, or be affected by, its outcome. Select individuals who have knowledge or skills relevant to the problem or who command organizational resources (time, budgets, other people, power, and influence) that you need to tap.

As you build your participant list, also give thought to the overall composition of the group. Identify the likely concerns and interests of the individual managers and the feelings they have about each other. Try to obtain a rough balance of power and status among subgroups or probable coalitions (unless you have clear reasons for wanting one group to be more powerful).

Do everything you can to keep the size of the group appropriate to your objectives. Although an information-exchange meeting can be almost any size, a problem-solving group should not exceed 10 people if at all possible.

Planning the Agenda   Even if you are planning an informal exploratory meeting, an agenda can be a valuable means of controlling the discussion and of giving the participants a sense of direction. The agenda defines the meeting's purpose for participants and places boundaries between relevant and irrelevant discussion topics. Furthermore, the agenda can serve as an important vehicle for premeeting discussions with participants.

Some important principles of building an agenda are listed here:

- Sequence items so they build on one another if possible.
- Sequence topics from easiest to most difficult or controversial.
- Keep the number of topics within reasonable limits.
- Avoid topics that can be better handled by subgroups or individuals.
- Separate information exchange from problem solving.
- Define a finishing time as well as a starting time.
- Depending on meeting length, schedule breaks at specific times when they will not disrupt important discussions.

Not every meeting requires a formal written agenda. Often you simply cannot predict where a discussion will lead or how long it will take. However, focusing your attention on these issues can help you anticipate controversy and be prepared to influence it in a productive manner. Even if you do not prepare a public written agenda, you should not begin the meeting without having a tentative private one.

Doing Your Homework   Your major objective in preparing for the meeting is to collect all relevant information you can and consider its implications. Some of this data may be in written documents, but much of it will probably be in other people's heads. The more important and the more controversial the subject, the more contact you should have with other participants before the actual meeting.

These contacts will help you anticipate issues and disagreements that may arise during the meeting. As you talk with the other participants, try to learn all you can about their personal opinions and objectives concerning the meeting topic. These personal objectives—often called hidden agendas—can have as big an impact on what happens during the meeting as your formal explicit agenda. Thus, the more you can discover about the other participants' goals for the meeting, the better prepared you will be to lead an effective discussion.

These premeeting contacts also give you an opportunity to encourage the other participants to do their homework. If there is enough time before the meeting to collect and circulate relevant data or background materials, the meeting itself will proceed much more quickly. Few events are as frustrating as a meeting of people who are unprepared to discuss or decide the issues on the agenda.

As part of your preparation you may want to brief your boss and other executives who will not be at the meeting but who have an interest in its outcomes.

Finally, circulate the agenda and relevant background papers a day or two before the meeting if you can. These documents help clarify your purposes and expectations and encourage the other participants to come to the meeting well prepared. Keep your demands on their time reasonable, however. People are more likely to read and think about brief memos than about long comprehensive reports.

Setting a Time and Place   The timing and location of your meeting can have a subtle but significant impact on the quality of the discussion. These choices communicate a surprising number of messages about the meeting's importance, style, and possible outcomes.

What time of day is best for your meeting? Often the work flow in the organization will constrain your freedom of choice. For example, you could not meet simultaneously with all of a bank's tellers during the regular business hours or with all the order-entry clerks just as the mail arrives. Within these kinds of constraints, however, you often have a wide choice of meeting times. How should you decide?

Early in the day participants will usually be fresher and will have fewer other problems on their minds. In contrast, late-afternoon meetings can be more leisurely, because there will usually be nothing else on anyone's schedule following your meeting. Perhaps the best question to ask is what the participants will be doing after the meeting. Will they be eager to end the meeting so they can proceed to other commitments, or will they be inclined to prolong the discussion? Which attitude better suits your purposes? There is no best time for a meeting, but you should consider which times would be most suitable for your particular objectives.

Two other factors may also influence when you schedule the meeting. First, try to ensure that there will be an absolute minimum of interruptions. Second, gear your starting time to the meeting's probable, or desirable, length. For example, if you want the meeting to last only one hour, a good time to schedule it is at 11 A.M.

Try not to plan meetings that last more than 90 minutes. Most people's endurance—or at least their creative capacity—will not last much longer than that. For complex or lengthy subjects that require more time, be sure to build in coffee-and-stretch breaks at least every 90 minutes.

Another key decision is where to hold the meeting. The setting can have a marked influence on the discussion's tone and content. Consider the difference between calling three subordinates to your office or meeting them for lunch in a restaurant. Each setting implies a particular level of formality and signals the kind of discussion you expect to have. Similarly, if you are meeting with several peers, a conference room provides a more neutral climate than would any of your offices. In each case, the appropriate setting depends on your purposes, and you should choose your location accordingly.

The discussion climate will also be affected by the arrangement of the furniture in the meeting room. In your office, you can stay behind your desk and thereby appear more authoritative or use a chair that puts you on a more equal basis with the other participants. In a conference room, you can sit at the head of the table to symbolize your control or in the center to be one of the group.

You should also be sure to arrange for any necessary mechanical equipment, such as an overhead or slide projector, an easel, or a blackboard. These visual aids can facilitate both information-exchange and problem-solving discussions.

Summary   These suggestions are intended to help you convene a meeting of people who have a common understanding of why they have come together and are prepared to contribute to the discussion. Of course, this kind of thorough preparation is often simply impossible. Nevertheless, the more preparation you do, the more smoothly the meeting will go. Although you can never anticipate *all* the issues and hidden agendas, you can clearly identify the major sources of potential disagreement. That anticipation enables you to control the meeting rather than be caught off guard. Even if you have to schedule a meeting only an hour in advance, you can still benefit from systematic attention to these kinds of details.

——— CONDUCTING THE MEETING

If you have done your homework, you probably have a good idea of where you want the group to be at the end of the meeting. However, remember that you called the meeting because you need something from the other participants—either information relevant to the problem or agreement and commitment to a decision. Your success in achieving those goals now depends not so much on what you know about the problem as on what you and the others can learn during the discussion. Thus, your primary concern as you begin the meeting should be with creating a healthy problem-solving atmosphere in which participants openly confront their differences and work toward a joint solution.

The following suggestions and leadership techniques should help you achieve that goal.

Beginning the Meeting   If you are well prepared, the chances are that no one else has thought as much about the meeting as you have. Thus, the most productive way to begin is with an explicit review of the agenda and your objectives. This discussion gives everyone an opportunity to ask questions, offer suggestions, and express opinions about why they are there. Beginning with a review of the agenda also signals its importance and gets the meeting going in a task-oriented direction.

Be careful not to simply impose the agenda on the group; others may have useful suggestions that will speed up the meeting or bring the problem into sharper focus. They may even disagree with some of your plans, but you will not learn about that disagreement unless you clearly signal that you consider the agenda open to revision. The more the others participate in defining the meeting, the more committed they will be to fulfilling that definition.

This initial discussion also permits participants to work out a shared understanding of the problem that brought them together and of what topics are and are not appropriate to discuss in the meeting.

Encouraging Problem Solving   As the formal leader of the meeting, you can employ a wide variety of techniques to keep the group in a problem-solving mode. Your formal authority as chairperson gives you a great deal of power to influence the group's actions. Often a simple comment, a pointed look, or even a lifted eyebrow is all you need to indicate approval or disapproval of someone's behavior.

Perhaps your best tool is simply your own style of inquiry. If you focus on facts and on understanding points of disagreement, to the exclusion of personalities, others will generally do the same. As the discussion progresses, try to keep differing points of view in rough balance. Do not let a few individuals dominate; when you sense an imbalance in participation, openly ask the quieter members for their opinions and ideas. Never assume that silence means agreement; more often, it signals some disagreement with the dominant theme of the discussion.

Effective problem-solving meetings generally pass through several phases. Early in the discussion, the group will be seeking to understand the nature of the problem. At that point you need to encourage factual nonevaluative discussion that emphasizes describing symptoms and searching for all possible causes. As understanding is gained, the focus will shift to a search for solutions. Again, you must discourage evaluative comments until the group has explored all potential alternatives. Only then should the discussion become evaluative, as the group moves toward a decision.

By being sensitive to the stages of problem solving (describing symptoms, searching for alternatives, evaluating alternatives, selecting a solution), you can vary your leadership style to fit the current needs of the group. At all times, however, keep the discussion focused on the problem, not on personalities or on unrelated issues, no matter how important they may be. Make your priorities clear, and hold the group to them. Finally, maintain a climate of honest inquiry in which anyone's assumptions (including yours) may be questioned and tested.

Keeping the Discussion on Track   When the meeting topic is controversial, with important consequences for the group members, you will have to work hard to keep the discussion focused on the issues.

Controversy makes most people uncomfortable, and groups will often avoid confronting the main issue by finding less important or irrelevant topics to talk about. If the discussion wanders too far from the agenda, bring the group back to the major topics.

Use your judgment in making these interventions, however. If the group is on the verge of splitting up in anger or frustration, a digression to a safe topic may be a highly functional way of reuniting. Generally, such digressions are most beneficial when they follow, rather than precede, open controversy. If you think the group has reached a decision on the main issue, even if it is only an implicit one, you may want to let the digression go on for a while. However, if the discussion is clearly delaying a necessary confrontation, then you will have to intervene to bring the discussion back to the main issue.

If you began the meeting with an explicit discussion of the agenda, you will find this focusing task easier to carry out. Often a simple reminder to the group, with a glance at the clock, is enough. Another useful technique for marking progress is periodically to summarize where you think the group has been and where it seems to be going. Again, treat your summaries as tentative and ask the group to confirm your assessments.

If the discussion seems to bog down or to wander too far afield, the group may need to take a short break. Even two minutes of standing and stretching can revitalize people's willingness to concentrate on the problem. The break also serves to cut off old conversations, making it easier to begin new ones.

Do everything you can to keep the discussion moving on schedule so that the meeting ends on time. The clock can be a useful taskmaster, and busy managers rarely have the luxury of ignoring it. If you have set a specific ending time, and everyone knows you mean it, members will be less likely to digress.

Controlling the Discussion   How authoritatively should you exercise control over the discussion? The answer depends so much on specific circumstances that a general response is almost impossible. The appropriate level of formality depends on the discussion topic, on the specific phase of the problem-solving cycle, and on your formal and informal relationships with the other participants. You will normally want to exercise greater control under the following circumstances:

- The meeting is oriented more toward information exchange;
- The topic generates strong, potentially disruptive feelings;
- The group is moving toward a decision;
- Time pressures are significant.

There are a whole range of techniques you can use to exert more formal control. For example, if you permit participants to speak only when you call on them or if you comment on or summarize each statement, direct confrontations between other individuals will be minimal. If you use a flip chart or blackboard to summarize ideas, you will also increase the level of formality and reduce the number of direct exchanges. In some circumstances, you may even want to employ formal parliamentary procedures, such as requiring motions, limiting debate, taking notes, and so on. These procedures might be appropriate, for example, in meetings of a board of directors, in union-management contract negotiations, or in policy-setting sessions that involve managers from several different parts of the organization.

Many of these techniques are clearly inappropriate for, and rarely used in, smaller management meetings. Although these techniques can give you a high degree of control, they cannot prevent participants from developing strong feelings about the issues—feelings that often become strong precisely because you have not permitted them to be openly expressed.

Thus, it is possible to control a meeting in a way that minimizes conflict. However, one result of that control may be increased tension and even hostility between the participants, leading to more serious future problems. Yet, if tension levels are already so high that a rational discussion will not evolve on its own, some of these controlling techniques may be essential.

Reaching a Decision Many management groups fall into decision-making habits without thinking carefully about the consequences of those habits. The two major approaches to reaching a group decision are voting and reaching a consensus. Each strategy has its advantages and disadvantages.

Voting is often used when the decision is important and the group seems deadlocked. A major benefit of taking a vote is that it guarantees you will get a decision. However, voting requires public commitment to a position and creates a win/lose situation for the group members. Some individuals will be clearly identified as having favored a minority position. Losers on one issue often try to balance their account on the next decision, or they may withdraw their commitment to the total group. Either way, you may have won the battle but lost the war.

Reaching a group consensus is generally a much more effective decision-making procedure. It is often more difficult, however, and is almost always more time-consuming. Working toward a genuine consensus means hearing all points of view and usually results in a better decision. This also results in greater individual commitment to the group decision, a condition that is especially important when the group members are responsible for implementing the decision. Even when individuals do not fully agree with the group decision, they are more likely to support it (or less likely to sabotage it) if they believe their positions have had a complete hearing.

Ending the Meeting Most important at the end of the meeting is to clarify what happens next. If the group has made a major decision, be certain all agree on who is responsible for its implementation and on when the work will be completed.

If the group has to meet again, you can save considerable time by scheduling your next meeting then and there. Have everyone check calendars and mark down the date and time of the next meeting.

Depending on the discussion topic and the decisions that have been made, either you or someone else should follow the meeting with a brief memo summarizing the discussion, the decisions, and the follow-up commitments each participant has made. This kind of document serves not only as a record of the meeting but also as a reminder to the participants of what they decided and what they committed themselves to doing.

If you can, spend the last several minutes of the meeting discussing how the meeting went. Although most managers are not accustomed to self-critiques, this practice can contribute significantly to improvements in group problem solving. The best time to share reactions to a meeting is right after it has ended. You evaluate the effectiveness of other management techniques all the time; why not apply the same criteria to your meetings?

——— SUMMARY

Management meetings occur frequently and have a significant impact on organizational productivity. By applying these techniques carefully, with sensitivity to the combination of people and problems you have brought together, you can make your meetings more effective and more interesting. The techniques are simple and require little more than systematic preparation before the meeting and sensitive observation and intervention while the meeting is in progress.

——— DISCUSSION QUESTIONS

1. Name other procedures that you can think of that would enhance the effectiveness of a meeting.
2. State your general opinion about meetings as well as the effectiveness of the meetings that you have attended. What have been their assets and drawbacks?
3. Should the structure of a meeting reflect the structure of the organization? For example, should a hierarchical company have hierarchically structured meetings?
4. What has been the most disruptive incident at a meeting that you have attended? How was it handled? What could have been done to prevent the disruption from occurring? What was done to control its effects?
5. What is your opinion about routine, regularly scheduled meetings? What might prevent them from being effective? How can they maintain their effectiveness?

20   Managing a Task Force

JAMES WARE

This reading describes how to establish, organize, and manage an effective task force. The author guides the reader through each stage of a task force's life cycle: starting up, conducting the first meeting, running the task force, and completing the project. He provides practical advice on how to achieve an outcome that serves the interests of task-force members as well as those of the organization itself.

Companies establish task forces to work on problems and projects that cannot be easily handled by the regular organization. Typically the problems cut across existing departmental boundaries or are simply so time-consuming that working on them would disrupt routine department tasks.

A task force can be a powerful management tool for resolving complex and challenging problems. Several factors contribute to this strength:

- The group is usually very task oriented because it was formed to solve a specific problem or achieve a well-defined outcome. When the problem is solved or the task is accomplished, the group disbands.
- If the task force brings together managers from the affected functional areas, it will possess a diversity of skills and understanding that can potentially produce a high-quality solution.
- If group members are selected on the basis of their individual competence relative to the problem, there is rarely any deadwood.

These same characteristics, however, can present a task-force leader with several difficult managerial problems:

- Because the group represents an inherent criticism of the regular organization's failure to deal with the problem, there may be significant tensions and even battles between members and non-members.
- Individual task-force members who come from different parts of the organization usually bring with them a wide diversity of viewpoints, goals, and loyalties. The task force can become a battleground for fighting out long-standing departmental conflicts.
- The temporary nature of the task force may limit members' willingness to commit personal time and energy to the project.

- Managers who are personally ambitious often view a task-force assignment as a major opportunity to impress upper management. These private agendas can seriously interfere with the group's problem-solving effectiveness.
- If the group members do not know each other well or are competing with each other either personally or as departmental representatives, the leader will find it difficult to create the shared sense of purpose and mutual respect necessary for issue-oriented problem solving.

Clearly, the success of a task force's efforts depends heavily on the way its activities are managed. This reading suggests some operating guidelines for increasing the effectiveness of any temporary management group. These suggestions have been grouped into four categories, based on the sequence in which the leader will confront the problems:

- Starting up the task force,
- Conducting the first meeting,
- Running the task force,
- Completing the project.

The guidelines apply primarily to a task-force leader. Often, however, the most effective groups are those in which several members carry out the leadership activities. Thus, you may find many of these ideas useful even in groups where you do not have formal leadership responsibilities.

▬▬ STARTING UP THE TASK FORCE

Your work as task-force leader begins the moment you accept responsibility for chairing the group. The period before the first formal meeting presents several opportunities for making decisions that will affect many of the group's later activities. Early attention to details will pay dividends as the group confronts tough issues during its deliberations. In fact, these front-end activities probably represent your greatest opportunity for defining the group's working style.

These start-up activities should focus on the following sequence of tasks:

1. Clarify Why the Task Force Is Being Formed Although the specific circumstances of each project will be unique, most task forces are established to accomplish one or more of the following general objectives:

- Investigate a poorly understood problem.
- Recommend and/or implement a high-quality solution to a recognized problem.
- Respond to a crisis that results from a sudden change in the organization's business conditions.

- Bring together people with the knowledge and skills to work on the problem.
- Gain commitment to a decision by involving the people who will be affected by its implementation.
- Develop managers by providing them with exposure to other functional areas and people.
- Force resolution of a long-standing problem, or work around an obstacle (such as a particular individual or group).

Usually the commissioning executives will have several purposes in mind. (*Commissioning executives* refers to the upper-level management group that determines a task force should be established.) For example, a new-product-development project can also be an excellent training experience for junior marketing managers. Similarly, a study of excessive inventories could be part of a strategy to reduce the power of an ineffective but well-entrenched purchasing manager.

Often, however, multiple objectives are incompatible, because one objective may be attainable only at the expense of another. Additionally, the various commissioning executives may have different objectives or different priorities for conflicting objectives. In many instances these differences will not be openly expressed or even recognized.

Thus, one of your first critical tasks will be to meet with the commissioning executives and with other managers who have an interest in the project's outcome. In those meetings you will want to explore the relevance and relative importance of each possible objective. You may even find it necessary to define alternative objectives and possible conflicts yourself. You can be an active participant in the process of clarifying the task force's mission.

You must also determine whether the task force will be expected to conduct a preliminary investigation, to engage in problem solving and decision making, or to implement an already agreed-upon change. The choice of emphasis will obviously depend upon the history and nature of the particular problem, but you should seek an explicit statement about the boundaries of the project.

The nature of the task will help determine who should be on the task force and what kinds of operating and decision-making procedures will be appropriate.

For example, an exploratory investigation of a customer-service department's efficiency would require very different analytic skills and working procedures than would the installation of a computerized invoicing and inventory-control system. Consequently, you will want to select task-force members whose skills match the project requirements.

A useful technique for confronting these issues is to write out a proposed statement of purpose and then to ask the commissioning executives how well your statement reflects their expectations. As the executives help you revise the statement, they will develop personal commitment to it and thus to the task force's success.

2. Define General Operating Procedures

- Will members be assigned to the group full-time or part-time?
- When should the task be completed?
- What will the group's budget be?
- What organizational reports and other information will be available to the group?
- How much decision-making power is being delegated to the group?
- What information should be reported to functional managers and how often?

You will not be able to anticipate all the procedural issues that the group will face, and many of those that can be anticipated will have to be worked out by the whole task-force group. Again, however, you should discuss these questions in advance with the executives who are establishing the task force. It is far better to be told explicitly that some topics and decisions are beyond the group's charter than to discover those boundaries only by crossing over them.

One of the most important procedural issues to be resolved is the way in which the group will make task-related decisions. The more exploratory and open-ended the basic project is, the more open and participative the decision-making procedures should be. Considerable research evidence suggests that task-oriented groups prefer relatively directive leaders and that decision making is usually more efficient in a structured climate. However, if the problem requires an imaginative or wholly new perspective, then a more unstructured climate will generally produce more innovative ideas.

You should discuss leadership and decision-making styles with both the commissioning executives and prospective task-force members; however, this is not a decision to make once for the entire project. The effectiveness of each style depends very much on the nature of the current problem, and you will probably want to vary your procedures as the project progresses.

3. Determine Who Should Be on the Task Force

As much as possible, individuals who are asked to join the task force should be people who

- Possess knowledge and skills relevant to the task,
- Are personally interested in the problem,
- Have, or can make, the time to devote to the task force,
- Enjoy working in groups and are effective in group settings,
- Will not dominate the meetings or decisions solely with their personality or power.

Although individual competence is important, it is not an adequate basis for constructing the project group. Equally important is the overall composition of the group. Does each member possess organizational credibility and influence relative to the problem? Are all the functional areas that will be affected by the group's work represented? The exclusion of important departments will not only generate resentment and resistance but also may reduce both the quality of the task force's recommendations and the probability that the recommendations will eventually be implemented.

A major dilemma in membership selection is whether to include persons who are likely to obstruct the group's investigations and slow down progress toward a consensus solution. Although including such individuals may reduce problem-solving efficiency, it will increase substantially the probability of their later supporting (or at least not actively opposing) the group's recommendations. Lowered efficiency in early deliberations is usually more than compensated for by a smoother implementation process. In addition, when individual resistance is based on valid information or experience, a solution that ignores the sources of that resistance is likely to be suboptimal or even unworkable.

It is vital that you be involved in the membership selection process. You may have information about prospective members that will have a direct bearing on the appropriateness of their involvement. In addition, your participation in the selection process adds your personal commitment to the group's effectiveness. Finally, your involvement in selecting task-force members provides you with another opportunity to learn about upper management's expectations for the task force.

4. Contact Prospective Members   Your first contact with each prospective task-force member is an opportunity to begin defining not only the problem the group will be addressing but also the procedures it will be using. Whenever possible, make this contact in person. Try to include the prospective member's functional boss in the same meeting so that all three of you can agree on the basic purpose of the task force and on the prospective member's level of involvement.

These first contacts also provide an opportunity for you to explore each person's current knowledge and feelings about the problem and to build a productive personal relationship if one does not already exist. This information and experience can prove invaluable as you prepare for the first full task-force meeting.

5. Prepare for the First Meeting   Because the first meeting sets the tone for all later activities, you will want to prepare a careful agenda. There are two major objectives for this first meeting:

- Reaching a common understanding of the group's task,
- Defining working procedures and relationships.

Because the most important function of the first meeting will be to define the problem and the organization's expectations for the group's output, the commissioning executives should attend the meeting if at all possible. Before the meeting, review everything you have learned about the problem and the group members with your boss.

You probably will not be able to carry out all these start-up activities as thoroughly as you would like. Time pressures, physical separation of group members, and prior relationships may prevent the kind of thorough, rational analysis these suggestions imply. In addition, the commissioning executives may find it difficult to give you a clear statement of the problem. After all, most task forces are established because the organization does not fully understand the nature of its problem.

You have to accept some of the responsibility for defining the problem. But you also have to know when to stop discussing and start doing. That is a difficult managerial judgment that you can make only within the context of a specific situation. These suggestions can get you off to a good start, but you may not be able to follow them all. Often you will have no choice; other decisions will limit your alternatives. But you can become aware of the risks you incur by omitting a preparatory step and thereby be more alert to potential future problems.

—— CONDUCTING THE FIRST MEETING

This meeting is important not only because it is the first time all task-force members will be together but also because patterns of interactions begun here will influence later group activities.

The two major objectives for this meeting are discussed here:

Reaching a Common Understanding of the Group's Task This goal is clearly the most important item on the agenda; yet in most instances, it will be the most difficult to accomplish. Few of the other members will have devoted as much time or attention to the task as you have. Until they get "up to speed" and see the problem in the same general terms that you do, they will be a group in name only.

Each manager will come to this meeting feeling a responsibility to represent his or her own department's interests. Each will interpret the problem in terms of those interests, and each will possess a unique combination of ideas and information about the problem. Furthermore, many of the group members will be feeling highly defensive, as they anticipate that other managers will blame their departments for the problems. These feelings are common and are often based on past personal experiences. If you know or suspect that such feelings exist within the group, try to find a positive way to bring them to the surface. Encourage group members to participate by expressing their opinions and offering their suggestions, but ask them to withhold judgments until all the relevant information has been heard. You can serve as a role model for other group members by asking questions that focus on facts, by maintaining strict neutrality on the issues, and by eliciting ideas from all members.

At this point the group probably does not possess enough information to achieve a deep understanding of the problem and its causes. Indeed, a lack of information and understanding is generally one of the major reasons for establishing a task force. Nevertheless, it is essential for the group to acknowledge the problem and to agree on its boundaries.

Your most difficult task at this first meeting, however, may be to prevent a premature consensus on an appropriate solution. Most experienced managers are sure they know what the problems are and what actions are required. Thus, although you are seeking some agreement on the nature of the *problem*, you do not want the group to settle on a *solution* yet.

You *do* want group members to develop a sense of their joint responsibilities and to begin considering the appropriate next steps. Be explicit about areas in which group members differ. A task-focused discussion of this kind will generate commitment to the group and its general goals, even when differences of opinion as to appropriate strategies exist and are openly recognized.

Defining Working Procedures and Relationships   The second topic for the first meeting is the question of how the group will work on its task. Among the issues that require explicit attention are the following:

- Frequency and nature of full task-force meetings,
- Structure of subgroups,
- Ground rules for communication and decision making within the task force between meetings,
- Ground rules or norms for decision making and conflict resolution,
- Schedules and deadlines for accomplishing subtasks and for completing the final report,
- Ground rules for dealing with sensitive issues; agreement on which ones require involving other managers,
- Procedures for monitoring and reporting progress to members of the task force and to functional area managers,
- Explicit processes for evaluating and modifying task-force working procedures.

Spending time on these procedural issues serves two primary purposes. First, the discussion will help group members form clear expectations concerning their projected activities and working relationships. These expectations will reduce the tensions inherent in an otherwise very unstructured situation. Second, the process of reaching agreement on procedural matters can become a model of how the task force will resolve other problems.

Resolution of these issues at the first meeting can provide all participants with a positive experience associated with the group; however, you may need to carry some of these topics over into subsequent meetings. Try to end the first meeting on a note of agreement: If you can achieve a solid consensus on some portion of these procedural matters, you will have taken a big step toward a successful project no matter how deeply divided the group is on substantive issues.

RUNNING THE TASK FORCE

Once you have completed front-end work, you should focus on keeping the project moving and on monitoring and reporting the group's progress. Although specific circumstances will vary, there are several general principles to keep in mind:

Hold Full Task-force Meetings Frequently Enough to Keep All Members Informed About Group Progress   Though each meeting should have a specific purpose, periodic meetings should be scheduled well in advance, and all members should be required to attend. A meeting can always be canceled if there is nothing substantial to discuss. However, full meetings do have an important symbolic value. They are the only time the full group is physically together, and anything said there is heard simultaneously by everyone. Very often the most valuable and creative discussions are those that evolve spontaneously in response to someone's raising a nonagenda item. For example, the most successful fund-raising project in the history of public television (the cast party following the final episode of *Upstairs, Downstairs*) grew out of two spontaneous comments during an informal staff meeting at WGBH in Boston.

Although you cannot plan that kind of creativity, you *can* create opportunities for unstructured exploratory discussions.

Unless the Task Force Is Very Small (Fewer Than 5 to 7 Members), Dividing Up into Groups Will Be Mandatory   You must manage this process carefully, however. Dividing the project into separate tasks that can be worked on simultaneously can be an efficient mechanism for achieving rapid progress. But remember that one of the virtues of the task-force approach is the synergy that results from new combinations of individuals investigating problems in areas that are unfamiliar to them. If you permit the task-force members to work only in their own areas or with persons they already know and work well with, you are throwing away an important advantage.

Of course, when managers go poking around in parts of the company that are unfamiliar to them, they may ask questions that insult or unintentionally threaten the functional managers with whom they work. Warn your group members of this danger, and then be prepared to spend some of your time telling functional managers about your group's work and smoothing ruffled feathers as they occur.

You must also recognize that working in subgroups can cause individuals to lose their overall perspective. If the task force becomes too differentiated, the various subgroups may form their own identities and develop an advocacy style of pushing for their own solutions. The more the total job is broken down for subgroup work, the more you must encourage formal intergroup sharing of problems, findings, and ideas as the project moves along.

Be Careful Not to Align Yourself Too Closely with One Position or Subgroup Too Early   This principle is particularly important if there are clearly opposing and mutually exclusive sides to the issue. Although you will eventually have to commit to a plan of action, you will serve the group most effectively by being as concerned with the problem-solving *process* as you are with the specific outcomes of that process.

Set Interim Project Deadlines and Demand Adherence to Them   When you are in charge of the schedule and know how arbitrarily some of the key checkpoints were set, it becomes far too easy to assume you can make up lost time later. No matter how arbitrary the interim deadlines are, however, if you miss them, you will miss your final deadline too.

Insistence on meeting deadlines is doubly important when the task-force members are assigned to the project only on a part-time basis. If they are continuing to carry out functional responsibilities, they will feel pressures to spend their time on tasks with immediate outcomes. The pressure to accomplish immediate tasks will always outweigh the needs of longer-range task-force projects. Part-time task-force members face a real dilemma and will be under continual stress. As the project leader, you must be prepared to spend a large portion of your time prodding group members to complete their tasks on schedule. At the same time, however, you must remain sympathetic with the legitimate needs of the functional areas and be careful not to antagonize either your members or their functional bosses. Your task will be especially delicate in situations where you have no formal authority over these part-time members or where the lines of authority are vague.

Be Sensitive to the Conflicting Loyalties Created by Belonging to the Task Force   As task-force members work together in group activities, they normally begin to develop commitments to the project and to each other. These commitments often become another source of stress, as members feel loyalties to both the task force and to their own departments. On the one hand, they continue to feel responsible for representing the interests of their functional areas, and on the other, they feel growing pressures to help the task force accomplish its goals.

Assisting the task force frequently requires group members to share confidential information with you or with other members. You must recognize the risk that this sharing involves. Whenever feasible, the source of confidential information should remain anonymous. As task-force leader you may be able to play a valuable intermediary role. But remember that once someone has entrusted you with confidential information, that person has become dependent on your integrity. If you are ever indiscreet, you are unlikely to be so trusted again, and your value to the organization will be seriously diminished.

Your Most Important Leadership Role Is That of Communicating Information Among Task-force Members and Between the Task Force and the Rest of the Organization   This communications role is time-consuming but essential to the success of the project. You must take personal responsibility for monitoring group progress, for bringing appropriate subgroups together to share information and ideas, and for reporting both progress and problems to your own boss and to the functional managers in whose areas the task force is working.

Very often your most important activities will involve listening to individual managers, passing information from one task-force member to another, and bringing together managers who must exchange or share information and ideas. Although these activities often seem inordinately time-consuming, they form the glue that binds the individual task-force members together. As individuals and subgroups pursue their investigative tasks, you will probably become the only manager who retains an overall understanding of the total project. Communicating that understanding to others and reminding them of their interdependence are critical responsibilities.

——— COMPLETING THE PROJECT

The work of an investigative task force typically culminates with a written report and a summary presentation of findings and recommendations to upper management. An implementation task force will normally have results that are more concrete to demonstrate its accomplishments, but even so, there is often a formal meeting at which the task force officially relinquishes its responsibilities to an operating group.

The written report documents the work of the task force, but its importance lies in the decision-making process it generated. In fact, the preparation of the final report can provide a structure and focus for the task force's concluding activities. You should prepare a tentative outline of this report early in the project and circulate it widely among group members. This outline can actually serve as a guide to the development of specific recommendations. The need to write the report will force the group to reach specific decisions.

Drafts of the report thus often become the basis for working out any differences remaining among the task-force members. Except in highly charged situations with major organizational consequences, you should strive to reach a group consensus before presenting any recommendations to upper management. Unless your group members agree on what actions are needed, you can hardly expect management acceptance or approval of the report.

The formal presentation of findings and recommendations to management is just as important as the task force's first meeting. The presentation should be carefully organized, with explicit attention to who will say what, in what sequence, and with what visual aids. If the recommendations are surprising, controversial, or expensive, these preparations need even greater attention.

You should brief your own boss and other key executives before the formal presentation. This briefing does not necessarily require their approval or agreement, but their advance understanding can help to prevent defensive reactions or categorical rejections of your group's recommendations. This kind of briefing can be especially important if your recommendations involve major changes in organization structure, budget allocations, or strategic focus for any of the executives who will be present at the formal presentation.

Although important, this formal presentation rarely constitutes an adequate wrap-up of the task-force project. Only if the recommendations are very straightforward and noncontroversial will the management group be able to understand and act on them at one sitting. A more-effective strategy will be to plan two meetings. In the first, you summarize the findings and recommendations and distribute the formal report. At the end of this presentation, you then schedule a second, decision-making meeting for the near future. The time period between the two meetings gives the executives an opportunity to read the report and consider its implications.

This period will be a busy time for the task-force members, who can meet individually and in subgroups with key executives to clarify the report. Only when the report has been acted upon can the task force consider its work actually finished.

▬▬ DISCUSSION QUESTIONS

1. Considering the changes taking place in the business world of the 1990s, do you think the task-force form of organization has more, less, or the same importance?
2. Describe the personality needed to manage a task force. What are some of the important qualities? What type of personality would be ill-suited to manage a task force?
3. What are the advantages and disadvantages of an in-house task force versus outside consultants? Does one seem preferable? If so, under what circumstances?
4. The reading gives four stages in the "life cycle" of a task force (e.g., starting up a task force). The reading provides management guidelines for each stage. Would you add any other guidelines?
5. Think of an instance from your professional experience when a task force might have been useful, but was never established. Why wasn't a task force used in that particular circumstance? What course of action was taken instead? Knowing what you now know, do you think that a task force would have resolved the problem more efficiently? Why or why not?

PART THREE

MANAGING ORGANIZATIONAL EFFECTIVENESS

DESIGNING ORGANIZATIONS
FOR EFFECTIVENESS

Organization Design 21

JAY W. LORSCH

This reading focuses on how managers use organization design to influence subordinates to work toward a firm's goals. It begins by describing the origins and elements of organizational contingency theory; it then examines the design issues managers face in the functional unit and in the single-business organization. The reading concludes by discussing leadership style and company culture—two other factors that play a role in how an organization influences its members.

$\mathbf{M}$anagers influence subordinates to work toward the goals of the firm in three primary ways: by personal contact (their actions and words in meetings and one-on-one sessions, their speeches, their tours of the plant); by substantive decisions about the allocation of resources; and by decisions about the definition of jobs, their arrangement on organization charts, measurement-and-reward schemes, selection criteria for personnel, and so forth. The latter set of decisions is the focus of this reading and is referred to as organization design.

To be more precise, the *organization design* consists of the structure, rewards, and measurement practices intended to direct members' behavior toward the organization's goals, as well as the criteria used to select persons for the organization. Structure means the pattern of job definition, authority, and communication relationships represented in organization charts, position descriptions, and so on. Rewards refer to financial compensation and benefits as well as career opportunities, interesting work, and even meaningful personal relationships. The criteria that managers use to select new employees are also important. Measurement includes the control and management-information system—that is, the procedures by which plans are made and results are measured and reported.

How much time and effort managers devote to decisions about these design elements depends upon the size of the firm and their own level in the hierarchy. As managers move up in the hierarchy, and/or as the size of their organization grows, they become more concerned with issues of organization design. With more subordinates, managers are less able to rely on personal contact to influence subordinates; therefore, they have to rely more on the organization-design elements of structure, rewards, measurement, and selection criteria. The focus here is more on issues of structure than on the other design elements.

───── THE GOALS OF ORGANIZATION DESIGN

Managers are concerned with three related goals when they make design decisions:

1. To create an organization design that provides a permanent setting in which managers can influence individuals to do their particular jobs.
2. To achieve a pattern of collaborative effort among individual employees, which is necessary for successful operations.
3. To create an organization that is cost effective—one that achieves the first two goals with a minimum of duplication of effort, payroll costs, and so on.

───── A BRIEF HISTORICAL PERSPECTIVE

Managers' concerns with these goals and the issues of organization design are not new. Many of the earliest management writers—Fayol, Urwick, Gulick—wrote about these matters in the first half of the twentieth century. What is new, however, is the increased understanding of organizations and their operations. Those early writers generalized from their own experiences as practitioners in a few basic industries—such as railroads, mining, and automobiles—and concluded that the principles they learned in those industries were applicable to other industries at other points in time. Furthermore, they believed that people are motivated solely by money. Researchers and practitioners since then have learned that employees' needs at work are more varied and complex. The goals of organization design discussed earlier are based on this recognition of the full range of rewards that motivate people to work. More recent studies have also indicated that there is no one best way for a firm to organize; the appropriate organizational form depends upon the human and business situation facing the firm.

Although it is easy to find flaws in the ideas of early management writers, it has not been easy for managers to discard the so-called principles that those early authors laid down: the span of control should be between six and nine subordinates; one boss for each man; authority must equal responsibility; the line does, the staff advises; and so on. Such statements have become part of the folklore of management, at least in the United States. Thus, many managers, when confronted with an organization-design decision, intuitively fall back on those early ideas. This tendency is not surprising, because the simplicity of the ideas gives them an intuitive appeal. It is a dangerous practice, however, because the principles ignore the infinitely varied and complex human, technological, and market conditions for which organizations must be designed. Recent managerial experience and organizational research have provided an approach for thinking about organization-design issues.

THE CONTINGENCY APPROACH

This approach emphasizes that the characteristics of an organization are contingent upon the nature of the environment in which it operates, the tasks that members must perform to accomplish the firm's strategy in this environment, and the psychological characteristics of the members.

DEFINITIONS

To be more precise, four terms need to be defined:

1. *Environment* refers to the forces and objects outside the firm with which its members must deal to achieve the organization's purposes. These may include competitors' actions, customer requirements, financial constraints, scientific and technological knowledge, and so forth. They are information that must be considered when making and implementing decisions inside the organization.
2. The organization's *strategy* is a statement of the environment(s) or business(es) relevant to the organization, the purposes of the organization within that context, and the specific means for achieving these goals. In a sense, then, the strategy defines the environment in which an organization operates. A strategy may be explicitly stated and even written down, or it may simply exist as an implicit idea based on the actions of the organization's managers over time.
3. *Task* refers to the activities that members must perform to achieve the organization's strategic goals in a particular environment. This reading generally uses task to refer to the activities of a particular set of individuals in dealing with the environment— that is, the task of a sales unit or the task of division general managers, and so on.
4. *Psychological characteristics of members* are the factors in an individual's personality that lead him or her to behave in a consistent fashion over time. It is not necessary to debate here whether these should be labeled needs, values, interests, or all three. The important point is that different individuals have different characteristics, and organization-design decisions must take these differences into account.

EXHIBIT 1
The Concept of Fit

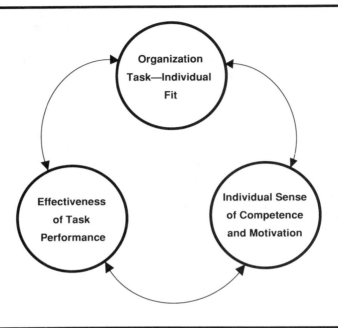

FIT

The first concept to be discussed is *fit*. If there is a three-way fit between an individual's psychological makeup, the nature of the task he or she is performing, and the organization design, the individual will be motivated to perform that task effectively (see *Exhibit 1*). Two examples illustrate the point:

> A production supervisor, such as a foreman, has a job in which his activities are well defined by the technology and product specifications. In essence, his job is to make sure that his subordinates do the same thing well today that they did yesterday. In this sense, the work is highly certain and predictable. Results here can be measured on a daily or possibly more frequent basis. This supervisor has a bachelor's degree in industrial engineering. He likes working with his supervisor, who provides him with clear directions and enjoys his frequent contact with other supervisors. The routine and the predictable work are also attractive to him. In fact, he is upset by too much ambiguity and confusion. For this manager and his colleagues, given their predictable tasks, an organization design that emphasizes tight control and procedures is appropriate. Tight spans of supervisory control, well-specified operating procedures, and specific and frequent measurement of results make sense in this situation.

A group leader in a research laboratory in a consumer products company has a job where results are *not* highly predictable. Her subordinates, who are Ph.D.'s, and their technical assistants are working on problems in food technology. Their progress is hard to measure, and meaningful results may take months or even years. The group leader, who is a Ph.D. biochemist herself, shares many personal characteristics with her subordinates. She likes to work with minimum direction and maximum autonomy and prefers to work alone. She also likes to work on complex and uncertain problems. These tasks and personal characteristics require an organization design with a wide span of management control and with infrequent measurement in relation to general progress. Detailed procedures, job descriptions, and so forth, are out of place here because so little of the work can be preprogrammed. An organization design that has these characteristics should be motivating for this technical manager, as well as her subordinates, and it should also lead to effective results for the laboratory.

As these two examples and *Exhibit 1* illustrate, the three-way fit produces two outcomes—motivation for the individual and performance for the organization. These results are interconnected. As individuals perform their jobs well and receive feedback, their needs for mastery are satisfied, which in turn encourages them to continue working to maintain these positive feelings. There is also a fit required between individual and task characteristics—that is, to be effective, the individual must have interests, skills, and needs that are consistent with the work required. One way to ensure this fit is to select personnel using criteria based on the need for fit. Finally, such a fit also enables the individual to achieve other goals, such as earning money, having an appropriate amount of social contact, and so on.

DIFFERENTIATION

The concept of *differentiation* follows from the notion of fit. It can be defined as the differences among the several units of the organization in organization design and members' behavior. These differences arise because of the variety of tasks various organizational units must accomplish to cope successfully with the firm's total environment. As each unit's organization is designed to achieve a fit with its task and the characteristics of its members, it becomes differentiated from the other units with their own tasks and members; how differentiated depends upon how similar the tasks of the several units are and how similar their members are.

Differentiation has positive and negative consequences simultaneously. Because differentiation stems from the fact that the several units in an organization have achieved a fit with their task and human situations—and this leads to motivation and performance—some degree of differentiation is critical to the effective functioning of organizations. This differentiation among units results from differences in their tasks or members and is therefore appropriate. (Differentiation, of course, can result from management action that is inappropriate to the units' tasks and members; in this instance, too much differentiation might be a liability.) The negative side is that the greater the differentiation among units of an organization, the more difficult it becomes for members to communicate across unit boundaries. For example, a factory supervisor may have great difficulty dealing with a laboratory group leader: One thinks in the short term, the other in the long term; one is concerned with costs and productivity, the other with innovation and knowledge building; one believes in an orderly unambiguous organization, the other relishes ambiguity and autonomy, and so on. Such differences between the individuals impede their understanding of each other's concerns and will probably lead to conflicting ideas about how to solve mutual problems. The fact that differentiation leads to such conflicts is connected to the third concept—integration.

INTEGRATION

Integration is the state of collaboration among organizational units. Integration usually manifests itself in specific conversations between the representatives of units. In thinking about organization design, however, it is possible and necessary to generalize about the state of integration required for the organization to be effective. To do this, we must consider various aspects of integration.

The first is the number and patterns of units that must collaborate to achieve the organization's purposes. In *Organizations in Action*, Thompson identifies one useful way to think about these patterns (see *Exhibit 2*).[1] *Pooled integration* is the simplest pattern, where the various subsidiary units (B,C,D) have no need for integration among themselves. They are all linked together only through their contact with the central unit (A). A holding company typically has this pattern of integration among its major components. *Sequential integration* is where each unit must integrate its activities only with units that precede or follow it in a process or task flow. Factories with work flow across departmental lines provide a good example of this pattern. *Reciprocal integration* means that collaboration is in both directions among all units; for this reason it is the most complex pattern. The integration required among marketing, research development, and manufacturing personnel in developing new products often follows this pattern. As one moves from the pooled to the sequential to the reciprocal pattern, achieving integration becomes more difficult.

---

1. James D. Thompson, *Organizations in Action* (New York: McGraw-Hill, 1967), p. 54.

EXHIBIT 2
Patterns of Required Integration

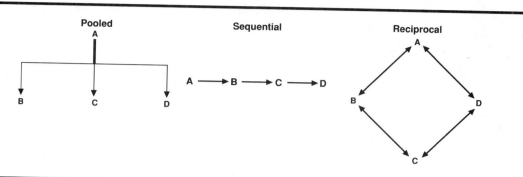

Note: These diagrams are the author's concepts based on Thompson's ideas.

Although this way of thinking can be useful, it is important to recognize that in the real world these pure types rarely exist.

A second aspect of integration is the frequency with which collaboration is necessary. For example, a sales organization usually requires a relatively low frequency of integration among various regional units. The national sales manager may want the regional units to collaborate occasionally in a national program, but generally the regions conduct their sales activity independently. In contrast, consider the electronic engineering and power systems departments of an aerospace firm that is trying to develop a new rocket for NASA. These engineers need to be in frequent contact across departmental lines to make certain that the components they are each developing for the total system will work in harmony.

Closely connected to the frequency of integration required is the importance of achieving it, but these two aspects are not necessarily identical. For example, the sales and manufacturing departments may meet only semiannually to develop an integrated production schedule, but the success of this decision making may have a major impact on the firm's success.

Another aspect of integration that must be considered in thinking about design issues is the certainty and predictability of the information involved. If the matters requiring integration are highly predictable, the managers can use plans and preestablished procedures to achieve integration; then, only infrequent face-to-face contact is necessary. If the information is uncertain and complex, however, more face-to-face contact, as in the aerospace example, may be necessary.

As the examples suggest, organization design can be used to achieve integration in several ways—for example, management hierarchy, regular meetings, coordinating roles such as product or program managers, incentives that reward integrative behavior, and so forth. Managers do have a choice about how much they orient their organization-design decisions to

EXHIBIT 3
Factors Affecting the Difficulty of Achieving Integration

DIFFICULTY OF ACHIEVING INTEGRATION	*LOW*	*HIGH*
Degree of differentiation	Small	Large
Number of units requiring integration	Few	Many
Pattern of integration	Pooled	Reciprocal
Frequency of integration required	Infrequent contact	Frequent contact daily or more often
Importance of integration to organization's strategy	Marginal	Critical
Complexity and uncertainty of information	Simple and highly certain	Uncertain and highly complex

achieving integration. To understand the appropriate choice, they need to answer the questions suggested by the factors just discussed:

- How many units require integration and in what pattern?
- How frequently is integration required?
- How important is integration among any set of these units?
- How complex and uncertain is the information being considered?

As *Exhibit 3* illustrates, the answers to these questions can be a rough guide to the difficulty of achieving the necessary integration and therefore to the proper mix of design elements devoted to achieving integration. For example, the more units that must be integrated and the more they are involved in reciprocal relationships, the more the organization design must provide mechanisms, such as teams' coordinating roles, plans, and so forth, to facilitate this integration. This, of course, assumes that achieving integration is important to the company's goals. Whether face-to-face contact or a formal planning scheme is the better means to achieve this integration depends on the complexity and uncertainty of the information that must be handled. If the data are relatively simple and predictable, a predetermined plan might be suitable, but if the information is more uncertain and complex, the organization design will have to provide mechanisms for integration that encourage more face-to-face contact.

Exhibit 3 includes one other issue that affects the difficulty of achieving integration—the degree of differentiation among units. The more differentiated the units are, the more difficult it becomes to achieve integration. Because differentiation and integration have this complex relationship, they are important to understand as tools for thinking about organization design. Together with the concept of fit, they give managers powerful tools for analyzing specific organization-design problems.

In dealing with organization-design issues, the suggested approach involves three steps. First, managers need to use the concepts of fit, differentiation, and integration to understand and assess what the environmental and human situations require of their organization. Second, they need to make design choices to meet these requirements. Finally, they need to consider how to implement necessary changes. (This reading emphasizes the first two steps.)

To illustrate how managers can deal with these diagnosis and design steps, the reading next focuses on some of the design issues managers face at two organizational levels—the functional unit and the single-business organization. This choice of examples is made for two reasons. First, most business firms build their organizations from functional units up. Second, managers at each of these levels of organization are faced with different design problems; therefore, the conceptual ideas discussed earlier must be applied somewhat differently at each level.

ORGANIZATION DESIGN IN FUNCTIONAL UNITS

Functional units are not only the basic building blocks on which larger organizations are constructed but also the home of most organization members. In fact, functional units are so pervasive in the business world that they have become institutionalized in the specialized training offered by business administration and engineering schools. Undergraduates and graduate students become specialized; they enter organizations with careers in these function areas as their goals. The average employee may spend an entire career in one function, but even the rising star on a fast career track to general management is likely to spend his or her early years in one function.

EMPLOYEE MOTIVATION

One of the major issues facing a functional manager is to create an organization design that provides a viable set of rewards for subordinates, including compensation and benefits, professionally stimulating work, and meaningful career opportunities. The concept of fit among task and individual characteristics and organization design is a useful way of thinking about how to create a psychological contract acceptable to both the members of a functional unit and the employing organization. It is a potent tool to ensure that the measurements, rewards, and structure of a unit together accomplish the goal of motivating employees to work toward the purposes of the firm.

DIVISION OF WORK

Another important aspect of achieving such a fit is the question of job design and the division of work within the function. Earlier, the reading examined job-design issues as they affected motivation. Job-design decisions also have an important bearing upon a second design goal—creating a cost-effective organization. For example, designing sales jobs to reduce an employee's travel time creates a more cost-effective organization; similarly, adding a second and/or third shift to a factory can ensure maximum machine utilization and lower manufacturing costs. As these examples suggest, the subunits within a function can be created on the basis of occupational specialty, time of workday, or territorial responsibility. The major rationale for occupationally based units is to maintain a differentiated home for specialized expertise. The major reason for creating geographic or temporal subunits is to bring down costs, as the prior examples also suggest.

Regardless of the basis for dividing work, differences in behavior and organization design may exist among members of different subunits within the same function. For example, the controller's function in many firms is made up of a diverse set of subunits, ranging from computer programmers and systems analysts dealing with relatively complex problem-solving tasks to clerical operations with routine and repetitive tasks. Similarly, within a manufacturing function, there are not only line manufacturing supervisors but also industrial engineers, production schedulers, quality control specialists, computer programmers, and so on. Although these different specialists all share some goals and behavior patterns common to their function, they may also have differentiated approaches to these issues, and their tasks and personal characteristics may make a somewhat different organization design appropriate. As functional managers consider the issues of job design and division of work, they must think about achieving a fit that will lead to a motivated and efficient organization. They should also consider how this will affect differentiation within the function and the potential difficulties of achieving integration.

ACHIEVING INTEGRATION

Such difficulties can be managed if the organization design provides a way of achieving integration among those subunits that must work together. Within most functional units the primary device for this is the management hierarchy. The hierarchy is not only a mechanism for directing the activities of individual subunits but also a means for achieving the integration required within the function. For example, if the industrial engineers and mechanical engineers within a manufacturing function have difficulty agreeing upon the production methods for a new product, their common boss would be expected to resolve the dispute.

EXHIBIT 4
Stratified Structures—Product Divisions' Structure

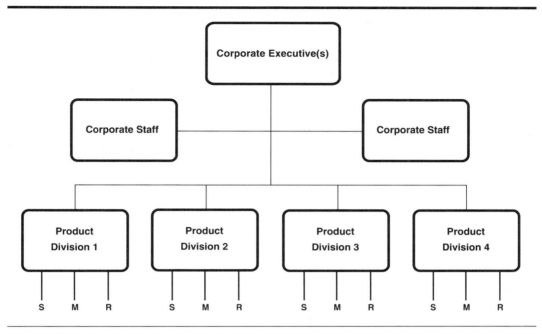

Note: S = Sales; M = Manufacturing; R = Research

Although the management hierarchy is usually capable of handling the information and decision making required for integration within a function, occasionally other means are also necessary. These other means must be employed when the difficulty of achieving integration becomes too great for the hierarchy to manage. This can happen because of any combination of factors mentioned previously and displayed in *Exhibit 4*. Perhaps the hierarchy must be supplemented because the impending start-up of a new-generation computer has increased the need for integrating a controller function; therefore, a special project team is created. Perhaps new pricing regulations make it necessary to create a new position of pricing coordinator on the national sales manager's staff to coordinate pricing decisions across all regions.

APPLYING DESIGN TOOLS

The specific issues that have been discussed show how the three major concepts of fit, differentiation, and integration can help functional managers think about the design problems they face. Before considering how these concepts can be used in single-business organizations, two other points, which apply to all that follows, should be emphasized:

1. *Creative invention can be very useful in solving design problems once they are understood.* An example of this is a factory that experienced difficulty with the integration of its three shifts, each of which operated seven days a week. The management tried all the standard remedies—log books, foremen meeting before the shift, the factory superintendent visiting all shifts, and so on. A more careful review revealed that the problem had arisen because foremen did not have time to grasp the situation on the production floor and then direct their workers. The solution was to put the foremen on a schedule that brought them into work early and allowed them to leave two hours before their subordinates. Thus, the foremen were on a schedule that allowed them time to grasp the problems of the prior shift before a new shift started. This simple scheduling change enabled the management hierarchy to become an effective integrative tool. Such a solution may seem obvious in retrospect; however, given the number of plants that have struggled with the same issue, it is clear that creativity is a necessary ingredient in handling such organizational issues.

2. *The design elements of structure, measurement, and reward need to be thought of as a package.* Changes in one may have to be accompanied by changes in others. If they do not give consistent signals to employees about what management expects, the results can range from confusion to chaos.

———— ORGANIZING THE SINGLE BUSINESS

Single-business organizations are those organizations that are in one primary business. They may be the product division of a multibusiness firm, or they may be a financially independent enterprise. In either case, the organization consists of a set of interrelated functional units whose activities aim at developing, producing, and marketing a common product or service to a particular set of customers.

DIFFERENTIATION OF FUNCTIONS

Because each function needs to achieve a fit with its particular task and human situation to be effective, one of the design issues facing managers of single-business organizations is to maintain and/or achieve the degree of differentiation among functions that is appropriate to their several tasks. If functional managers are allowed to handle the design issues facing them without interference, the necessary differentiation might be a natural consequence of their independent actions. The general managers of single businesses often feel compelled, however, to limit such independent action on the part of their functional managers for two reasons. First, they become concerned about the issue of equity and fairness across functions. Second, uniformity and standardization of practice make it easier for the manager to administer and be certain of what is happening in the organization. Although it is important to maintain a sense of equity in compensation and benefits among various occupational groups in an organization, too much emphasis on standardization can reduce differentiation and harm the organization's effectiveness.

For example, higher management often imposes the same rigid working hours on research scientists that are required of production personnel. Coming and going on time makes sense when the personnel involved are operating a highly interdependent factory where scheduling is critical. In the case of research scientists, however, their problem solving and creative activity does not adhere to any schedule. Thus, the focus on regular hours is inappropriate, and the scientist may become annoyed with such unnecessary rules. The scientist's attitude is then expressed: "If they are so insistent about my being here on time, I'll be sure to quit on time. No more working at night or on weekends to finish experiments." This example is typical of the problems managers can encounter if they do not understand the importance of maintaining differentiation among the functions in their business.

The amount of differentiation required among functions will vary, of course, depending upon the nature of the organization's environment. In most cases, however, the differences across functions will be much more pronounced than those within functional units. The following examples may help the reader understand the range of such cross-functional differentiation.

As an example of minimal differentiation required across functions, consider a firm in the business of producing corrugated containers—boxes or cartons. Only two major functions are involved in this business—selling and manufacturing—and they have different goals: The sales personnel focus on prompt customer delivery and high quality as well as on competitive pricing. The manufacturing managers are concerned with low cost and want to avoid quality and delivery requirements that adversely affect costs. Beyond these varying goals, there are few differences between these two functions. Both are focused on short-term results and are involved in relatively predictable tasks. Thus, a more formal organization design and directive leadership would make sense for both production and sales personnel.

Next, consider a business requiring greater amounts of differentiation—a basic plastic materials business (polystyrene, polyvinylchloride). Here the functions are sales, manufacturing, research, and technical services. The manufacturing personnel, like those in the previous example, are primarily concerned with near-term results in the areas of cost and quality. But because they are operating a more capital-intensive technology, they may be less flexible than their counterparts in other businesses about interrupting product flows or process changes. The sales personnel are concerned with customer relations, competitive pricing, and so forth. Again, their focus is largely on the near term, but they also attend to the future and new products. The technical-services group focuses on providing technical service to the customer in support of the sales force, and thus is concerned with immediate results. At the same time, this group has responsibility for applied research aimed at developing new and improved products and processes; therefore, it also may be focused on the long term. Members of the research unit are involved in more basic research—understanding the structure of the materials and using this understanding to improve existing products and processes and develop entirely new ones. Their time horizon may extend over several years. These units will need widely different organization designs and management styles, which allow each to match its highly differentiated task and members.

These examples demonstrate the range of differences that occurs in different businesses. Although they are all drawn from manufacturing enterprises, similar examples can be found in service industries. Of course, these illustrations are overly simplified. The financial function has been omitted, for example, even though any joint decision involving the functions mentioned will also involve discussions of the appropriate allocation of financial resources.

Using these concepts, managers need to look at each function and determine what characteristics of organization design and behavior are necessary for that function to be performed, and what will motivate the individuals who work in it. From this analysis of each function, the pattern of differences among the functions will become apparent. These questions can be useful when making such an analysis:

- What are the goals that each unit should focus upon?
- What is the time period for each unit to obtain some definitive feedback about the results of its members' efforts?
- What pattern of leadership behavior is appropriate for each unit?
- What pattern of structure, measurement, and rewards will encourage behavior directed toward the goals, time horizon, and other aspects of the unit's task, while also meeting the members' personal expectations?

If managers concern themselves with how much differentiation they want to encourage in their organizations, they will find a useful starting point in considering these questions.

GROUPING FUNCTIONS

The issue of differentiation has an important bearing on another design issue that concerns the manager of a single-business organization—what functions to group together under a common manager. In thinking about this issue, like other design questions, managers often tend to rely on conventional wisdom and/or to emulate what other firms do.

Managers consider grouping activities together for two essential reasons: either they want to get similar activities under a manager who understands them or they want to place activities requiring close integration under one manager to facilitate collaboration. Therefore, the concepts of differentiation and integration can be helpful tools for such decisions. Just by being aware of these concepts, one is forced to ask, "Am I considering grouping these activities together because I want to encourage integration among them, or because they are similar (not highly differentiated), or for both reasons?" If the answer to this question is "both," clearly the decision to group activities together is a sound and easy one. However, if the answer to all parts of the question is "no," one does not want to group the units together.

The more frequently encountered and more difficult problems occur with low differentiation and few requirements for integration or with a large amount of differentiation but also a great need for integration. Here, the organizational designer must make a trade-off about what is to be accomplished. Should the hierarchy be used to achieve integration in this instance? Or should similar activities be grouped together, perhaps facilitating their differentiation from other activities and certainly easing the job of supervisors? In the latter instance, other means would have to be found to achieve integration between the units grouped together and those parts of the organization with which they needed to be integrated.

INTEGRATION OF FUNCTIONS

Using the hierarchy is only one of several means to facilitate integration. Even in single-business units, however, the hierarchy is often the fundamental mechanism for achieving integration. In fact, in businesses with low differentiation and relatively simple integrative requirements (e.g., the corrugated container business), the hierarchy may be the only integrative device necessary. As the requirements for differentiation and integration become greater, however, other integrative devices must supplement the hierarchy. Thus, greater differentiation and a more complex requirement for integration might call for product managers who play an integrating role, and/or a management committee made up of the heads of the several functions.

As with most organization-design issues, there are no simple rules to define what mix of integrative devices is appropriate in a particular situation. Thinking of an organization as a system for taking in bits of information from the business environment and then combining the information to reach and implement decisions can help clarify when certain integrative devices will be appropriate. From this perspective, a review of the factors identified in *Exhibit 3* that affect the difficulty of achieving integration follows:

- Number of units requiring integration,
- Pattern of integration (pooled, sequential, reciprocal),
- Frequency of integration required,
- Importance of integration to organizational results,
- Complexity and uncertainty of information,
- Degree of differentiation.

All of these factors, in theory, could affect the flow of information among functional units, which in turn would affect the difficulty of achieving integration. The more problems these factors suggest, the more supplements the hierarchy will need. Just what form these other devices should take will depend upon the frequency of integration required and the complexity and uncertainty of information. Both of these factors, which frequently are closely connected, will have important influence on whether face-to-face contact is necessary to achieve integration or whether predetermined plans, schedules, and so on, once arrived at, will allow units to operate in an integrated fashion without such direct contact.

There are two types of integrative devices that allow face-to-face contact:

1. *Integrating roles* include positions such as product managers, brand managers, program managers, project managers, account executives, and so on. A major responsibility of these employees is to integrate their activities with those of their peers in other functions. Such an approach makes sense when the information is sufficiently certain and simple so that one person can achieve integration with his or her counterparts on a one-to-one basis.
2. *Cross-functional groups of managers* may be labeled teams, committees, task forces, and so on. Such groups make sense as integrative devices when the information is so complex and uncertain that representatives from the several functions need to sit down together to understand each other's data and reach joint decisions.

Individual integrating positions and cross-functional groups are not mutually exclusive. In some organizations, where the requirements for integration are particularly acute, both devices are used simultaneously. Another reason for establishing a cross-functional group, in addition to an individual integrating role, is that the group builds commitment to the success of integrated effort among the functional specialists assigned to it. For example, artists, copywriters, market information specialists, and others assigned to an account team in an advertising agency become concerned with the overall goals of serving the account, in addition to their own particular functions.

Besides these structural devices, reward and measurement practices can also be utilized to encourage integration. The most common example of this is tying the compensation of functional executives not just to the results of their function but also to business profits.

—— CULTURE AND LEADERSHIP STYLE—THE MISSING LINKS

This reading has used three major concepts—fit, differentiation, and integration—to consider organization-design issues. The focus has been on designing organizations to be consistent with the environment, strategy, and tasks of the organization on the one hand, and the members' characteristics on the other. Such an emphasis is consistent with the present state of knowledge (see *Exhibit 5*). The clearest knowledge exists about the relationship between these factors and organization design. Even in these areas, however, knowledge is limited, and there is still room for managerial judgment and creativity. The shaded area of *Exhibit 5* includes two other major factors about which much less is known but which also must be considered if the organization-design variables are to have their intended impact on members' behavior. In a broad sense the organization design must also be compatible with the style and experience of top management and the company's traditional culture.

MANAGERIAL STYLE

The manager in charge of any organization has a persistent style of leading others with which he or she is comfortable and presumably has had some success. This style is a direct outgrowth of his or her personality and is not likely to be altered easily. Therefore, although there has been little

EXHIBIT 5
Organization-Design Considerations

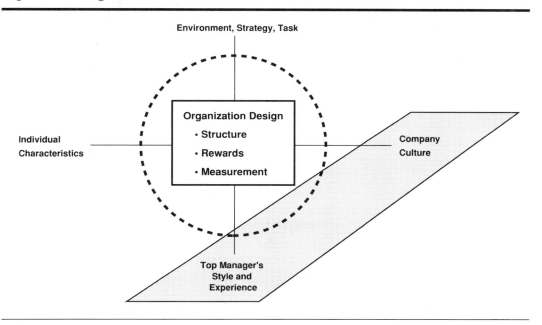

Note: Shading indicates those areas where little systematic research has been completed.

systematic research in this direction, it seems clear that whatever design choices are made must not only fit the external conditions facing the firm and the expectations of its members but also be consistent with the style of the person(s) leading the organization.

The organization design must also be compatible with the experience and talents of the top manager(s). The organization designer should start by using the ideas discussed here; however, the resulting design may have to be altered to accommodate the strengths and weaknesses of available top managers. This approach is preferable to the alternative—tailoring the organization to the style and experience of top managers with little or no regard to the other factors.

COMPANY CULTURE

Company culture consists of the shared implicit and explicit assumptions that members make about what is legitimate behavior in the organization. For example, some organizations place a value on being self-reliant and making decisions alone. Others place more emphasis on holding meetings to reach decisions. As a manager in one such company said, "Here, work is attending meetings." The culture includes not only such norms about how people should behave but also the values they are expected to hold. Further, it includes general understandings about the corporate pecking order. For example, in some companies the technical-research people have high status and influence, while in other firms the product manager reigns. Similarly, in some companies the president of a particular division is understood to be the heir apparent to the presidency of the corporation, and others treat him or her with the deference due such status. Although such expectations are not written down in procedure manuals or drawn on organization charts, they can have an important impact on people's behavior in a particular company. Some researchers have labeled such sets of expectations as the informal organization. This label may suggest, however, that there is a choice between the formal and informal organization and that these organizations are in opposition. In fact, the opposite appears to be true: Organization-design changes can have more immediate impact if they are consistent with the existing culture. Of course, changing the organization design in a way that is inconsistent with the existing culture can be one way of trying to bring about change in an organization's culture, but such efforts are likely to encounter stiff resistance from organization members.

—— **DISCUSSION QUESTIONS**

1. The reading describes the concept of fit and gives two examples of successful fits. Give an example from your personal experience of a fit that worked. Give an example of one that didn't work. Using the examples in the reading as a guide, provide specifics about what worked and didn't work for you.

2. Name other design issues besides those discussed in this reading that you feel are important or that you have experienced in your professional life.

3. Are design issues always under the control of management? Give an example from your experience in which design was not responsive to management. What are the implications of such situations for company managers?

4. Identify social issues that have surfaced in the 1980s that have had an effect on organization design. Suggest others that may surface in the 1990s.

22   Organization Design: Fashion or Fit?

HENRY MINTZBERG

This reading argues that many organizations fall into one of five configurations: the simple structure, the machine bureaucracy, the professional bureaucracy, the divisionalized form, and the adhocracy. When managers and organizational designers try to mix and match elements of different configurations, they may emerge with a misfit—an organization whose design is no longer suited to its task. The key to organizational design, says the author, is consistency and coherence. He concludes by considering how the five configurations can serve as tools in diagnosing organizational problems.

- **A** conglomerate takes over a small manufacturer and tries to impose budgets, plans, organizational charts, and untold systems on it. The result: declining sales and product innovation—and near bankruptcy—until the division managers buy back the company and promptly turn it around.
- Consultants make constant offers to introduce the latest management techniques. Years ago LRP and OD were in style, later QWL and ZBB.
- A government sends in its analysts to rationalize, standardize, and formalize citywide school systems, hospitals, and welfare agencies. The results are devastating.

These incidents suggest that a great many problems in organizational design stem from the assumption that organizations are all alike: mere collections of component parts to which elements of structure can be added and deleted at will, a sort of organizational bazaar.

The opposite assumption is that effective organizations achieve a coherence among their component parts, that they do not change one element without considering the consequences to all of the others. Spans of control, degrees of job enlargement, forms of decentralization, planning systems, and matrix structure should not be picked and chosen at random. Rather, they should be selected according to internally consistent groupings. And these groupings should be consistent with the situation of the organization—its age and size, the conditions of the industry in which it operates, and its production technology. In essence, like all phenomena from atoms to stars, the characteristics of organizations fall into natural clusters, or *configurations*. When these characteristics are mismatched—when the wrong ones are put together—the organization does not function effectively, does not achieve a natural harmony.

If managers are to design effective organizations, they need to pay attention to the fit.

If we look at the enormous amount of research on organizational structuring in light of this idea, a lot of the confusion falls away and a striking convergence is revealed. Specifically, five clear configurations emerge that are distinct in their structures, in the situations in which they are found, and even in the periods of history in which they first developed. They are the simple structure, machine bureaucracy, professional bureaucracy, divisionalized form, and adhocracy.

DERIVING THE CONFIGURATIONS

An adaptable picture of five component parts (see part A, *Exhibit 1*) descibes the five configurations. An organization begins with a person who has an idea. This person forms the strategic apex or top management. He or she hires people to do the basic work of the organization, in what can be called the operating core. As the organization grows, it acquires intermediate managers between the chief executive and the workers. These managers form the middle line. The organization may also find that it needs two kinds of staff personnel. First are the analysts who design systems concerned with the formal planning and control of the work; they form the technostructure. Second is the support staff, providing indirect services to the rest of the organization—everything from the cafeteria and the mail room to the public relations department and the legal counsel.

These five parts together make the whole organization (see part B, *Exhibit 1*). Not all organizations need all of these parts. Some use few and are simple, others combine all in rather complex ways. The central purpose of structure is to coordinate the work divided in a variety of ways; how that coordination is achieved—by whom and with what—dictates what the organization will look like (see *Exhibit 2*):

- In the simplest case, coordination is achieved at the strategic apex by direct supervision—the chief executive officer gives the orders. The configuration called *simple structure* emerges, with a minimum of staff and middle line.
- When coordination depends on the *standardization of work,* an organization's entire administrative structure—especially its technostructure, which designs the standards—needs to be elaborated. This gives rise to the configuration called *machine bureaucracy.*
- When, instead, coordination is through the *standardization of skills* of its employees, the organization needs highly trained professionals in its operating core and considerable support staff to back them up. Neither its technostructure nor its middle line is very elaborate. The resulting configuration is called *professional bureaucracy.*

- Organizations will sometimes be divided into parallel operating units, allowing autonomy to the middle-line managers of each, with coordination achieved through the *standardization of outputs* (including performance) of these units. The configuration called the *divisionalized form* emerges.
- Finally, the most complex organizations engage sophisticated specialists, especially in their support staffs, and require them to combine their efforts in project teams coordinated by *mutual adjustment*. This results in the *adhocracy* configuration, in which line and staff as well as a number of other distinctions tend to break down.

The elements of structure include the following:

- Specialization of tasks.
- Formalization of procedures (job descriptions, rules, and so forth).

EXHIBIT 1
The Five Basic Parts of the Organization

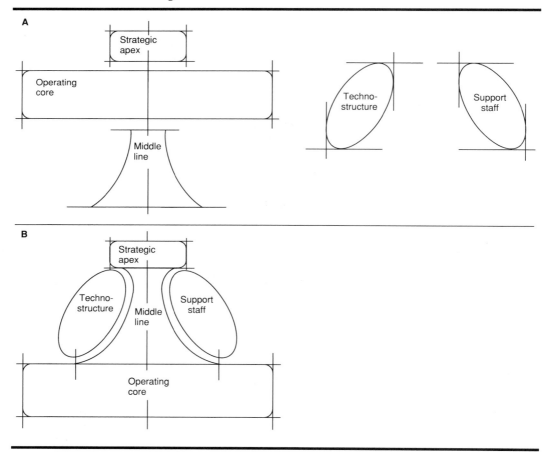

- Formal training and indoctrination required for the job.
- Grouping of units (notably by function performed or market served).
- Size of each of the units (that is, the span of control of its manager).
- Action planning and performance control systems.
- Liaison devices, such as task forces, integrating managers, and matrix structure.

EXHIBIT 2
The Five Configurations

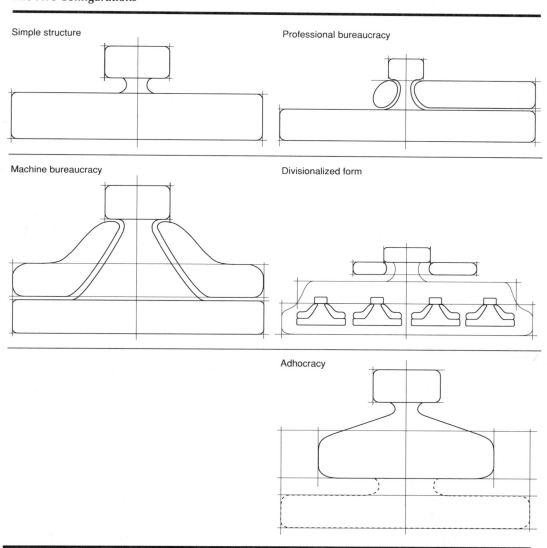

- Delegation of power down the chain of authority (called *vertical decentralization*).
- Delegation of power out from that chain of authority to nonmanagers (called *horizontal decentralization*).

I describe how all of these elements cluster into the five configurations in the sections that follow and summarize these descriptions in *Exhibit 3,* where all the elements are displayed in relation to the configurations. In the discussion of each configuration, it should become evident how all of its elements of structure and situation form themselves into a tightly knit, highly cohesive package. No one element determines the others; rather, all are locked together to form an integrated system.

SIMPLE STRUCTURE

The name tells all, and *Exhibit 2* shows all. The structure is simple—not much more than one large unit consisting of one or a few top managers and a group of operators who do the basic work. The most common simple structure is, of course, the classic entrepreneurial company.

What characterizes this configuration above all is what is missing. Little of its behavior is standardized or formalized, and minimal use is made of planning, training, or the liaison devices. The absence of standardization means that the organization has little need for staff analysts. Few middle-line managers are hired because so much of the coordination is achieved at the strategic apex by direct supervision. That is where the real power in this configuration lies. Even the support staff is minimized to keep the structure lean and flexible—simple structures would rather buy than make.

The organization must be flexible because it operates in a dynamic environment, often by choice because that is the one place it can outmaneuver the bureaucracies. And that environment must be simple, as must the organization's system of production, so that the chief executive can retain highly centralized control. In turn, centralized control makes the simple structure ideal for rapid, flexible innovation, at least of the simple kind. With the right chief executive, the organization can turn on a dime and run circles around the slower-moving bureaucracies. That is why so much innovation comes not from the giant mass producers but from small entrepreneurial companies. But where complex forms of innovation are required, the simple structure falters because of its centralization. As we shall see, that kind of innovation requires another configuration, one that engages highly trained specialists and gives them considerable power.

Simple structures are often young and small, in part because aging and growth encourage them to bureaucratize but also because their vulnerability causes many of them to fail. They never get a chance to grow old and large. One heart attack can wipe them out—as can a chief executive so obsessed with innovation that he or she forgets about the operations, or vice versa. The corporate landscape is littered with the wrecks of entrepreneurial companies whose leaders encouraged growth and mass production yet could never accept the transition to bureaucratic forms of structure that these changes required. Yet some simple structures have managed to grow very large under the tight control of clever, autocratic leaders, the most famous example being the Ford Motor Co. in the later years of its founder.

Almost all organizations begin their lives as simple structures, granting their founding chief executives considerable latitude to set them up. And most revert to simple structure—no matter how large or what other configuration normally fits their needs—when they face extreme pressure or hostility in their environment. In other words, systems and procedures are suspended as power reverts to the chief executive to give him or her a chance to set things right.

The heyday of the simple structure probably occurred during the period of the great American trusts, late in the nineteenth century. Although today less in fashion and to many a relic of more autocratic times, the simple structure remains a widespread and necessary configuration—for building up most new organizations and for operating those in simple, dynamic environments and those facing extreme, hostile pressures.

MACHINE BUREAUCRACY

Just as the simple structure is prevalent in pre-Industrial Revolution industries such as agriculture, the machine bureaucracy is the offspring of industrialization, with its emphasis on the standardization of work for coordination and its resulting low-skilled, highly specialized jobs. *Exhibit 2* shows that, in contrast to simple structure, the machine bureaucracy elaborates its administration. First, it requires many analysts to design and maintain its systems of standardization—notably those that formalize its behaviors and plan its actions. And by virtue of the organization's dependence on these systems, these analysts gain a degree of informal power, which results in a certain amount of horizontal decentralization.

A large hierarchy emerges in the middle line to oversee the specialized work of the operating core and to keep the lid on conflicts that inevitably result from the rigid departmentalization, as well as from the alienation that often goes with routine, circumscribed jobs. That middle-line hierarchy is usually structured on a functional basis all the way up to the top, where the real power of coordination lies. In other words, machine bureaucracy tends to be centralized in the vertical sense—formal power is concentrated at the top.

And why the large support staff shown in *Exhibit 2*? Because machine bureaucracies depend on stability to function (change interrupts the smooth functioning of the system), they tend not only to seek out stable environments in which to function but also to stabilize the environments they find themselves in. One way they do this is to envelop within their structures all of the support services possible, ones that simple structures prefer to buy. For the same reason they also tend to integrate vertically—to become their own suppliers and

EXHIBIT 3
Dimensions of the Five Configurations

	SIMPLE STRUCTURE	MACHINE BUREAUCRACY	PROFESSIONAL BUREAUCRACY	DIVISIONAL-IZED FORM	ADHOCRACY
Key Means of Coordination	Direct supervision	Standardization of work	Standardization of skills	Standardization of outputs	Mutual adjustment
Key Part of Organization	Strategic apex	Technostructure	Operating core	Middle line	Support staff (with operating core in operating adhocracy)
STRUCTURAL ELEMENTS					
Specialization of Jobs	Little specialization	*Much horizontal and vertical specialization*	*Much horizontal specialization*	Some horizontal and vertical specialization (between divisions and headquarters)	*Much horizontal specialization*
Training and Indoctrination	Little training and indoctrination	Little training and indoctrination	*Much training and indoctrination*	Some training and indoctrination (of division managers)	Much training
Formalization of Behavior— Bureaucratic/ Organic	*Little formalization— organic*	*Much formalization— bureaucratic*	*Little formalization— bureaucratic*	Much formalization (within divisions)— bureaucratic	*Little formalization— organic*
Grouping	Usually functional	*Usually functional*	Functional and market	*Market*	Functional and market
Unit Size	Wide	Wide at bottom, narrow elsewhere	Wide at bottom, narrow elsewhere	Wide at top	Narrow throughout
Planning and Control Systems	Little planning and control	Action planning	Little planning and control	*Much performance control*	Limited action planning (esp. in administrative adhocracy)
Liaison Devices	Few liaison devices	Few liaison devices	Liaison devices in administration	Few liaison devices	*Many liaison devices throughout*
Decentraliza-tion	*Centralization*	*Limited horizontal decentralization*	*Horizontal and vertical decentralization*	*Limited vertical decentralization*	*Selective decentralization*

EXHIBIT 3
Dimensions of the Five Configurations (Continued)

	SIMPLE STRUCTURE	MACHINE BUREAUCRACY	PROFESSIONAL BUREAUCRACY	DIVISIONAL-IZED FORM	ADHOCRACY
SITUATIONAL ELEMENTS					
Age and Size	Typically young and small	Typically old and large	Varies	Typically old and very large	Typically young (operating adhocracy)
Technical System	Simple, not regulating	Regulating but not automated, not very complex	Not regulating or complex	Divisible, otherwise like machine bureacracy	Very complex, often automated (in administrative adhocracy), not regulating or complex (in operating adhocracy)
Environment	Simple and dynamic; sometimes hostile	Simple and stable	Complex and stable	Relatively simple and stable; diversified markets (esp. products and services)	Complex and dynamic; sometimes disparate (in administrative adhocracy)
Power	Chief executive control; often owner man- aged; not fashionable	Technocratic and external control; not fashionable	Professional operator control; fashionable	Middle-line control; fashionable (esp. in industry)	Expert control; very fashionable

Note: Italic type in columns 2–6 indicates key design parameters.

customers. And that of course causes many machine bureaucracies to grow very large. So we see the two-sided effect of size here: size drives the organization to bureaucratize ("We do that every day; let's standardize it!"), but bureaucracy also encourages the organization to grow larger. Aging also encourages this configuration; the organization standardizes its work because "we've done that before."

To enable the top managers to maintain centralized control, both the environment and the production system of the machine bureaucracy must be fairly simple. In fact, machine bureaucracies fit most naturally with mass production, where the products, processes, and distribution systems are usually rationalized and thus easy to comprehend. And so machine bureaucracy is most common among large, mature mass-production companies, such as automobile manufacturers, as well as the largest of the established providers of mass services, such as insurance companies and railroads. Thus McDonald's is a classic example of this configuration—achieving enormous success in its simple industry through meticulous standardization.

Because external controls encourage bureaucratization and centralization, this configuration is often assumed by organizations that are tightly controlled from the outside. That is why government agencies, which are subject to many such controls, tend to be driven toward the machine bureaucracy structure regardless of their other conditions.

The problems of the machine bureaucracy are legendary—dull and repetitive work, alienated employees, obsession with control (of markets as well as workers), massive size, and inadaptability. These are machines suited to specific purposes, not to adapting to new ones. For all of these reasons, the machine bureaucracy is no longer fashionable. Bureaucracy has become a dirty word. Yet this is the configuration that gets the products out cheaply and efficiently. And here too there can be a sense of harmony, as in the Swiss railroad system whose trains depart as the second hand sweeps past the twelve.

In a society consumed by its appetite for mass-produced goods, dependent on consistency in so many spheres (how else to deliver millions of pieces of mail every day?), and unable to automate a great many of its routine jobs, machine bureaucracy remains indispensable—and probably the most prevalent of the five configurations.

PROFESSIONAL BUREAUCRACY

This bureaucratic configuration relies on the standardization of skills rather than work processes or outputs for its coordination and so emerges as dramatically different from the machine bureaucracy. It is the structure hospitals, universities, and accounting firms tend most often to favor. Most important, because it relies for its operating tasks on trained professionals—skilled people who must be given considerable control over their own work—the organization surrenders a good deal of its power not only to the professionals themselves but also to the associations and institutions that select and train them in the first place. As a result, the structure emerges as very decentralized; power over many decisions, both operating and strategic, flows all the way down the hierarchy to the professionals of the operating core. For them this is the most democratic structure of all.

Because the operating procedures, although complex, are rather standardized—taking out appendixes in a hospital, teaching the American Motors case in a business school, doing an audit in an accounting firm—each professional can work independently of his or her colleagues, with the assurance that much of the necessary coordination will be effected automatically through standardization of skills. Thus a colleague of mine observed a five-hour open-heart operation in which the surgeon and anesthesiologist never exchanged a single word!

As can be seen in *Exhibit 2*, above the operating core we find a unique structure. Since the main standardization occurs as a result of training that takes place outside the professional bureaucracy, a technostructure is hardly needed. And because the professionals work independently, the size of operating units can be very large, and so few first-line managers are needed. (I work in a business school where 55 professors report directly to one dean.) Yet even those few managers, and those above them, do little direct supervision; much of their time is spent linking their units to the broader environment, notably to ensure adequate financing. Thus to become a top manager in a consulting firm is to become a salesperson.

On the other hand, the support staff is typically very large in order to back up the high-priced professionals. But that staff does a very different kind of work—much of it the simple and routine jobs that the professionals shed. As a result, parallel hierarchies emerge in the professional bureaucracy—one democratic with bottom-up power for the professionals, a second autocratic with top-down control for the support staff.

Professional bureaucracy is most effective for organizations that find themselves in stable yet complex environments. Complexity requires that decision-making power be decentralized to highly trained individuals, and stability enables these individuals to apply standardized skills and so to work with a good deal of autonomy. To further ensure that autonomy, the production system must be neither highly regulating, complex, nor automated. Surgeons use their scalpels and editors their pencils; both must be sharp but are otherwise simple instruments that allow their users considerable freedom in performing their complex work.

Standardization is the great strength as well as the great weakness of professional bureaucracy. That is what enables the professionals to perfect their skills and so achieve great efficiency and effectiveness. But that same standardization raises problems of adaptability. This is not a structure to innovate but one to perfect what is already known. Thus, so long as the environment is stable, the professional bureaucracy does its job well. It identifies the needs of its clients and offers a set of standardized programs to serve them. In other words, pigeonholing is its great forte; change messes up the pigeonholes. New needs arise that fall between or across the slots, and the standard programs no longer apply. Another configuration is required.

Professional bureaucracy, a product of the middle years of this century, is a highly fashionable structure for two reasons. First, it is very democratic, at least for its professional workers. And second, it offers them considerable autonomy, freeing the professionals even from the need to coordinate closely with each other. To release themselves from the close control of administrators and analysts, not to mention their own colleagues, many people seek to have themselves declared "professional"—and thereby turn their organizations into professional bureaucracies.

DIVISIONALIZED FORM

Like the professional bureaucracy, the divisionalized form is not so much an integrated organization as a set of rather independent entities joined together by a loose administrative overlay. But whereas those entities of the professional bureaucracy are individuals—professionals in the operating core—in the divisionalized form they are units in the middle line, called divisions.

The divisionalized form differs from the other four configurations in one central respect: it is not a complete but a partial structure, superimposed on others. Those others are in the divisions, each of which is driven toward machine bureaucracy.

An organization divisionalizes for one reason above all—because its product lines are diversified. (And that tends to happen most often in the largest and most mature organizations, those that have run out of opportunities or become stalled in their traditional markets.) Such diversification encourages the organization to create a market-based unit, or division, for each distinct product line (as indicated in *Exhibit 2*) and to grant considerable autonomy to each division to run its own business.

That autonomy notwithstanding, divisionalization does *not* amount to decentralization, although the terms are often equated with each other. Decentralization is an expression of the dispersal of decision-making power in an organization. Divisionalization refers to a structure of semiautonomous market-based units. A divisionalized structure in which the managers at the heads of these units retain the lion's share of the power is far more centralized than many functional structures where large numbers of specialists get involved in the making of important decisions.

In fact, the most famous example of divisionalization involved centralization. Alfred Sloan adopted the divisionalized form at General Motors to *reduce* the power of the different units, to integrate the holding company William Durant had put together. That kind of centralization appears to have continued to the point where the automotive units in some ways seem closer to functional marketing departments than true divisions.[1]

But how does top management maintain a semblance of control over the divisions? Some direct supervision is used—headquarters managers visit the divisions periodically and authorize some of their more important decisions. But too much of that interferes with the necessary autonomy of the divisions. So headquarters relies on performance control systems or, in other words, on the standardization of outputs. It leaves the operating details to the divisions and exercises control by measuring their performance periodically. And to design these control systems, headquarters creates a small technostructure. It

---

1. *See* Leonard Wrigley, "Diversification and Divisional Autonomy," DBA thesis, Harvard Business School, 1970.

also establishes a small central support staff to provide certain services common to the divisions (such as legal counsel and external relations).

This performance control system has an interesting effect on the internal structure of the division. First, the division is treated as a single integrated entity with one consistent, standardized, and quantifiable set of goals. Those goals tend to get translated down the line into more and more specific subgoals and, eventually, work standards. In other words, they encourage the bureaucratization of structure. And second, headquarters tends to impose its standards through the managers of the divisions, whom it holds responsible for divisional performance. That tends to result in centralization within the divisions. And centralization coupled with bureaucratization gives machine bureaucracy. That is the structure that works best in the divisions.

Simple structures and adhocracies make poor divisions because they abhor standards—they operate in dynamic environments where standards of any kind are difficult to establish. And professional bureaucracies are not logically treated as integrated entities, nor can their goals be easily quantified. (How does one measure cure in a psychiatric ward or knowledge generated in a university?)

This conclusion is, of course, consistent with the earlier argument that external control (in this case, from headquarters) pushes an organization toward machine bureaucracy. The point is invariably illustrated when a conglomerate takes over an entrepreneurial company and imposes a lot of bureaucratic systems and standards on its simple structure.

The divisionalized form was created to solve the problem of adaptability in machine bureaucracy. By overlaying another level of administration that could add and subtract divisions, the organization found a way to adapt itself to new conditions and to spread its risk. But there is another side to these arguments. Some evidence suggests that the control systems of these structures discourage risk taking and innovation, that the division head who must justify his or her performance every month is not free to experiment the way the independent entrepreneur is.[2]

Moreover, to spread risk is to spread the consequences of that risk; a disaster in one division can pull down the entire organization. Indeed, the fear of this is what elicits the direct control of major new investments, which is what often discourages ambitious innovation. Finally, the divisionalized form does not solve the problem of adaptability of machine bureaucracy, it merely deflects it. When a division goes sour, all that headquarters seems able to do is change the management (as an independent board of directors would do) or divest it. From society's point of view, the problem remains.

Finally, from a social perspective, the divisionalized form raises a number of serious issues. By enabling organizations to grow very large, it leads to the concentration of a great deal of economic power in a few hands. And there is some evidence that it sometimes encourages that power to be

---

2. *See* Wrigley, "Diversification and Divisional Autonomy."

used irresponsibly. By emphasizing the measurement of performance as its means of control, a bias arises in favor of those divisional goals that can be operationalized, which usually means the economic ones, not the social ones. That the division is driven by such measures to be socially unresponsive would not seem inappropriate—for the business of the corporation is, after all, economic.

The problem is that in big businesses (where the divisionalized form is prevalent) every strategic decision has social as well as economic consequences. When the screws of the performance control system are turned tight, the division managers, in order to achieve the results expected of them, are driven to ignore the social consequences of their decisions. At that point, *un*responsive behavior becomes *ir*responsible.[3]

The divisionalized structure has become very fashionable in the past few decades, having spread in pure or modified form through most of the *Fortune* "500" in a series of waves and then into European companies. It has also become fashionable in the nonbusiness sector in the guise of "multiversities," large hospital systems, unions, and government itself. And yet it seems fundamentally ill suited to these sectors for two reasons.

First, the success of the divisionalized form depends on goals that can be measured. But outside the business sector, goals are often social in nature and nonquantifiable. The result of performance control, then, is an inappropriate displacement of social goals by economic ones.

Second, the divisions often require structures other than machine bureaucracy. The professionals in the multiversities, for example, often balk at the technocratic controls and the top-down decision making that tends to accompany external control of their campuses. In other words, the divisionalized form can be a misfit just as can any of the other configurations.

ADHOCRACY

None of the structures discussed so far suits the industries of our age—industries such as aerospace, petrochemicals, think-tank consulting, and filmmaking. These organizations need above all to innovate in complex ways. The bureaucratic structures are too inflexible, and the simple structure is too centralized. These industries require "project structures" that fuse experts drawn from different specialties into smoothly functioning creative teams. Hence they tend to favor our fifth configuration, adhocracy, a structure of interacting project teams.

Adhocracy is the most difficult of the five configurations to describe because it is both complex and nonstandardized. Indeed, adhocracy contra-

---

3. For a full discussion of the problems of implementing social goals in the divisionalized form, *see* Robert W. Ackerman, *The Social Challenge to Business* (Cambridge: Harvard University Press, 1975).

dicts much of what we accept on faith in organizations—consistency in output, control by administrators, unity of command, strategy emanating from the top. It is a tremendously fluid structure, in which power is constantly shifting and coordination and control are by mutual adjustment through the informal communication and interaction of competent experts. Moreover, adhocracy is the newest of the five configurations, the one researchers have had the least chance to study. Yet it is emerging as a key structural configuration, one that deserves a good deal of consideration.

These comments notwithstanding, adhocracy is a no less coherent configuration than any of the others. Like the professional bureaucracy, adhocracy relies on trained and specialized experts to get the bulk of its work done. But in its case, the experts must work together to create new things instead of working apart to perfect established skills. Hence, for coordination adhocracy must rely extensively on mutual adjustment, which it encourages by the use of the liaison devices—integrating managers, task forces, and matrix structure.

In professional bureaucracy, the experts are concentrated in the operating core, where much of the power lies. But in adhocracy, they tend to be dispersed throughout the structure according to the decisions they make—in the operating core, middle line, technostructure, strategic apex, and especially support staff. Thus, whereas in each of the other configurations power is more or less concentrated, in adhocracy it is distributed unevenly. It flows, not according to authority or status but to wherever the experts needed for a particular decision happen to be found.

Managers abound in the adhocracy—functional managers, project managers, integrating managers. This results in narrow "spans of control" by conventional measures. That is not a reflection of control but of the small size of the project teams. The managers of adhocracy do not control in the conventional sense of direct supervision; typically, they are experts too who take their place alongside the others in the teams, concerned especially with linking the different teams together.

As can be seen in *Exhibit 2*, many of the distinctions of conventional structure disappear in the adhocracy. With power based on expertise instead of authority, the line/staff distinction evaporates. And with power distributed throughout the structure, the distinction between the strategic apex and the rest of the structure also blurs. In a project structure, strategy is not formulated from above and then implemented lower down; rather, it evolves by virtue of the multitude of decisions made for the projects themselves. In other words, the adhocracy is continually developing its strategy as it accepts and works out new projects, the creative results of which can never be predicted. And so everyone who gets involved in the project work—and in the adhocracy that can mean virtually everyone—becomes a strategy maker.

There are two basic types of adhocracy, operating and administrative. The *operating* adhocracy carries out innovative projects directly on behalf of its clients, usually under contract, as in a creative advertising agency, a think-tank consulting firm, a manufacturer of engineering prototypes. Professional bureaucracies work in some of these industries too, but with a different orientation. The operating adhocracy treats each client problem as a unique one to be solved in creative fashion; the professional bureaucracy pigeonholes it so that it can provide a standard skill.

For example, there are some consulting firms that tailor their solutions to the client's order and others that sell standard packages off the rack. When the latter fits, it proves much cheaper. When it does not, the money is wasted. In one case, the experts must cooperate with each other in organic structures to innovate; in the other, they can apply their standard skills autonomously in bureaucratic structures.

In the operating adhocracy, the operating and administrative work blend into a single effort. That is, the organization cannot easily separate the planning and design of the operating work—in other words, the project—from its actual execution. So another classic distinction disappears. As shown above the dotted lines in *Exhibit 2*, the organization emerges as an organic mass in which line managers, staff, and operating experts all work together on project teams in ever-shifting relationships.

The *administrative* adhocracy undertakes projects on its own behalf, as in a space agency—NASA, for example, during the Apollo era—or a producer of electronic components. In this type of adhocracy, in contrast to the other, we find a sharp separation of the administrative from the operating work—the latter shown by the dotted lines in *Exhibit 2*. This results in a two-part structure. The administrative component carries out the innovative design work, combining line managers and staff experts in project teams. And the operating component, which puts the results into production, is separated or "truncated" so that its need for standardization will not interfere with the project work.

Sometimes the operations are contracted out altogether. Other times, they are set up in independent structures, as in the printing function in newspapers. And when the operations of an organization are highly automated, the same effect takes place naturally. The operations essentially run themselves, while the administrative component tends to adopt a project orientation concerned with change and innovation, with bringing new facilities on line. Note also the effects of automation—a reduction in the need for rules, since these are built right into the machinery, and a blurring of the line/staff distinction, since control becomes a question more of expertise than authority. What does it mean to supervise a machine? Thus the effect of automation is to reduce the degree of machine bureaucracy in the administration and to drive it toward administrative adhocracy.

Both kinds of adhocracy are commonly found in environments that are complex as well as dynamic. These are the two conditions that call for sophisticated innovation, which requires the cooperative efforts of many different kinds of experts. In the case of administrative adhocracy, the production system is also typically complex and, as noted, often automated. These production systems create the need for highly skilled support staffers, who must be given a good deal of power over technical decisions.

For its part, the operating adhocracy is often associated with young organizations. For one thing, with no standard products or services, organizations that use it tend to be highly vulnerable, and many of them disappear at an early age. For another, age drives these organizations toward bureaucracy, as the employees themselves age and tend to seek an escape from the instability of the structure and its environment. The innovative consulting firm converges on a few of its most successful projects, packages them into standard skills, and settles down to life as a professional bureaucracy; the manufacturer of prototypes hits on a hot product and becomes a machine bureaucracy to mass-produce it.

But not all adhocracies make such a transition. Some endure as they are, continuing to innovate over long periods of time. We see this, for example, in studies of the National Film Board of Canada, famous since the 1940s for its creativity in both films and the techniques of filmmaking.

Finally, fashion is a factor associated with adhocracy. This is clearly the structure of our age, prevalent in almost every industry that has grown up since World War II (and none I can think of established before that time). Every characteristic of adhocracy is very much in vogue today—expertise, organic structure, project teams and task forces, diffused power, matrix structure, sophisticated and often automated production systems, youth, and dynamic, complex environments. Adhocracy is the only one of the five configurations that combines some sense of democracy with an absence of bureaucracy.

Yet, like all the others, this configuration too has its limitations. Adhocracy in some sense achieves its effectiveness through inefficiency. It is inundated with managers and costly liaison devices for communication; nothing ever seems to get done without everyone talking to everyone else. Ambiguity abounds, giving rise to all sorts of conflicts and political pressures. Adhocracy can do no ordinary thing well. But it is extraordinary at innovation.

CONFIGURATIONS AS A DIAGNOSTIC TOOL

What in fact are these configurations? Are they (1) abstract ideals, (2) real-life structures, one of which an organization had better use if it is to survive, or (3) building blocks for more complex structures? In some sense, the answer is a qualified yes in all three cases. These are certainly abstract ideals, simplifications of the complex world of structure. Yet the abstract ideal can come to life too. Every organization experiences the five pulls that underlie these configurations: the pull to centralize by the top management, the pull to formalize by the technostructure, the pull to professionalize by the operators, the pull to balkanize by the managers of the middle line, and the pull to collaborate by the support staff.

Where one pull dominates—where the conditions favor it above all—then the organization will tend to organize itself close to one of the configurations. I have cited examples of this throughout my discussion—the entrepreneurial company, the hamburger chain, the university, the conglomerate, the space agency.

But one pull does not always dominate; two may have to exist in balance. Symphony orchestras engage highly trained specialists who perfect their skills, as do the operators in professional bureaucracy. But their efforts must be tightly coordinated, hence, the reliance on the direct supervision of a leader—a conductor—as in simple structure. Thus a hybrid of the two configurations emerges that is eminently sensible for the symphony orchestra (even if it does generate a good deal of conflict between leader and operators).

Likewise, we have companies that are diversified around a central theme that creates linkages among their different product lines. As a result, they continually experience the pull to separate, as in the divisionalized form, and also integrate, as in machine bureaucracy or perhaps adhocracy. And what configuration should we impute to an IBM? Clearly, there is too much going on in many giant organizations to describe them as one configuration or another. But the framework of the five configurations can still help us to understand how their different parts are organized and fit together—or refuse to.

The point is that managers can improve their organizational designs by considering the different pulls their organizations experience and the configurations toward which they are drawn. In other words, this set of five configurations can serve as an effective tool in diagnosing the problems of organizational design, especially those of the *fit* among component parts. Let us consider four basic forms of misfit to show how managers can use the set of configurations as a diagnostic tool.

ARE THE INTERNAL ELEMENTS CONSISTENT?

Management that grabs at every structural innovation that comes along may be doing its organization great harm. It risks going off in all directions: yesterday long-range planning to pin managers down, today Outward Bound to open them up. Quality of working life programs as well as all those fashionable features of adhocracy—integrating managers, matrix structure, and the like—have exemplary aims: to create more satisfying work conditions and to increase the flexibility of the organization. But are they appropriate for a machine bureaucracy? Do enlarged jobs really fit with the requirements of the mass production of automobiles? Can the jobs ever be made large enough to really satisfy the workers—and the cost-conscious customers?

I believe that in the fashionable world of organizational design, fit remains an important characteristic. The *hautes structurières* of New York—the consulting firms that seek to bring the latest in structural fashion to their clients—would do well to pay a great deal more attention to that fit. Machine bureaucracy functions best when its reporting relationships are sharply defined and its operating core staffed with workers who prefer routine and stability. The nature of the work in this configuration—managerial as well as operating—is rooted in the reality of mass production, in the costs of manual labor compared with those of automated machines, and in the size and age of the organization.

Until we are prepared to change our whole way of living—for example, to pay more for handcrafted instead of mass-produced products and so to consume less—we would do better to spend our time trying not to convert our machine bureaucracies into something else but to ensure that they work effectively as the bureaucracies they are meant to be. Organizations, like individuals, can avoid identity crises by deciding what it is they wish to be and then pursuing it with a healthy obsession.

ARE THE EXTERNAL CONTROLS FUNCTIONAL?

An organization may achieve its own internal consistency and then have it destroyed by the imposition of external controls. The typical effect of those controls is to drive the organization toward machine bureaucracy. In other words, it is the simple structures, professional bureaucracies, and adhocracies that suffer most from such controls. Two cases of this seem rampant in our society: one is the takeover of small, private companies by larger divisionalized ones, making bureaucracies of entrepreneurial ventures; the other is the tendency for governments to assume increasingly direct control of what used to be more independent organizations—public school systems, hospitals, universities, and social welfare agencies.

As organizations are taken over in these ways—brought into the hierarchies of other organizations—two things happen. They become centralized and formalized.[4] In other words, they are driven toward machine bureaucracy. Government administrators assume that just a little more formal control will bring this callous hospital or that weak school in line. Yet the cure—even when the symptoms are understood—is often worse than the disease. The worst way to correct deficiencies in professional work is through control by technocratic standards. Professional bureaucracies cannot be managed like machines.

In the school system, such standards imposed from outside the classroom serve only to discourage the competent teachers, not to improve the weak ones. The performance of teachers—as that of all other professionals—depends

---

4. There is a good deal of evidence for this conclusion. *See,* for example, Yitzhak Samuel and Bilha F. Mannheim, "A Multidimensional Approach Toward a Typology of Bureaucracy," *Administrative Science Quarterly* (June 1970): 216; Edward A. Holdaway, John F. Newberry, David J. Hickson, and R. Peter Heron, "Dimensions of Organizations in Complex Societies: The Educational Sector," *Administrative Science Quarterly* (March 1975): 37; D. S. Pugh, D. J. Hickson, C. R. Hinnings, and C. Turner, "The Context of Organization Structures," *Administrative Science Quarterly* (March 1969): 91; Bernard C. Reimann, "On the Dimensions of Bureaucratic Structure: An Empirical Reappraisal," *Administrative Science Quarterly* (December 1973): 462.

primarily on their skills and training. Retraining or, more likely, replacing them is the basic means to improvement.

For almost a century now, the management literature—from time study through operations research to long-range planning—has promoted machine bureaucracy as the "one best way." That assumption is false; it is one way among a number suited to only certain conditions.

IS THERE A PART THAT DOES NOT FIT?

Sometimes an organization's management, recognizing the need for internal consistency, hives off a part in need of special treatment—establishes it in a pocket off in a corner to be left alone. But the problem all too often is that it is not left alone. The research laboratory may be built out in the country, far from the managers and analysts who run the machine bureaucracy back home. But the distance is only physical.

Standards have a long administrative reach: it is difficult to corner off a small component and pretend that it will not be influenced by the rest. Each organization, not to mention each configuration, develops its own norms, traditions, beliefs—in other words, its own ideology. And that permeates every part of it. Unless there is a rough balance among opposing forces—as in the symphony orchestra—the prevailing ideology will tend to dominate. That is why adhocracies need especially tolerant controllers, just as machine bureaucracies must usually scale down their expectations for their research laboratories.

IS THE RIGHT STRUCTURE IN THE WRONG SITUATION?

Some organizations do indeed achieve and maintain an internal consistency. But then they find that it is designed for an environment the organization is no longer in. To have a nice, neat machine bureaucracy in a dynamic industry calling for constant innovation or, alternately, a flexible adhocracy in a stable industry calling for minimum cost makes no sense. Remember that these are configurations of situation as well as structure. Indeed, the very notion of configuration is that all the elements interact in a system. One element does not cause another; instead, all influence each other interactively. Structure is no more designed to fit the situation than situation is selected to fit the structure.

The way to deal with the right structure in the wrong environment may be to change the environment, not the structure. Often, in fact, it is far easier to shift industries or retreat to a suitable niche in an industry than to undo a cohesive structure. Thus the entrepreneur goes after a new, dynamic environment when the old one stabilizes and the bureaucracies begin to move in. When a situation changes suddenly—as it did for oil companies some years ago—a rapid change in situation or structure would seem to be mandatory. But what of a gradual change in situation? How should the organization adapt, for example, when its long-stable markets slowly become dynamic?

Essentially, the organization has two choices. It can adapt continuously to the environment at the expense of internal consistency—that is, steadily redesign its structure to maintain external fit. Or it can maintain internal consistency at the expense of a gradually worsening fit with its environment, at least until the fit becomes so bad that it must undergo sudden structural redesign to achieve a new internally consistent configuration. In other words, the choice is between evolution and revolution, between perpetual mild adaptation, which favors external fit over time, and infrequent major realignment, which favors internal consistency over time.

In his research on configuration, Danny Miller found that effective companies usually opt for revolution. Forced to decide whether to spend most of their time with a good external fit or with an established internal consistency, they choose consistency and put up with brief periods of severe disruption to realign the fit occasionally. It is better, apparently, to maintain at least partial configuration than none at all. Miller called this process, appropriately enough, a "quantum" theory of structural change.[5]

—— FIT OVER FASHION

To conclude, consistency, coherence, and fit—harmony—are critical factors in organization design, but they come at a price. An organization cannot be all things to all people. It should do what it does well and suffer the consequences. Be an efficient machine bureaucracy where that is appropriate and do not pretend to be highly adaptive. Or be an adaptive adhocracy and do not pretend to be highly efficient. Or create some new configuration to suit its own needs. The point is not really *which* configuration; it is *that* configuration is achieved.

---

5. Danny Miller, *Revolution and Evolution: A Quantum View of Organizational Adaptation*, working paper, McGill University, 1980.

——— DISCUSSION QUESTIONS

1. Are there other organizational configurations besides the five described in this reading? If so, are they specific to an industry or a particular type of work?
2. What is the relationship between a firm's configuration and its strategy?
3. Choose a company that you know well and identify its configuration, according to Mintzberg's types. Does the configuration seem coherent? If not, how would you modify it to achieve "fit"?
4. The author refers to "the pull to centralize by . . . top management." What are the advantages of centralization? How would you balance this tendency in order to achieve a harmonious configuration?

Functional Integration: Getting All the Troops to Work Together

23

BENSON P. SHAPIRO

This reading begins by explaining the need for functional integration. The focus then turns to cross-functional coordination and the six approaches necessary to achieve it: a strategy, the structural hierarchy, the management processes and systems, the management information system, the informal social systems and culture, and the selection and promotion of employees. The author next examines the four groups of people, in addition to the functional line manager, who contribute to interfunctional coordination: the staff engineering group, cost accounting experts, human resource managers, and top-level general management. The reading concludes with a word about the total system versus "the home team."

Sales is customer oriented. Marketing takes a more long-term perspective, but operations, by definition, needs to keep all systems functioning. Manufacturing wants the product out the door; engineering's interest is to develop new technologically exciting and sophisticated products; but field service wants to keep the customers' earlier purchases running. These line-operating departments, or functions, have different objectives, perspectives, and even cultures. Furthermore, each group, the manager and the workers, often has its own predilections, interests, and culture. It is no wonder that the functions have problems with integration.

Many company decisions can be made only with input from several different functional departments. Making good product-design decisions, for example, requires information from all departments. More important, the inputs cannot be provided sequentially but must occur simultaneously and interactively. Otherwise, effective trade-offs and compromises cannot be made. Engineering may overdesign a product in response to its understanding of customer desires as reported by sales. Had sales recognized the added cost of the attributes it requested, its request might have been different. Desires and constraints, approaches and solutions must constantly be discussed and shared; however, this sharing is difficult to achieve.

The following section describes where interfunctional coordination is most needed. The next section discusses the nature of coordination. The final sections present six different approaches to achieving integration and four adjudicating roles.

WHERE IS FUNCTIONAL INTEGRATION NEEDED?

The importance of functional integration is determined by the company and decisions it makes. Some companies need more functional integration than others; unfortunately, functional integration is generally hardest to achieve in the companies that need it most.

The more dispersed the functions, the harder they are to integrate. The dispersion may be organizational: Different functions may reside in different operating units, profit centers, or divisions. It is more difficult to coordinate a sales function in one division with an engineering function in another than to coordinate sales and engineering functions in the same division. Each time a jurisdictional boundary is crossed, a "coordination toll" must be paid. If the two functional departments to be coordinated are in the same jurisdiction, there is only one boundary to cross and one toll to pay.

Geographical distance, even within the same country, but particularly across national borders, adds to problems in functional integration. National cultural differences amplify functional cultural differences; suspicion festers and miscommunication becomes more routine. The logistics of communication also grow more difficult with geographical distance as travel becomes harder and time-zone differences disrupt easy telephone communication. Although voice and electronic mail can help, problems can still remain.

Functional integration is also more problematic in larger companies. There are larger groups of people, and more of them, to pull together and generally greater differences in culture and location among groups. Communication becomes exponentially more difficult as the number of people or groups who must communicate grows.

A company's products and markets have a significant influence on the importance of functional integration. Specialty products require much more intimate cross-functional integration than do commodity products.[1] By and large, specialities depend upon value-added features provided through close functional cooperation. Commodity businesses are generally run in a "lean-and-mean" fashion, which does not require as much cross-functional integration. In addition, the tight margins of a commodity business cannot generously provide for cross-functional integration.

Companies that market systems or programs whose different parts must work together also need exceptional levels of cross-functional integration. A company selling capital equipment through a program based on strong

---

1. For further information, *see* "Specialties vs. Commodities: The Battle for Profit Margins," Harvard Business School Case No. 9-587-120.

service must effectively coordinate engineering, manufacturing, and field service around repair problems and their avoidance; it must also coordinate sales, with its close customer contact, and service so that the customer feels important. A system works only if the individual products are designed in conjunction with one another; however, sometimes parts are engineered and/or produced in different operating units or divisions. Thus, simultaneous cross-division and cross-functional integration is needed for the sales function in one division to talk to the engineering function in another.

Finally, service companies often require more interdepartmental coordination than do product companies because the customer is especially dependent upon it. Many services are performed in the presence of the customer and under intense time pressure. Interfunctional conflicts can become obvious and have immediate and dramatic competitive impact.

By their nature some decisions demand much more functional integration than others. Product-policy decisions are among those requiring the highest degree of functional integration. Each function has a major impact upon product-policy decisions, and as mentioned earlier, the impact must be simultaneous rather than sequential.

Functional integration is also needed in the order-fulfillment cycle, which consists of sales forecasting and capacity planning, shipping, installation, service and repair, and billing. The receipt and entry of the order alone often involves three different functions: Sales accepts the order and hands it over to the customer-service department for credit checking and entry, which hands it over to operations and/or production for scheduling. To make the organizational situation even more complex, the customer-service function, which sits amidst all the order activity, is typically low in status and powerless. Particular activities or parts of the order-fulfillment cycle have traditionally generated exceptional interdepartmental conflict.

Effective cross-functional communication about short-term promotions, for example, can make policies and programs much more profitable. If the sales department, either alone or with the marketing department, schedules promotions without considering their impact on warehouse and factory, the promotions will be suboptimal. Because promotions create a short-term peak in sales, often preceded and followed by an exaggerated trough, they must be carefully integrated into inventory management and production scheduling. Ideally, promotions enable the warehouse and factory to be more efficient, not less. If planning is done separately by function, the promotions will invariably result in lower profits.

Cross-functional policies regarding human resources management will also decrease cross-functional jealousy and backbiting and make transferring individuals across functional jurisdictions easier. When each function designs its own personnel policies, cultural differences among various functions are highlighted. Of course, optimal corporatewide personnel policies can be created only with input from the various functions.

Finally, all operating functions should participate in developing a basic company strategy. If the marketing function mandates that the company will have a strong field-service component in its basic strategy, the field-service department must be committed to developing such strength. A major flaw in the design, and certainly the execution, of many corporate strategies is the absence of some critical functions that have insufficient power to take part in strategy development. Field service and other, generally smaller, functions, such as customer service or order processing, are examples. Few top-level executives spend much thought on order processing; yet ineffective order processing can destroy the finest corporate strategy and waste the work of even the best sales force.

To summarize, interfunctional coordination is most important for specialty products and companies that market systems and programs. Interfunctional coordination is most difficult to achieve in large and/or dispersed companies. It is most necessary when dealing with product-policy decisions, the order-fulfillment cycle, basic human resources policies, and broad corporate strategies.

——— TYPES OF CROSS-FUNCTIONAL COORDINATION

Most people intuitively divide coordination in a company into vertical and horizontal components. The vertical component involves issues such as leadership and delegation. That form of coordination, though important, is not the subject of this reading.

The horizontal dimension of integration and communication typically includes lateral cross-functional aspects. How can sales and manufacturing work together to develop a delivery schedule for a particular customer, for example? Most of this reading will focus on lateral, cross-functional communication and integration. This type of coordination, though simple on paper, is difficult to accomplish.

Other types of cross-functional integration are generally even harder to accomplish. One type is diagonal cross-functional integration, where the people involved reside simultaneously in different functions and at different levels in the organization. This type of coordination involves both vertical communication and lateral cross-functioning. Diagonal communication is fairly common in companies operating in specialty markets. The regional sales manager, for example, might need to talk to a bench engineer, a shipping clerk, or a field-service technician about a particular problem. Or, an engineering manager may want to discuss a particular customer need with a salesperson. The vertical component of the communication makes coordination even harder than when the communication is merely cross-functional.

Finally, as briefly described above, some cross-functional communication must also break through other jurisdictional barriers—for example, those of integrated or partially integrated profit centers or such boundaries as country operating units. Sometimes the communication might involve people in the same function who reside in different divisions—for example, two engineers from different divisions who design components that eventually combine into a finished product or system. At other times, communication is both cross-functional and cross-jurisdictional. One division might provide field-service or technical support for the products of another division. Here, the salesperson of the receiving division might make requests of the technicians of the supplying division. Situations also arise in which the communication is cross-functional, cross-jurisdictional, or cross-divisional, and vertical. For example, an engineering or a manufacturing manager in one division might need to talk with salespeople in other divisions.

In general, as the number of jurisdictional boundaries and the number of levels to be crossed increase so does the difficulty of coordination. The next section shows how cross-functional coordination can be achieved.

THE SIX APPROACHES

There are six approaches to achieving cross-functional coordination:

- A unified, holistic strategy;
- The organization structure or management hierarchy;
- Management processes and systems;
- The management information system and related electronic communications systems;
- The informal social systems and culture;
- The selection and promotion of employees.

These six approaches appear in every organization. Every company has a strategy, for example—even if it is not explicit or written. The point here, however, is to harness these approaches to improve interjurisdictional coordination. These approaches can be "mixed and matched," but this can only happen by first making clear and explicit the role of each in interjurisdictional coordination and the relationships among the six. Most managers, because of their proclivities or experience, tend to depend more heavily on one of the six approaches than on the others. Making trade-offs among the different approaches and among specific elements within each approach is important. In addition, integrating the six approaches is imperative; otherwise, each approach will contribute to interfunctional warfare rather than to coordination. If all the troops are to pull in the same direction, the approaches involved must also pull in the same direction.

A UNIFIED HOLISTIC STRATEGY

Functional coordination begins with the creation of "marching orders" and priorities—the unified, holistic strategy. The strategy is unified because all functional departments have contributed to its development; it is holistic because it describes each major function's role. The strategy document becomes a map as the company threads its way through the competitive maze. Each department understands its role in the strategy and how that role relates to its sibling functions. An effective document offers clear priorities so that all functions share a set of objectives. Limitations, such as resource constraint, should also be clear. Thus, each department has reasonable expectations about what it will receive from other departments and what human and financial resources will be available.

An effective strategy document begins with a clear statement about which customers the unit will serve and which customer needs it will address. These customers and needs will be ranked; because different customers have varying and often conflicting needs, the document must include priorities. When the customer base is small, individual customers can be dealt with. When the customer base is large, the customers must be considered in groups or segments. Customer selection and ranking is probably the most important single topic in the strategy document. It defines the nature and importance of functional contributions and, if done properly, leads to a sustainable, distinctive competitive competence.

The customer-ranking process, though difficult, must be part of a strategy session; it certainly will never happen in the day-to-day hassle of customer complaints, salesperson and customer service lobbying, production and operations expediting, and logistics and service limitations. The clearer the strategy, the customer priorities, and the functional expectations are, the more likely each function will be able to understand and respond to its strategic role.

The strategy-development process offers a wonderful opportunity for introducing and inculcating the concept of cross-jurisdictional coordination. A deliberate, open, and equitable process can be emblematic of the day-to-day interaction to be encouraged among functions, divisions, and other jurisdictions.

Finally, the strategy document and the development process are the foundation upon which to build appropriate organizational structure and management processes. If the strategy is fuzzy, the remaining coordination approaches will not be well defined and smoothly applied.

THE ORGANIZATION STRUCTURE OR MANAGEMENT HIERARCHY

The traditional approach to functional-integration issues has been the organization structure. The organization structure is indeed a powerful way to encourage integration—so powerful that it creates problems. People are anxious about organization structure because it defines their position, and in fact, has a large impact on their power and privileges. The issue thus becomes highly political, with each person typically supporting the structure that most benefits him or her. In addition, executives often analyze structures for the impact they have on organizational protégés and friends. This, combined with the apparent clarity and symbolism of the organization structure, often leads to heated discussions and battles. Consultants may be brought in to provide a more balanced and unbiased view. Though they sometimes succeed, other times they too become embroiled in political wars.

The stakes in structuring decisions have been particularly high in the past because restructuring was relatively infrequent. People feared they would be placed in a permanent, or close to permanent, position. Lately, as companies more frequently restructure in response to more rapid environmental and strategic change, the stakes seem lower, the battles less intense, and companies somewhat more supple organizationally.

In addition to its political sensitivity, the organization structure has major limitations as an integrating mechanism. A natural adversarial relationship seems to exist between specialization and integration, for example. The more specialized two functions are, the more difficult it is to integrate them. Specialization will be necessary when a function must create its own culture, skills, or operating methods that are substantially different from those of other functions. Thus, in many senses, specialization is good. However, increased specialization almost invariably leads to decreased integration.[2]

Nonetheless, the management hierarchy can be used to improve functional coordination. One approach is to separate large functional organizations into parts, which are then grouped around products, geography, or divisions. Thus, a company might be organized to have separate sales and manufacturing functions within each product division. This solution is not perfect because each function does not develop the strong specialization that can make it more efficient. The company might have five different manufacturing functions instead of one more powerful, perhaps better-run, manufacturing department. Furthermore, it is often impossible to separate functions into smaller pieces and still have them well coordinated within the function across operating units and above minimum-efficient scale. Let us look briefly at sales and manufacturing as examples.

Within the sales function, it is important to coordinate all the salespeople calling on a particular account or person.[3] If the company has a single sales force, obtaining that coordination is easier. However, the large single sales force is in direct counterpoint to the concept of having separate sales forces within separate divisions for each product or geography. Choosing between the single sales force and multiple sales forces is difficult and complex. Furthermore, the political sensitivities and personal ambitions of high-level sales executives make it hard to approach this decision in a deliberate and unbiased fashion.

2. Jay W. Lorsch and Paul R. Lawrence, "Organizing for Product Innovation," *Harvard Business Review* (January–February 1965): 114–115.

3. Frank V. Cespedes, Stephen X. Doyle, and Robert J. Freedman, "Teamwork for Today's Selling," *Harvard Business Review* (March–April 1989): 44.

The manufacturing function faces much the same problem, although in a somewhat different form. It is often most economical to operate high-speed specialized equipment that requires a substantial product flow. If divisions have their own manufacturing operations, each of the smaller manufacturing operations may fall below this minimum-efficient scale. In addition, divisions often end up being suppliers or customers to one another for components and parts, a situation that opens up new problems of transfer pricing and cross-divisional coordination. Thus, divisionalizing is not a full-blown integration solution. It is merely another partial approach in which compromise and trade-off are necessary.

Another integration technique, the interfunctional coordinating unit, can be used when functions are quite specialized. The interfunctional unit attempts to tie together two functions. Consumer-packaged-goods companies often have sales-promotion groups to connect the sales force and the marketing people (product managers). Some interfunctional groups operate well because they understand both cultures and address a limited number of issues. In other situations, the interfunctional group becomes another group of people to be coordinated. Instead of sales and marketing working together, sales, marketing, and the sales-promotion group must work together. Sometimes, in fact, the coordinating unit adds organizational distance between the two departments it is supposed to coordinate. And, the proliferation of coordinating units can add new jurisdictional boundaries leading to more, rather than fewer, coordination problems. Interfunctional coordinating units must be introduced with careful attention to clarity of objectives, structural design, and streamlined operating procedures.

Another approach is matrix management, an attempt to gain some of the advantages of both the functional and the divisional organization. It arose in the defense industry where project managers formed one side of the matrix and functional managers the other. The hope was that specialization would be nurtured within the functions and integration within the projects. For many companies and industries this approach has been good; for others, it has been an unmitigated disaster. When it has been applied in a true system sense, utilizing sensible management processes and systems, the informal social systems, and the right people, it has tended to work. When used as a panacea, it has tended to fail. The matrix by itself will not solve all the problems of interfunctional or interdivisional conflict.

Because a matrix structure is so hard to work within, it should be used only when a company already has an organization structure that works fairly effectively. Although change to a matrix structure can sometimes improve a strong organization, it will only stress and confound a weak, ineffective organization.

Although the organization structure is a powerful tool for promoting interfunctional coordination, changing the hierarchy frequently, particularly in cultures not used to upheaval, can be difficult. Some companies have found that constant changes help to prevent the creation of oversized barriers between different operating functions and to make the whole structure limber and supple. Other companies have found that frequent organization change leads to constant turmoil. It takes time for each manager and each person to understand where they fit in the new structure. If the structure is constantly changing, people have little chance to learn their jobs.

Finally, there is no perfect organization structure, only important trade-offs and temporary optimums. It is impossible to obtain all the benefits of specialization and integration at the same time, using only the management hierarchy. A move in one direction invariably means that a company gains some things and loses others. If the organization is to be responsive to the environment and to its own strategy, it must change as the environment and strategy change. Thus, even an optimum approach is only a temporary optimum.

The strategy and the structure provide a basis for the application of a rich set of formal management processes and systems, which are presented in the next section.

MANAGEMENT PROCESSES AND SYSTEMS

Formal management process and systems and the informal social system (discussed later) are the two most underused interfunctional coordination approaches among the six. Formal management processes and systems include everything a company can formally do outside of the organization structure and all the people within the organization structure. This section includes only a few of the many ways of using this approach.

The goal-setting process and the system for measuring performance and allocating rewards are closely related. If manufacturing is rewarded for having low inventory levels, while sales is rewarded for obtaining additional sales based on good customer service and high inventory levels, the differing rewards for the two departments will generate intense arguments over inventory and service levels. The explicit differences in the goal-setting process, the measurement system, and the rewards system are much easier to identify then other subtle, more cultural aspects of an organization. At the same time, the goal-setting process, measurement system, and rewards system tend to make the culture and tone of the organization more tangible by emphasizing either cross-functional goals and rewards or single-department goals and rewards. To the extent that the goals and rewards are interfunctional, they tend to foster coordination across departments.

Task forces and committees are other management processes and systems related to the organization structure. A task force tends to be temporary, while a committee can be permanent. Both encourage people from different parts of the organization to come together and jointly solve problems or take advantage of an opportunity.

If the task forces and committees become a focal point of rancor, they may contribute to interfunctional warfare rather than to coordination. Membership, agendas, and processes must be carefully determined if task forces and committees are to work well. Putting a group of people in a room, locking the door, and telling them to work together does not ensure that they will. The task must be clear, and mechanisms must be developed to bring ideas as well as people together.

Another formal management process and system that contributes to interfunctional coordination is career paths. In many companies an individual moves from function to function, gaining background and perspective along the way. In addition, someone who has worked in functions will have political connections there. People in these career paths can help turn a formal system into an effective informal social network.

The interfunctional career path can be overdone, however. A manager who constantly changes function, with no clear progression in one or two primary departments, almost invariably becomes a "jack-of-all-trades but master of none" with little functional depth. An organization staffed with such people tends to lack the subtle judgment and well-honed skills that come from extensive experience in one function. Thus, the interfunctional-career-path approach should include deep experience in one or two functions complemented by broadening exposure to one or perhaps two others. The combinations should make sense for the individual and be related to the natural grouping of functions in the business.

As the interfunctional-career-path approach indicates, some management processes and systems can be a double-edged sword. Each approach and component must be used with moderation and care because each has advantages and disadvantages. The overuse of interfunctional career paths is no better than the underutilization.

THE MANAGEMENT INFORMATION SYSTEM

One formal management process, the information system, has become so pervasive and powerful that it deserves separate attention as the fourth coordination approach. The information system helps the corporation to define what is important and to frame how different departments and divisions view one another and the whole company. Often, the information system is structured to provide functional managers with information in a format customized to their function. This customization tends to exacerbate the cultural differences among functions and to encourage managers in each function to focus on different key success factors. By the same token, the information system can harmonize perspectives of different jurisdictions. A unified information system can be particularly useful to top-level functional managers, encouraging them to focus on the whole company rather than on their individual areas.

The information system is also a powerful communications tool and a potent aid in managing important interfunctional activities, such as order fulfillment. Communication methods, such as shared databases using computer networks, electronic mail, voice mail, and teleconferencing, reduce the barriers of distance, time, and jurisdictional boundaries. Voice mail enables workers and managers in different time zones to share thoughts and keep each other informed. A teleconference has some of the feel and tone of a face-to-face meeting without the travel and hassle. Such technology can foster a sense of unification and togetherness that is otherwise hard to develop in a large multinational, multidivisional organization.

Of course, electronic connectors do not replace the human warmth and feel of a face-to-face meeting; often, electronic get-togethers are more structured and formal. But, they are important and efficient links to face-to-face gatherings and allow the organization to operate without time delays. With electronic communication, the day-to-day flow of information goes faster and more smoothly, thereby diminishing annoyance and irritation.

Finally, the information system is critical to the order-fulfillment process, which is often a primary source of interdepartmental conflict. As the order flows from the sales department, to customer service, to finance/credit, to operations, to logistics, to service, and finally to the finance/billing department, objectives, cultures, evidence, thought processes, and outlooks easily clash. An integrated order-fulfillment system with a shared database can identify points of likely conflict earlier so more time for resolution is available. Shared databases can minimize arguments over the quality of evidence and different people's views of the same situation. Important policy-level issues can be highlighted for high-level decision making. A good order-fulfillment system can also eliminate problems that arise from poor communication and faulty or outdated information.

Much like a strategy document, an integrated order-fulfillment system enables functions to work together with some relief from the tension of on-line decision making. Even the analysis needed to develop the system encourages sharing views and mutual understanding.

The information system is one of the most important tools for coping with the increasing complexity of customer relationships and functional coordination and with the vast growth in transaction volume. And, it has not yet reached its limit as a jurisdictional integrator.

INFORMAL SOCIAL SYSTEMS AND CULTURE

When asked about interfunctional coordination, managers think naturally of organization structure and formal management processes and systems; these approaches are visible, tangible, and enforceable. However, the informal social system can also be helpful. It is an old and effective method of encouraging the parts of an organization to work together.

Geography is important to the information social system. By and large, people tend to work most closely with those who are near them. Thus, a strong way to encourage interfunctional coordination is to move the offices of the people in different functions close to one another. Of course, there are physical limits as well as conflicting pulls to keep the members of a single department close together because they must cooperate to accomplish everyday work.

However, even joint cafeteria facilities, parking lots, restrooms, coffee pots, and water fountains have a big impact on the informal social system. Whenever people see one another or congregate informally, they can converse about business or other joint interests. Such constant, low-key communication is very useful in building interfunctional coordination, and informal goodwill can help limit the work-related conflicts.

Other forms of team building exist, some more subtle than others. At the company picnic, for example, a volleyball game of sales against manufacturing tends to hinder interfunctional coordination. If, however, the two teams each have players from sales and manufacturing, coordination and a sense of working together are engendered. Identifying a wide range of opportunities for such informal team building is possible with careful and creative thought. If the sales vice president and manufacturing vice president go on a series of plant tours and customer visits together, they will tend to work better together over time. In addition, the symbolism is powerful. Their subordinates will understand that working cross-functionally is acceptable and admirable. In fact, it is vital for top functional managers to be seen together publicly; it helps set the culture and tone of the organization.

Many formal management processes have informal social-system consequences that are relevant to interfunctional coordination. For example, as corporate life has grown more complex, corporate training and development programs have increased. Some are designed to help participants learn about other parts of the company and the company's strategy and culture. This formal mechanism helps engender interfunctional coordination and a holistic sense of the firm. However, perhaps most powerful from an interfunctional perspective are the relationships and networks that arise in such settings. By sharing travel, meals, discussion groups, and occasional recreational activities, the representatives of different departments build valuable contacts and resources throughout the organization; their viewpoints broaden. They also have colleagues to contact when they need information or help from other jurisdictions. Almost all face-to-face corporate meetings allow information networks to develop, and these opportunities should be carefully and deliberately nurtured.

A major part of an organization's culture and tone comes from how interfunctional coordination is considered and accomplished. If the president turns to functional subordinates and says, "Work it out among yourselves" and walks away from interfunctional contention, the tone of the meeting is likely to be negative and adversarial. If the president makes all the interfunctional decisions, various top functional managers will not learn how to work together. However, if the president actively brings the various functional leaders together and helps them work out their problems in a constructive, mutually beneficial way, the culture of interfunctional cooperation will be encouraged. Even informal slurs greeted as humor can add to the problem. Top general management must help different functions understand, rather than attack, one another.

THE SELECTION AND PROMOTION OF EMPLOYEES

Culture is set and decisions are made by people. One critical way to encourage interfunctional cooperation is by choosing people with broad perspectives, interfunctional experience, and the ability to work together toward a common vision. All too often, managers are promoted solely on their ability to perform their jobs within their functions. Instead, promotions and hiring should be based not only on functional competence but also on an ability to coordinate and cooperate across jurisdictional boundaries and to engender such behavior from subordinates. Not only will the organization be populated with interdepartmental team players but also a tone of interfunctional communication and working together will be encouraged. In essence, the promotion process becomes part of the formal reward system.

Promotions are related to the reward system and also to career paths. If a company makes a conscious effort to develop people with interfunctional perspectives, it will have a stockpile of promotable managers with broad views and interfunctional experience.

Unfortunately, some people cannot deal psychologically with the conflict accompanying interfunctional coordination. These people do not see conflict as healthy and natural but avoid it at all costs and force their subordinates to do the same. It is most difficult to help such "team destroyers" embrace the need for open communication, honest dissent, and joint compromise.[4] These people can harm an organization; however, should their skills be necessary, they can be placed in special nonmanagement positions. Some companies create positions for those with great functional talent but limited coordination ability.

At a minimum, the people an organization hires must be competent in their own functions. If they are not, the organization will suffer interjurisdictional coordination problems because people coordinate best with those who are able and respected. Functional incompetence breeds interfunctional problems.

—— THE FOUR ADJUDICATORS

In addition to the functional line managers, there are four groups of people that can contribute to interfunctional coordination: the staff engineering group, cost-accounting experts, human resource managers, and top-level

---

4. The term *team destroyers* was coined by Suzanne Wetlaufer in "Anatomy of a 'Team Destroyer'," Harvard Business School Case No. 9-589-038.

general management. The engineers can help by providing clear technical trade-offs that illuminate conflicting points of view and encourage an intellectual dialogue rather than a power struggle. Sometimes, creative engineering ideas can resolve apparently conflicting goals. The engineers can inform people and affect outcomes if they are willing to participate in business decisions. They cannot run from the important issues by hiding behind a veil of formulas and purely technical contributions. Similarly, the line functions must be willing to welcome staff engineering input and to help the engineers incorporate business concerns into their technical analyses.

Cost-accounting experts can also give carefully formed opinions on heated conflicts. Good cost accounting, which focuses on realistic accuracy rather than imagined precision, can help line-operating managers weigh the impact of different options and understand the real cost of various approaches. The cost accountants must understand the economic consequences of decisions and be able to communicate them if they are to be useful in decision making. Most important, they must understand the whole business, and how each function operates. A unified cost system can be an important integrative tool.

Human resources managers can identify and attract to the company highly competent people capable of cross-functional integration. In addition, they can participate in the development of formal management systems and processes and organization structures that contribute to integration. Among these should be training and development programs that include exposure and respect for differing functional responsibilities and perspective. Human resources specialists can also demonstrate a continuing commitment to building a team spirit and mediating functional conflicts. As respected neutral parties, often privy to confidential and sensitive personal information, they can help each line function to understand differing objectives and perspectives.

Staff functions, such as staff engineering, cost accounting, and human resources, are a potentially influential force in interdepartmental coordination. If the staff people see their job as bringing the operating departments together, they can be very helpful. If they believe their power increases when the line functions must deal through them, rather than directly, the staff groups can be very disruptive. It is difficult yet important to inculcate staff values that nurture cooperation with and among line-operating departments.

Finally, top-level general managers can have a great impact on interfunctional coordination. Only they can provide a clear statement of a unified strategy and explicit policies for accomplishing it. The strategy becomes the core of shared goals that supersede individual department goals for the good of the total business. General managers can consistently demonstrate their commitment to building a unified interfunctional team through assignments that foster cooperation, meetings that stress sharing and cooperation, a tone of equity, and an orientation toward results rather than politics and internal power. Finally, top-level general managers can set high standards of competence for high-level functional managers.

—— THE TOTAL SYSTEM

No single aspect or approach to interfunctional coordination is as important as the total system. Over the years different companies have developed a wide variety of techniques, such as particular organizational structures and management processes for engendering interfunctional coordination. Many of these techniques have failed because they were not part of a total system. If top management makes interfunctional coordination a major priority, it can become a part of the strategy, culture, and tone and will be supported by the organization structure, formal management processes and information systems, informal social systems, and the choice of people. All this, however, must be managed continually. Interfunctional coordination is not a problem to be solved; it is constantly being challenged by new environmental demands, new strategic imperatives, and the desire to form closed units. People, and perhaps particularly Americans, tend to "root for the home team." Thus, the members of a function can easily become insular and make themselves the home team.

Top general management must constantly provide the focus, rewards, and systems that inculcate interfunctional coordination, particularly for companies determined to provide specialties and not commodities.

Top management tends to be preoccupied with leadership, but perhaps as important as leadership, which implies a vertical dimension in working within the organization, is team building, which concerns the horizontal dimension. Some managers seem more eager to develop teams than do others. However, if the strategy and the environment require interfunctional coordination, a manager could not find a more worthwhile activity than team building.

—— BIBLIOGRAPHY

Aicklen, Chad, "Development Team Approach to New Product Introductions," *Business Marketing* (November 1985) , p. 114.

Bartlett, Christopher A., and Sumantra Ghoshal, *Managing Across Borders: The Transnational Solution,* (Boston, Mass.: Harvard Business School Press, 1989).

Couretas, John, "The Challenge to Marketing of Integrated Manufacturing Databases," *Business Marketing* (March 1985), p. 40.

Davis, Stanley M., *Future Perfect,* (Reading, Mass.: Addison-Wesley, 1987).

Davis, Stanley M., and Paul R. Lawrence, *Matrix,* (Reading, Mass.: Addision-Wesley, 1977).

Dyer, William G., *Team Building: Issues and Alternatives,* (Reading, Mass.: Addison-Wesley, 1977).

Eccles, Robert G., and Dwight B. Crane, *Doing Deals: Investment Banks at Work,* (Boston, Mass.: Harvard Business School Press, 1988).

Flood, Robert L., and Ewart R. Carson, *Dealing with Complexity: An Introduction to the Theory and Application of Systems*, (New York: Plenum Press, 1988).

Galbraith, Jay, *Designing Complex Organizations*, (Reading, Mass.: Addision-Wesley, Inc., 1973).

Gemmill, Gary R., and David L. Wilemon,"The Product Manager as an Influence Agent," *Journal of Marketing*, Vol 36 (January 1972), pp. 26–33.

Gupta, Ashok K., Raj S.P. Gupta, and David L. Wilemon, "The R & D-Marketing Interface in High-Technology Firms," *Journal of Product Innovation Management*, 2:12–24 (New York: Elsevier Science Publishing Co., Inc., 1985).

Kanter, Rosabeth Moss, "When a Thousand Flowers Bloom: Structural, Collective, and Social Conditions for Innovation in Organizations," Division of Research, Harvard Business School, Working Paper, No. 87-018.

Kanter, Rosabeth Moss, *When Giants Learn to Dance: Mastering the Challenges of Strategy, Management, and Careers in the 1990s*, (New York: Simon and Schuster, 1989).

Lawrence, Paul R., and Jay W. Lorsch, *Developing Organizations: Diagnosis and Action*, (Reading, Mass.: Addison-Wesley, 1969).

Lawrence, Paul R., and Jay W. Lorsch, "New Management Job: The Integrator," *Harvard Business Review* (November–December 1967), pp. 142–151.

Lawrence, Paul R., and Jay W. Lorsch, *Organization and Environment Managing Differentiation and Integration*, (Boston, Mass.: Harvard Business School Press, 1967).

Lorsch, Jay W., "Note on Organization Design," Harvard Business School, Case No. 476-094 (1975).

Lorsch, Jay W., and Paul R. Lawrence, "Organizing for Product Innovation," *Harvard Business Review* (January–February 1965), pp. 109–122.

Mitchell, Russell, "How Ford Hit the Bull's-Eye with Taurus," *Business Week,* (June 30, 1986), p. 69.

Nadler, David, and Michael Tushman, *Strategic Organization Design: Concepts, Tools, Processes*, (Glenview, Ill.: Scott, Foresman and Company, 1988).

Peters, Tom, "The Destruction of Hierarchy," *Industry Week* (August 15, 1988), p. 33.

Ruekert, Robert W., and Orville C. Walker, Jr., "Marketing's Interaction with Other Functional Units: A Conceptual Framework and Empirical Evidence," *Journal of Marketing*, Volume 51 (January 1987), pp. 1–19.

Ruekert, Robert W., Orville C. Walker, Jr., and Kenneth J. Roering, "The Organization of Marketing Activities: A Contingency Theory of Structure and Performance," *Journal of Marketing*, Volume 49 (Winter 1985), pp. 13–25.

Seiler, John A., "Diagnosing Interdepartmental Conflict," *Harvard Business Review* (September–October 1963), pp. 121–132.

Shapiro, Benson P., "Can Marketing and Manufacturing Coexist?," *Harvard Business Review* (September–October 1977), pp. 104–114.

Stefflre, Volney, "Organization Obstacles to Innovation: A Formulation of the Problem," *Journal of Product Innovation Management*, 2:3–11, (New York: Elsevier Science Publishing Co., 1985).

Tekeuchi, Hirotaka, and Ikujiro Nonaka, "The New Product Development Game," *Harvard Business Review* (January–February 1986), pp. 137–146.

Venkatesh, Alladi, and David L. Wilemon, "Interpersonal Influence in Product Management," *Journal of Marketing* (October 1976), pp. 33–40.

Walker, Arthur H., and Jay W. Lorsch, "Organizational Choice: Product vs. Function," *Harvard Business Review* (November–December 1968), pp. 129–138.

Walton, Richard E., *Up and Running: Integrating Information Technology and the Organization,* (Boston, Mass.: Harvard Business School Press, 1989).

Ware, James, "Managing a Task Force," Harvard Business School, Case No. 478-002 (1977).

Wetlaufer, Suzanne, "Anatomy of a 'Team Destroyer'," Harvard Business School, Case No. 589-038 (1988).

DISCUSSION QUESTIONS

1. Is functional integration appropriate, to the degree suggested by this reading, for all organizations? When is functional integration beneficial? When is it harmful?

2. Some organizations operate by the philosophy of each tub on its own bottom. Would this interfere with functional integration? Explain whether or not an individualistic style can be just as effective as a highly cooperative style.

3. Are certain societies more culturally suited to functional integration than other societies? Compare and contrast two societies and how you think they would be more or less responsive to functional integration. For example, near the end of the reading the author states, "People, and perhaps particularly Americans, tend to 'root for the home team.'" What might be some of the aspects of the cultures that you have chosen that would encourage or hinder functional integration?

4. Considering the trends that some business authorities see developing—a lessening of hierarchy and a broader dispersion of authority and responsibility—what are the implications for integration as a management concern? Under the influence of these trends, will integration become easier or more difficult?

24 Matrix Management: Not a Structure, a Frame of Mind

CHRISTOPHER A. BARTLETT AND SUMANTRA GHOSHAL

In many companies, argue these authors, strategic thinking has outdistanced organizational capability. These companies adopt elaborate organizational matrices that actually impair their ability to implement sophisticated strategies. Keeping a company strategically agile while still coordinating its activities across divisions, functions, and even continents means eliminating parochialism, improving communication, and weaving the decision-making process into the company's social fabric.

This reading describes techniques that successful companies have used to manage complex strategies. The key is to build a matrix of corporate values and priorities in the minds of managers and let them make the judgments and negotiate the deals that make the strategy pay off.

Top-level managers in many of today's leading corporations are losing control of their companies. The problem is not that they have misjudged the demands created by an increasingly complex environment and an accelerating rate of environmental change, nor even that they have failed to develop strategies appropriate to the new challenges. The problem is that their companies are organizationally incapable of carrying out the sophisticated strategies they have developed. Over the past 20 years, strategic thinking has far outdistanced organizational capabilities.

All through the 1980s, companies everywhere were redefining their strategies and reconfiguring their operations in response to such developments as the globalization of markets, the intensification of competition, the acceleration of product life cycles, and the growing complexity of relationships with suppliers, customers, employees, governments, even competitors. But as companies struggled with these changing environmental realities, many fell into one of two traps—one strategic, one structural.

The strategic trap was to implement simple, static solutions to complex and dynamic problems. The bait was often a consultant's siren song promising to simplify or at least minimize complexity and discontinuity. Despite the new demands of overlapping industry boundaries and greatly altered value-added chains, managers were promised success if they would "stick to their knitting." In a swiftly changing international political economy, they were urged to rein in dispersed overseas operations and focus on the triad markets, and in an increasingly intricate and sophisticated competitive environment, they were encouraged to choose between alternative generic strategies—low cost or differentiation.

Yet the strategic reality for most companies was that both their business and their environment really *were* more complex, while the proposed solutions were often simple, even simplistic. The traditional telephone company that stuck to its knitting was trampled by competitors who redefined their strategies in response to new technologies linking telecommunications, computers, and office equipment into a single integrated system. The packaged-goods company that concentrated on the triad markets quickly discovered that Europe, Japan, and the United States were the epicenters of global competitive activity, with higher risks and slimmer profits than more protected and less competitive markets such as Australia, Turkey, and Brazil. The consumer electronics company that adopted an either-or generic strategy found itself facing competitors able to develop cost and differentiation capabilities at the same time.

In recent years, as more and more managers recognized oversimplification as a strategic trap, they began to accept the need to manage complexity rather than seek to minimize it. This realization, however, led many into an equally threatening organizational trap when they concluded that the best response to increasingly complex strategic requirements was increasingly complex organizational structures.

The obvious organizational solution to strategies that required multiple, simultaneous management capabilities was the matrix structure that became so fashionable in the late 1970s and the early 1980s. Its parallel reporting relationships acknowledged the diverse, conflicting needs of functional, product, and geographic management groups and provided a formal mechanism for resolving them. Its multiple information channels allowed the organization to capture and analyze external complexity. And its overlapping responsibilities were designed to combat parochialism and build flexibility into the company's response to change.

In practice, however, the matrix proved all but unmanageable—especially in an international context. Dual reporting led to conflict and confusion; the proliferation of channels created informational log-jams as a proliferation of committees and reports bogged down the organization; and overlapping responsibilities produced turf battles and a loss of accountability. Separated by barriers of distance, language, time, and culture, managers found it virtually impossible to clarify the confusion and resolve the conflicts.

In hindsight, the strategic and structural traps seem simple enough to avoid, so one has to wonder why so many experienced general managers have fallen into them. Much of the answer lies in the way we have traditionally thought about the general manager's role. For decades, we have seen the general manager as chief strategic guru and principal organizational architect. But as the competitive climate grows less stable and less predictable, it is harder for one person alone to succeed in that great visionary role. Similarly, as formal, hierarchical structure gives way to networks of personal relationships that work through informal, horizontal communication channels, the image of top management in an isolated corner office moving boxes and lines on an organization chart becomes increasingly anachronistic.

Paradoxically, as strategies and organizations become more complex and sophisticated, top-level general managers are beginning to replace their historical concentration on the grand issues of strategy and structure with a focus on the details of managing people and processes. The critical strategic requirement is not to devise the most ingenious and well-coordinated plan but to build the most viable and flexible strategic process; the key organizational task is not to design the most elegant structure but to capture individual capabilities and motivate the entire organization to respond cooperatively to a complicated and dynamic environment.

───── BUILDING AN ORGANIZATION

Although business thinkers have written a great deal about strategic innovation, they have paid far less attention to the accompanying organizational challenges. Yet many companies remain caught in the structural-complexity trap that paralyzes their ability to respond quickly or flexibly to the new strategic imperatives.

For those companies that adopted matrix structures, the problem was not in the way they defined the goal. They correctly recognized the need for a multidimensional organization to respond to growing external complexity. The problem was that they defined their organizational objectives in purely structural terms. Yet the term *formal structure* describes only the organization's basic anatomy. Companies must also concern themselves with organizational physiology—the systems and relationships that allow the lifeblood of information to flow through the organization. They also need to develop a healthy organizational psychology—the shared norms, values, and beliefs that shape the way individual managers think and act.

The companies that fell into the organizational trap assumed that changing their formal structure (anatomy) would force changes in interpersonal relationships and decision processes (physiology), which in turn would reshape the individual attitudes and actions of managers (psychology).

But as many companies have discovered, reconfiguring the formal structure is a blunt and sometimes brutal instrument of change. A new structure creates new and presumably more useful managerial ties, but these can take months and often years to evolve into effective knowledge-generating and decision-making relationships. And because the new job requirements will frustrate, alienate, or simply overwhelm so many managers, changes in individual attitudes and behavior will likely take even longer.

As companies struggle to create organizational capabilities that reflect rather than diminish environmental complexity, good managers gradually stop searching for the ideal structural template to impose on the company from the top down. Instead, they focus on the challenge of building up an appropriate set of employee attitudes and skills and linking them together with carefully developed processes and relationships. In other words, they begin to focus on building the organization rather than simply on installing a new structure.

Indeed, the companies that are most successful at developing multi-dimensional organizations begin at the far end of the anatomy-physiology-psychology sequence. Their first objective is to alter the organizational psychology—the broad corporate beliefs and norms that shape managers' perceptions and actions. Then, by enriching and clarifying communication and decision processes, companies reinforce these psychological changes with improvements in organizational physiology. Only later do they consolidate and confirm their progress by realigning organizational anatomy through changes in the formal structure.

No company we know of has discovered a quick or easy way to change its organizational psychology to reshape the understanding, identification, and commitment of its employees. But we found three principal characteristics common to those that managed the task most effectively:

1. They developed and communicated a clear and consistent corporate vision.
2. They effectively managed human resource tools to broaden individual perspectives and to develop identification with corporate goals.
3. They integrated individual thinking and activities into the broad corporate agenda by a process we call co-option.

——— BUILDING A SHARED VISION

Perhaps the main reason managers in large, complex companies cling to parochial attitudes is that their frame of reference is bounded by their specific responsibilities. The surest way to break down such insularity is to develop and communicate a clear sense of corporate purpose that extends into every corner of the company and gives context and meaning to each manager's particular roles and responsibilities. We are not talking about a slogan, however catchy and pointed. We are talking about a company vision, which must be crafted and articulated with clarity, continuity, and consistency. We are talking about clarity of expression that makes company objectives understandable and meaningful; continuity of purpose that underscores their enduring importance; and consistency of application across business units and geographical boundaries that ensures uniformity throughout the organization.

Clarity There are three keys to clarity in a corporate vision: simplicity, relevance, and reinforcement. NEC's integration of computers and communications—C&C—is probably the best single example of how simplicity can make a vision more powerful. Top management has applied the C&C concept so effectively that it describes the company's business focus, defines its distinctive source of competitive advantage over large companies like IBM and AT&T, and summarizes its strategic and organizational imperatives.

The second key, relevance, means linking broad objectives to concrete agendas. When Wisse Dekker became CEO at Philips, his principal strategic concern was the problem of competing with Japan. He stated this challenge in martial terms—the U.S. had abandoned the battlefield; Philips was now Europe's last defense against insurgent Japanese electronics companies. By focusing the company's attention not only on Philips's corporate survival but also on the protection of national and regional interests, Dekker heightened the sense of urgency and commitment in a way that legitimized cost-cutting efforts, drove an extensive rationalization of plant operations, and inspired a new level of sales achievements.

The third key to clarity is top management's continual reinforcement, elaboration, and interpretation of the core vision to keep it from becoming obsolete or abstract. Founder Konosuke Matsushita developed a grand, 250-year vision for his company, but he also managed to give it immediate relevance. He summed up its overall message in the "Seven Spirits of Matsushita," to which he referred constantly in his policy statements. Each January he wove the company's one-year operational objectives into his overarching concept to produce an annual theme that he then captured in a slogan. For all the loftiness of his concept of corporate purpose, he gave his managers immediate, concrete guidance in implementing Matsushita's goals.

Continuity   Despite shifts in leadership and continual adjustments in short-term business priorities, companies must remain committed to the same core set of strategic objectives and organizational values. Without such continuity, unifying vision might as well be expressed in terms of quarterly goals.

It was General Electric's lack of this kind of continuity that led to the erosion of its once formidable position in electrical appliances in many countries. Over a period of 20 years and under successive CEOs, the company's international consumer-product strategy never stayed the same for long. From building locally responsive and self-sufficient "mini-GEs" in each market, the company turned to a policy of developing low-cost offshore sources, which eventually evolved into a de facto strategy of international outsourcing. Finally, following its acquisition of RCA, GE's consumer electronics strategy made another about-face and focused on building centralized scale to defend domestic share. Meanwhile, the product strategy within this shifting business emphasis was itself unstable. The Brazilian subsidiary, for example, built its TV business in the 1960s until it was told to stop; in the early 1970s, it emphasized large appliances until it was denied funding, then it focused on housewares until the parent company sold off that business. In two decades, GE utterly dissipated its dominant franchise in Brazil's electrical products market.

Unilever, by contrast, made an enduring commitment to its Brazilian subsidiary, despite volatile swings in Brazil's business climate. Company chairman Floris Maljers emphasized the importance of looking past the latest political crisis or economic downturn to the long-term business potential. "In those parts of the world," he remarked, "you take your management cues from the way they dance. The samba method of management is two steps forward then one step back." Unilever built—two steps forward and one step back—a profitable $300 million business in a rapidly growing economy with 130 million consumers, while its wallflower competitors never ventured out onto the floor.

Consistency The third task for top management in communicating strategic purpose is to ensure that everyone in the company shares the same vision. The cost of inconsistency can be horrendous. It always produces confusion and, in extreme cases, can lead to total chaos, with different units of the organization pursuing agendas that are mutually debilitating.

Philips is a good example of a company that, for a time, lost its consistency of corporate purpose. As a legacy of its wartime decision to give some overseas units legal autonomy, management had long experienced difficulty persuading North American Philips (NAP) to play a supportive role in the parent company's global strategies. The problem came to a head with the introduction of Philips's technologically first-rate videocassette recording system, the V2000. Despite considerable pressure from world headquarters in the Netherlands, NAP refused to launch the system, arguing that Sony's Beta system and Matsushita's VHS format were too well established and had cost, feature, and system-support advantages Philips couldn't match. Relying on its legal independence and managerial autonomy, NAP management decided instead to source products from its Japanese competitors and market them under its Magnavox brand name. As a result, Philips was unable to build the efficiency and credibility it needed to challenge Japanese dominance of the VCR business.

Most inconsistencies involve differences between what managers of different operating units see as the company's key objectives. Sometimes, however, different corporate leaders transmit different views of overall priorities and purpose. When this stems from poor communication, it can be fixed. When it's a result of fundamental disagreement, the problem is serious indeed, as illustrated by ITT's problems in developing its strategically vital System 12 switching equipment. Continuing differences between the head of the European organization and the company's chief technology officer over the location and philosophy of the development effort led to confusion and conflict throughout the company. The result was disastrous. ITT had difficulty transferring vital technology across its own unit boundaries and so was irreparably late introducing this key product to a rapidly changing global market. These problems eventually led the company to sell off its core telecommunications business to a competitor.

But formulating and communicating a vision—no matter how clear, enduring, and consistent—cannot succeed unless individual employees understand and accept the company's stated goals and objectives. Problems at this level are more often related to receptivity than to communication. The development of individual understanding and acceptance is a challenge for a company's human resource practices.

——— DEVELOPING HUMAN RESOURCES

Although top managers universally recognize their responsibility for developing and allocating a company's scarce assets and resources, their focus on finance and technology often overshadows the task of developing the scarcest resource of all—capable managers. But if there is one key to regaining control of companies that operate in fast-changing environments, it is the ability of top management to turn the perceptions, capabilities, and relationships of individual managers into the building blocks of the organization.

One pervasive problem in companies whose leaders lack this ability—or fail to exercise it—is getting managers to see how their specific responsibilities relate to the broad corporate vision. Growing external complexity and strategic sophistication have accelerated the growth of a cadre of specialists who are physically and organizationally isolated from each other, and the task of dealing with their consequent parochialism should not be delegated to the clerical staff that administers salary structures and benefit programs. Top managers inside and outside the human resource function must be leaders in the recruitment, development, and assignment of the company's vital human talent.

Recruitment and Selection   The first step in successfully managing complexity is to tap the full range of available talent. It is a serious mistake to permit historical imbalances in the nationality or functional background of the management group to constrain hiring or subsequent promotion. In today's global marketplace, domestically oriented recruiting limits a company's ability to capitalize on its worldwide pool of management skill and biases its decision-making processes.

After decades of routinely appointing managers from its domestic operations to key positions in overseas subsidiaries, Procter & Gamble realized that the practice not only worked against sensitivity to local cultures—a lesson driven home by several marketing failures in Japan—but also greatly underutilized its pool of high-potential non-American managers. (Fortunately, our studies turned up few companies as shortsighted as one that made overseas assignments on the basis of *poor* performance, because foreign markets were assumed to be "not as tough as the domestic environment.")

Not only must companies enlarge the pool of people available for key positions, they must also develop new criteria for choosing those most likely to succeed. Because past success is no longer a sufficient qualification for increasingly subtle, sensitive, and unpredictable senior-level tasks, top management must become involved in a more discriminating selection process. At Matsushita, top management selects candidates for international assignments on the basis of a comprehensive set of personal characteristics, expressed for simplicity in the acronym SMILE: specialty (the needed skill, capability, or knowledge); management ability (particularly motivational ability); international flexibility (willingness to learn and ability to adapt); language facility; and endeavor (vitality, perseverance in the face of difficulty). These attributes are remarkably similar to those targeted by NEC and Philips, where top executives also are involved in the senior-level selection process.

Training and Development   Once the appropriate top-level candidates have been identified, the next challenge is to develop their potential. The most successful development efforts have three aims that take them well beyond the skill-building objectives of classic training programs: to inculcate a common vision and shared values; to broaden management perspectives and capabilities; and to develop contacts and shape management relationships.

To build common vision and values, white-collar employees at Matsushita spend a good part of their first six months in what the company calls "cultural and spiritual training." They study the company credo, the "Seven Spirits of Matsushita," and the philosophy of Konosuke Matsushita. Then they learn how to translate these internalized lessons into daily behavior and even operational decisions. Culture-building exercises as intensive as Matsushita's are sometimes dismissed as innate Japanese practices that would not work in other societies, but in fact, Philips has a similar entry-level training practice (called "organization cohesion training"), as does Unilever (called, straightforwardly, "indoctrination").

The second objective—broadening management perspectives—is essentially a matter of teaching people how to manage complexity instead of merely to make room for it. To reverse a long and unwieldy tradition of running its operations with two- and three-headed management teams of separate technical, commercial, and sometimes administrative specialists, Philips asked its training and development group to de-specialize top management trainees. By supplementing its traditional menu of specialist courses and functional programs with more intensive general management training, Philips was able to begin replacing the ubiquitous teams with single business heads who also appreciated and respected specialist points of view.

The final aim—developing contacts and relationships—is much more than an incidental byproduct of good management development, as the comments of a senior personnel manager at Unilever suggest: "By bringing managers from different countries and businesses together at Four Acres [Unilever's international management-training college], we build contacts and create bonds that we could never achieve by other means. The company spends as much on training as it does on R&D not only because of the direct effect it has on upgrading skills and knowledge but also because it plays a central role in indoctrinating managers into a Unilever club where personal relationships and informal contacts are much more powerful than the formal systems and structures."

Career-Path Management   Although recruitment and training are critically important, the most effective companies recognize that the best way to develop new perspectives and thwart parochialism in their managers is through personal experience. By moving selected managers across functions, businesses, and geographic units, a company encourages cross-fertilization of ideas as well as the flexibility and breadth of experience that enable managers to grapple with complexity and come out on top.

Unilever has long been committed to the development of its human resources as a means of attaining durable competitive advantage. As early as the 1930s, the company was recruiting and developing local employees to replace the parent-company managers who had been running most of its overseas subsidiaries. In a practice that came to be known as "-ization," the company committed itself to the Indianization of its Indian company, the Australization of its Australian company, and so on.

Although delighted with the new talent that began working its way up through the organization, management soon realized that by reducing the transfer of parent-company managers abroad, it had diluted the powerful glue that bound diverse organizational groups together and linked dispersed operations. The answer lay in formalizing a second phase of the -ization process. While continuing with Indianization, for example, Unilever added programs aimed at the "Unileverization" of its Indian managers.

In addition to bringing 300 to 400 managers to Four Acres each year, Unilever typically has 100 to 150 of its most promising overseas managers on short- and long-term job assignments at corporate headquarters. This policy not only brings fresh, close-to-the-market perspectives into corporate decision making but also gives the visiting managers a strong sense of Unilever's strategic vision and organizational values. In the words of one of the expatriates in the corporate offices, "The experience initiates you into the Unilever Club and the clear norms, values, and behaviors that distinguish our people—so much so that we really believe we can spot another Unilever manager anywhere in the world."

Furthermore, the company carefully transfers most of these high-potential individuals through a variety of different functional, product, and geographic positions, often rotating every two or three years. Most important, top management tracks about 1,000 of these people—some 5% of Unilever's total management group—who, as they move through the company, forge an informal network of contacts and relationships that is central to Unilever's decision-making and information-exchange processes.

Widening the perspectives and relationships of key managers as Unilever has done is a good way of developing identification with the broader corporate mission. But a broad sense of identity is not enough. To maintain control of its global strategies, Unilever must secure a strong and lasting individual commitment to corporate visions and objectives. In effect, it must co-opt individual energies and ambitions into the service of corporate goals.

———— CO-OPTING MANAGEMENT EFFORTS

As organizational complexity grows, managers and management groups tend to become so specialized and isolated and to focus so intently on their own immediate operating responsibilities that they are apt to respond parochially to intrusions on their organizational turf, even when the overall corporate interest is at stake. A classic example, described earlier, was the decision by North American Philips's consumer electronics group to reject the parent company's VCR system.

At about the same time, Philips, like many other companies, began experimenting with ways to convert managers' intellectual understanding of the corporate vision—in Philips's case, an almost evangelical determination to defend Western electronics against the Japanese—into a binding personal commitment. Philips concluded that it could co-opt individuals and organizational groups into the broader vision by inviting them to contribute to the corporate agenda and then giving them direct responsibility for implementation.

In the face of intensifying Japanese competition, Philips knew it had to improve coordination in its consumer electronics among its fiercely independent national organizations. In strengthening the central product divisions, however, Philips did not want to deplete the enterprise or commitment of its capable national management teams.

The company met these conflicting needs with two cross-border initiatives. First, it created a top-level World Policy Council for its video business that included key managers from strategic markets—Germany, France, the United Kingdom, the United States, and Japan. Philips knew that its national companies' long history of independence made local managers reluctant to take orders from Dutch headquarters in Eindhoven—often for good reason, because much of the company's best market knowledge and technological expertise resided in its offshore units. Through the council, Philips co-opted their support for company decisions about product policy and manufacturing location.

Second, in a more powerful move, Philips allocated global responsibilities to units that previously had been purely national in focus. Eindhoven gave NAP the leading role in the development of Philips's projection television and asked it to coordinate development and manufacture of all Philips television sets for North America and Asia. The change in the attitude of NAP managers was dramatic.

A senior manager in NAP's consumer electronics business summed up the feelings of U.S. managers: "At last, we are moving out of the dependency relationship with Eindhoven that was so frustrating to us." Co-option had transformed the defensive, territorial attitude of NAP managers into a more collaborative mind-set. They were making important contributions to global corporate strategy instead of looking for ways to subvert it.

In 1987, with much of its TV set production established in Mexico, the president of NAP's consumer electronics group told the press, "It is the commonality of design that makes it possible for us to move production globally. We have splendid cooperation with Philips in Eindhoven." It was a statement no NAP manager would have made a few years earlier, and it perfectly captured how effectively Philips had co-opted previously isolated, even adversarial, managers into the corporate agenda.

——— THE MATRIX IN THE MANAGER'S MIND

Since the end of World War II, corporate strategy has survived several generations of painful transformation and has grown appropriately agile and athletic. Unfortunately, organizational development has not kept pace, and managerial attitudes lag even farther behind. As a result, corporations now commonly design strategies that seem impossible to implement, for the simple reason that no one can effectively implement third-generation strategies through second-generation organizations run by first-generation managers.

Today the most successful companies are those where top executives recognize the need to manage the new environmental and competitive demands by focusing less on the quest for an ideal structure and more on developing the abilities, behavior, and performance of individual managers. Change succeeds only when those assigned to the new transnational and interdependent tasks understand the overall goals and are dedicated to achieving them.

One senior executive put it this way: "The challenge is not so much to build a matrix structure as it is to create a matrix in the minds of our managers." The inbuilt conflict in a matrix structure pulls managers in several directions at once. Developing a matrix of flexible perspectives and relationships within each manager's mind, however, achieves an entirely different result. It lets individuals make the judgments and negotiate the trade-offs that drive the organization toward a shared strategic objective.

——— DISCUSSION QUESTIONS

1. What aspects of American culture support participation in a shared vision? What aspects of American culture might hinder a company's employees from participation in a company's shared vision?

2. An international company is encouraged to create loyalty to the organization among its managers. What are some of the difficulties an organization might encounter from its overseas managers? Within the world at large, what social implications, both positive and negative, might result from creating a matrix of the mind?

3. The authors state that matrix management is a way of thinking. What are some possible disadvantages to this approach that relies heavily on developing an organization's human resource?

4. Does this reading suggest that the organization is taking a place similar to that of a country in the loyalties of its managers? Explain why or why not.

25   In Praise of Hierarchy

ELLIOTT JAQUES

Hierarchy, the most effective organizational form that a big company can employ, has been widely misunderstood and abused, according to this author. Pay grades are confused with real layers of responsibility, for example, and incompetent bosses abound. Nevertheless, the key to organizational success is individual accountability, and hierarchy preserves unambiguous accountability for getting work done. This reading describes the uses and misuses of hierarchy, demonstrating that it can serve as a powerful tool for understanding how an organization ought to work and how it ought to perform.

A t first glance, hierarchy may seem difficult to praise. Bureaucracy is a dirty word even among bureaucrats, and in business there is a widespread view that managerial hierarchy kills initiative, crushes creativity, and has therefore seen its day. Yet 35 years of research have convinced me that managerial hierarchy is the most efficient, the hardiest, and in fact the most natural structure ever devised for large organizations. Properly structured, hierarchy can release energy and creativity, rationalize productivity, and actually improve morale. Moreover, I think most managers know this intuitively and have only lacked a workable structure and a decent intellectual justification for what they have always known could work and work well.

As currently practiced, hierarchy undeniably has its drawbacks. One of business's great contemporary problems is how to release and sustain among the people who work in corporate hierarchies the thrust, initiative, and adaptability of the entrepreneur. This problem is so great that it has become fashionable to call for a new kind of organization to put in place of managerial hierarchy, an organization that will better meet the requirements of what is variously called the Information Age, the Services Age, or the Post-Industrial Age.

As vague as the description of the age is the definition of the kind of new organization required to suit it. Theorists tell us it ought to look more like a symphony orchestra or a hospital or perhaps the British raj. It ought to function by means of primus groups or semiautonomous work teams or matrix overlap groups. It should be organic or entrepreneurial or tight-loose. It should hinge on skunk works or on management by walking around or perhaps on our old friend, management by objective.

All these approaches are efforts to overcome the perceived faults of hierarchy and find better ways to improve morale and harness human creativity. But the theorists' belief that our changing world requires an alternative to hierarchical organization is simply wrong, and all their proposals are based on an inadequate understanding of not only hierarchy but also human nature.

Hierarchy is not to blame for our problems. Encouraged by gimmicks and fads masquerading as insights, we have burdened our managerial systems with a makeshift scaffolding of inept structures and attitudes. What we need is not simply a new, flatter organization but an understanding of how managerial hierarchy functions—how it relates to the complexity of work and how we can use it to achieve a more effective deployment of talent and energy.

The reason we have a hierarchical organization of work is not only that tasks occur in lower and higher degrees of complexity—which is obvious—but also that there are sharp discontinuities in complexity that separate tasks into a series of steps or categories—which is not so obvious. The same discontinuities occur with respect to mental work and to the breadth and duration of accountability. The hierarchical kind of organization we call bureaucracy did not emerge accidentally. It is the only form of organization that can enable a company to employ large numbers of people and yet preserve unambiguous accountability for the work they do. And that is why, despite its problems, it has so doggedly persisted.

Hierarchy has not had its day. Hierarchy never did have its day. As an organizational system, managerial hierarchy has never been adequately described and has just as certainly never been adequately used. The problem is not to find an alternative to a system that once worked well but no longer does; the problem is to make it work efficiently for the first time in its 3,000-year history.

▬▬▬ WHAT WENT WRONG . . .

There is no denying that hierarchical structure has been the source of a great deal of trouble and inefficiency. Its misuse has hampered effective management and stifled leadership, while its track record as a support for entrepreneurial energy has not been exemplary. We might almost say that successful businesses have had to succeed despite hierarchical organization rather than because of it.

One common complaint is excessive layering—too many rungs on the ladder. Information passes through too many people, decisions through too many levels, and managers and subordinates are too close together in experience and ability, which smothers effective leadership, cramps accountability, and promotes buck passing. Relationships grow stressful when managers and subordinates bump elbows, so to speak, within the same frame of reference.

Another frequent complaint is that few managers seem to add real value to the work of their subordinates. The fact that the breakup value of many large corporations is greater than their share value shows pretty clearly how much value corporate managers can *subtract* from their subsidiary businesses, but in fact few of us know exactly what managerial added value would look like as it was occurring.

Many people also complain that our present hierarchies bring out the nastier aspects of human behavior, like greed, insensitivity, careerism, and self-importance. These are the qualities that have sent many behavioral scientists in search of cooperative, group-oriented, nonhierarchical organizational forms. But are they the inevitable companions of hierarchy, or perhaps a product of the misuse of hierarchy that would disappear if hierarchy were properly understood and structured?

—— . . . AND WHAT CONTINUES TO GO WRONG

The fact that so many of hierarchy's problems show up in the form of individual misbehavior has led to one of the most widespread illusions in business, namely, that a company's managerial leadership can be significantly improved solely by doing psychotherapeutic work on the personalities and attitudes of its managers. Such methods can help individuals gain greater personal insight, but I doubt that individual insight, personality matching, or even exercises in group dynamics can produce much in the way of organizational change or an overall improvement in leadership effectiveness. The problem is that our managerial hierarchies are so badly designed as to defeat the best efforts even of psychologically insightful individuals.

Solutions that concentrate on groups, on the other hand, fail to take into account the real nature of employment systems. People are not employed in groups. They are employed individually, and their employment contracts—real or implied—are individual. Group members may insist in moments of great esprit de corps that the group as such is the author of some particular accomplishment, but once the work is completed, the members of the group look for individual recognition and individual progression in their careers. It is not groups but individuals whom the company will hold accountable. The only true group is the board of directors, with its corporate liability.

None of the group-oriented panaceas face this issue of accountability. All the theorists refer to group authority, group decisions, and group consensus, none of them to group accountability. Indeed, they avoid the issue of accountability altogether, for to hold a group accountable, the employment contract would have to be with the group, not with the individuals, and companies simply do not employ groups as such.

To understand hierarchy, first you must understand employment. To be employed is to have an ongoing contract that holds you accountable for doing work of a given type for a specified number of hours per week in exchange for payment. Your specific tasks within that given work are assigned to you by a person called your manager (or boss or supervisor), who *ought to be held accountable* for the work you do.

If we are to make our hierarchies function properly, it is essential to place the emphasis on *accountability for getting work done.* This is what hierarchical systems ought to be about. Authority is a secondary issue and flows from accountability in the sense that there should be just that amount of authority needed to discharge the accountability. So if a group is to be given authority, its members must be held accountable as a group, and unless this is done, it is very hard to take so-called group decisions seriously. If the CEO or the manager of the group is held accountable for outcomes, then in the final analysis, he or she will have to agree with group decisions or have the authority to block them, which means that the group never really had decision-making power. Alternatively, if groups are allowed to make decisions without their manager's seal of approval, then accountability as such will suffer, for if a group does badly, the group is never fired. (And it would be shocking if it were.)

In the long run, therefore, group authority *without* group accountability is dysfunctional, and group authority *with* group accountability is unacceptable. So images of organizations that are more like symphony orchestras or hospitals or the British raj are surely nothing more than metaphors to express a desired feeling of togetherness—the togetherness produced by a conductor's baton, the shared concern of doctors and nurses for their patients, or the apparent unity of the British civil service in India.

In employment systems, after all, people are not mustered to play together as their manager beats time. As for hospitals, they are the essence of everything bad about bureaucratic organization. They function in spite of the system, only because of the enormous professional devotion of their staffs. The Indian civil service was in many ways like a hospital, its people bound together by the struggle to survive in a hostile environment. Managers do need authority, but authority based appropriately on the accountabilities they must discharge.

⎯⎯⎯ WHY HIERARCHY?

The bodies that govern companies, unions, clubs, and nations all employ people to do work, and they all organize these employees in managerial hierarchies, systems that allow organizations to hold people accountable for getting assigned work done. Unfortunately, we often lose sight of this goal and set up the organizational layers in our managerial hierarchies to accommodate pay brackets and facilitate career development instead. If work happens to get done as well, we consider that a useful bonus.

But if our managerial hierarchical organizations tend to choke so readily on debilitating bureaucratic practices, how do we explain the persistence and continued spread of this form of organization for more than 3,000 years? And why has the determined search for alternatives proved so fruitless?

The answer is that managerial hierarchy is and will remain the *only* way to structure unified working systems with hundreds, thousands, or tens of thousands of employees, for the very good reason that managerial hierarchy is the expression of two fundamental characteristics of real work. First, the tasks we carry out are not only more or less complex but they also become more complex as they separate out into discrete categories or types of complexity. Second, the same is true of the mental work that people do on the job, for as this work grows more complex, it too separates out into distinct categories or types of mental activity. In turn, these two characteristics permit hierarchy to meet four of any organization's fundamental needs: to add real value to work as it moves through the organization, to identify and nail down accountability at each stage of the value-adding process, to place people with the necessary competence at each organizational layer, and to build a general consensus and acceptance of the managerial structure that achieves these ends.

——— HIERARCHICAL LAYERS

The complexity of the problems encountered in a particular task, project, or strategy is a function of the variables involved—their number, their clarity or ambiguity, the rate at which they change, and overall, the extent to which they are distinct or tangled. Obviously, as you move higher in a managerial hierarchy, the most difficult problems you have to contend with become increasingly complex. The biggest problems faced by the CEO of a large corporation are vastly more complex than those encountered on the shop floor. The CEO must cope not only with a huge array of often amorphous and constantly changing data but also with variables so tightly interwoven that they must be disentangled before they will yield useful information. Such variables might include the cost of capital; the interplay of corporate cash flow; the structure of the international competitive market; the uncertainties of Europe in the next decade; the future of Pacific Rim development; social developments with respect to labor; political developments in Eastern Europe, the Middle East, and the Third World; and technological research and change.

That the CEO's and the lathe operator's problems are different in quality as well as quantity will come as no surprise to anyone. The question is—and always has been—where does the change in quality occur? On a continuum of complexity from the bottom of the structure to the top, where are the discontinuities that will allow us to identify layers of hierarchy that are distinct and separable, as different as ice is from water and water from steam? I spent years looking for the answer, and what I found was somewhat unexpected.

My first step was to recognize the obvious, that the layers have to do with manager-subordinate relationships. The manager's position is in one layer and the subordinate's is in the next layer below. What then sets the necessary distance between? This question cannot be answered without knowing just what it is that a manager does.

The managerial role has three critical features. First, and *most* critical, every manager must be held accountable not only for the work of subordinates but also for adding value to their work. Second, every manager must be held accountable for sustaining a team of subordinates capable of doing this work. Third, every manager must be held accountable for setting direction and getting subordinates to follow willingly, indeed enthusiastically. In brief, every manager is accountable for work and leadership.

In order to make accountability possible, managers must have enough authority to ensure that their subordinates can do the work assigned to them. This authority must include at least these four elements:

1. The right to veto any applicant who, in the manager's opinion, falls below the minimum standards of ability;
2. The power to make work assignments;
3. The power to carry out performance appraisals and, within the limits of company policy, to make decisions—not recommendations—about raises and merit rewards;
4. The authority to initiate removal—at least from the manager's own team—of anyone who seems incapable of doing the work.

But defining the basic nature of the managerial role reveals only part of what a managerial layer means. It cannot tell us how wide a managerial layer should be, what the difference in responsibility should be between a manager and a subordinate, or most important, where the break should come between one managerial layer and another. Fortunately, the next step in the research process supplied the missing piece of the puzzle.

⎯⎯ RESPONSIBILITY AND TIME

This second step was the unexpected and startling discovery that the level of responsibility in any organizational role—whether a manager's or an individual contributor's—can be objectively measured in terms of the target completion time of the *longest* task, project, or program assigned to that role. The more distant the target completion date of the longest task or program, the heavier the weight of responsibility is felt to be. I call this measure the responsibility time span of the role. For example, a supervisor whose principal job is to plan tomorrow's production assignments and next week's work schedule but who also has ongoing responsibility for uninterrupted production supplies for the month ahead has a responsibility time span of one month. A foreman who spends most of the time riding herd on this week's production quotas but who must also develop a program to deal with the labor requirements of next year's retooling has a responsibility time span of a year or a little more. The advertising vice president who stays late every night working on next week's layouts but who also has to begin making contingency plans for the expected launch of two

EXHIBIT 1
Managerial Hierarchy in Fiction and in Fact

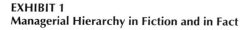

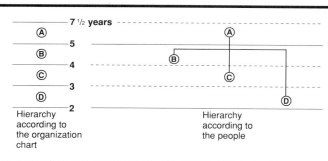

new local advertising media campaigns three years away has a responsibility time span of three years.

To my great surprise, I have found, over the past 35 years, that in all types of managerial organizations in many different countries, people in roles that have the same time spans experience the same weight of responsibility and declare the same level of pay to be fair, regardless of their occupation or actual pay. The time-span range runs from a day at the bottom of a large corporation to more than 20 years at the top, while the felt-fair pay ranges from $15,000 to $1 million and more.

Armed with my definition of a manager and my time-span measuring instrument, I then bumped into the second surprising finding—repeatedly confirmed—about layering in managerial hierarchies: the boundaries between successive managerial layers occur at certain specific time-span increments, just as ice changes to water and water to steam at certain specific temperatures. And the fact that everyone in the hierarchy, regardless of status, seems to see these boundaries in the same places suggests that the boundaries reflect some universal truth about human nature.

Exhibit 1, "Managerial Hierarchy in Fiction and in Fact," shows the hierarchical structure of part of a department at one company I studied, along with the approximate responsibility time span for each position. The longest task for manager A was more than five years, while for B, C, and D, the longest tasks fell between two and five years. Note also that according to the organization chart, A is the designated manager of B, B of C, and C of D.

In reality, the situation was quite different. Despite the managerial roles specified by the company, B, C, and D all described A as their "real" boss. C complained that B was "far too close" and "breathing down my neck." D had the same complaint about C. B and C also admitted to finding it very difficult to manage their immediate subordinates, C and D respectively, who seemed to do better if treated as colleagues and left alone.

In short, there appeared to be a cutoff at five years, such that those with responsibility time spans of less than five years felt they needed a manager with a responsibility time span of more than five years. Manager D, with a time span of two to three years, did not feel that C, with a time span of three to four, was distant enough hierarchically to take orders from. D felt the same way about B. Only A filled the bill for *any* of the other three.

As the responsibility time span increased in the example from two years to three to four and approached five, no one seemed to perceive a qualitative difference in the nature of the responsibility that a manager discharged. Then, suddenly, when a manager had responsibility for tasks and projects that exceeded five years in scope, everyone seemed to perceive a difference not only in the scope of responsibility but also in its quality and in the kind of work and worker required to discharge it.

I found several such discontinuities that appeared consistently in more than 100 studies. Real managerial and hierarchical boundaries occur at time spans of three months, 1 year, 2 years, 5 years, 10 years, and 20 years.

These natural discontinuities in our perception of the responsibility time span create hierarchical strata that people in different companies, countries, and circumstances all seem to regard as genuine and acceptable. The existence of such boundaries has important implications in nearly every sphere of organizational management. One of these is performance appraisal. Another is the capacity of managers to add value to the work of their subordinates.

The only person with the perspective and authority to judge and communicate personal effectiveness is an employee's accountable manager, who in most cases, is also the only person from whom an employee will accept evaluation and coaching. This accountable manager must be the supervisor one real layer higher in the hierarchy, not merely the next higher employee on the pay scale.

As I suggested earlier, part of the secret to making hierarchy work is to distinguish carefully between hierarchical layers and pay grades. The trouble is that companies need two to three times as many pay grades as they do working layers, and once they've established the pay grades, which are easy to describe and set up, they fail to take the next step and set up a different managerial hierarchy based on responsibility rather than salary. The result is too many layers.

My experience with organizations of all kinds in many different countries has convinced me that effective value-adding managerial leadership of subordinates can come only from an individual one category higher in cognitive capacity, working one category higher in problem complexity. By contrast, wherever managers and subordinates are in the same layer— separated only by pay grade—subordinates see the boss as too close, breathing down their necks, and they identify their "real" boss as the next manager at a genuinely higher level of cognitive and task complexity. This kind of overlayering is what produces the typical symptoms of bureaucracy in its worst form—too much passing problems up and down the system, bypassing, poor task setting, frustrated subordinates, anxious managers, wholly inadequate performance appraisals, "personality problems" everywhere, and so forth.

LAYERING AT COMPANY X

Companies need more than seven pay grades—as a rule, many more. But seven hierarchical layers is enough or more than enough for all but the largest corporations.

Let me illustrate this pattern of hierarchical layering with the case of two divisions of Company X, a corporation with 32,000 employees and annual sales of $7 billion. As shown in *Exhibit 2*, the CEO sets strategic goals that look ahead as far as 25 years and manages executive vice presidents with responsibility for 12- to 15-year development programs. One vice president is accountable for several strategic business units, each with a president who works with critical tasks of up to 7 years duration.

One of these units (Y Products) employs 2,800 people, has annual sales of $250 million, and is engaged in the manufacture and sale of engineering products, with traditional semiskilled shop-floor production at Layer I. The other unit (Z Press) publishes books and employs only 88 people. Its funding and negotiations with authors are in the hands of a general editor at Layer IV, assisted by a small group of editors at Layer III, each working on projects that may take up to 18 months to complete.

So the president of Y Products manages more people, governs a greater share of corporate resources, and earns a lot more money for the parent company than does the president of Z Press. Yet the two presidents occupy the same hierarchical layer, have similar authority, and take home comparable salaries. This is neither coincidental nor unfair. It is natural, correct, and efficient.

It is the level of responsibility, *measured in terms of time span*, that tells you how many layers you need in an enterprise—not the number of subordinates or the magnitude of sales or profits. These factors may have a marginal influence on salary; they have no bearing at all on hierarchical layers.

CHANGES IN THE QUALITY OF WORK

The widespread and striking consistency of this underlying pattern of true managerial layers leads naturally to the question of why it occurs. Why do people perceive a sudden leap in status from, say, 4½ years to 5 and from 9 to 10?

The answer goes back to the earlier discussion of complexity. As we go higher in a managerial hierarchy, the most difficult problems that arise grow increasingly complex, and as the complexity of a task increases, so does the

EXHIBIT 2
Two Divisions of Corporation X

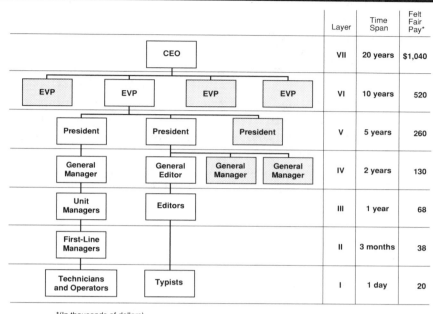

	Layer	Time Span	Felt Fair Pay*
CEO	VII	20 years	$1,040
EVP EVP EVP EVP	VI	10 years	520
President President President	V	5 years	260
General Manager General Editor General Manager General Manager	IV	2 years	130
Unit Managers Editors	III	1 year	68
First-Line Managers	II	3 months	38
Technicians and Operators Typists	I	1 day	20

*(In thousands of dollars)

complexity of the mental work required to handle it. What I found when I looked at this problem over the course of 10 years was that this complexity, like responsibility time span, also occurs in leaps or jumps. In other words, the most difficult tasks found within any given layer are all characterized by the same type or category of complexity, just as water remains in the same liquid state from 0° to 100° Celsius, even though it ranges from very cold to very hot. (A few degrees cooler or hotter and water changes in state, to ice or steam.)

It is this suddenly increased level of necessary mental capacity, experience, knowledge, and mental stamina that allows managers to add value to the work of their subordinates. What they add is a new perspective, one that is broader, more experienced, and most important, one that extends further in time. If the Z Press editors at Layer III find and develop manuscripts into books with market potential, it is their general editor at Layer IV who fits those books into the press's overall list, who thinks ahead to their position on next year's list and later allocates resources to their production and marketing, and who makes projections about the publishing and book-buying trends of the next two to five years.

It is also this sudden change in the quality, not just the quantity, of managerial work that subordinates accept as a natural and appropriate break in the continuum of hierarchy. It is why they accept the boss's authority and not just the boss's power.

So the whole picture comes together. Managerial hierarchy or layering is the only effective organizational form for deploying people and tasks at complementary levels, where people can do the tasks assigned to them, where the people in any given layer can add value to the work of those in the layer below them, and finally, where this stratification of management strikes everyone as necessary and welcome.

What we need is not some new kind of organization. What we need is managerial hierarchy that understands its own nature and purpose. Hierarchy is the best structure for getting work done in big organizations. Trying to raise efficiency and morale without first setting this structure to rights is like trying to lay bricks without mortar. No amount of exhortation, attitudinal engineering, incentive planning, or even leadership will have any permanent effect unless we understand what hierarchy is and why and how it works. We need to stop casting about fruitlessly for organizational Holy Grails and settle down to the hard work of putting our managerial hierarchies in order.

━━━ DISCUSSION QUESTIONS

1. Hierarchy or bureaucracy has always been a feature of organizational life, and according to the author, hierarchy has never been adequately used. In the rush for innovation in the business world, what other traditional aspects of organizational life are being considered a problem when indeed they may be the solution?
2. The author addresses the issue of accountability. What are some of the factors that contribute to a lack of accountability in many businesses?
3. In your opinion, how effectively does the author make the case for hierarchy? Do his ideas about hierarchy hold up for the organization of the 1990s? How does his argument hold up against those promoting flatter organizations?
4. Relate your work experience in a hierarchical organization. In your experience, what have the positive aspects of hierarchy been? The negative aspects?
5. Would you rather work in a hierarchical or a flat organization? Explain the basis of your preference.

MANAGING ORGANIZATIONAL CHANGE

Choosing Strategies for Change

26

JOHN P. KOTTER AND LEONARD A. SCHLESINGER

As the business environment becomes more competitive, organizations cannot afford not to change; yet, people in organizations understandably fear and resist change. A major task of managers is to implement change, which means overcoming the resistance. The authors of this reading describe four basic reasons why people resist change and offer various methods for dealing with the different types of resistance.

In 1973, The Conference Board asked 13 eminent authorities to speculate what significant management issues and problems would develop over the next 20 years. One of the strongest themes that runs through their subsequent reports is a concern for the ability of organizations to respond to environmental change. As one person wrote: "It follows that an acceleration in the rate of change will result in an increasing need for reorganization. Reorganization is usually feared, because it means disturbance of the status quo, a threat to people's vested interests in their jobs, and an upset to established ways of doing things. For these reasons, needed reorganization is often deferred, with a resulting loss in effectiveness and an increase in costs."[1]

Subsequent events have confirmed the importance of this concern about organizational change. Today, more and more managers must deal with new government regulations, new products, growth, increased competition, technological developments, and a changing work force. In response, most companies or divisions of major corporations find that they must undertake moderate organizational changes at least once a year and major changes every four or five.[2]

Few organizational change efforts tend to be complete failures, but few tend to be entirely successful either. Most efforts encounter problems; they often take longer than expected and desired; they sometimes kill morale, and they often cost a great deal in terms of managerial time or emotional upheaval. More than a few organizations have not even tried to initiate needed changes because

---

1. Marvin Bower and C. Lee Walton, Jr., "Gearing a Business to the Future," in *Challenge to Leadership* (New York: The Conference Board, 1973), p. 126.

2. For recent evidence on the frequency of changes, *see* Stephen A. Allen, "Organizational Choice and General Influence Networks for Diversified Companies," *Academy of Management Journal*, September 1978, p. 341.

the managers involved were afraid that they were simply incapable of success-fully implementing them.

In this reading, we first describe various causes for resistance to change and then outline a systematic way to select a strategy and set of specific approaches for implementing an organizational change effort. The methods described are based on our analyses of dozens of successful and unsuccessful organizational changes.

——— DIAGNOSING RESISTANCE

Organizational change efforts often run into some form of human resistance. Although experienced managers are generally all too aware of this fact, surprisingly few take time before an organizational change to assess systematically who might resist the change initiative and for what reasons. Instead, using past experiences as guidelines, managers all too often apply a simple set of beliefs—such as "engineers will probably resist the change because they are independent and suspicious of top management." This limited ap-proach can create serious problems. Because of the many different ways in which individuals and groups can react to change, correct assessments are often not intuitively obvious and require careful thought.

Of course, all people who are affected by change experience some emotional turmoil. Even changes that appear to be "positive" or "rational" involve loss and uncertainty.[3] Nevertheless, for various reasons, individuals or groups can react very differently to change—from passively resisting it, to aggressively trying to undermine it, to sincerely embracing it.

To predict what form their resistance might take, managers need to be aware of the four most common reasons people resist change. These include a desire not to lose something of value, a misunderstanding of the change and its implications, a belief that the change does not make sense for the organization, and a low tolerance for change.

PAROCHIAL SELF-INTEREST

One major reason people resist organizational change is that they think they will lose something of value as a result. In these cases, because people focus on their own best interests and not on those of the total organization, resistance often results in "politics" or "political behavior."[4] Consider these two examples:

---

3. For example, *see* Robert A. Luke, Jr., "A Structural Approach to Organizational Change," *Journal of Applied Behavioral Science*, September–October 1973, p. 611.

4. For a discussion of power and politics in corporations, *see* Abraham Zaleznik and Manfred F. R. Kets de Vries, *Power and the Corporate Mind* (Boston: Houghton Mifflin, 1975), Chapter 6; and Robert H. Miles, *Macro Organizational Behavior* (Pacific Palisades, Calif.: Goodyear, 1978), Chapter 4.

After several years of rapid growth, the president of an organization decided that its size demanded the creation of a new staff function— New-Product Planning and Development—to be headed by a vice president. Operationally, this change eliminated most of the decision-making power that the vice presidents of marketing, engineering, and production had over new products. Inasmuch as new products were very important in this organization, the change also reduced the vice presidents' status which, together with power, was very important to them.

During the two months after the president announced his idea for a new-product vice president, the existing vice presidents each came up with six or seven reasons why the new arrangement might not work. Their objections grew louder and louder until the president shelved the idea.

A manufacturing company had traditionally employed a large group of personnel people as counselors and "father confessors" to its pro-duction employees. This group of counselors tended to exhibit high morale because of the professional satisfaction they received from the helping relationships they had with employees. When a new perfor-mance-appraisal system was installed, every six months the counsel-ors were required to provide each employee's supervisor with a written evaluation of the employee's emotional maturity, promotional potential, and so forth.

As some of the personnel people immediately recognized, the change would alter their relationships from a peer and helper to more of a boss and evaluator with most of the employees. Predictably, the personnel counselors resisted the change. While publicly arguing that the new system was not as good for the company as the old one, they privately put as much pressure as possible on the personnel vice president until he significantly altered the new system.

Political behavior sometimes emerges before and during organizational change efforts when what is in the best interests of one individual or group is not in the best interests of the total organization or of other individuals and groups.

Although political behavior sometimes takes the form of two or more armed camps publicly fighting things out, it usually is much more subtle. In many cases, it occurs completely under the surface of public dialogue. Although initiators of power struggles are sometimes scheming and ruthless individuals, more often than not they are people who view their potential loss from change as an unfair violation of their implicit, or psychological, contract with the organization.[5]

---

5. *See* Edgar H. Schein, *Organizational Psychology* (Englewood Cliffs, N.J.: Prentice-Hall, 1965), p. 44.

MISUNDERSTANDING AND LACK OF TRUST

People also resist change when they do not understand its implications and perceive that it might cost them much more than they will gain. Such situations often occur when trust is lacking between the person initiating the change and the employees.[6] Here is an example:

When the president of a small midwestern company announced to his managers that the company would implement a flexible working schedule for all employees, it never occurred to him that he might run into resistance. He had been introduced to the concept at a management seminar and decided to use it to make working conditions at his company more attractive, particularly to clerical and plant personnel.

Shortly after the announcement, numerous rumors began to circulate among plant employees—none of whom really knew what flexible working hours meant and many of whom were distrustful of the manufacturing vice president. One rumor, for instance, suggested that flexible hours meant that most people would have to work whenever their supervisors asked them to—including evenings and weekends. The employee association, a local union, held a quick meeting and then presented the management with a nonnegotiable demand that the flexible hours concept be dropped. The president, caught completely by surprise, complied.

Few organizations can be characterized as having a high level of trust between employees and managers; consequently, it is easy for misunderstandings to develop when change is introduced. Unless managers surface misunderstandings and clarify them rapidly, they can lead to resistance. And that resistance can easily catch change initiators by surprise, especially if they assume that people only resist change when it is not in their best interest.

DIFFERENT ASSESSMENTS

Another common reason people resist organizational change is that they assess the situation differently from their managers or those initiating the change and see more costs than benefits resulting from the change, not only for themselves but for their company as well. For example:

The president of one moderate-size bank was shocked by his staff's analysis of the bank's real estate investment trust (REIT) loans. This complicated analysis suggested that the bank could easily lose up to $10 million, and that the possible losses were increasing each month by 20%. Within a week, the president drew up a plan to reorganize the

---

6. See Chris Argyris, *Intervention Theory and Method* (Reading, Mass.: Addison-Wesley, 1970), p. 70.

part of the bank that managed REITs. Because of his concern for the bank's stock price, however, he chose not to release the staff report to anyone except the new REIT section manager.

The reorganization immediately ran into massive resistance from the people involved. The group sentiment, as articulated by one person, was, "Has he gone mad? Why in God's name is he tearing apart this section of the bank? His actions have already cost us three very good people [who quit], and have crippled a new program we were implementing [which the president was unaware of] to reduce our loan losses."

Managers who initiate change often assume both that they have all the information required to conduct an adequate organization analysis and that those who will be affected by the change have the same facts, when neither assumption may be correct. In either case, the difference in information that each group works with often leads to different analyses, which in turn can lead to resistance. Moreover, if the analysis made by those not initiating the change is more accurate than that derived by the initiators, resistance is obviously "good" for the organization. But this likelihood is not obvious to some managers who assume that resistance is always bad and therefore always fight it.[7]

LOW TOLERANCE FOR CHANGE

People also resist change because they fear they will not be able to develop the new skills and behavior that will be required of them. All human beings are limited in their ability to change, with some people much more limited than others.[8] Organizational change can inadvertently require people to change too much, too quickly.

Peter F. Drucker has argued that the major obstacle to organizational growth is managers' inability to change their attitudes and behavior as rapidly as their organizations require.[9] Even when managers intellectually understand the need for changes in the way they operate, they sometimes are emotionally unable to make the transition.

It is because of people's limited tolerance for change that individuals will sometimes resist a change even when they realize it is a good one. For example, those who receive significantly more important jobs as a result of an organizational change will probably be very happy. But it is just as possible for such people to also feel uneasy and to resist giving up certain aspects of the current situation. New and very different jobs will require new and different

---

7. *See* Paul R. Lawrence, "How to Deal with Resistance to Change," *Harvard Business Review* (May–June 1954): 49; reprinted as *Harvard Business Review Classic* (January–February 1969): 4.

8. For a discussion of resistance that is personality based, *see* Goodwin Watson, "Resistance to Change," in *The Planning of Change*, eds. Warren G. Bennis, Kenneth F. Benne, and Robert Chin (New York: Holt, Rinehart, and Winston, 1969), p. 489.

9. Peter F. Drucker, *The Practice of Management* (New York: Harper and Row, 1954).

behaviors, new and different relationships, as well as the loss of some satisfactory current activities and relationships. If the changes are significant and the tolerance for change is low, people might begin actively to resist the change for reasons even they do not consciously understand.

People also sometimes resist organizational change to save face; to go along with the change would be, they think, an admission that some of their previous decisions or beliefs were wrong. Or they might resist because of peer group pressure or because of a supervisor's attitude. Indeed, there are probably an endless number of reasons why people resist change.[10]

Assessing which of the many possibilities might apply to those who will be affected by a change is important because it can help a manager select an appropriate way to overcome resistance. Without an accurate diagnosis of possibilities of resistance, a manager can easily get bogged down during the change process with very costly problems.

───── DEALING WITH RESISTANCE

Many managers underestimate not only the variety of ways people can react to organizational change but also the ways they can positively influence specific individuals and groups during a change. And, again because of past experiences, managers sometimes do not have an accurate understanding of the advantages and disadvantages of the methods with which they are familiar.

EDUCATION AND COMMUNICATION

One of the most common ways to overcome resistance to change is to educate people about it beforehand. Communication of ideas helps people see the need for and the logic of a change. The education process can involve one-on-one discussions, presentations to groups, or memos and reports. For example:

> As a part of an effort to make changes in a division's structure and in measurement and reward systems, a division manager put together a one-hour audiovisual presentation that explained the changes and the reasons for them. Over a four-month period, she made this presentation no less than a dozen times to groups of 20 or 30 corporate and division managers.

---

10. For a general discussion of resistance and reasons for it, *see* Chapter 3 in Gerald Zaltman and Robert Duncan, *Strategies for Planned Change* (New York: John Wiley, 1977).

An education and communication program can be ideal when resistance is based on inadequate or inaccurate information and analysis, especially if the initiators need the resistors' help in implementing the change. But some managers overlook the fact that a program of this sort requires a good relationship between initiators and resistors or that the latter may not believe what they hear. It also requires time and effort, particularly if a lot of people are involved.

PARTICIPATION AND INVOLVEMENT

If the initiators involve the potential resistors in some aspect of the design and implementation of the change, they can often forestall resistance. With a participative change effort, the initiators listen to the people the change involves and use their advice. To illustrate:

> The head of a small financial services company once created a task force to help design and implement changes in his company's reward system. The task force was composed of eight second- and third-level managers from different parts of the company. The president's specific charter to them was that they recommend changes in the company's benefit package. They were given six months and asked to file a brief progress report with the president once a month. After they had made their recommendations, which the president largely accepted, they were asked to help the company's personnel director implement them.

We have found that many managers have quite strong feelings about participation—sometimes positive and sometimes negative. That is, some managers feel that there should always be participation during change efforts, while others feel this is always a mistake. Both attitudes can create problems for a manager, because neither is very realistic.

When change initiators believe they do not have all the information they need to design and implement a change or when they need the whole-hearted commitment of others to do so, involving others makes very good sense. Considerable research has demonstrated that, in general, participation leads to commitment, not merely compliance.[11] In some instances, commitment is needed for the change to be a success. Nevertheless, the participation process does have its drawbacks. Not only can it lead to a poor solution if the process is not carefully managed, but also it can be enormously time consuming. When the change must be made immediately, it might take too long to involve others.

---

11. *See,* for example, Alfred J. Marrow, David F. Bowers, and Stanley E. Seashore, *Management by Participation* (New York: Harper and Row, 1967).

FACILITATION AND SUPPORT

Another way that managers can deal with potential resistance to change is by being supportive. This process might include providing training in new skills or giving employees time off after a demanding period or simply listening and providing emotional support. For example:

> Management in one rapidly growing electronics company devised a way to help people adjust to frequent organizational changes. First, management staffed its human resource department with four counselors who spent most of their time talking to people who were feeling burnt out or who were having difficulty adjusting to new jobs. Second, on a selective basis, management offered people four-week mini-sabbaticals that involved some reflective or educational activity away from work. And, finally, it spent a great deal of money on in-house education and training programs.

Facilitation and support are most helpful when fear and anxiety lie at the heart of resistance. Seasoned, tough managers often overlook or ignore this kind of resistance, as well as the efficacy of facilitative ways of dealing with it. The basic drawback of this approach is that it can be time consuming and expensive and still fail.[12] If time, money, and patience are not available, then using supportive methods will not be very practical.

NEGOTIATION AND AGREEMENT

Another way to deal with resistance is to offer incentives to active or potential resistors. For instance, management could give a union a higher wage rate in return for a rule change; it could increase an individual's pension benefits in return for an early retirement. Here is an example of negotiated agreements:

> In a large manufacturing company, the divisions were very interdependent. One division manager wanted to make some major changes in her organization. Yet, because of the interdependence, she recognized that she would be forcing some inconvenience and change on other divisions as well. To prevent top managers in other divisions from undermining her efforts, the division manager negotiated a written agreement with each manager. The agreement specified the outcomes the other division managers would receive and when, as well as the kinds of cooperation that she would receive from them in return during the change process. Later, whenever the division managers complained about her changes or the change process itself, she could point to the negotiated agreements.

---

12. Zaltman and Duncan, *Strategies for Planned Change,* Chapter 4.

Negotiation is particularly appropriate when someone is going to lose out as a result of a change, and his or her power to resist is significant. Negotiated agreements can be a relatively easy way to avoid major resistance though, like some other processes, they may become expensive. And once a manager makes it clear that he or she will negotiate to avoid major resistance, the manager is vulnerable to the possibility of blackmail.[13]

MANIPULATION AND CO-OPTATION

In some situations, managers also resort to covert attempts to influence others. Manipulation, in this context, normally involves the very selective use of information and the conscious structuring of events.

One common form of manipulation is co-optation. Co-opting an individual usually involves giving him or her a desirable role in the design or implementation of the change. Co-opting a group involves giving one of its leaders, or someone it respects, a key role in the design or implementation of a change. This is not a form of participation, however, because the initiators do not want the advice of the co-opted, merely his or her endorsement. For example:

> One division manager in a large multibusiness corporation invited the corporate human relations vice president, a close friend of the president, to help him and his key staff diagnose some problems the division was having. Because of his busy schedule, the corporate vice president was not able to do much of the actual information gathering or analysis himself, thus limiting his own influence on the diagnoses. But his presence at key meetings helped commit him to the diagnoses as well as the solutions the group designed. The commitment was subsequently very important because the president, at least initially, did not like some of the proposed changes. Nevertheless, after a discussion with his human relations vice president, he did not try to block them.

Under certain circumstances co-optation can be a relatively inexpensive and easy way to gain an individual's or a group's support (cheaper, for example, than negotiation and quicker than participation). Nevertheless, it has its drawbacks. If people feel they are being tricked into not resisting, are not being treated equally, or are being lied to, they may respond unfavorably. More than one manager has found that, by his effort to give some subordinate a sense of participation through co-optation, he created more resistance than if he had done nothing. In addition, co-optation can create a different kind of problem if those co-opted use their ability to influence the design and implementation of changes in ways that are not in the best interests of the organization.

---

13. For an excellent discussion of negotiation, *see* Gerald I. Nierenberg, *The Art of Negotiating* (Birmingham, Ala.: Cornerstone, 1968).

Other forms of manipulation have drawbacks also, sometimes to an even greater degree. Most people are likely to greet what they perceive as covert treatment and/or lies with a negative response. Furthermore, if a manager develops a reputation as a manipulator, it can undermine his ability to use needed approaches such as education/communication and participation/involvement. At the extreme, it can even ruin his career.

Nevertheless, people do manipulate others successfully—particularly when all other tactics are not feasible or have failed.[14] Having no other alternative and not enough time to educate, involve, or support people and without the power or other resources to negotiate, coerce, or co-opt them, managers have resorted to manipulating information channels in order to scare people into thinking there is a crisis coming which they can avoid only by changing.

EXPLICIT AND IMPLICIT COERCION

Finally, managers often deal with resistance coercively. Here they essentially force people to accept a change by explicitly or implicitly threatening them (with the loss of jobs, promotion possibilities, and so forth) or by actually firing or transferring them. As with manipulation, using coercion is a risky process because inevitably people strongly resent forced change. But in situations where speed is essential and where the changes will not be popular, regardless of how they are introduced, coercion may be the manager's only option.

Successful organizational change efforts are always characterized by the skillful application of a number of these approaches, often in very different combinations. However, successful efforts share two characteristics: managers employ the approaches with a sensitivity to their strengths and limitations (see *Exhibit 1*) and appraise the situation realistically.

The most common mistake managers make is to use only one approach or a limited set of them regardless of the situation. A surprisingly large number of managers have this problem. This would include the hard-boiled boss who often coerces people, the people-oriented manager who constantly tries to support and involve people, the cynical boss who always manipulates and co-opts others, the intellectual manager who relies heavily on education and communication, and the lawyerlike manager who usually tries to negotiate.[15]

A second common mistake that managers make is to approach change in a disjointed and incremental way that is not a part of a clearly considered strategy.

---

14. *See* John P. Kotter, "Power, Dependence, and Effective Management," *Harvard Business Review* (July–August 1977): 125.

15. Ibid., p. 135.

EXHIBIT 1
Methods for Dealing with Resistance to Change

APPROACH	COMMONLY USED IN SITUATIONS	ADVANTAGES	DRAWBACKS
Education + communication	Where there is a lack of information or inaccurate information and analysis	Once persuaded, people will often help with the implementation of the change	Can be very time consuming if many people are involved
Participation + involvement	Where the initiators do not have all the information they need to design the change and where others have considerable power to resist	People who participate will be committed to implementing change, and any relevant information they have will be integrated into the change plan	Can be very time consuming if participators design an inappropriate change
Facilitation + support	Where people are resisting because of adjustment problems	No other approach works as well with adjustment problems	Can be time consuming, expensive, and still fail
Negotiation + agreement	Where someone or some group will clearly lose out in a change and where that group has considerable power to resist	Sometimes it is a relatively easy way to avoid major resistance	Can be too expensive in many cases if it alerts others to negotiate for compliance
Manipulation + co-optation	Where other tactics will not work or are too expensive	It can be a relatively quick and inexpensive solution to resistance problems	Can lead to future problems if people feel manipulated
Explicit + implicit coercion	Where speed is essential and the change initiators possess considerable power	It is speedy and can overcome any kind of resistance	Can be risky if it leaves people mad at the initiators

CHOICE OF STRATEGY

In approaching an organizational change situation, managers explicitly or implicitly make strategic choices regarding the speed of the effort, the amount of preplanning, the involvement of others, and the relative emphasis they will give to different approaches. Successful change efforts seem to be those where these choices both are internally consistent and fit some key situational variables.

The strategic options available to managers can be usefully thought of as existing on a continuum (see *Exhibit 2*).[16] At one end of the continuum, the

---

16. *See* Larry E. Greiner, "Patterns of Organization Change," *Harvard Business Review* (May–June 1967): 119; and Larry E. Greiner and Louis B. Barnes, "Organization Change and Development," in *Organizational Change and Development*, eds. Gene W. Dalton and Paul R. Lawrence (Homewood, Ill.: Irwin, 1970), p. 3.

EXHIBIT 2
Strategic Continuum

FAST	SLOWER
Clearly planned	Not clearly planned at the beginning
Little involvement of others	More involvement of others
Attempt to overcome any resistance	Attempt to minimize any resistance

Key Situational Variables

The amount and type of resistance anticipated

The position of the initiators vis-à-vis the resistors (in terms of power, trust, etc.)

The locus of relevant data for designing the change and of needed energy for implementing it

The stakes involved (e.g., the presence or lack of presence of a crisis, the consequences of resistance and lack of change)

change strategy calls for a very rapid implementation, a clear plan of action, and little involvement of others. This type of strategy mows over any resistance and, at the extreme, would result in a fait accompli. At the other end of the continuum, the strategy would call for a much slower change process, a less clear plan, and the involvement of many people other than the change initiators. This type of strategy is designed to reduce resistance to a minimum.[17]

The further to the left one operates on the continuum in *Exhibit 2*, the more one tends to be coercive and the less one tends to use the other approaches—especially participation; the converse also holds.

Organizational change efforts that are based on inconsistent strategies tend to run into predictable problems. For example, efforts that are not clearly planned in advance and yet are implemented quickly tend to become bogged down owing to unanticipated problems. Efforts that involve a large number of people, but are implemented quickly, usually become either stalled or less participative.

SITUATIONAL FACTORS

Exactly where a change effort should be strategically positioned on the continuum in *Exhibit 2* depends on four factors:

17. For a good discussion of an approach that attempts to minimize resistance, *see* Renato Tagiuri, "Notes on the Management of Change: Implication of Postulating a Need for Competence," in John P. Kotter, Vijay Sathe, and Leonard A. Schlesinger, *Organization* (Homewood, Ill.: Irwin, 1979).

1. *The amount and kind of resistance that is anticipated.* All other factors being equal, the greater the anticipated resistance, the more difficult it will be simply to overwhelm it, and the more a manager will need to move toward the right on the continuum to find ways to reduce some of it.[18]

2. *The position of the initiator vis-à-vis the resistors, especially regarding power.* The less power the initiator has with respect to others, the more the initiating manager *must* move to the right on the continuum.[19] Conversely, the stronger the initiator's position, the more he or she can move to the left.

3. *The person who has the relevant data for designing the change and the energy for implementing it.* The more the initiators anticipate that they will need information and commitment from others to help design and implement the change, the more they must move to the right.[20] Gaining useful information and commitment requires time and the involvement of others.

4. *The stakes involved.* The greater the short-run potential for risks to organizational performance and survival if the present situation is not changed, the more one must move to the left.

Organizational change efforts that ignore these factors inevitably run into problems. A common mistake some managers make, for example, is to move too quickly and involve too few people despite the fact that they do not have all the information they really need to design the change correctly.

Insofar as these factors still leave a manager with some choice of where to operate on the continuum, it is probably best to select a point as far to the right as possible for both economic and social reasons. Forcing change on people can have too many negative side effects over both the short and the long term. Change efforts using the strategies on the right of the continuum can often help develop an organization and its people in useful ways.[21]

In some cases, however, knowing the four factors may not give a manager a comfortable and obvious choice. Consider a situation where a manager has a weak position vis-à-vis the people whom she thinks need a change and yet is faced with serious consequences if the change is not implemented immediately. Such a manager is clearly in a bind. If she somehow is not able to increase her power in the situation, she will be forced to choose some compromise strategy and to live through difficult times.

---

18. Jay W. Lorsch, "Managing Change," in *Organizational Behavior and Administration,* eds. Paul R. Lawrence, Louis B. Barnes, and Jay W. Lorsch (Homewood, Ill.: Irwin, 1976), p. 676.

19. Ibid.

20. Ibid.

21. Michael Beer, *Organization Change and Development: A Systems View* (Santa Monica, Calif.: Goodyear, 1980).

IMPLICATIONS FOR MANAGERS

Managers can improve their chance of success in an organizational change effort by doing the following:

1. *Conducting an organizational analysis that identifies the current situation, problems, and the forces that are possible causes of those problems.* The analysis should specify the actual importance of the problems, the speed with which the problems must be addressed if additional problems are to be avoided, and the kinds of changes that are generally needed.

2. *Conducting an analysis of factors relevant to producing the needed changes.* This analysis should focus on questions of who might resist the change, why, and how much; who has information that is needed to design the change, and whose cooperation is essential in implementing it; and what is the position of the initiator vis-à-vis other relevant parties in terms of power, trust, normal modes of interaction, and so forth.

3. *Selecting a change strategy, based on the previous analysis.* This analysis should specify the speed of change, the amount of preplanning, and the degree of involvement of others; select specific tactics for use with various individuals and groups; and be internally consistent.

4. *Monitoring the implementation process.* No matter how good a job one does of initially selecting a change strategy and tactics, something unexpected will eventually occur during implementation. Only by carefully monitoring the process can one identify the unexpected in a timely fashion and react to it intelligently.

Interpersonal skills, of course, are the key to using this analysis. But even the most outstanding interpersonal skills will not make up for a poor choice of strategy and tactics. And in a business world that continues to become more and more dynamic, the consequences of poor implementation choices will become increasingly severe.

—— DISCUSSION QUESTIONS

1. The reading mentions education and communication as "one of the most common ways to overcome resistance to change." What are the positive attitudes about change that you would want to instill in employees? What are negative attitudes toward change that you would want to acknowledge?

2. Considering your personal temperament, what method of dealing with resistance to change suggested by the authors would you be prone to choose? What action would you take to verify your decision?

3. What steps can an organization take to incorporate healthier attitudes toward change in its corporate culture?
4. Resistance to change is not necessarily wrong. Give an example—hypothetical or one from your own experience—when resistance could actually be the proper outcome to a proposed change.
5. What are changes that American businesses need to make to remain competitive? What aspects of American culture promote change? What aspects resist change?
6. Compare and contrast factors that might influence (1) a national company versus a multinational company regarding change; (2) a single business versus multibusiness; and (3) a manufacturing business versus a service business.

27

Evolution and Revolution as Organizations Grow

LARRY E. GREINER

This author maintains that growing organizations move through five distinguishable phases of development, each of which contains a calm period of growth that ends with a management crisis. He argues, moreover, that because each phase is strongly influenced by the previous one, a management with a sense of its own organization history can anticipate and prepare for the next developmental crisis. This reading provides a prescription for appropriate management action in each of the five phases, and it shows how companies can turn organizational crises into opportunities for future growth.

A small research company chooses too complicated and formalized an organization structure for its young age and limited size. It flounders in rigidity and bureaucracy for several years and is finally acquired by a larger company.

Key executives of a retail store chain hold on to an organization structure long after it has served its purpose, because their power is derived from this structure. The company eventually goes into bankruptcy.

A large bank disciplines a "rebellious" manager who is blamed for current control problems, when the underlying causes are centralized procedures that are holding back expansion into new markets. Many younger managers subsequently leave the bank, competition moves in, and profits are still declining.

The problems of these companies, like those of many others, are rooted more in past decisions than in present events or outside market dynamics. Historical forces do indeed shape the future growth of organizations. Yet management, in its haste to grow, often overlooks critical developmental questions such as Where has our organization been? Where is it now? And what do the answers to these questions mean for where we are going? Instead, management's gaze is fixed outward toward the environment and the future—as if more precise market projections will provide a new organizational identity.

Companies fail to see that many clues to their future success lie within their own organizations and their evolving states of development. Moreover, the inability of management to understand its organization-development problems can result in a company becoming frozen in its current stage of evolution or, ultimately, in failure, regardless of market opportunities.

My position in this reading is that the future of an organization may be determined less by outside forces than it is by the organization's history. In stressing the force of history on an organization, I have drawn from the legacies of European psychologists (their thesis being that individual behavior is determined primarily by previous events and experiences, not by what lies ahead). Extending this analogy of individual development to the problems of organization development, I shall discuss a series of developmental phases through which growing companies tend to pass. But, first, let me provide two definitions:

- The term *evolution* is used to describe prolonged periods of growth where no major upheaval occurs in organization practices.
- The term *revolution* is used to describe those periods of substantial turmoil in organization life.

As a company progresses through developmental phases, each evolutionary period creates its own revolution. For instance, centralized practices eventually lead to demands for decentralization. Moreover, the nature of management's solution to each revolutionary period determines whether a company will move forward into its next stage of evolutionary growth. As I shall show later, there are at least five phases of organization development, each characterized by both an evolution and a revolution.

—— KEY FORCES IN DEVELOPMENT

During the past few years a small amount of research knowledge about the phases of organization development has been building. Some of this research is very quantitative, such as time-series analyses that reveal patterns of economic performance over time.[1] The majority of studies, however, are case-oriented and use company records and interviews to reconstruct a rich picture of corporate development.[2] Yet both types of research tend to be heavily empirical without attempting more generalized statements about the overall process of development.

A notable exception is the historical work of Alfred D. Chandler, Jr., in his book *Strategy and Structure*.[3] This study depicts four very broad and general phases in the lives of four large U.S. companies. It proposes that outside market opportunities determine a company's strategy, which in turn determines the company's organization structure. This thesis has a valid ring for the four companies examined by Chandler, largely because they developed in a time of

---

1. *See*, for example, William H. Starbuck, "Organizational Metamorphosis," in *Promising Research Directions*, edited by R. W. Millman and M. P. Hottenstein (Tempe, Arizona: Academy of Management, 1968), p. 113.

2. *See*, for example, the *Grangesberg* case series, prepared by C. Roland Christensen and Bruce R. Scott, IMEDE, Lausanne, Switzerland.

3. *Strategy and Structure: Chapters in the History of the American Industrial Enterprise* (Cambridge, Mass., The M.I.T. Press, 1962).

explosive markets and technological advances. But more recent evidence suggests that organization structure may be less malleable than Chandler assumed; in fact, structure can play a critical role in influencing corporate strategy. It is this reverse emphasis on how organization structure affects future growth which is highlighted in the model presented in this reading.

From an analysis of various studies, five key dimensions emerge as essential for building a model of organization development:[4]

1. The age of the organization
2. The size of the organization
3. The stages of evolution
4. The stages of revolution
5. The growth rate of the industry

Each of these elements will be discussed separately, but first note their combined effect as illustrated in *Exhibit 1*. Note especially how each dimension influences the other over time; when all five elements begin to interact, a more complete and dynamic picture of organizational growth emerges.

After describing these dimensions and their interconnections, each evolutionary/revolutionary phase of development will be discussed. Next the reading will discuss how each stage of evolution breeds its own revolution and how management solutions to each revolution determine the next stage of evolution.

AGE OF THE ORGANIZATION

The most obvious and essential dimension for any model of development is the life span of an organization (represented as the horizontal axis in *Exhibit 1*). All historical studies gather data from various points in time and then make comparisons. From these observations, it is evident that the same organization practices are not maintained throughout a long time span. This makes a most basic point: management problems and principles are rooted in time. The concept of decentralization, for example, can have meaning for describing corporate practices at one time period but loses its descriptive power at another.

---

4. I have drawn on many sources for evidence: a) numerous cases collected at the Harvard Business School; b) *Organization Growth and Development*, edited by William H. Starbuck (Middlesex, England: Penguin Books, Ltd., 1971), where several studies are cited; and c) articles published in journals, such as Lawrence E. Fouraker and John M. Stopford, "Organization Structure and the Multinational Strategy," *Administrative Science Quarterly*, Vol. 13, No. 1 (1968): 47; and Malcolm S. Salter, "Management Appraisal and Reward Systems," *Journal of Business Policy*, Vol. 1, No. 4 (1971).

EXHIBIT 1
Model of Organization Development

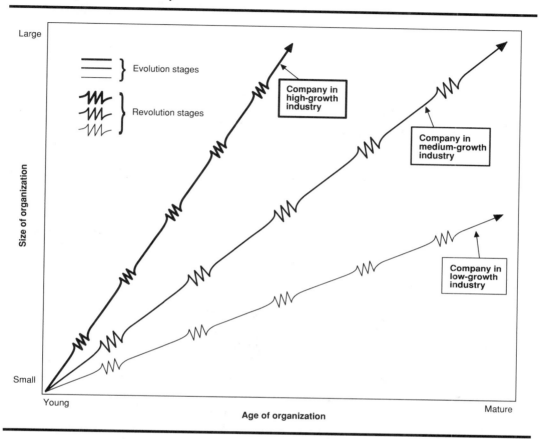

The passage of time also contributes to the institutionalization of managerial attitudes. As a result, employee behavior becomes not only more predictable but also more difficult to change when attitudes are outdated.

SIZE OF THE ORGANIZATION

This dimension is depicted as the vertical axis in *Exhibit 1*. A company's problems and solutions tend to change markedly as the number of employees and sales volume increase. Thus, time is not the only determinant of structure; in fact, organizations that do not grow in size can retain many of the same management issues and practices over lengthy periods. In addition to increased size, however, problems of coordination and communication magnify, new functions emerge, levels in the management hierarchy multiply, and jobs become more interrelated.

STAGES OF EVOLUTION

As both age and size increase, another phenomenon becomes evident: the prolonged growth that I have termed the evolutionary period. Most growing organizations do not expand for two years and then retreat for one year; rather, those that survive a crisis usually enjoy four to eight years of continuous growth without a major economic setback or severe internal disruption. The term *evolution* seems appropriate for describing these quieter periods because only modest adjustments appear necessary for maintaining growth under the same overall pattern of management.

STAGES OF REVOLUTION

Smooth evolution is not inevitable; it cannot be assumed that organization growth is linear. *Fortune's* "500" list, for example, has had significant turnover during the last 50 years. Thus we find evidence from numerous case histories that reveals periods of substantial turbulence spaced between smoother periods of evolution.

I have termed these turbulent times the periods of revolution because they typically exhibit a serious upheaval of management practices. Traditional management practices, which were appropriate for a smaller size and earlier time, are brought under scrutiny by frustrated top managers and disillusioned lower-level managers. During such periods of crisis, a number of companies fail—those unable to abandon past practices and effect major organization changes are likely either to fold or to level off in their growth rates.

The critical task for management in each revolutionary period is to find a new set of organization practices that will become the basis for managing the next period of evolutionary growth. Interestingly enough, these new practices eventually sow their own seeds of decay and lead to another period of revolution. Companies therefore experience the irony of seeing a major solution in one time period become a major problem at a later date.

GROWTH RATE OF THE INDUSTRY

The speed at which an organization experiences phases of evolution and revolution is closely related to the market environment of its industry. For example, a company in a rapidly expanding market will have to add employees rapidly; hence, the need for new organization evolutions to accommodate large staff increases is accelerated. While evolutionary periods tend to be relatively short in fast-growing industries, much longer evolutionary periods occur in mature or slowly growing industries.

Evolution can also be prolonged, and revolutions delayed, when profits come easily. For instance, companies that make grievous errors in a rewarding industry can still look good on their profit-and-loss statements; thus, they can avoid a change in management practices for a longer period. The aerospace industry in its infancy is an example. Yet revolutionary periods still occur, as one did in aerospace when profit opportunities began to dry up. Revolutions seem to be much more severe and difficult to resolve when the market environment is poor.

―― PHASES OF GROWTH

With the foregoing framework in mind, let us now examine in depth the five specific phases of evolution and revolution. As shown in *Exhibit 2*, each evolutionary period is characterized by the dominant *management style* used to achieve growth, while each revolutionary period is characterized by the dominant *management problem* that must be solved before growth can continue. The patterns presented in *Exhibit 2* seem to be typical for companies in industries with moderate growth over a long time period; companies in faster-growing industries tend to experience all five phases more rapidly, while those in slower-growing industries encounter only two or three phases over many years.

It is important to note that *each phase is both an effect of the previous phase and a cause for the next phase.* For example, the evolutionary management style in Phase 3 of the exhibit is "delegation," which grows out of and becomes the solution to demands for greater "autonomy" in the preceding Phase 2 revolution. The style of delegation used in Phase 3, however, eventually provokes a major revolutionary crisis that is characterized by attempts to regain control over the diversity created through increased delegation.

The principal implication of each phase is that management actions are narrowly prescribed if growth is to occur. For example, a company experiencing an autonomy crisis in Phase 2 cannot return to directive management for a solution—it must adopt a new style of delegation in order to move ahead.

PHASE 1: CREATIVITY

In the birth stage of an organization, the emphasis is on creating both a product and a market. Here are the characteristics of the period of creative evolution:

- The company's founders are usually technically or entrepreneurially oriented, and they disdain management activities; their physical and mental energies are absorbed entirely in making and selling a new product.
- Communication among employees is frequent and informal.
- Long hours of work are rewarded by modest salaries and the promise of ownership benefits.
- Control of activities comes from immediate marketplace feedback; the management acts as the customers react.

The Leadership Crisis   All of the foregoing individualistic and creative activities are essential for the company to get off the ground. But therein lies the problem. As the company grows, larger production runs require knowledge about the efficiencies of manufacturing. Increased numbers of employees cannot be managed exclusively through informal communication; new employees are not motivated by an intense dedication to the product or organization. Additional capital must be secured, and new accounting procedures are needed for financial control.

Thus the founders find themselves burdened with unwanted management responsibilities. So they long for the good old days, still trying to act as they did in the past. And conflicts between the harried leaders grow more intense.

EXHIBIT 2
The Five Phases of Growth

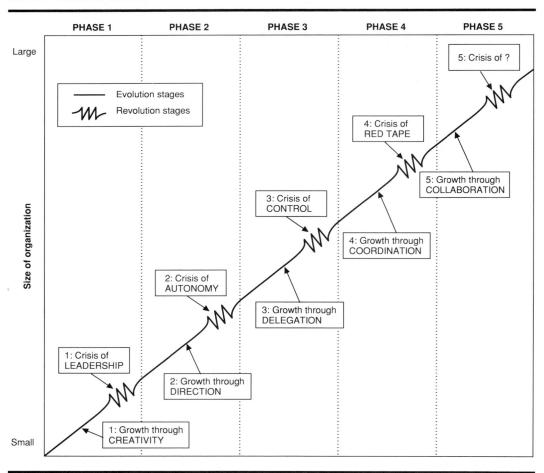

At this point a crisis of leadership occurs, which is the onset of the first revolution. Who is to lead the company out of confusion and solve the managerial problems confronting it? Quite obviously, a strong manager is needed who has the necessary knowledge and skill to introduce new business techniques. But this is easier said than done. The founders often hate to step aside even though they are probably temperamentally unsuited to be managers. So here is the first critical developmental choice—to locate and install a strong business manager who is acceptable to the founders and who can pull the organization together.

PHASE 2: DIRECTION

Those companies that survive the first phase by installing a capable business manager usually embark on a period of sustained growth under able and directive leadership. Here are the characteristics of this evolutionary period:

- A functional organization structure is introduced to separate manufacturing from marketing activities, and job assignments become more specialized.
- Accounting systems for inventory and purchasing are introduced.
- Incentives, budgets, and work standards are adopted.
- Communication becomes more formal and impersonal as a hierarchy of titles and positions builds.
- The new manager and his or her key supervisors take most of the responsibility for instituting direction, while lower-level supervisors are treated more as functional specialists than as autonomous decision-making managers.

The Autonomy Crisis   Although the new directive techniques channel employee energy more efficiently into growth, they eventually become inappropriate for controlling a larger, more diverse and complex organization. Lower-level employees find themselves restricted by a cumbersome and centralized hierarchy. They have come to possess more direct knowledge about markets and machinery than do the leaders at the top; consequently, they feel torn between following procedures and taking initiative on their own.

Thus the second revolution is imminent as a crisis develops from demands for greater autonomy on the part of lower-level managers. The solution adopted by most companies is to move toward greater delegation. Yet it is difficult for top managers who previously were successful at being directive to give up responsibility. Moreover, lower-level managers are not accustomed to making decisions for themselves. As a result, numerous companies flounder during this revolutionary period, adhering to centralized methods while lower-level employees grow more disenchanted and leave the organization.

PHASE 3: DELEGATION

The next era of growth evolves from the successful application of a decentralized organization structure. It exhibits these characteristics:

- Much greater responsibility is given to the managers of plants and market territories.
- Profit centers and bonuses are used to stimulate motivation.
- The top executives at headquarters restrain themselves to managing by exception, based on periodic reports from the field.
- Management often concentrates on making new acquisitions that can be lined up beside other decentralized units.
- Communication from the top is infrequent, usually by correspondence, telephone, or brief visits to field locations.

The delegation stage proves useful for gaining expansion through heightened motivation at lower levels. Decentralized managers with greater authority and incentive are able to penetrate larger markets, respond faster to customers, and develop new products.

The Control Crisis   A serious problem eventually evolves, however, as top executives sense that they are losing control over a highly diversified field operation. Autonomous field managers prefer to run their own shows without coordinating plans, money, technology, and personnel with the rest of the organization. Freedom breeds a parochial attitude.

Hence, the Phase 3 revolution is under way when top management seeks to regain control over the total company. Some top management teams attempt a return to centralized management, which usually fails because of the vast scope of operations. Those companies that move ahead find a new solution in the use of special coordination techniques.

PHASE 4: COORDINATION

During this phase, the evolutionary period is characterized by the use of formal systems for achieving greater coordination and by top executives taking responsibility for the initiation and administration of these new systems, for example:

- Decentralized units are merged into product groups.
- Formal planning procedures are established and intensively reviewed.
- Numerous staff members are hired and located at headquarters to initiate companywide programs of control and review for line managers.
- Capital expenditures are carefully weighed and parceled out across the organization.

- Each product group is treated as an investment center where return on invested capital is an important criterion used in allocating funds.
- Certain technical functions, such as data processing, are centralized at headquarters, while daily operating decisions remain decentralized.
- Stock options and companywide profit sharing are used to encourage identity with the firm as a whole.

All of these new coordination systems prove useful for achieving growth through more efficient allocation of a company's limited resources. They prompt field managers to look beyond the needs of their local units. Although these managers still have much decision-making responsibility, they learn to justify their actions more carefully to a watchdog audience at headquarters.

The Red-Tape Crisis   A lack of confidence gradually builds between line and staff and between headquarters and the field, however. The proliferation of systems and programs begins to exceed its utility; a red-tape crisis is created. Line managers, for example, increasingly resent heavy staff direction from those who are not familiar with local conditions. Staff people, on the other hand, complain about uncooperative and uninformed line managers. Together both groups criticize the bureaucratic paper system that has evolved. Procedures take precedence over problem solving, and innovation is dampened. In short, the organization has become too large and complex to be managed through formal programs and rigid systems. The Phase 4 revolution is under way.

PHASE 5: COLLABORATION

The last observable phase in previous studies emphasizes strong interpersonal collaboration in an attempt to overcome the red-tape crisis. Where Phase 4 was managed more through formal systems and procedures, Phase 5 emphasizes greater spontaneity in management action through teams and the skillful confrontation of interpersonal differences. Social control and self-discipline take over from formal control. This transition is especially difficult for those experts who created the old systems as well as for those line managers who relied on formal methods for answers.

The Phase 5 evolution, then, builds around a more flexible and behavioral approach to management. Here are its characteristics:

- The focus is on solving problems quickly through team action.
- Teams are combined across functions for task-group activity.
- Headquarters staff experts are reduced in number, reassigned, and combined in interdisciplinary teams to consult with, not to direct, field units.
- A matrix-type structure is frequently used to assemble the right teams for the appropriate problems.

- Previous formal systems are simplified and combined into single multipurpose systems.
- Conferences of key managers are held frequently to focus on major problem issues.
- Educational programs are utilized to train managers in behavioral skills for achieving better teamwork and conflict resolution.
- Real-time information systems are integrated into daily decision making.
- Economic rewards are geared more to team performance than to individual achievement.
- Experiments in new practices are encouraged throughout the organization.

The Crisis   What will be the revolution in response to this stage of evolution? Many large U.S. companies are now in the Phase 5 evolutionary stage, so the answers are critical. Although there is little clear evidence, I imagine the revolution will center around the psychological saturation of employees who grow emotionally and physically exhausted by the intensity of teamwork and the heavy pressure for innovative solutions.

My hunch is that the Phase 5 revolution will be solved through new structures and programs that allow employees to periodically rest, reflect, and revitalize themselves. We may even see companies with dual organization structures: a "habit" structure for getting the daily work done, and a "reflective" structure for stimulating perspective and personal enrichment. Employees then could move back and forth between the two structures as their energies are dissipated and refueled.

One European organization has implemented just such a structure. Five reflective groups have been established outside the regular structure for the purpose of continuously evaluating five task activities basic to the organization. They report directly to the managing director, although their reports are made public throughout the organization. Membership in each group includes all levels and functions, and employees are rotated through these groups every six months.

Other concrete examples now in practice include providing sabbaticals for employees, moving managers in and out of "hot-spot" jobs, establishing a four-day workweek, ensuring job security, building physical facilities for relaxation during the working day, making jobs more interchangeable, creating an extra team on the assembly line so that one team is always off for reeducation, and switching to longer vacations and more flexible working hours.

The Chinese practice of requiring executives to spend time periodically on lower-level jobs may also be worth a nonideological evaluation. For too long U.S. management has assumed that career progress should be equated with an upward path toward title, salary, and power. Could it be that some vice presidents of marketing might just long for, and even benefit from, temporary duty in the field sales organization?

IMPLICATIONS OF HISTORY

Let me now summarize some important implications for practicing managers. First, the main features of this discussion are depicted in *Exhibit 3,* which shows the specific management actions that characterize each growth phase. These actions are also the solutions that ended each preceding revolutionary period.

In one sense, I hope that many readers will react to my model by calling it obvious and natural for depicting the growth of an organization. To me this type of reaction is a useful test of the model's validity.

But at a more reflective level I imagine some of these reactions are more hindsight than foresight. Those experienced managers who have been through a developmental sequence can empathize with it now, but how did they react when in the middle of a stage of evolution or revolution? They can probably recall the limits of their own developmental understanding at that time. Perhaps they resisted desirable changes or were even swept emotionally into a revolution without being able to propose constructive solutions. So let me offer some explicit guidelines for managers of growing organizations to keep in mind.

Know Where You Are in the Developmental Sequence   Every organization and its component parts are at different stages of development. The task of top management is to be aware of these stages; otherwise, it may not recognize when the time for change has come, or it may act to impose the wrong solution.

Top leaders should be ready to work with the flow of the tide rather than against it; yet they should be cautious, because it is tempting to skip phases out of impatience. Each phase results in certain strengths and learning experiences in the organization that will be essential for success in subsequent phases. A child prodigy, for example, may be able to read like a teenager, but he cannot behave like one until he ages through a sequence of experiences.

I also doubt that managers can or should act to avoid revolutions. Rather, these periods of tension provide the pressure, ideas, and awareness that afford a platform for change and the introduction of new practices.

Recognize the Limited Range of Solutions   In each revolutionary stage it becomes evident that this stage can be ended only by certain specific solutions; moreover, these solutions are different from those that were applied to the problems of the preceding revolution. Too often it is tempting to choose solutions that were tried before, which makes it impossible for a new phase of growth to evolve.

Management must be prepared to dismantle current structures before the revolutionary stage becomes too turbulent. Top managers, realizing that their own managerial styles are no longer appropriate, may even have to take themselves out of leadership positions. A good Phase 2 manager facing Phase 3 might be wise to find another Phase 2 organization that better fits his or her talents, either outside the company or with one of its newer subsidiaries.

EXHIBIT 3
Organization Practices During Evolution in the Five Phases of Growth

CATEGORY	PHASE 1	PHASE 2	PHASE 3	PHASE 4	PHASE 5
Management Focus	Make and sell	Efficiency of operations	Expansion of market	Consolidation of organization	Problem solving and innovation
Organization Structure	Informal	Centralized and functional	Decentralized and geographical	Line-staff and product groups	Matrix of teams
Top Management Style	Individualistic and entrepreneurial	Directive	Delegative	Watchdog	Participative
Control System	Market results	Standards and cost centers	Reports and profit centers	Plans and investment centers	Mutual goal setting
Management Reward Emphasis	Ownership	Salary and merit increases	Individual bonus	Profit sharing and stock options	Team bonus

Finally, evolution is not an automatic affair; it is a contest for survival. To move ahead, companies must consciously introduce planned structures that not only are solutions to a current crisis but also are fitted to the *next* phase of growth. This requires considerable self-awareness on the part of top management, as well as great interpersonal skill in persuading other managers that change is needed.

Realize That Solutions Breed New Problems   Managers often fail to realize that organizational solutions create problems for the future, such as when a decision to delegate eventually causes a problem of control. Historical actions are very much determinants of what happens to the company at a much later date.

An awareness of this effect should help managers to evaluate company problems with greater historical understanding instead of pinning the blame on a current development. Better yet, managers should be in a position to *predict* future problems, and thereby to prepare solutions and coping strategies before a revolution gets out of hand.

A management that is aware of the problems ahead could well decide *not* to grow. Top managers may, for instance, prefer to retain the informal practices of a small company, knowing that this way of life is inherent in the organization's limited size, not in their congenial personalities. If they choose to grow, they may do themselves out of a job and a way of life they enjoy.

And what about the managements of very large organizations? Can they find new solutions for continued phases of evolution? Or are they reaching a stage where the government will act to break them up because they are too large?

——— CONCLUDING NOTE

Clearly, there is still much to learn about processes of development in organizations. The phases outlined here are only five in number and are still only approximations. Researchers are just beginning to study the specific developmental problems of structure, control, rewards, and management style in different industries and in a variety of cultures.

One should not, however, wait for conclusive evidence before educating managers to think and act from a developmental perspective. The critical dimension of time has been missing for too long from our management theories and practices. The intriguing paradox is that by learning more about history we may do a better job in the future.

Copyright © 1972; revised 1991.

——— DISCUSSION QUESTIONS

1. The author states that growth through collaboration or teamwork characterizes evolution in Phase 5. Social control and self-discipline mark the transition. Based on cultural history, what are possible difficulties that Americans might have with this approach? What characteristics of American culture support this approach?

2. The author has provided a scenario for the next revolution. Do you agree? If you do, what do you see as the next scenario for the revolution arising out of this evolution? If you disagree, what scenario would you propose as an alternative to the one the author has suggested?

3. How could the phases of organization development based on evolution and revolution be used to assist human resource management in its hiring decisions? In the reassignment of personnel? In other practices?

4. The author stresses the force of history on an organization. Give examples from your work life when you have been influenced by the force of your own work history. How have you changed? Were the changes you made internal (new behaviors or outlooks) or external (new careers or companies)?

5. Is it possible to apply the theory of evolution and revolution to a country's competitive position? For example, compare American and Japanese competitiveness based on this theory.

28   Leading Change

MICHAEL BEER

Dissatisfaction with the status quo is the source of motivation for change. This reading describes how company leaders can "create" dissatisfaction in their organization and define a vision of how the organization can improve both its internal and competitive performance. Change is inevitably painful and must be carried out with care and deliberation. The author offers a variety of insights on managing transitions effectively, emphasizing the importance of helping individuals and groups understand the reasons for the change as well as involving them in its implementation.

Leading change has become a crucial competence for managers. International competition and deregulation have forced corporations to seek and adopt more effective approaches to management, strategic planning, marketing, and manufacturing. In many firms these changes amount to major shifts in the culture, or in the basic behavior and belief system, of the organization.

This reading presents a conceptual formula incorporating the critical dimensions of change that must be considered by managers.[1] The formula can be summarized as follows:

$$\text{Amount of Change} = (\text{Dissatisfaction} \times \text{Model} \times \text{Process}) > \text{Cost of Change}$$

——— DISSATISFACTION

For change to take place, key organization members must be dissatisfied with the status quo and lack confidence in themselves and their organization. This dissatisfaction is the source of energy or motivation for the change. That energy is essential because change demands extraordinary commitment.

What conditions lead executives to be dissatisfied with the status quo? A survey of the contemporary business scene quickly leads to the conclusion that crisis is the most frequent condition that energizes change. But must companies approach the precipice before major adaptation to new conditions

---

1. This change formula was developed by me based on discussions with Dr. Alan Burns many years ago. I subsequently learned that the formula came from David Gleicher. It is also discussed in Michael Beer, *Organization Change and Development: A Systems View* (Santa Monica, Calif.: Goodyear, 1980).

is possible? Are the human and economic costs of a crisis an inevitable by-product of major change? The answer to these questions is no. Change can be stimulated and managed without crisis, though managers should be ready to use external crisis, when it presents itself, as a vehicle for managing planned change.

What, then, is the alternative to crisis as the stepping-stone to change? If dissatisfaction is necessary for change, then corporate leaders must create dissatisfaction in their organizations. They may use one or more of the following methods:

1. Managers can use information about the organization's competitive environment to generate discussions of current or prospective problems. Top management often does not understand why employees are not as concerned as it is about productivity, customer service, or cost. Often this situation is created because management has not provided employees with the same data that have led to management dissatisfaction. Sometimes this information is kept from employees because it is thought to be confidential. Companies trying to be more competitive have begun communicating this information to employee groups and union leaders.

2. Similarly, information about the concerns of employees and their perceptions about how the company is being run can be a powerful tool for creating dissatisfaction among managers. Just as competitive information can be a tool for creating dissatisfaction downward so attitude surveys (through interviews and questionnaires) can be a powerful tool for creating dissatisfaction upward. Consider managers who do not know their subordinates feel uninvolved because these managers control too closely, or top management that does not understand how the vitality of the organization is being sapped by overmanagement from corporate staff groups.

3. There must be a dialogue between managers and employees about the meaning of the data. Through dialogue, managers and employees can inform each other about their underlying assumptions and reach a joint understanding of the organization's problems. A shared explanation of root causes is key to a process of mutual adaptation by all stakeholders.

4. Managers can also create the energy for change by setting high, but realistic, standards and expecting employees to meet them. The managerial act of stating expectations is an effective means of creating dissatisfaction as long as the manager is trusted and seen as credible. Although managers often state expectations for profit performance, they rarely demand specific behaviors, even when the behaviors necessary to turn a situation around are known. Specifying organizational and individual behaviors is important to successful change.

These methods can individually or in concert unleash discontent and mobilize energy for change. But if managers are to channel this discontent into focused efforts, they must concern themselves with the model in the change formula.

———— MODEL

A vision of the future state of the organization—its behaviors and attitudes as well as structure and systems—is necessary for change to occur. Such a vision not only serves the purpose of energizing change but also provides a model toward which employees and managers can work. Management should design the model based on its own diagnosis of root causes of organizational problems, examples of excellent practice observed in visits to other companies, and the ideas of leading consultants and academics.

The envisioned state should reflect the multidimensionality of organizations. The model should specify hard aspects of organization design, strategy, structure, and systems, as well as the soft elements of style, staff, skills, and shared values.[2] Too often, change efforts to improve the organization specify only one or two of these dimensions, usually strategy and structure, and ignore the behaviors, attitudes, and competencies required for the new organization to work. Moreover, the specification of a multidimensional model forces managers to examine the fit between elements. Ignoring the multiple elements of organization is one of the reasons for failure to change organizational behavior and culture.

The multidimensional model must also fit the diagnosis of the organization's problems. The organizational arrangements contemplated for the future should induce those behaviors that are keys to its success. Much theory and experience support the proposition that organizational arrangements (structure, systems, style, etc.) differ for companies that compete through low cost as compared with companies that compete through innovation and differentiation. At the same time, the organizational arrangements contemplated must match the needs and expectations of employees and the social culture of the country in which the company is embedded. Through analysis and discussion, the designers of the model must determine that their vision of the future is viable.

As the change effort unfolds, it is extremely beneficial to have an organizational unit within the firm that represents successful application of the new practice from which others can learn and become convinced. Most companies undergoing transformations toward employee involvement have at least one leading-edge plant that serves as their model. Prospective change managers visit these plants or are transferred into them for a period of time so that they

---

2. Waterman, Robert, T. Peters, and J. Philips, "Structure Is Not Organization," *Business Horizons*, June 1980.

can learn new management approaches and apply them in their own assignments as change managers.

—— PROCESS

Organizational change is not instantaneous. A model of how the organization is to be structured does not quickly translate into change in the behaviors of large aggregates of employees. Managers sometimes make the mistake of assuming that announcing the change is the same as making it happen. How often is a Friday memorandum expected to translate into change on Monday morning?

The process for change is a sequence of events, speeches, meetings, educational programs, personnel decisions, and other actions aimed at helping employees, including top management, learn new perspectives, skills, attitudes, and behaviors. The elements of the process required to gain commitment and/or compliance need attention. Although commitment is clearly the more desirable means for achieving change, doses of compliance are inevitably part of the change process even when employees have been involved in developing the new model. Often change that starts with compliance becomes change to which individuals become committed as they engage in the new management practice.

All things being equal, people will become committed to that which they help create. Effective processes of change involve those affected in planning the change and executing it. The direction of the change may be set by the general manager, but many significant aspects of the change can be determined by individuals at lower levels. Executives often underestimate the amount of involvement in change employees can constructively undertake or the types of decisions in which employees can participate.

Despite the possibilities for participation when trust exists, the politics of change must be understood and managed. Even individuals who want to put the interest of the organization ahead of their own, succeed in doing so only partially and only some of the time. It is, therefore, important for managers to recognize the realities of self-interest and to cultivate support from individuals and groups. Coalitions must be formed to support change and the voice of support must be louder than the voice of resistance to change. Managers succeed in making participation work by placing supporters on key task forces or committees and by developing sufficient political support for them to be taken seriously by those who might otherwise resist.

Because behavioral change is required, the process of organizational change demands that change managers discuss ineffective or inappropriate behavior with managers and workers. In effective organizational transformation, change managers confront ineffective or inappropriate behavior early. That discussion leads to adaptation or replacement. Too often, however, managers who are leading a change do not confront these difficult problems, thus calling into question management's commitment to the new model.

Difficult personnel decisions are an important part of every major cultural change. When participation, politics, and performance appraisal fail, replacement becomes the only option if momentum is to be maintained. The transfer or termination of some individuals and the promotion of others who fit the new model is common in most organizational changes. The consistency of this finding leads to this rule of thumb: if no replacements are taking place, there is probably no major cultural change occurring.

More important, effective change requires careful planning for succession. Are the candidates for promotion consistent with the new model? If they are not, how can the corporation hire or develop these types of managers? How can the corporation most effectively use the limited number of managers who fit the new model?

Major organizational change is a matter of years—not days or months. Therefore, the capacity of the change manager to be patient and persistent is a key ingredient in managing change. Transforming an organization can be frustrating; other problems are always demanding attention. Managers often lose the will to confront difficult problems that arise or to continue expending the necessary energy for keeping the change effort alive. The proper time perspective helps as does the development of a change process that can maintain focus, organize the activities that are part of the effort, and provide emotional support for change leaders. Developing a network of change managers who periodically meet and consult with each other is one way to persist.

━━━ THE COST OF CHANGE

The change formula suggests that if organizational change is to occur, D, M, and P must all be present in sufficient strength to overcome the cost of change. The cost of change is the *losses* employees and other stakeholders anticipate as a result of the change. What are the typical losses incurred?

Power   Major change involves a shift in power. That power may be from manufacturing to marketing, from first-line supervisors to production workers, from staff to line, or from distributors to the direct sales force. Groups and their managers who will be losing power typically resist such shifts because of the implications for influence, careers, and status in the organization.

Competence   New models require new competencies and make old ones obsolete. A shift in marketing focus from the sale of products to the sale of systems will require systems-oriented salespersons and will make narrower-product salespeople obsolete. A shift to more participative management will devalue the skills of first-line supervisors who rely on technical competence to direct others. A new set of people and process skills will be required. The fear of losing competencies relied on to be successful can be very threatening; people feel a loss of mastery and dignity.

Relationships   Security and comfort in daily work come from a network of dependable relationships. Changes in organizational arrangement typically require new relationships and therefore make obsolete this network of people.

Rewards   Most major organizational changes involve the reassignment of individuals, changes in title and perquisites, changes in pay grades, and consequently, changes in actual compensation. Thus, major change threatens the tangible and intangible rewards of some individuals. A smaller office, the loss of a vice president's title, the loss of points, the loss of a company car, the loss of a private parking space, exclusion from eligibility for a bonus—all these can cause resistance to the change. This may occur even when the change is not intended to signal demotion.

Identity   Many of these losses amount in whole or in part to a change in the role of the individual manager or worker in the organization's social fabric. Thus, changes in the workplace often mean a crisis in personal identity. Managers and other professionals for whom work is central to a concept of self are particularly vulnerable to this loss of self-esteem.

───── BALANCING DRIVING FORCES WITH REDUCTION OF LOSSES

The fear of losses is the cause of resistance to change. The change formula, *Change = (D × M × P) > Cost*, suggests that the greater the potential losses, the stronger the $D \times M \times P$ must be. Major changes require considerable dissatisfaction, a clear vision of the future model, and a well-planned process. Alternatively, change momentum may be increased by working on the loss side of the equation, by reducing resistance through a reduction in perceived losses. How might losses be reduced?

Losses of competence may be reduced by strong efforts to develop employees in the newly required skills. Development means not only training but also counseling and coaching from supervisors and human resource professionals. The development of new career paths that support the change can also pave the way. If all this is done well before the actual rearrangement of the organization, the threat of the change can be reduced. Similarly, people can be helped to establish new relationships before having to permanently break the old.

These efforts require substantial deviation from the accepted practice of announcing the change and making it immediately. Corporations usually do not provide an interim period when people are still in their old jobs but know what their new positions will be and with whom they will work. Allowing people to participate in planning changes is, of course, another way to establish new relationships and develop competencies. As people discuss the future, they begin to make necessary adaptations in attitude and to anticipate competencies required.

Losses in power and rewards are harder to face. Nevertheless, a manager can help individuals adapt to these losses through empathy and listening and by helping them reorient their perceptions of themselves. By emphasizing the value of the new role, a manager can help an employee develop a new professional identity. Individuals who experience losses can adapt to them faster if they are allowed a legitimate outlet for their initial anger and then are helped, through dialogue, to go through a rationalization process, which will help them create meaning out of their new circumstances.

The role of losses in creating resistance to change has implications for the design of adaptive organizations. Organizations that have fewer distinctions in power and rewards—in other words, more egalitarian organizations—give people fewer things to lose. In such organizations people are more willing to take jobs and roles called for by the changes in competitive circumstances. Similarly, losses in relationships and competence are less likely to be experienced in organizations that have high trust and that naturally encourage lateral job mobility, collaboration, and integration. Finally, change will be less threatening to a sense of competence if employees have multiple skills and a broad corporate perspective developed through cross-functional career paths.

Leading change is not easy and cannot be reduced to simple or quick fixes. Change leaders must persist over a long time in involving many individuals and groups in understanding why change is needed, formulating a new approach to organizing and managing, and selecting and developing employees who fit the vision.

——— DISCUSSION QUESTIONS

1. Do you agree with the formula for change offered in this reading? Are there elements that you would change, leave out, or add? Apply this model to your own personal experience with a change in your life.
2. There are inevitable changes facing companies in the 1990s, such as the changing demographics of the work force. Give an example of a change that is not inevitable but that a company might decide to make rather than *have to* make.
3. Imagine that you are working for a company and you hit upon an idea for change that would make your organization more effective. There is no crisis, you are ahead of your time. Discuss how you would approach handling this change as the company's president, as a middle manager, and as a line worker or regular employee.

4. The reading mentions elements of design that are important for organizational change. What might an organization's design look like when it is successfully implementing change? Can an organization have a different design and still implement successful change?
5. In the past, tradition has been considered important to an organization's identity and unity. What is the role of tradition in an organization that is leading change?

29   Speed, Simplicity, Self-Confidence: An Interview with Jack Welch

NOEL TICHY AND RAM CHARAN

Jack Welch, chairman and CEO of General Electric, believes that a large company must operate with the flexibility and agility of a small company. In this interview, he discusses the companywide drive he has implemented to eliminate unproductive work and energize employees. The centerpiece of Welch's transformation process is Work-Out—a program through which representatives of GE's 14 businesses meet regularly to identify and resolve problems. In describing his goals for GE and his means of attaining them, Welch offers a variety of insights into the qualities of effective leaders and effective organizations.

John F. Welch, Jr., chairman and CEO of General Electric, leads one of the world's largest corporations. It is a very different corporation from the one he inherited in 1981. GE is now built around 14 distinct businesses—including aircraft engines, medical systems, engineering plastics, major appliances, NBC television, and financial services. They reflect the aggressive strategic redirection Welch unveiled soon after he became CEO.

By now the story of GE's business transformation is familiar. In 1981, Welch declared that the company would focus its operations on three "strategic circles"—core manufacturing units such as lighting and locomotives, technology-intensive businesses, and services—and that each of its businesses would rank first or second in its global market. GE has achieved world market-share leadership in nearly all of its 14 businesses. In 1988, its 300,000 employees generated revenues of more than $50 billion and net income of $3.4 billion.

GE's strategic redirection had essentially taken shape by the end of 1986. Since then, Welch has embarked on a more imposing challenge: building a revitalized "human engine" to animate GE's formidable "business engine."

His program has two central objectives. First, he is championing a companywide drive to identify and eliminate unproductive work in order to energize GE's employees. It is neither realistic nor useful, Welch argues, to expect employees of a decidedly leaner corporation to complete all the reports, reviews, forecasts, and budgets that were standard operating procedure in more forgiving times. He is developing procedures to speed decision cycles, move information through the organization, provide quick and effective feedback, and evaluate and reward managers on qualities such as openness, candor, and self-confidence.

Second, and perhaps of even greater significance, Welch is leading a transformation of attitudes at GE—struggling, in his words, to release "emotional energy" at all levels of the organization and encourage creativity and feelings of ownership and self-worth. His ultimate goal is to create an enterprise that can tap the benefits of global scale and diversity without the stifling costs of bureaucratic controls and hierarchical authority and without a managerial focus on personal power and self-perpetuation. This requires a transformation not only of systems and procedures, he argues, but also of people themselves.

What makes a good manager?

Jack Welch: I prefer the term "business leader." Good business leaders create a vision, articulate the vision, passionately own the vision, and relentlessly drive it to completion. Above all else, though, good leaders are open. They go up, down, and around their organization to reach people. They don't stick to the established channels. They're informal. They're straight with people. They make a religion out of being accessible. They never get bored telling their story.

Real communication takes countless hours of eyeball to eyeball, back and forth. It means more listening than talking. It's not pronouncements on a videotape, it's not announcements in a newspaper. It is human beings coming to see and accept things through a constant interactive process aimed at consensus. And it must be absolutely relentless. That's a real challenge for us. There's still not enough candor in this company.

What do you mean by "candor"?

I mean facing reality, seeing the world as it is rather than as you wish it were. We've seen over and over again that businesses facing market downturns, tougher competition, and more demanding customers inevitably make forecasts that are much too optimistic. This means they don't take advantage of the opportunities change usually offers. Change in the marketplace isn't something to fear; it's an enormous opportunity to shuffle the deck, to replay the game. Candid managers—leaders—don't get paralyzed about the fragility of the organization. They tell people the truth. That doesn't scare them because they realize their people know the truth anyway.

We've had managers at GE who couldn't change, who kept telling us to leave them alone. They wanted to sit back, to keep things the way they were. And that's just what they did—until they and most of their staffs had to go. That's the lousy part of this job. What's worse is that we still don't understand why so many people are incapable of facing reality, of being candid with themselves and others.

But we are clearly making progress in facing reality, even if the progress is painfully slow. Take our locomotive business. That team was the only one we've ever had that took a business whose forecasts and plans were headed straight up, and whose market began to head straight down, a virtual collapse, and managed to change the tires while the car was moving. It's the team that forecast the great locomotive boom, convinced us to invest $300 million to renovate its plant in Erie, and then the market went boom all right—right into a crater. But when it did, that team turned on a dime. It reoriented the business.

Several of our other businesses in the same situation said, "Give it time, the market will come back." Locomotive didn't wait. And today, now that the market *is* coming back, the business looks great. The point is, what determines your destiny is not the hand you're dealt; it's how you play the hand. And the best way to play your hand is to face reality—see the world the way it is—and act accordingly.

What makes an effective organization?

For a large organization to be effective, it must be simple. For a large organization to be simple, its people must have self-confidence and intellectual self-assurance. Insecure managers create complexity. Frightened, nervous managers use thick, convoluted planning books and busy slides filled with everything they've known since childhood. Real leaders don't need clutter. People must have the self-confidence to be clear, precise, to be sure that every person in their organization—highest to lowest—understands what the business is trying to achieve. But it's not easy. You can't believe how hard it is for people to be simple, how much they fear being simple. They worry that if they're simple, people will think they're simpleminded. In reality, of course, it's just the reverse. Clear, tough-minded people are the most simple.

Soon after you became CEO, you articulated GE's now-famous strategy of "number one or number two globally." Was that an exercise in the power of simplicity?

Yes. In 1981, when we first defined our business strategy, the real focus was Japan. The entire organization had to understand that GE was in a tougher, more competitive world, with Japan as the cutting edge of the new competition. Nine years later, that competitive toughness has increased by a factor of 5 or 10. We face a revitalized Japan that's migrated around the world—to Thailand, Malaysia, Mexico, the United States—and responded successfully to a massive yen change. Europe is a different game today. There are great European business people, dynamic leaders, people who are changing things. Plus you've got all the other Asian successes.

So being number one or number two globally is more important than ever. But scale alone is not enough. You have to combine financial strength, market position, and technology leadership with an organizational focus on speed, agility, and simplicity. The world moves so much faster today. You can be driving through Seoul, talking to France on the phone and making a deal, and have a fax waiting for you when you get back to the United States with the deal in good technical shape. Paolo Fresco, senior vice president of GE International, has been negotiating around-the-clock for the past two days on a deal in England. Last night I was talking with Larry Bossidy, one of our vice chairmen, who was in West Germany doing another deal. We never used to do business this way. So you can be the biggest, but if you're not flexible enough to handle rapid change and make quick decisions, you won't win.

How have you implemented your commitment to simplicity at the highest levels of GE, where you can have the most direct impact on what happens?

First, we took out management layers. Layers hide weaknesses. Layers mask mediocrity. I firmly believe that an overburdened, overstretched executive is the best executive because he or she doesn't have the time to meddle, to deal in trivia, to bother people. Remember the theory that a manager should have no more than 6 or 7 direct reports? I say the right number is closer to 10 or 15. This way you have no choice but to let people flex their muscles, let them grow and mature. With 10 or 15 reports, a leader can focus only on the big important issues, not on minutiae.

We also reduced the corporate staff. Headquarters can be the bane of corporate America. It can strangle, choke, delay, and create insecurity. If you're going to have simplicity in the field, you can't have a big staff at home. We don't need the questioners and the checkers, the nitpickers who bog down the process, people whose only role is to second-guess and kibitz, the people who clog communication inside the company. Today people at headquarters are experts in taxes, finance, or some other key area that can help people in the field. Our corporate staff no longer just challenges and questions; it assists. This is a mind-set change; staff essentially reports to the field rather than the other way around.

So many CEOs disparage staff and middle management—you know, "If only those bureaucrats would buy into my vision." When you talk about "nitpickers" and "kibitzers," are you talking about lousy people or about good people forced into lousy jobs?

People are not lousy, period. Leaders have to find a better fit between their organization's needs and their people's capabilities. Staff people, whom I prefer to call individual contributors, can be tremendous sources of added value in an organization. But each staff person has to ask, How do I add value? How do I help make people on the line more effective and more competitive? In the past, many staff functions were driven by control rather than adding value. Staffs with that focus have to be eliminated. They sap emotional energy in the organization. As for middle managers, they can be the stronghold of the organization. But their jobs have to be redefined. They have to see their roles as a combination of teacher, cheerleader, and liberator, not controller.

You've dismantled GE's groups and sectors, the top levels of the corporate organization to which individual strategic business units once reported. That certainly makes the organization chart more simple—you now have 14 separate businesses reporting directly to you or your two vice chairmen. How does the new structure simplify how GE operates on a day-to-day basis?

Cutting the groups and sectors eliminated communications filters. Today there is direct communication between the CEO and the leaders of the 14 businesses. We have very short cycle times for decisions and little interference by corporate staff. A major investment decision that used to take a year can now be made in a matter of days.

We also run a Corporate Executive Council, the CEC. For two days every quarter, we meet with the leaders of the 14 businesses and our top staff people. These aren't stuffy, formal strategic reviews. We share ideas and information candidly and openly, including programs that have failed. The important thing is that at the end of those two days everyone in the CEC has seen and discussed the same information. The CEC creates a sense of trust, a sense of personal familiarity and mutual obligation at the top of the company. We consider the CEC a piece of organizational technology that is very important for our future success.

Still, how can it be "simple" to run a $50 billion enterprise? Doesn't a corporation as vast as GE need management layers, extensive review systems, and formal procedures—if for no other reason than to keep the business under control?

People always overestimate how complex business is. This isn't rocket science; we've chosen one of the world's more simple professions. Most global businesses have three or four critical competitors, and you know who they are. And there aren't that many things you can do with a business. It's not as if you're choosing among 2,000 options.

You mentioned review systems. At our 1986 officers' meeting, which involves the top 100 or so executives at GE, we asked the 14 business leaders to present reports on the competitive dynamics in their businesses. How'd we do it? We had them each prepare one-page answers to five questions: What are your market dynamics globally today, and where are they going over the next several years? What actions have your competitors taken in the last three years to upset those global dynamics? What have you done in the last three years to affect those dynamics? What are the most dangerous things your competitor could do in the next three years to upset those dynamics? What are the most effective things you could do to bring your desired impact on those dynamics?

Five simple charts. After those initial reviews, which we update regularly, we could assume that everyone at the top knew the plays and had the same playbook. It doesn't take a genius. Fourteen businesses each with a playbook of five charts. So when Larry Bossidy is with a potential partner in Europe, or I'm with a company in the Far East, we're always there with a competitive understanding based on our playbooks. We know exactly what makes sense; we don't need a big staff to do endless analysis. That means we should be able to act with speed.

Probably the most important thing we promise our business leaders is fast action. Their job is to create and grow new global businesses. Our job in the executive office is to facilitate, to go out and negotiate a deal, to make the acquisition, or get our businesses the partners they need. When our business leaders call, they don't expect studies—they expect answers.

Take the deal with Thomson, where we swapped our consumer electronics business for their medical equipment business. We were presented with an opportunity, a great solution to a serious strategic problem, and we were able to act quickly. We didn't need to go back to headquarters for a strategic analysis and a bunch of reports. Conceptually, it took us about 30 minutes to decide that the deal made sense and then a meeting of maybe two hours with the Thomson people to work out the basic terms. We signed a letter of intent in five days. We had to close it with the usual legal details, of course, so from beginning to end it took five months. Thomson had the same clear view of where it wanted to go—so it worked perfectly for both sides.

Another of our jobs is to transfer best practices across all the businesses, with lightning speed. Staff often put people all over the place to do this. But they aren't effective lightning rods to transfer best practice; they don't have the stature in the organization. Business leaders do. That's why every CEC meeting deals in part with a generic business issue—a new pay plan, a drug-testing program, stock options. Every business is free to propose its own plan or program and present it at the CEC, and we put it through a central screen at corporate, strictly to make sure it's within the bounds of good sense. We don't approve the details. But we want to know what the details are so we can see which programs are working and immediately alert the other businesses to the successful ones.

You make it sound so easy.

Simple *doesn't* mean easy, especially as you try to move this approach down through the organization. When you take out layers, you change the exposure of the managers who remain. They sit right in the sun. Some of them blotch immediately; they can't stand the exposure of leadership.

We now have leaders in each of the businesses who *own* those businesses. Eight years ago, we had to sell the idea of ownership. Today the challenge is to move that sense of ownership, that commitment to relentless personal interaction and immediate sharing of information, down through the organization. We're very early in this, and it's going to be anything but easy. But it's something we have to do.

From an organizational point of view, how are the 14 businesses changing? Are they going through a delayering process? Are their top people communicating as the CEC does?

In addition to locomotives, which I've already discussed, we've had major delayering and streamlining in almost all of our businesses, and they have made significant improvements in total cost productivity.

The CEC concept is flowing down as well. For example, each of the businesses has created its own executive committee to meet on policy questions. These committees meet weekly or monthly and include the top staff and line people from the businesses. Everyone in the same room, everyone with the same information, everyone buying into the targets. Each business also has an operations committee. This is a bigger group of maybe 30 people for each business: 5 staffers, 7 people from manufacturing, 6 from engineering, 8 from marketing, and so on. They get together every quarter for a day and a half to thrash out problems, to get people talking across functions, to communicate with each other about their prospects and programs. That's 30 people in 14 businesses, more than 400 people all together, in a process of instant communication about their businesses and the company.

You see, I operate on a very simple belief about business. If there are six of us in a room, and we all get the same facts, in most cases, the six of us will reach roughly the same conclusion. And once we all accept that conclusion, we can force our energy into it and put it into action. The problem is, we don't get the same information. We each get different pieces. Business isn't complicated. The complications arise when people are cut off from information they need. That's what we're trying to change.

> *That brings us to Work-Out, which you've been championing inside GE since early this year. Why are you pushing it so hard?*

Work-Out is absolutely fundamental to our becoming the kind of company we must become. [See the *Appendix* at end of reading for an example of Work-Out.] That's why I'm so passionate about it. We're not going to succeed if people end up doing the same work they've always done, if they don't feel any psychic or financial impact from the way the organization is changing. The ultimate objective of Work-Out is so clear. We want 300,000 people with different career objectives, different family aspirations, different financial goals, to share directly in this company's vision, the information, the decision-making process, and the rewards. We want to build a more stimulating environment, a more creative environment, a freer work atmosphere, with incentives tied directly to what people do.

Now, the business leaders aren't particularly thrilled that we're so passionate about Work-Out. In 1989, the CEO is going to every business in this company to sit in on a Work-Out session. That's a little puzzling to them. "I own the business, what are you doing here?" they say. Well, I'm not there to tell them how to price products, what type of equipment they need, whom to hire; I have no comments on that.

But Work-Out is the next generation of what we're trying to do. We had to put in a process to focus on and change how work gets done in this company. We have to apply the same relentless passion to Work-Out that we did in selling the vision of number one and number two globally. That's why we're pushing it so hard, getting so involved.

What is the essence of Work-Out, the basic goal?

Work-Out has a practical and an intellectual goal. The practical objective is to get rid of thousands of bad habits accumulated since the creation of General Electric. How would you like to move from a house after 112 years? Think of what would be in the closets and the attic—those shoes that you'll wear to paint next spring, even though you know you'll never paint again. We've got 112 years of closets and attics in this company. We want to flush them out, to start with a brand new house with empty closets, to begin the whole game again.

The second thing we want to achieve, the intellectual part, begins by putting the leaders of each business in front of 100 or so of their people, 8 to 10 times a year, to let them hear what their people think about the company, what they like and don't like about their work, about how they're evaluated, about how they spend their time. Work-Out will expose the leaders to the vibrations of their business—opinions, feelings, emotions, resentments, not abstract theories of organization and management.

Ultimately, we're talking about redefining the relationship between boss and subordinate. I want to get to a point where people challenge their bosses every day: "Why do you require me to do these wasteful things? Why don't you let me do the things you shouldn't be doing so you can move on and create? That's the job of a leader—to create, not to control. Trust me to do my job, and don't make me waste all my time trying to deal with you on the control issue."

Now, how do you get people communicating with each other with that much candor? You put them together in a room and make them thrash it out.

These Work-Out sessions—and I've already done several of them—create all kinds of personal dynamics. Some people go and hide. Some don't like the dinner in the evening because they can't get along with the other people. Some emerge as forceful advocates. As people meet over and over, though, more of them will develop the courage to speak out. The norm will become the person who says, "Dammit, we're not doing it. Let's get on with doing it." Today the norm in most companies, not just GE, is not to bring up critical issues with a boss, certainly not in a public setting, and certainly not in an atmosphere where self-confidence has not been developed. This process will create more fulfilling and rewarding jobs. The quality of work life will improve dramatically.

> *It's one thing to insist that the people who report directly to you, or who work one or two layers below you, become forceful advocates and criticize the status quo. They've got your support. But what about people lower in the organization, people who have to worry how their bosses will react?*

You're right on the hottest issue—when a boss reacts to criticism by saying, "I'll get that guy." Now, hopefully, that guy is so good he quits that same week and shows the boss where that attitude gets him. That's not the best result for GE, of course, but that's what it may take to shake people up.

It's not going to be easy to get the spirit and intent of Work-Out clear throughout the company. I had a technician at my house to install some appliances recently. He said, "I saw your videotape on Work-Out. The guys at my level understand what you're talking about: we'll be free to enjoy our work more, not just do more work, and to do more work on our own. But do you know how our supervisors interpreted it? They pointed to the screen and said, 'You see what he's saying, you guys better start busting your butts.'" We have a long way to go!

The potential for meanness in an organization, for a variety of reasons, is often in inverse proportion to level. People at the top have more time and resources to be fair. I wasn't trained to be a judge, but I spend a lot of time worrying about fairness. The data I get generally favor the manager over the employee. But we have two people at headquarters, fairness arbitrators so to speak, who sift the situation. So when I get a problem, I can smell it and feel it and try to figure out what's really happening. Managers down in the organization don't have the time or help for that. They too often say, "This is how we do it here, go do it." Work-Out is going to break down those attitudes. Managers will be in front of their people, challenged in a thousand different ways, held to account.

To change behavior, you must also change how people are compensated and rewarded. Are those systems being changed at GE?

We let every business come up with its own pay plan. It can create bonus plans in any way that makes sense. We're also doing all kinds of exciting things to reward people for their contributions, things we've never done before. For example, we now give out $20 to $30 million in management awards every year—cash payments to individuals for outstanding performance. We're trying desperately to push rewards down to levels where they never used to be. Stock options now go to 3,000 people, up from 400 ten years ago, and that's probably still not enough.

Another way to influence behavior is to promote people based on the characteristics you want to encourage. How can you evaluate executives on qualities as subjective as candor and speed?

Not only can we do it, we *are* doing it. Again, we're starting at the top of the company and, as the new systems prove themselves, we'll drive them down. We took three years to develop a statement on corporate values, what we as a company believe in. It was a brutal process. We talked to 5,000 people at our management development center in Crotonville. We sweated over every word. This will be the first year that our Session C meetings, the intensive process we use to evaluate the officers of the company, revolve around that value statement. We've told the business leaders that they must rank each of their officers on a scale of one to five against the business and individual characteristics in that statement (see the *Exhibit*). Then I, Larry Bossidy, and Ed Hood, our other vice chairman, will rate the officers and see where we agree or disagree with the business leaders.

We had a long discussion about this in the CEC. People said just what you said: "How can you put a number on how open people are, on how directly they face reality?" Well, they're going to have to—the best numbers they can come up with, and then we'll argue about them. We have to know if our people are open and self-confident, if they believe in honest communication and quick action, if the people we hired years ago have changed. The only way to test our progress is through regular evaluations at the top and by listening to every audience we appear before in the company.

> *All corporations, but especially giant corporations like GE, have implicit social and psychological contracts with their employees—mutual responsibilities and loyalties by which each side abides. What is GE's psychological contract with its people?*

Like many other large companies in the United States, Europe, and Japan, GE has had an implicit psychological contract based on perceived lifetime employment. People were rarely dismissed except for cause or severe business downturns, like in Aerospace after Vietnam. This produced a paternal, feudal, fuzzy kind of loyalty. You put in your time, worked hard, and the company took care of you for life.

That kind of loyalty tends to focus people inward. But given today's environment, people's emotional energy must be focused outward on a competitive world where no business is a safe haven for employment unless it is winning in the marketplace. The psychological contract has to change. People at all levels have to feel the risk-reward tension.

My concept of loyalty is not "giving time" to some corporate entity and, in turn, being shielded and protected from the outside world. Loyalty is an affinity among people who want to grapple with the outside world and win. Their personal values, dreams, and ambitions cause them to gravitate toward each other and toward a company like GE that gives them the resources and opportunities to flourish.

The new psychological contract, if there is such a thing, is that jobs at GE are the best in the world for people who are willing to compete. We have the best training and development resources and an environment committed to providing opportunities for personal and professional growth.

> *How deeply have these changes penetrated? How different does it feel to be a GE manager today versus five years ago?*

It depends how far down you go. In some old-line factories, they probably feel it a lot less than we would like. They hear the words every now and then, but they don't feel a lot of difference. That's because the people above them haven't changed enough yet. Don't forget, we built much of this company

EXHIBIT
GE Value Statement

BUSINESS CHARACTERISTICS	INDIVIDUAL CHARACTERISTICS
Lean	**Reality**
What – Reduce tasks and the people required to do them.	What – Describe the environment as it is—not as we hope it to be.
Why – Critical to developing world cost leadership.	Why – Critical to developing a vision and a winning strategy, and to gaining universal acceptance for their implementation.
Agile	**Leadership**
What – Delayering.	What – Sustained passion for and commitment to a proactive, shared vision and its implementation.
Why – Create fast decision making in rapidly changing world through improved communication and increased individual response.	Why – To rally teams toward achieving a common objective.
Creative	**Candor/Openness**
What – Development of new ideas—innovation.	What – Complete and frequent sharing of information with individuals (appraisals, etc.) and organization (everything).
Why – Increase customer satisfaction and operating margins through higher-value products and services.	Why – Critical to employees knowing where they, their efforts, and their business stand.
Ownership	**Simplicity**
What – Self-confidence to trust others. Self-confidence to delegate to others the freedom to act while, at the same time, self-confidence to involve higher levels in issues critical to the business and the corporation.	What – Strive for brevity, clarity, the "elegant, simple solution"—less is better.
	Why – Less complexity improves everything, from reduced bureaucracy to better product designs to lower costs.
Why – Support concept of more individual responsibility, capability to act quickly and independently. Should increase job satisfaction and improve understanding of risks and rewards. Although delegation is critical, there is a small percentage of high-impact issues that need or require involvement of higher levels within the business and within the corporation.	**Integrity**
	What – Never bend or wink at the truth, and live within both the spirit and letter of the laws of every global business arena.
	Why – Critical to gaining the global arenas' acceptance of our right to grow and prosper. Every constituency: shareowners who invest; customers who purchase; community that supports; and employees who depend on, expect, and deserve our unequivocal commitment to integrity in every facet of our behavior.
Reward	**Individual Dignity**
What – Recognition and compensation commensurate with risk and performance—highly differentiated by individual, with recognition of total team achievement.	What – Respect and leverage the talent and contribution of every individual in both good and bad times.
Why – Necessary to attract and motivate the type of individuals required to accomplish GE's objectives. A #1 business should provide #1 people with #1 opportunity.	Why – Teamwork depends on trust, mutual understanding, and the shared belief that the individual will be treated fairly in any environment.

in the 1950s around the blue books and POIM: plan, organize, integrate, measure. We brought people in buses over to Crotonville and drilled it into them. Now we're saying, "Liberate, trust," and people look up and say, "What?" We're trying to make a massive cultural break. This is at least a 5-year process, probably closer to 10.

What troubles you about what's happened to date?

First, there's a real danger of the expectation level getting ahead of reality. I was at Crotonville recently, talking about Work-Out, and someone said, "I don't feel it yet." Well, we're only a few months into it, it's much too early.

No matter how many exciting programs you implement, there seems to be a need for people to spend emotional energy criticizing the administration of the programs rather than focusing on the substance. I can sit in the Crotonville pit and ask, "How many of you are part of a new pay plan?" More than half the hands go up. "How many of you have received a management award in the last year?" More than 90% of the hands go up. "How many of you are aware of stock options?" All the hands go up. And yet many of these people don't see what we're trying to do with the programs, why we've put them in place. The emotional energy doesn't focus often enough on the objectives of the bonus plan or the excitement of the management award; it focuses on the details. The same is true of Work-Out. We'll have too much discussion on the Work-Out "process" and not enough on the "objective" to instill speed, simplicity, and self-confidence in every person in the organization.

When will we know whether these changes have worked? What's your report card?

A business magazine recently printed an article about GE that listed our businesses and the fact that we were number one or number two in virtually all of them. That magazine didn't get one complaint from our competitors. Those are the facts. That's what we said we wanted to do, and we've done it.

Ten years from now, we want magazines to write about GE as a place where people have the freedom to be creative, a place that brings out the best in everybody. An open, fair place where people have a sense that what they do matters, and where that sense of accomplishment is rewarded in both the pocketbook and the soul. That will be our report card.

APPENDIX
Work-Out: A Case Study

GE Medical Systems (GEMS) is the world leader in medical diagnostic imaging equipment, including CT scanners, magnetic resonance equipment, and X-ray mammography. Its more than 15,000 employees face formidable international competition. Despite positive financial results, GEMS is working to transform its human organization. Work-Out is designed to identify sources of frustration and bureaucratic inefficiency, eliminate unnecessary and unproductive work, and overhaul how managers are evaluated and rewarded.

Work-Out began last fall when some 50 GEMS employees attended a five-day offsite session in Lake Lawn, Wisconsin. The participants included senior vice president and group executive John Trani, his staff, six employee relations managers, and informal leaders from technology, finance, sales, service, marketing, and manufacturing. Trani selected these informal leaders for their willingness to take business risks, challenge the status quo, and contribute in other key ways to GEMS. We participated as Work-Out faculty members and have participated in follow-up sessions that will run beyond 1989.

The Lake Lawn session took place after two important preliminary steps. First, we conducted in-depth interviews with managers at all levels of GEMS. Our interviews uncovered many objections to and criticisms of existing procedures, including measurement systems (too many, not focused enough on customers, cross-functional conflicts); pay and reward systems (lack of work goals, inconsistent signals); career development systems (ambiguous career paths, inadequate performance feedback); and an atmosphere in which blame, fear, and lack of trust overshadowed team commitments to solving problems. Here are some sample quotes from our interviews:

- I'm frustrated. I simply can't do the quality of work that I want to do and know how to do. I feel my hands are tied. I have no time. I need help on how to delegate and operate in this new culture.

- The goal of downsizing and delayering is correct. The execution stinks. The concept is to drop a lot of 'less important' work. This just didn't happen. We still have to know all the details, still have to follow all the old policies and systems.

- I'm overwhelmed. I can and want to do better work. The solution is not simply adding new people; I don't even want to. We need to team up on projects and work. Our leaders must stop piling on more and help us set priorities.

Second, just before the first Work-Out session, Jack Welch traveled to GEMS headquarters for a half-day roundtable with the Work-Out participants. Here are some sample quotes from middle managers:

APPENDIX
Work-Out: A Case Study (Continued)

- To senior management: "Listen! Think carefully about what the middle managers say. Make them feel like they are the experts and that their opinions are respected. There appear to be too many preconceived beliefs on the part of Welch and Trani."

- To senior management: "Listen to people, don't just pontificate. Trust people's judgment and don't continually second-guess. Treat other people like adults and not children."

- About themselves: "I will recommend work to be discontinued. I will try to find 'blind spots' where I withhold power. Any person I send to speak for me will 'push' peers who resist change."

- About themselves: "I will be more bold in making decisions. I will no longer accept the status quo. I will ask my boss for authority to make decisions. In fact, I will make more decisions on my own."

The five-day Work-Out session was an intense effort to unravel, evaluate, and reconsider the complex web of personal relationships, cross-functional interactions, and formal work procedures through which the business of GEMS gets done. Cross-functional teams cooperated to address actual business problems. Each functional group developed a vision of where its operations are headed.

John Trani participated in a roundtable where he listened and responded to the concerns and criticisms of middle managers. Senior members of the GEMS staff worked to build trust and more effective communication with the functional managers. All the participants focused on ways to reorganize work and maximize return on organization time, on team time, and on individual time.

The five-day session ended with individuals and functional teams signing close to 100 written contracts to implement the new procedures. There were contracts between functional teams, contracts between individuals, contracts between function heads an their staffs, and businesswide contracts with John Trani and his staff.

Work-Out has picked up steam since Lake Lawn. Managers from different product lines have participated in workshops to review and implement the attitudes, values, and new work procedures discussed at Lake Lawn. A Work-Out steering committee has held cross-functional information meetings for field employees around the world. Managers throughout GEMS are reviewing and modifying their reward and measurement systems. And Welch continues to receive regular briefings on Work-Out's progress.

No two GE businesses approach Work-Out in the same way; a process this intensive can't be cloned successfully among vastly different businesses. But Work-Out at GEMS offers a glimpse of the change process taking place throughout General Electric.

——— DISCUSSION QUESTIONS

1. Jack Welch mentions the importance of candor, which he defines as "facing reality, seeing the world as it is rather than as you wish it were." Do you feel that American businesses are practicing candor? Why or why not? What contribution can an individual make in a corporation that isn't facing reality?

2. What do you think Welch means by simplicity? Why is it important?

3. What changes in the business world have created the need for a leader with Welch's philosophy? What conditions could make his leadership style obsolete? What philosophy could replace his? Compare Welch with another dynamic business leader that you admire.

4. "GE has had an implicit psychological contract based on perceived lifetime employment," states Welch. Discussing GE's new psychological contract he says, " . . . jobs at GE are the best in the world for people who are willing to compete. . . . [they] provid[e] opportunities for personal and professional growth." Do you believe that this psychological contract is more appropriate in today's business context? Why or why not?

5. Do you think Welch has the formula that will keep American business competitive? Choose two or three of Welch's ideas on maintaining competitiveness and comment on why you either agree or disagree with them.

PART FOUR

MANAGING THE HUMAN RESOURCE

Planning with People in Mind
30

D. QUINN MILLS

This reading focuses on the need for companies to incorporate human resource planning into their long-term strategy making. It provides a firsthand report on the changes occurring in the management of human resources. Drawing on a survey of human resource activities at large companies as well as experience in the field, the author analyzes current practice, illustrates the diversity that characterizes the planning processes at sophisticated companies, and provides an inside view of people planning that works. As the author shows, top-level officers at the companies studied are likely to credit people planning for its part in raising morale, improving performance, and boosting profits.

General Electric had been engaged in formal business planning for several years before it began to take a longer-term view of human resources. In the interim, GE had faced a big problem as its business plans directed corporate resources to new products and technologies. "I didn't realize it at the time [that is, in 1970]," Reginald Jones, GE's former chairman, told me, "but we were a company with 30,000 electromechanical engineers becoming a company that needed electronics engineers. We didn't plan for this change in 1970, and it caused us big problems by the mid-1970s." Partly as a result of this experience, in the late 1970s GE began to ask its managers to plan for its human resource needs.

Similar costly hitches attributable to a lack of "people planning" are easily found. Consider, for example, the experience of a large multinational aluminum company planning to build a sophisticated computerized smelter in Brazil. The new technology had been a great success in the company's home country. But management ultimately realized that in Brazil it would be unable to find or train the computer technicians and service people needed to run such a facility. Plans were then revised at considerable cost to adapt the facility to the local labor force.

A large defense company faced its "people" crisis when it received a demanding government contract for which it had done little personnel planning. The company was forced to drain engineers and managers from other divisions, give them responsibilities far above their competence, and mount a costly rapid-hiring effort. The project survived, but the excess strain and high costs led top management to include a human resource component in its

449

business plans. Since then, the company has also used human resource planning to avoid abrupt layoffs that could adversely affect the whole community.

Partly because of experiences like these, many American companies have begun to plan for their professional, managerial, and technical personnel. The scope of this activity varies widely, of course, and at some companies planning still means little more than head-count forecasts and a succession plan for the CEO. But a growing number of senior executives have been rethinking their companies' human resource planning in two important regards. First, they are supplementing familiar hiring and promotion activities with innovative efforts to enhance corporate performance and boost employee morale. And second, they are forging new links between these activities and their long-term business goals.

How a company forges these links depends in large part on how its management views planning. As we will see, some executives like informal methods, while others prefer written memos and plans. But whatever form the process takes, the most critical element is management's appreciation for the ways in which its human resource decisions affect the company's ability to achieve its business plans—and vice versa. Thus corporate blueprints, however roughly drawn, are likely to contain some version of the feedback loops that characterize my model of the people-planning process.

In the pages that follow, I will examine instances of successful people planning and discuss its implications at greater length. First, however, let us review current practice in the field.

——— WHY COMPANIES PLAN FOR PEOPLE

The trend toward human resource planning emerges clearly from my survey of planning practices in large companies as well as from other studies and conversations with corporate officers.[1] (See *Exhibit 1*.)

Among respondents to my survey, 40% include a human resource component in their long-term business plans. A somewhat larger group, just below 50%, draws up a formal management-succession plan, and a similar proportion prepares training and development plans for managerial employees. In contrast, only 15% of the respondents reported that they do no people planning at all.

Typically, planning horizons fall into industry-related patterns, with formal human resource plans following the time line established by a company's business plan. (Some 89% of the respondents prepare a long-term business plan.) Business plans in construction and service companies, for example, tend to be short term, while in mining, transportation, communications, and utilities,

---

1. *See*, for example, Harriet Gorlin and Lawrence Schein, *Innovations in Managing Human Resources* (New York: Conference Board, 1984).

EXHIBIT 1
A Survey of Human Resource Planning in Large Companies

To ensure that the sample would be characteristic of large American companies as a whole, I chose approximately 11% of the 2,625 U.S. parent companies listed in Dun's *Directory of American Corporate Families*. Each of the randomly selected 291 companies in the sample reported sales of $50 million or more, conducted business from 10 or more locations, and had a controlling interest in one or more subsidiaries.

Because I also wished to minimize the possibility that professional attachments would color the respondents' replies, I directed the survey mostly to line managers, as the following breakdown indicates:

President	28.6%
Vice president—operations	23.7%
Vice president—manufacturing	14.3%
Senior executive vice president	10.7%
Vice president—planning or business development	9.4%
Vice president—personnel	5.3%
Vice president—sales administration or finance	8.0%

Executives at the sample companies received telephone calls during the summer of 1983. Some 77% replied to inquiries in 20- to 30-minute conversations. While this rate of response would be high in any case, it is especially striking in contrast to the 14% to 50% response rates usually registered in surveys.

managers are likely to plan five or more years ahead. (*Exhibit 2* gives the planning horizons by industry for companies in the survey.)

I based the survey on the notion that people planning is mainly a matter of challenge and response: companies facing occupational shortages or anticipating major business changes would respond by taking a careful look at their human resource needs. So in interviews I asked managers about their expectations. Were personnel shortages anticipated? Were competitors pressing hard on the company's heels? Were technological changes altering the skills their people needed? If so, then planning would surely follow.

And to a degree this hypothesis is correct: managers who anticipate competitive and technological challenges do plan for the effects of these changes on their people. But other managers, equally aware of coming changes, do not engage in people planning. Challenge alone is not enough to elicit a response.

Corporate size and strategic intent also fail to differentiate companies that plan from those that do not. Larger companies are no more likely to plan than smaller ones; and companies pursuing rapid growth are no more likely to plan than those that are simply trying to hold their own. What then explains the difference?

The explanation, I find, lies less in how a company's managers perceive the challenges facing them than in how they perceive planning. The companies engaged in people planning do it because their top executives are convinced it gives them a competitive advantage in the marketplace. Thus they adopt

EXHIBIT 2
Business Plan Horizons for Sample Companies

	TWO YEARS	THREE TO FIVE YEARS	MORE THAN FIVE YEARS
Mining		67%	33%
Construction	17%	83	
Nondurable-goods manufacturing	2	88	10
Durable-goods manufacturing		88	12
Transportation, communication, utilities*		67	27
Wholesale trade		88	12
Retail trade		95	5
Finance, insurance, real estate		89	11
Services	8	84	8

*6% not applicable.

planning because they believe it makes their company more flexible and entre-preneurial, not because the environment forces it on them.

Managers involved in human resource planning have difficulty under-standing how other companies can do without it. "Our growth is related to talent and training," said one executive. "We prepare for the future to eliminate surprises," added another. "It is basic to the planning process," said a third, "because it is easier to save capital than people." "It is our number-one priority," said a bank president, "absolute, unquestioned. It is the most important thing we do in terms of our productivity. How can a company be successful without people planning?"

In contrast, managers who resist planning do so because they believe it is costly and ineffective. They often associate planning with bureaucracy, and many remember unhappy planning experiences from years past. "I've told my staff to quit talking to me about human resource planning," said one executive. "We can't plan for people because we do a miserable job of business planning. And I don't want another nest of strategic planners in the company."

When planning gives the wrong directions or becomes too bureaucratic, of course it deserves to be condemned. But companies that do the best job of people planning usually avoid these problems by keeping the process as infor-mal as possible and leaving the responsibility in the hands of line officers. Moreover, managers who dismiss people planning out of hand may be short-changing their companies and their employees.

During the 1981–1982 recession, for example, more than half the com-panies in the survey had to lay off middle managers. But those companies in which people planning is most developed minimized these reductions, partly through hiring freezes, attrition, and other forms of advance action.

Similarly, 72% of the survey respondents who practice human resource planning are certain that it improves profitability. And 39%, or more than half of the human resource planners, insist that they can measure the difference on the bottom line. (It is probably no surprise that the companies doing the most wide-range planning are also the most likely to measure quantitatively the impact of their human resource efforts.)

Survey data also allowed me to analyze the profitability of the companies that include human resource goals in their business plans compared with those that do not. Profitability rests on many factors other than planning, of course. Yet on balance, when I compared companies in the same broad industrial categories, those that have such goals in their business plans are the more profitable. Thus the survey corroborates the intuitive judgment of those who link people with profits.

——— EVOLVING PROCESSES

For comparative purposes, I grouped the sample companies into five stages, based on three criteria: 1) the number of people-planning elements used in the company, 2) the degree to which human resource plans are integrated into the business plan, and 3) the expressed amount of interest in and commitment to the planning process. The greater the number of elements, the degree of integration, and the degree of interest, the higher the stage to which I assigned the company.

Each stage represents a point along a continuum. At one end are the companies that do little or no people planning; at the other are those that integrate long-range human resource planning into their strategic business plans. The majority of the survey companies fall between these two extremes, as *Exhibit 3* indicates.

Stage 1 companies have no long-term business plans, and they do little or no human resource planning. Several are family companies and tend to be run paternalistically. Their managers often build morale by traditional methods such as parties and picnics and show little interest in planning. "There are plenty of people in the local labor market," said one executive, "We go on faith."

Senior managers at Stage 2 companies tend to be skeptical of human resource planning, even though each of their companies has a long-term business plan. Some, especially those "managing for survival" in declining industries, think people planning is not very realistic, while others see it in limited terms and equate it with head-count forecasts. "To most companies, human resource planning is basically forecasting," said one executive. Still, a number of Stage 2 company managers see that people planning is becoming more important and believe there is a need to do more.

Respondents at all Stage 3 companies cited several people-planning components in addition to longer-term staff forecasts that project human resource

EXHIBIT 3
Five Stages in Human Resource Planning

	NUMBER OF COMPANIES	PERCENT OF RESPONDENTS	CHARACTERISTIC ACTIVITIES
Traditional			
1	34	15%	Company picnic
2	81	36	Short-term head-count forecasting
Moderate			
3	60	27	Longer-term head-count forecasting
Advanced			
4	27	14	Skills inventories and succession planning as part of a long-term business plan
5	18	8	Scenarios, trend analysis, management development, morale management

needs three to five years out. For the most part, however, they do not integrate these activities into the long-range business plan.

Stage 4 companies do a good deal of people planning, and their senior managers typically are enthusiastic about the process. "People are our principal asset," said one. "Without good people our company can't do a thing." "A well-managed company *must* emphasize it," said another. "We should be doing more. We often fall short of having qualified people ready when we need them." All Stage 4 companies practice long-term planning, and 87% have at least one human resource component integrated into the long-range plan.

At Stage 5 companies, human resource components are an important part of the long-term business plan. Almost all do formal management-succession planning, and 94% engage in forecasting activities of some kind. Predictably, all these companies are highly enthusiastic about human resource planning. As one corporate executive commented, "HRP is our number-one priority—the most important thing we do relative to productivity. To get people involved, HRP has to be alive and credible."

To illustrate the differences among companies at various stages, consider the pattern that emerges from the respondents' replies to questions about their hiring and retraining practices. As *Exhibit 4* indicates, there is a quite steady progression from Stage 1 companies' focus on hiring and training as needed to Stage 5 companies' emphasis on anticipatory action.

Thus managers at Stage 1 and 2 companies tend to hire or retrain people only when they have immediate vacancies, while those at Stage 4 and 5 companies often look as far as three to six years ahead. These differences are marked for scientific and technical positions, and they are even more dramatic for

EXHIBIT 4
Time Frames for Personnel Decisions

Human resource planning stage	*HIRE OR RETRAIN TO FILL SCIENTIFIC AND TECHNICAL POSITIONS* *Percent of Respondents*			
	As needed	*Six months to one year in advance*	*Two years in advance*	*Three to six years in advance*
1	66%	31%	0%	3%
2	63	26	4	7
3	49	36	2	13
4	47	40	0	13
5	44	19	6	31
	HIRE OR RETRAIN TO FILL MANAGERIAL AND PROFESSIONAL POSITIONS *Percent of Respondents*			
1	55%	26%	0%	19%
2	34	33	1	32
3	36	24	5	35
4	23	27	3	47
5	11	25	6	58

managerial and professional personnel. For example, some large companies have recruited a number of graduating electronics engineers, with the expectation that the payoff from their contributions will come in 5 to 10 years. Thus the managers at these Stage 5 companies seem to be applying the same time frame to their human resource investments that they have commonly used for research and development projects and large-scale capital investments.

Succession planning, or the identification of people to fill key administrative positions, is probably the most widely used building block in human resource planning. And it, too, reflects a full range of responses. At one extreme are the companies that do no succession planning other than replacement planning. At the other are Stage 4 and Stage 5 companies that gain competitive advantage from planning for all their employees, not just top executives.

Despite the widespread use of formal and informal succession plans, only about one company in ten integrates succession into its long-term strategic plan. Apparently many executives conceive of succession plans as nothing more than a way of coping with possible crises such as resignations or serious illnesses. If these executives thought about the plans' potential for orderly career advancement, however, the wisdom of incorporating them in their business plans (which identify opportunities and therefore promotion possibilities) would be obvious.

Beyond preparing for disasters, succession planning has two important advantages. First, it spotlights people in the ranks, potentially enhancing their careers by calling them to top management's attention. Second, and even more critical, it identifies and directs management's attention to possible costly vacancies that cannot readily be filled.

Like all aspects of planning, succession planning has its pitfalls, of course, including the possibility that a key subordinate will be listed for several management slots. But these snares should not deter executives from using them to develop a more competitive work force.

——— VIEW FROM WITHIN

Although I have used human resource policies and practices as criteria for categorizing companies, these activities are only building blocks for individual systems. In practice, people planning has many sources and takes various forms, as companies develop distinctive ways to meet their needs, experience, and business strategies.

The ways in which companies link people planning to long-term strategic business planning vividly reflect these differences. For example, some companies request formal human resource plans from their division managers and review them at regional or group-level corporate planning meetings. At other companies, where people planning is woven into day-to-day operations, the link may be nothing more formal than the fact that the corporate vice president of personnel sits in on strategic planning meetings and raises human resource issues.

Even companies that do the most advanced people planning show considerable divergence in their planning processes. Some carefully build the process around sophisticated components, such as computerized personnel-data systems, skills inventories, career and organizational development plans, environmental-scanning and trend analyses, competitive work force analyses, and alternative-future scenarios. In other companies, however, the process may focus on one or two components, such as succession planning or executive selection and development. (The range of planning practices among Stage 5 companies is described in *Exhibit 5.*)

Whatever form a company's people planning takes, however, the involvement of line managers is a must. People planning may benefit significantly from staff support, of course. Usually, in the best-organized processes, staff people analyze problems and identify options. But in the end, people planning is a line responsibility.

"People and Productivity," a study published by the New York Stock Exchange in 1982, suggests one reason for line managers' involvement. Based primarily on a survey of American industrial corporations, the report identifies 15 common human resource activities. Although some are training matters, a

EXHIBIT 5
No One Way to Plan

People planning takes many forms. Some Stage 5 companies find an informal and decentralized approach best suited to their needs, while others opt for more structure. What matters most is achieving a fit between top management's style and the planning process it chooses so that the company's human resource activities mesh with its culture.

To illustrate, consider these two examples of sophisticated people planning.

The James Company is a large, decentralized multinational with divisions and subsidiaries throughout the world. Each operating company does its own planning, while the CEO has the job of conceptualizing corporate strategy. A small staff with expertise in finance, technology, and personnel turns these concepts into plans.

The company's human resource planning is likewise decentralized and informal; discussions and minimal reporting constitute the planning process. An international skills group works with company and regional personnel to coordinate skills inventories. And people planners from each division and subsidiary meet all over the world through the company's personnel network to discuss human resource issues.

Human resource planning at the corporate level focuses on policy development in three key areas: 1) the identification and appointment of senior managers to implement business strategies, 2) the incorporation of people-related information into strategic, operational, and succession planning, and 3) the design and review of personnel policies to support strategy implementation.

Human resource building blocks used at the corporate level and by the individual companies include head-count planning and forecasting, environmental monitoring, and training and development programs. These are not formally related to the strategic-planning process, which focuses on management-succession planning and the worldwide skills inventory only.

Rising managers receive profit-and-loss responsibilities early in their careers, and their candidacy for high-level, general management positions is measured by how well the units perform.

The planning process at Webb Company, a large, successful high-tech company, is highly centralized and carefully structured. Formal links between the human resource function and the strategic-

large number, such as individual goal setting, appraisal and feedback, job redesign, quality circles, and so forth, affect the organization's day-to-day relations with its employees. Thus line management has to be part of the people-planning system.

Involvement can occur in different ways, however. Line management may submit a business plan to the corporate staff analysts who then request modifications. Alternatively, the staff may prepare reports on expected developments (such as occupational shortages and surpluses, life-style changes that could affect attitudes and performance, and government regulations) that it circulates to division managers. Then these line officers, with their staff, prepare a plan to deal with the identified issues and send it back to corporate staff for review.

EXHIBIT 5
No One Way to Plan (Continued)

planning process go back to the late 1960s, when management devised a concurrence/nonconcurrence option for corporate personnel. Under this system, personnel is a decision-pushing function with real influence on decision making. If the corporate staff disagrees strongly with a business strategy, it can stop the plan until the issues are resolved by top management. By using the "silver bullet" of nonconcurrence, the staff can even kill an unfit program; if it chooses not to do so, it commits itself to the plan by default.

The company separated strategic and operational planning during the mid-1970s and in 1982 introduced a new business-planning system to encourage entrepreneurship and minimize bureaucracy. With this reorganization strategic planning became a corporate-level, top-down process, limited in detail and focused on the investment-planning cycle. At the same time, the company replaced its old divisional operating blueprints with bottom-up, detailed commitment plans. Proposals developed by the divisions in the commitment-planning process go to all major functional vice presidents for review. The human resources staff retains its concurrence option and prepares strategy

reviews to identify disadvantages. If it finds issues that cannot be resolved informally, personnel sends the plan to the top-level business operations committee for resolution.

To give promising executives wide exposure to the company, Webb rotates them through varied assignments that can include staff positions designed to give them a look at top-level management. Its commitment to getting, keeping, and developing the very best people is evident in a recent decision to authorize yearly hiring of the top 5% of new graduates in certain engineering specialties. This philosophy is also reflected in the company's full-employment no-layoff policy for full-time permanent employees. This policy, in turn, is an important feature in other decisions, such as the ongoing need to find new projects for talented employees.

Among Webb's well-executed human resource activities are management-succession planning, extensive management-development efforts, and training programs in effective management. The company is also beginning to apply strategic thinking to its compensation systems so that they support its business goals, strategies, and culture.

Getting operating managers to invest time in the planning process can be difficult. Helping managers look beyond numbers or head-counts to development, morale, and performance issues, breaking away from job descriptions in thinking about future skill needs, and escaping the tyranny of sales forecasts with their implicit message that people are simply a derived demand are among the problems senior executives cite. To make human resource plans more than shallow appendages to the strategic business plan, however, managers must master these difficulties.

Identifying the payoff from human resource planning in improved organizational performance is one way to try to overcome resistance. If line executives see plans as "a graphics exercise," in GE Chairman John Welch's words, they simply will not support the process.[2] Also, managers need adequate information about legal developments, employee mores, and other external factors to plan intelligently for hiring, motivation, performance, and morale.

Significantly, companies that show the highest commitment to human resource planning are also those that share the most information with their managers and are the most likely to help them make sense of their environment. For example, managers at Stage 1 companies reported that, for the most part, they try to keep up with legal, legislative, and life-style trends on their own. Conversely, 77% of those at Stage 5 companies rely on their organizations for half or even most of their information.

────── PEOPLE PLANNING THAT WORKS

Many companies incorporate human resource goals in their long-term business planning, and about half of those surveyed require staffing forecasts. But few include the development activities and costs that are a crucial part of long-term staffing strategies. Thus the people-planning process is often seriously incomplete.

When planning stops with objectives and short of implementation, the business advantages it provides are likely to be lost. Consider, therefore, how one high-tech company avoided this common pitfall in its approach to a crucial sales-force planning issue.

For years this big company had prospered by hiring large numbers of young liberal arts graduates and giving them extensive training. As product technology advanced, however, salespeople lacking a technical background were less and less able to grasp it. By 1983 management faced an important decision: In the years ahead should the company alter its strategy and recruit more heavily among technical college graduates? If so, how fast should the company move, and how should the transition be managed?

Representatives from marketing, field sales, product development, and personnel formed a task force to devise a program for identifying future sales-force candidates. The assignment proved extraordinarily complicated, and days of discussion followed. A flow chart, prepared to assist the task force's deliberations, demonstrated the complexity of careful human resource planning and the virtue of organizing the process into a series of manageable steps (see *Exhibit 6*).

The task force began by identifying the chief factors that were determining future salespeople's capabilities. It then used these factors to establish the

2. John F. Welch, Jr., "Managing Change," dedication convocation, Fuqua School of Business, Duke University, April 21, 1983.

company's needs and to determine objectives for the sales force. At this point, too, the task force requested an inventory of the company's current sales team to see how it balanced against the identified needs.

Having determined that the company lacked the people it needed, the task force identified its alternatives. This brainstorming phase was a logical follow-up to the forecasting, modeling, and data collection that had gone on before, and it represented the task force's entry into the decision stage. However, at the same time the alternatives made further analysis essential. For example, because hiring from the outside was one alternative, the company had to survey the available job seekers. And because internal development was another avenue, the task force had to know more about the company's willingness to retrain and relocate its employees.

At this point, the task force faced crucial "make-or-buy" decisions. What should it recommend? The decision to look outside for more technically trained people could be easily implemented. But, as the task force realized, its options were also constrained by previous decisions. New hires could strengthen the sales force, but they could not substitute for it. The company had a large number of salespeople already and could not seriously think about replacing them in a short time. What, then, could the company do?

The task force recommended that the company detail technically trained people to sales and supplement them with a large-scale retraining program for the existing staff. Options such as reorganization of the company's sales efforts, job redesign, and changes in the compensation system were held for further study. Implementation of the task force's recommendations occurred during the next three years.

EXHIBIT 6
The Planning Process for a Sales Force Change

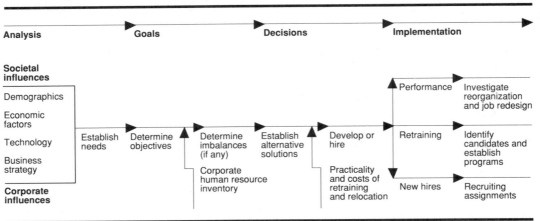

MODEL PROCESS

Every company organizes its people-planning process in its own way, and some use only parts of the model shown in *Exhibit 7*. Yet this sequential and idealized version of the people-planning process both accurately reflects current practice at several highly successful companies and reveals the logical order that ties these activities together.

As the model makes clear, the most important development in human resource planning is not the creation of many elements but rather their integration into a decision-making process that combines three important activities: 1) identifying and acquiring the right number of people with the proper skills, 2) motivating them to achieve high performance, and 3) creating interactive links between business objectives and people-planning activities.

Thinking ahead begins with a company's multiyear business plan, which establishes both its overall organization structure and goals and objectives for each business. Then the planning process divides to reflect the two factors that make any business successful in human terms.

A company's skill and staffing forecasts are set by both its organization structure and its business goals. Then company managers must decide whether to meet forecasted needs by hiring new people or retraining and reassigning the

EXHIBIT 7
The Human Resource Planning Process

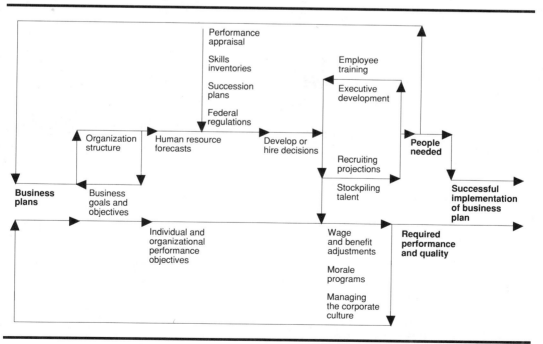

current staff. Performance appraisals, skills inventories, management succession plans, and equal opportunity programs all provide input for this choice. For current personnel, employee training and executive-development programs come into play, while recruiting projections, advance hiring, and even stockpiling of key talent are used for new hires.

Business goals also generate the productivity and quality requirements that are translated into performance objectives for individuals and organizational units. Designing and strengthening work programs, assessing the corporate culture, and, if necessary, modifying or reinforcing it from the top are among the ways human resource planners target performance objectives. They also adjust wages and benefits as necessary to preserve morale and promote recruiting and retention of employees.

Companies that have the people in place to meet their performance objectives are well-equipped to implement their business plans successfully. If, however, the right people are unavailable or if the performance goals cannot be met, the plans themselves may require revision, as the feedback loops in the model show. Many companies would have spared themselves embarrassing marketplace failures if they had first recognized that the human resource implications of their strategic plans were unrealizable. And in fact, astute managers no longer assume that every plan is doable, nor do they simply derive their people plans from their long-term business plans.

Personnel and skills forecasts are common in business organizations, and this aspect of people planning has received much attention in recent years. Newer and quite important are the human resource activities designed to evoke high performance from individuals and groups within the company. This morale management bodes well for the future, since it is people's performance and productivity that help create the lower costs and higher quality essential for profitability.

The people-planning process described here is taking shape in many companies throughout the country. In some it has evolved, beginning with one or two components and the gradual addition of others. In a smaller group of companies it began in reaction to environmental challenges. But in the largest group by far, people planning has resulted from the leadership, vision, and purpose of top management.

—— DISCUSSION QUESTIONS

1. The reading points out how people planning benefits companies. How might it benefit individuals? How might people planning influence an individual's career development? What other benefits might this approach to planning have for the individual?

2. This reading focuses on the advantages of people planning. What might be some drawbacks to people planning?

3. Few companies involve themselves in people planning. What message does this send to employees of companies? Does the scarcity of people planning reveal particular attitudes that companies hold toward the work force?

4. As an employee of a company that does not take the approach to planning advocated in the reading, would your job performance be affected in any way? Would your commitment to the company be stronger, weaker, or unaffected?

31   Career Systems and Strategic Staffing

JEFFREY A. SONNENFELD AND MAURY A. PEIPERL

This reading begins by defining career systems as the sets of policies and procedures firms use to provide staff to meet human resource requirements. It examines the basic elements of career systems and explains how human resource management policy relates to the overall strategy of a firm. The authors discuss the three stages of a career system: entry, development, and exit. They then describe the two fundamental properties of career systems: supply flow and assignment flow. Also covered are different methods that groups use to maintain membership: the academy, the club, the baseball team, and the fortress. This four-cell typology of career systems links staffing policy with business strategy.

A small but successful software company faces a severe turnover problem. Because its labor market is so competitive, employees whom it has spent hundreds of hours and thousands of dollars recruiting and training are leaving more rapidly than it can replace them. Besides the obvious personnel shortage, the firm is receiving little or no return for its substantial investment in these employees' development.

A second firm—a retailer—finds that its staff is mismatched to its needs: It has too many merchandisers and not enough store-operations personnel. Should the firm—already running on extremely tight margins—retrain and relocate its employees or cut its surplus merchandisers and try to bring in experienced operations talent?

A third firm—a professional-services company—is experiencing a drop in productivity as both its technical and sales managers reach performance plateaus. Although there is room for growth in its market, the firm is unable to take advantage of these external opportunities without further developing and revitalizing its people. How does it approach this task?

All three of these companies face strategic staffing problems that depend on the firm's career system for solutions. A *career system* is the set of policies and practices an organization uses to provide staff to meet its human resource requirements. The firm is a production system as well as a social system. Three general system events—input, throughput, and output—are the basic dynamics behind entry, development, and exit. Within these areas, specific career-system functions include the hiring and firing of employees, training and development, performance evaluation, succession planning, and retirement provisions. Career systems may be the result of careful planning and construction, or they may be de facto products of organizational evolution.

Why study career systems? The successful manager recognizes that human resource management is not merely the assignment of the right people to the right jobs, but that it also includes responsibility for helping employees manage their careers within (and occasionally beyond) the company's career system.

HUMAN RESOURCE FLOWS: THREE BASIC STAGES

Career systems involve the flow of people through the organization.[1] As in any system, the flows take place in three stages: entry, development, and exit. In a career system, entry corresponds to recruitment and selection; development to assignment, promotion, and training; and exit to layoff, firing, retirement, or resignation.

ENTRY

Recruitment is the means of attracting candidates for hire, while *selection* is the process of evaluating the fit of the candidate to the position and the firm. Because these processes go hand in hand, they are frequently managed together. The first step in the recruitment and selection process is the determination of human resource requirements. The firm must decide what sort of people are required to support current and future strategic directions. Firms will vary, for example, in their needs for technological expertise and management skill. Firms organized along product lines and functional areas may recruit by product or function with fairly specialized criteria. More diversified or regionally organized firms may require more general talent with greater variation in recruiting criteria.

Having decided on the human resource requirements behind recruitment, the firm must next consider which executives should be involved in the selection process. Often senior managers become involved in specifications but not in the initial screening process. The initial phases are generally guided by professional recruiters. These recruiters disseminate information about the firm and manage the initial contact and follow-through. The better informed the recruiters are about organizational needs, the higher the quality of the recruitment decision.

Firms must then decide on recruitment methods. These will depend on the type of recruit desired. Executive search firms are usually used to fill senior

1. Jeffrey A. Sonnenfeld, *Managing Career Systems: Channeling the Flow of Executive Careers* (Homewood, Ill.: Richard D. Irwin, 1984), Chapter 1.

positions when the labor market is tight. Technical experts are most effectively located through word-of-mouth channels and professional associations. Employee referrals are also an important source of information and candidates.

After a pool of candidates has been recruited, the final selection occurs. Although this process may include sophisticated procedures, such as assessment centers and physical and/or psychological examinations, the more common procedure for selection is a series of interviews with department heads, peers, and likely bosses. It is important that, during this process, candidates not become the victims of internal feuds, biases derived from initial impressions (e.g., physical attractiveness, sex, religion, race), or poor listening skills on the part of interviewers.

Interviews in the final stage often blend into early socialization, in an effort to provide candidates with realistic job previews. Meetings with current employees, site visits, job descriptions, and company literature on its history, performance, and career paths can supplement the more costly and more time-consuming interview process.

DEVELOPMENT

Assignment and promotion are two key elements of the development process. Research has shown that initial job assignments significantly affect a manager's later career; thus, a new employee's first assignment should be neither too easy nor too difficult. Employees spend much of their time in the first assignment adjusting to the realities of the workplace and the culture.

Competition for promotion may begin early. Those who fail in early tournament competitions are not likely to be included in later contests. Although the losers of promotion contests may not travel much farther on the career path, they may still face peer-level contests in order to maintain the same position. Their immobility may make them feel stagnant and frustrated. Monitoring the direction and pace of individual careers can help minimize problems of immobility. Companies such as IBM, which pace people through career paths, can ensure that one undesirable or dead-end post does not block an employee's further development.

Career momentum, the pace at which people advance, varies by company. Culture and strategy influence what constitutes being "on, ahead of, or behind schedule." Overall company growth and strategy will affect employees' opportunities for career growth by helping to determine how many and what kinds of jobs are open, and with what frequency. Also, different types of individuals will seek different types of mobility. For instance, younger, early-career workers may be disappointed with lateral movement, while older ones may prefer lateral moves to hierarchical moves that would require relocating.

Organizations can assist their members in their career planning through formal career-development programs that take some of the control away from the supervisor. Firms with centralized career programs can (1) minimize hoarding of talent, (2) reduce drifts toward obsolescence, and (3) improve equal-opportunity provisions for women and minorities. Often career-development programs include an employee self-assessment and a developmental review with the boss. Yet in order to have effective career-development programs, companies must go beyond the self-assessment tools and employee-superior meetings. They must assess themselves to determine the changing human resource needs of the company and the career paths likely to be followed by those who will fill those needs in the future.

Training programs are the other half of the development process. They can serve many purposes. Most generally they serve as key interventions in large organizational changes or as individual development efforts designed to improve the immediate performance or longer-term preparedness of particular workers. Examples of training for organizational change include teaching new techniques and explaining new products; individual development programs might include new-employee orientation, functional-skills training, and preparation for retirement or outplacement.

The steps in developing training programs are, first, to assess the organization's training goals and the training requirements of individuals; second, to plan a curriculum, taking into account the time frame (will the training have immediate or longer-term applicability?); and third, to choose pedagogical techniques appropriate to the people being trained and the ideas being taught. Techniques might include self-study workbooks, videos, lectures, class discussions, group work, and intergroup competitions. Fourth, the firm must select instructors appropriate to the material and the audience. Lastly, the firm must evaluate the success of the training effort: Was the proper material taught? Were the right people involved? Did the training address the immediate needs of the firm? The long-term needs? Company training staffs can play critical roles as educational brokers or intermediaries, and with managers, as evaluators of the training process.

EXIT

Organizational exit is typically the single worst-managed process in the career system. Even when the reasons for exit are logical and clear-cut—a plant closing, a retirement, a resignation in order to pursue a better opportunity—the processes are unnecessarily destructive to the departing individual and the organization he or she leaves behind.

Losing or leaving a job can be extremely difficult on an individual, whose life in some degree revolves around the job. The change spills over into other life sectors; the loss of a work identity often shatters one's self-confidence in dealing with future challenges. People suffer from job loss as much from the way the event transpires as from its actual occurrence. Managers who lack the courage to address the facts surrounding the firing of a subordinate allow a cloud of suspicion about one's honesty or competence to haunt an employee upon dismissal. The lack of directness, the anger, and the abruptness may reflect a manager's fear of reprisal from friends of the fired employee. Such behavior may also reflect a manager's own feelings of guilt. Such poor management of organizational exit not only damages the lives and careers of those departing but also hurts the internal culture of the firm.

To manage exits effectively, firms must understand the reason for a worker's departure. High turnover may be symptomatic of underlying problems in the organization (alternatively, it may be typical of certain industries or markets). Exit interviews and research on resignations may help determine causes. When an employee is dismissed, firms must learn whether the firing was fair, appropriate, and necessary. Was the employee consistently receiving honest performance feedback?

Firms must also be certain which workers they are better off losing and which are hard to replace. Carefully tailored approaches to exits can improve a firm's ability to keep the employees it needs and remove those it does not. Selective salary cuts, job redesign, changes in hours, and retraining of experienced and motivated personnel may all be more effective than broad-based exit plans in management of the workforce.

Finally, managing exits means easing the transition. Advance notice and outplacement counseling can better prepare employees for their disengagement. If the explanation for the termination is clear and assistance is genuine, the likelihood of retaliation and sabotage is not greater than for any other source of disgruntlement. Programs for flextime, job sharing, part-time employment, and phased retirement allow workers to learn and become increasingly involved in activities outside of the firm.

CAREER SYSTEMS: AN ORGANIZATIONAL PERSPECTIVE

A firm's labor supply is subject to the external environment in the basic processes of entry and exit and is internally interdependent among its components in the process of development.[2] This approach implies two fundamental properties of career systems: first, the movement into and out of the firm, the *supply flow*; and second, the movement across job assignments and through promotions within the firm, the *assignment flow*. By positioning firms along these two dimensions, many of the variations in career systems can be profiled.

---

2. Jeffrey A. Sonnenfeld and Maury A. Peiperl, "Staffing Policy as a Strategic Response: A Typology of Career Systems," *Academy of Management Review* (October 1988): 588–600.

SUPPLY FLOW

The supply-flow dimension is measured by the openness of the career system to the external labor market at other than entry levels. For example, IBM has an almost total reliance on its internal labor market, creating a closed supply flow except at the entry level. In contrast, most semiconductor, advertising, broadcasting, and entertainment firms rely on extensive mid-career recruitment; therefore, positions other than those at entry level are more open to outside supply. It follows that these firms also see a higher level of mid-career exits or outflow. Supply flow thus reflects the degree to which a firm staffs itself from external sources. It can be seen in the level of employment security and loyalty to long-service employees on the one hand, and receptiveness to new members and turnover on the other.

ASSIGNMENT FLOW

The assignment-flow dimension describes the criteria by which assignment and promotion decisions are made. It reflects the pace and pressure in the career pipeline and the criteria for promotion: technical versus political. The vacancy rate, growth rate, and demographics also affect this dimension. In particular, the choice of individuals for assignments can be made primarily on the basis of their individual performance or on the basis of their contribution to the general group. Although some career systems favor the star performer, others prefer the solid contributor.

The *Exhibit* on the next page displays these two dimensions and the resultant four-cell typology, with entry, development, and exit characteristics for each cell. The cells have been given distinctive labels that evoke groups with distinctly different methods of maintaining membership.

THE ACADEMY

The key career-system objective of an academy is development. The academy is often a dominant or core competitor. Workers in these firms see themselves as members of a modern guild. They see professional growth as a personal goal and a community obligation. They value skillful teamwork rather than solo performance. Important to these systems are such contextual qualities as task uncertainty, firm-specific knowledge, related job sequences, and competition for scarce skills. These systems seek to develop and retain their own talent.

Within the academy, IBM is a good example. At IBM, point of entry is restricted to early-career positions. An employee entering any given management group has an 80% chance of staying with IBM through to retirement. By contrast, at a major New York City bank that same individual would have an

EXHIBIT
Models of Career Systems

	FORTRESS—Retrenchment	BASEBALL TEAM—Recruitment
External	*Entry*	*Entry*
	Passive recruitment Drawn to industry by own interests/background Selective turnaround recruitment	Primary human resources practice Emphasis on credentials, expertise Recruit at all career stages
	Development	*Development*
	Effort to retain core talent	On-the-job Little formal training Little succession planning
	Exit	*Exit*
	Layoffs frequent Respects seniority	High turnover Cross-employer career paths
SUPPLY FLOW	CLUB—Retention	ACADEMY—Development
	Entry	*Entry*
	Early career Emphasis on reliability	Strictly early career Ability to grow
	Development	*Development*
	As generalists Slow paths Required steps Emphasis on commitment	Primary human resources practice Extensive training for specific jobs Tracking and sponsorship of high-potential employees Elaborate career paths/job ladders
	Exit	*Exit*
	Low turnover Retirement	Low turnover Retirement Dismissal for poor performance
Internal		

Group Contribution	ASSIGNMENT FLOW	Individual Contribution

80% chance of quitting by the end of his or her first decade of employment. To understand the reasons behind these kinds of statistics, keep in mind that disparate corporate objectives have resulted in a wide variety of career-systems policies.

THE CLUB

The key career-system task for a club is retention. Security and membership are the essence of commitment. Status attainment prior to employment, such as schooling, contributes to an employee's perceived value. The club is frequently shielded by regulatory buffers or a monopoly situation. Workers often see their employer (e.g., a public utility) as an institution with a mission—to serve the public interest—that transcends marketplace concerns.

THE BASEBALL TEAM

A baseball team's career system focuses on recruitment. In firms where innovation is at a premium, the lack of employment security heightens the pressure for creativity. The pool of risk takers is not limited to the internal labor market. The spirit in the baseball team is upbeat; employees see themselves as minor celebrities, each with a shot at becoming a true star. Commitment is at a lower level than in either academies or clubs. When complacency sets in at baseball types of firms (such as advertising, broadcasting, or semiconductor companies), professional networks, trade associations, and recruiters seek new talent.

THE FORTRESS

A fortress career system focuses on retrenchment. The fortress is in a struggle for survival. This type of firm may have hired and fired in reaction to market conditions. These may be firms never in control of their strategic environment because of the intense competition or the shortage of key resources. They may also be firms caught in crises, facing turnaround challenges. Sometimes such crises are intentionally brought to a head by a shift in career systems. For instance, a commercial bank attempting to shed the people and businesses acquired during a different regulatory environment may lead the firm into a fortress career system as a planned transitional phase. Similarly, a film studio or advertising firm with long-service, but poor-performing, talent may elect to streamline before restaffing in ways that resemble its baseball-team competitors. Workers in these fortress industries may have been attracted to the presumed glamour in the business (e.g., publishing, hotels, retail). They may also have joined the firms in a healthier period. Or, they may have backed in by mistake. Employees here see themselves as soldiers locked in combat.

STRATEGIC CHOICE AND CAREER SYSTEMS

The differing management practices of each career-system profile are frequently the product of strategic intentions. To create the needed pool of labor to accomplish distinct missions, firms will vary in their emphasis upon such membership qualities as professional expertise, competitiveness, loyalty, flexibility, and company-specific knowledge.

Each of the four strategic types corresponds to a different set of career-system practices that provides the requisite degree of skill and continuity in the workforce. Academies, for example, survey their context carefully and inventory their internal resources before plunging into new activities. They are most skillful at execution and rarely lead the market with new ideas. Their career systems must be anticipatory so that they have the infrastructure to ensure reliable delivery upon their commitments. The more feisty baseball teams attract innovative talent that often has a more cosmopolitan commitment to the occupation or profession than to the firm. The clubs are concerned more with maintaining their strategic domain than with seeking new expansion. Regulatory protection and general community support are often important. Hence, their employment practices are often managed in ways that promote their identity as benevolent public institutions. Finally, the fortresses' strategic style suggests that they have lost control over their environment. These firms may be academies, clubs, or baseball teams that failed at their mission. Many firms may pass through this style while retrenching or turning themselves around. Some spend a long time as fortresses before reviving; others institute quick and drastic changes; still others never break out of fortress mode. Although persisting in a boom-or-bust fashion may be natural in certain industries (e.g., retail), it may indicate a performance problem in others.

Thus the staffing difficulties experienced by the three firms at the beginning of this reading may be better understood in light of the models just described. The software company that keeps investing in people only to lose them is an example of a baseball team, where people regularly move from firm to firm. Rather than pouring money into employees' development, this company should consider buying the skills it needs in the open labor market. Of course, it will have to ensure that its reward systems address the pay-for-performance expectations of its workforce, or else it may not be able to keep any employees for long. The retailer is probably a fortress, under so much competitive pressure that it cannot afford the costs of job security and retraining. It may find it necessary to lay off its surplus merchandisers and hire operations talent from outside. The mature professional-services company may want to be an academy but is finding itself more like a club. To foster the continued development of its plateaued managers, the company should focus more on pay-for-performance and targeted training. Only by aligning career systems with overall corporate strategy can firms achieve satisfactory management of human resource flows.

DISCUSSION QUESTIONS

1. Should a company be concerned with the three stages of human resource flows? Why not simply focus on the stage best suited for that particular company?

2. What is a more effective philosophy for a company's career planning system—one based on paternalism or one based on each employee for himself or herself? Does this depend on certain factors such as the kind of business or industry in which a company is engaged?

3. Given your career choices, what sort of company would you be attracted to as described in the *Exhibit*—the fortress, the baseball team, the club, or the academy? Explain why.

32 Reward Systems and the Role of Compensation

MICHAEL BEER AND RICHARD E. WALTON

This reading examines reward systems and their effects on employee satisfaction and motivation. It explores how employees' and management's attitudes toward money make designing a reward system problematic. It then considers systems for maintaining pay equity, internally and externally, as well as the advantages and disadvantages of determining pay levels by evaluating the worth of a job or an individual's abilities and skill level. Seniority and pay for performance are also considered as the bases for rewards.

The design and management of reward systems present the general manager with one of the most difficult HRM (human resource management) tasks. This HRM policy area contains the greatest contradictions between the promise of theory and the reality of implementation. Consequently, organizations sometimes go through cycles of innovation and hope as reward systems are developed, followed by disillusionment as these reward systems fail to deliver.[1]

REWARDS AND EMPLOYEE SATISFACTION

Gaining an employee's satisfaction with the rewards given is not a simple matter. Rather, employee satisfaction is a function of several factors that organizations must learn to manage:

- *The individual's satisfaction with rewards is, in part, related to what is expected and how much is received.* Feelings of satisfaction or dissatisfaction arise when individuals compare their input—job skills, education, effort, and performance—with output—the mix of extrinsic and intrinsic rewards they receive.
- *Employee satisfaction is also affected by comparisons with other people in similar jobs and organizations.* In effect, employees compare their own

---

1. This reading consists of material adapted from *Managing Human Assets* by Michael Beer, Bert Spector, Paul Lawrence, D. Quinn Mills, and Richard Walton (New York: The Free Press, 1984).

input/output ratio with that of others. People vary considerably in how they weigh various inputs in that comparison. They tend to weigh their strong points more heavily, such as certain skills or a recent incident of effective performance. Individuals also tend to give their own performance a higher rating than the one they receive from their supervisors. The problem of unrealistic self-ratings exists partly because supervisors in most organizations do not communicate a candid evaluation of their subordinates' performances to them. Such candid communication to subordinates, unless done skillfully, seriously risks damaging self-esteem. The bigger dilemma is that failure by managers to communicate a candid appraisal of performance makes it difficult for employees to develop a realistic view of their own performance, thus increasing the possibility of dissatisfaction with the pay they are receiving.

- *Employees often misperceive the rewards of others.* Evidence shows that individuals tend to overestimate the pay of fellow workers doing similar jobs and to underestimate their performance (a defense or self-esteem-building mechanism). Misperceptions of the performance and rewards of others also occur because organizations do not generally make available accurate information about the salary or performance of others.
- *Overall satisfaction results from a mix of rewards rather than from any single reward.* The evidence suggests that both intrinsic rewards and extrinsic rewards are important and cannot be directly substituted for each other. Employees who are paid well for repetitious, boring work will be dissatisfied with the lack of intrinsic rewards, just as employees who are paid poorly for interesting, challenging work may be dissatisfied with extrinsic rewards.

REWARDS AND MOTIVATION

From the organization's point of view, rewards are intended to motivate certain behaviors. But under what conditions will rewards actually motivate employees? To be useful, rewards must be seen as timely and tied to effective performance.

One theory suggests that the following conditions are necessary for employee motivation:[2]

- Employees must believe effective performance (or certain specified behavior) will lead to certain rewards. For example, attaining certain results will lead to a bonus or approval from others.
- Employees must feel that the rewards offered are attractive. Although some employees may desire promotions because they seek

2. Edward E. Lawler, *Pay and Organizational Effectiveness: A Psychological View* (New York: McGraw-Hill, 1971): 267–272.

power, others may want a fringe benefit, such as a pension, because they are older and want retirement security.
- Employees must believe a certain level of individual effort will lead to achieving the corporation's standards of performance.

As indicated, motivation to exert effort is triggered by the prospect of desired rewards: money, recognition, promotion, and so forth. If effort leads to performance and performance leads to desired rewards, the employee is satisfied and motivated to perform again.

As previously mentioned, rewards fall into two categories: extrinsic and intrinsic. *Extrinsic rewards* come from the organization as money, perquisites, or promotions or from supervisors and co-workers as recognition. *Intrinsic rewards* accrue from performing the task itself and may include the satisfaction of accomplishment or a sense of influence. The process of work and the individual's response to it provide the intrinsic reward. But the organization seeking to increase intrinsic rewards must provide a work environment that allows these satisfactions to occur; therefore, more organizations are redesigning work and delegating responsibility to enhance employee involvement.

EQUITY AND PARTICIPATION

The ability of a reward system to both motivate and satisfy depends on who influences and/or controls the system's design and implementation. Even though considerable evidence suggests that participation in decision making can lead to greater acceptance of decisions, participation in both the design and administration of reward systems is rare. Such participation is time-consuming.

Perhaps a greater roadblock is that pay has been one of the last strongholds of managerial prerogatives. Concerned about employee self-interest and compensation costs, corporations do not typically allow employees to participate in pay-system design or decisions. Thus, it is not possible to test thoroughly the effects of widespread participation on acceptance of and trust in reward systems.

—— COMPENSATION SYSTEMS: THE DILEMMAS OF PRACTICE

A body of experience, research, and theory has been developed about how money satisfies and motivates employees. Virtually every study on the importance of pay compared with other potential rewards has shown that pay is important. It consistently ranks among the top five rewards. Many factors, however, affect the importance of pay and other rewards. Money, for example, is likely to be viewed differently at various points in one's career, because the need for money versus other rewards (status, growth, security, and so forth) changes at each stage. National culture is another important factor. U.S. managers and employees emphasize pay for individual performance more than do their European or Japanese counterparts. European and Japanese companies, however, rely more on slow promotions and seniority as well as some degree of employment security. Even within a single culture, shifting national forces may alter people's needs for money versus other rewards.

Companies have developed various compensation systems and practices to achieve pay satisfaction and motivation. In manufacturing firms, payroll costs can run as high as 40% of sales revenues, whereas in service organizations payroll costs can top 70%. General managers, therefore, take an understandable interest in payroll costs and how these dollars are spent.

The traditional view of managers and compensation specialists is that the right system would solve most problems. This assumption is not plausible because there is no one right answer or objective solution to what or how someone should be paid. What people will accept, be motivated by, or perceive as fair is highly subjective. Pay is a matter of perceptions and values that often generate conflict.

MANAGEMENT'S INFLUENCE ON ATTITUDES TOWARD MONEY

Many organizations are caught in a vicious cycle that they partly create. In their recruitment and internal communications, firms often emphasize compensation levels and a belief in individual pay for performance. This is likely to attract people with high needs for money as well as to heighten that need in those already employed. Thus, the meaning employees attach to money is partly shaped by management's views. If merit increases, bonuses, stock options, and perquisites are held out as valued symbols of recognition and success, employees will come to see them in this light even more than they might have at first. Having heightened money's importance as a reward, management must then respond to employees who may demand more money or better pay-for-performance systems.

Firms must establish a philosophy about rewards and the role of pay in the mix of rewards. Without such a philosophy, the compensation practices that happen to be in place will continue to shape employees' expectations, and those expectations will sustain the existing practices. If money has been emphasized as an important symbol of success, that emphasis will continue even though a compensation system with a slightly different emphasis might have equal motivational value with fewer administrative problems and perhaps even lower cost. Money is important, but its degree of importance is influenced by the type of compensation system and philosophy that management adopts.

PAYROLL STRATIFICATION: A ONE- OR TWO-CLASS SOCIETY?

An organization with different compensation systems for different levels of the organization that offer different fringe benefits, pay-for-performance rewards, and administrative procedures is sending employees a message about more than just the specific behavior the compensation system is intended to reward. That message is that there are differences in the company's expectations of the commitment and role of employees at different levels and the degree to which they are full and responsible members of the organization.

Several understandable reasons exist for these differences. To circumvent the intended effects of progressive tax laws, corporations pay managers in a form different from that of lower-level employees. Deferred compensation, stock options, and various perquisites protect executives from taxation that reduces the value of their rewards.

In the United States, all organizations must distinguish between *exempt employees* (those who, according to the wage-and-hour laws, have significant decision-making responsibility—typically, managers and professional employees) and *nonexempt employees* (all other regular members of the organization—typically clerical white-collar and hourly blue-collar employees). Federal law requires nonexempt employees to receive overtime pay for a workweek that exceeds 40 hours; exempt employees are, as the name implies, exempt from such legislative protection. Because of this legal requirement, organizations must maintain records of time worked by nonexempt employees, which often results in the use of time clocks. These groups are also given different payroll labels: salaried payroll for exempt employees and hourly payroll for production employees. Thus, a two-class language is created.

Federal law governing overtime pay for nonexempt employees was created in the 1930s to protect employees from exploitation by management. It can, and often does, have the unintended result of creating or reinforcing certain assumptions made by managers about their employees' commitment to the organization. It might also affect employees' perceptions of their roles in the organization and thereby alter their commitment. A two-class society is subtly reinforced within the organization.

All-Salaried System   Some organizations have attempted to overcome this legislated division of the work force through an all-salaried compensation system. Workers traditionally paid by the hour join management in receiving a weekly or monthly salary (nonexempt employees are still paid on an hourly basis for overtime work).

Although an all-salaried system cannot eliminate the legislated distinction between exempt and nonexempt employees, it can at least remove one symbolic, but nonetheless important, difference: Workers join managers in having more flexibility, because time can be taken off from work with no loss in pay. Thus, workers can be given more responsibility for their hours. Such treatment, in turn, could increase their commitment and loyalty to the organization.

Some managers fear that adopting a salaried system across the board will lead to greater absenteeism, but this does not appear to have happened. Such a system by itself will not increase commitment; nevertheless, as part of an overall shift in corporate philosophy and style, it can play an important supporting role. Companies such as Hewlett-Packard and IBM as well as participative nontraditional plants at Procter & Gamble, Dana, TRW, and Cummins Engine have successfully used the all-salaried payroll in this way.

SYSTEMS FOR MAINTAINING EQUITY

To maintain employee satisfaction with pay, corporations have developed systems to maintain pay equity with comparable internal and external persons and groups.

The consequences of inequity in employee pay regarding the external labor markets are potentially severe for a corporation, which would be unable to attract and keep the talent required. The costs of maintaining that equity, however, are also high. Meeting all competitive wage offers obtainable by employees—the extreme form of maintaining external equity—can encourage employees to search for the highest job offers to convince management to increase their pay. This results in a market system for determining compensation much like the free-agent system in sports—a time-consuming and expensive proposition for employers that can lead to internal inequities. It can also lead an employee to a self-centered orientation toward career and pay.

Some companies, such as IBM, intentionally position their total compensation package at the high end of the market range. High total compensation does not, however, ensure that the best employees are retained. To keep them, a company must also pay its better performers more than it pays poorer performers, and the difference must be significant in the judgment of individual employees.

The potential consequences of internal pay inequity are employee dissatisfaction, withholding of effort, and lack of trust in the system. Internal inequity can result in conflict within the organization, which consumes the time and energy of managers and personnel. Maintaining high internal equity, however, can result in overpaying some people compared to the market, while underpaying others—thus destroying external equity.

There is continual tension in an organization between concerns for external and internal equity. Line personnel may be willing to sacrifice corporate internal equity to attract and keep the talent they want for their departments. Because they perceive efforts to pay whatever is needed to attract a candidate as a threat to internal equity, human resource personnel, with their corporate perspectives, often oppose such efforts by line managers. Human resource personnel insist on the integrity of the job-evaluation and wage-survey systems to avoid the costly conflicts that they fear will result from numerous exceptions to the job-evaluation system. This dilemma remains insoluble; no new system will eliminate it. The balance must be continually managed to reduce problems and maintain a pay system that yields equity and cost effectiveness.

Job Evaluation   In the United States, most firms determine pay levels by evaluating the worth of a job to the organization through a job-evaluation system.

Job evaluations begin by describing the various jobs within an organization. Then jobs are evaluated by considering several job factors: working conditions, necessary technical knowledge, required managerial skills, and importance to the organization. A rating for each factor is made on a standard scale, and the total rating points are used to rank jobs. Next, a salary survey identifies comparable jobs in other organizations and learns what those organizations are paying for similarly rated jobs.

The salary survey and other considerations—such as legislation, job-market conditions, and the organization's willingness to pay—establish pay ranges for jobs. (The tighter the labor market, the more closely wages will be tied to the going rate. In a loose labor market, the other factors will tend to dominate.) Jobs may then be grouped into a smaller number of classifications and assigned a salary range. The level of the individual employee within his or her particular range is determined by a combination of job performance, seniority, and experience or any other combination of factors selected by the organization.

Job-evaluation plans, along with wage surveys, have been used in wage-and-salary administration for over 50 years. They have proved useful for maintaining internal and external equity.

Even if these steps are taken, however, no job-evaluation system can solve the problem of salary compression, or inequities, that inevitably occur when new employees are hired. To recruit successfully in the labor market, firms must offer competitive wages, and these competitive wages sometimes create inequities with the salaries of employees who have been with the firm for some time. These inequities occur because corporations usually do not raise the salaries of incumbents when salary surveys result in an upward movement of the salary range. To do so would be costly; not doing so also allows the firms to keep the pay of poorer performers behind the market by denying merit increases.

Some analysts argue that companies should solve inequities due to compression by regularly raising wages for everyone when salary surveys so indicate and by managing poor performers through other means. Some companies ask managers to position their subordinates within the appropriate pay range according to performance, providing larger increases for good performers over several years so they will be near the top of their range and giving poor performers lower increases or no increases to keep them at the bottom of the range.

The conflicting objectives of keeping costs down and rewarding good performers—not the job-evaluation system itself—cause inequity and dissatisfaction. Of these objectives, cost effectiveness is the critical factor, because good performance can be rewarded and poor performance discouraged in other monetary and nonmonetary ways. General managers must decide if the cost of across-the-board increases is worth the benefits of greater internal and external equity. To solve the equity problems, they must clarify their philosophy and make choices between objectives of cost and equity, a process determined more by values and financial constraints than by systems.

Pay systems structured by job evaluation have special problems. Salary ranges associated with jobs limit the pay increases an individual can obtain. Thus, significant advancements in status and pay can come only through promotions. This need for promotion can cause technical people to seek promotions to management positions, even though their real skills and interests might be in technical work. If no promotions are available, individuals' needs for advancement and progress are frustrated.

Additionally, job-evaluation systems cause a certain loss of flexibility in transferring people within an organization. If that transfer is to a job with a lower pay grade, fear of lower pay and status will reduce the individual's willingness to transfer. Although companies usually make an exception and maintain the individual's salary above the range of the new job, the perception of loss and the reality of an actual loss of pay over time makes such a transfer difficult.

To solve problems of job-evaluation systems, some companies have come up with an alternative: a person- or skill-based evaluation system. This system promises to solve the flexibility and limited growth problem of job evaluation, but it does not solve all the equity problems already discussed.

Person/Skill Evaluation   Person- or skill-based evaluation systems base salary on the person's abilities. Pay ranges are arranged in steps, from least skilled to most skilled. Employees come into the organization at an entry-level pay grade and, after demonstrating competence at that level, begin to move up the skill-based ladder. Such a system should lead to higher pay for the most skilled individuals and encourage the acquisition of new skills.

Skill-based systems generally allow more flexibility in moving people from one job to another and in introducing new technology. A skill-based compensation system can also change management's orientation. Rather than limit assignments to be consistent with job level, managers must try to utilize the available skills of people, since employees are being paid for those skills. Moreover, a skill-based evaluation system's greatest benefit is that it communicates to employees a concern for their development. This concern leads management to develop competence and utilize it, resulting in greater employee well-being and organizational effectiveness.

Person-based evaluation systems that have been applied to technical personnel in R&D organizations are often called *technical ladders*. Technical ladders could be applied to other technical specialists, such as lawyers, sales personnel, and accountants. Their use might encourage good specialists to stay in these roles rather than seek management jobs that pay more but for which they may not have talent. The organizations would avoid losing good technical specialists and gaining poor managers.

Skill-based pay systems have also been applied to production-level employees. In some of their more progressive plants, companies such as Procter & Gamble, General Motors, and Cummins Engine have introduced plans that pay workers for the skills they possess rather than for the jobs they hold. The benefits of flexibility and employee growth and satisfaction, mentioned earlier, have been experienced in these plants.

Some problems exist in a person- or skill-based approach, however. For example, many individual employees may, after several years, reach the top skill level and find themselves with no place to go. At this point, the organization might consider some type of profit-sharing scheme to encourage these employees to continue to seek ways of improving organizational effectiveness. Another problem is that a skills-evaluation program calls for a large investment in training, because pay increases depend upon the learning of new skills. Furthermore, external equity is more difficult to manage. Because each organization has its own unique configurations of jobs and skills, it is unlikely that individuals with similar skills can be found elsewhere, particularly in the same community, which is where production workers typically look for comparisons. This is less of a problem for professional employees whose jobs are more similar across companies. Because skill-based systems emphasize learning new tasks, employees may come to feel that their higher skills call for higher pay than the system provides, particularly when they compare their wages with those of workers in traditional jobs. Without effective comparisons expectations could rise, unchecked by a good reality test.

The most difficult problem facing a skills-evaluation plan is its administration. To make the system work properly, attention must be paid to the skill level of every employee. Some method must be devised, first, to determine how many and what new skills must be learned to receive a pay boost and, second, to determine whether or not the individual employee has, in fact, mastered those new skills. The ease with which the first point is achieved depends on how measurable or quantifiable the necessary skills are. Identification of particular skills is more easily accomplished for lower-level positions than for top management or professional positions.

Skill-based pay systems hold out some promise of improving competence in a cost-effective way and enhancing both organizational effectiveness and employee well-being. They are not solutions for all situations and depend heavily on solving the problem of measuring and assessing skills or competencies. Only an organization with a climate of trust is likely to use the system successfully. Moreover, skill-based compensation systems work only in those organizations where skilled workers are essential and where flexibility is required. They are also hard to introduce in organizations where a traditional job-evaluation system exists.

SENIORITY

Seniority has been accepted as a valid criterion for pay in some countries. Japanese companies, for instance, use seniority-based pay along with other factors, such as slow-but-steady promotion, to help achieve a desired organizational culture. In the United States, proponents of a seniority-based pay system tend to be trade unions. Distrustful of management, unions often feel that any pay-for-performance system will end up increasing paternalism, unfairness, and inequities. Thus, unions often prefer a strict seniority system. Many U.S. managers, however, feel that seniority runs contrary to the country's individualistic ethos, which maintains that individual effort and merit should be rewarded above all else.

PAY FOR PERFORMANCE

Some reasons organizations pay their employees for performance are as follows:

- Under the right conditions, a pay-for-performance system can motivate desired behavior.
- A pay-for-performance system can help attract and keep achievement-oriented individuals.
- A pay-for-performance system can help to retain good performers while discouraging the poor performers.
- In the United States, at least, many employees, both managers and workers, prefer a pay-for-performance system, although white-collar workers are significantly more supportive of the notion than are blue-collar workers.

However, there is a wide gap between the desire to devise a pay-for-performance system and the ability to make such a system work.

The most important distinction among various pay-for-performance systems is the level of aggregation at which performance is defined—individual, group, and organization-wide.[3] The *Exhibit* summarizes several pay-for-performance systems.

Historically, pay for performance has meant pay for individual performance. Piece-rate incentive systems for production employees and merit salary increases or bonus plans for salaried employees have been the dominant means of paying for performance. In the past, piece-rate incentive systems have dramatically declined because managers have discovered that such systems result in dysfunctional behavior, such as low cooperation, artificial limits on

---

3. Edward E. Lawler, *Pay and Organization Development* (Reading, Mass.: Addison-Wesley, 1981): 82–85.

EXHIBIT
Pay-for-Performance Systems

INDIVIDUAL PERFORMANCE	GROUP PERFORMANCE	ORGANIZATION-WIDE PERFORMANCE
Merit system	Productivity incentive	Profit sharing
Piece rate	Cost effectiveness	Productivity sharing
Executive bonus		(Scanlon Plan)

production, and resistance to changing standards. Similarly, more questions are being asked about individual bonus plans for executives as top managers discover their negative effects.

Meanwhile, organization-wide incentive systems are becoming more popular, particularly because managers are finding that these systems foster cooperation, which leads to productivity and innovation. To succeed, however, these plans require certain conditions. A review of the key considerations for designing a pay-for-performance plan and a discussion of the problems that arise when these considerations are not observed follow.

Individual Pay for Performance   The design of an individual pay-for-performance system requires an analysis of the task. Does the individual have control over the performance (result) that is to be measured? Is there a significant effort-to-performance relationship? For motivational reasons already discussed, such a relationship must exist. Unfortunately, many individual bonus, commission, or piece-rate incentive plans fall short in meeting this requirement. An individual may not have control over a performance result, such as sales or profit, because economic cycles or competitive forces beyond his or her control affect that result. Indeed, few outcomes in complex organizations are not dependent on other functions or individuals, and fewer still are not subject to external factors.

Choosing an appropriate measure of performance on which to base pay is a related problem incurred by individual bonus plans. For reasons discussed earlier, effectiveness on a job can include many facets not captured by cost, units produced, or sales revenues. Failure to include all activities that are important for effectiveness can lead to negative consequences. For example, sales personnel who receive a bonus for sales volume may push unneeded products, thus damaging long-term customer relations, or they may push an unprofitable mix of products just to increase volume. These same salespeople may also take orders and make commitments that cannot be met by manufacturing. Instead of rewarding salespeople for volume, why not reward them for profits, a more inclusive measure of performance? The obvious problem with this measure is that sales personnel do not have control over profits.

These dilemmas are constantly encountered and have led to the use of more subjective but inclusive behavioral measures of performance. Why not observe whether the salesperson or executive is performing all aspects of the job well? Most merit salary increases are based on subjective judgments and so are some individual bonus plans. Subjective evaluation systems, though they can be all-inclusive if based on a thorough analysis of the job, require deep trust in management, good manager-subordinate relations, and effective interpersonal skills. Unfortunately, these conditions are not fully met in many situations, though they can be developed if judged to be sufficiently important.

Group and Organization-wide Pay Plans   Organizational effectiveness depends on employee cooperation in most instances. An organization may elect to tie pay, or at least some portion of pay, indirectly to individual performance. Seeking to foster teamwork, a company may tie an incentive to some measure of group performance, or it may offer some type of profit- or productivity-sharing plan for the whole plant or company.

Gain-sharing plans have been used for years and in many varieties. The real power of a gain-sharing plan comes when it is supported by a climate of participation.[4] Various structures, systems, and processes involve employees in decisions that improve the organization's performance and result in a bonus throughout the organization. The Scanlon Plan is one such example. When the plan is installed in cooperation with workers and unions, a management-labor committee is created. Then committees seek and review suggestions for reducing costs. Payout is based on improvements in the sales-to-cost ratio of the plant compared to some agreed-upon base period before the adoption of the plan.

Organization-wide incentive plans that are part of a philosophy of participation require strong labor-management cooperation in design and administration. For example, the Scanlon Plan requires a direct employee vote with 75% approval before implementation. Without joint participation, commitment to any organization-wide incentive plan system will be low, and its symbolic and motivational value will be minimal.

Several critical decisions influence the effectiveness of a gain-sharing plan:

- Who should participate in the plan's design and administration, and how much participation will be allowed by management and union?
- What will be the size of the unit covered? Small units obviously offer easier identification with the organization's performance and the bonuses that result.
- What standard will be used to judge performance? Employees, the union (if involved), and management must agree on this for strong commitment. There are inevitable disagreements.
- How will the gains be divided? Who shares in the gains? What percentage of the gains goes to the company and what percentage to employees?

---

4. Christopher S. Miller and Michael H. Schuster, "Gain-sharing Plan: A Comparative Analysis," *Organizational Dynamics* (Summer 1987): 44–67.

When management and employees have gone through a process of discussion and negotiation, allowing a consensus to emerge on these questions, a real change in management-employee and union relations can occur. A top-down process would not yield the same benefits. Gain-sharing approached participatively can create a fundamental change in the psychological and economic ownership of the firm. Therein lies its primary motivational and satisfactional value; however, only a management that embraces values consistent with participation can make it work.

——— DISCUSSION QUESTIONS

1. In the United States, future employees may earn less than those currently working. How will this affect the design of reward systems and the role of compensation?
2. What business conditions might cause a company to redesign its reward system?
3. As observed in the reading, there are many different ways to design reward systems. Is there a design not mentioned in the reading that you can suggest?
4. Name a company and describe its reward system that you believe should be emulated. Explain why the system is effective in the organization.
5. How have you felt about the compensation you've received for the work you've done? Have you felt overpaid, underpaid, or fairly paid? How important is compensation to you relative to the other factors of your career? What is the source of your view?

From Control to Commitment in the Workplace

RICHARD E. WALTON

The author of this reading focuses on two different strategies for managing a work force. One is based on imposing control; the other relies on eliciting the commitment of workers. The traditional control model attempts to "establish order, exercise control, and achieve efficiency." In the commitment strategy, jobs are designed more broadly; planning and implementation are combined; operations are upgraded, not simply maintained; individual responsibilities vary as conditions vary; the focus is on teams rather than on the individual; and the organization is flatter. Workers are encouraged to fulfill their potential, and the company offers employees the assurance of security.

Eliciting worker commitment—and providing the environment in which it can flourish—pays tangible dividends for the individual and for the company. The author describes these opposing strategies toward employees and points out the key challenges in moving from one to the other.

The larger shape of institutional change is always difficult to recognize when one stands right in the middle of it. Today, throughout American industry, a significant change is under way in long-established approaches to the organization and management of work. Although this shift in attitude and practice takes a wide variety of company-specific forms, its larger shape—its overall pattern—is already visible if one knows where and how to look.

Consider, for example, the marked differences between two plants in the chemical products division of a major U.S. corporation. Both make similar products and employ similar technologies, but that is virtually all they have in common.

The first, organized by businesses with an identifiable product or product line, divides its employees into self-supervising 10- to 15-person work teams that are collectively responsible for a set of related tasks. Each team member has the training to perform many or all of the tasks for which the team is accountable, and pay reflects the level of mastery of required skills. These teams have received assurances that management will go to extra lengths to provide continued employment in any economic downturn. The teams have also been thoroughly briefed on such issues as market share, product costs, and their implications for the business.

Not surprisingly, this plant is a top performer economically and rates well on all measures of employee satisfaction, absenteeism, turnover, and safety. With its employees actively engaged in identifying and solving problems, it operates with fewer levels of management and fewer specialized departments than do its sister plants. It is also one of the principal suppliers of management talent for these other plants and for the division manufacturing staff.

In the second plant, each employee is responsible for a fixed job and is required to perform up to the minimum standard defined for that job. Peer pressure keeps new employees from exceeding the minimum standards and from taking other initiatives that go beyond basic job requirements. Supervisors, who manage daily assignments and monitor performance, have long since given up hope for anything more than compliance with standards, finding sufficient difficulty in getting their people to perform adequately most of the time. In fact, they and their workers try to prevent the industrial engineering department, which is under pressure from top plant management to improve operations, from using changes in methods to "jack up" standards.

A management campaign to document an "airtight case" against employees who have excessive absenteeism or sub-par performance mirrors employees' low morale and high distrust of management. A constant stream of formal grievances, violations of plant rules, harassment of supervisors, wildcat walkouts, and even sabotage has prevented the plant from reaching its productivity and quality goals and has absorbed a disproportionate amount of division staff time. Dealings with the union are characterized by contract negotiations on economic matters and skirmishes over issues of management control.

No responsible manager, of course, would ever wish to encourage the kind of situation at this second plant, yet the determination to understand its deeper causes and to attack them at their root does not come easily. Established modes of doing things have an inertia all their own. Such an effort is, however, in process all across the industrial landscape. And with that effort comes the possibility of a revolution in industrial relations every bit as great as that occasioned by the rise of mass production the better part of a century ago. The challenge is clear to those managers willing to see it—and the potential benefits, enormous.

APPROACHES TO WORK-FORCE MANAGEMENT

What explains the extraordinary differences between the plants just described? Is it that the first is newer and the other old? Yes and no. Not all new plants enjoy so fruitful an approach to work organization; not all older plants have such intractable problems. Is it that one plant is not unionized and the other is? Again, yes and no. The presence of a union may institutionalize conflict and lackluster performance, but it seldom causes them.

At issue here is not so much age or unionization but two radically different strategies for managing a company's or a factory's work force, two incompatible views of what managers can reasonably expect of workers and of the kind of partnership they can share with them. For simplicity, I will speak of these profound differences as reflecting the choice between a strategy based on imposing *control* and a strategy based on eliciting *commitment*.

THE 'CONTROL' STRATEGY

The traditional—or control-oriented—approach to work-force management took shape during the early part of this century in response to the division of work into small, fixed jobs for which individuals could be held accountable. The actual definition of jobs, as of acceptable standards of performance, rested on "lowest common denominator" assumptions about workers' skill and motivation. To monitor and control effort of this assumed caliber, management organized its own responsibilities into a hierarchy of specialized roles buttressed by a top-down allocation of authority and by status symbols attached to positions in the hierarchy.

For workers, compensation followed the rubric of "a fair day's pay for a fair day's work" because precise evaluations were possible when individual job requirements were so carefully prescribed. Most managers had little doubt that labor was best thought of as a variable cost, although some exceptional companies guaranteed job security to head off unionization attempts.

In the traditional approach, there was generally little policy definition with regard to employee voice unless the work force was unionized, in which case damage-control strategies predominated. With no union, management relied on an open-door policy, attitude surveys, and similar devices to learn about employees' concerns. If the work force was unionized, then management bargained terms of employment and established an appeal mechanism. These activities fell to labor relations specialists, who operated independently from line management and whose very existence assumed the inevitability and even the appropriateness of an adversarial relationship between workers and managers. Indeed, to those who saw management's exclusive obligation to be to a company's shareowners and the ownership of property to be the ultimate source of both obligation and prerogative, the claims of employees were constraints, nothing more.

At the heart of this traditional model is the wish to establish order, exercise control, and achieve efficiency in the application of the work force. Although it has distant antecedents in the bureaucracies of both church and military, the model's real father is Frederick W. Taylor, the turn-of-the-century "father of scientific management," whose views about the proper organization of work have long influenced management practice as well as the reactive policies of the U.S. labor movement.

Recently, however, changing expectations among workers have prompted a growing disillusionment with the apparatus of control. At the same time, of course, an intensified challenge from abroad has made the competitive obsolescence of this strategy clear. A model that assumes low employee commitment and that is designed to produce reliable if not outstanding performance simply cannot match the standards of excellence set by world-class competitors. Especially in a high-wage country like the United States, market success depends on a superior level of performance, a level that, in turn, requires the deep commitment, not merely the obedience—if you could obtain it—of workers. And as painful experience shows, this commitment cannot flourish in a workplace dominated by the familiar model of control.

THE 'COMMITMENT' STRATEGY

Over the past 20 years, companies have experimented at the plant level with a radically different work-force strategy. The more visible pioneers—among them, General Foods at Topeka, Kansas; General Motors at Brookhaven, Mississippi; Cummins Engine at Jamestown, New York; and Procter & Gamble at Lima, Ohio—have shown how great and productive the contribution of a truly committed work force can be. For a time, all new plants of this sort were nonunion, but by 1980 the success of efforts undertaken jointly with unions—GM's cooperation with the UAW at the Cadillac plant in Livonia, Michigan, for example—was impressive enough to encourage managers of both new and existing facilities to rethink their approach to the work force.

Local managers and union officials increasingly talk about common interests, working to develop mutual trust, and agreeing to sponsor quality-of-work-life (QWL) or employee involvement (EI) activities. Although most of these ventures have been initiated at the local level, there have been major exceptions.

More recently, a growing number of manufacturing companies have begun to remove levels of plant hierarchy, increase managers' spans of control, integrate quality and production activities at lower organizational levels, combine production and maintenance operations, and open up new career possibilities for workers. Some corporations have even begun to chart organizational renewal for the entire company. Cummins Engine, for example, has ambitiously committed itself to inform employees about the business, to encourage participation by everyone, and to create jobs that involve greater responsibility and more flexibility.

In this commitment-based approach to the work force, jobs are designed to be broader than before, to combine planning and implementation, and to include efforts to upgrade operations, not just maintain them. Individual responsibilities are expected to change as conditions change, and teams, not individuals, often are the organizational units accountable for performance. With management hierarchies relatively flat and differences in status minimized, control and lateral coordination depend on shared goals, and expertise rather than formal position determines influence.

Under the commitment strategy, performance expectations are high and serve not to define minimum standards but to provide "stretch objectives," emphasize continuous improvement, and reflect the requirements of the marketplace. Accordingly, compensation policies reflect less the old formulas of job evaluation than the heightened importance of group achievement, the expanded scope of individual contribution, and the growing concern for such questions of "equity" as gain sharing, stock ownership, and profit sharing.

Equally important to the commitment strategy is the challenge of giving employees some assurance of security, perhaps by offering them priority in training and retraining as old jobs are eliminated and new ones are created. Guaranteeing employees access to due process and providing them the means to be heard on such issues as production methods, problem solving, and human resources policies and practices is also a challenge. In unionized settings, the additional tasks include making relations less adversarial, broadening the agenda for joint problem solving and planning, and facilitating employee consultation.

Underlying all these policies is a management philosophy, often embodied in a published statement, that acknowledges the legitimate claims of a company's multiple stakeholders—owners, employees, customers, and the public. At the center of this philosophy is a belief that eliciting employee commitment will lead to enhanced performance. The evidence shows this belief to be well-grounded. In the absence of genuine commitment, however, new management policies designed for a committed work force may well leave a company distinctly more vulnerable than would older policies based on the control approach. The advantages—and risks—are considerable.

THE COSTS OF COMMITMENT

Because the potential leverage of a commitment-oriented strategy on performance is so great, the natural temptation is to assume the universal applicability of that strategy. Some environments, however, especially those requiring intricate teamwork, problem solving, organizational learning, and self-monitoring, are better suited than others to the commitment model. Indeed, the pioneers of the deep commitment strategy—a fertilizer plant in Norway, a refinery in the United Kingdom, a paper mill in Pennsylvania, a pet-food-processing plant in Kansas—were all based on continuous process technologies and were all capital- and raw-material intensive. All provided high economic leverage to improvements in workers' skills and attitudes, and all could offer considerable job challenge.

Is the converse true? Is the control strategy appropriate whenever—as with convicts breaking rocks with sledgehammers in a prison yard—work can be completely prescribed, remains static, and calls for individual, not group,

EXHIBIT
Work-Force Strategies

	CONTROL	TRANSITIONAL	COMMITMENT
Job Design Principles	Individual attention limited to performing individual job.	Scope of individual responsibility extended to upgrading system performance, via participative problem-solving groups in QWL, EI, and quality circle programs.	Individual responsibility extended to upgrading system performance.
	Job design deskills and fragments work and separates doing and thinking.	No change in traditional job design or accountability.	Job design enhances content of work, emphasizes whole task, and combines doing and thinking.
			Frequent use of teams as basic accountable unit.
	Accountability focused on individual.		
	Fixed job definition.		Flexible definition of duties, contingent on changing conditions.
Performance Expectations	Measured standards define minimum performance. Stability seen as desirable.		Emphasis placed on higher, "stretch objectives," which tend to be dynamic and oriented to the marketplace.
Management Organization: Structure, Systems, and Style	Structure tends to be layered, with top-down controls.	No basic changes in approaches to structure, control, or authority.	Flat organization structure with mutual influence systems.
	Coordination and control rely on rules and procedures.		Coordination and control based more on shared goals, values, and traditions.
	More emphasis on prerogatives and positional authority.		Management emphasis on problem solving and relevant information and expertise.
	Status symbols distributed to reinforce hierarchy.	A few visible symbols change.	Minimum status differentials to de-emphasize inherent hierarchy.

effort? In practice, managers have long answered yes. Mass production, epitomized by the assembly line, has for years been thought suitable for old-fashioned control.

But not any longer. Many mass producers, not least the automakers, have recently been trying to reconceive the structure of work and to give employees a significant role in solving problems and improving methods. Why?

EXHIBIT
Work-Force Strategies (Continued)

	CONTROL	TRANSITIONAL	COMMITMENT
Compensation Policies	Variable pay where feasible to provide individual incentive.	Typically no basic changes in compensation concepts.	Variable rewards to create equity and to reinforce group achievements: gain sharing, profit sharing.
	Individual pay geared to job evaluation.		Individual pay linked to skills and mastery.
	In downturn, cuts concentrated on hourly payroll.	Equality of sacrifice among employee groups.	Equality of sacrifice.
Employment Assurances	Employees regarded as variable costs.	Assurances that participation will not result in loss of job.	Assurances that participation will not result in loss of job.
		Extra effort to avoid layoffs.	High commitment to avoid or assist in reemployment.
			Priority for training and retaining existing work force.
Employee-Voice Policies	Employee input allowed on relatively narrow agenda. Attendant risks emphasized. Methods include open-door policy, attitude surveys, grievance procedures, and collective bargaining in some organizations.	Addition of limited, ad hoc consultation mechanisms. No change in corporate governance.	Employee participation encouraged on wide range of issues. Attendant benefits emphasized. New concepts of corporate governance.
	Business information distributed on strictly defined "need to know" basis.	Additional sharing of information.	Business data shared widely.
Labor-Management Relations	Adversarial labor relations; emphasis on interest conflict.	Thawing of adversarial attitudes; joint sponsorship of QWL or EI; emphasis on common fate.	Mutuality in labor relations; joint planning and problem solving on expanded agenda.
			Unions, management, and workers redefine their respective roles.

For many reasons, including to boost in-plant quality, lower warranty costs, cut waste, raise machine utilization and total capacity with the same plant and equipment, reduce operating and support personnel, reduce turnover and absenteeism, and speed up implementation of change. In addition, some managers place direct value on the fact that the commitment policies promote the development of human skills and individual self-esteem.

The benefits, economic and human, of worker commitment extend not only to continuous process industries but to traditional manufacturing industries as well. What, though, are the costs? To achieve these gains, managers have had to invest extra effort, develop new skills and relationships, cope with higher levels of ambiguity and uncertainty, and experience the pain and discomfort associated with changing habits and attitudes. Some of their skills have become obsolete, and some of their careers have been casualties of change. Union officials, too, have had to face the dislocation and discomfort that inevitably follow any upheaval in attitudes and skills. For their part, workers have inherited more responsibility and, along with it, greater uncertainty and more open-ended possibility of failure.

Part of the difficulty in assessing these costs is the fact that so many of the following problems inherent to the commitment strategy remain to be solved.

EMPLOYMENT ASSURANCES

As managers in heavy industry confront economic realities that make such assurances less feasible and as their counterparts in fiercely competitive high-technology areas are forced to rethink early guarantees of employment security, pointed questions await.

Will managers give lifetime assurances to the few, those who reach, say, 15 years' seniority, or will they adopt a general no-layoff policy? Will they demonstrate by policies and practices that employment security, though by no means absolute, is a higher-priority item than it was under the control approach? Will they accept greater responsibility for outplacement?

COMPENSATION

In one sense, the more productive employees under the commitment approach deserve to receive better pay for their better efforts, but how can managers balance this claim on resources with the harsh reality that domestic pay rates have risen to levels that render many of our industries uncompetitive internationally? Already, in such industries as trucking and airlines, new domestic competitors have placed companies that maintain prevailing wage rates at a significant disadvantage. Experience shows, however, that wage freezes and concession bargaining create obstacles to commitment, and new approaches to compensation are difficult to develop at a time when management cannot raise the overall level of pay.

Which approach is really suitable to the commitment model is unclear. Traditional job classifications place limits on the discretion of supervisors and encourage workers' sense of job ownership. Can pay systems based on employees' skill levels, which have long been used in engineering and skilled crafts, prove widely effective? Can these systems make up in greater mastery, positive motivation, and workforce flexibility what they give away in higher average wages?

In capital-intensive businesses, where total payroll accounts for a small percentage of costs, economics favors the move toward pay progression based on deeper and broader mastery. Still, conceptual problems remain with measuring skills, achieving consistency in pay decisions, allocating opportunities for learning new skills, trading off breadth and flexibility against depth, and handling the effects of "topping out" in a system that rewards and encourages personal growth.

There are also practical difficulties. Existing plants cannot, for example, convert to a skill-based structure overnight because of the vested interests of employees in the higher classifications. Similarly, formal profit- or gain-sharing plans like the Scanlon Plan (which shares gains in productivity as measured by improvements in the ratio of payroll to the sales value of production) cannot always operate. At the plant level, formulas that are responsive to what employees can influence, that are not unduly influenced by factors beyond their control, and that are readily understood, are not easy to devise. Small stand-alone businesses with a mature technology and stable markets tend to find the task least troublesome, but they are not the only ones trying to implement the commitment approach.

TECHNOLOGY

Computer-based technology can reinforce the control model or facilitate movement to the commitment model. Applications can narrow the scope of jobs or broaden them, emphasize the individual nature of tasks or promote the work of groups, centralize or decentralize the making of decisions, and create performance measures that emphasize learning or hierarchical control.

To date, the effects of this technology on control and commitment have been largely unintentional and unexpected. Even in organizations otherwise pursuing a commitment strategy, managers have rarely appreciated that the side effects of technology are not somehow "given" in the nature of things or that they can be actively managed. In fact, computer-based technology may be the least deterministic, most flexible technology to enter the workplace since the industrial revolution. As it becomes less hardware-dependent and more software-intensive and as the cost of computer power declines, the variety of ways to meet business requirements expands, each with a different set of human implications. Management has yet to identify the potential role of technology policy in the commitment strategy, and it has yet to invent concepts and methods to realize that potential.

SUPERVISORS

The commitment model requires first-line supervisors to facilitate rather than direct the work force, to impart rather than merely practice their technical and administrative expertise, and to help workers develop the ability to manage themselves. In practice, supervisors are to delegate away most of their traditional functions—often without having received adequate training and support for their new team-building tasks or having their own needs for voice, dignity, and fulfillment recognized.

These dilemmas are even visible in the new titles many supervisors carry—"team advisers" or "team consultants," for example—most of which imply that supervisors are not in the chain of command, although they are expected to be directive if necessary and assume functions delegated to the work force if they are not being performed. Part of the confusion here is the failure to distinguish the behavioral style required of supervisors from the basic responsibilities assigned them. Their ideal style may be advisory, but their responsibilities are to achieve certain human and economic outcomes. With experience, however, as first-line managers become more comfortable with the notion of delegating what subordinates are ready and able to perform, the problem will diminish.

Other difficulties are less tractable. The new breed of supervisors must have a level of interpersonal skill and conceptual ability often lacking in the present supervisory work force. Some companies have tried to address this lack by using the position as an entry point to management for college graduates. This approach may succeed where the work force has already acquired the necessary technical expertise, but it blocks a route of advancement for workers and sharpens the dividing line between management and other employees. Moreover, unless the company intends to open up higher-level positions for these college-educated supervisors, they may well grow impatient with the shift work of first-line supervision.

Even when new supervisory roles are filled—and filled successfully—from the ranks, dilemmas remain. With teams developed and functions delegated, to what new challenges do they turn to utilize fully their own capabilities? Do these capabilities match the demands of the other managerial work they might take on? If fewer and fewer supervisors are required as their individual span of control extends to a second and third work team, what promotional opportunities exist for the rest? Where do they go?

UNION-MANAGEMENT RELATIONS

Some companies, as they move from control to commitment, seek to decertify their unions and, at the same time, strengthen their employees' bond to the company. Others pursue cooperation with their unions, believing that they need their active support.

These developments open up new questions. Where companies are trying to preserve the nonunion status of some plants and yet promote collaborative union relations in others, will unions increasingly force the company to choose? After General Motors saw the potential of its joint QWL program with the UAW, it signed a neutrality clause and then an understanding about automatic recognition in new plants. If forced to choose, what will other managements do? Further, where union and management have collaborated in promoting QWL, how can the union prevent management from using the program to appeal directly to the workers about issues, such as wage concessions, that are subject to collective bargaining?

And if, in the spirit of mutuality, both sides agree to expand their joint agenda, what new risks will they face? Do union officials have the expertise to deal effectively with new agenda items like investment, pricing, and technology? To support QWL activities, they already have had to expand their skills and commit substantial resources at a time when shrinking employment has reduced their membership and thus their finances.

—— THE TRANSITIONAL STAGE

Although some organizations have adopted a comprehensive version of the commitment approach, most initially take on a more limited set of changes, a "transitional" stage or approach. The challenge here is to modify expectations, to make credible the leaders' stated intentions for further movement, and to support the initial changes in behavior. These transitional efforts can achieve a temporary equilibrium, provided they are viewed as part of a movement toward a comprehensive commitment strategy.

The cornerstone of the transitional stage is the voluntary participation of employees in problem-solving groups like quality circles. In unionized organizations, union-management dialogue leading to a jointly sponsored program is a condition for this type of employee involvement, which must then be supported by additional training and communication and by a shift in management style. Managers must also seek ways to consult employees about changes that affect them and to assure them that management will make every effort to avoid, defer, or minimize layoffs from higher productivity. When volume-related layoffs or concessions on pay are unavoidable, the principle of "equality of sacrifice" must apply to all employee groups, not just the hourly work force.

As a rule, during the early stages of transformation, few immediate changes can occur in the basic design of jobs, the compensation systems, or the management system itself. It is easy, of course, to attempt to change too much too soon. A more common error, especially in established organizations, is to make only "token" changes that never reach a critical mass. All too often managers try a succession of technique-oriented changes one by one: job enrichment, sensitivity training, management by objectives, group brainstorming, quality circles, and so on. Whatever the benefits of these techniques, their value to the organization will rapidly decay if the management philosophy—and practice—does not shift accordingly.

A different type of error—"overreaching"—may occur in newly established organizations based on commitment principles. In one new plant, managers allowed too much peer influence in pay decisions; in another, they underplayed the role of first-line supervisors as a link in the chain of command; in a third, they overemphasized learning of new skills and flexibility at the expense of mastery in critical operations. These design errors by themselves are not fatal, but the organization must be able to make mid-course corrections.

—— RATE OF TRANSFORMATION

How rapidly is the transformation in work-force strategy occurring? (See the *Exhibit* on pages 492–493 for a summary of work-force strategies.) Early change focused on the blue-collar work force and on those clerical operations that most closely resemble the factory. Although clerical change has lagged somewhat—because the control model has not produced such overt employee disaffection, and because management has been slow to recognize the importance of quality and productivity improvement—there are signs of a quickened pace of change in clerical operations.

Only a small fraction of U.S. workplaces today can boast of a comprehensive commitment strategy, but the rate of transformation continues to accelerate, and the move toward commitment via some explicit transitional stage extends to a still larger number of plants and offices. This transformation may be fueled by economic necessity, but other factors are shaping and pacing it—individual leadership in management and labor, philosophical choices, organizational competence in managing change, and cumulative learning from change itself.

—— DISCUSSION QUESTIONS

1. Is a commitment strategy economically feasible for most firms? What are the hidden costs of implementing such a strategy?
2. Are some elements of the traditional control strategy still essential to competitiveness? Would a mix of the two strategies better serve some companies, or should all firms seek to move from control to commitment?
3. With a commitment strategy, "Compensation policies reflect less the old formulas of job evaluation than the heightened importance of group achievement . . ." Does a commitment strategy remove individual incentive to perform well?
4. Should a commitment strategy change the way managers approach their work? Would it affect their perceived status?

From Affirmative Action to Affirming Diversity

34

R. ROOSEVELT THOMAS, JR.

To compete globally, America needs to create workplaces that tap the full potential of every employee, says this author. Affirmative action programs, although appropriate, fail to deal with the root causes of prejudice and inequality and do little to develop people and strengthen organizations. In this reading, the author examines affirmative action programs and their shortcomings, contrasting them with more suitable contemporary approaches that affirm and make full use of an openly multicultural workplace.

Sooner or later, affirmative action will die a natural death. Its achievements have been stupendous, but if we look at the premises that underlie it, we find assumptions and priorities that look increasingly shopworn. Thirty years ago, affirmative action was invented on the basis of these five appropriate premises:

1. Adult, white males make up something called the U.S. business mainstream.
2. The U.S. economic edifice is a solid, unchanging institution with more than enough space for everyone.
3. Women, blacks, immigrants, and other minorities should be allowed in as a matter of public policy and common decency.
4. Widespread racial, ethnic, and sexual prejudice keeps them out.
5. Legal and social coercion are necessary to bring about the change.

Today all five of these premises need revising. Over the past six years, I have tried to help some 15 companies learn how to achieve and manage diversity, and I have seen that the realities facing us are no longer the realities affirmative action was designed to fix.

To begin with, more than half the U.S. work force now consists of minorities, immigrants, and women, so white, native-born males, though undoubtedly still dominant, are themselves a statistical minority. In addition, white males will make up only 15% of the increase in the work force over the next 10 years. The so-called mainstream is now almost as diverse as the society at large.

Second, while the edifice is still big enough for all, it no longer seems stable, massive, and invulnerable. In fact, American corporations are scrambling,

499

doing their best to become more adaptable, to compete more successfully for markets and labor, foreign and domestic, and to attract all the talent they can find. (*Exhibits 1* to *5* show what a number of U.S. companies are doing to manage diversity.)

Third, women and minorities no longer need a boarding pass, they need an upgrade. The problem is not getting them in at the entry level; the problem is making better use of their potential at every level, especially in middle-management and leadership positions. This is no longer simply a question of common decency, it is a question of business survival.

Fourth, although prejudice is hardly dead, it has suffered some wounds that may eventually prove fatal. In the meantime, American businesses are now filled with progressive people—many of them minorities and women themselves—whose prejudices, where they still exist, are much too deeply suppressed to interfere with recruitment. The reason many companies are still wary of minorities and women has much more to do with education and perceived qualifications than with color or gender. Companies are worried about productivity and well aware that minorities and women represent a disproportionate share of the undertrained and undereducated.

Fifth, coercion is rarely needed at the recruitment stage. There are very few places in the United States today where you could dip a recruitment net and come up with nothing but white males. Getting hired is not the problem—women and blacks who are seen as having the necessary skills and energy can get *into* the work force relatively easily. It's later on that many of them plateau and lose their drive and quit or get fired. It's later on that their managers' inability to manage diversity hobbles them and the companies they work for.

In creating these changes, affirmative action had an essential role to play and played it very well. In many companies and communities it still plays that role. But affirmative action is an artificial, transitional intervention intended to give managers a chance to correct an imbalance, an injustice, a mistake. Once the numbers mistake has been corrected, I don't think affirmative action alone can cope with the remaining long-term task of creating a work setting geared to the upward mobility of *all* kinds of people, including white males. It is difficult for affirmative action to influence upward mobility even in the short run, primarily because it is perceived to conflict with the meritocracy we favor. For this reason, affirmative action is a red flag to every individual who feels unfairly passed over and a stigma for those who appear to be its beneficiaries.

Moreover, I doubt very much that individuals who reach top positions through affirmative action are effective models for younger members of their race or sex. What, after all, do they model? A black vice president who got her job through affirmative action is not necessarily a model of how to rise through the corporate meritocracy. She may be a model of how affirmative action can work for the people who find or put themselves in the right place at the right time.

If affirmative action in upward mobility meant that no person's competence and character would ever be overlooked or undervalued on account of

EXHIBIT 1
Out of the Numbers Game and into Decision Making

Like many other companies, Avon practiced affirmative action in the 1970s and was not pleased with the results. The company worked with employment agencies that specialized in finding qualified minority hires, and it cultivated contacts with black and minority organizations on college campuses. Avon wanted to see its customer base reflected in its work force, especially at the decision-making level. But while women moved up the corporate ladder fairly briskly—not so surprising in a company whose work force is mostly female—minorities did not. So in 1984, the company began to change its policies and practices.

"We really wanted to get out of the numbers game," says Marcia Worthing, the corporate vice president for human resources. "We felt it was more important to have five minority people tied into the decision-making process than ten who were just heads to count."

First, Avon initiated awareness training at all levels. "The key to recruiting, retaining, and promoting minorities is not the human resource department," says Worthing. "It's getting line management to buy into the idea. We had to do more than change behavior. We had to change attitudes."

Second, the company formed a Multicultural Participation Council that meets regularly to oversee the process of managing diversity. The group includes Avon's CEO and high-level employees from throughout the company.

Third, in conjunction with the American Institute for Managing Diversity, Avon developed a diversity-training program. For several years, the company has sent racially and ethnically diverse groups of 25 managers at a time to Institute headquarters at Morehouse College in Atlanta, where they spend three weeks confronting their differences and learning to hear and avail themselves of viewpoints they initially disagreed with. "We came away disciples of diversity," says one company executive.

Fourth, the company helped three minority groups—blacks, Hispanics, and Asians—form networks that crisscrossed the corporation in all 50 states. Each network elects its own leaders and has an adviser from senior management. In addition, the networks have representatives on the Multicultural Participation Council, where they serve as a conduit for employee views on diversity issues facing management.

race, sex, ethnicity, origins, or physical disability, then affirmative action would be the very thing we need to let every corporate talent find its niche. But what affirmative action means in practice is an unnatural focus on one group, and what it means too often to too many employees is that someone is playing fast and loose with standards in order to favor that group. Unless we are to compromise our standards, a thing no competitive company can even contemplate, upward mobility for minorities and women should always be a question of pure competence and character unmuddled by accidents of birth.

And that is precisely why we have to learn to manage diversity—to move beyond affirmative action, not to repudiate it. Some of what I have to say may strike some readers—mostly those with an ax to grind—as directed at the majority white males who hold most of the decision-making posts in our economy. But I am speaking to all managers, not just white males, and I certainly don't mean to suggest that white males somehow stand outside diversity. White males are as odd and as normal as anyone else.

——— THE AFFIRMATIVE ACTION CYCLE

If you are managing diverse employees, you should ask yourself this question: Am I fully tapping the potential capacities of everyone in my department? If the answer is no, you should ask yourself this follow-up: Is this failure hampering my ability to meet performance standards? The answer to this question undoubtedly will be yes.

Think of corporate management for a moment as an engine burning pure gasoline. What's now going into the tank is no longer just gas, it has an increasing percentage of, let's say, methanol. In the beginning, the engine will still work pretty well, but by and by it will start to sputter, and eventually it will stall. Unless we rebuild the engine, it will no longer burn the fuel we're feeding it. As the work force grows more and more diverse at the intake level, the talent pool we have to draw on for supervision and management will also grow increasingly diverse. So the question is: Can we burn this fuel? Can we get maximum corporate power from the diverse work force we're now drawing into the system?

Affirmative action gets blamed for failing to do things it never could do. Affirmative action gets the new fuel into the tank, the new people through the front door. Something else will have to get them into the driver's seat. That something else consists of enabling people, in this case minorities and women, to perform to their potential. This is what we now call managing diversity. Not appreciating or leveraging diversity, not even necessarily understanding it. Just managing diversity in such a way as to get from a heterogeneous work force the same productivity, commitment, quality, and profit that we got from the old homogeneous work force.

The correct question today is not, How are we doing on race relations? or Are we promoting enough minority people and women? but rather, Given the diverse work force I've got, am I getting the productivity, does it work as smoothly, is morale as high, as if every person in the company was the same sex and race and nationality? Most answers will be, Well, no, of course not! But why shouldn't the answer be, You bet!?

When we ask how we're doing on race relations, we inadvertently put our finger on what's wrong with the question and with the attitude that underlies affirmative action. So long as racial and gender equality is something we grant to minorities and women, there will be no racial and gender equality. What we must do is create an environment where no one is advantaged or disadvantaged, an environment where "we" is everyone. What the traditional approach to diversity did was to create a cycle of crisis, action, relaxation, and disappointment that companies repeated over and over again without ever achieving more than the barest particle of what they were after.

Affirmative action pictures the work force as a pipeline and reasons as follows: If we can fill the pipeline with *qualified* minorities and women, we can solve our upward mobility problem. Once recruited, they will perform in accordance with our promotional criteria and move naturally up our regular developmental ladder. In the past, where minorities and women have failed to progress, they were simply unable to meet our performance standards. Recruiting qualified people will enable us to avoid special programs and reverse discrimination.

This pipeline perspective generates a self-perpetuating, self-defeating, recruitment-oriented cycle with six stages:

1. Problem Recognition   The first time through the cycle, the problem takes this form—We need more minorities and women in the pipeline. In later iterations, the problem is more likely to be defined as a need to retain and promote minorities and women.

2. Intervention   Management puts the company into what we may call an Affirmative Action Recruitment Mode. During the first cycle, the goal is to recruit minorities and women. Later, when the cycle is repeated a second or third time and the challenge has shifted to retention, development, and promotion, the goal is to recruit *qualified* minorities and women. Sometimes, managers indifferent or blind to possible accusations of reverse discrimination will institute special training, tracking, incentive, mentoring, or sponsoring programs for minorities and women.

3. Great Expectations   Large numbers of minorities and women have been recruited, and a select group has been promoted or recruited at a higher level to serve as highly visible role models for the newly recruited masses. The stage seems set for the natural progression of minorities and women up through the pipeline. Management leans back to enjoy the fruits of its labor.

4. Frustration   The anticipated natural progression fails to occur. Minorities and women see themselves plateauing prematurely. Management is upset (and embarrassed) by the failure of its affirmative action initiative and begins to resent the impatience of the new recruits and their unwillingness to give the company credit for trying to do the right thing. Depending on how high in the hierarchy they have plateaued, alienated minorities and women either leave the company or stagnate.

5. Dormancy   All remaining participants conspire tacitly to present a silent front to the outside world. Executives say nothing because they have no solutions. As for those women and minorities who stayed on, calling attention to affirmative action's failures might raise doubts about their qualifications. Do

EXHIBIT 2
"It Simply Makes Good Business Sense"

Corning characterizes its 1970s affirmative action program as a form of legal compliance. The law dictated affirmative action and morality required it, so the company did its best to hire minorities and women.

The ensuing cycle was classic: recruitment, confidence, disappointment, embarrassment, crisis, more recruitment. Talented women and blacks joined the company only to plateau or resign. Few reached upper-management levels, and no one could say exactly why.

Then James R. Houghton took over as CEO in 1983 and made the diverse work force one of Corning's three top priorities, alongside Total Quality and a higher return on equity. His logic was twofold:

First of all, the company had higher attrition rates for minorities and women than for white males, which meant that investments in training and development were being wasted. Second, he believed that the Corning work force should more closely mirror the Corning customer base.

In order to break the cycle of recruitment and subsequent frustration, the company established two quality-improvement teams headed by senior executives, one for black progress and one for women's progress. Mandatory awareness training was introduced for some 7,000 salaried employees—a day and a half for gender awareness, two-and-a-half days for racial awareness. One goal of the training is to identify unconscious company values that work against minorities and women. For example, a number of awareness groups reached the conclusion that working late had so much symbolic value that managers tended to look more at the quantity than at the quality of time spent on the job, with predictably negative effects on employees with dependent-care responsibilities.

The company also made an effort to improve communications by printing regular stories and articles about the diverse work force in its in-house newspaper and by publicizing employee success stories that emphasized diversity. It worked hard to identify and publicize promotion criteria. Career-planning systems were introduced for all employees.

With regard to recruitment, Corning set up a nationwide scholarship program that provides renewable grants of $5,000 per year for college in exchange for a summer of paid work at some Corning installation. A majority of program participants have come to work for Corning full-time after graduation, and very few have left the company so far, though the program has been in place only four years.

The company also expanded its summer intern program, with an emphasis on minorities and women, and established formal recruiting contacts with campus groups such as the Society of Women Engineers and the National Black MBA Association.

Corning sees its efforts to manage diversity not only as a social and moral issue but also as a question of efficiency and competitiveness. In the words of Mr. Houghton, "It simply makes good business sense."

they deserve their jobs, or did they just happen to be in the right place at the time of an affirmative action push? So no one complains, and if the company has a good public relations department, it may even wind up with a reputation as a good place for women and minorities to work.

If questioned publicly, management will say things like "Frankly, affirmative action is not currently an issue," or "Our numbers are okay," or "With respect to minority representation at the upper levels, management is aware of this remaining challenge."

In private and off the record, however, people say things like "Premature plateauing is a problem, and we don't know what to do," and "Our top people don't seem to be interested in finding a solution," and "There's plenty of racism and sexism around this place—whatever you may hear."

6. Crisis   Dormancy can continue indefinitely, but usually it is broken by a crisis of competitive pressure, government intervention, external pressure from a special interest group, or internal unrest. One company found that its pursuit of a Total Quality program was hampered by the alienation of minorities and women. Senior management at another corporation saw the growing importance of minorities in their customer base and decided they needed minority participation in their managerial ranks. In another case, growing expressions of discontent forced a break in the conspiracy of silence even after the company had received national recognition as a good place for minorities and women to work.

Whatever its cause, the crisis fosters a return to the Problem Recognition phase, and the cycle begins again. This time, management seeks to explain the shortcomings of the previous affirmative action push and usually concludes that the problem is recruitment. This assessment by a top executive is typical:

> The managers I know are decent people. While they give priority to performance, I do not believe any of them deliberately block minorities or women who are qualified for promotion. On the contrary, I suspect they bend over backward to promote women and minorities who give some indication of being qualified.
>
> However, they believe we simply do not have the necessary talent within those groups, but because of the constant complaints they have heard about their deficiencies in affirmative action, they feel they face a no-win situation. If they do not promote, they are obstructionists. But if they promote people who are unqualified, they hurt performance and deny promotion to other employees unfairly. They can't win. The answer, in my mind, must be an ambitious new recruitment effort to bring in quality people.

And so the cycle repeats. Once again blacks, Hispanics, women, and immigrants are dropped into a previously homogeneous, all-white, all-Anglo, all-male, all native-born environment, and the burden of cultural change is placed on the newcomers. There will be new expectations and a new round of frustration, dormancy, crisis, and recruitment.

EXHIBIT 3
Turning Social Pressures into Competitive Advantage

Like most other companies trying to respond to the federal legislation of the 1970s, Digital Equipment Corp. started off by focusing on numbers. By the early 1980s, however, company leaders could see it would take more than recruitment to make Digital the diverse workplace they wanted it to be. Equal Employment Opportunity (EEO) and affirmative action seemed too exclusive—too much "white males doing good deeds for minorities and women." The company wanted to move beyond these programs to the kind of environment where every employee could realize his or her potential, and Digital decided that meant an environment where individual differences were not tolerated but valued, even celebrated.

The resulting program and philosophy, called Valuing Differences, has two components:

First, the company helps people get in touch with their stereotypes and false assumptions through what Digital calls Core Groups. These voluntary groupings of 8 to 10 people work with company-trained facilitators whose job is to encourage discussion and self-development and, in the company's words, "to keep people safe" as they struggle with their prejudices. Digital also runs a voluntary two-day training program called "Understanding the Dynamics of Diversity," which thousands of Digital employees have now taken.

Second, the company has named a number of senior managers to various Cultural Boards of Directors and Valuing Differences Boards of Directors. These bodies promote openness to individual differences, encourage younger managers committed to the goal of diversity, and sponsor frequent celebrations of racial, gender, and ethnic differences such as Hispanic Heritage Week and Black History Month.

In addition to the Valuing Differences program, the company preserved its EEO and affirmative action functions. Valuing Differences focuses on personal and group development, EEO on legal issues, and affirmative action on systemic change. According to Alan Zimmerle, head of the Valuing Differences program, EEO and Valuing Differences are like two circles that touch but don't overlap—the first representing the legal need for diversity, the second the corporate desire for diversity. Affirmative action is a third circle that overlaps the other two and holds them together with policies and procedures.

Together, these three circles can transform legal and social pressures into the competitive advantage of a more effective work force, higher morale, and the reputation of being a better place to work. As Zimmerle puts it, "Digital wants to be the employer of choice. We want our pick of the talent that's out there."

TEN GUIDELINES FOR LEARNING TO MANAGE DIVERSITY

The traditional American image of diversity has been assimilation: the melting pot, where ethnic and racial differences were standardized into a kind of American puree. Of course, the melting pot is only a metaphor. In real life, many ethnic and most racial groups retain their individuality and express it energetically. What we have is perhaps some kind of American mulligan stew; it is certainly no puree.

At the workplace, however, the melting pot has been more than a metaphor. Corporate success has demanded a good deal of conformity, and employees have voluntarily abandoned most of their ethnic distinctions at the company door.

Now those days are over. Today the melting pot is the wrong metaphor even in business, for three good reasons. First, if it ever was possible to melt down Scotsmen and Dutchmen and Frenchmen into an indistinguishable broth, you can't do the same with blacks, Asians, and women. Their differences don't melt so easily. Second, most people are no longer willing to be melted down, not even for eight hours a day—and it's a seller's market for skills. Third, the thrust of today's nonhierarchical, flexible, collaborative management requires a ten- or twentyfold increase in our tolerance for individuality.

So companies are faced with the problem of surviving in a fiercely competitive world with a work force that consists and will continue to consist of *unassimilated diversity*. And the engine will take a great deal of tinkering to burn that fuel.

What managers fear from diversity is a lowering of standards, a sense that anything goes. Of course, standards must not suffer. In fact, competence counts more than ever. The goal is to manage diversity in such a way as to get from a diverse work force the same productivity we once got from a homogeneous work force, and to do it without artificial programs, standards—or barriers.

Managing diversity does not mean controlling or containing diversity, it means enabling every member of your work force to perform to his or her potential. It means getting from employees, first, everything we have a right to expect, and, second—if we do it well—everything they have to give. If the old homogeneous work force performed dependably at 80% of its capacity, then the first result means getting 80% from the new heterogeneous work force too. But the second result, the icing on the cake, the unexpected upside that diversity can perhaps give as a bonus, means 85% to 90% from everyone in the organization.

For the moment, however, let's concentrate on the basics of how to get satisfactory performance from the new diverse work force. There are few adequate models. So far, no large company I know of has succeeded in managing diversity to its own satisfaction. But any number have begun to try.

On the basis of their experience, here are my 10 guidelines:

1. Clarify Your Motivation   A lot of executives are not sure why they should want to learn to manage diversity. Legal compliance seems like a good reason. So does community relations. Many executives believe they have a social and moral responsibility to employ minorities and women. Others want to placate an internal group or pacify an outside organization. None of these are bad reasons, but none of them are business reasons, and given the nature and scope of today's competitive challenges, I believe only business reasons will supply the necessary long-term motivation. In any case, it is the business reasons I want to focus on here.

In business terms, a diverse work force is not something your company ought to have; it's something your company does have, or soon will have. Learning to manage that diversity will make you more competitive.

2. Clarify Your Vision   When managers think about a diverse work force, what do they picture? Not publicly, but in the privacy of their minds?

One popular image is of minorities and women clustering on a relatively low plateau, with a few of them trickling up as they become assimilated into the prevailing culture. Of course, they enjoy good salaries and benefits, and most of them accept their status, appreciate the fact that they are doing better than they could do somewhere else, and are proud of the achievements of their race or sex. This is reactionary thinking, but it's a lot more common than you might suppose.

Another image is what we might call heightened sensitivity. Members of the majority culture are sensitive to the demands of minorities and women for upward mobility and recognize the advantages of fully utilizing them. Minorities and women work at all levels of the corporation, but they are the recipients of generosity and know it. A few years of this second-class status drives most of them away and compromises the effectiveness of those that remain. Turnover is high.

Then there is the coexistence-compromise image. In the interests of corporate viability, white males agree to recognize minorities and women as equals. They bargain and negotiate their differences. But the win-lose aspect of the relationship preserves tensions, and the compromises reached are not always to the company's competitive advantage.

Diversity and equal opportunity is a big step up. It presupposes that the white male culture has given way to one that respects difference and individuality. The problem is that minorities and women will accept it readily as their operating image, but many white males, consciously or unconsciously, are likely to cling to a vision that leaves them in the driver's seat. A vision gap of this kind can be a difficulty.

In my view, the vision to hold in your own imagination and to try to communicate to all your managers and employees is an image of fully tapping the human resource potential of every member of the work force. This vision sidesteps the question of equality, ignores the tensions of coexistence, plays down the uncomfortable realities of difference, and focuses instead on individual enablement. It doesn't say, "Let *us* give *them* a chance." It assumes a diverse work force that includes us and them. It says, "Let's create an environment where everyone will do their best work."

Several years ago, an industrial plant in Atlanta with a highly diverse work force was threatened with closing unless productivity improved. To save their jobs, everyone put their shoulders to the wheel and achieved the results they needed to stay open. The senior operating manager was amazed.

EXHIBIT 4
Discovering Complexity and Value in P&G's Diversity

Because Procter & Gamble fills its upper-level management positions only from within the company, it places a premium on recruiting the best available entry-level employees. Campus recruiting is pursued nationwide and year-round by line managers from all levels of the company. Among other things, the company has made a concerted—and successful—effort to find and hire talented minorities and women.

Finding first-rate hires is only one piece of the effort, however. There is still the challenge of moving diversity upward. As one top executive put it, "We know that we can only succeed as a company if we have an environment that makes it easy for all of us, not just some of us, to work to our potential."

In May 1988, P&G formed a Corporate Diversity Strategy Task Force to clarify the concept of diversity, define its importance for the company, and identify strategies for making progress toward successfully managing a diverse work force.

The task force, composed of men and women from every corner of the company, made two discoveries: First, diversity at P&G was far more complex than most people had supposed. In addition to race and gender, it included factors such as cultural heritage, personal background, and functional experience. Second, the company needed to expand its view of the value of differences.

The task force helped the company to see that learning to manage diversity would be a long-term process of organizational change. For example, P&G has offered voluntary diversity training at all levels since the 1970s, but the program has gradually broadened its emphasis on race and gender awareness to include the value of self-realization in a diverse environment. As retiring board chairman John Smale put it, "If we can tap the total contribution that everybody in our company has to offer, we will be better and more competitive in everything we do."

P&G is now conducting a thorough, continuing evaluation of all management programs to be sure that systems are working well for everyone. It has also carried out a corporate survey to get a better picture of the problems facing P&G employees who are balancing work and family responsibilities and to improve company programs in such areas as dependent care.

For years he had seen minorities and women plateauing disproportionately at the lower levels of the organization, and he explained that fact away with two rationalizations. "They haven't been here that long," he told himself. And "This is the price we pay for being in compliance with the law."

When the threat of closure energized this whole group of people into a level of performance he had not imagined possible, he got one fleeting glimpse of people working up to their capacity. Once the crisis was over, everyone went back to the earlier status quo—white males driving and everyone else sitting back, looking on—but now there was a difference. Now, as he put it himself, he had been to the mountaintop. He knew that what he was getting from minorities and women was nowhere near what they were capable of giving. And he wanted it, crisis or no crisis, all the time.

3. Expand Your Focus   Managers usually see affirmative action and equal employment opportunity as centering on minorities and women, with very little to offer white males. The diversity I'm talking about includes not only race, gender, creed, and ethnicity but also age, background, education, function, and personality differences. The objective is not to assimilate minorities and women into a dominant white male culture but to create a dominant heterogeneous culture.

The culture that dominates the United States socially and politically is heterogeneous, and it works by giving its citizens the liberty to achieve their potential. Channeling that potential, once achieved, is an individual right but still a national concern. Something similar applies in the workplace, where the keys to success are individual ability and a corporate destination. Managing disparate talents to achieve common goals is what companies learned to do when they set their sights on, say, Total Quality. The secrets of managing diversity are much the same.

4. Audit Your Corporate Culture   If the goal is not to assimilate diversity into the dominant culture but rather to build a culture that can digest unassimilated diversity, then you had better start by figuring out what your present culture looks like. Because what we're talking about here is the body of unspoken and unexamined assumptions, values, and mythologies that make your world go round, this kind of cultural audit is impossible to conduct without outside help. It's a research activity, done mostly with in-depth interviews and a lot of listening at the water cooler.

The operative corporate assumptions you have to identify and deal with are often inherited from the company's founder. "If we treat everyone as a member of the family, we will be successful" is not uncommon. Nor is its corollary "Father Knows Best."

Another widespread assumption, probably absorbed from American culture in general, is that "cream will rise to the top." In most companies, what passes for cream rising to the top is actually cream being pulled or pushed to the top by an informal system of mentoring and sponsorship.

Corporate culture is a kind of tree. Its roots are assumptions about the company and about the world. Its branches, leaves, and seeds are behavior. You can't change the leaves without changing the roots, and you can't grow peaches on an oak. Or rather, with the proper grafting, you *can* grow peaches on an oak, but they come out an awful lot like acorns—small and hard and not much fun to eat. So if you want to grow peaches, you have to make sure the tree's roots are peach friendly.

5. Modify Your Assumptions   The real problem with this corporate culture tree is that every time you go to make changes in the roots, you run into terrible opposition. Every culture, including corporate culture, has root guards that turn out in force every time you threaten a basic assumption.

Take the family assumption as an example. Viewing the corporation as a family suggests not only that father knows best; it also suggests that sons will inherit the business, that daughters should stick to doing the company dishes, and that if Uncle Deadwood doesn't perform, we'll put him in the chimney corner and feed him for another 30 years regardless. Each assumption has its constituency and its defenders. If we say to Uncle Deadwood, "Yes, you did good work for 10 years, but years 11 and 12 look pretty bleak; we think it's time we helped you find another chimney," shock waves will travel through the company as every family-oriented employee draws a sword to defend the sacred concept of guaranteed jobs.

But you have to try. A corporation that wants to create an environment with no advantages or disadvantages for any group cannot allow the family assumption to remain in place. It must be labeled dishonest mythology.

Sometimes the dishonesties are more blatant. When I asked a white male middle manager how promotions were handled in his company, he said, "You need leadership capability, bottom-line results, the ability to work with people, and compassion." Then he paused and smiled. "That's what they say. But down the hall there's a guy we call Captain Kickass. He's ruthless, mean-spirited, and he steps on people. That's the behavior they really value. Forget what they say."

In addition to the obvious issue of hypocrisy, this example also raises a question of equal opportunity. When I asked this young middle manager if he thought minorities and women could meet the Captain Kickass standard, he said he thought they probably could. But the opposite argument can certainly be made. Whether we're talking about blacks in an environment that is predominantly white, whites in one predominantly black, or women in one predominantly male, the majority culture will not readily condone such tactics from a member of a minority. So the corporation with the unspoken kickass performance standard has at least one criterion that will hamper the upward mobility of minorities and women.

Another destructive assumption is the melting pot I referred to earlier. The organization I'm arguing for respects differences rather than seeking to smooth them out. It is multicultural rather than culture blind, which has an important consequence: When we no longer force people to "belong" to a common ethnicity or culture, then the organization's leaders must work all the harder to define belonging in terms of a set of values and a sense of purpose that transcend the interests, desires, and preferences of any one group.

6. Modify Your Systems   The first purpose of examining and modifying assumptions is to modify systems. Promotion, mentoring, and sponsorship comprise one such system, and the unexamined cream-to-the-top assumption I mentioned earlier can tend to keep minorities and women from climbing the corporate ladder. After all, in many companies it is difficult to secure a promotion above a certain level without a personal advocate or sponsor. In the context of managing diversity, the question is not whether this system is maximally

EXHIBIT 5
The Daily Experience of Genuine Workplace Diversity

Chairman David T. Kearns believes that a firm and resolute commitment to affirmative action is the first and most important step to work-force diversity. "Xerox is committed to affirmative action," he says. "It is a corporate value, a management priority, and a formal business objective."

Xerox began recruiting minorities and women systematically as far back as the mid-1960s, and it pioneered such concepts as pivotal jobs (described later). The company's approach emphasizes behavior expectations as opposed to formal consciousness-raising programs because, as one Xerox executive put it, "It's just not realistic to think that a day-and-a-half of training will change a person's thinking after 30 or 40 years."

On the assumption that attitude changes will grow from the daily experience of genuine workplace diversity, the Xerox Balanced Work Force Strategy sets goals for the number of minorities and women in each division and at every level. (For example, the goal for the top 300 executive-level jobs in one large division is 35% women by 1995, compared with 15% today.) "You *must* have a laboratory to work in," says Ted Payne, head of Xerox's Office of Affirmative Action and Equal Opportunity.

Minority and women's employee support groups have grown up in more than a dozen locations with the company's encouragement. But Xerox depends mainly on the three pieces of its balanced strategy to make diversity work.

First are the goals. Xerox sets recruitment and representation goals in accordance with federal guidelines and reviews them constantly to make sure they reflect work-force demographics. Any company with a federal contract is required to make this effort. But Xerox then extends the guidelines by setting diversity goals for its upper-level jobs and holding division and group managers accountable for reaching them.

The second piece is a focus on pivotal jobs, a policy Xerox adopted in the 1970s when it first noticed that minorities and women did not have the upward mobility the company wanted to see. By examining the backgrounds of top executives, Xerox was able to identify the key positions that all successful managers had held at lower levels and to set goals for getting minorities and women assigned to such jobs.

The third piece is an effort to concentrate managerial training not so much on managing diversity as on just plain managing people. What the company discovered when it began looking at managerial behavior toward minorities and women was that all too many managers didn't know enough about how to manage anyone, let alone people quite different from themselves.

---

efficient but whether it works for all employees. Executives who only sponsor people like themselves are not making much of a contribution to the cause of getting the best from every employee.

Performance appraisal is another system where unexamined practices and patterns can have pernicious effects. For example, there are companies where official performance appraisals differ substantially from what is said informally, with the result that employees get their most accurate performance feedback through the grapevine. So if the grapevine is closed to minorities and women, they are left at a severe disadvantage. As one white manager observed, "If the blacks around here knew how they were really perceived, there would be a revolt." Maybe so. More important to your business, however, is the fact that without an accurate appraisal of performance, minority and women employees will find it difficult to correct or defend their alleged shortcomings.

7. Modify Your Models   The second purpose of modifying assumptions is to modify models of managerial and employee behavior. My own personal hobgoblin is one I call the Doer Model, often an outgrowth of the family assumption and of unchallenged paternalism. I have found the Doer Model alive and thriving in a dozen companies. It works like this:

Because father knows best, managers seek subordinates who will follow their lead and do as they do. If they can't find people exactly like themselves, they try to find people who aspire to be exactly like themselves. The goal is predictability and immediate responsiveness because the doer manager is not there to manage people but to do the business. In accounting departments, for example, doer managers do accounting, and subordinates are simply extensions of their hands and minds, sensitive to every signal and suggestion of managerial intent.

Doer managers take pride in this identity of purpose. "I wouldn't ask my people to do anything I wouldn't do myself," they say. "I roll up my sleeves and get in the trenches." Doer managers love to be in the trenches. It keeps them out of the line of fire.

But managers aren't supposed to be in the trenches, and accounting managers aren't supposed to do accounting. What they are supposed to do is create systems and a climate that allow accountants to do accounting, a climate that enables people to do what they've been charged to do. The right goal is doer subordinates, supported and empowered by managers who manage.

8. Help Your People Pioneer   Learning to manage diversity is a change process, and the managers involved are change agents. There is no single tried-and-tested "solution" to diversity and no fixed right way to manage it. Assuming the existence of a single or even a dominant barrier undervalues the importance of all the other barriers that face any company, including, potentially, prejudice, personality, community dynamics, culture, and the ups and downs of business itself.

While top executives articulate the new company policy and their commitment to it, middle managers—most or all of them still white males, remember—are placed in the tough position of having to cope with a forest of problems and simultaneously develop the minorities and women who represent their own competition for an increasingly limited number of promotions. What's more, every time they stumble they will themselves be labeled the major barriers to progress. These managers need help, they need a certain amount of sympathy, and most of all, perhaps, they need to be told that they are pioneers and judged accordingly.

In one case, an ambitious young black woman was assigned to a white male manager, at his request, on the basis of her excellent company record. They looked forward to working together, and for the first three months, everything went well. But then their relationship began to deteriorate, and the harder they worked at patching it up, the worse it got. Both of them, along with their superiors, were surprised by the conflict and seemed puzzled as to its causes. Eventually, the black woman requested and obtained reassignment. But even though they escaped each other, both suffered a sense of failure severe enough to threaten their careers.

What could have been done to assist them? Well, empathy would not have hurt. But perspective would have been better yet. In their particular company and situation, these two people had placed themselves at the cutting edge of race and gender relations. They needed to know that mistakes at the cutting edge are different—and potentially more valuable—than mistakes elsewhere. Maybe they needed some kind of pioneer training. But at the very least they needed to be told that they were pioneers, that conflicts and failures came with the territory, and that they would be judged accordingly.

9. Apply the Special Consideration Test   I said earlier that affirmative action was an artificial, transitional, but necessary stage on the road to a truly diverse work force. Because of its artificial nature, affirmative action requires constant attention and drive to make it work. The point of learning once and for all how to manage diversity is that all that energy can be focused somewhere else.

There is a simple test to help you spot the diversity programs that are going to eat up enormous quantities of time and effort. Surprisingly, perhaps, it is the same test you might use to identify the programs and policies that created your problem in the first place. The test consists of one question: Does this program, policy, or principle give special consideration to one group? Will it contribute to everyone's success, or will it only produce an advantage for blacks or whites or women or men? Is it designed for *them* as opposed to *us*? Whenever the answer is yes, you're not yet on the road to managing diversity.

This does not rule out the possibility of addressing issues that relate to a single group. It only underlies the importance of determining that the issue you're addressing does not relate to other groups as well. For example, management in one company noticed that blacks were not moving up in the organization. Before instituting a special program to bring them along, managers conducted interviews to see if they could find the reason for the impasse. What blacks themselves reported was a problem with the quality of supervision. Further interviews showed that other employees too—including white males— were concerned about the quality of supervision and felt that little was being done to foster professional development. Correcting the situation eliminated a problem that affected everyone. In this case, a solution that focused only on blacks would have been out of place.

Had the problem consisted of prejudice, on the other hand, or some other barrier to blacks or minorities alone, a solution based on affirmative action would have been perfectly appropriate.

10. Continue Affirmative Action   Let me come full circle. The ability to manage diversity is the ability to manage your company without unnatural advantage or disadvantage for any member of your diverse work force. The fact remains that first you must have a work force that is diverse at every level, and if you don't, you're going to need affirmative action to get from here to there.

The reason you then want to move beyond affirmative action to managing diversity is because affirmative action fails to deal with the root causes of prejudice and inequality and does little to develop the full potential of every man and woman in the company. In a country seeking competitive advantage in a global economy, the goal of managing diversity is to develop our capacity to accept, incorporate, and empower the diverse human talents of the most diverse nation on earth. It's our reality. We need to make it our strength.

⸻ DISCUSSION QUESTIONS

1. Examine your attitudes toward people who are different. In the workplace, what are your attitudes toward people of another race or the other gender?
2. As a general manager, would you consider it important to encourage diversity in your work force? Explain your principal reasons for your position, pro or con.
3. Do the issues that this reading addresses apply only to large corporations? Should smaller businesses also strive for diversity?
4. The reading touches on modifying assumptions about the corporate culture. What assumptions do you have about the workplace culture, or what assumptions have you had to modify since you began working?
5. Should affirming diversity be an issue that is addressed by other institutions besides business corporations? If so, what other institutions can help to promote diversity?

35 Management Women and the New Facts of Life

FELICE N. SCHWARTZ

Women managers cost more to employ than men, asserts this author. Management women range from those whose careers come first—often to the exclusion of family—to those who try to balance family and career. The chances are that turnover among women managers will be higher and that they will be more likely to interrupt their careers.

In this reading, the author explores ways to retain the best women and eliminate the extra cost of employing them. She advocates a combination of opportunity and flexibility. Opportunity means judging and promoting ambitious women on the same terms as men. Flexibility means allowing women to share jobs or work part-time while their children are young.

The cost of employing women in management is greater than the cost of employing men. This is a jarring statement, partly because it is true, but mostly because it is something people are reluctant to talk about. A new study by one multinational corporation shows that the rate of turnover in management positions is 2½ times higher among top-performing women than it is among men. A large producer of consumer goods reports that one half of the women who take maternity leave return to their jobs late or not at all. And we know that women also have a greater tendency to plateau or to interrupt their careers in ways that limit their growth and development. But we have become so sensitive to charges of sexism and so afraid of confrontation, even litigation, that we rarely say what we know to be true. Unfortunately, our bottled-up awareness leaks out in misleading metaphors ("glass ceiling" is one notable example), veiled hostility, lowered expectations, distrust, and reluctant adherence to Equal Employment Opportunity requirements.

Career interruptions, plateauing, and turnover are expensive. The money corporations invest in recruitment, training, and development is less likely to produce top executives among women than among men, and the invaluable company experience that developing executives acquire at every level as they move up through management ranks is more often lost.

The studies just mentioned are only the first of many, I'm quite sure. Demographic realities are going to force corporations all across the country to analyze the cost of employing women in managerial positions, and what they will discover is that women cost more.

But here is another startling truth: The greater cost of employing women is not a function of inescapable gender differences. Women *are* different from men, but what increases their cost to the corporation is principally the clash of their perceptions, attitudes, and behavior with those of men, which is to say, with the policies and practices of male-led corporations.

It is terribly important that employers draw the right conclusions from the studies now being done. The studies will be useless—or worse, harmful—if all they teach us is that women are expensive to employ. What we need to learn is how to reduce that expense, how to stop throwing away the investments we make in talented women, how to become more responsive to the needs of the women that corporations *must* employ if they are to have the best and the brightest of all those now entering the work force.

The gender differences relevant to business fall into two categories: those related to maternity and those related to the differing traditions and expectations of the sexes. Maternity is biological rather than cultural. We can't alter it, but we can dramatically reduce its impact on the workplace and in many cases eliminate its negative effect on employee development. We can accomplish this by addressing the second set of differences, those between male and female socialization. Today, these differences exaggerate the real costs of maternity and can turn a relatively slight disruption in work schedule into a serious business problem and a career derailment for individual women. If we are to overcome the cost differential between male and female employees, we need to address the issues that arise when female socialization meets the male corporate culture and masculine rules of career development—issues of behavior and style, of expectation, of stereotypes and preconceptions, of sexual tension and harassment, of female mentoring, lateral mobility, relocation, compensation, and early identification of top performers.

The one immutable, enduring difference between men and women is maternity. Maternity is not simply childbirth but a continuum that begins with an awareness of the ticking of the biological clock, proceeds to the anticipation of motherhood, includes pregnancy, childbirth, physical recuperation, psychological adjustment, and continues on to nursing, bonding, and child rearing. Not all women choose to become mothers, of course, and among those who do, the process varies from case to case depending on the health of the mother and baby, the values of the parents, and the availability, cost, and quality of child care.

In past centuries, the biological fact of maternity shaped the traditional roles of the sexes. Women performed the home-centered functions that related to the bearing and nurturing of children. Men did the work that required great physical strength. Over time, however, family size contracted, the community assumed greater responsibility for the care and education of children, packaged foods and household technology reduced the work load in the home, and technology eliminated much of the need for muscle power at the workplace.

Today, in the developed world, the only role still uniquely gender related is childbearing. Yet men and women are still socialized to perform their traditional roles.

Men and women may or may not have some innate psychological disposition toward these traditional roles—men to be aggressive, competitive, self-reliant, risk taking; women to be supportive, nurturing, intuitive, sensitive, communicative—but certainly both men and women are capable of the full range of behavior. Indeed, the male and female roles have already begun to expand and merge. In the decades ahead, as the socialization of boys and girls and the experience and expectations of young men and women grow steadily more androgynous, the differences in workplace behavior will continue to fade. At the moment, however, we are still plagued by disparities in perception and behavior that make the integration of men and women in the workplace unnecessarily difficult and expensive.

Let me illustrate with a few broadbrush generalizations. Of course, these are only stereotypes, but I think they help to exemplify the kinds of preconceptions that can muddy the corporate waters.

Men continue to perceive women as the rearers of their children so they find it understandable, indeed appropriate, that women should renounce their careers to raise families. Edmund Pratt, CEO of Pfizer, once asked me in all sincerity, "Why would any woman choose to be a chief financial officer rather than a full-time mother?" By condoning and taking pleasure in women's traditional behavior, men reinforce it. Not only do they see parenting as fundamentally female, they see a career as fundamentally male—either an unbroken series of promotions and advancements toward CEOdom or stagnation and disappointment. This attitude serves to legitimize a woman's choice to extend maternity leave and even, for those who can afford it, to leave employment altogether for several years. By the same token, men who might want to take a leave after the birth of a child know that management will see such behavior as a lack of career commitment, even when company policy permits parental leave for men.

Women also bring counterproductive expectations and perceptions to the workplace. Ironically, although the feminist movement was an expression of women's quest for freedom from their home-based lives, most women were remarkably free already. They had many responsibilities, but they were autonomous and could be entrepreneurial in how and when they carried them out. And once their children grew up and left home, they were essentially free to do what they wanted with their lives. Women's traditional role also included freedom from responsibility for the financial support of their families. Many of us were socialized from girlhood to expect our husbands to take care of us, while our brothers were socialized from an equally early age to complete their educations, pursue careers, climb the ladder of success, and provide dependable financial support for their families. To the extent that this tradition of freedom lingers subliminally, women tend to bring to their employment a sense that they can choose to change jobs or careers at will, take time off, or reduce their hours.

Finally, women's traditional role encouraged particular attention to the quality and substance of what they did, specifically to the physical, psychological, and intellectual development of their children. This traditional focus may explain women's continuing tendency to search for more than monetary reward—intrinsic significance, social importance, meaning—in what they do. This too makes them more likely than men to leave the corporation in search of other values.

The misleading metaphor of the glass ceiling suggests an invisible barrier constructed by corporate leaders to impede the upward mobility of women beyond the middle levels. A more appropriate metaphor, I believe, is the kind of cross-sectional diagram used in geology. The barriers to women's leadership occur when potentially counterproductive layers of influence on women—maternity, tradition, socialization—meet management strata pervaded by the largely unconscious preconceptions, stereotypes, and expectations of men. Such interfaces do not exist for men and tend to be impermeable for women.

One result of these gender differences has been to convince some executives that women are simply not suited to top management. Other executives feel helpless. If they see even a few of their valued female employees fail to return to work from maternity leave on schedule or see one of their most promising women plateau in her career after the birth of a child, they begin to fear there is nothing they can do to infuse women with new energy and enthusiasm and persuade them to stay. At the same time, they know there is nothing they can do to stem the tide of women into management ranks.

Another result is to place every working woman on a continuum that runs from total dedication to career at one end to a balance between career and family at the other. What women discover is that the male corporate culture sees both extremes as unacceptable. Women who want the flexibility to balance their families and their careers are not adequately committed to the organization. Women who perform as aggressively and competitively as men are abrasive and unfeminine. But the fact is, business needs all the talented women it can get. Moreover, as I will explain, the women I call career-primary and those I call career-and-family each have particular value to the corporation.

Women in the corporation are about to move from a buyer's to a seller's market. The sudden, startling recognition that 80% of new entrants in the work force over the next decade will be women, minorities, and immigrants has stimulated a mushrooming incentive to "value diversity."

Women are no longer simply an enticing pool of occasional creative talent, a thorn in the side of the EEO officer, or a source of frustration to corporate leaders truly puzzled by the slowness of their upward trickle into executive positions. A real demographic change is taking place. The era of sudden population growth of the 1950s and 1960s is over. The birth rate has dropped about 40%, from a high of 25.3 live births per 1,000 population in 1957, at the peak of the baby boom, to a stable low of a little more than 15 per 1,000 over the last 16 years, and there is no indication of a return to a higher rate. The tidal wave of baby boomers that swelled the recruitment pool to overflowing seems to have been a one-time phenomenon. For 20 years, employers had the pick of a very large crop and were able to choose males almost exclusively for the executive track. But if future population remains fairly stable while the economy continues to expand and if the new information society simultaneously creates a greater need for creative, educated managers, then the gap between supply and demand will grow dramatically and, with it, the competition for managerial talent.

The decrease in numbers has even greater implications if we look at the traditional source of corporate recruitment for leadership positions—white males from the top 10% of the country's best universities. Over the past decade, the increase in the number of women graduating from leading universities has been much greater than the increase in the total number of graduates, and these women are well represented in the top 10% of their classes.

The trend extends into business and professional programs as well. In the old days, virtually all MBAs were male. I remember addressing a meeting at the Harvard Business School as recently as the mid-1970s and looking out at a sea of exclusively male faces. Today, about 25% of that audience would be women. The pool of male MBAs from which corporations have traditionally drawn their leaders has shrunk significantly.

Of course, this reduction does not have to mean a shortage of talent. The top 10% is at least as smart as it always was—smarter, probably, because it's now drawn from a broader segment of the population. But it now consists increasingly of women. Companies that are determined to recruit the same number of men as before will have to dig much deeper into the male pool, while their competitors will have the opportunity to pick the best people from both the male and female graduates.

Under these circumstances, there is no question that the management ranks of business will include increasing numbers of women. There remains, however, the question of how these women will succeed—how long they will stay, how high they will climb, how completely they will fulfill their promise and potential, and what kind of return the corporation will realize on its investment in their training and development.

There is ample business reason for finding ways to make sure that as many of these women as possible will succeed. The first step in this process is to recognize that not all women are alike. Like men, they are individuals with differing talents, priorities, and motivations. For the sake of simplicity, let me focus on the two women I referred to earlier, on what I call the career-primary woman and the career-and-family woman.

Like many men, some women put their careers first. They are ready to make the same trade-offs traditionally made by the men who seek leadership positions. They make a career decision to put in extra hours, to make sacrifices in their personal lives, to make the most of every opportunity for professional development. For women, of course, this decision also requires that they remain single or at least childless or, if they do have children, that they be satisfied to have others raise them. Some 90% of executive men but only 35% of executive women have children by the age of 40. The *automatic* association of all women with babies is clearly unjustified.

The secret to dealing with such women is to recognize them early, accept them, and clear artificial barriers from their path to the top. After all, the best of these women are among the best managerial talent you will ever see. And career-primary women have another important value to the company that men and other women lack. They can act as role models and mentors to younger women who put their careers first. Because upwardly mobile career-primary women still have few role models to motivate and inspire them, a company with women in its top echelon has a significant advantage in the competition for executive talent.

Men at the top of the organization—most of them over 55, with wives who tend to be traditional—often find career women "masculine" and difficult to accept as colleagues. Such men miss the point, which is not that these women are just like men but that they are just like the *best* men in the organization. And there is such a shortage of the best people that gender cannot be allowed to matter. It is clearly counterproductive to disparage in a woman with executive talent the very qualities that are most critical to the business and that might carry a man to the CEO's office.

Clearing a path to the top for career-primary women has four requirements:

1. Identify them early.
2. Give them the same opportunity you give to talented men to grow and develop and contribute to company profitability. Give them client and customer responsibility. Expect them to travel and relocate, to make the same commitment to the company as men aspiring to leadership positions.
3. Accept them as valued members of your management team. Include them in every kind of communications. Listen to them.
4. Recognize that the business environment is more difficult and stressful for them than for their male peers. They are always a minority, often the only woman. The male perception of talented, ambitious women is at best ambivalent, a mixture of admiration, resentment, confusion, competitiveness, attraction, skepticism, anxiety, pride, and animosity. Women can never feel secure about how they should dress and act, whether they should speak out or grin and bear it when they encounter discrimination, stereotyping, sexual harassment, and paternalism. Social interaction and travel with male colleagues and with male clients can be charged. As they move up, the normal increase in pressure and responsibility is compounded for women because they are women.

Stereotypical language and sexist day-to-day behavior do take their toll on women's career development. Few male executives realize how common it is to call women by their first names while men in the same group are greeted with surnames, how frequently female executives are assumed by men to be secretaries, how often women are excluded from all-male social events where business is being transacted. With notable exceptions, men are still generally more comfortable with other men, and as a result women miss many of the career and business opportunities that arise over lunch, on the golf course, or in the locker room.

The majority of women, however, are what I call career-and-family women, women who want to pursue serious careers while participating actively in the rearing of children. These women are a precious resource that has yet to be mined. Many of them are talented and creative. Most of them are willing to trade some career growth and compensation for freedom from the constant pressure to work long hours and weekends.

Most companies today are ambivalent at best about the career-and-family women in their management ranks. They would prefer that all employees were willing to give their all to the company. They believe it is in their best interests for all managers to compete for the top positions so the company will have the largest possible pool from which to draw its leaders.

"If you have both talent and motivation," many employers seem to say, "we want to move you up. If you haven't got that motivation, if you want less pressure and greater flexibility, then you can leave and make room for a new generation." These companies lose on two counts. First, they fail to amortize the investment they made in the early training and experience of management women who find themselves committed to family as well as to career. Second, they fail to recognize what these women could do for their middle management.

The ranks of middle managers are filled with people on their way up and people who have stalled. Many of them have simply reached their limits, achieved career growth commensurate with or exceeding their capabilities, and they cause problems because their performance is mediocre but they still want to move ahead. The career-and-family woman is willing to trade off the pressures and demands that go with promotion for the freedom to spend more time with her children. She's very smart, she's talented, she's committed to her career, and she's satisfied to stay at the middle level, at least during the early child-rearing years. Compare her with some of the people you have there now.

Consider a typical example, a woman who decides in college on a business career and enters management at age 22. For nine years, the company invests in her career as she gains experience and skills and steadily improves her performance. But at 31, just as the investment begins to pay off in earnest, she decides to have a baby. Can the company afford to let her go home, take another job, or go into business for herself? The common perception now is yes, the corporation can afford to lose her unless, after six or eight weeks or even three months of disability and maternity leave, she returns to work on a full-time schedule with the same vigor, commitment, and ambition that she showed before.

But what if she doesn't? What if she wants or needs to go on leave for six months or a year or, heaven forbid, five years? In this worst-case scenario, she works full-time from age 22 to 31 and from 36 to 65—a total of 38 years as opposed to the typical male's 43 years. That's not a huge difference. Moreover, my typical example is willing to work part-time while her children are young, if only her employer will give her the opportunity. There are two rewards for companies responsive to this need: higher retention of their best people and greatly improved performance and satisfaction in their middle management.

The high-performing career-and-family woman can be a major player in your company. She can give you a significant business advantage as the competition for able people escalates. Sometimes too, if you can hold on to her, she will switch gears in mid-life and reenter the competition for the top. The price you must pay to retain these women is threefold: you must plan for and manage maternity, you must provide the flexibility that will allow them to be maximally productive, and you must take an active role in helping to make family supports and high-quality, affordable child care available to all women.

The key to managing maternity is to recognize the value of high-performing women and the urgent need to retain them and keep them productive. The first step must be a genuine partnership between the woman and her boss. I know this partnership can seem difficult to forge. One of my own senior executives came to me recently to discuss plans for her maternity leave and subsequent return to work. She knew she wanted to come back. I wanted to make certain that she would. Still, we had a somewhat awkward conversation, because I knew that no woman can predict with certainty when she will be able to return to work or under what conditions. Physical problems can lengthen her leave. So can a demanding infant, a difficult family or personal adjustment, or problems with child care.

I still don't know when this valuable executive will be back on the job full-time, and her absence creates some genuine problems for our organization. But I do know that I can't simply replace her years of experience with a new recruit. Since our conversation, I also know that she wants to come back, and that she *will* come back—part-time at first—unless I make it impossible for her by, for example, setting an arbitrary date for her full-time return or resignation. In turn, she knows that the organization wants and needs her and, more to the point, that it will be responsive to her needs in terms of working hours and child care arrangements.

In having this kind of conversation it's important to ask concrete questions that will help to move the discussion from uncertainty and anxiety to some level of predictability. Questions can touch on everything from family income and energy level to child care arrangements and career commitment. Of course you want your star manager to return to work as soon as possible, but you want her to return permanently and productively. Her downtime on the job is a drain on her energies and a waste of your money.

For all the women who want to combine career and family—the women who want to participate actively in the rearing of their children and who also want to pursue their careers seriously—the key to retention is to provide the flexibility and family supports they need in order to function effectively.

Time spent in the office increases productivity if it is time well spent, but the fact that most women continue to take the primary responsibility for child care is a cause of distraction, diversion, anxiety, and absenteeism—to say nothing of the persistent guilt experienced by all working mothers. A great many women, perhaps most of all women who have always performed at the highest levels, are also frustrated by a sense that while their children are babies they cannot function at their best either at home or at work.

In its simplest form, flexibility is the freedom to take time off—a couple of hours, a day, a week—or to do some work at home and some at the office, an arrangement that communication technology makes increasingly feasible. At the complex end of the spectrum are alternative work schedules that permit the woman to work less than full-time and her employer to reap the benefits of her experience and, with careful planning, the top level of her abilities.

Part-time employment is the single greatest inducement to getting women back on the job expeditiously and the provision women themselves most desire. A part-time return to work enables them to maintain responsibility for critical aspects of their jobs, keeps them in touch with the changes constantly occurring at the workplace and in the job itself, reduces stress and fatigue, often eliminates the need for paid maternity leave by permitting a return to the office as soon as disability leave is over, and, not least, can greatly enhance company loyalty. The part-time solution works particularly well when a work load can be reduced for one individual in a department or when a full-time job can be broken down by skill levels and apportioned to two individuals at different levels of skill and pay.

I believe, however, that shared employment is the most promising and will be the most widespread form of flexible scheduling in the future. It is feasible at every level of the corporation except at the pinnacle, for both the short and the long term. It involves two people taking responsibility for one job.

Two red lights flash on as soon as most executives hear the words "job sharing": continuity and client-customer contact. The answer to the continuity question is to place responsibility entirely on the two individuals sharing the job to discuss everything that transpires—thoroughly, daily, and on their own time. The answer to the problem of client-customer contact is yes, job sharing requires reeducation and a period of adjustment. But as both client and supervisor will quickly come to appreciate, two contacts means that the customer has continuous access to the company's representative, without interruptions for vacation, travel, or sick leave. The two people holding the job can simply cover for each other, and the uninterrupted, full-time coverage they provide together can be a stipulation of their arrangement.

Flexibility is costly in numerous ways. It requires more supervisory time to coordinate and manage, more office space, and somewhat greater benefits costs (though these can be contained with flexible benefits plans, prorated benefits, and, in two-paycheck families, elimination of duplicate benefits). But the advantages of reduced turnover and the greater productivity that results from higher energy levels and greater focus can outweigh the costs.

A few hints:

- Provide flexibility selectively. I'm not suggesting private arrangements subject to the suspicion of favoritism but rather a policy that makes flexible work schedules available only to high performers.
- Make it clear that in most instances (but not all) the rates of advancement and pay will be appropriately lower for those who take time off or who work part-time than for those who work full-time. Most career-and-family women are entirely willing to make that trade-off.
- Discuss costs as well as benefits. Be willing to risk accusations of bias. Insist, for example, that half time is half of whatever time it takes to do the job, not merely half of 35 or 40 hours.

The woman who is eager to get home to her child has a powerful incentive to use her time effectively at the office and to carry with her reading and other work that can be done at home. The talented professional who wants to have it all can be a high performer by carefully ordering her priorities and by focusing on objectives rather than on the legendary 15-hour day. By the time professional women have their first babies—at an average age of 31—they have already had nine years to work long hours at a desk, to travel, and to relocate. In the case of high performers, the need for flexibility coincides with what has gradually become the goal-oriented nature of responsibility.

Family supports—in addition to maternity leave and flexibility—include the provision of parental leave for men, support for two-career and single-parent families during relocation, and flexible benefits. But the primary ingredient is child care. The capacity of working mothers to function effectively and without interruption depends on the availability of good, affordable child care. Now that women make up almost half the work force and the growing percentage of managers, the decision to become involved in the personal lives of employees is no longer a philosophical question but a practical one. To make matters worse, the quality of child care has almost no relation to technology, inventiveness, or profitability but is more or less a pure function of the quality of child care personnel and the ratio of adults to children. These costs are irreducible. Only by joining hands with government and the public sector can corporations hope to create the vast quantity and variety of child care that their employees need.

Until quite recently, the response of corporations to women has been largely symbolic and cosmetic, motivated in large part by the will to avoid litigation and legal penalties. In some cases, companies were also moved by a genuine sense of fairness and a vague discomfort and frustration at the absence of women above the middle of the corporate pyramid. The actions they took were mostly quick, easy, and highly visible—child care information services, a three-month parental leave available to men as well as women, a woman appointed to the board of directors.

When I first began to discuss these issues 26 years ago, sometimes I was able to get an appointment with the assistant to the assistant in personnel, but it was only a courtesy. Over the past decade, I have met with the CEOs of many large corporations, and I've watched them become involved with ideas they had never previously thought much about. Until recently, however, the shelf life of that enhanced awareness was always short. Given pressing, short-term concerns, women were not a front-burner issue. In the past few months, I have seen yet another change. Some CEOs and top management groups now take the initiative. They call and ask us to show them how to shift gears from a responsive to a proactive approach to recruiting, developing, and retaining women.

I think this change is more probably a response to business needs—to concern for the quality of future profits and managerial talent—than to uneasiness about legal requirements, sympathy with the demands of women and minorities, or the desire to do what is right and fair. The nature of such business motivation varies. Some companies want to move women to higher positions as role models for those below them and as beacons for talented young recruits. Some want to achieve a favorable image with employees, customers, clients, and stockholders. These are all legitimate motives. But I think the companies that stand to gain most are motivated as well by a desire to capture competitive advantage in an era when talent and competence will be in increasingly short supply. These companies are now ready to stop being defensive about their experience with women and to ask incisive questions without preconceptions.

Even so, incredibly, I don't know of more than one or two companies that have looked into their own records to study the absolutely critical issue of maternity leave—how many women took it, when and whether they returned, and how this behavior correlated with their rank, tenure, age, and performance. The unique drawback to the employment of women is the physical reality of maternity and the particular socializing influence maternity has had. Yet to make women equal to men in the workplace we have chosen on the whole not to discuss this single most significant difference between them. Unless we do, we cannot evaluate the cost of recruiting, developing, and moving women up.

Now that interest is replacing indifference, there are four steps every company can take to examine its own experience with women:

1. Gather quantitative data on the company's experience with management-level women regarding turnover rates, occurrence of and return from maternity leave, and organizational level attained in relation to tenure and performance.
2. Correlate these data with factors such as age, marital status, and presence and age of children, and attempt to identify and analyze why women respond the way they do.
3. Gather qualitative data on the experience of women in your company and on how women are perceived by both sexes.
4. Conduct a cost-benefit analysis of the return on your investment in high-performing women. Factor in the cost to the company of

women's negative reactions to negative experience, as well as the probable cost of corrective measures and policies. If women's value to your company is greater than the cost to recruit, train, and develop them—and of course I believe it will be—then you will want to do everything you can to retain them.

We have come a tremendous distance since the days when the prevailing male wisdom saw women as lacking the kind of intelligence that would allow them to succeed in business. For decades, even women themselves have harbored an unspoken belief that they couldn't make it because they couldn't be just like men, and nothing else would do. But now that women have shown themselves the equal of men in every area of organizational activity, now that they have demonstrated that they can be stars in every field of endeavor, now we can all venture to examine the fact that women and men are different.

On balance, employing women is more costly than employing men. Women can acknowledge this fact today because they know that their value to employers exceeds the additional cost and because they know that changing attitudes can reduce the additional cost dramatically. Women in management are no longer an idiosyncrasy of the arts and education. They have always matched men in natural ability. Within a very few years, they will equal men in numbers as well in every area of economic activity.

The demographic motivation to recruit and develop women is compelling. But an older question remains: Is society better for the change? Women's exit from the home and entry into the work force has certainly created problems—an urgent need for good, affordable child care; troubling questions about the kind of parenting children need; the costs and difficulties of diversity in the workplace; the stress and fatigue of combining work and family responsibilities. Wouldn't we all be happier if we could turn back the clock to an age when men were in the workplace and women in the home, when male and female roles were clearly differentiated and complementary?

Nostalgia, anxiety, and discouragement will urge many to say yes, but my answer is emphatically no. Two fundamental benefits that were unattainable in the past are now within our reach. For the individual, freedom of choice—in this case the freedom to choose career, family, or a combination of the two. For the corporation, access to the most gifted individuals in the country. These benefits are neither self-indulgent nor insubstantial. Freedom of choice and self-realization are too deeply American to be cast aside for some wistful vision of the past. And access to our most talented human resources is not a luxury in this age of explosive international competition but rather the barest minimum that prudence and national self-preservation require.

—— DISCUSSION QUESTIONS

1. The reading quotes a CEO asking the author, "Why would any woman choose to be a chief financial officer rather than a full-time mother?" Do you think that this is a commonly asked question? If someone were to ask you the same question, how would you respond?
2. Do you think that special provisions ought to be made in order to keep working mothers in the work force? Why or why not?
3. Can you think of other groups of people who would also benefit from the types of considerations and policies that the author discusses?
4. Is it possible that the use of special policies within an organization might cause hostility among employees? Explain. How would you manage the situation if hostility *did* develop?

Business and the Facts of Family Life

36

FRAN SUSSNER RODGERS AND CHARLES RODGERS

The shift of women out of the home and into the workplace has not been matched by an adjustment in business policies and practices. Gradually, however, organizations are becoming more interested in work-and-family issues. This reading examines the reasons why companies must find ways to help employees balance their professional and personal responsibilities and reports on the progress some companies have made in addressing these concerns.

Business is a good thing. Family is also a good thing. These are simple, self-evident propositions.

Yet the awkward fact is that when we try to combine these two assertions in the new labor force, they stop being safe, compatible, and obvious and become difficult, even antagonistic. Sometimes the most complex and controversial challenges we face have commonsense truths at their roots.

Consider these variations on the same theme:

- Our economy needs the most skilled and productive work force it can possibly find in order to remain competitive.
- That same work force must reproduce itself and give adequate care to the children who are the work force of the future.
- People with children—women especially—often find themselves at a serious disadvantage in the workplace.
- Among Western democracies, the United States ranks number three in dependence on women in the work force, behind only Scandinavia and Canada.

In short, we value both business and family, and they are increasingly at loggerheads.

THE FAMILY AS A BUSINESS ISSUE

At one time, women provided the support system that enabled male breadwinners to be productive outside the home for at least 40 hours every week. That home-based support system began to recede a generation ago and is now more the exception than the rule. The labor force now includes more than 70% of all women with children between the ages of 6 and 17 and more than half the women with children less than 1 year old. This new reality has had a marked effect on what the family requires of each family member—and on what employers can expect from employees. It is not only a question of who is responsible for very young children. There is no longer anyone home to care for adolescents and the elderly. There is no one around to take in the car for repair or to let the plumber in. Working families are faced with daily dilemmas: Who will take care of a sick child? Who will go to the big soccer game? Who will attend the teacher conference?

Yet employees from families where all adults work are still coping with rules and conditions of work designed, as one observer put it, to the specifications of Ozzie and Harriet. These conditions include rigid adherence to a 40-hour workweek, a concept of career path inconsistent with the life cycle of a person with serious family responsibilities, notions of equity formed in a different era, and performance-evaluation systems that confuse effort with results by equating hours of work with productivity.

Despite the growing mismatch between the rules of the game and the needs of the players, few companies have made much effort to accommodate changing lifestyles. For that matter, how serious can the problem really be? After all, employees still get to work and do their jobs. Somehow the plumber manages to find the key. We know that children and the elderly are somewhere. Why start worrying now? Women's entry into the labor force has been increasing for 20 years, and the system still appears to function.

Nevertheless, we are seeing a rapidly growing corporate interest in work-and-family issues. There are four principal *business* reasons:

First, work-force demographics are changing. Most of the increase in the number of working women has coincided with the baby boom. Any associated business fallout—high turnover, lost productivity, absenteeism—occurred in the context of a large labor surplus. Most people were easily replaced, and there was plenty of talent willing to make the traditional sacrifices for success—such as travel, overtime work, and relocation. With the baby boom over and a baby bust upon us, there are now higher costs associated with discouraging entry into the labor force and frustrating talented people who are trying to act responsibly at home as well as at work. In some parts of the country, labor is already so scarce that companies are using progressive family policies as a means of competing for workers.

Second, employee perceptions are changing. Unless we rethink our traditional career paths, the raised aspirations of many women are now clearly on a collision course with their desire to be parents. Before the emergence of the women's movement in the 1960s, many suburban housewives thought their frustrations were uniquely their own. Similarly, for 20 years corporate women who failed to meet their own high expectations considered it a personal failing. But now the invisible barriers to female advancement are being named, and the media take employers to task for their inflexibility.

This shift in women's perceptions greatly changes the climate for employers. Women and men in two-career and single-parent families are much better able to identify policies that will let them act responsibly toward their families and still satisfy their professional ambitions. Companies that don't act as partners in this process may lose talent to companies that do rise to the challenge. No one knows how many women have left large companies because of cultural rigidity. It is even harder to guess at the numbers of talented women who have never even applied for jobs because they assume big companies will require family sacrifices they are unwilling to make.

And it's not just women. In two studies at Du Pont, we found that men's reports of certain family-related problems nearly doubled from 1985 to 1988. (Interestingly, on a few of these items, women's reported problems decreased proportionally, which suggests that one reason women experience such great difficulty with work-and-family issues is that men experience so little.)

In fact, men's desire for a more active role in parenting may be unacceptable to their peers. Numerous reports show that few men take advantage of the formal parental leave available to them in many companies. Yet a recent study shows that many men do indeed take time off from work after the birth of a child, but that they do so by piecing together other forms of leave—vacation, personal leave, sick leave—that they see as more acceptable.[1]

A third reason why more companies are addressing work-and-family issues is increasing evidence that inflexibility has an adverse effect on productivity. In a study at Merck in 1984, employees who perceived their supervisors as unsupportive on family issues reported higher levels of stress, greater absenteeism, and lower job satisfaction.[2] Other studies show that supportive companies attract new employees more easily, get them back on the job more quickly after maternity leave, and benefit generally from higher work-force morale.[3]

Fourth, concern about America's children is growing fast. Childhood poverty is up, single-parent families are on the increase, SAT scores are falling, and childhood literacy, obesity, and suicide rates are all moving in the wrong direction.

So far, the business community has expressed its concern primarily through direct efforts to improve schools. Yet in our studies, one-third to one-half of parents say they do not have the workplace flexibility to attend teacher conferences and important school events. It is certainly possible that adapting work rules to allow this parent-school connection—and trying to

---

1. Joseph Pleck, "Family-Supportive Employer Policies and Men's Participation," Wheaton College (1989), unpublished paper.

2. From research conducted by Ellen Galinsky at Merck and Company, Rahway, New Jersey, 1983, 1984, and 1986.

3. Terry Bond, *Employer Supports for Child Care*, report for the National Council of Jewish Women, Center for the Child, New York (August 1988).

influence schools to schedule events with working parents in mind—might have as great a positive effect on education as some direct interventions.

For companies that want to use and fully develop the talents of working parents and others looking for flexibility, the agenda is well defined. There are three broad areas that require attention:

- Dependent care, including infants, children, adolescents, and the elderly.
- Greater flexibility in the organization, hours, and location of work, and creation of career paths that allow for family responsibility as well as professional ambition.
- Validation of family issues as an organizational concern by means of company statements and manager training.

Few companies are active in all three areas. Many are active in none. The costs and difficulties are, after all, considerable, and the burden of change does not fall only on employers. There is plenty for government to do. Individual employees too will have to take on new responsibilities. Corporate dependent-care programs often mean purchasing benefits or programs from outside providers and may entail substantial community involvement. Workplace flexibility demands reexamination of work assumptions by employees as well as employers and often meets with line resistance. A corporate commitment to family takes time to work its way down to the front-line supervisory levels where most of the work force will feel its effects.

DEPENDENT CARE

Dependent care is a business issue for the obvious reason that employees cannot come to work unless their dependents are cared for. Study after study shows that most working parents have trouble arranging child care, and that those with the most difficulty also experience the most frequent work disruptions and the greatest absenteeism. Moreover, the lack of child care is still a major barrier to the entry of women into the labor force.

Child-care needs vary greatly in any employee population, and most companies have a limited capacity to address them. But, depending on the company's location, financial resources, the age of its work force, and the competitiveness of its labor market, a corporate child-care program might include some or all of the following:

- Help in finding existing child care and efforts to increase the supply of care in the community, including care for sick children.
- Financial assistance for child care, especially for entry-level and lower-level employees.
- Involvement with schools, Ys, and other community organizations to promote programs for school-age children whose parents work.

- Support for child-care centers in locations convenient to company employees.
- Efforts to move government policies—local and federal—toward greater investment in children.

Existing child care is often hard to find because so much of the country's care is provided by the woman down the street, who does not advertise and is not usually listed in the yellow pages or anywhere else. Even where lists do exist—as the result, say, of state licensing requirements—they are often out-of-date. (Turnover in family day care, as this form of child care is called, is estimated at 50% per year.) And lists don't give vacancy information, so parents can spend days making unsuccessful phone calls. Sometimes existing care is invisible because it operates in violation of zoning rules or outside of onerous or inefficient regulatory systems.

In other places—suburban neighborhoods where many women work outside the home or where family income is so high that few need the extra money—there is virtually no child care. Often, too, land prices make centers unaffordable. Infant care is especially scarce because it requires such a high ratio of adults to children. Care for children before and after school and during the many weeks when school is out is in short supply just about everywhere, as is care for "off hour" workers such as shift workers, police officers, and hospital employees.

In addition to the difficulty of finding child care, quality and afford-ability are always big questions. Cost depends greatly on local standards. In Massachusetts, for example, infant care in centers runs from $150 to more than $200 per week per child due to a combination of high labor costs and strict state licensing standards. Even the highest standards, however, still mean that an infant-care staff member has more to do all day—and more responsibility—than a new parent caring for triplets. In states with lower standards, one staff member may care for as many as eight infants at a time. Up to now, child care in many places has been made affordable by paying very low wages—the national average for child-care staff is $5.35 an hour—and by reducing the standards of quality and safety below what common sense would dictate.[4]

Given all these problems, is it any wonder the companies that want to help feel stymied? Although few companies provide significant child-care support today, a very large number are exploring the possibility. We think that number will increase geometrically as the competition for labor grows and more members of the labor force need such support.

One increasingly popular way for companies to address these issues is through resource and referral services. Typically, such services do three things: they help employees find child care suited to their circumstances; they make an

---

4. Marcy Whitebook, Carollee Howes, and Deborah Phillips, "Who Cares: Child Care Teachers and the Quality of Care in America," National Child Care Staffing Study, Child Care Employee Project, Oakland, California (1989).

effort to promote more care of all types in the communities where employees live; and they try to remove regulatory and zoning barriers to care facilities. Resource and referral services (R&Rs) meet standards of equity by assisting parents regardless of their incomes and their children's ages. And R&Rs work as well for a few workers as for thousands. When the service is delivered through a network of community-based R&Rs, moreover, corporate involvement also can strengthen the community at large.

Although R&R programs can be very helpful, they have limitations. By themselves, they have little effect on affordability, for example, and only an indirect effect on quality, primarily through consumer education and provider training. Also, R&Rs cannot dig up a supply of care where market conditions are highly unfavorable.

A small but growing number of companies provide, subsidize, or contract with outside providers to operate on-site or near-site centers that are available to employees at fees covering at least most of the cost. A North Carolina software company, SAS Institute Inc., provides child care at an on-site center at no cost to employees. The company reports that its turnover rates are less than half the industry average and feels the center's extra expense is justified because it decreases the extremely high cost of training new workers.[5]

Companies that get involved with child-care centers, however, find themselves making difficult trade-offs as a result of the high cost of good care. Many companies won't associate themselves even indirectly with any child care that doesn't meet the highest standards, which means that without a subsidy, only higher-income employees can afford the service. But if a company does subsidize child care, it must justify giving this considerable benefit to one group of parents while other parents, who buy child care in some other place or way, get none. One way of avoiding this dilemma is to give child-care subsidies to all lower-income employees as an extension of the R&R service, the approach recently announced by NCNB, the banking corporation.

Companies sometimes capitalize centers by donating space or land along with renovation costs or by providing an initial subsidy until the centers are self-supporting. In this way, Du Pont helped a number of community not-for-profit organizations establish and expand existing child-care centers in Delaware. Of course, costs can vary hugely. If a building is already available, renovation and startup costs could be as low as $100,000. In most cases, the bill will run from several hundred thousand to several million dollars.

Businesses also are working more closely with schools to encourage before-school, after-school, and vacation care programs. Such a partnership has been established between the American Bankers Insurance Group and the Dade

---

5. "On-site Child Care Results in Low Turnover at Computer Firm," *National Report on Work and Family,* vol. 2, no. 13 (Washington, D.C.: Buraff Publications, June 9, 1989): 3.

County, Florida, school system. The school system actually operates a kindergarten and a first- and second-grade school in a building built by the insurance company. In Charlotte, North Carolina, the 19 largest employers have joined forces with the public sector to expand and improve the quality of care.

In any case, employee interest in child care is great, and employees often fix on the issue of on-site care as a solution to the work-and-family conflicts they experience. But helping employees with child care, given the enormity of the problem in the society at large, is a complicated question. More and more companies are taking the kinds of steps described here, but as the pressure grows, business as a whole is likely to focus more attention on public policy.

Of course, dependent care is not just a question of care for children. Studies at Travelers Insurance Company and at IBM show that 20% to 30% of employees have some responsibility for the care of an adult dependent. Traditionally, the wife stayed home and cared for the elderly parents of both spouses, but as women entered the work force, this support system began to disappear. Because the most recent growth in the female work force involves comparatively younger women whose parents are not yet old enough to require daily assistance, the workplace has probably not yet felt the full effects of elder-care problems.

As in the case of child care, studies show that productivity suffers when people try to balance work and the care of parents. Some people quit their jobs entirely. The most immediate need is for information about the needs and problems of the aging and about available resources. Most young people know nothing at all about government programs like Medicare and Medicaid. More often than not, children know very little about their own parents' financial situations and need help simply to open communication.

Unlike child care, elder care is often complicated by distance. In our experience with some 12,000 employees with elderly dependents, more than half lived more than 100 miles from the person they were concerned about. Crises are common. The elderly suffer unexpected hospitalizations, for example, and then come out of the hospital too weak to care for themselves. A service that can help with referrals and arrangements in another city can spare employees time, expense, and anguish. Also, people often need to compare resources in several states where different siblings live in order to make decisions about such things as where parents should live when their health begins to deteriorate.

CONDITIONS OF WORK

A study at two high-tech companies in New England showed that the average working mother logs in a total workweek of 84 hours between her home and her job, compared with 72 hours for male parents and about 50 hours for married men and women with no children. In other words, employed parents—

women in particular—work the equivalent of two full-time jobs.[6] No wonder they've started looking for flexible schedules, part-time employment, and career-path alternatives that allow more than one model of success. For that matter, is it even reasonable to expect people who work two jobs to behave and progress along exactly the same lines as those with no primary outside responsibilities?

Until now, most companies have looked at job flexibility on a case-by-case basis and have offered it sparingly to valued employees as a favor. But increasing competition for the best employees will make such flexibility commonplace. A smaller labor supply means that workers will no longer have to take jobs in the forms that have always been offered. Companies will have to market their own employment practices and adapt their jobs to the demands of the work force.

We all know that the way we did things in the past no longer works for many employees. Our research shows that up to 35% of working men and women with young children have told their bosses they will not take jobs involving shift work, relocation, extensive travel, intense pressure, or lots of overtime. Some parents are turning down promotions that they believe might put a strain on family life. Women report more trade-offs than men, but even the male numbers are significant and appear to be increasing. In our study, nearly 25% of men with young children had told their bosses they would not relocate.

Interestingly enough, few employees seem angry about such trade-offs. They value the rewards of family life, and by and large, they don't seem to expect parity with those willing to sacrifice their family lives for their careers. Nevertheless, they are bothered by what they see as unnecessary barriers to success. Most believe they could make greater contributions and go farther in their own careers—despite family obligations—if it weren't for rigid scheduling, open-ended expectations, and outmoded career definitions. They long for alternative scenarios that would allow them more freedom to determine the conditions of their work and the criteria for judging their contributions.

The question is whether a willingness to sacrifice family life is an appropriate screen for picking candidates for promotions. It would be wrong to suppose that these employees are any less talented or less ambitious than those who don't make the family trade-off. One study we conducted at NCNB showed no evidence of any long-term difference in ambition between people with and without child-care responsibilities. Because fewer and fewer people in our diverse labor force are willing to pay the price for traditional success, to insist on it is only to narrow the funnel of opportunity and, eventually, to lower the quality of the talent pool from which we draw our leaders.

---

6. Dianne Burden and Bradley Googins, *Boston University Balancing Job and Homelife Study* (Boston: Boston University School of Social Work, 1986).

FLEXIBLE SCHEDULES

In addition to time away from work to care for newborn or newly adopted children, employees with dependent-care responsibilities have two different needs for flexibility. One is the need for working hours that accommodate their children's normal schedules and their predictable special requirements such as doctor's appointments, school conferences, and soccer championships. The other is the need to deal with the emergencies and unanticipated events that are part and parcel of family life—sudden illness, an early school closing due to snow, a breakdown in child-care arrangements.

The most common response to both needs has been flextime. Flextime can be narrowly designed to permit permanent alterations of a basically rigid work schedule by, say, half an hour or an hour, or it can be more broadly defined to allow freewheeling variations from one workday to the next.

Pioneered in this country by Hewlett-Packard, flextime is now used by about 12% of all U.S. workers, while half the country's large employers offer some kind of flextime arrangement. Its effects on lateness, absenteeism, and employee morale have been highly positive.[7] The effects on the family are not as easily measured, but most employees say they find it helpful, and the more scheduling latitude it offers, the more helpful they seem to find it.

A number of companies are considering ways of further expanding the notion of flextime. One alternative, called *weekly balancing,* lets employees set their own hours day-to-day as long as the weekly total stays constant. In Europe, some companies offer monthly and yearly balancing. Clearly, this is most difficult to do in situations where production processes require a predictable level of staffing.

In November 1988, Eastman Kodak announced a new work-schedule program that permits four kinds of alternative work arrangements:

1. Permanent changes in regular, scheduled hours.
2. Supervisory flexibility in adjusting daily schedules to accommodate family needs.
3. Temporary and permanent part-time schedules at all levels.
4. Job sharing.

Aetna Life and Casualty also recently launched an internal marketing effort and training program to help its supervisors adapt to, plan for, and implement unconventional work schedules.

Employees also must assume new roles. In the job-sharing program at Rolscreen Company, for example, employees are responsible for locating compatible partners for a shared job and for ensuring that the arrangement

---

7. Kathleen Christensen, *A Look at Flexible Staffing and Scheduling in U.S. Corporations* (New York: Conference Board, 1989); and Jon L. Pierce et al., *Alternative Work Schedules* (Newton, Mass.: Allyn and Bacon, 1988).

works and that business needs are met.[8] Also, employees are often expected to make themselves available when business emergencies arise. In the best flexible arrangements, employers and employees work as partners.

PART-TIME EMPLOYMENT

Studies show that a third to half of women with young children want to work less than full time for at least a while, despite the loss of pay and other benefits. Yet we have found in our work with dozens of companies that managers at all levels show firm resistance to part-time work. They seem to regard the 40-hour week as sacred and cannot imagine that anyone working fewer hours could be doing anything useful. Even in companies that accept the need for part-time work, we see managers who refuse to believe it will work in their own departments. Indeed, even the term "part-time" seems to have a negative connotation.

Research on part-time productivity is sometimes hard to interpret, but the studies we've seen indicate that the productivity of part-time workers is, in certain cases, better than their full-time counterparts and, in all cases, no worse. One study comparing part-time and full-time social workers found that, hour for hour, the part-time employees carried greater caseloads and serviced them with more attention.[9]

Part-time is not necessarily the same as half-time, as many managers assume. Many parents want 4-day or 30-hour workweeks. Many other assumptions about less than full-time employment are also unwarranted. For example, managers often insist that customers will not work with part-time employees, but few have asked their customers if this is true.

Another axiom is that supervisory and managerial personnel must always be full-time, because it is a manager's role to "be there" for subordinates. This article of faith ignores the fact that managers travel, attend meetings, close their doors, and are otherwise unavailable for a good part of every week.

CAREER-PATH ALTERNATIVES

It takes a lot of ingenuity and cultural adaptability to devise meaningful part-time work opportunities and to give employees individual control of their working hours. But an even greater challenge is to find ways of fitting these flexible arrangements into long-term career paths. If the price of

---

8. *Work and Family: A Changing Dynamic* (Washington, D.C.: Bureau of National Affairs Special Report, 1986): 78–80.

9. *Part-Time Social Workers in Public Welfare* (New York: Catalyst, 1971), cited in *Alternative Work Schedules*, p. 81.

family responsibility is a label that reads "Not Serious About Career," frustrations will grow. But if adaptability and labor-market competitiveness are the goals, then the usual definition of fast-track career progression needs modification.

The first step, perhaps, is to find ways of acquiring broad business experience that are less disruptive to the family. For example, Mobil Oil has gradually concentrated a wide range of facilities at hub locations, partly in order to allow its employees a greater variety of work experience without relocation.

Another essential step is to reduce the tendency to judge productivity by time spent at work. Nothing is more frustrating to parents than working intensely all day in order to pick up a child on time, only to be judged inferior to a coworker who has to stay late to produce as much. For many hardworking people, hours certainly do translate into increased productivity. Not for all. And dismissing those who spend fewer hours at the workplace as lacking dedication ignores the fact that virtually all employees go through periods when their working hours and efficiency rise or fall, whether the cause is family, health, or fluctuating motivation.

▬▬ CORPORATE MISSION

Fertility in the United States is below replacement levels. Moreover, the higher a woman's education level, the more likely she is to be employed and the less likely to have children. The choice to have a family is complex, yet one study shows that two-thirds of women under 40 who have reached the upper echelons in our largest companies and institutions are childless, while virtually all men in leadership positions are fathers.[10] If we fail to alter the messages and opportunities we offer young men and women and if they learn to see a demanding work life as incompatible with a satisfying family life, we could create an economy in which more and more leaders have traded family for career success.

There are four steps a company needs to take in order to create an environment where people with dependents can do their best work without sacrificing their families' welfare:

- Develop a corporate policy that it communicates to all its employees;
- Train and encourage supervisors to be adaptable and responsible;
- Give supervisors tools and programs to work with;
- Hold all managers accountable for the flexibility and responsiveness of their departments.

---

10. *The Corporate Woman Officer* (Chicago, Ill.: Heidrick and Struggles, Inc., 1986); *Korn/Ferry International's Executive Profile: Corporate Leaders in the Eighties* (New York: Korn/Ferry International, 1986).

The key people in all this are first-line managers and supervisors. All the policies and programs in the world don't mean much to an employee who has to deal with an unsupportive boss, and the boss is often unsupportive because of mixed signals from above.

We have seen companies where the CEO went on record in support of family flexibility but where supervisors were never evaluated in any way for their sensitivity to family issues. In one company, managers were encouraged to provide part-time work opportunities, yet head-count restrictions reckoned all employees as full-time. In another, maternity leave was counted against individual managers when measuring absenteeism, a key element in their performance appraisals. As a general rule, strict absenteeism systems designed to discourage malingerers often inadvertently punish the parents of young children. Yet such systems coexist with corporate admonitions to be flexible. Where messages are mixed and performance measurement has not changed since the days of the "give them an inch, they'll take a mile" personnel policy, it is hardly surprising that supervisors and managers greet lofty family-oriented policy statements with some cynicism.

Training is critical. IBM, Johnson & Johnson, Merck, and Warner-Lambert have all established training programs to teach managers to be more sensitive to work-and-family issues. The training lays out the business case for flexibility, reviews corporate programs and policies, and presents case studies that underline the fact that there are often no right answers or rule books to use as guides in the complicated circumstances of real life.

Perhaps the thorniest issue facing businesses and managers is that of equity. Most managers have been trained to treat employees identically and not to adjudicate the comparative merits of different requests for flexibility. But what equity often means in practice is treating everyone as though they had wives at home. On the other hand, it is difficult to set up guidelines for personalized responses, since equity is a touchstone of labor relations and human resource management. Judging requests individually, on the basis of business and personal need, is not likely to lead to identical outcomes.

Seniority systems also need rethinking. Working second or third shift is often the only entry to a well-paying job for nonprofessional employees, but for a parent with a school-age child, this can mean not seeing the child at all from weekend to weekend. Rotating shifts wreak havoc with child-care arrangements and children's schedules. Practices that worked fine when the labor force consisted mostly of men with wives at home now have unintended consequences.

Finally, the message top management sends to all employees is terribly important. In focus groups at various large companies, we hear over and over again a sense that companies pay lip service to the value of family and community but that day-to-day practice is another story altogether. We hear what we can only describe as a yearning for some tangible acknowledgment from top management that family issues are real, complex, and important.

EXHIBIT
Companies That Lead the Way

For years, IBM has steadily increased its efforts to adapt to family needs. It pioneered child-care and elder-care assistance programs. A national resource and referral service network originally put together for IBM in 1984 now serves about 900,000 employees of more than 35 national companies. In 1988, IBM expanded its flextime program to allow employees to adjust their workdays by as much as two hours in either direction and adopted an extended leave-of-absence policy permitting up to a three-year break from full-time employment with part-time work in the second and third years. The company has also been experimenting with work-at-home programs. And earlier this year, it introduced family-issues sensitivity training for more than 25,000 managers and supervisors.

Johnson & Johnson recently announced an extremely broad work-and-family initiative that includes support for elder care and child care, greater worktime flexibility, management training, and a change in its corporate credo.

AT&T recently negotiated a contract with two of its unions that established a dependent-care referral service and provides for leaves of up to one year, with guaranteed reinstatement, for new parents and for workers with seriously ill dependents.

At NCNB, a program called Select Time allows employees at all levels in the company, including managers, to reduce their time and job commitments for dependent-care purposes without cutting off current and future advancement opportunities.

Apple Computer operates its own employee-staffed child-care center and gives "baby bonuses" of $500 to new parents. Du Pont has helped to establish child-care centers in Delaware with contributions of money and space. Eastman Kodak has adopted new rules permitting part-time work, job sharing, and informal situational flextime.

For reasons partly societal and partly strategic, these and scores of other businesses are building work environments that let people give their best to their jobs without giving up the pleasures and responsibilities of family life.

Johnson & Johnson, which sees its 40-year-old corporate credo as central to its culture, recently added the statement, "We must be mindful of ways to help our employees fulfill their family obligations." Du Pont has developed a mission statement that commits it, in part, to "making changes in the workplace and fostering changes in the community that are sensitive to the changing family unit and the increasingly diverse work force." (See the *Exhibit*.)

Throughout Europe, governments have required companies to treat the parenting of babies as a special circumstance of employment and have invested heavily in programs to support the children of working parents. In this country, recent surveys indicate almost universal popular support for parental leave. But our instincts oppose government intervention into internal business practices. We leave decisions about flexibility and the organization of work to individual companies, which means that the decisions of first-line managers in large part create our national family policy.

In this, the United States is unique. But then we are also unique in other ways, including the depth of our commitment to business, to fairness, to equal opportunity, to common sense. Many of our young women now strive to become CEOs. No one intended that the price for business success should be indifference to family or that the price of having a family should be to abandon professional ambition.

DISCUSSION QUESTIONS

1. In your opinion, can an individual be both an involved family member and an active, committed participant in the work force? Why or why not?

2. Imagine that your company is moving to another state and your supervisor tells you that you must relocate in order to keep your job. Assume also that this new situation conflicts with the needs of your family. What would you decide to do? What factors would influence your decision?

3. How have the organizations you have worked for accommodated the needs of employees who have dependents? Could these organizations have done more to accommodate the needs of families? Should they do more?

4. The authors state that "Women and men in two-career and single-parent families are much better able to identify policies that will let them act responsibly toward their families and still satisfy their professional ambitions." They stress that employees and management must work together to create flexible policies. Do you find leaders in the organizations you have worked for open to suggestions from employees? Has management been open to this type of collaboration with employees? How would you foster this approach as a senior manager in a company?

Beyond Testing: Coping with Drugs at Work

37

JAMES T. WRICH

Drug abuse costs American business billions of dollars a year in lost productivity. Many companies have adopted drug-testing initiatives as a way of identifying drug abusers for treatment or disciplinary action. But these initiatives often create more problems than they solve.

This reading explores a more effective method for dealing with chemical dependency—employee assistance programs. It describes their history, how they work, and what they can accomplish. Acknowledging that "a drug-free workplace in a drug-filled society is an illusion," the author offers hope rather than a panacea.

It is hard to overestimate the impact of substance abuse on the workplace. Even the most conservative estimates are staggering. The National Institute on Drug Abuse (NIDA) and the National Institute on Alcohol Abuse and Alcoholism (NIAAA) estimate that at least 10% of the work force is afflicted with alcoholism or drug addiction. Another 10% to 15% is affected by the substance abuse of an immediate family member. Still more bear the scars of having grown up with an addicted or alcoholic parent.

All in all, even after eliminating duplicates, at least 25% of any given work force suffers from substance abuse—their own or someone else's. As a chronic alcoholic from the ages of 15 to 27, I have personal experience with the problem and know the devastation it can cause. Managers are right to be apprehensive about drugs in the workplace, but a punitive response is inappropriate. Drug testing may be necessary where compelling issues of safety or national security are involved, but drug testing alone will not make the problem go away. Inexplicably, our efforts to deal with drug abuse ignore nearly 50 years of experience in the workplace treatment of alcoholism. We have had Broadbrush employee assistance programs for more than 15 years, and they continue to be used with great effectiveness to reduce absenteeism, promote recovery, minimize relapse, cut treatment costs, and improve productivity among drug abusers as well as alcoholics.

━━━ ASSESSING THE PROBLEM

For practical purposes, alcoholics and addicts are not two groups of people but one. Alcoholics cannot safely use drugs, and drug addicts cannot safely use alcohol. Moreover, treatment centers have reported for at least 10 years that a majority of patients under the age of 40 are dually addicted to alcohol and at least one other drug. Because it is legal, we seem to find alcohol less frightening, but the effects of alcoholism are at least as devastating.

A recent estimate by the Alcohol, Drug Abuse and Mental Health Administration indicates that alcohol and drug abusers together cost the country more than $140 billion annually, including $100 billion in lost productivity. And these are only the direct costs. If we include family members in our calculation, the total will rise still higher.

An NIDA survey indicates that 19% of Americans over the age of 12 have used illicit drugs during the past year. Among 18- to 25-year-olds—the population now entering the work force—65% have used illicit drugs, 44% in the past year.

Given these figures, it is hardly surprising that many companies have opted for hardball methods, heeding the law and conventional notions of human rights only when faced with unequivocal prohibitions. In general, managers are not only extremely concerned about drugs, they are also convinced that fast action can solve the problem quickly and that they have the muscle and the means to do it. They have been encouraged by the attorney general's drug-testing initiative and by testimony from the commissioner of baseball claiming that the drug problem in the major leagues has been resolved. First Lady Nancy Reagan's "Just Say No!" slogan gave the effort an appealing simplicity that encouraged everyone to overlook the complexities involved. In essence, many *managers* just said "No!" They resolved to get drug abusers out of the workplace one way or another, and drug-testing initiatives (DTIs) became their weapon of choice (see *Exhibit 1*).

Drug-testing initiatives usually employ the following sequence of elements. The company does the following:

1. Prepares a written policy and procedure statement;
2. Trains supervisors to recognize the signs and symptoms that would justify reasonable suspicion of drug use;
3. Instructs supervisors to refer employees for testing if these criteria are met;
4. Obtains and tests a sample of the employee's urine;
5. Confirms all positive test results with a second, more accurate test;
6. Gives those who are confirmed positive a second time the choice between treatment and disciplinary action up to and including termination;
7. Requires retesting without notice for those who complete treatment;
8. Establishes serious disciplinary measures, often termination, for those who test positive after undergoing treatment.

More than 35% of the country's largest companies have DTIs, and the number is growing fast. This overwhelming response may be seen as a clear indication that business is ready to tackle the problem. Nevertheless, I believe these programs are based on a number of questionable assumptions, many of which were proven false by programs instituted as long ago as the 1940s to deal with alcoholism. Drug-testing initiatives make the following assumptions.

- We can adequately train supervisors to recognize the telltale signs and symptoms of substance abuse.
- Supervisors will find reasonable suspicion an adequate basis for referral.
- Supervisors can be motivated to make such referrals.
- Testing will be accurate.
- The positive tests will be accurately interpreted.
- The imposition of treatment or disciplinary action will be appropriate, and employees will respond appropriately to whichever course is pursued.

——— OUR EXPERIENCE WITH ALCOHOLISM

Substance abuse is nothing new. Heroin was once considered a wonder drug to cure morphine addiction in soldiers returning from Civil War hospitals.

EXHIBIT 1
When DTIs Are Called For

The value of drug testing is so questionable and the drawbacks so great that no organization should even consider a DTI without compelling safety or national security reasons. An airline, for example, might decide to saddle itself with a DTI to increase the safety of its passengers, and a defense contractor might consider weapons secrets worth the small extra protection that an expensive and troublesome DTI could provide. Even in such cases, however, careful planning and administration are essential if the DTI is to solve more problems than it creates.

To set up a workable drug-testing program, an organization should

1. Have an effective employee assistance program already in place.

2. Familiarize itself with the technical and legal limitations of a DTI and consider the possible negative effect on employee relations.

3. Place control and direction of the DTI in the hands of its human resource department, with input from its legal department—not the other way around.

4. Convince supervisors and employees of the need for drug testing and give them reason to trust and support the program.

5. Require drug testing of everyone in the organization from the CEO on down.

6. Establish criteria in advance for maintaining confidentiality and evaluating effectiveness.

Cocaine was first used in the United States in the 1880s—not the 1980s—and was outlawed in 1914, whereupon amphetamines more or less took its place until recently.

Alcohol, our national legal drug of choice, has been with us practically forever and, with 11 million alcoholics and another 7 million alcohol abusers, is by far our most serious chemical dependency. Employers who recognized the problems that alcohol creates in the workplace have tried a number of remedies over the past 45 years. Employee assistance programs have been the most effective.

Until the 1970s, the great majority of companies addressed employee alcoholism with an informal policy of concealment and denial. When the alcoholic employee's condition became so severe as to be obvious to everyone, he or she was fired or retired or died. Some companies have tried to weed out alcoholics before they reached that stage, but managerial naivete and a lack of supervisory cooperation have usually thwarted such efforts.

The problem has always been twofold: how to identify afflicted employees and what to do with them. The success of identification programs depended greatly on what the work force perceived to be the consequences to the employee. Progressive companies such as Eastman Kodak and the Northern Pacific Railroad (now part of the Burlington Northern) launched formal efforts decades ago to help alcoholics. Program staff usually consisted of a recovering alcoholic and sometimes a sympathetic company doctor or nurse who encouraged the employee to attend meetings of Alcoholics Anonymous.

These early efforts greatly helped those few alcoholics who were referred, but the vast majority went unidentified and untreated. Naturally, employees were concerned about confidentiality, job security, the possible stigma, and the quality of case handling.

Experience brought other problems to light through the 1940s and 1950s. Training was difficult to deliver, and its impact was short-lived. In the course of their regular work, supervisors had scant opportunity to practice what little they had learned. The training taught them to look for bloodshot eyes, slurred speech, and the smell of alcohol on the breath, but supervisors were neither comfortable nor proficient as amateur sleuths and pseudo-diagnosticians. Much of the current DTI training to help supervisors establish "reasonable suspicion" resembles those early efforts to cope with alcoholism.

In those early programs, the training was seldom offered to managers above the supervisory level, and instructional anecdotes focused almost exclusively on nonmanagement employees, which implied that no one above that level had a problem. Addicted supervisors rarely saw the problem anywhere. Supervisors with a strong bias against alcohol tended to see it everywhere.

All the while, the alcoholic senior manager remained completely hidden. These inconsistencies did not go unnoticed by employees and unions. They are also analogous to situations found in many of today's DTIs. It is rare for company officers to be tested, even though the problem is certainly present at that level.

Finally, there was the dimension of the disease that still amazes experts—the alcoholic's profound capacity for denial and deception. By the time addicted people were confronted, they had often spent years developing their alibi systems and their unique capacity to manipulate. Matching an alcoholic against a supervisor with one or two hours of training in late-stage symptoms was usually no contest. Moreover, when alcoholic employees learned what supervisors were looking for, they stopped displaying those symptoms, at least until the very latest stages when they completely lost control. When today's addicted employees learn their company's criteria for "reasonable suspicion," they too will work hard to avoid such behavior. Today's addicts are at least as cunning as yesterday's.

In the 1960s, programs shifted their focus from symptoms to job performance. Because supervisors were so often outmaneuvered, the experts decided to take the game out of the alcoholic's ballpark and put it into the supervisor's. Job performance became the principal criterion for referral. Supervisors were told to stop diagnosing and, moreover, not even to discuss alcohol. Of course if they thought an employee had a drinking problem, they were to refer him or her to the company program.

This ambiguous message confused everyone. Obviously, if supervisors did not make some kind of diagnosis, however amateurish, they certainly were not going to refer the employee to an alcoholism program.

On the positive side, these programs were sincere efforts at rehabilitation, recovery rates were encouraging, and the testimonials of participants were glowing. Even so, feelings of suspicion ran high among employees. Confidentiality was so often compromised that laws were later written to safeguard it. Supervisors disliked the confrontational role, and they feared sending someone to the program who wasn't really an alcoholic, thus hurting the employee and damaging their own credibility. A 1976 review showed that only one-third of 1% of all employees made use of such programs each year. In addition, those who used the programs tended to be in late stages of the disease and had already experienced great personal suffering and productivity loss. Because of the denial inherent in the disease, and because coercion as a method of referral so closely resembled punitive action, there seemed little hope of seeing significant numbers of self-referrals without a change in approach.

Ironically, had there then been a test to prove conclusively that an employee had been drinking on the job, it is doubtful that it would have improved overall program effectiveness. Then, as now, you can't test what you can't refer; you can't refer what you can't find; you can't find what you're not trained to find; and training alone will not inspire those with a vested interest in the status quo. Experience indicates that a disproportionate number of chemically dependent employees end up working for others who are addicts, substance abusers, or the untreated adult children of alcoholics. Such individuals—perhaps as many as a third of all supervisors—are unlikely to do well as police officers.

───── BROADBRUSH EMPLOYEE ASSISTANCE PROGRAMS

In 1972, NIAAA launched a new workplace alcoholism program called the Broadbrush approach and sent 100 program consultants, of whom I was one, into the field to sell the idea to management and labor.

The Broadbrush approach—what we now call employee assistance programs or EAPs—took into account the limitations of earlier efforts as well as the nature of addiction. Knowing that alcoholic denial and manipulation were more than the typical supervisor could learn to cope with, it likewise stressed that supervisors were not to diagnose.

But for the first time, it also provided a structure for implementation. Rather than focus only on alcoholism, the program was broadened to cover a wide range of personal problems including emotional, marital, family, and financial difficulties, and of course, drug abuse. The alcoholic label was no longer automatically attached to anyone using the program. The new approach not only reduced the stigma but also encouraged supervisors to refer a troubled employee without first trying to figure out the nature of the problem. Previously, when alcoholic employees argued that the problem wasn't really drinking but a bad marriage, say, or indebtedness, they generally got off the hook. Now there was a program that dealt with these other, "respectable" issues as well. EAP staff assessed the nature and severity of problems, referred employees to appropriate care in the community, and followed up (see *Exhibit 2*).

EXHIBIT 2
Developing an Effective EAP

Building an effective EAP requires time, insight, and a lot of work. We cannot simply slap together a few outmoded ideas, dress them up with word processors, add a testing gimmick, and peddle them as a package.

For the most part, an EAP should be custom designed for its specific workplace. To be effective, it should see and refer for drug-abuse treatment at least 1% of the work force each year. To do this, the program must be properly staffed. Generally this means one full-time equivalent assessment and referral (A&R) resource professional for every 3,500 to 4,200 employees, plus adequate clerical support.

The A&R staff must have considerable training and experience working with chemically dependent people. Whatever their academic degrees, professionals without vast experience working with alcoholics and drug addicts can do as much harm as good. Resourceful addicts and alcoholics often can deceive them, which leads to inappropriate care and drives up employee health-care costs without solving the problem.

A sufficient budget, an effective training and communications program, a good management information system, a valid outcome evaluation program, a credible benefit-to-cost analysis, an appropriately designed benefits package, ongoing education for EAP staff, and lots of attention and support from senior management are among the other key ingredients for a successful EAP.

By the late 1970s, employees could get help even without a documented job performance problem. In addition, EAP professionals had developed new outreach and intervention techniques to generate referrals by peers and to identify substance abusers at an earlier stage of their dependency. For the first time, self-referrals began to outnumber referrals from supervisors.

The results were gratifying. Employees were getting experienced, professional help, and getting it sooner, which reduced both personal suffering and productivity losses. Earlier treatment also meant lower costs, because someone in the later stages of any problem is less likely to respond to outpatient care. Both diagnosis and treatment were confidential. Managers liked the idea of attacking a wider range of problems, because their goal was to reduce losses in productivity regardless of their cause. Many managers had wanted to address alcoholism more aggressively for years but had hesitated because previous approaches so often looked like witch-hunts.

Most important, the programs were reaching nearly three times as many alcoholics as before. Burlington Northern changed from a straight alcoholism program to the Broadbrush approach and achieved utilization rates of more than 1% for alcohol and 2% to 3% for other problems. This meant that the time required to reach a number of alcoholics equivalent to the population at risk had been reduced to as little as seven years in some programs. We thought we had discovered pure gold.

The new approach had its detractors, of course. Some alcoholism professionals feared that alcoholism would get lost in the shuffle if it weren't the sole focus of the program. Some managers disdained rehabilitation as an organized form of coddling undesirables. Some unions thought that EAPs infringed on their turf. But EAPs worked, and by 1979, more than half of the country's largest companies had EAPs in one form or another, and about 80% of new programs were some variation of the Broadbrush approach.

My own experience is representative. From 1978 to 1984, I was director of the EAP at United Airlines. Of the first 5,100 employees using the program, 65% came in on their own or on the encouragement of their family, friends, or unions. About 2,000 of these were in trouble with alcohol or drugs, often both. Of the 35% referred by management, less than half had developed job-performance problems. Our evaluation showed the following:

- Absenteeism among program participants, measured from one year before entering the program to one year after, went down 74% in Chicago and 80% in San Francisco, to cite two cities.
- Recovery rates the first time through the program were 74% for ground employees, 82% for flight attendants, and 92% for pilots and copilots.
- Recovery rates for those who relapsed and reentered the program were about 40%.
- The benefit-to-cost ratio, based on reduction in sick leave and including cost of program operations, treatment, and time off work while receiving treatment, was 7 to 1 projected over five

years and nearly 17 to 1 when projected over the expected career of participants.

- Job performance improvement, rated by supervisors on an 11-point scale ranging from -5 to +5, was 3.5 points on average.

Other companies have reported equally encouraging results.

- Kimberly-Clark documented a 43% reduction in absenteeism and a 70% reduction in accidents among a sample of employees who had participated in its employee assistance program.
- Chairman Roger Smith of General Motors announced in 1983 that, of some 60,000 employees who had taken part in its EAP, between 60% and 70% were still abstaining from alcohol or drugs one year later.
- Phillips Petroleum reported that its EAP had netted more than $8 million a year in reduced accidents and sick leave, and in higher productivity.
- The Kelsey-Hayes EAP tracked 58 plant workers involved in its program and documented the recovery of 18,325 hours in one year, an average of 316 hours per employee.
- An AT&T study in 1982 showed declines of 78% in overall absenteeism, 87% in absence due to disability, 81% in on-the-job accidents, and 58% in off-the-job accidents.

——— THE SOLUTION THAT ACTS LIKE A PROBLEM

In our eagerness to attack the current crop of devastating drugs—particularly cocaine—we have ignored not only the pitfalls of the past but also the effectiveness of our present employee assistance programs. We have somehow convinced ourselves that the solution should be easy—an inference easily drawn from the Reagan administration's simplistic approach and the blandishments of those consultants who market DTIs.

But solving tough problems is seldom easy. Even a superficial study of past efforts suggests a number of hard questions. It was difficult to train supervisors to identify late-stage alcoholics whose drug was familiar and whose problems developed slowly. How difficult will it be to train supervisors in the various effects of a wide spectrum of unfamiliar drugs that can cause extreme problems in the course of a few months? If it was difficult for supervisors to overcome their fear of stigmatizing subordinates with an alcoholic label, how hard will they find it to refer employees for possible termination? If the alcoholic supervisors of the past failed to refer alcoholic subordinates for fear of exposing themselves, what are the chances today that a supervisor who abuses illegal drugs will refer an employee for testing?

The basic approach and underlying philosophy of many DTIs pose serious obstacles to their effectiveness. Although EAPs generally assure employees that only substandard performance or rule violations—not EAP participation—will jeopardize their jobs, drug testing can mean job loss even where performance problems and rules violations are not evident. DTIs are essentially punitive and therefore legalistic in tone and approach. They are often based on several misjudgments.

For example, we take it for granted that supervisors will support tough tactics because the problem is so serious, but experience shows that supervisors often identify more closely with the subordinates they work with every day than they do with top management.

We figure that if we can make examples of the worst offenders, others will change their behavior. This may work with some people, but not with alcoholics and other addicts. Addicts believe they can get away with it because they nearly always do. Until the late stages of the illness, their deception skills will be much more effective than the detection skills of the company.

We assume that a positive or negative test result will help us to identify problems and limit their effects. But the tests in use today are not entirely reliable, and many practiced drug abusers know how to beat them. Even a true positive can mean many things. The employee could be an addict, an abuser, an occasional user, or merely someone who likes a sandwich on a poppy-seed roll. Moreover, a nonaddicted employee who smoked marijuana 10 days ago could test positive, while a chronic alcoholic who was drunk 10 hours ago might very well test negative. Even error-free test results would need professional assessment (see *Exhibit 3*).

We argue that cocaine and other drugs require special attention and effort because they are against the law, but alcohol is legal and does no less damage in the workplace. The problem for businesses and their employees is chemical dependency, and fortunately, that is a problem we know how to address with EAPs.

We tell ourselves that drug testing can't hurt so we may as well try it. But if drug testing ignores the human element and damages employee relations, it can hurt greatly. Worst of all may be the mistaken belief that something of value has been done.

Finally, we tend to assume that as long as drug testing is legal, it is all right. But the tone, approach, and perceived objectives of DTIs are adversarial, and the courts and legislatures have not yet spoken their final words on the subject. Drug-test procedures are essentially legal treatises designed to defend the company in a grievance hearing or courtroom, but that is the last place anyone but a lawyer wants to be.

The fact that DTIs emphasize "reasonable suspicion" as a basis for referral reveals the essential combativeness of such programs and explains why they are so ineffective. Establishing reasonable suspicion requires a focus on the more obvious, late-stage symptoms—the more conclusive the evidence, the safer the process legally. But winning in court is not the same as winning in the workplace. Later and fewer referrals mean a return to the intake levels of the 1940s.

Moreover, skewing tests to avoid the legal fallout of false positives will only produce more false negatives. And these particular false negatives are

EXHIBIT 3
The Medical Case Against Drug Testing

A drug's detectability depends on many variables: dosage, absorption rate, location of entry, drug purity, individual metabolism, frequency of use, and whether drugs are consumed singly or in combination. A urine test does not test for the presence or absence of the drug, but for a critical quantity of it. If the concentration drops below a certain level, the test usually will not detect it. Knowing how long it takes for abstinence to reduce concentrations below these critical thresholds—2 to 4 days for cocaine, heroin, and amphetamines; 3 to 10 days for occasional use of marijuana; 5 to 13 hours for alcohol—allows chronic users to feign illness and postpone their tests long enough to free their bodies of the drug and its metabolites.

Abstinence is not the only way to beat the tests. Employees have been known to smuggle in clean urine (and to keep it at body temperature to fool the medical attendant), to drink large quantities of water to dilute their samples, even to obtain prescriptions for legal drugs known to test positive in order to provide themselves with a "legitimate" explanation of their own more genuine positives. Marijuana users can add salt, sweat, or Drano to increase the pH of their urine samples. Besides, there is a 5% to 10% chance that drug abusers will falsely test negative despite the drugs in their bodies.

There is also a chance that positive tests will be false. Even if the test is accurate, the mere indication of the drug does not tell us whether the employee has used the drug once or a hundred times—or at all.

Most laboratories screen for illegal drugs with the so-called EMIT method, which is hardly foolproof. A number of harmless—or in any case legal—substances have molecular and electrochemical patterns similar to the hard drugs EMIT was designed to identify. Over-the-counter cough and cold preparations may test positive for amphetamines. The opiate-like drugs and alcohol found in other legal medications may also confound test findings. Poppy seeds eaten in quantity may produce a trace opiate indication. Some herbal teas have been associated with positive tests for various illegal drugs.

Ibuprofen, a painkiller found in Advil, Datril, Rufen, and other over-the-counter medications, can cause a false positive result for marijuana. Ephedrine, an ingredient of Nyquil, can test positive for amphetamines. Dextromathorphon, found in many cough suppressants, has tested positive for opiates. False positives may also result from laboratory errors such as mislabeling urine or transposing results, or from improperly cleaned equipment, incompetence, or out-and-out fraud.

Several years ago, the Navy found that more than 30% of positives were erroneous. In one methadone maintenance program, accuracy was no better than 50%. In a litigious society, employers are well-advised to do two confirmatory tests. Even so, they run the risk of lawsuits. In May 1987, San Diego Gas and Electric lost a court case to a "false positive." The cost of defending the suit, settlement, and other fees was publicly stated as $80,000.

Even without litigation, testing is expensive. Besides the costs of the tests, companies must add the costs of administration, supervision, and lost work time. Last but hardly least, the cost to employee morale cannot be measured.

– David Bearman, M.D.

likely to render the DTI ineffective, because the people we most want to catch in a drug-testing net are the very people who are most skilled at achieving negative or ambiguous results by devious means.

Drug testing, even when necessary, should not be seen as a program in itself but rather as one element in a larger effort, an effort that begins with a properly designed and staffed EAP.

Our leaders suggest that we may be able to eliminate this problem in two or three years if we really get tough. But until we find a way to prevent 10% of the population from becoming addicted, the problem will continue. If all employers were able to prescreen with 100% accuracy, the resulting rise in unemployment would be staggering, and we would also find an increase in the suffering and disruption of other family members still in the work force. By the same token, if all employed alcoholics and addicts could be identified in the next three years, our current treatment capacity could not possibly handle the load.

Creation of a drug-free workplace in a drug-filled society is an illusion. It emphasizes supply rather than demand. It suggests that eradication of cocaine and other hard drugs will solve the problem generally. It insists that drug addicts and alcoholics are separable groups, the former far more intractable than the latter.

Our goal should be an *addiction-free* workplace. That means focusing on all addictive substances, not just those portrayed in the scariest colors. It means treatment of the whole problem, not just punitive measures for the small portion currently in the spotlight. It means concern for all employees at all levels, not just those in the lower echelons. We could have a drug-free workplace today if that were the only freedom we valued. We certainly would not be free of addiction. Untreated addiction will always resurface in some new and equally destructive form.

—— DISCUSSION QUESTIONS

1. What should a corporation's policy be regarding employees' personal problems? How involved should a company become in the personal problems of its employees?
2. Suppose you've discovered that your boss or a coworker has a serious drinking/drug problem. What action would you take?
3. What steps can a company take to educate employees about such issues as drug abuse? What other issues that affect an employee's productivity might a company want to address?
4. Do you think that companies and organizations in the future will become more or less involved with the general well-being of their employees, or will their involvement remain the same? Explain the reasons for your view.

INDEX

Absenteeism
   family issues and, 531
   flextime and, 537
   salaried system and, 478
Academy (career-system model),
   469–470, 472
Acceptance, group problem-solving
   and, 267
Accountability, hierarchy and, 384–385
Accounting system, at Semco, 79–80
Achievement, motivation and, 163, 164
Ackerman, Robert W., 344n
Addiction, 553. *See also* Alcoholism;
   Drug abuse
Adhocracy, 334, 338–339, 344–347
Administrative adhocracy, 346–347
Aetna Life and Casualty, 537
Affirmative action, 499–505
   at Corning, 504
   cycle in, 503, 505
   at DEC, 506
   managing diversity and, 501, 502,
   515
Agenda, for meeting, 290–291
Agenda control, as motivation, 67

Agreement, change resistance overcome
   by, 402–403, 405
Aguilar, Francis J., 15n
Alan Patricof Associates, 119
Albrook, Robert C., 191n
Alcan, 59
Alcoholism, 543–544, 546–547
   Broadbrush employee assistance
      programs for, 548–550
   drug testing and, 550–553
Aligning of people, 107–109
Allen, Stephen A., 395n
Allis-Chalmers Corp., 79, 80
All-salaried compensation system,
   478–479
Alternative career paths, 538–540
Alternative work schedules, career-and-
   family women and, 524. *See also*
   Flexible scheduling
Ambiguity, leadership pattern and, 133
Ambivalence, in performance appraisal,
   199–200
American Bankers Insurance Group,
   534–535
American Express, 58, 106–107

Anderson, John, 209n
Andrews, Kenneth R., 18n
Apple Computer, 120, 541
Appraisal process or interview, 196, 204–211
  guidelines for assessing, 211–212
Appraisal system, 196, 203–204. *See also* Performance appraisal or evaluation
Apprenticeship, in leadership development, 97–98
Argyris, Chris, 133n, 398n
Assignment (human resources), 466
Assignment flow (human resources), 468, 469
Athos, Anthony G., 241n
Atkinson, John W., 185n
AT&T Co., 176, 541, 550
Authority
  accountability and, 385
  dependence and, 36
  formal, 42
  in leadership pattern, 127–128, 132
Authority figures, relationship with boss and, 233
Autonomy crisis, 417
Avoidance
  in group conflict resolution, 270–271, 272, 273
  in performance appraisal, 199–200, 201
Avon Products, Inc., 501

Banc One, 58
Banfield, Edward C., 48, 48n
Bargaining
  in group conflict resolution, 271, 272–273
  interpersonal conflict and, 221–222
Barnard, Chester I., 65, 145
Barnes, Louis B., 92n, 405n, 407n
Barrett, Diana, 241n
Baseball team (career-system model), 470, 471, 472
Bass, Bernard, 116n
Beech-Nut Nutrition Corporation, 149
Beer, Michael, 197n, 203n, 407n, 424n, 474n
Behavioral modification, 174

Behavioral science, personnel management and, 166–167
Behavior model, of work-group, 257–258, 261
Benne, Kenneth F., 399n
Bennis, Warren G., 192, 193, 399n
Berlew, David E., 181, 185n, 187, 187n, 188n
Blake, Robert R., 221n, 270n
Bond, Terry, 531n
Bossidy, Larry, 434, 436, 441
Boss-imposed time, 50
Bower, Marvin, 395n
Bowers, David F., 401n
Brazil, Semco in, 70
Bridge club, as participative mechanism, 118
Broadbrush employee assistance programs, 548–550
Brophy, Paul, 143n
Buchanan, Paul C., 137n
Budgeting, 103
  at Semco, 80
Burden, Dianne, 536n
Bureaucracy. *See also* Hierarchy
  machine, 333, 337–340, 349
  professional, 333, 338–339, 340–341, 346
Burlington Northern Railroad, 546, 549
Burnham, David H., 48n
Burns, Alan, 424n
Burns, James McGregor, 116n
Burns, Robert K., 203n
Burns, Tom, 16n
Business plans, human resources planning and, 450–451, 452
Buy-make decision. *See* Make-or-buy decision

Candor
  in GE value statement, 442
  Welch on GE and, 433–434
Capital budgeting, managerial decisions and, 24
Caplan, Frieda, 118–119, 121
Career momentum, 466
Career paths
  alternatives in, 538–540

interfunctional coordination and, 362, 365

management of, 378

mentors in, 98–99, 511–512

temporary lower-level jobs, 420

for women, 521, 522–523, 530

Career system, 464–465

assignment flow, 468, 469

basic stages, 465–468

strategic choice and, 471–472

supply flow, 468, 469

typology of groups defined through, 469-471

Carlson, Sune, 15n

Carlzon, Jan, 104

Carnegie, Andrew, 98

Cartwright, Dorwin, 38n

CEOs, contacts of, 20–21, 22. *See also* Senior managers

Cespedes, Frank V., 359n

Chandler, Alfred D., 411–412

Change, 395–396

choice of strategy for, 405–408

cost of, 428–429

dealing with resistance to, 400–405

diagnosing resistance to, 396–400

formula for, 424–430

leadership and, 103

in managerial work, 57–62

quantum theory of, 351

in society, 138–139

women's opportunities and, 124

Chemical dependency. *See* Alcoholism; Drug abuse

Chew, Pat, 143n

Child care, 525, 532–535

Chin, Robert, 399n

Choran, Irving, 16n

Christensen, C. Roland, 411n

Christensen, Kathleen, 537n

Chrysler Corp., 193

Circle, organizational, 73

Civil disobedience, 75

Civil rights movement, leadership pattern and, 138

Clarifying, in group process, 286

Clarity, in corporate vision, 373–374

Cloherty, Patricia M., 119

Club (career-system model), 470–471, 472

Coaching, performance appraisal and, 197, 203

Coercion, change resistance overcome by, 404, 405

Coleman, Debi, 120

Collaboration period of organizational growth, 419–420, 422

Collaborative ventures, 64

Commissioning executives, 300

Commitment

of followers, 147–148

group problem-solving and, 267

group-process influence and, 282

new management work and, 69

Commitment strategy in work-force management, 490–497, 498

Communication

aligning as, 107–108

change resistance overcome by, 400–401, 405

cross-functional, 356–357; *see also* Interfunctional coordination

informational roles and, 21–22

of managerial expectations, 183–186

motivation and, 162–163

preferences on forms of, 235

two-way, 163

Welch on, 433

Communications media, managers' use of, 16–18

Communications role, of task-force leader, 307

Company culture, 330

Compensation systems, 476–477. *See also* Rewards and rewards systems

equity and, 479–482

management philosophy and, 477

pay-for-performance, 483–486

payroll stratification, 477–478

seniority and, 483

wages as motivation, 161

Competence

change and, 428–429

of followers, 148

Complexity, group problem-solving and, 266–267

Compromising, in group process, 286

Computer, managers' work procedures and, 18, 30

Conditions of work. See Working conditions

Confidence in subordinates, 133

Confidential information, task force and, 306

Configurations, organization design. See Organization design configurations

Conflict
adjudicators of, 365–366
group problem-solving, 266–267
interdepartmental, 274
in interfunctional coordination, 365
in task forces, 298, 306

Conflict, interpersonal, 213–220
action questions, 225–226
managing, 214, 220–225
managing your boss and, 229; see also Managing your boss

Conflict resolution in groups. See Group conflict resolution

Confrontation
authority vs. issues, 100
constructive, 221, 224–225
in group conflict resolution, 271–272, 273

Confronting norms, 269

Connor, Fox, 98

Consensus testing, in group process, 286

Consistency, in corporate vision, 375

Consumer movement, leadership pattern and, 138

Context, group, 243–244

Contingency approach, to organization design, 315–321

Continuity, in corporate vision, 374–375

Continuum of leadership behavior, 128–130, 138, 139

Continuum of manager-nonmanager behavior, 140–141

Control
as configuration element, 338
external (over divisions), 340, 342–343, 349–350
in growth phases, 422
vs. motivation, 109–110

Control crisis, 418

Controlling
actual managerial work and, 13
interpersonal conflict and, 221, 222–224

Control strategy in work-force management, 489–490, 492–493

Co-opting
change resistance, 403–404, 405
management efforts, 379–380

Coordinating, actual managerial work and, 13

Coordination, interfunctional or cross-functional. See Interfunctional coordination

Coordination period of organizational growth, 418–419, 422

Copeman, George H., 16n

Corning Glass Works, 504

Corporate Executive Council (General Electric), 436, 437–438

Corporate mission, family concerns and, 539–542

Corporation Man (Jay), 72

Cost-accounting experts, as interfunctional adjudicators, 366

Counseling
interpersonal conflict and, 224
motivation and, 163

Counterdependence, 233–234

Courage, of followers, 149

Crandall, Bob, 108–109

Creativity
in GE value statement, 442
organizational design and, 324

Creativity period in organizational development, 415–417, 422

Critical Incident Method, 203

Cross-functional coordination. See Interfunctional coordination

Cross-functional groups of managers, 328

Culture
group, 252–256, 257, 260, 261–262
of leadership, 111–114
managerial, 86

Culture, company or corporate, 330
diversity and, 510
interfunctional coordination and, 363–365

Culture, national, compensation systems and, 476–477
Cummins Engine Co., 479, 482, 490
Customer-ranking process, 358

Dalton, Gene W., 92n, 405n
Dana Corp., 479
Data bank, in managers' minds, 18, 26
Davis, Robert T., 16n, 189n
Deadlines, task–force membership and, 306
Decentralization
  as configuration element, 338
  vs. divisionalization, 342
  horizontal, 336
  leadership development and, 112
  vertical, 336
Decisional roles, 23
  disturbance handler, 23–24
  entrepreneur, 23
  negotiator, 24
  resource allocator, 24
Decision making
  in continuum of leadership behavior, 128
  delegation of, 18, 64–65, 131, 152
  in group problem-solving, 277
  intergroup and interdepartmental, 274–276
  in meeting, 296
Decision-making style, managing your boss and, 235
Defensiveness, in performance appraisal, 201
de Gaulle, Charles, 91
Dekker, Wisse, 374
Delegation
  followership encouragement, 152
  hierarchy and, 64–65
  information dilemma, 18
  risk, 131
Delegation period of organizational growth, 418, 422
Democracy, in leadership pattern, 127–128, 132
Democracy, work-force. See Employee involvement; Participation
Department representatives, 274–276

Dependability, in managing your boss, 237
Dependency
  leadership and, 87
  mutual, 229–230
  perception of, 40–42, 43, 44–45
Dependency relationships of manager, 34–38
Dependent care, 532–535
Design, organization. See Organization design
Design tools, 323–324
Development
  of managers, 377–378
  performance appraisal and, 197, 203
DeVries, David L., 195n
Differentiation, 317–318
  of single-business organizations, 324–328
Digital Equipment Corp. (DEC), 58, 506
Direction period of organizational growth, 417, 422
Direction-setting, leadership as, 103, 104–105
Discretionary time, 50
Dissatisfaction, change and, 424–426
Disseminator role, 22
Disturbance handler role, 23–24
Diversity, managing, 502, 506–515. See also Women managers
  affirmative action and, 501, 502, 515; see also Affirmative action
  at Avon, 501
  at DEC, 506
  family concerns in, 529–542
  future work-force entrants and, 519
  inability at, 500
Divisionalized form, 334, 338–339, 342–344
Division of work, 322
Donner, Frederic G., 88
Doyle, Stephen X., 359n
Dress code, Semco abolition of, 75–76
Drucker, Peter F., 235, 399, 399n
Drug abuse, 543–544
  Broadbrush employee assistance programs, 548–550
Drug testing, 543, 544–545
  medical case against, 552

Drug testing (continued)
obstacles to, 550–551
senior managers and, 546
unreliability of, 551–553
Dual membership problem, 275–276
Duncan, Robert, 400n, 402n
du Pont, Pierre, 88, 90
Du Pont (E. I.) De Nemours and Co.,
531, 534, 541
Durant, William, 342

Eastman Kodak Co., 59, 108–109, 537,
541, 546
Ecology, leadership pattern and, 138
Education. *See also* Training
change resistance overcome by,
400–401, 405
of managers, 29
Einstein, Albert, 97
Eisenhower, Dwight D., 97–98, 98n
Elaborating, in group process, 286
Elder care, 535
Electronic mail, 363
Elliott, Susan S., 119, 120–121
Emotional issues, 217
in relationship with boss, 232–233
Empathy, 64, 93
Employee assistance programs (EAPs),
Broadbrush, 548–550
Employee involvement (EI). *See also*
Participation
commitment strategy, 490
at Semco, 72–75
Employee motivation, organization
design and, 321
Employees, at Semco, 75–77
Employee satisfaction, rewards and,
474–475
Empowerment, through aligning, 108
Engineers, as interfunctional adjudi-
cators, 366
Entrepreneurial company, as simple
structure, 336
Entrepreneur role, 23
Environment, 315
as configuration element, 339
organization design and, 350–351

Equity
child care and, 534
family concerns and, 540
systems for maintaining, 479–482
Ethics, followership and, 149
Evaluation
job, 480–481
person/skill, 481–482
Evaluation goals, of performance
appraisal, 197
Evolution, as growth period, 411, 414
Exempt employees, 478
Exit from firm, 467–468
Expectations
group, 268–269
in managing your boss, 236
Expectations by managers, 179–181
communication of, 183–186
early years, 186–190
new hires, 190–192
as Pygmalion effect, 192–193
realistic vs. unrealistic, 185
as self-fulfilling prophecies, 181–183,
186, 187
Expertise, power and, 39, 43, 44
Extrinsic rewards, 476

Face-to-face influence, 42–45
Facilitation, change resistance overcome
by, 402, 405
Family and business, 529–532. *See also*
Women; Women managers
corporate mission and, 539–542
dependent care, 532–535
working conditions, 535–539
Fayol, Henri, 13, 314
Feedback
firing of employee and, 468
for followership, 151
in groups, 257, 287
in performance appraisal, 200, 201,
209
Feelings
in appraisal interview, 206
group process and, 285
Festinger, Leon, 198n
Figurehead role, 19–20
Firing of employees, 467–468

Fit in organization design, 106, 315–317, 348–349
Flanagan, John C., 203n
Flexible scheduling
  career-and-family women and, 524–525
  family concerns and, 536, 537–538
  at Semco, 77
Flextime
  family concerns and, 537
  outside activities and, 468
  at Semco, 76
Focus, of followers, 148
Followers, 143–146
  cultivating, 150–153
  qualities of, 146–149
Forcing, in group conflict resolution, 271, 272–273
Ford Motor Co., 337
Formal authority, 42
Formal organization, as group design factor, 248–249
Formal structure, 372
Fortress (career-system model), 470, 471, 472
Fouraker, Lawrence E., 412n
Freedman, Robert J., 359n
French, John R. P., Jr., 38n, 203n
Fresco, Paolo, 434
Freud, Sigmund, 40
Frieda's Finest, 118–119
Fringe benefits, motivation and, 162
Functional integration. See Interfunctional coordination; Integration
Functional units, organization design in, 321–324

Gabarro, John J., 227n, 273
Gain-sharing plans, 485–486
Galinsky, Ellen, 531n
Gate keeping, in group process, 286
General Electric Co., 67–68, 112, 374, 432–445, 449
  continuity lacking in, 374
  Corporate Executive Council, 436, 437–438
  decentralization, 112
  human resources, 449

as training ground, 67–68
  Value statement, 442
  Welch interview on, 432–445
  Work-Out program, 438–440, 443, 444–445
General Foods Corp., 64, 490
General Motors Corp., 65, 90, 342, 482, 490, 497, 550
Gerstner, Lou, 106–107
Glass ceiling, 516, 519
Gleicher, David, 424n
Goals
  in boss's world, 230–231
  managers vs. leaders, 88–89
  social vs. economic, 344
Googins, Bradley, 536
Gorlin, Harriet, 450n
Grapevine, diversity and, 512–513
Grayson, C. Jackson, Jr., 19n
Great Western Forum, 119
Greiner, Larry E., 405n
Group climate, group process and, 283–284
Group conflict resolution, 269–270
  bargaining and forcing, 271, 272–273
  confronting and problem solving, 271–272, 273
  smoothing and avoidance, 270–271, 272, 273
Group culture, 252–256, 257, 260, 261–262
Group effectiveness, leadership pattern and, 135
Grouping of functions, for single-business organizations, 326–327
Group process, 279–287
Groups, work, 241
  behavior model of, 257–258, 261
  context of, 243–244
  design factors, 246–249
  interdepartmental, 274–276
  leaderless, 152
  Merit Corp. case, 241–243, 244–246, 249–252, 256, 259–261
  outcomes, 256–257
  as problem solvers, 264–269, 276–277
  at Semco, 77
  task forces, 298–308
  with temporary and rotating leadership, 152

Growth, organizational, 410–411
  implications of history of, 421–422
  key forces in, 411–415
  phases, 415–420
Guest, Robert H., 14n, 20, 21
Gulick, Charles A., Jr., 314

Hackman, Richard J., 196n, 199
Half-time employment, 538
Hall, Adrienne, 120
Hall, Douglas T., 181, 185n, 187, 187n,
  188n, 200n
Harmonizing, in group process, 286
Hawthorne Effect and experiment, 163,
  169
Hecht, Lee, 65
Hekimian, James S., 28n
Heron, R. Peter, 349n
Hewlett-Packard Co., 112, 479, 537
Hickson, David J., 349n
Hierarchy, 382–383, 392. *See also*
  Bureaucracy
  delegation and, 64–65
  faults, 383–385
  intellectual complexity, 390–391
  layers, 386–387
  managerial change and, 58, 59, 60, 63
  new managerial work and, 65
  vs. participatory management, 74
  reason for, 385–386
  responsibility time span, 387–390
Hinnings, C. R., 349n
Hodgson, Richard C., 25n
Hoffmann, Inge, 91, 91n
Hoffmann, Stanley, 91, 91n
Holdaway, Edward A., 349n
Homans, George C., 21, 21n
Honesty, in managing your boss, 237
Hood, Ed, 441
Horizontal job loading, 167–168, 172
Hottenstein, M. P., 411n
Houghton, James R., 504
Howes, Carollee, 533n
HRM. *See* Human resources manage-
  ment
Hubris, 100
Human relations training, motivation
  and, 162

Human resources management
  assignment, 466
  career systems, 464–472
  diversity and, 502, 506–515; *see also*
    Diversity, managing of
  exit, 467–468
  family concerns and, 529–542
  organizational psychology and,
    376–379
  planning, 449–462
  promotion, 466–467; *see also* Promotion
  recruitment, 376, 465–466, 500
  rewards, 474–486; *see also* Rewards
    and reward systems
  selection, 365, 376–377, 466
  training, 29, 150–151, 377–378, 467
  women managers and, 115–118,
    124–125, 516–527; *see also* Women
    managers
Human resources managers, as interfunctional adjudicators, 366
Hygiene vs. motivators, 164–166, 173

Iacocca, Lee A., 193
IBM Corp., 59, 72, 76, 469–470, 479, 535,
  540, 541
Identification, with manager, 40, 43
Identity, change and, 429, 430
Implementation, dissident individuals
  and, 302
Incentives, innovative types of, 67
Incentive system, 483–486
  as motivation, 160
Indirect influence methods, 43, 45–46
Industrial engineering, personnel management and, 166–167
Industrial revolution, big-group functioning and, 72
Influence, 42
  face-to-face, 42–45
  in group process, 282–283
  indirect, 43, 45–46
  managerial ways of, 313
  as necessary, 48
Informal relationships. *See also* Networks
  coordination through, 110–111
  interfunctional coordination and,
    363–365

Information
   confidential, 306
   hard vs. soft, 17
   privileged, 26
   women managers as sharing, 120–121
Information access, at Semco, 71, 78–80
Information Age, 382
Informational roles, 21–22
Information-exchange meeting, 290
Information flow, managing your boss
   and, 236–237
Information seeking, in group process,
   286
Information system, 16, 362–363
Initiative, 54, 55
Insight, of managers, 25
Inspiration, through leadership, 104
Integrating roles, 328
Integration, 318–321, 353–356. *See also*
   Interfunctional coordination
   functional units and, 322–323
   in single-business organizations,
   327–328
Interactive leadership
   vs. command-and-control, 125
   by women, 118–122, 123, 124–125
Interdepartmental conflict, 274
Interdependence, 105–106
   in forces affecting leadership pattern,
   139
   group problem-solving and, 267
Interfunctional (cross–functional)
   coordination, 356–357
   adjudicators in, 365–366
   through informal social systems and
   culture, 363–365
   through management information
   system, 362–363
   through management processes or
   systems, 361–362
   through organization structure
   or management hierarchy,
   358–361
   through selection and promotion,
   365
   total system and, 367
   unified holistic strategy for,
   357–358
International Women's Forum, 116

Interpersonal conflict. *See* Conflict,
   interpersonal
Interpersonal roles, 19
   figurehead, 19–20
   leader, 20
   liaison, 20–21
Intrinsic rewards, 476
Involvement, change resistance overcome by, 401, 405
Issues, substantive vs. emotional, 217
ITT Corp., 375

Jacobson, Lenore, 182n, 186n
James, William, 95, 95n
Jay, Antony, 72, 77
Job design, 176
   work-force strategies and, 492
Job enlargement, 167
Job enrichment, 167, 173–174,
   176–178
   steps, 170–173
   successful experiment in, 168–170
Job evaluation, 480–481
Job loading, 167–168, 172
Job participation. *See* Participation
Job rotation, at Semco, 76
Job satisfaction
   family issues and, 531
   motivation vs. hygiene, 164
Job security, at Semco, 76
Job sharing
   for career-and-family women, 524
   outside activities and, 468
Johnson, George, 186
Johnson & Johnson, 112, 540, 541
Jones, Reginald, 449

Kay, Emanuel, 203n
Kearns, David T., 512
Kelsey-Hayes, 550
Kennedy, John F., 91–92
Kets de Vries, Manfred F. R., 97n,
   396n
Kettering, Charles, 90
Kimberly-Clark Corp., 550
KITA, as motivator, 159–164, 174–175
Kotter, John P., 227n, 404n, 406n

Labor force, demographic change and, 519–520, 530
Labor-management relations, work-force strategies and, 493, 496–497
Land, Edwin, 89
Language, in group culture, 254–255
Lawler, Edward E. III, 196n, 199, 200n, 475n, 483n
Lawrence, Paul R., 270, 270n, 359n, 399n, 405n, 407n, 474n
Leader role, 20
Leaders, group norms and, 253
Leadership, 85, 126–127
  command-and-control type, 125
  creating culture of, 111–114
  deciding on pattern of, 132–136
  democracy vs. authority in, 127–128, 132
  development, 96–100
  followers and, 143–153
  in GE value statement, 442
  group process and, 282
  human needs and, 110
  insight and, 137
  interactive, 118–122, 123, 124–125
  key questions, 130–132
  long-run strategy and, 136–137
  need for, 102
  range of behavior in, 128–130
  social changes and, 138–141
  vs. technical ability (Semco), 74
  transformational, 117, 125
  by women, 115–125; see also Women managers
Leadership crisis, 416–417
Leadership-management differences, 102–104
  alignment of people vs. organizing or staffing, 105–109
  in attitudes toward goals, 88–89
  direction-setting vs. planning, 103, 104–105
  motivating vs. control or problem solving, 109–111
  in personality, 86–88
  relations with others, 92–95
  senses of self, 95–96
  in work conceptions, 89–92

Learning
  cognitive vs. skills, 29
  as motivational tool, 67–68
Levine, J. D., 198n
Levinson, Daniel J., 25n
Levitt, Theodore, 86, 86n
Liaison role, 20–21
LiCari, Jerome, 149
Life Insurance Agency Management Association, 189
Lifetime employment, Welch on, 441
Livingston, J. Sterling, 29n
Lorsch, Jay W., 270, 270n, 359n, 407n
Loyalty, Welch on, 441
Luke, Robert A., Jr., 396n

McAllister, Daniel, 116
McCall, Morgan W., 195n
McClelland, David, 48n, 185
McDonald's Corp., 340
Machine bureaucracy, 333, 337–340
  external control and, 340, 349
McWhinney, Will, 140
Maier, Norman R. F., 205, 205n, 207n, 263n, 280, 280n
Maintenance functions, group process and, 286–287
Make-or-buy decision
  on human resources, 460
  simple structure and, 336
Maljers, Floris, 375
Management by Objectives (MBO), 196, 203
Management hierarchy, interfunctional coordination and, 358–361
Management information system (MIS), 16, 362–363
Management-leadership differences. See Leadership-management differences
Management processes and systems, 361–362
Management time, 50. See also Subordinate-imposed time
Management training. See Training
Managerial culture, 86
Managerial expectations. See Expectations by managers

Managerial style, 329–330
  in growth phases, 422
Managerial work, 13–14
  change in, 57–62; see also New managerial work
  decisional roles in, 23–24
  description of, 19
  folklore vs. fact, 14–19
  ignorance, 13–14, 31
  informational roles, 21–22
  integration of roles, 25
  interpersonal roles, 19–21
  issues in effectiveness of, 25–28
  managers vs. leaders and, 89–92; see also Leadership-management differences
  two faces of, 30–31
Managers
  development and training, 29, 376–379
  expectations of, 179–194
  regular duties, 15–16
  vs. technical experts (Semco), 74
  Welch on, 433
Managing your boss, 227–229
  boss's world, 230–232
  developing relationship, 234–238
  misreading boss-subordinate relationship, 229–230
  own needs and, 232–234
Manipulation, change resistance overcome by, 403–404, 405
Manipulation of environment, 43, 45–46
Mannheim, Bilha F., 349n
Maps, in group culture, 255–256
Marrow, Alfred J., 401n
Massarik, Fred, 132n
Maternity, women managers and, 517–518
Maternity leave, 526
Matrix management, 360, 371, 372, 380
Matsushita, 377
Matsushita, Konosuke, 374, 377
Mechlin, Ellen, 143n
Mechlin, Stuart, 143n
Meetings
  conducting, 293–297
  preparing for, 290–293
Membership, in group process, 284–285

Mentors, 98–99
  diversity and, 511–512
Merck & Co., Inc., 531, 540
Merit Corp. case, 241–243, 244–246, 249–252, 256, 259–261
Messages, vs. signals, 94
Metropolitan Life Insurance Co., 189
Meyer, Herbert Henry, 203n, 207n
Miles, Robert H., 396n
Miller, Christopher S., 485n
Miller, Danny, 351, 351n
Millman, R. W., 411n
Mills, D. Quinn, 474n
Minorities, affirmative action and, 500
Mintzberg, Henry, 14n, 28n, 36n
MIS (management information system), 16, 362–363
Mission, as motivational tool, 67
Mixed-model interview, 207–211
Mobil Oil, 539
Models
  mental, 17
  as specialists, 28
Moll, Albert, 181–182
Monitor role, 22
Monkey-on-the-back analogy, 51–56
Moore, Leo, 130n
Motivation
  conditions necessary for, 475–476
  vs. control, 109–110
  employee (organization design), 321
  expectancy and, 184, 185
  in high-producing group, 180
  vs. hygiene, 164–166, 173
  through job enrichment, 167, 168–174, 176–178
  KITA as, 159–164, 174–175
  through leadership, 104; see also Leadership
  vs. movement, 174
  myths, 161–164
  new managerial work and, 66–69
  at Procter & Gamble, 112–113
  rewards and, 475–476
  snake-oil speculation on, 159
  by women managers, 122
Mouton, Jane S., 221n, 270n
Multicultural Participation Council (Avon), 501

Nanus, Burt, 192, 193
National Film Board of Canada, 347
NCNB, 534, 536, 541
NEC, 377
Needs
    biological vs. psychological, 164
    leadership as satisfying, 110
Negative physical KITA, 160
Negative psychological KITA, 160
Negotiation, change resistance overcome by, 402–403, 405
Negotiator role, 24
Networks. *See also* Informal relationships
    coordination through, 110–111
    new managerial work and, 63, 65
Neustadt, Richard E., 17, 17n, 22, 22n, 41n
Newberry, John F., 349n
New managerial work, 57–62
    motivation sources and, 66–69
    power bases and, 62–66
New-venture teams, 65
New York Stock Exchange, "People and Productivity" study by, 456
Nicolosi, Richard, 112–113
Nielsen, Eric H., 279n
Nierenberg, Gerald I., 403n
Nonexempt employees, 478
Nontraditional leadership style, 124
Nonverbal cues, in group process, 285
Nordin, Janet, 143n
Nordstrom's, 152
Norms
    confronting, 269
    in group culture, 252–253, 265
North American Philips Corp. (NAP), 375, 379–380
Northern Pacific Railroad, 546

Oberlander, Alfred, 180, 189, 189n
Obligation
    managerial effectiveness and, 28
    power and, 38–39, 43, 47
One Enterprise program (American Express), 58
One-to-one relationships, 100
Open-system theory, 139

Operating adhocracy, 345–346, 347
Operating systems, as group design factor, 248–249
Opinion seeking, in group process, 286
Order-fulfillment system, integrated, 363
Organizational change. *See* Change
Organizational circle, 73
Organizational growth. *See* Growth, organizational
Organizational psychology, 372, 373
    co-opting and, 379–380
    human resource development and, 376–379
    shared vision and, 373–376
Organizational pyramid, 73
Organizational structure
    for followership encouragement, 151–153
    as group design factor, 248–249
    in growth phases, 422
    interfunctional coordination and, 358–361
    and organizational psychology, 372–373
    at Semco, 77
    strategic requirements, 370–371
    work-force strategies and, 492
Organizational theory, personnel management and, 166–167
Organization design, 313
    coherence, 332
    company culture and, 330
    consistency, 348–349, 351
    contingency approach to, 315–321
    external controls and, 349–350
    in functional units, 321–324
    goals, 314
    historical perspective on, 314
    hived-off parts in, 350
    managerial style and, 329–330
    single businesses and, 324–328
    and situation, 350–351
Organization design configurations, 332–336, 338–339
    adhocracy, 334, 338–339, 344–347
    as diagnostic tool, 347–348
    divisionalized form, 334, 338–339, 342–344

machine bureaucracy, 333, 337–340, 349

professional bureaucracy, 333, 338–339, 340–341, 346

simple structure, 333, 336–337, 338

Organizations

conservatism of, 85–86

leadership development and, 99–100

Organizing, 103–104

actual managerial work and, 13

vs. aligning, 106

Outplacement counseling, 468

Overreaching, commitment strategy and, 498

Parental leave, 526, 531

Participation. *See also* Employee involvement

change and, 401, 405, 427

in group process, 280–282

in interactive leadership, 118–120

motivation and, 163

in reward systems, 476

Part-time employment

family concerns and, 524, 538

outside activities and, 468

Patricof, Alan, Associates, 119

Payne, Ted, 512

Pay for performance, 483–486

Payroll stratification, 477–478

Peer training, 99

Peiperl, Maury A., 468n

People, as group design factor, 247

People planning, 449–462. *See also* Human resources

Performance appraisal or evaluation, 195–196

ambivalence and avoidance, 199–200

appraisal interview and, 196, 204–211

appraisal system, 196, 203–204

combined avoidance and defensiveness in, 201

diversity and, 512–513

factors influencing outcomes, 202

feedback and defensiveness, 201

for followership, 151

goals, 196–199

nonevaluative evaluation as dilemma, 202

overall supervisor-subordinate relations and, 204

Performance control systems, 342–343

Personal relations

change and, 429

managers vs. leaders, 92–95

Personnel management, general philosophies of, 166–167. *See also* Human resources management

Person/skill evaluation, 481–482

Persuasion, 36, 43

Peters, Tom, 31, 426n

Pettigrew, T. F., 198n

Philips Industries, N.V., 99, 374, 375, 377, 379

Philips, J., 426n

Phillips, Deborah, 533n

Phillips Petroleum Company, 550

Piece-rate incentive systems, 483–484

Pierce, Jon L., 537n

Placebo effect, 182

Planning, 103

actual managerial work and, 13, 14–15

as configuration element, 338

for human resources, 449–462

vs. setting direction, 104, 105

Planning dilemma, 28

Pleck, Joseph, 531n

Polaroid, 89

Pondy, Louis R., 221n

Pooled integration, 318

Porter, Lyman W., 196n, 199, 200n

Positive KITA, 160–161

Postentrepreneurial corporation, 57, 62–69

Post-industrial Age, 382

Power, 33–34

belief in manager's expertise and, 39, 43, 44

change and, 428, 430

as configuration element, 339

dependence and, 36–38

through identification with manager, 40

influencing others through, 42

investing of, 48

Power (continued)
new managerial work and, 58, 62–66
perceived dependence on manager and, 40–42, 43, 44–45
sense of obligation and, 38–39, 43
use of, 47–48
women managers as sharing, 120–121
Pratt, Edmund, 518
Predictability, leadership pattern and, 133
Prejudice, decline of, 500
Presidents, U.S., information-collecting habits, 17, 21–22
Pressures, in boss's world, 230–231
Privileged information, sharing, 26
Problem-solving
in group conflict resolution, 271–272, 273
by groups, 264–269, 276–277
interview, 206–207
managers vs. leaders, 109
manager's presence and, 131, 277
meetings and, 290, 294
Process observation, group process and, 287
Procter & Gamble Co., 65, 112–113, 376, 479, 482, 490, 509
Productivity
expectancy and, 181
vs. time at work, 539
Professional bureaucracy, 333, 338–339, 340–341
operating adhocracy and, 346
Professions, management and, 18
Profit sharing, 485
at Semco, 71, 77–78, 80
Promotion of employees, 466–467
diversity and, 511–512
family life and, 536
interfunctional coordination through, 365
Psychological saturation, 420
Psychology, organizational. *See* Organizational psychology
Pugh, D. S., 349n
Pygmalion (Shaw), 179
Pygmalion effect, 192–193
Pyramid, organizational, 73

Quality circles, 497
Quality-of-work-life (QWL), 138, 177
commitment strategy and, 490
at GM, 497

Raven, Bertram, 38n
Raytheon Co., New Products Center, 63
Reagan administration, drug abuse and, 550
Reagan, Nancy, 544
Reciprocal integration, 318
Recruitment, 465–466
affirmative action and, 500
of managers, 376
Red-tape crisis, 419
Reflective structure, 420
Reimann, Bernard C., 349n
Relations, personal. *See* Personal relations
Representatives, department, 274–276
Reputation, as motivator, 68
Resource allocator role, 24
Resource and referral services (R&Rs), 534
Resources
affecting perceptions of, 41–42
finding and acquiring, 40–41
in managing your boss, 237–238
Responsibility, in groups, 265
Responsibility time span, 387–390
Retirement, phased, 468
Revolution, as growth period, 411, 414
Rewards and reward systems
change and, 429, 430
compensation systems, 161, 476–486; *see also* Compensation systems
employee satisfaction and, 474–475
followership and, 152
in GE value statement, 442
in growth phases, 422
motivation and, 475–476
participation in, 476
Rituals, in group culture, 254–255
Rockefeller, John D. 3rd, 85–86, 86n
Rogers, Carl R., 206n

Roles, 254
  communications (task force), 307
  decisional, 23–24
  in group culture, 253–254
  informational, 21–22
  as integrated whole, 25
  integrating, 328
  interpersonal, 19–21
  responsibility time span of, 387–389
Rolscreen Co., 537
Roosevelt, Franklin, 22
Rosenthal, Robert, 182, 182n, 186n, 187
Rothman, Claire, 119, 121, 122
Ruh, Robert A., 197n, 203n
Rynd, Mary Jane, 119–120, 121–122

Salter, Malcolm S., 412n
Samuel, Yitzhak, 349n
San Diego Gas and Electric Co., 552
SAS Institute Inc., 534
Sather, Vijay, 406n
Satisfaction, employee, 474–475
Sayles, Leonard R., 23, 23n, 34n
Scandinavian Airline Systems (SAS),
    104–105
Scanlon Plan, 484, 485, 495
Schedules, alternate or flexible,
    524–525, 536, 537–538
Schein, Edgar H., 397n
Schein, Lawrence, 450n
Schlesinger, Leonard A., 406n
Schmidt, Warren H., 137n
Schuster, Michael H., 485n
Science, management and, 18
Scientific management, 489
Scott, Bruce R., 411n
Scott, Thomas A., 98
Seashore, Stanley E., 401n
Seckler, Howard, 143n
Second American Revolution, The
    (Rockefeller), 85
Security, of employment vs. employ-
    ability, 69
Security Pacific National Bank, 58
Selection of employees, 466
  interfunctional coordination through,
    365
Selection of managers, 376–377

Selection of subordinates, 189–190
Self, senses of, managers vs. leaders
    and, 95–96
Self-esteem, managers' effect on, 192,
    193
Self-image
  manager's effect on, 192, 193
  productivity and, 181
Self-imposed time, 50
Self-interest, change and, 396–397, 427
Self-management, followership and,
    146–147
Self-worth, woman managers as
    enhancing, 121–122
Semco, 70–80
Seniority, 483
  family concerns and, 540
Senior (top-level) managers
  alcoholism testing and, 546
  interfunctional coordination and,
    364–365, 366
  in leadership development, 113–114
  organizational tasks, 372
  organization design and, 330
Sensitivity training, motivation and,
    162
Sequential integration, 318
Shariq, Syed, 143n
Shaw, George Bernard, Pygmalion, 179
Signals, vs. messages, 94
Simple structure, 333, 336–337, 338
Single-business organizations, 324–328
Sloan, Alfred P., Jr., 88, 88n, 90, 342
SMILE (specialty, management ability,
    international flexibility, language
    facility, endeavor), 377
Smoothing, in group conflict resolution,
    270–271, 272, 273
Social changes, and leadership,
    138–141
Social consequences, and divisionalized
    form, 344
Socialization process
  leaders and, 96
  women managers and, 122, 123
Social systems, interfunctional coordina-
    tion and, 363–365
Sonnenfeld, Jeffrey A., 465n, 468n
Special consideration test, 514

Specialization
  as configuration element, 338
  integration and, 359
Spector, Bert, 474n
Spokesperson role, 22
Sponsorship, diversity and, 511–512
Stability, leadership pattern and, 133
Staffing, 103–104, 106
Staffs
  interdepartmental coordination and,
    366
  Welch on, 435
Stakeholders, commitment strategy
    and, 491
Starbuck, William H., 411n, 412n
Stephens, Gregory, 116
Stewart, Rosemary, 15n, 16n, 20, 34n
Stopford, John M., 412n
Stories, in group culture, 254–255
Strategic choice, and career systems,
    471–472
Strategy, 315
  leadership pattern and, 136–137
  organizational structure and, 370,
    371–372, 380
Strategy document, 357–358
Stress, family issues and, 531
Structure, formal, 372
Style, in relationship with boss, 231–232,
    234–236
Subordinate-imposed time, 50–51
  monkey-on-the-back analogy and,
    51–56
Subordinates
  firing, 467–468
  as followers, 143–153
  generation gap and, 191
  GE Work-Out program and, 439
  leader role of managers and, 20
  managers' influence on, 313
  managing of boss by, 227–238
  selection of, 189–190
Substance abuse, 543, 545–546. *See also*
    Alcoholism; Drug abuse
Substantive issues, 217
Succession planning, 455–456
Summarizing, in group process, 286
Superficiality, managerial work and,
    27, 31

Supervisors
  in commitment strategy, 496
  drug-abuse measures and, 545,
    546–547, 550, 551
Supply flow (human resources), 468,
    469
Support, change resistance overcome
    by, 402, 405
Sweeney, James, 186
System-imposed time, 50
System Service Enterprises, 119

Tannenbaum, Robert, 132n
Task, 315
Task forces, 298–299
  first meeting of, 303–305
  project completion and, 307–308
  running of, 305–307
  start-up activities, 299–303
Task functions, in group process, 286
Task requirements, as group design
    factor, 247–248
Taylor, Frederick W., 489
Team destroyers, 365
Team management, problems of, 25
Technical ladders, 481
Technology, commitment strategy and,
    495
Teknowledge, Inc., 65
Teleconferencing, 363
Tell-and-listen interview, 205–206
Tell-and-sell method in appraisal inter-
    view, 205
Termination of employment, 467–468
Thompson, James D., 318, 318n, 319
3M Co. (Minnesota Mining & Mfg. Co.),
    112
Time pressure
  leadership pattern and, 136
  managing your boss and, 237–238
Time span, responsibility, 387–390
Top-level managers. *See* Senior managers
Total information system, 16
Training, 467
  for followership, 150–151
  of managers, 29, 76, 377–378
Trani, John, 444, 445

Transformational leadership, 117, 125
Transitional stage in work-force management, 492–493, 497–498
Travelers Insurance Co., 535
Travel Related Services (TRS) arm of American Express, 106–107
Trowbridge, Chuck, 108–109
Trust, change and, 398
TRW Inc., 479
Turner, C., 349n

Uncertainty
  group problem-solving and, 266–267
  leadership pattern and, 133
Unilever, 375, 377–379
Union-management relations. See Labor-management relations
United Airlines, 549
Upward appraisal, 204
Urwick, Lyndall, 314

Valence effect, 280
Value creation, sharing of, 67
Value statement, GE, 442
Value system, leadership continuum and, 132–133
Valuing Differences program (DEC), 506
Varieties of Religious Experience, The (James), 95
Vertical job loading, 167, 168, 172
Vietnam War, leadership excess and, 92
Viteles, Morris S., 137n
Voice mail, 363

Wages, motivation and, 161. See also Compensation system
Walters, R. W., Jr., 190
Walton, C. Lee, Jr., 395n
Walton, Richard, 221n, 474n
Warner-Lambert Co., 540
Waterman, Robert, 31, 426n
Watson, Goodwin, 399n
Watson, Thomas, 76

Weber, Max, 38n
Weekly balancing, 537
Welch, John F., Jr., 432–445, 458–459, 459n
Wetlaufer, Suzanne, 365n
WGBH, 305
Whitebook, Marcy, 533n
Whyte, William F., 21n
Win-win situation, 93–94
Women. See also Diversity, managing of
  affirmative action and, 500; see also Affirmative action
  family and, 530–531; see also Family and business
  work-plus-home burden, 535–536
Women managers, 115–118, 124–125, 516–527
  career-primary vs. career-and-family, 519, 520–523
  child care and, 525
  flexible scheduling and, 524–525
  interactive leadership by, 118–122, 123, 124–125
  maternity and, 517–518
  as part-time workers, 538
  in paths of least resistance, 122–123
  societal issues concerning, 527
Work, division of, 322
Work ethic, decline of, 177
Work-force democracy. See Employee involvement; Participation
Work-force management, 487–498
  commitment strategy in, 490–497, 498
  control strategy in, 489–490, 492–493
  transitional stage in, 492–493, 497–498
Work groups. See Groups, work
Working conditions
  alternate or flexible schedules, 524–525, 536, 537–538
  employee involvement in, 72–75, 490; see also Participation
  family concerns and, 535–539
  job enrichment, 167, 168–174, 176–178
  quality-of-work-life (QWL), 138, 177, 490, 497
  at Semco, 75–76
  three philosophies of, 166–167
Work-Out (GE program), 438–440, 443, 444–445

Work schedules, alternate or flexible, 524–525, 536, 537–538
Work style, in relationship with boss, 231–232, 234–236
Work time, motivation and, 161
Worthing, Marcia, 501
Wrapp, H. Edward, 17n
Wrigley, Leonard, 342n, 343n

Xerox Corp., 512

Youth revolution, leadership pattern and, 138

Zaleznik, Abraham, 25n, 92n, 97n, 396n
Zaltman, Gerald, 400n, 402n
Zandler, Alvin, 38n, 201n
Zimmerle, Alan, 506